Robert John (Bob) Hunter was born in rural Meath in 1938 and was educated at Wesley College and Trinity College, Dublin. After graduation in 1960, he began research on the Ulster Plantation in the counties of Armagh and Cavan, 1608–41. This interest in the Plantation, and early modern Irish history generally, was to dominate his life.

In 1963 he was appointed Assistant Lecturer in History at Magee College, thus beginning an association with the city of Derry/Londonderry that was to continue for the rest of his life. The creation of what was to become the University of Ulster also saw him teaching regularly in Coleraine.

Through his meticulous research, he developed an encyclopaedic knowledge of his subject, traversing such themes as the development of towns, the role of the English planters, the history of trade and migration and the intellectual and cultural life of Ulster more generally.

Though his untimely death in 2007 was to cut short his ambitions for further writing, he was nevertheless to leave behind more than sixty articles, essays, reviews, etc., which were the result of painstaking study conducted with a careful eye for detail and relevance.

* * * * *

John Morrill FBA HonMRIA is Professor of British and Irish History at Cambridge University and an Honorary Fellow of Trinity College Dublin. He has written prolifically on the early modern period and was one of the four principal investigators who prepared the 1641 Depositions for its web edition (1641.tcd.ie). He became a good friend and admirer of Bob Hunter while he was external examiner for an MA course at the (New) University of Ulster from 1981–9.

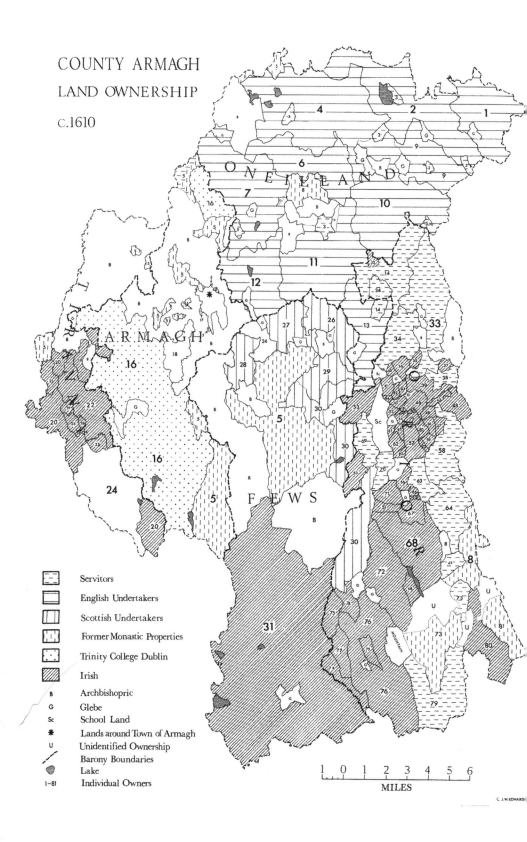

COUNTY ARMAGH
LAND OWNERSHIP
c.1610

Servitors
English Undertakers
Scottish Undertakers
Former Monastic Properties
Trinity College Dublin
Irish
B   Archbishopric
G   Glebe
Sc   School Land
✳   Lands around Town of Armagh
U   Unidentified Ownership
     Barony Boundaries
     Lake
1–81 Individual Owners

1 0 1 2 3 4 5 6
         MILES

C. J.W. EDWARDS

Ulster Transformed
Plantation in early modern Ireland
c.1590–1641

R.J. Hunter

Prepared for publication
and introduced by

John Morrill

ULSTER HISTORICAL FOUNDATION
in association with Geography Publications

Published in association with the R.J. Hunter Committee.
The Committee works to acknowledge the contribution R.J. Hunter made to
the study of our past by making more widely known the results of his research,
as well as giving limited support to others engaged in associated endeavours.

The Committee is grateful for the assistance of Professor John Morrill
in producing this volume.

COVER ILLUSTRATIONS
Front: Termon McGrath Castle, near Pettigo, County Donegal
(Photograph by William Roulston)

Back: Map of Ulster attributed to Willem Blaeu, *c.* 1603–10
(PRONI)

Page i: R.J. 'Bob' Hunter at Monasterboice during the
Dublin University History Society's Annual Outing in June 1963
(Photograph by Dr Jonathan Bardon (1941–2020) as an eighteen-year-old first year student)

First published by Ulster Historical Foundation in 2012 as:
Ulster Transformed c. 1590–1641:
Essays on Plantation and Print Culture

This edition published 2020.

www.ancestryireland.com
www.booksireland.org.uk

ISBN 2020 edition: 978-1-909556-81-2
ISBN First edition: 978-1-903688-97-7

PRINTED IN IRELAND BY
SPRINTprint

DESIGN
J. P. Morrison

CONTENTS

ACKNOWLEDGEMENTS

Ulster Historical Foundation is pleased to acknowledge the co-operation and goodwill of the joint-authors, editors and publishers of these collected essays of R.J. Hunter. Thanks are due to F.H.A. Aalen (with whom Robert co-wrote 'Two Early Seventeenth-Century Maps of Donegal'), Raymond Gillespie (with whom Robert co-wrote the unpublished essay, 'The Ulster Plantation'), David McConaghy, Joanne Taggart, and in particular, to Willie Nolan of Geography Publications for his personal interest in the project. The Foundation is grateful to the R.J. Hunter Committee for their guidance and support in the course of preparing these projects for publication.

Without the assistance of the following publishers this publication would not have been possible.

GEOGRAPHY PUBLICATIONS
'The End of O'Donnell Power', *Donegal: history and society*, William Nolan, Liam Ronayne and Máiread Dunleavy (eds), 1995

'Plantation in Donegal', *Donegal: history and society*, William Nolan, Liam Ronayne and Máiread Dunleavy (eds), 1995

'The Fishmongers' Company of London and the Londonderry Plantation, 1609–41', *Derry & Londonderry: history and society*, Gerard O'Brien (ed.), 1999

'Style and Form in Gravestone and Monumental Sculpture in County Tyrone in the seventeenth and eighteenth centuries', *Tyrone: history and society*, Henry A. Jefferies and Charles Dillon (eds), 2000

'County Armagh: A map of plantation, *c.* 1610', *Armagh: history and society*, A.J. Hughes and William Nolan (eds), 2001

'Sir William Cole, the Town of Enniskillen and Plantation County Fermanagh', *Fermanagh: history and society*, Eileen Murphy and William Roulston (eds), 2004

BLACKSTAFF PRESS
'Sir Ralph Bingley *c.* 1570–1627: Ulster Planter', *Plantation to partition: essays in Ulster history in honour of J.L. McCracken*, Peter Roebuck (ed.), 1981

DONEGAL HISTORICAL SOCIETY
'The Settler Population of an Ulster Plantation County', *Donegal Annual*, vol. x, 1971–3

THE ROYAL SOCIETY OF ANTIQUARIES OF IRELAND
'Two Early Seventeenth-Century Maps of Donegal', *The Journal of the Royal Society of Antiquaries of Ireland*, Vol. 94, No. 2, 1964

CLOGHER HISTORICAL SOCIETY
'Sir William Cole and Plantation Enniskillen, 1607–41', *Clogher Record*, Vol. 9, No. 3, 1978

CUMANN SEANCHAIS BHREIFNE (BREIFNE HISTORICAL SOCIETY)
'The English Undertakers in the Plantation of Ulster: A Cavan Case Study, 1610–41', *Breifne*, Vol. IV, No. 16, 1973–5

'An Ulster Plantation Town, Virginia', *Breifne*, Vol. IV, No. 13, 1970

APPLETREE PRESS
'Ulster Plantation Towns 1609–41', *The Town in Ireland*, D.W. Harkness and Mary O'Dowd (eds), 1981

STUDIA HIBERNICA
'Towns in the Ulster Plantation', *Studia Hibernica*, No. 11, 1971

LILLIPUT PRESS AND THE LIBRARY ASSOCIATION OF IRELAND
'John Franckton (d. 1620): Printer, Publisher and Bookseller in Dublin', *That Woman – Studies in Irish Bibliography: A Festschrift for Mary 'Paul' Pollard*, Charles Benson and Siobhán Fitzpatrick (eds), 2005

CAMBRIDGE UNIVERSITY PRESS
'The Bible and the Bawn: an Ulster Planter Inventorised', *British Interventions in Early Modern Ireland*, Ciaran Brady and Jane Ohlmeyer (eds), 2005

THE ECONOMIC AND SOCIAL HISTORY SOCIETY OF IRELAND
'Chester and the Irish Book Trade', *Irish Economic and Social History* 15, 1988

John Morrill would like to thank Dr Elaine Murphy for bibliographical help and Ms Nvard Chalikyan for assistance in decoding and preparing a typescript of chapter 11 from some difficult and much amended handwritten drafts.

INTRODUCTION:
BOB HUNTER'S ULSTER

By John Morrill

Robert J. Hunter was born in 1938, on 22 October, an auspicious day for any Ulsterman, and died just before his 69th birthday, on 24 September 2007. He was educated in Dublin and then spent nearly half a century in the north of Ireland, teaching in Magee College and in Coleraine. He was a man of profound learning. He was a man with a deep sense of *la comédie humaine* and the ironies of human life. He could be a curmudgeon. He was a wry observer of his own paranoia. He was a man to whom things happened which were slightly sad and very funny, and he could turn any minor tragedy into a major source of laughter. Typically, when I last saw him, a fortnight before he died, he pulled out an envelope containing a card I had written in response to a query he had put to me some time in the 1980s, when I was external examiner at the then New University of Ulster. He had asked me to send him the size of the shot used in the different artillery pieces in the civil war and I had sent a list. He pointed out that the envelope had been twice opened and re-sealed and he maintained, with a delicious half-conviction, that it must have been intercepted and opened by Special Branch, and that we had both been marked men ever since. Entering into the spirit of this fantasy, I refrained from pointing out that I had manifestly added information about the demi-culverin, as an afterthought that required unsealing and resealing. He liked to tease himself.

He yearned to write big books and to complete great projects. Even when I saw him for that last time, in great pain and exhausted, he wanted to impress upon me that if only he was granted another eighteen months to live, his great projects would be completed. He needed to say it, at some level he may have believed it; but the truth is that while he lamented all the obstacles that people and events had thrown in his path (the denial of a doctorate, the shabby treatment meted out to him by the University of Ulster, especially in his later years, the daily enforced commute from Derry to Coleraine by a deteriorating public transport system), in truth he himself had always erected the biggest of those obstacles. He set himself impossible goals and could never recognise the magnitude of the achievements he did have. He lived with terrible and unnecessary regrets. In a mid-career c.v. prepared as the New University of Ulster morphed into the University of Ulster with the merger of the NUU with the Ulster Polytechnic in Jordanstown and Magee College in Derry/Londonderry, Bob wrote that

'I still retain some hope of producing these books', listing 'The English and the Ulster Plantation', 'a study of Derry, the principal plantation town', 'an edition of the Ulster Port Books 1612–15' and 'essays on the Anglicization in Ireland'. In the event, most of these are now being completed by others as a memorial to him after his death but the frank truth is that he would never have published them himself. The perfectionism, rooted in a range of insecurities, that made him such a remarkable scholar, also inhibited all sense of ripeness.

Amongst the temperamental reasons why the bigger projects were never brought to conclusion, Bob's radical commitment to teaching must be prominent. In a long letter written in the early 1980s to Brian Manning, Pro-Vice-Chancellor of the new University, Bob pleaded for the integration of the School of Humanities with Extra-Mural Studies, the creation of structures for lifelong learning for the province. He went on to detail his own teaching in Omagh, Strabane, Portstewart, Derry, Buncrana, Clogher, Letterkenny (all in historic Ulster but some not in post-1921 'Ulster'), teaching undertaken for TCD, for Magee College, for Queen's University Belfast and for the Inishowen Adult Education Board and he spoke with passion about his work with 80 adult-learners in Omagh helping them to reconstruct their history or more accurately histories. He pleaded to be allowed to teach one semester at Coleraine and one in Derry and to be funded to set up a project in Inishowen like the one he had overseen in Omagh. (He clearly chose not to recognise the partition treaty of 1921 or at least he preferred to overlook the North's lack of responsibility for counties ripped away from the province). It was not to be, of course. But it reminds us that, as Keith Lindley, in his funeral address, said, 'Bob was a victim of his own popularity' with students of all ages.[1] The self-revelations in this letter to Brian Manning include not only the tipping of the teaching/research balance in favour of teaching but also the deep commitment to what Keith Lindley called 'a meticulous eye for detail and relevance'. Both are vital, and first and foremost in that search for relevance was a search for a sense of place, the interaction not only of inhabitants and colonists, but their interactions in very specific landscapes.

Bob was not a man of Ulster; but he was a man born close to the soil. He was born on 22 October 1938, a farmer's son brought up on a farm close to Ashbourne, County Meath, 17 miles north of Dublin, a village, then, of less than one hundred dwellings midway between Dublin and Navan, south of the Boyne Valley. At one end of its high street was a memorial commemorating a notable engagement in 1916 in which British forces finally surrendered to the volunteers led by Thomas Ashe. It is a monument with a notable dual image – on one side the figure is in the form of Christ, on the other an insurgent.[2] It was a village where people knew their history.

The farm was not small (171 lush Meath acres) but his father was disabled and money hard to come by. Bob had to work long hours and return to a house with few amenities, certainly no electricity or running water. A friend from childhood speaks of a family that was proud, independent, frugal, one of the few Protestant families in the farming community.[3] Bob grew up very much as the only child of elderly parents, much loved and over-protected, the cause of some of the later insecurities. At the age of 13, he won a Church of Ireland scholarship to Wesley College, and for five years he made the 30-mile round-trip from Ashbourne to school. He had almost three hours to kill between the end of school and the 17:30 Navan bus which dropped him back into Ashbourne, just in time for tea and the Archers on an old battery radio before an evening of reading. He spent those afternoon hours in the YMCA library in Middle Abbey Street, and came across to his contemporaries as 'bookish and preoccupied'. And it was in that library that he formed a lifetime's fascination with maps, with what old maps could *unintentially* tell us as well as intentionally tell us. This deep concern with material culture and a sense of place went deep, almost certainly informed by childhood on a farm and in a spartan farmhouse. One contemporary remembers that as a schoolboy, walking from school to the YMCA, Bob would regularly stop at every travel agency and collect as many brochures as possible so that he could find out about, and visualise, exotic places hither and yon.

He moved on from Wesley to TCD, still commuting from home (by bus or bicycle) until he won the first foundation scholarship in History in 1959, and completing a distinguished undergraduate career by winning the Dunbar Ingram Prize in 1960 and the Alison Phillips Medal, although a First Class degree (still almost as rare as a hen's tooth) eluded him. He wrote for (and edited) student magazines and boasted of his journalistic achievements in later c.v.s.[4]

In 1961, he began research at TCD for a doctorate with Theo Moody on Plantation (1607–41) in the counties of Armagh and Cavan, and from 1962 he combined research with piecemeal and part-time work at Magee, then linked to TCD, and Queen's University Belfast. His papers contain carbon-copies of letters of applications to universities across the island of Ireland as he looked for a permanent position in the golden age of many posts, already complaining (as in a c.v. dated 1964) that 'material gathering has now reached an advanced stage. The demands of lecturing have this year imposed a halt, but I hope after the intensive round up of sources during the coming summer to complete the thesis in about a year.' This hyper-conscientiousness was to be a blessing and a curse over the next 45 years. In the event, the dissertation was submitted five years later for a TCD PhD. It was awarded an MLitt as a superior kind of antiquarianism. The magnitude of this injustice can now be seen by us all, since the dissertation, warts and all, is being published simultaneously with this collection, edited by Dr David Edwards. But for a humble and anxiety-ridden personality like Bob's, it was a devastating blow. Nothing could kill his passion for history and for the love of the chase, but it further limited his ability to complete and to let go of his work. What is surprising is not that he never completed the books he so much wanted to write, but that he published so much.

This volume brings together a selection of his more significant scholarly works. There are many more, however these are, on the whole, shorter (one to three pages in length) or designed for the wider public, not strictly academic.[5] The most extraordinary of these is the lavishly-illustrated 80 page account of the Strabane barony during the Ulster Plantation. This was one of those projects on which Bob had worked with local enthusiasts and 'amateurs' (as Bob called them) and indeed there are eight authors altogether of 28 short sections, ten written by Bob and four others co-written by him and one or more of the others. This too has now happily been republished and is a handsome pendant to this volume.[6] To those scholarly essays previously published, I have added one major unpublished essay which was in an editable form. It offers a summary of Bob's view of the impact of plantation on two counties about which he otherwise did not write – Antrim and Down – and precisely because a central theme of his work is to look at the distinctive impact of plantation on people and land in each part of Ulster, the essay is of first importance. It is also one of his best pieces. There is a saying in Cambridge that students need to learn supervisor hand as well as secretary and court hands; and Bob's handwriting was deceptively elegant, concealing many ambiguities. I am grateful to Ms Nvard Chalikyan for her help in deciphering this text. That her own homeland of Nagorno Karabakh (Armenia) has a history of occupation and plantation even more bloodstained than Ulster was a help. He would have made something of the irony.

There were other manuscripts of unpublished lectures and essays in Bob's papers that were considered for publication, but none was complete, and all broke off at a certain point into jottings and bullet-points, at which juncture footnoting also broke down. There is an especially interesting lecture on 'The origins of tobacco in Ireland, 1600–41' but seven pages of text degenerate into seven more of jottings. That this 'hobby' and 'sideline'[7] should get such thorough treatment from Exchequer Papers (TNA, E190), State Papers Ireland, English and Irish Port records, Carew Papers and much else, is evidence of what constituted a 'hobby'. Amongst the many very short essays not included here, but representative of the breadth of Bob's interest are pieces on 'a detail in Donegal transport history' (1964), 'the disruption of a Munster plantation exercise' (1970), 'a seventeenth-century Mill in Tyrhugh' (1970), an account of 'Dublin to Boston, 1719' (1971), 'Carew's Survey of Ulster, 1611' (1975), 'John Gwillim and the Dublin Book Trade in 1614' (1991), and 'Scotland and the Atlantic: the voyage of the *Jonet* of Leith, December 1611' (1993). He also contributed seven short entries to the *Oxford Dictionary of National Biography*, including lives of the Protestant settlers and native chieftains.[8]

There were then, tangential ventures into other subjects but always an overwhelming tug back to the story of Ulster between the Flight of the Earls and the rebellion of 1641. This collection reflects the centrifugal force of Plantation Ulster and two of its aspects: patterns of settlement in particular rural and agrarian contexts, and the planting of towns. Both involve a strong sense of material culture and the physicality of cultural engagement. One of the longest essays is a study of a relatively small number of gravestones surviving from the colonial period in just one of the counties (Tyrone). Each had been sought out on heroic expeditions. One friend reports a trip to Inishowen in search of one such gravestone, a trip delayed by cups of tea in Bob's house in Clarendon Street, L'derry[9] and a stop for fish and chips in Moville. By the time Bob and his companion reached the graveyard and, clambering over a wall armed with shovels, began to hack at the ivy covering the grave, it was getting dark. A crowd, suspicious and not a little hostile, gathered. But then a voice from the back called out: 'that's Bob Hunter who lectured me in Coleraine'. Hostility dissolved and collaboration took its place.[10]

He had a lifetime passion for libraries and for the preservation of records of all kinds. He fought tigerishly to preserve the old library at Magee, and I was one of those who suffered as a result of not observing the injunction referred to by Keith Lindley in his funeral address for Bob: 'those in the know found themselves warning others "don't mention the library"'. When Bob's financial fortunes were transformed by the sale of his family farmland for housing development, he became a generous benefactor of a number of libraries, not least in a substantial donation to the Derry and Raphoe Diocesan Library. And he had a very substantial and significant library of his own. I was given a guided tour two weeks before Bob's death and can testify that while the house itself and all its furnishings were much neglected (to put it mildly), the library was magnificently housed. (The chaos and disorder is wonderfully captured in the story of what happened when an RUC officer, investigating a burglary next door, came round to see if Bob had seen or heard anything that might help the investigation. Bob opened the door and the officer, looking beyond Bob, called out to his colleague: 'you had better get round here. You should see what the bastards have done to this house …').[11]

What is published in this volume is, then, the nineteen essays of real substance that Bob produced over a 40-year period from 1964 and the onset of a horrid cancer in 2005. We have arranged them thematically rather than chronologically and between them they cover seven counties in historic pre-partition Ulster together with a cluster of articles on the print trade, focused on Dublin. There can be no doubt that they are emphatically more than the sum of their parts. While Bob was undoubtedly (in terms of a famous distinction made by Laurence Stone in relation to himself and Geoffrey Elton) a truffle-pig rather than a parachutist – that is he found treasure buried deep in the records more than he took in the big picture with a sweep of the eye across a vast landscape, there are insistent themes that come through the very different questions he asked of very different types of evidence for different parts of the province. And so very often, the devil (and the delight) is in the detail. He noticed in Cartwright's muster roll of 1630 not only a concentration of English and Scottish names, but also, as he put it 'the interesting appearance of a body of Welsh names in the estate of the servitor Robert Davies and occasionally elsewhere'.[12] The precision of that sentence, and especially of the appropriately cautious 'occasionally' should be noted. More dramatic is the discussion in the course of his analysis of Donegal Plantation records of the development of clusters of new buildings (long vanished) along riverbanks ('a village of twelve houses and cottages at Ballybofey "inhabited for the most part with British" … [and an] estate on the opposite side of the River Finn "near unto the ford"' (still an identifiable location)), evidence that he walked the area before he wrote about it.[13] And so he was able to notice that a small four-acre plot withheld from the grant made to a former sheriff, Sir Richard Hansard and retained for the Crown, consisted of the land immediately along the riverbank at the confluence of the Deele and the Finn, a crucial strategic point.[14]

This preoccupation with telling detail, the synecdoches that open up the social and cultural history of the Plantation are to be found throughout these essays. Writing about Sir William Cole and the construction of the new plantation town of Enniskillen, he worried away at the sources until they revealed that:

> The town itself mainly followed the line of one main street. By the 1740s, when the first map to survive was published,[15] there was an

intersection not only, necessarily, at the Diamond, but also (nearer the Church) at Middleton Street and Paget Street, but the pre-1641 settlement can scarcely have exceeded fifty houses, many probably of one storey with attic accommodation lit by dormer windows above a second floor which would have been one and half storeys. The detail of one house survives, building having proceeded apace.[16]

The careful use of adverbs and subjunctives allows the careful underlying scholarship to retain its integrity.

Once a detail had been found which needed interrogation, he would research and read away exponentially until he was able to achieve analytical precision. Here he is resolving a puzzle about the date of building of the substantial house at Richhill, County Armagh. Surviving estate evidence is unhelpful, so Bob focused on the chimneys:

Chimneys with recessed semi-circular-headed panels were mainly current in England during the middle decades of the seventeenth century, but the style had a long history. It may have been in the brick style buildings of Francis I (1515–45) around Paris, and earlier in the Loire (Chateaudun, on a wing begun 1502), while Blois itself has a wing finished in 1503, with Gothic tracery in the chimney panels. Though it seems to have a French origin, in Britain it is English and not Scottish, perhaps because French brick styles did not find much favour among the stone-building Scottish patrons and their masons. The style was thus already time-honoured when used at Swakeleys (1629–38), Scole (1655), Moyles Court (Hants, 1660), and in Ireland it must be considered an English style, seen at Brazeel House near Dublin (probably 1650) as well as Richhill. In England a few examples are later seventeenth century, and one (without imposts on the panels) occurs on an early eighteenth-century building (*c.* 1715) at Bourton-on-the-Hill, Glos. The close comparison between Richhill and Brazeel and the English mid-seventeenth-century group – Swakeleys, Scols, Moyles Court – are the strongest reasons for considering Richhill a house of the later seventeenth century.

He concludes his account with comments on imitation houses built in New England.[17] Here is virtuoso (and relentless) scholarship indeed.

Places and built environment were tactile reminders of the history he studied. But people mattered too: and not just the nobs. Let us return to Enniskillen:

Now as for the town, [Sir William Cole] had taken bonds from twelve burgesses to build their houses this next summer, while 'divers carpenters and other artificers that purpose to settle there' were about the works then in hand. He had himself provided for the making of 300,000 bricks and 'tile proportionate', with 'good store' of timber for the works of the corporation. For all this work in fact, quite a number of craftsmen – possibly even from London – must have been engaged by Cole; Irish labourers may also have been employed there. Some hint as to who might have had a part in laying out the town comes from a witness to an Enniskillen deed in April 1616; one John Widdowes. Widdowes, or Woodhouse, now in Ireland, was a man with a new scientific training of the age with some link to Gresham College in London, and may have been at this stage in some way in Cole's employ.[18]

So locating people in their precise time and space was another passion and imperative. No-one has captured with such precision the interlocking economic, geopolitical and cultural forces bearing down on Rory O'Donnell between 1603 and 1607 which culminated in his catastrophic miscalculation in leaving Ireland;[19] or got close to the heart of the mental worlds of disappointed military adventurers like Ralph Bingley, destabilising a world that was in danger of being pacified, rendering him redundant. Bob revelled in detail and in how unexpected conjunctions or contingencies explain puzzles in the past.[20] Here he is unravelling how we need to get beyond simple lists of freeholders to understand why what happened was not what was supposed to happen. He looks first at a list of six names proposed for 3,000 acres of Fishmongers' Company land in 1617. Some were military men, like 'Captain' Vaughan, others were merchants owed money by the company (Thomas Haward or Hayward). Some never arrived to make good their claim, some were objected to by the Irish Society, and there was great squabbling among them about who got the best land, aided by the fact that one of them was a skilled cartographer. Painful and painstaking reconstruction allows Bob to conclude that

> What happened presents a pattern of substitution, with many of the actual freeholders not being exclusively linked to the estate but rather mainly being people who lived in or near Derry and having also other interests. Thus although Captain Vaughan was indeed denied a freehold, his relative James received one – at Ballyrory – but immediately in 1619 he sold it to Thomas Skipton who, himself a building contractor it would seem, was at this point establishing himself with many acres of land on both the Goldsmiths' and Grocers' estates a few miles opposite Derry and who, a persistent tradition has it, had been killed by some of the Irish in the early 1620s. Certainly he was dead by 1624, leaving a son, also Thomas,

a child under age who in the 1630s was to attend Sidney Sussex College, Cambridge and then to follow the law at Gray's Inn in London. These were not the conditions for establishing a subplantation of settler tenant farmers in the southern part of the estate and it looks likely that the former owners, the O Harrons, remained in occupation as rent payers of some kind up to 1641.[21]

Wow! And so it goes on. Bob revelled in the detail and sometimes was overwhelmed by it. But most of the time it gave him an entirely unique and persuasive ability not simply to describe but to evaluate a society at a pivotal point in its history, an irruption with profound consequences for the present as well as for the past.

Bob was a driven man, who set himself impossible goals and set up even more obstacles in his own path than others put there. He yoked a droll precision to a deep love of communicating what he knew to very different audiences. He had a gift for friendship, a generosity to those who had 'the root of the matter in them', a passion for truth. Only twice did he try to pull all that he knew together, first in the essay we publish here for the first time as chapter 1 and simply entitled 'The Ulster Plantation', an essay co-written with Raymond Gillespie around 1984 and intended as the introduction to a collection of photocopied documents being prepared for the Teachers' Centre in Belfast. The other is a mere 676 words written by Bob for a BBC website. The text is still to be found online, as is a recording of Bob reading those 676 words, and summarising his life's work.[22] To hear again that voice, so characteristic, so inimitable, at once warm and wily, slow and deliberate and yet so anxious to say more than there is time for, so full of droll precision, is a vital way to remember him as it was to get to know him. We print off the words themselves below. But we encourage anyone who knew Bob or, having read this book, wishes he or she had known him, to listen to him reading these words. They are at http://www.bbc.co.uk/history/british/plantation/transcripts/sm01_t01.shtml.*

---

* As of the time of the reprint of this volume, the link provided above is no longer operational. The associated webpage www.bbc.co.uk/history/british/plantation/settlement/index.shtml is archived and readers may also have trouble accessing the audio file contained therein. Please refer to www.therjhcollection.com (forthcoming) for any alternative audiovisual records for as long as they remain available.

APPENDIX

Settlement Map
By R.J. Hunter

We are looking at a map of Ulster as a whole which throws light on change in land ownership there in the early seventeenth century. In the first place, it gives a summary outline of the distribution of the land to the different categories of grantees across the six counties involved in the formal plantation in Ulster in 1610. In these counties, the undertakers and the Londoners received probably somewhat over 40 per cent of the acreage of the land. The servitors received about 15 per cent of the acreage and the native Irish were restored to perhaps some 20 per cent of the land. Church-owned land of various forms accounted for perhaps 20 per cent of the acreage also. Small areas of land were also provided for various cultural purposes – to endow a grammar school in each county and to support the new university, Trinity College in Dublin. (Provision made for the establishment of towns was also very important).

Of the undertakers, about 60 were of English origin, some 60 were Scottish from the lowlands, and there were also about 60 servitor grantees, mainly former military men. The Irish grantees numbered about 290 in all, but very many of these were people restored to just small estates, with perhaps only about 20 or 30 receiving really large grants.

In organisational terms, the individual grantees – for example the Scottish and the English undertakers – were grouped together in sub-divisions of counties known as 'baronies' and this gives the Ulster plantation its regional character. The Londonderry Plantation embraced one newly-created county, granted to the city of London which, through a committee known as the Irish Society, built the two towns of Coleraine and Londonderry, and which allocated the rest of the land in estates to the London mercantile organisations – the twelve livery companies, such as the Grocers, Fishmongers etc – who were themselves undertaker equivalents.

The ownership of the land is different from its occupation and some areas of land and estates became more highly-colonised by tenantry than others. County Monaghan was not included in the official plantation because in 1591 its land ownership had been reorganised, mainly amongst the Irish themselves, though with a significant number of new English owners too, and their numbers were to increase in the early seventeenth century. The rationale for this reorganisation in 1591 had been to diminish the autonomy and independent power of an Ulster Gaelic lord, MacMahon.

Two other counties, both close to England and Scotland, did not form part of the official plantation because their ownership had already been redesigned beforehand in the years from 1603. McDonnell, the Earl of Antrim, was confirmed in the ownership of a massive area (about a third of a million acres) in County Antrim – the area known as The Glens and The Route – stretching from just north of Carrickfergus to Dunluce. The ownership of Clandeboye, an O'Neill acquisition from earlier times, and stretching both north and south of Belfast where there had been an O'Neill castle, was radically changed at this time: because English landowners, including Sir Arthur Chichester and other military men (many of them like himself from County Devon) acquired estates here in the northern part of it. While in the southern part of Clandeboye, which includes Bangor and Newtownards, two Lowland Scots Sir James Hamilton and Sir Hugh Montgomery, both minor courtiers to James I, received massive estates. The former O'Neill chieftains of Clandeboye were restored to about a third of this area at the same time.

In south County Down, much land remained in Irish ownership – for example, by the McCartans and Magennises – but some English owners were also establishing themselves there and their share gradually increased; while based in Newry, the Bagenals (there since the middle of the sixteenth century) retained a large estate. The descendants of some old Anglo-Norman settlers retained land in south County Down also. Where ownership actually changed in these counties, very substantial colonisation of the land ensued both by Lowland Scots and indeed English tenantry.

---

[1] I am grateful to Keith Lindley for allowing me to draw on his funeral address given in St Columb's Cathedral, Londonderry in October 2007.

[2] http://www.meath.ie/Tourism/MeathsTownandVillages/Ashbourne/

[3] For stories about Bob's early life I am grateful to Laura Houghton (Bob's daughter) for sharing with me letters written by George Matthews and Biddy Philip as well as Keith Lindley's funeral address.

[4] Laura Houghton has made available to me c.v.s for jobs and for promotions (denied) in 1963, 1964, 1965, 1981, 1984, 1986 and 1995.

[5] A selection of his remaining articles will soon be available for viewing at www.therjhuntercollection.com, while his research notes are held at the Public Record Office of Northern Ireland (PRONI).

[6] Robert J. Hunter (ed.), *Strabane Barony during the Ulster Plantation 1607–1641* (Ulster Historical Foundation, 2011).

[7] There is a characteristic pencil note in the top right-hand corner of the MS: 'tell them this has just been a hobby of mine pursued as a sideline in London. They will discover that I haven't got very far with it.' (He understates the case!) The paper was given to the Post-medieval archaeology conference in Derry, 2004, organised by the Carrickfergus Excavations Project.

[8] His essays in the *Oxford Dictionary of National Biography* are of: Caulfeild, Toby, first Baron Caulfeild of Charlemont; Cole, Sir William; Hamilton, James, first Viscount Clandeboye; Lambert [Lambart], Oliver, first Baron Lambart of Cavan; O'Cahan, Sir Donnell

Ballagh [Domhnall Ballach Ó Catháin]; Paulet, Sir George. (I have viewed them at http://www.oxforddnb.com/). Curiously he wrote only one life for the *Dictionary of Irish Biography*, a 1,000 word life of John Robinson Leebody, one of the fathers of Magee College, a man who, in Bob's droll and self-referential words, 'he worked at one of the peripheries of academic life in Ireland for over sixty years' .

9 L'derry was Bob's invariable way of dealing with the Derry/Londonderry problem.

10 I am grateful to Laura Houghton, Bob's daughter, for this anecdote, which she in turn got from Sam Burnside.

11 I owe this wonderful story to Billy Kelly.

12 See below, ch. 5, p. 105.

13 See below, ch. 3, p. 67. And at ch. 3, p. 85 see his lavish thanks to thirteen persons for their help 'in various ways, as well as to many people in Donegal who assisted with investigations on the ground'.

14 Ibid, pp 53–4 and 83, n27.

15 Reproduced below, ch. 8, p. 213–14.

16 Ibid, ch. 8, pp 212–14.

17 See below, ch. 12, pp 328–30.

18 See below, ch. 8, p. 214.

19 See below, ch. 2, pp 11–39.

20 See below, ch. 4. pp 88–98.

21 See below, ch. 7, p. 155.

22 Archived at http://www.bbc.co.uk/history/british/plantation/transcripts/sm01_t01.shtml. This is from the BBC British History website, and consists of a map of early seventeenth-century Ulster, with both text and audio accompaniments.

PUBLICATIONS
OF R.J. HUNTER
(1964–2009)

Works published in this collection are in **bold**

(with F.H.A. Aalen), 'The estate maps of Trinity College: an introduction and annotated catalogue, *Hermathena* 98 (1964), pp 85–96.

(with F.H.A. Aalen), **'Two Early Seventeenth-Century Maps of Donegal'**, *Journal of the Royal Society of Antiquaries of Ireland* 94 (1964), pp 199–202 [below, ch. 6].

'A detail in Donegal transport history', *Donegal Annual* 4:1 (1964), pp 83–6.

'Rowan Hamilton's *Lectures on Quaternions*', *The Irish Book* 3 (1964), pp 14–16.

'Fragments of the civil survey of counties Kerry, Longford and Armagh', *Analecta Hibernica* 24 (1967), pp 227–31.

'An Ulster Plantation Town, Virginia', *Breifne: Journal of the Cumann Seanchais Bhreifne*, 4 (1970), pp 43–51 [below ch. 16].

'The disruption of a Munster Plantation enterprise', *Journal of the Cork Historical and Archaeological Society,* 75 (1970), pp 158–60.

'A seventeenth-century mill in Tyrugh', *Donegal Annual* 9 (1970), pp 238–40.

'Dublin in Boston, 1719', *Eire-Ireland* 6 (1971), pp 18–24.

'Catholicism in Meath, *c.* 1622', *Collecteana Hibernica,* 14 (1972 for 1971), pp 7–12.

'Towns in the Ulster Plantation', *Studia Hibernica* 11 (1971), pp 40–79 [below ch. 15].

'The settler population in an Ulster Plantation County' *Donegal Annual* 10:2 (1972), pp 124–54 [below ch. 5].

(with C.J. Woods), 'Libraries and Archives: 10, Ireland', *History* 58 (1973), pp 392–6.

'Plantations in Ulster', *PRONI, Education Facsimile series* (1975)

'The English Undertakers in the Plantation of Ulster', *Breifne: Journal of the Cumann Seanchais Bhreifne* 4:16 (1973–5), pp 471–99 [below, ch. 10].

(with T.W. Moody), 'The Ulster Plantation 1609–13: map and commentary', in (eds) T.W. Moody, F.X. Martin and F.J. Byrne, *A new history of Ireland: III, 1534–1691* (Oxford, 1976), pp 198–9.

'Carew's survey of 1611: the voluntary works', *Ulster Journal of Archaeology,* 38 (1975), pp 81–2

(with M. Perceval-Maxwell), 'The muster roll of 1630: county Cavan', *Breifne: Journal of the Cumann Seanchais Bhreifne,* 5 (1978), pp 206–22.

'Sir William Cole and Plantation in Enniskillen, 1607–41', *Clogher Record, Journal of the Clogher Historical Society* 9:3 (1978), pp 336–50 [below, ch. 9]

'Sir Ralph Bingley *c.* **1570–1627: Ulster Planter',** in P. Roebuck (ed.), *Plantation to Partition: essays in Ulster History in honour of J.L. McCracken* (Belfast, 1981), pp 14–28 [below, ch. 4].

(with others: an extra-mural workshop team), *The plantation in Ulster in Strabane Barony, County Tyrone* (NUU, 1982).

'Chester and the Irish Book Trade', *Irish Economic and Social History* 15 (1988), pp 89–93 [below, ch. 19].

'John Gwillim and the Dublin Book Trade in 1614', *The Long Room* 36 (1991), pp 17–18.

'The water bastion and urban renewal in Derry', *The Foyle Civic Trust* 1 (1990), pp 6–8.

'Scotland and the Atlantic', *Mariner's Mirror* 79 (1993), pp 83–4.

'The end of O'Donnell Power' in W. Nolan, L. Ronayne, M. Dunleavy (eds), *Donegal: history and society. Interdisciplinary essays on the history of an Irish county* (Dublin, 1995), pp 229–66 [below, ch. 2].

'Plantation in Donegal', in W. Nolan, L. Ronayne, M. Dunleavy (eds), *Donegal: history and society. Interdisciplinary essays on the history of an Irish county* (Dublin, 1995), pp 283–326 [below, ch. 3]

'Plantation' in R. Welch (ed.), *The Oxford Companion to Irish Literature* (Oxford, 1996), p. 474.

'The Fishmongers' Company of London and the Londonderry Plantation, 1609–41', in G. O'Brien (ed.), *Derry and Londonderry: history and society. Interdisciplinary essays on the history of an Irish county* (Dublin, 1999), pp 205–58 [below, ch. 7].

'Style and Form in Gravestone and Monumental Sculpture in County Tyrone in the seventeenth and eighteenth century', in C. Dillon, H.A. Jefferies (eds), *Tyrone: history and society. Interdisciplinary essays on the history of an Irish county* (Dublin, 2000), pp 291–325 [below, ch. 13].

'County Armagh: A map of plantation', in A.J. Hughes and W. Nolan (eds), *Armagh: history and society. Interdisciplinary essays on the history of an Irish county* (Dublin, 2001), pp 265–294 [below, ch. 10].

'Sir William Cole, the town of Enniskillen and Plantation County Fermanagh', in E. Murphy, W. Roulston (eds), *Fermanagh: history and society. Interdisciplinary essays on the history of an Irish county* (Dublin, 2004), pp 105–45 [below, ch. 8].

'The Bible and the Bawn: an Ulster planter inventorised', in C. Brady and J. Ohlmeyer (eds), *British Interventions in Early Modern Ireland* (Cambridge, 2005), pp 116–34 [below, ch. 18].

'John Franckton (d. 1620): printer, publisher and bookseller in Dublin', in C. Benson, S. Fitzpatrick (eds), *That woman: studies in Irish bibliography – a festschrift for Mary 'Paul' Pollard* (Dublin, 2005), pp 2–26 [below, ch. 17].

(1) Toby Caulfeild, 1st Baron Caulfeild of Charlemont; (2) Sir George Paulet (1553–1608); (3) Sir Donnell Dallagh O'Cahan (d. 1626); (4) Oliver Lambert, 1st Baron Lambert of Cavan (*c.* 1560–1628); (5) James Hamilton, 1st Viscount Clandeboye (*c.* 1560–1644); (6) Cole, Sir William (1563–1653) in C. Matthew and B. Harrison (eds) *Oxford Dictionary of National Biography* (Oxford, 2003), http://www.oxforddnb.com

John Robinson Leebody, in J. McGuire and J. Quinn (eds), *Dictionary of Irish Biography* (9 vols., Cambridge, 2009), http://dib.cup.org

The Ulster Plantation[1]

1. Ulster and the crown in the sixteenth century

The Tudor inheritance in Ireland was not a simple one. Rather than being a unified society by the standards of the day, Ireland in fact was a diverse mix of a number of elements. As far as rural Ireland goes, these can be reduced to two – the areas in which the Norman conquest had proved lasting (the Anglo-Irish areas) and the areas in which Gaelic society survived. In addition, there were the port towns – Limerick, Cork, Waterford for example – Anglo-Irish in culture, governed by mayors and corporations under medieval royal charters, none very large but all of them focuses of trade for their hinterlands (Norman and Gaelic) with England and continental Europe. The pattern of local government based on the county which was familiar to most of England, operated only in small areas of Ireland and indeed in much of Ireland, counties, which symbolised a relationship between central and local, had not been created at all. Also, at this time, the provinces – themselves the descendants of the pre-Norman Gaelic regional balance of power – had not emerged in their modern form and had no pronounced importance in their own right.

There was indeed a central administration, based on Dublin castle built by King John just after the Norman conquest, but the area directly answerable to it was restricted to the Anglo-Irish parts of Leinster nearby, while much of Norman Ireland, for example the earldoms of Ormond and Desmond, was organised in lordships or liberties, which had parallels with the lordships in the north of England or on the English borders with Wales.

Beyond this amorphous frontier lay the world of Gaelic Ireland – a series of autonomous Gaelic lordships. In these, political authority was exercised by a chief or lord and the chieftainship was likely to be disputed, often with violence, between various branches of the ruling family. Under them were the smaller landowning families, called freeholders by the English, from whom they exacted customary dues and services, though the chieftains had no right of ownership over their lands. Furthermore as Gaelic society had evolved a small group of more powerful lords had established regional dominances thereby making some of the lords their sub-chieftains or *uirrí*.

Changes in power could result in some of these smaller lords becoming the vassals of a different overlord. There were thus numerous sources of tension within the Gaelic world. The assimilation of this Gaelic world, operating under its own legal system, into a centralised system based on English law was the most intractable problem the sixteenth-century Tudor regime in Ireland encountered. Yet that is what they sought to do from the 1540s when, after the downfall of the earls of Kildare as royal governors, the crown had already adopted a policy of ruling Ireland directly by means of English-born lord deputies.

A number of factors made early sixteenth-century Ulster a local variant on the pattern so far outlined: the Anglo-Irish area was very limited, the Gaelic lordships were perhaps stronger and had perhaps been less influenced by Anglo-Norman culture than elsewhere, Ulster was less urbanised and had less contact with England and Ulster was prone to be deeply influenced by its contacts with highland and island Scotland. The contraction of the Anglo-Irish area – the old Earldom of Ulster essentially in Antrim and Down – resulted from the Gaelic resurgence of the later middle ages and, more significantly, the simultaneous intrusion of the Scottish MacDonnells into Antrim. To drive out these Scots and to revive the earldom was a pre-occupation of government during much of the sixteenth century, accounting for the strong garrisoning of Carrickfergus, the granting of monastic land at Newry to Nicholas Bagnal in 1549 and a range of plantation plans in the 1560s and 1570s as well. The major Gaelic lordships within Ulster, both O Neill and O Donnell, had also established dynastic alliances with Scottish clans from whom they drew mercenary forces. Thus much of Ulster fitted into the often hostile and internationalised relations of England and Scotland as a whole, though these were to improve from the late 1580s under James VI who also had an interest in finding means, including plantation, of subordinating his own outlying subjects. However in the 1590s Ulster was to become a factor in Anglo-Spanish relations.

The initial expansionist thrust of government, in the 1540s, towards the Gaelic lords was assimilative: the threat of conquest would be removed if they took out land titles under the crown. But this fell foul of the internal dynastic tensions when Shane O Neill disputed the succession to his father Conn, first Earl of Tyrone and the more impatient lord deputies of the 1550s and '60s waged war against him. Thereafter the move towards Anglicisation in Ulster faltered, the plantation schemes, intended to be examples of English civility, proved abortive and Turlogh Luineach O Neill, head of another collateral branch of the dynasty, assumed the chieftainship and dominance in mid-Ulster. Administrative innovation for the regions concentrated on Munster and Connacht where presidential councils, headed by Englishmen, were established, c. 1570. By the mid 1580s substantial progress for English authority in these provinces seemed to be assured when in the former a major government-planned plantation was introduced while in Connacht lords and landowners alike had been got both to pay a land tax to government and to agree to financial arrangements between themselves which were designed to demilitarise the lordships and to replace the lord/client relationship of the past with one whereby the client (or freeholder) paid instead a money rent to the lord.

Lord Deputy Perrott (1584–88) sought to apply something like the Connacht framework to Ulster, though it was really his successor, Fitzwilliam, who applied it radically in the case of Monaghan in 1591. Perrott, by creating Hugh O Neill earl of Tyrone, effectively divided the O Neill lordship in two. He also detached some of the smaller lords from their overlords – O Hanlon and O Doherty for example – when they received knighthoods and patents of their 'countries' to hold from the crown and he proceeded with the creation of counties. It was the Monaghan 'settlement' which embodied the most dramatic policy of integrating a lordship under the crown. The chieftainship was terminated with the execution of McMahon. Substantial estates were confirmed to some half dozen landowners, mainly the heads of the leading branches of the McMahons (who might otherwise have competed for the lordship) to hold from the crown in perpetuity with an annual payment, and 200–300 of the lesser owners were likewise confirmed as freeholders with an annual payment both to the crown and to one or other of the greater grantees. Only a few settlers were introduced but the lands which directly supported the chieftainship were allocated to the garrison at Monaghan.

The fear that social engineering on the Monaghan model, which might gain acceptance through the vested interest in it of the smaller landowners, might be extended over all Ulster precipitated the Nine Years' War. With the land question resolved through the substitution of the crown for the chieftainship, the basic programme of Anglicisation might be advanced: English law introduced, the reformation promoted, an education programme developed and firm controls established. O Neill, who meanwhile was fighting a succession battle with Turlogh Luineach and seeking to subordinate the other collateral O Neills, clung for long to an older model of integration whereby he would hold extensive lands as earl under the crown but with minimum changes. O Donnell's position was simpler: encouraged by the local bishops, he turned directly to Spain for military assistance. The outcome was a confederacy to offer the crown of Ireland to a Spanish king. But they lost the war.

2. The plantation plan

It had been the threat of change and mistrust of government intention which brought about the Nine Years' War. Support for 'natural' leaders in a traditionalist society made the war possible, but as it went on the internal tensions showed and a number of sub-chiefs and collateral heads surrendered on promise of their lands from the crown. A few received them. The peace after 1603, however, restored Hugh O Neill as earl with control over a very extensive area and created Rory O Donnell, Earl of Tyrconnell. But victory in the war had enhanced the control of Dublin and now significant changes were introduced. The assize judges began circuits into the Ulster counties, where small garrisons ware retained in some of the forts established during the war period. Monastic dissolutions were carried out. Protestant episcopal appointments were made, notably George Montgomery as bishop of Derry, Raphoe and Clogher to replace unreformed Catholic bishops who had died or been killed, as was Redmond O Gallagher of Derry, in the course of the war. These were expected to engage in the conversion of the Ulster Irish. In particular, the military and political authority of the lords over their followers based on the customary duties and services was to be terminated and the lords got to recognise the smaller landholders as freeholders paying money rents in return for a guaranteed security of tenure. In short, something not unlike the Monaghan 'settlement' of 1591 should be extended over all of Gaelic Ulster.

But the prospects for the transformation (or Anglicisation) of Ulster and its people in accordance with these specific strategies were not to be tested. In response to these pressures and burdened by post-war financial problems, the earls fled in 1607. Their flight was adjudged to be treason and preparations for plantation were immediately put in hand. Six counties – Donegal, Derry, Tyrone, Armagh, Cavan and Fermanagh – were considered to have escheated, or forfeited, to the crown mainly because of the Flight of the Earls and the rights of the freeholders were disregarded. Why the draconic decision for plantation? Security was a major factor. Although Ulster was now quiet and peace had been made with Spain (allowing the American colony in Virginia to go forward at the same time) circumstances might change and insurrection and invasion recur. Plantation was, anyhow, not a new policy. The precedent of the Munster scheme indicates that governments were quite prepared to adopt it when a legal opportunity presented itself. It was in fact expected to serve several ends at once: the assured introduction of English common law and the regular system of local government, a sure foothold for the reformation and the English language, economic development and a consequent sound basis for taxation and both the submergence and transformation of the native population deprived of their own leadership.

After some two years of planning the new order was inaugurated in 1610. In five counties (excluding Londonderry) a highly systematic plan was followed. The new settler owners – English and Lowland Scots – were grouped together by type in baronies which were sub-divisions of the counties. They were to receive estates ranging from 1,000 to 2,000 acres. There were two types – undertakers and servitors. The servitors, some 60 in all, were mainly English ex-army officers and they were to be allowed to take the Irish as tenants on their estates. The undertakers were civilian grantees, 110 in all, half from Scotland and half from England, coming new to Ireland and baronies were allocated to groups of them either English or Scottish, together.

The Londonderry plantation was a special case. Here the forfeited land was allocated to the London merchant companies under the supervision of an umbrella body, the Irish Society, itself responsible for the new towns at Derry and Coleraine. These new owners between them appear to have got almost 50 per cent of the land, varying from county to county. In all counties former church land was confirmed to the Protestant bishops and glebe land was specially set aside to be allocated to the parish clergy. Provision through landed endowment was also made for the establishment of settler towns, mostly at traditional sites and for a grammar school in each county and, in addition, the new university at Dublin (TCD) was granted a substantial acreage. Irish grantees were also included but the grants made to them were in most cases very small and their number across all the six counties, some 300, was no greater than the total of freeholders in the one county of Monaghan in 1591. They got almost one-fifth of the land but, since for security reasons they were placed in the same baronies as the servitors, many had to transplant from their former homes.

So much for the ownership arrangements. The actual responsibility for colonisation fell to the undertakers in their baronies and to the London companies. The Irish population as a whole was to be removed entirely from these areas (they might live under any of the other owners) and a replacement English and Lowland Scottish colony introduced. Thus not only were the Irish landowners to be segregated within each county but the tenant and landless Irish were to be segregated as well. The colony the undertakers and companies should introduce was to be on the scale of 10 families or 24 adult males for each 1,000 acres of their estates and rules governing the kinds of tenancies these should receive, following English models, were laid down. Furthermore they were to be planted in villages near the strongholds the landlords were to build. The minimum size of colony thus to be introduced was in the order of 5,000 adult males.

3. Antrim and Down

Antrim and Down were not included in the official plantation plan. In the sixteenth century they were not ruled by the great Gaelic lords – O Neill, O Donnell, Maguire – but by numerous smaller lords, the McCartans and Magennises in south Down, the O Neills of Clandeboy in north Down and south Antrim and the Scottish MacDonnells in north Antrim. At the end of the war in 1603 many of these lords were confirmed in possession of their lands, but some were subsequently forced to sell part of them through indebtedness. They found ready markets in Scots and Englishmen keen to avail of new opportunities in Ulster at a time when the main plantation scheme was not yet conceived. Sir James Hamilton and Sir Hugh Montgomery established themselves in north Down and in south-west Antrim, Sir Fulke Conway and Sir Hugh Clotworthy, both ex-army officers, received grants of land.

As the parts of Ulster nearest to Scotland, Antrim and Down were the natural places for Scottish migrants to settle, making them generally better settled than the rest. The settlers mainly lived near the coast, in north Down and the Ards and along the Antrim coastline, moving down the Six Mile Water valley and the Lagan valley to live on the better land inland. As they established themselves they began to develop the countryside. New towns were built, including Belfast and Bangor, and older towns such as Carrickfergus and Newry redeveloped.

The Scottish and English settlers brought with them ideas and practices from their homes. In particular, the Scots brought their religion: presbyterianism. At first the liberal anglican archbishop of Armagh, James Ussher, accepted presbyterian clergy into his churches as they had many points in common with the anglicans. Gradually, because of developments in England and Scotland, presbyterians were less welcome. Governments feared they might be disloyal since they did not acknowledge the King as head of the church and tried to impose an oath of loyalty on them, the Black Oath, in 1638. In 1638–40 there were widespread riots in Down and many Scots left Ulster to return home A few years earlier one group under their minister, Robert Blair, had tried to go to America in a ship, the *Eagle's Wing* built in Belfast, but were forced back by storms.

The main difference between the settlement in Antrim and Down and elsewhere was that it was not shackled by the formal government regulations for the planted counties. This gave the settlers considerable freedom to exploit their lands according to their ambitions. With no controls on the size of estates as in the planted counties, one man, the earl of Antrim, could hold almost all of north County Antrim, and two, Hamilton and Montgomery, could run north Down between them. Thus because of these differences, men could become extremely wealthy – more so than in the other counties – and hence the success of the east Ulster settlement was assured, so that even into the nineteenth century Antrim and Down were the heartland of the Ulster Scots.

4. The countryside

We know little about the Ulster countryside before the settlers arrival. The evidence of late sixteenth-century maps and descriptions suggests a mixed landscape. Large areas of south Derry, the shores of Lough Neagh and the Lagan valley were densely wooded and large bogs extended over much of mid-Antrim and mid-Tyrone. The population was low and the workforce too small to reclaim these areas. There was much good land also. In mid-Armagh, north Antrim and Derry corn was grown extensively. Its destruction by the English army during the war against Hugh O Neill had caused famines. Livestock, mainly cattle, were the most important part of farming; in livestock farming areas there were few enclosed fields and cattle were often driven between summer and winter pastures. Where corn was grown the land was fenced to keep out livestock.

When the settlers arrived they began to alter this countryside dramatically. Since timber was profitable large areas of forest were cleared and exported as timber for barrels. They also used timber to build their own houses. Irish houses, to judge by drawings on maps, were relatively simple in design with poor chimney systems, although there were also stone castles built by the great lords in the sixteenth century following the medieval tower house model. There were also some fine monastic buildings.

By 1641 the Ulster landscape was dotted with a variety of house types. In some areas where stone was available this was used while elsewhere, where timber was plentiful, it gave rise to 'Tudor' style half-timbered houses. On the farms attached to these houses more fields were enclosed so that in some areas the landscape began to take on the patchwork appearance of the fields today. The English landlords built houses conforming to current styles protected by bawns, the Scots more after the castellated tower house model.

The settlers also brought agricultural practices and ideas from their homes. They recognised, for example the need for maps to know the exact extent of their estates. One of the most important map-makers, Thomas Raven, worked for a number of planters. They introduced new breeds of cattle and sheep from England and Scotland which produced better meat and more corn was grown. This does not mean that the settlers abandoned the older Gaelic agricultural practices, including ploughing by attaching the plough to a horse's tail, but where appropriate they continued them. They also kept the old land divisions, the ballyboes, which were often the same as the townland divisions operated by the settlers.

Others apart from farmers lived in the countryside. Many people carried on small industries to supplement their farming income. Linen yarn was being produced in some quantities. Iron working was carried on on a large scale in the Lagan valley and Tyrone, areas with an abundance of the necessary materials of timber, iron ore and water. Tanning of leather was also widely practiced in the countryside, using the skins of cattle and the bark of trees rejected by the iron workers.

The early seventeenth century, then, saw significant developments in rural Ulster when both economy and landscape were changed to form the basis of the modern countryside.

5. Towns

Sixteenth-century Ulster was amongst the least urbanised areas of Ireland. There were some important medieval towns such as the ecclesiastical centres of Armagh and Downpatrick, the ports of Ardglass, Newry and Carrickfergus and the market towns of Cavan and Dungannon. Many of the Gaelic lords probably also had small settlements around their principal castles, as in the case of Enniskillen. Most of the early towns were small groups of buildings around a church, a monastery or a castle. It was at many of these places, in decline or virtual extinction since the late medieval population contraction, that the planters built their new urban settlements. Only a few, such as Charlemont and Mount Norris which originated as military bases in the 1590s, were on sites without some such tradition, though many of the villages the planters were required to build must have been on new sites.

With the coming of the new plantation order, towns became more important. Towns were necessary for local and national government. As boroughs, many returned MPs to the Dublin parliament and in a local context towns were the location of jails and the meeting place for the lord's manor courts and the central government's court of quarter sessions and assizes. As the economy grew markets were needed in which both settlers and natives could sell surplus produce to pay the rent and buy goods they could not produce themselves. As a result over 150 small market centres grew up in Ulster between plantation and the rising in 1641.

Some of the new towns were planned such as Derry and Coleraine. The Irish Society laid out these by the most modern standards of town planning so that they had a regular 'grid iron' pattern of streets. Both also were walled towns – a form that had already disappeared in the rest of Europe. Other towns were extensions of older settlements such as Carrickfergus which met the increase in town size by expanding its walls. A third group were new creations which lacked formal planning. Belfast, for example, built by the Chichester landlords, developed along the river Farset, a tributory of the Lagan, with little planning. The pattern was much the same with villages. In some areas, such as County Londonderry, where there was relatively tight landlord control villages were built around a crossroads in a '+' plan or along a street from the landlord's house, to form the centre of the estate. Elsewhere they could be more haphazardly arranged.

Most of the plantation towns were small by contemporary standards – with the exceptions of Derry, Coleraine, Belfast and Carrickfergus, they rarely exceeded 30–40 houses. Yet they offered a wide range of services. Schools were established in many and there were even a few lawyers and medical doctors in the main Ulster towns. At a lower social level, carpenters, masons, shoemakers, tanners, weavers, tailors, butchers and more general 'shopkeepers' all featured in most Ulster towns. The stocks of one shop keeper in Belturbet were hops, iron, steel, stockings, tobacco and various types of cloth. Also a merchant class was emerging in the ports.

While the early seventeenth-century Ulster towns were small they had a wide range of services available. They were handicapped in many ways – for example unlike most English towns they had no land attached to them from which to draw income – yet they managed to establish themselves firmly to become an enduring legacy of the Ulster plantation.

6. The impact of plantation
Politically, the importance of the plantation lies just in the government decision to confiscate. The Ulster scheme was a major stage in the development of the policy of plantation which had the result that by 1641 over one-third of the land of Ireland had passed into settler ownership. Since landownership was a source of power, each increase in the share of the emerging settler class enhanced its position. So if plantation integrated Ulster into a unified Ireland it was an Ireland of which the new settler class increasingly had the control. Furthermore, plantation achieved one of the central aims of government: through it Ulster became a guaranteed source of government taxation. Also both the English system of law and the reformation church became effective in Ulster. Plantation thus brought very fundamental change.

Over the entire planted area the colony had grown to some 15,000 adult males by 1630 and continued to grow for much of that decade. The immigration, with its own natural increase, may then have been in the order of 40,000 men, women and children by 1641. That may have placed it somewhere between 1:5 and 1:10 in the population as a whole. In the six escheated counties serious errors in the measurement of the land in 1609 meant the estates the settlers received were substantially larger than the 1,000–2,000 acres intended. The result was fewer grantees and a consequently overall lower tenant requirement than there might have been. Also, the colony as it actually became established tended to bunch or group with some areas becoming more densely settled than others. In addition the Irish population was not in practice uniformly removed from the undertakers' estates. Thus while as the colony increased on these estates their position worsened, it did not result in their total exclusion.

The plantation introduced the whole system of English land law – the lease, the manor, the manor court. It also produced a much more commercially-orientated society in Ulster. While we cannot separate out the share of settler and native in productive activity, it is clear that there was a substantial increase in productivity in the period 1610–41. This is indicated by the growth in the export trade of the ports. It is more difficult to assess its effect in transforming the Ulster Irish, however the English language made some progress in Ulster at this time and there were some conversions to Protestantism. At the same time, the reformation church that emerged in early seventeenth-century Ulster was largely staffed by English and Scottish clergy and largely concentrated its efforts on the English and Scottish settlers.

Plantation overturned the ways of the Gaelic world and produced a controlled society but not, ultimately, a stable one. While the outbreak of the rising in 1641 was due more to the breakdown in relations between king and subjects in England and Scotland than to the merely local effects of the plantation, many of the Ulster Irish were unhappy with the new order in Ulster as well. To that extent plantation had failed as a method of Anglicisation. Had the earls not fled the slower persuasive processes, under a government strengthened by victory in the Nine Years' War, might well have produced an anglicised Ulster without dispossession. But that is to beg too many questions.

---

[1] Typescript by R.J. Hunter and Raymond Gillespie.

2

The End of O'Donnell Power

When Rory O'Donnell, created earl of Tyrconnell in September 1603, received a patent from the crown of 'all the territories or countries in the precinct of Tyrconnell' the following February, it could appear that he had been handsomely endowed in the pacification which ended the Nine Years' War.[1] To a substantial extent this was, of course, true. The O'Donnells had been, with the O'Neills, leading confederates in a major rebellion (and one which had drawn the Spaniards into Ireland as well) which, though defeated, was being terminated, not with confiscation and plantation but with restoration and the creation of an earldom. The explanation is not far to find. The crown was seeking a way to end the Irish dimension of the broader, protracted and expensive Anglo-Spanish war; it was not inflexibly committed to large-scale plantation as the only solution to its Irish problems.[2]

An examination of the patent reveals, however, that it represented, in a variety of ways, a very substantial curb on O'Donnell power. In the first place, the long-established O'Donnell pretensions to overlordship in areas beyond the main land mass of Donegal (west and south of Lough Swilly) were being overturned. The patent contained specific 'injunction' that the earl and his successors 'should renounce and relinquish all claim or right which they had or might pretend to have over O'Doghertie's and O'Connor Sligoe's countries'. In fact, these claims to political overlordship over a grander region, based on the historic powers of earlier O'Donnell kings but analogous in royal eyes to an exercise of the overmighty practice of bastard feudalism, had extended even further, both southwards and eastwards, than the restriction in the patent would suggest. In 1607 Rory himself asserted that he had been deprived, southwards into Connacht, of long accustomed tributes not only from Sligo but from Tirawley (in Mayo) and Moylurg (in Roscommon), and also from Dartry (in Monaghan) and Fermanagh, both in south Ulster.[3] The claim to overlordship in North Connacht had, indeed, been the breaking point in the crown's negotiations with Manus O'Donnell at the time of surrender and regrant in the early 1540s and the principle was established then that the crown would not normally concede to one lord a permanent overlordship over others beyond the bounds of his own territory.[4] While the establishment of that principle meant that Manus

11

O'Donnell received no patent, the attempt to make it effective in practice proved a slow and protracted one. However, with the establishment of the presidency and council of Connacht and more particularly the composition there in 1585, O'Donnell influence in north Connacht was being curtailed. Similarly, the crown's policy towards the *uirrí* lordships in south Ulster and especially its success in bringing about the 'settlement' of Monaghan in 1591 had major implications for the exercise of any overlordship there by either of the two bigger lords to the north: O'Neill or O'Donnell. These progressive changes being brought about by the crown had contributed to the outbreak of the Nine Years' War, and in the course of it, Rory's brother, Red Hugh, had re-asserted O'Donnell overlordship in north Connacht.[5]

The claim to overlordship, eastward, in O'Doherty's country of Inishowen had been but part of the longstanding dispute of the O'Donnells with the O'Neills as to which of them, Ceneál Conaill or Ceneál nEogain, should control both it and a long stretch of territories on either side of the river Foyle.[6] In the sixteenth century each had sought to maintain their authority on either side of that river by lines of small castles or tower houses. Thus, for example, the O'Donnell strongholds at Carrigans and Mongavlin matched the O'Neill Dunnalong on the Tyrone side.[7] The right to collect tribute from O'Doherty, however, had oscillated between O'Neill and O'Donnell, but apparently, in the early sixteenth century, O'Donnell had secured one strategic advantage: the establishment of a footing in the ecclesiastical enclave at Derry. The building of a small O'Donnell castle at Derry (erected, according to a later account, by O'Doherty on behalf of O'Donnell in lieu of certain duties, on a piece of ground acquired from one of the erenachs there)[8] may possibly have been also done to secure for O'Donnell control of the trade of Lough Foyle.[9] But here too recent change by the government had reduced O'Donnell power. In June 1588 John O'Doherty had been brought to engage in a surrender and regrant agreement whereby he would hold Inishowen directly from the crown,[10] though again Red Hugh O'Donnell won O'Doherty back, 'by the point and edge of the sword' in the words of his biographer Lughaidh O'Clery, in 1592.[11] However, with the landing of an army under Sir Henry Docwra at Lough Foyle in 1600, in what proved to be a decisive strategic move by the crown in the latter stages of the Nine Years' War, Derry became a base from which military operations against the confederates radiated.[12] Also, the military settlement at Derry itself evolved quickly into a small urban plantation which received a charter in July 1604.[13] The loss of this O'Donnell foothold – 'a house in Derry' as Rory later described it[14] – was to be permanent. Furthermore, just as Docwra's military force contributed to the defeat of the confederate rebellion, so also did his diplomacy, which unbared the tensions existing within the Gaelic world. Hence many of the minor adherents to the confederation were brought to surrender on promise of restoration to their lands. In the case of O'Doherty's country, the situation was complicated by the death of Shane (or Sir John) O'Doherty in 1601. Exercising his right of overlordship, Red Hugh O'Donnell nominated one candidate for the succession, while the supporters of another, Cahir, son of Sir John, procured Docwra's backing for him.[15] The subsequent pardon and patent to Sir Cahir of a slightly reduced Inishowen was designed to ensure the termination, once and for all, of O'Donnell influence over it.[16]

Much of the aim of the leading Ulster confederates in rebellion in the 1590s – themselves previously effectively ungoverned lords – had been to procure from the crown in some new form a legitimacy for claims to regional dominance which had been systematically under threat in the 1580s, while they were later to offer their allegiance to Spain, then the most powerful country in the world, promising to obey a Spanish king of Ireland.[17] Apart from the varied political influences over the dependent countries which these claims implied (cemented often by marriage alliances though often difficult to sustain), their implications for the smaller lordships in financial terms have been lost sight of because of the paucity of surviving evidence concerning them. Accounts surviving from the 1620s suggest that the costs of dependency, where it could be enforced, were high: in tribute, O'Doherty's Inishowen should supply O'Donnell with 120 cattle (beeves and milch cows) in the year; in military service, it must provide 60 horse and 120 foot and maintain O'Donnell's bonaghts (mercenary soldiers) 'be they ever so numerous for the space of nine nights'; and in the profits of justice, the *éiric* for killing a man was 168 cows.[18] Put simply, O'Donnell was greatly strengthened while he could enjoy this authority over satellite lords.[19] Now he was to be stripped of these claims.

More important, perhaps, was the nature of the settlement within Tyrconnell itself. The restoration of Rory O'Donnell (the first formally-completed surrender and regrant between the O'Donnells and the crown) needs, then, to be approached from two angles: to see what was granted to him and what was withheld. The two most important reservations in his patent concerned forts and monastic lands. Ever since direct rule in the 1530s, it had been recurrently suggested that the authority of the Dublin government on behalf of the crown over the outlying regions could best be made effective in those areas by a policy of fortification and related small-scale urban plantation within them. While the crown normally baulked at the cost of these proposals,[20] such progress as was made to this end in Ulster was bitterly resented by the Gaelic lords. However, the exigencies of the Nine

Years' War made garrisons and fortifications imperative. Originally intended to be two parts of a single operation directed to both Derry and Ballyshannon, under two military commanders, Sir Henry Docwra and Sir Matthew Morgan (both with experience in the Netherlands), a military intervention in Donegal was brought about in two stages instead. Sir Henry Docwra's naval expedition, from Chester via Carrickfergus, with some 4,000 troops, which landed and fortified at Derry in May 1600 was all that could be achieved then,[21] but after Kinsale, in 1602, the castle at Ballyshannon was occupied by forces under Sir Henry Folliott, who, as a captain from Worcestershire, had been sent to Ireland in 1596 and had succeeded Morgan as colonel of a regiment in October 1601.[22]

Docwra's strategy, both militarily and diplomatically, played a major part in ending the Nine Years' War. Diplomatically, he secured the adhesion, of, amongst others, Niall Garbh O'Donnell, a dynastic competitor of Red Hugh's for power in Donegal; militarily, he occupied or built crucial strongholds in the area stretching between Derry and Lifford and took over other places of strength including the MacSweeney castle at Rathmullan, placing captains with forces within them.[23] Folliott, from his Ballyshannon base, pursued a similar military strategy which included the use of boats on the Erne to assault Maguire.[24]

Although financial constraints ensured that massive military reductions followed the peace in 1603, the importance of this initiative has to be stressed: the crown had now for the first time acquired footholds within the O'Donnell lordship and since these were mostly not new forts in new locations, it had deprived the O'Donnells and also some of their sub-lords of strongholds of immense practical and symbolic importance. When Lord Deputy Mountjoy returned to England in May 1603, he brought with him recommendations about army dispositions which he hoped to 'persuade' were essential; despite the ending of the rebellion and the failure of the associated Spanish invasion, for the future government of Ireland until a programme of social change, 'the reformation of religion and due obedience to the magistrate', were to he 'at least in some good measure settled' there.[25] In the north-west, along with Ballyshannon, Derry, Culmore, Rathmullan and Doe (which must all have been seen as essential against invasion), he felt that Lifford was a place 'most necessary to be held … and guardable with 100 men to be maintained by land annexed to the town' while Coolmacatrean (near Newtowncunningham) was less essential. This question of government installations had to be decided on in London in the autumn of 1603 when the terms for the restoration of Rory O'Donnell, who, along with O'Connor Sligo ('two rebels of greatest power in those parts'), had submitted unconditionally to Mountjoy at Athlone on 14

December 1602,[26] were worked out. The outcome, conveyed in September to the Dublin government (which would have to deal with the implementation), was a compromise. The crown retained Ballyshannon castle and lands annexed to it 'adjoining the fishing there', assessed as 1,000 acres – Derry and Inishowen were, of course, excluded from the regrant – but reserved the right to build in the future any such forts as should he necessary for the 'service of the country'.[27]

The other significant change concerned monastic land. For Ireland, the Henrician policy for the dissolution of the monasteries had not proceeded at the pace of its English equivalent, leaving monasticism, in some form, to survive in the remoter localities. In the later sixteenth century it had furthermore become a recognised tenet of government policy that grants of monastic land, if they could be made effective, could provide one means of inserting controls into these localities. The termon (*tearmann*) lands, with origins in early Irish Christianity, were seen to have the same capacity. However, to the O'Donnells and presumably also their sub-lords, notably the MacSweeneys, monasticism served a dual utility. The lands of the older orders and the termon lands were a source of taxation. Thus it was claimed that the termon of Derry had rendered Red Hugh O'Donnell a tribute of 18 beeves apparently three times a year and Kilmacrenan a 'supply of food' ('24 methers of butter and 40 methers of meal') in each quarter of the year.[28] The newer houses founded and endowed (however sparsely) by the chieftains, such as the Observant Franciscan friary dating from the 1470s at Donegal, as exercises in ecclesiastical patronage, served much wider cultural functions ranging from being places of burial for the O'Donnells to their members being found as part of the lordship's intelligensia engaged in its diplomacy.[29] On this matter, London's decision was an interim one: the earl-to-be should have a custodiam of them 'till we shall otherwise dispose of them'.[30] He should not receive, however, the presentation of 'spiritual livings'. Thereby such rights of patronage as the O'Donnells had enjoyed over the secular church would be severed, to remain at the disposal of the crown in accordance with the organisational principles of the English reformation.

These were the exceptions made on behalf of the crown. Finally, an exception was made on behalf of Niall Garbh O'Donnell, who should hold his own land around Castlefinn directly from the crown. Niall Garbh, a close relative of Rory's, was a competitor, in the Gaelic way, for the chieftainship. Linked with Docwra, the locally-placed agent of the crown, he had been granted a custodiam of Tir Chonaill in March 1601 on much the same terms as those now made with Rory[31] but had rebelled early in 1603[32] when it had become clear (to Docwra's subsequent regret) that the lord deputy in Dublin favoured his rival. Now, in satisfying one so relatively fully, the crown, however, had not solved the problem created by the aspirations of the other; it had, as it turned out, merely postponed it. Beyond that no precise guarantees were introduced at this stage governing the rights to land under the earl of the other occupiers, great or small, within Donegal.

It was left to Dublin to implement London's decisions. These it necessarily amplified, but also, at least in practice, slightly varied. The creation of the earldom followed quickly, Rory to have a seat in all parliaments and 'general' councils.[33] The patent of the land defined some important specifics which the outline decision of general principles in London had not attended to. The quit rent to be paid annually into the exchequer was set at 300 marks (£200 stg). The tenure was *in capite*, by the service of four knights' fees, and the military service required of him was 60 horse and 120 foot to serve in all general hostings.[34] Therein would lie the principal financial implications of tenure under the crown. However, before the patent was issued, commissioners (out of chancery) had to be appointed – on 24 October 1603 – to take inquisitions to record boundaries and to produce extents of the excluded lands.[35] In this way, while their work was far from complete, a record and valuation of some of the areas of monastic land was brought into existence and one which equated those of the termon lands (peculiar to the Gaelic parts of Ireland) as had been investigated with monastic property.[36] To these may be added the inquisitions taken at an earlier stage, in 1601 and 1602, recording other areas of such land in a piecemeal way (into one of which a piece of lay land – O'Doherty's rich island of Inch – got extra-legally slipped), the impulse behind which must have derived from the desire of a number of the captains in Docwra's Derry command, himself included, to obtain crown leases of the lands involved, and indeed also the recording of the property of the Cistercian abbey of St Bernard of Assaroe made as early as 1588.[37] In some of these inquisitions as well, the regalities (i.e. rights of royal authority) and the fisheries in both Lough Foyle and Lough Swilly were defined as crown property. When O'Donnell's patent was issued to him in February 1604, the crown specifically reserved the fishery both of the port of Ballyshannon and also of all rivers and lakes belonging to the castle 'or town' there.[38]

The process of granting out both the monastic land and some of the termon land which followed was a complex one but the ultimate beneficiaries were a small group of the local military commanders. The Dublin government did not have the initiative to dispose of major accretions of forfeited land unless authorised by commission from London. However, a practice grew up whereby grants of land in Ireland to various favoured individuals (often recompensing past service), which should amount to a specified valuation, were authorised by the king's signet. Their patents usually contained accumulated pieces of land ('books' of land) dispersed throughout Ireland, including at this time small areas formerly belonging to individuals attainted for their part in the recent rebellion. Commonly the beneficiary sold many of these pieces to somebody anxious to consolidate a holding in a particular area.

Ecclesiastical land in Donegal (which included at this time Termon Derry) was granted out in perpetuity in this way in patents to some six people between 1603 and 1609. They included two presidents of Munster, Sir George Carew and his successor Sir Henry Brouncker. One Robert Leycester, whose father had held land in King's County, was favoured on the recommendation of Mountjoy and the Irish privy council. A grant authorised to the old English countess of Delvin and her son, Richard, to compensate for the escheated lands of Gaelic owners in Longford and Cavan promised much earlier to her deceased husband, Christopher Nugent, baron Delvin but not realised, came, in 1609, after elaborate dealings, to include not monastic land but the valuable fisheries at Ballyshannon. Another beneficiary who received monastic land in Donegal in one of his many patents was a Scot, James Fullerton, who had come to Dublin as a schoolteacher in the later 1580s and had acted as an informant to James VI on Irish affairs prior to his succession and was now at court as one of James's numerous Scottish suitors. Finally, and exemplifying the advantage of holding office under the crown in London, a grant was made to Francis Gaston, one of the auditors of the imprests (a financial official) of the abbey of Assaroe.[39]

Those who actually acquired the benefit of this land were, with one exception,[40] a small persistent group of the English military officers who managed to remain on (many, of course, got nothing and sought other outlets) as the war was brought to a close: principally Sir Henry Docwra (at Derry), Captain Ralph Bingley, Sir Henry Folliott, Captain Basil Brooke. Some of these had also acquired leases of the lands in question from the Dublin government.[41] Their entitling represented the tentative probes of Englishmen into one area of English expansion, Donegal (however limited its scope at this time), in the revival of a process, delayed by the Anglo-Spanish war, which now also included the early New England voyages and the establishment of the colony at Jamestown, Virginia. Bingley, whose connections included a relative, Sir John, an exchequer official, sought to act on this wider stage himself. However, his participation in an intended trans-Atlantic voyage with the *Triall* of London in 1606, financed by some London merchants, which degenerated into piratical activity in the Bay of

Biscay, resulted in a trial before the high court of admiralty.[42] By contrast, Sir Henry Folliott was much more single-minded in approach. In June 1606, he was given a crown lease of Ballyshannon and the lands associated with it – that is to say, the area of secular land reserved from Rory O'Donnell's patent – and also of various fishing rights and tithes and a rectory which had belonged to the abbey of Assaroe, for the term of forty-one years. He was also given the valuable fishing rights of the ports and bays of Ballyshannon, Killybegs and Bundrowes and thereabouts, 'wherein fishes were accustomed to be taken'. In addition, to give him access to the centre of authority in Dublin, his lease included Tassagard (Saggart), County Dublin, the property of an owner recently attainted. In devolving away the 'castle or fortilage' of Ballyshannon with this lease, the only security provision made was that it should be held only for Sir Henry's lifetime.[43] The lease was renewed to him the following year, in July 1607.[44] By 1622, when he was granted a new patent, Folliott, who had become baron of Ballyshannon, had secured for himself, now in outright ownership, a substantial estate in this area (Tirhugh), which also included the lands of Assaroe abbey.[45] Two elements in his patent – the abbey of Assaroe and the bay of Ballyshannon 'from the sea to the salmon leap near the castle' and also an eel-weir 'called O'Donnell's weir' in the Erne – derived respectively from the earlier patents to Goston and to Lady Delvin and her son. It is not possible to establish what payment Folliott (or the others in like case) had made for these purchases.

What was being attempted more generally at this time was both simple and fundamental: the absorption of a major Gaelic Irish polity, the O'Donnell lordship, into a unitary administration of Ireland with forms and structures of power, central and local, deriving in part from those implanted in some areas of Ireland with the Anglo-Norman conquest and in part from refinements and modifications of these devised in the later sixteenth century. The changes that this process would require were extensive and would demand considerable adjustment on the part of a formerly quasi-autonomous lord. Thus appointments of customs officials to the ports took away rights formerly enjoyed by the lords and integrated the collection of this form of revenue into the crown's customs system. The first two appointments were made as early as November 1603: Richard Bingley (brother of Ralph) received a lease of the customs and subsidies on the imports and exports of the ports of Derry and Ballyshannon and their creeks and a certain Robert Kinsman was made searcher and gauger of these ports.[46] In a more limited way, further economic restrictions on local power, either of the O'Donnells or their vassal lords such as the MacSweeneys, are to be found in various grants of markets and fairs (more trivial, however, because of the crown rents laid down for them), made to some of these new figures, for example to Sir Henry Docwra at Lifford and to Sir Ralph Bingley at Rathmullan, at this time.[47] At another level entirely, the crown exercised the royal supremacy over the church, effectively here for the first time, in appointing the Protestant George Montgomery, a Scot who had moved to England in the 1580s and who had played some part in facilitating James VI's succession to the throne (rewarded with the office of one of the king's chaplains) and an administrator of marked ability, to be bishop of Raphoe, Derry and Clogher in February 1605.[48] This not only severed the relationship which had prevailed between the bishops of Raphoe and the lords, but had great potential importance for an area with leadership both lay and clerical which in recent times had been committed to a religiously-inspired ideology which had led them to seek in war a Spanish and Catholic rather than English and Protestant ruler for Ireland.[49]

Attempts at administrative change, to substitute the norms of county government in the place of lordly autonomy, also began to take some effect. County Donegal had already been created in 1585 under Lord Deputy Perrot, an amalgamation of O'Donnell's and O'Doherty's countries with the recommendation that Donegal become the county town, but the government had been incapable of making it effective then.[50] Two of the first recorded sheriffs of the county, Oliver Scurlock, a palesman probably of Scurlockstown, County Meath, and very possibly a relation of Martin Scurlock, attorney in the council of Connacht, who appears before February 1605, and MacSweeney Banagh, one of the Donegal sub-lords, who appears in 1606 are, however, unlikely to have made much impact.[51] Nevertheless, there were probes by the assize judges into Donegal in 1603 and 1605, the first prior to the arrival in Ireland of solicitor-general Sir John Davies when, on his account, the chief baron, Sir Edward Pelham, was reverenced by 'the multitude ... as if he had been a good angel sent from heaven.'[52] Also in 1605 when, on Rory O'Donnell's account Captain Henry Vaughan, another of the military officers, was sheriff, beginnings were made towards erecting a sessions house, probably at Lifford, by levying £150 on the county.[53] However, it was probably effectively from 1607 when Sir Richard Hansard, who had been moved there late in 1606, was sheriff – a merging of civil and military functions in the hands of a man who commanded fifty horse – that Lifford came to be defined as the county town.[54] Behind Hansard's appointment, too, lay a more general point (not lost on the Earl of Tyrconnell who had written to principal secretary Salisbury in London from Donegal in May 1606 to petition that he be allowed the nomination of the office): the conviction of Sir Arthur Chichester, then lord deputy in Dublin, that a significant sprinkling of such new English figures – men of 'civility and understanding' was required in the remoter localities if the transition to county government was to be successfully achieved.[55] It had, however, been decided in England in 1605 that the earl himself should be awarded the important office of county lieutenant, whose functions were concerned primarily with the organisation of a militia, and should also be a justice of the peace.[56]

There, arguably, it was scarcely intended that matters should rest. In the later sixteenth century the Dublin government had decided on a policy for the remodelling of Irish landed society beyond the pale, degenerate Anglo-Norman and Gaelic Irish alike, along manorial lines. The lord would retain demesne, to use as he wished, and the heads of the other major landholding families the 'ancient followers of the country' – would be redefined as freeholders, to owe to the lord no other major obligation than a fixed annual money rent. Although there were variations in this in practice, rents to the crown also from both lord and freeholder were normally part of it, thereby to satisfy the growing taxation requirements of an expanding administration. Revenue would arise as well, incrementally, from the tenures under which the land would be held. The purposes behind it in the composition of Connacht were lucidly summed up by one commentator:

> The plot of this composition was devised ... of purpose to take away the greatness of the Irish lords, with their names, macks and oes, that the inferior subject might be freed from their Irish customs, cuttings and unreasonable exactions, and (by knowing what was their own) be drawn to depend ever after upon the state (sic) and not on those Irish lords or gentlemen; which also might not only much avail her Majesty in time of any stirs or revolts, by drawing the common people from following the great chief lords, but also bring a more certainer yearly rent, or revenue, into her highness coffers than formerly was accustomed.[57]

In this way, then, the warlord of the late medieval *ancien regime* would be transformed into a landlord aristocrat, to exist within a framework embodying the controls and regulations of early modern government.[58] This was seen as the essential mechanism for the introduction of political stability through the demilitarisation of the localities. Since the process involved a detailed investigation of existing landownership, alongside it could go many other changes: monastic dissolutions, with the beneficiaries being normally new English; the defining and allocation of church lands, with the possibility that thereby the reformation might be advanced; the endowing of an occasional discoverer of 'concealed' land. In addition, counties could be created or resurrected, and seneschals or governors –

themselves usually given small areas (so re-organisation could entail some loss of land) – could be appointed to stifle resistance. In the cases of Connacht and Munster, presidencies and councils had been instituted to regulate the new order. For their part, the freeholders would, amongst other things, provide the county electorate and be expected to fulfill, generally, the role of a gentry of large landholders in the affairs of their county. The response the scheme evoked amongst the lords varied: some indeed complied (seeing advantage in a fixed rental), many opposed. As far as Gaelic lords were concerned, it made chieftainship, with all its political claims, redundant, by introducing tenure under the crown. For them, too, given the tendency in the Gaelic lordships for the ruling family to branch into different segments, the outcome might be a division of the lordship amongst the heads of its various branches, each with freeholders under them. Also, the very bringing of definition of ownership, secular and ecclesiastical, in this way would be likely to cause considerable initial contention about who owned what.

While the government lacked the strength to introduce this universally in Ulster, some beginnings were also made there in the later 1580s and early 1590s, though these were confined to the lesser lordships. Thus, in the north-west, O'Doherty's patent of 1588 had divided Inishowen into six manors and laid down a crown rent of thirty beeves, though no freeholders were actually designated at that time.[59] Much more systematic had been the 'settlement' of Monaghan in 1591 where the land had been divided between six heads of the ruling MacMahon family and McKenna (the principal non-MacMahon landholder in the lordship) with freeholders assigned to each, to pay him a rent, grantee and freeholder to also pay an annual rent to Dublin. In addition, a seneschal was appointed and received the lands around Monaghan which had always appertained to the office of chieftain, on a twenty-one year lease. Finally, the erenach lands were granted to a number of people, both old English and new English, with the stipulation that each should build castles on them within five years.[60] It was the attempt to bring about similar changes in Fermanagh by the sending in there as sheriff of Captain Humphrey Willis (who had been in Donegal the previous year), in 1593, that had precipitated the Nine Years' War.[61]

The fundamental principle behind the restoration of O'Donnell and O'Neill as earls in the aftermath of the war was that they should not only sever their connections with Spain, but that, in turn, they would be capable of delivering an ordered and pacified society in Ulster and co-operate with what changes should be introduced. The beginnings of some of these changes in Donegal have already been detailed. The pressing urgency to end the war (Mountjoy's opportunist strategy) at a time of political and economic crisis in England, which had led to the restoration of O'Donnell and O'Neill, had meant that the detailed and systematic investigation of landholding through which only the manorialised structure of ownership with freeholders might have been brought into being, had not been carried out. Hence the brevity of O'Donnell's patent. That, arguably, it was not intended thereby to concede to him an untrammelled ownership of the entire territory seems, however, clear both from the use of the word 'manor' within it and also in the cautious phrase that he was granted it only 'in as large and ample manner' as his predecessors had enjoyed it.[62] By contrast, it was easy to insert the manorial divisions into Sir Cahir O'Doherty's patent of January 1605 which was essentially a re-issue of that of 1588, while O'Donnell's was the first ever to be granted.[63]

Where a thorough-going reorganisation had begun to be addressed, it was, again, in the smaller lordship of Fermanagh. A group of commissioners (including the judge Sir Edward Pelham) was, in June 1603, appointed by the lord deputy, Sir George Carey, Mountjoy's successor, to, amongst other things, investigate the landownership there and record the 'freeholders', and by January 1604 two leading members of the Maguire ruling family, Connor Roe and Cú Chonnacht, had been brought to agree in outline to a division of that 'country' between them.[64] It was not, however, until after Sir Arthur Chichester, whose background in Ireland had been a military one and who was energetically committed to the functions of the office, took over as lord deputy in 1605, that a more systematic 'reformation' of Ulster, including the greater lordships, was attempted over the years 1605 to 1607. In this he was backed by his law officer, Sir John Davies, who adopted the policies for social reconstruction of his sixteenth-century predecessors. Davies consistently argued the case that anyhow the real position of the lesser landholders in the Gaelic world approximated nearest to the English status of freeholder and so that they should not with propriety be treated by their lords as mere tenants-at-will.[65] To take away any ambiguity on which the lords – who had sought in the sixteenth century to negotiate on behalf of themselves and their 'followers' – might play, a proclamation was issued in Dublin in 1605 which hit at the whole separate basis of the Gaelic lordships as political entities. The lesser people were to be 'the free, natural and immediate subjects' of the king, not subjects of the lords: they were 'not to be reputed or called the natives or natural followers of any other lord or chieftain'.[66] In two major tours in the summers of 1605 and 1606, the former including Donegal, the latter Fermanagh, Chichester attempted to bring a reorganisation of Ulster into being involving efforts to establish freeholders: 'the honest liberty of that sort of man' he saw as being very much bound up with 'his Majesty's service and the commonwealth's'.[67]

Throughout these years Rory O'Donnell found himself confronted by numerous problems. Apart altogether from the presence of new men in his midst, with all the special tensions that engendered, his most immediate problem was that posed by Niall Garbh. Writing in April 1604, Sir John Davies contrasted the Earl of Tyrone's position with that of the Earl of Tyrconnell. While O'Neill appeared to be successfully reasserting himself, O'Donnell was not. Thus '... in Tirconnell,' Davies reported, 'Neale Garve O'Donnell ... hath gotten many followers, hath possessed himself of the tenants and herds of cattle, and has grown so strong that the earl seems to hold it not safe to return thither, but lies here within the Pale very meanly attended.'[68] It was a classic situation of a challenger, Rory's rival as he had been his brother's (dissatisfied as well with his allocation under the crown) and himself no mean exponent of the rights of a Gaelic lord, competing for power.[69] Thus from the crown's point of view, it seemed that the two pillars of Mountjoy's restoration were proving to be of unequal stability. However, in August 1604, when he was still in Dublin, O'Donnell sent his secretary, Matthew Tully, to London to present a petition to the privy council[70] and by the end of that year he was in London himself, where he remained into the next year.[71] There he was seeking a clarification of his rights and the issuing of a new patent. The matters at issue, discussed between London and Dublin until July, reveal Rory's concerns: amongst them that the garrison be removed from Lifford, which had not been excepted from his patent, and that he should recover it; that his quit rent should be reduced; that he should receive the abbeys and their estates; that his complaints against Niall Garbh be upheld; that he should decide which land should be allocated to Ballyshannon; that he should receive payments for the fishing rights and that he should have the right to nominate the sheriffs.[72]

His attempts to assert his authority within Donegal also brought their tensions. His approach to the sub-lords appears to be borne out by his own evidence as well as that of government figures. 'The three McSwynes and O'Boyle,' he was to assert after the flight, 'who always held their lands from O'Donnell (sic) paying what rent he pleased to impose upon them and who consequently ought to hold from the earl (sic) on the same terms,' had been supported by the lord deputy against him, despite the fact that on foot of his patent and through recourse to English legal procedures they had been brought to 'make over all their estates and rights' to him and had 'taken their said lands again' from him 'by lease of years for certain rent'.[73] Thus he was seeking to become a landlord on his own terms. His attempts to raise a rental income emerge also from another tactic: between February 1604 and July 1607, he made mortgages and leases of considerable areas of land and fisheries to a group of Dublin merchants (newcomers of his own)

23

– Nicholas Weston, John Arthur and Patrick Conley – which included MacSweeney's Doe castle and lands near Rathmullan, lands at Coolmacatrain and a substantial area in Portlough and Tirbrassil.[74] These commercialising decisions can scarcely have endeared the earl to the occupiers of these lands and they would seem to account for a number of incidents between him and some of the lesser figures which come to light in 1607. Thus it was reported in July 1607 that (*Cathbharr Óg*) O'Donnell had gone to the Scottish isle of Islay 'with thirty men in company', leading to fears that he would return with forces, 'for he is a malcontent and unsatisfied with the earl of Tyrconnell, who withholds most of his land from him, against right, as he affirms,' and that that had also been the cause of 'his and Neale McSwyne's last stirs', at the beginning of the year.[75] They may also go some way to account for the unexplained fracas at Rathmullan in September 1607, after the earls had boarded ship for the flight, between boatmen sent for water and firewood and MacSweeney Fanad's son and a patty of supporters.[76]

It was into this context that Chichester, whose entourage included the assize judges, intervened in his northern journey of August 1605. Operating within the limits of the original decision, he sought, sitting at Lifford, to resolve the conflict between Rory and Niall Garbh, both of whom appeared with lawyers, by defining the latter's share (forty-three quarters in Glan Fyn and Munganagh) to him.[77] A central issue also was O'Donnell's relations with the MacSweeneys, O'Boyle and 'other ancient gents', because it raised the question of freeholders. The earl (whom Chichester found more compliant than he had been after his return from England) did not deny that he had 'procured' them 'to surrender their several estates in their lands' to him, but he was persuaded to name 'such of them as he deemed fit to be freeholders of part thereof, reserving their ancient rents in certainty'.[78] Sir Cahir O'Doherty was also asked to give the names of those to be created freeholders in Inishowen.[79]

On the issues raised by O'Donnell's petition, both London and Dublin had shown a willingness to make some little concessions, for example on the important appointment of the lieutenant. Some concessions proposed were also well-considered: he should only receive a regrant on condition that he relinquish all claim to the freeholders, and, he might suggest the names of six gentlemen from whom the sheriff would be chosen provided that they were 'freeholders of the country'.[80] On one point, however, the lord deputy, concerned as of first necessity he must be with security, would make no concession. Although O'Donnell's protest about Lifford had received a somewhat sympathetic response from the king, the lord deputy's judgement (which followed Mountjoy's that it was essential for security reasons) prevailed. The fact that he 'reserved' it (as a 'place, of special importance to be kept and preserved in his Majesty's own hands' even preferable to Derry) and a small area of good lowland land nearby had the effect of depriving the earl of a strategic and economic resource in the north of the county.[81] The public purse, however, still heavily dependent on subvention from an England determined on financial retrenchment, was unable to stretch to his and the privy council's grander aspirations for Lifford that, in addition to the fort, it be 'walled about' and developed like Derry as an incorporated urban plantation, with houses and inns built and with merchants, tradesmen and artificers from England and Scotland commanded 'by authority' to come and work there, whereby (and this was a common belief about the value of urbanisation to bring about a change in life-style) 'obedience, peace, civility and plenty' would be established in the surrounding area, both on 'Tyrone and Tirconnell's side' of the river.[82] Eventually and in conjunction with the subsequent plantation, as will be seen, this goal was in fact to be devolved to private enterprise. Lifford and the adjacent land was subsequently leased[83] and later given in outright grant to Sir Richard Hansard, in a fall-back reliance on individual effort, on condition that he should bring about urban development there.[84] This was, however, to be in the future. Meanwhile, Chichester and the Dublin government furthermore recommended to London in 1605 that Culmore should also be retained and a small ward established there, to include a few cannoniers, as a means of challenging any invading vessels.[85] Finally, they claimed to have 'taken an exact note' of all the quarters of land in County Donegal with the intention of dividing them into six baronies. The precision of such a hasty survey must be doubted. If the intent behind it was indeed also to produce a record by which freeholds could be defined in a new patent, this did not happen. Chichester came to the view from the 'wastes and desolution' he had seen on his tour that the people were too poor to pay composition in the sense of the land tax to Dublin, and Rory's 1604 patent remained in operation.[86]

The northern tour of 1605 had, at any rate, set out the broad parameters within which the earl and Sir Cahir O'Doherty were expected to operate. The tour of 1606 into the small lordships, including Fermanagh, bade fair to bring about there – where after all beginnings had already been initiated – a land re-organisation with freeholders and left Cú Chonnacht Maguire particularly disaffected.[87] Also in 1606 a closeness was detected between him and Rory O'Donnell in what has all the appearance of a revival of the traditional relationship of *uirrí* to overlord and at this time Dublin government suspicions were aroused by rumours that both intended to go to Spain or the Spanish Netherlands.[88] The departure of Maguire to

Spanish Flanders the following year set in motion one of those chains of circumstances which culminated in the Flight of the Earls in September. The precise purpose of Maguire's secret journey is necessarily hard to determine: while on the one hand it may merely have been to seek employment in the newly-formed Irish regiment there, on the other, and perhaps more plausibly, it may well have been to test the waters, since the Archduke Albert (who with his wife, the Infanta Isabella, was now joint ruler there under Spain) had been the candidate proposed to be king of Ireland in 1596, for a possible renewed invasion of Ireland.[89]

The question is immediately raised as to whether the Ulster lords had indeed retained contact with Spain in the intervening years since 1603. In O'Donnell's case, at any rate, such a thread of contact can be found, mediated principally through Matthew Tully, a layman rather than an ecclesiastic – though the militant Franciscan intellectual Fr Florence Conry (formerly confessor to Hugh O'Donnell and subsequently absentee Catholic archbishop of Tuam) and various priests and friars can be found in the background – and a conspirator who had been in the pay of both the Spaniards and the O'Donnells.[90] Much of this contact had revolved around the quest for pensions for O'Neill and O'Donnell from a somewhat reluctant Spain, or even the suggestion that they might go to the Spanish court 'for protection and favour', with the skilful Matthew Tully arguing in February 1606, in a petition on behalf of both, that the former would be the preferable option, 'for if the earls come to Spain ... they would not be of such service if the opportunity arose'.[91] As early as December 1604, when O'Donnell, then in London, had himself approached the Spanish ambassador on this matter, he suggested that both he and O'Neill would be willing to renew the war in Ireland should the Spanish peace with England not hold, and the ambassador, conscious of Spain's recent grander aspirations with regard to England as well as Ireland, in reporting this to Spain, pointed to the fact that O'Donnell, through his marriage to Bridget, daughter of the deceased Earl of Kildare whose wife had been a daughter of the Earl of Nottingham, lord high admiral of England, had 'both in Ireland and in England ... relatives and rank'.[92] Eventually, in November 1606, a decision was made in Spain to grant a subvention to them, given the fact that 'should war break out again they could be of great use and so it is well to keep them well disposed,' and the resulting process for the payment of' this through the Spanish Netherlands was underway in the spring of 1607, all dictated no doubt in part by wider issues in the current state of Anglo-Spanish relations, of which the formation of' the English Virginia Company in April 1606 was one, as well as sympathy for their past actions and current decline.[93]

If, however, this new-found tentative Spanish interest, through which they might hope to achieve power as great potentates in Ireland, were to be converted to advantage, the earls must seek, as they had done in the later 1590s, to recreate a military alliance extending beyond the north which might attract Spanish armed intervention. It seems clear that O'Donnell at least was engaged in some explorations along these lines – towards the formation of a new Irish 'Catholic league' – at this time. In a powerfully-constructed essay in propaganda sent as a petition jointly by both earls to Philip III from Louvain in December 1607, after the flight, urging on him the ease with which he could take up their renewed request to be 'our lord and our king' and the advantages to Spain which would as a consequence accrue, they stated that 'one of us, the Earl O'Donnel, had secret dealings' with many of the 'nobles and the chief gentlemen' – except a few whom he did not trust – who had served Queen Elizabeth in the last war (that is, many of the old English), and that they, out of fidelity to Catholicism, would now be willing, should Philip send 'some aid to them', to change allegiance 'and help us so that, by common consent, we should deliver the kingdom to your Majesty'.[94] In other words, they were seeking to argue that a crucial change had now taken place in Irish circumstances.

In fact O'Donnell's conspirings may not have gone as deeply or at any rate, perhaps, have evoked as positive a response as this memorial sought to suggest. His most well-known overture appears to have been made to Sir Richard Nugent, baron Delvin, a young old English landowner living on the borders of the pale. At this time Delvin had good reason for disaffection. In May 1597 his father had received royal authorisation for a grant of attainted native Irish lands in Cavan or in the Anally, County Longford, to the value of £100.[95] However, no grant could be made until after the peace in 1603 and the Delvin claim to lands in Longford, which was engendering considerable ill-feeling just at this time, was ultimately not accepted, with the king ordering finally, in July 1607, that the O'Farrells in Longford be repossessed, Delvin and his widowed mother to receive escheated lands 'in Cavan and elsewhere.[96] Such was the context of O'Donnell's meetings with Nugent one of which had taken place, on the latter's confession of 6 November 1607, 'about Christmas twelve month' in the garden at Maynooth, Rory's wife's home. Nugent's confession also provides an outline of what was apparently being aired. Their discussions allegedly revolved around their discontents over land and also religion, with Rory accountedly complaining of his losses of Ballyshannon, Lifford and the fishings and expressing his determination to 'attempt something which might regain him his country in the same state his brother held it'. To this end Rory apparently proposed a coup to take Dublin castle when the lord deputy and council should be meeting there, and also some of the strongholds in the outlying localities including Ballyshannon and Lifford, arguing that O'Neill and Maguire and others, equally discontented, would join with him in doing so, and that in the resulting situation, 'the kingdom without other government than their own', he would have his 'lands and countries as [he] desire[d] it and make [his] friends peace with the king'. When pressed, at a later meeting, on the impracticality of the attempt, Rory, he said, stated that he had sent a messenger, a priest, to Fr Florence Conry in Spain to 'deal' with the king of Spain for 10,000 troops.[97] It was recognised therefore that success for such scheming would be contingent on Spanish intervention.

While it would be reasonable to assume that the earls had exaggerated the extent of Rory's conspirings in their December submission to Spain, Chichester's anxieties were aroused, when, conscious of the greatly reduced forces that were available to him, he received information, in the summer, from Sir Christopher St Lawrence, 22nd Baron of Howth, one of the lords of the pale and recently returned from Flanders, which suggested that a 'general revolt', with nobility (including some of the Mayo Burkes, Sir Randal McDonnell and the Earl of Tyrone as well as O'Donnell) and townsmen alike allegedly involved, had been planned and was intended, under promise of substantial Spanish military aid, to follow 'within twenty days after the peace should be broken', in order to 'shake off the yoke of the English government and adhere to the Spaniard' and that Fr Florence Conry had been employed by O'Donnell as his go-between with Spain and that the Spaniards had 'fed' O'Donnell with 'hope of great advancement and reward'. St Lawrence hoped to elicit more from O'Donnell, who was expected to come from the north for his countess early in September, and advised that he should be questioned on the matter. He expressed the view, however, that no pressing danger was presented since Spanish forces could not be ready to come for another year.[98]

On the strength of these allegations, made also in England, by St Lawrence, Chichester went down 'towards the borders of Ulster' in an effort to investigate and also perhaps, partly, to mollify O'Neill 'proceeding tenderly and slowly as with intemperate and desperate patients whom he could neither safely deal with nor yet abandon without imputation' and had decided to arrest and question O'Donnell when he should come into the pale.[99] At this point events overtook him. A ship with Maguire, Matthew Tully and Donagh O'Brien (a relative of the Earl of Thomond who had been in the Spanish service for some time) aboard arrived at Rathmullan. It was apparently promoted by the Archduke,[100] acting on the belief that O'Neill (who was just then about to go to England to defend a suit with his *uirrí* O'Cahan, whose lands he had been granted in his patent) was also to be arrested and perhaps even executed since the plotting had been discovered, and it apparently offered the earls refuge in Flanders or Spain pending negotiations on their behalf with James I.[101] It became known, however, that only if the negotiations then in hand with the Dutch, to whom the Spaniards and the Archdukes' dependent government in Brussels were at this precise time, 1607–9, gradually capitulating, were to result in some English intervention on the Dutch side would the Spaniards, also coming to grips with the English landing in Virginia in April, break their peace with England.[102] As it happened, England and Spain remained at peace until 1625.

In the event, then, the earls sailed off, unaware perhaps of the declining power of Spain or, at any rate, its lack now of European imperial ambition, into a wider European politics in which they proved to be in some measure an embarrassment to their would-be deliverers. Their intended destination was Spain but they were blown ashore in France and went to the Spanish Netherlands which they left on 18 February 1608 and ended up in Rome two months later, where O'Donnell died on 18 July.[103] On their departure rumour was spread in Ireland that they would be returned. Thus Owen Groome Magrath, deputy to Fr Florence Conry as provincial of the Irish Franciscans, anxious to keep the conspiracy in Ireland alive, visited Nugent shortly after the flight to inform him (on the latter's account) that the earls would return by St Bridget's day bringing with them 'sufficient forces to make good their designs', and expressing confidence that although the king of Spain had refused to give assistance, the pope and the archduke would, 'at which the king of Spain will wink and perchance give some assistance under hand'.[104] However, the returning proved more difficult than the departure, although the earls bent their efforts to achieve it.

In their joint petition to Philip III, already referred to, they set out their case for Spanish reintervention. They stressed the benefits that had accrued to Spain through their involvement by its 'order and persuasions' in the last war, presented themselves as the 'principal leaders' in a 'kingdom consisting entirely of Catholics' then under great pressure from 'heretics' to conform in religion,[105] and, in calling for his renewed assistance, asserted that he was under a moral obligation to provide it because their present troubles' had arisen from the fact that they had refused 'the honourable conditions which the heretics offered us many times during the war' on account of royal letters from his father and himself. Spanish intervention now would not only conduce to a religious good, the advancement of Catholicism against Protestantism, but would lead as well to the expansion of the Spanish monarchy. They also pressed that it would serve much more transcendent Spanish ambitions, 'because once your Majesty is lord of Ireland, within a short time you will also be lord of England and of Scotland and you will have peace in the States of Flanders'. Nor would it be a disadvantage tactically that they were 'now away from our country': they could still control its responses from abroad. Militarily too, their proposal was feasible because the king of England had 'neither the experienced soldiers nor the financial resources' to oppose successfully. Also they argued that James was disliked by all his 'vassals' in England and Scotland, especially the Catholic ones, with those of Scotland being the earls' 'kinsfolk, friends and neighbours' to boot, and claimed that the Catholics of the 'three kingdoms' had placed all their hopes in the earls' intercession with him. Thus, then, if he would intervene he would become 'master of all the north, where you will establish the Catholic faith'.[106]

It was precisely this kind of strategy – however much it was, perhaps, now an anachronistic vision – that the English Protestant government must seek to pre-empt: that through Irish circumstances a new assault on their religion and independence was again gestating and might be launched.[107] Accordingly, English diplomacy was directed towards the forestalling of the earls' plans, with, amongst other things, the argument being advanced that, unlike Elizabeth, James I 'being possessed of Scotland' had in that country, itself 'near adjoining to the north part of Ireland', a people – 'of their own fashion, diet and disposition that can walk their bogs as well as themselves' – well qualified to repress any Spanish-incited Ulster rebellion.[108]

In these circumstances, with the Archdukes, anxious above all things that the peace negotiations with the United Provinces would not be impeded by the earls' presence, arguing that the earls had been received in Spanish Flanders as 'refugees' for religion and not as 'traitors',[109] and with them seeking to go by some route to a Spain which was reluctant to receive them, the question of what should be done with, let alone what should be done for, them became an issue between Spain and the papacy, reminiscent of the earlier contretemps between them in 1585–7 over the payment for an armada against England.[110] For their part, the earls sought not just Spanish, but also papal, military assistance. In a submission to Pope Paul V, which is couched in similar terms to that addressed to Philip III and in which they presented themselves again as leaders in the Catholic cause, they insisted that 'empty expressions of compassion' would be inadequate to their needs and asserted that they had 'special claims' upon him – a reference to the old papal claim to sovereignty over Ireland – since 'all their misfortunes' were due 'to the grant of Ireland to England by the Holy See'.[111] In coming to their aid militarily, the pope then would 'hand down to posterity a name that [could] never be forgotten'.[112]

However, it was the immediate problem of where the earls should go, with its implications of who should take responsibility for them, which occupied some months after their arrival in Flanders, and the papal nuncio to Brussels, Cardinal Bentivoglio, found himself in the middle of the affair. His reports to the papal secretary of state, Cardinal Barberini, throw light on the predicament of the earls in Flanders prior to their departure to Rome. Acting on instructions of 17 November, Bentivoglio conveyed to Tyrone – who at that point had been forbidden to go to Spain pending further consideration, and who had indicated to him the earls' wish to go to Rome and from thence to Spain, in order to gain the pope's 'favour' and, through him, that of 'other Catholic princes' and especially Spain's, for their proposals – the 'great needs and difficulties of the Holy See', and made known to him that all hope must be placed in the king of Spain.[113] In a later interview with Conry, acting on behalf of the earls, Bentivoglio re-inforced the point. On Conry's admission that it was really the Spaniards who were seeking to direct the earls to Rome, Bentivoglio persuaded him of the 'artful cunning which lay behind this advice': were Tyrone to show a willingness to go to Rome, then the Spaniards would argue that 'since the earl wished to have recourse to the pope, it remained for the pope to help him' and thereby rid themselves of all future responsibility.[114] However by January–February 1608 the Spanish council of state had decided that they must go to Rome (where Spain would give them a monthly allowance), arguing that the pope should he persuaded to protect those who had lost their possessions 'for the Catholic faith'. Their presence in Rome could be used as a lever diplomatically to reduce pressure on Catholics in the English dominions to conform, while in the 'case of a break with England, the result will be the same as if they had come to Spain'.[115] Their eventual going to Rome, then, constituted a victory of the Spanish over the papal viewpoint. Not surprisingly, a mood of uncertainty and disillusion set in amongst the earls and their entourages as they awaited these decisions in Flanders, despite the sympathetic nature of their treatment there.[116]

In Rome the earls found themselves, despite persistent efforts, in a cul-de-sac from which there was neither exit nor return. Since the rebellion of old Irish and old English in Ireland, contingent anyhow in their view on Spanish support, did not materialise, it is difficult to judge the accuracy of the earls' assessment of its potential. In view of the expansionist tendencies of the O'Neills,[117] some doubt may perhaps be retained that the old English borderers of the pale would have been willing to risk themselves to a governance under Spain in which the old Irish lords of Ulster would expect to play such a prominent part.

The outcome for some of the principal figures drawn into O'Donnell's pre-flight conspirings throws light on how the affair was handled in Ireland. Delvin, initially destabilised, was arrested in November but escaped from Dublin castle and fled with a small following to Cloughowter in Cavan. He submitted, however, on 5 May 1608 and having been sent over to London was pardoned there in July.[118] When patronage was renewed to him, he (and his mother) did not refrain from accepting in a number of patents between 1 July 1609 and January 1613 substantial areas of land which, as has been seen, included property in Donegal.[119] For his part, St Lawrence was transferred to London but had been released by 1611.[120] The first of his family to become Protestant, he arranged a marriage between his son and heir, Nicholas, and the daughter of George Montgomery, now bishop of Meath. The Howth family estate of some 5,000 acres was retained up to 1641 and confirmed to them at the restoration.[121] The friar Owen Groome Magrath, sentenced to execution for high treason, was pardoned and released from Dublin castle in November 1609.[122] Pressure for religious conformity was also relaxed.

The rebellion which did break out was a purely local affair. O'Doherty's rising (18 April–5 July 1608), an attempt to expel both Captain Henry Harte from Culmore and the growing urban plantation from Derry, in which Bishop Montgomery was based and of which O'Doherty himself had been made one of the governing body, had arisen through ill-feeling with Docwra's successor there, Paulet, and because of delay in resolving his dispute over the possession of Inch island. Although causing limited upheavals elsewhere in Ulster (for example Oghy oge (*Eohbaidh Óg*) O'Hanlon's rebellion in Armagh, which did not peter out until September 1609)[124] and provoking Chichester to recriminations that his proposals for expenditure on fortifications had not received favour, O'Doherty's rising had been effectively suppressed with his death on 5 July.[125]

Seeking to seize on the opportunity thus presented, the earls, now in Rome, brought pressure on both Spain and the papacy to intervene and we are provided, as a result, with an interesting case of Spanish and papal interplay. In two submissions to Spain, on 30 June and 12 July, calling for armed assistance, they claimed that 4,000 of their 'vassals' had revolted in 'our province of Ulster' and that, crucially, the rising was spreading to the other provinces and causing reverberations in Scotland and England too.[126] The latter submission arose from a papal initiative: the pope had asked the Spanish ambassador to convey to Philip III the earls' proposal that Spain send forces to Ireland surreptitiously, 'doing so in the name of the pope'.[127] Spain's response to that was, however, dismissive: given the 'present lack of money and troops', there was too much in hand 'without undertaking anything new at the request of those who may be directly interested'.[128] However, for the next few months the issue was debated between Spain and the papacy. Thus, arising from a report from the Spanish ambassador in England which had spoken of financial difficulties and religious tensions there as well as events in Ireland, Philip III concluded that efforts now to 're-establish the holy faith in those parts' might succeed, and decided to urge the pope to take on the responsibility. The Spanish ambassador to Rome was accordingly instructed, on 19 July, to get both the English Jesuit Fr Robert Parsons (then employed in Rome) and the earls to test the pope's willingness to launch an assault to 'recover this patrimony of the church' (a reference it seems only to Ireland), given that 'Ireland belongs to the Apostolic See from ancient times' and given the precedent of Pope Gregory XIII's 'similar enterprise': the sending of a papal force to Ireland in 1580.[129] By September, however, the pope had made his decision: while in principle he would be 'glad to undertake this matter of Ireland', he could not in his present circumstances, being in conflict with Venice, levy the taxes for such a 'distant expedition' or offer any subvention to the Spaniards were they to take action.[130] At the same time the Spanish council of state and Philip III re-affirmed their earlier decision on the matter of Ireland.[131] Both instead sought to fall back on diplomacy – that because it was judged (with much exaggeration) that the English crown had been severely stretched by O'Doherty's rising, the restoration of O'Neill (O'Donnell had died in Rome on 18 July) could be negotiated and liberty of conscience achieved for at least Connacht and Ulster.[132] By now in fact, however, the process of planning a plantation for the lands in Ulster was already well underway. While it is impossible to know what the Spaniards might have done had the pope offered financial support, it is clear that they for their part had now fully accepted that their conflict with England, in which Ireland had, it can be seen, played a subordinate part, was over.[133] The death of O'Donnell (and Maguire) had also weakened the earls' effectiveness as a force for generating foreign involvement; however, the fear that O'Neill would be returned caused periodic anxieties in London and Dublin while he remained alive and indeed the ups and downs of Anglo-Spanish relations were to have reverberations in Ulster long after his death.

Plotting then, if manifestly not full-scale planning, on O'Donnell's part with a consequent fear of arrest and conviction for foreign conspiracy, had been a primary cause of the Flight of the Earls. That their fears of arrest or worse could have been very real ones can be seen in parallel with the treatment of the suspect north of England magnate, Henry Percy, ninth Earl of Northumberland, in the hardened atmosphere in the aftermath of the Gunpowder plot of 1605: he was imprisoned for life, only to be released in 1621.[134] To understand O'Donnell's actions, however, it is necessary to review briefly his position in the run-up to departure.

Although the broad outlines of his position in landholding were being laid down, as we have seen, they had not been confirmed in final detail. In the interim, as has also been shown, he had been actively seeking both a more favourable and a less regulated settlement, Thus in the summer of 1606 while Chichester was in Fermanagh, and at a time when the death of Mountjoy had taken away what the earl perceived as his 'patron' at court,[135] Rory approached him seeking arbitration of his land rights in south Donegal, a crucial area to him because much of the O'Donnell demesne land was located there. The matters at issue concerned the ownership of Bundrowes (and, effectively also, the defining of the county boundary there), boundary disputes arising from Folliott's lease, and in particular the future ownership of the large estate (15,768 acres) of the abbey of Assaroe. Rory, who up to this time still held much of the monastic property 'in commendam', was particularly anxious to procure a crown lease of this valuable estate. But Chichester, on visiting the area, was initially reluctant, as he informed Salisbury in London on 12 September, for security reasons, that this request be conceded: the abbey buildings stood in a valley close to Ballyshannon castle, with a hill rising between them 'by reason whereby the castle can discover nothing done in the abbey, which hath been a goodly house, and may yet shelter many people, who may in times of advantage lodge themselves within a caliver shot of the castle undiscovered …'[136] By the end of November, he had, however, adopted a different attitude. If Rory, who remained 'very earnest' with him for this estate, could be got in return to disclaim his demand for Lifford and agree to demolish the abbey buildings (because of their proximity to Ballyshannon castle) and build elsewhere – a compromise which he hoped to bring him to – he would recommend London's approval for the grant.[137] Speed of decision-making now came into play. Although the matter was listed for discussion in London at the end of January 1607, London had not responded prior to the flight.[138] However, the decision, communicated to the lord deputy on 26 October 1607, to grant the estate to Goston was made after, rather than before, the Flight of the Earls.[139]

It is obvious, then, that Rory was actively seeking to recast O'Donnell power even in the altered circumstances of these years and it may be that his conspiratorial activities were engaged in as little more than a bargaining counter (or a threat as the astute Sir John Davies perceived them) to secure a more advantageous settlement. His problems were not, however, one-sided. The feud with Niall Garbh O'Donnell surfaced to full light also at this time, when the latter sought advantage through government contact.

Hence in a statement made by him in Fermanagh in August 1606 to Chichester and chief justice Sir James Ley, on rumours then prevailing that Tyrconnell and Cú Connacht Maguire were about to depart the kingdom, he asserted that they and the earl of Tyrone and others had formed plans to seize the forts in Ulster, which they feared had now been discovered, and had links, through clerical agency, to Spain to boot.[140] However, whereas in the past such disputes between contestants for power would have been resolved by civil war with the stronger assuming control, the government now acted to pre-empt that by itself intervening in it. As a result, Rory and Niall Garbh, having 'submitted themselves to the order and arbitrament of the council table for all personal causes and variances … between them' were obliged, early in December, to enter into recognisances in £3,000, each to the other, to abide by the order and decision of the lord deputy and privy council concerning 'all differences, controversies and challenges of goods' between them.[141] By this means (an example of government by recognisance),[142] Rory was debarred from the normal trial by strength which such circumstances threw up, and in agreeing to abide by Dublin's arbitration might possibly have had to accept a territorial adjustment in Niall Garbh's favour as well.[143] To Rory, whose personal financial circumstances were ones of considerable indebtedness, the forfeiture of that penalty would have presented an unsustainable burden: after the flight, Chichester expressed the view that 'that needy earl of Tyrconnell' had debts to the sum of £3,000.[144]

It is clear also, however, that O'Donnell's conspiratorial activities, which made the Flight of the Earls necessary (and in which his indebtedness may well have played some part), were ill-judged since the desired Spanish or papal army did not materialise and it looks likely that he had received a false impression about the prospects for Spanish intervention through the enthusiasm of his channels of communication with Spain, many of them priests, themselves with an interest in frustrating the extension of the reformation into Ulster now clearly signalled both by Montgomery's appointment as bishop and by the monastic dissolutions.[145] Conformity and compliance might have left O'Donnell in a position in landholding at least approaching to that which the astute Earl of Antrim (though by no means an entirely parallel figure) secured and sustained for himself in these years.[146] However, the loss of *uirrí*, taxation through the quit rent; the loss of some castles; the insistence that the lesser lords must be freeholders paying only their 'ancient rents'; the loss of valuable fishing rights; the belief that some garrisons and some new owners must be an essential part of the new order as mechanisms of control all meant that in the Ireland whose 'settlement' was now being completed, the Earl of Tyrconnell's role, both politically and economically, would be a much restricted and transformed one. More a landlord now than a warlord, he would retain a personal estate (possibly enhanced by the 15,000 acres of Assaroe abbey lands) along with his principal castle at Donegal and (after a difficult transition) draw rents or services from much of the rest of the land as well. He could no longer, however, aspire to fill the role, embracing military virtues, personalised power and rights of patronage, of the 'independent' regional prince of the Gaelic world evoked so fulsomely in O'Clery's finely-honed obituary of his brother:

> … He was the head of support and planning, of counsel and disputation of the greater number of the Gaels of Ireland whether in peace or in war. He was a mighty bountiful lord with the attributes of a prince and the maintenance of justice, a lion in strength and force, with threatening and admonishing so that it was not allowed to gainsay his word, for whatever he ordered had to be done on the spot, a dove in meekness and gentleness to privileged men of the church and the arts, and every one who did not oppose him. A man who impressed fear and terror of him on everyone far and near, and on whom no man at all put dread. A man who banished brigands, crushed evildoers, exalted the sons of life, and hanged the sons of death. A man who did not allow himself to be injured or afflicted, cheated or insulted without repaying and avenging it immediately; a determined, fierce, and bold invader of districts; a warlike, aggressive plunderer of others' territories; a destroyer of any of the English and Irish that opposed him; a man who never failed to do all that befitted a prince so long as he lived; a sweet-sounding trumpet, with power of speech and eloquence, sense and counsel, with a look of affection on his face according to all who beheld him; a prophesied chosen one whom the prophets foretold long before his birth.[147]

There was, however, to be an aftermath to the earls' departure. Shortly after the outbreak of O'Doherty's rising, Niall Garbh, whose son Neachtan had gone to Trinity College, Dublin in what appears to have been a significant effort at adjustment, and who now professed his 'allegiance towards his king and country', sought the lord deputy's support with the king for a patent of 'the whole country and territory of Tyrconnell' ('the possessions of his ancestors'). In it he sought, on foot of a claimed previous promise of Chichester's, to have O'Doherty's Inishowen as well, and requested also a grant of the Lough Foyle fisheries. He avoided entirely the question of freehold status for the lesser owners, but was prepared to accept the exception of Lifford, Ballyshannon, Derry and, in effect, Culmore from his grant. He also sought patronage in various forms: the command, during the rebellion, of 300 foot and 50 horse which he would distribute to some of his supporters; the wardship of O'Boyle's son (which would give him power in south Donegal); and a pension for life.[148]

Chichester, in his replies, while temporising with him on the military command and offering some encouragement with regard to Inishowen, pointed out to Niall Garbh that since the earl was not yet attainted and the lands of the greater lordship not yet surveyed, whereby 'the king may know what he gives and that all subjects' rights may be preserved', he could not convey to him a sure estate of any more than had been formerly promised, and stressed also to him his need for loyalty and action in the context of the revolt.[149] He was reminded, too, that the king was now more powerful than Elizabeth had been 'by a populous and bordering kingdom' and urged not to so 'capitulate' with him 'as to cause his Majesty to believe him an ambitious and insatiable man, but one that would draw on his Majesty to do for him as a good and well-deserving subject'.[150] Also, in the ensuing correspondence with London, in May, Chichester expressed his concern about the deal Niall Garbh was attempting to negotiate. Referring to his 'spirit and vast desires', seeking by demanding the 'whole country' of Tyrconnell 'without any respect of other inferior rights and interests whatsoever' to become therein 'a Roytelett', he asked the privy council to direct him on 'how far to give him some reasonable satisfaction', and its view was that he should not make his 'fortune so great as may prove unfit should he show an evil mind hereafter'. Should he prove his loyalty by action against the rebels, they would, however, consent to his estate being enlarged (at Dublin's discretion) but he should not be made 'too powerful over his Majesty's other subjects'.[151] In fact, the effectiveness of the standing army in dealing with the revolt made Niall Garbh's proffered services redundant. In a campaign lasting from early May to late June, led by Sir Richard Wingfield, marshal of the army, lord treasurer Sir Thomas Ridgeway and Sir Oliver Lambert, a soldier of much experience, the revolt was brought under control through the recovery of the forts and the taking of O'Doherty's castles.[152] When they arrived (after a 'march so far and into such places of the North as no army has ever gone by land before'), they found Niall Garbh to be 'wavering and irresolute which side to take'.[153] By mid-June he had been arrested under suspicion and was conveyed to Dublin on the king's ship *Tramontane* to be eventually, after an abortive trial, transferred with his son to London where he died in the Tower.[154]

Thus ended O'Donnell power and with it a long crisis of integration between Gaelic lords and crown government. Direct-rule English government in sixteenth-century Ireland found itself confronted, beyond the pale, by a varying pattern of lordly power often expressed, as in the case of O'Donnell, through elaborate linkages which had created systems of regional dominance – which it sought to transform by creating a significantly disempowered nobility absorbed into a unitary administration with interlocking central and local elements. In secular terms, the model for change in Ulster lay in the arrangements for landownership devised in the 'settlement' of Monaghan in 1591, combined with its designation as a county in 1588.[155] A central assumption was that the ordinary people could only be ruled effectively if the barrier of lordly power was significantly reduced. Another aim was to achieve religious uniformity through the extension of the reformation to Ireland as well. At the time when social and political change was being attempted in Ulster in the 1580s and early 1590s, renewed and equally piecemeal efforts were made to extend the reformation into it also. In the course of the resulting Nine Years' War, religion and aristocratic power had come to be intertwined and eventually, and even more significantly, internationalised through the involvement of Spain.

Confronted by this gathering intensification of Tudor change, political and religious, the Ulster lords had been forced to think beyond the previous confines of regional power, and their own model for a unitary Ireland was put forward, without success, in 1599. The framework produced in a document ascribed to O'Neill, bears some of the character of the 'aristocratic constitutionalism' which surfaced from time to time elsewhere, as it had done, for example, in Sweden during a period of crisis in the monarchy in 1593–4.[156] The essence of the O'Neill proposal was simple: that, crucially, under a member of the English nobility representing the queen as lord deputy,[157] the nobility of Ireland should have access to all the offices of state and so form its government[158] and that the church of Ireland be 'wholly governed by the pope', in short, that the reformation should be reversed.[159] By now, therefore, the Ulster lords had come to a confirmed view that Catholicism rather than Protestantism was attuned 'best' to a right 'worldly policy' in which their kind of power should have its place.[160] However, as has been shown in the case of O'Donnell, Lord Deputy Chichester had, in the tense aftermath of the rebellion, renewed the programme for the 'settlement' of Ireland along opposing lines. Much of the 'lure of Spain' (by which one contemporary sought to explain the attempt at renewed conspiracy spearheaded by O'Donnell) must have resided in the expectation that under a Spanish dispensation the former kind of outcome might be achieved. Hence the strongly Catholic tone and aristocratic flavour of the appeals to Spain. However, a dispensation so favourable to aristocratic liberties was no longer easy to obtain in a period which tended everywhere in western Europe to be a 'time of collision between the authority of kings and local or national privileges, liberties and constitutions',[161] and least of all in Ireland which England still feared might become a base for Spanish aggression. The conjoining of aristocratic power with a requirement for religious diversity was an even more difficult demand to sustain. At first sight, it might appear that the Protestant Huguenot aristocracy in France had achieved it: the Edict of Nantes in 1598 conceded religious toleration. However, this privilege was gradually whittled away in Cardinal Richelieu's France, to he eventually revoked in 1685.[162] The outcome for the O'Donnells in Donegal may perhaps be understood more easily in this context. If Rory O'Donnell had hoped indeed to regain 'his country in the same state his brother held it' through a *coup d'etat* or by Spanish intervention he was to be disappointed, while Niall Garbh's attempts to achieve something slightly less through negotiation also proved abortive. Plantation followed.

---

1   *Cal. Pat. Rolls Ire., Jas I*, pp 10, 13. He was pardoned in October 1603 (ibid., p. 35).
2   The peace with Spain was agreed in the Treaty of London in August 1604.
3   *Cal. S.P. Ire., 1606–8*, p. 365. For a careful examination of O'Donnell overlordship in Sligo see Mary O'Dowd, *Power, politics and land: early modern Sligo, 1568–1688* (Belfast, 1991), pp 20–44.
4   I intend to examine this point in more detail elsewhere.
5   H. Morgan, *Tyrone's rebellion: the outbreak of the Nine Years' War in Tudor Ireland* (Dublin, 1993), passim. I have benefited greatly from discussions with Dr Morgan.
6   On this see K. Simms, 'Niall Garbh II O'Donnell, king of Tir Conaill, 1422–39' in *Donegal Annual* 12 (1977–9), pp 7–21.
7   The castle at Dunnalong was built by Turlough Luineach O'Neill in 1568 (TNA, S.P. 63/23, no. 74, ix).
8   *Inq. Cancell. Hib. Repert.*, II, App. IV.
9   For a discussion of the O'Donnells and Derry in the early sixteenth century see B. Lacy, *Siege city: the story of Derry and Londonderry* (Belfast, 1990), pp 61–5.
10 *Fiants Ire., Eliz.*, nos 5190 and 5207.
11 P. Walsh (ed), *The life of Aodh Ruadh Ó Domhnaill transcribed front the Book of Lughaidh Ó Cléirigh* (Dublin, 1948, 1957), 1, 55.
12 Sir Henry Docwra, 'A narration of the services done by the army employed to Lough Foyle' in John O'Donovan (ed.), *Miscellany of the Celtic Society*, passim.
13 *Cal. Pat. Rolls Ire., Jas I*, p. 52.
14 *Cal. S.P. Ire., 1606–8*, p. 365.
15 *AFM*, 1601.
16 *Fiants Ire., Eliz.*, no. 6655; *Cal. Pat. Rolls Ire., Jas I*, p. 59.
17 For a full discussion of the issues at stake in the Nine Years' War see Morgan, *Tyrone's rebellion* (Dublin, 1993).
18 RIA, MS 14.B.7., pp 423–4. These accounts of the 'old customs' of O'Donnell, one by Teige McLinchy who had been steward to Red Hugh O'Donnell, suggest that the later O'Donnells had had difficulty in drawing revenue from North Connacht. There, only Tirawley is mentioned, where O'Donnell's 'rent' was 'ten pence in lieu of each cow'. Political influence might, of course, be exercised nonetheless. The document seems to imply, by mentioning it, that O'Donnell should receive the *eric*.
19 Interestingly, the conditions in Sir Cahir O'Doherty's patent under the crown in 1605 were less onerous than the ones demanded by O'Donnell had been: he should pay a rent of 30 beeves and provide a rising out of 6 horse and 20 foot; however, his tenure in capite would allow of the incidents of fiscal feudalism.

[20] Lord Deputy Perrott was informed by the privy council in August 1584 of 'how loth we are to be carried into charges and how we would rather spend a pound, forced by necessity, than a penny for prevention' (*Cal. S.P. Ire., 1574–85*, p. 525).

[21] For his own account of this see Docwra, 'Narration'.

[22] *Cal. S.P. Ire., 1596–7* pp 108, 146; *Cal. Carew MSS, 1603–24*, pp 284, 299, 397.

[23] G.A. Hayes-McCoy (ed.), *Ulster and other Irish maps* (Dublin, 1964) pp 26–7.

[24] *Cal. Carew MSS, 1601–3*, pp 284, 299, 397.

[25] F. Moryson, *An history of Ireland from the year 1599 to 1603* (Dublin, 1735), ii, 347–51.

[26] Ibid., p. 231.

[27] Erck (ed.), *Pat. Rolls Ire., Jas I*, pp 24–5.

[28] RIA, MS 14.B.7, p. 424.

[29] B. Lacy et al., *Archaeological survey of county Donegal* (Lifford, 1983), pp 330–2. The friars of Donegal were witnesses of the agreement between O'Donnell and O'Connor Sligo in 1539 (M. Carney, 'Agreement between Ó Domhnaill and Tadhg Ó Conchobhair concerning Sligo castle (23 June 1539)' in *IHS*, 3 (1942–3), pp 282–96.

[30] Erck (ed.), *Pat Rolls Ire., Jas 1*, pp 24–5.

[31] *Cal. Pat. Rolls Ire., Eliz.*, p. 587.

[32] For accounts of these events see *AFM*, 1603; F. Moryson, *An history of Ireland front the year 1599 to 1603*, ii, 154, 167, 256, 284, 335–6; Docwra, 'Narration', pp 263–81.

[33] Erck, *Rep. Pat. Rolls Ire., Jas I*, p. 47; *Cal. Pat. Rolls Ire., Jas I*, p.10. He received a pardon on 15 October (ibid., p. 35).

[34] *Cal. Pat. Rolls Ire., Jas I*, p. 13; Erck, *Rep. Pat. Rolls Ire., Jas I*, pp 59–60.

[35] Erck, *Rep. Pat. Rolls Ire., Jas I*, pp 106–7; *Cal. Pat. Rolls Ire., Jas I*, pp 47–8. The commissioners were some of the local military commanders along with William Parsons, surveyor-general and Nicholas Kenney, escheator-general.

[36] Ibid.; *Inq. Cancell. Hib. Repert.*, II, Donegal (2), (3) Jas I.

[37] TNA, R.C.9/1, pp 141–9.

[38] *Cal. Pat. Rolls Ire., Jas I*, p. 13. A crown lease of some of the regalities was made to John Bingley, then of Dublin, in October 1603 (ibid., p. 14).

[39] *Cal. Pat. Rolls Ire., Jas I*, pp 12, 48, 57–8, 113, 129, 145; Erck, *Rep. Pat. Rolls Ire., Jas I*, pp 223, 40–1, 53, 54, 107–9, 112–14, 132–4.

[40] The lands of St Patrick's Purgatory, Termon Magrath and Termonnemongan found by inquisition in November 1603 and granted to Robert Leicester in 1604, were granted to James Magrath in December 1610 (*Cal. Pat. Rolls Ire., Jas I*, p. 187). The influence of Archbishop Miler Magrath of Cashel is probably to be found here.

[41] The commission to the lord deputy and other government officers empowering them to grant leases was dated 12 April 1603 (Erck, *Rep. Pat. Rolls Ire., Jas I*, pp 18–19).

[42] R.J. Hunter, 'Sir Ralph Bingley, c. 1570–1627: Ulster planter' in P. Roebuck (ed), *Plantation to partition* (Belfast, 1981), pp 14–28, 253–6. For the *Triall* episode see D.B. Quinn, 'The voyage of *Triall* 1606–7: an abortive Virginia venture' in *The American Neptune*, XXXI, no. 2 (1971), 85–103.

[43] *Cal. Pat. Rolls Ire., Jas I*, p. 95. Tassagard is modern Saggart, approximately 500 acres and 11 miles from Dublin.

[44] Ibid., pp 101–2. On this occasion too, a fairly standard provision was inserted with regard to Ballyshannon castle, which again was granted only for Folliott's lifetime, that lie should make no assignment of it to any person except of English birth or born in the Pale, without the deputy's consent.

[45] Ibid., pp 541–2.

[46] Ibid., p. 14 (bis).

[47] Ibid., pp 10, 15.

[48] *Cal. Pat. Rolls Ire., Jas I*, pp 84–5.

[49] For the most recent exposition see H. Morgan, 'Hugh O'Neill and the Nine Years' War in Tudor Ireland' in *Historical Journal*, 36 (1993), 21–37. Niall O'Boyle who was Catholic bishop of Raphoe, 1591–1611, was therefore the last single bishop of the diocese.

[50] *Inq. Cancell. Hib. Repert.*, II, xvii.

[51] HMC, *Egmont MSS* i, 1, 29–30; *Fiants Ire., Eliz.*, no. 6501; *Cal. S.P. Ire., 1603–6*, pp 432, 567. There had been one appointment of sheriff prior to the Nine Years' War.

[52] *Cal. S.P. Ire., 1603–6*, p. 111.

[53] *Cal. S.P. Ire., 1606–8*, p. 369.

[54] *Cal. S.P. Ire., 1606–8*, pp 2, 35.

[55] HMC, *Salisbury [=Cecil] MSS* 18, 140–41; *Cal. S.P. Ire. 1603–6*, p. 562.

[56] *Cal. S.P. Ire., 1603–6*, pp 268, 296.

[57] J. O'Donovan (ed.), *Miscellany of the Celtic Society* (Dublin, 1849), pp 190–1. The author, it may be noted, was Sir Henry Docwra.

[58] I have adopted the term 'warlord' from Katharine Simms's important study *From kings to warlords: the changing political structure of Gaelic Ireland in the later middle ages* (Woodbridge, 1987), and suggest that the term 'landlord' conveys something useful about the changes that were intended. This paragraph is based on a reading of the sources for this policy in Connacht and Monaghan.

[59] *Fiants Ire, Eliz*, no. 5207.

[60] *Inq. Cancell. Hib. Repert.*, 2, xxi–xxxi.

[61] H. Morgan, *Tyone's rebellion*, pp 130, 143–4.

[62] *Cal. Pat. Rolls Ire., Jas I*, p. 13.

[63] Ibid., p. 59.

[64] *Inq. Cancell. Hib. Repert.*, 2, xxxi–xl; HMC, *Hastings MSS*, iv, 153.

[65] G.A. Hayes-McCoy, 'Sir John Davies in Cavan in 1606 and 1610' in *Breifne*, i, no. 3 (1960), pp 177–91.

[66] Printed in M.J. Bonn, *Die englische kolonisation in Ireland* i (Stuttgart & Berlin, 1906) 394–7; Aidan Clarke in *N.H.I.* iii, 193.

[67] *Cal. S.P. Ire., 1606–8*, p. 262.

[68] *Cal. S.P. Ire., 1603–6*, p. 161.

[69] K. Simms, *From kings to warlords*, p. 146; *Cal. S.P. Ire., 1600–1*, pp 289–90. Rory had, of course, been neither elected nor inaugurated, Gaelic-style, as lord. His brother Hugh had by will disponed the lordship to him (J.J. Silke, 'The last will of red Hugh O'Donnell' in *Studia Hibernica*, 24 (1984–8), 58.

[70] *Cal. S.P. Ire., 1603–6*, p. 192.

[71] Walsh, *Destruction by peace*, pp 152–3. His cause was finally heard by the privy council at Greenwich on 28 March 1605.

[72] *Cal. S.P. Ire., 1603–6*, pp 296–8, 303–5. O'Donnell made no reference to religion in these articles. He was seeking the right to nominate the sheriff again in May 1606 (HMC, *Salisbury [=Cecil] MSS* 18, 140–41).

[73] *Cal. S.P. Ire., 1606–8*, p. 373.

[74] *Cal. S.P. Ire., 1608–10*, pp 571–2.

[75] *Cal. S.P. Ire., 1606–8*, pp 85, 124, 225.

[76] T. Ó Cianáin, *The Flight of the Earls*, (ed.) P. Walsh (Dublin, 1916), p. 9.

[77] *Cal. S.P. Ire., 1603–6*, p. 319.

[78] Ibid., p. 320. The most recent 'ancient rent' of MacSweeney Fanad appears to have been 18 beeves and 10 milch cows and 10 marks for the support of bonaghts, though he must send to the field 120 gallowglasses in time of warfare (RIA, MS 14.8.7., p. 423). The early sixteenth-century historian of the MacSweeneys claimed that an agreement had been reached a century earlier between MacSweeney Fanad and O'Donnell for the payment of a *martaigheacht* of six beeves no more than three times a year and an earlier MacSweeney, he asserted, had given no cows at all to O'Donnell, 'for he was strong and powerful and his own tribe was in submission to him' (P. Walsh (ed.) *Leabhar Chlainne Suibne* (Dublin, 1920), pp 51, 59). For analysis see K. Simms, *From kings to warlords*, pp 142–3. No wonder, then, that Rory should seek, in Englished circumstances, to reduce them to leaseholders for years.

[79] *Cal. S.P. Ire., 1603–6*, p. 320.

[80] Ibid., pp 297, 304.

[81] Ibid., pp 319–20. For the loss of castles to the nobility in England see P. Williams, *The Tudor regime* (Oxford, 1979), p. 438. A segment at Carrigans was also retained though it is not mentioned at this time.

[82] *Cal. S.P. Ire., 1603–6*, pp 319–20. Some sums of money were however spent in those years on improvements to the fortifications here and at Ballyshannon and Culmore (J. Buckley (ed),

'Report of Sir Josias Bodley on some Ulster fortresses in 1608' in *Ulster Journal of Archaeology*, 2nd ser. 16 (1910), 61–4).

[83] *Cal. Pat. Rolls Ire., Jas I*, p. 182.

[84] Ibid., pp 206–7.

[85] *Cal. S.P. Ire., 1603–6*; p. 322. Captain Henry Harte received a lease for twenty-one years of the castle and fort of Culmore and some 300 acres adjoining, reserved to the crown out of O'Doherty's patent in February 1606 (*Cal. Pat. Rolls Ire., Jas I*, p. 83).

[86] *Cal. S.P. Ire., 1603–6*, pp 320, 322. This exact note, which must have been very hastily done, does not appear to have survived. It could scarcely have been an adequate record on which to base land titles.

[87] *Cal. S.P. Ire., 1603–6*, pp 558–68; N.P. Canny, 'The flight of the earls, 1607' in *IHS*, 17 (1970–71), 386–7.

[88] *Cal. S.P. Ire., 1603–6*, pp 542, 560.

[89] For the government of the Spanish Netherlands under the Archdukes and its relationship to Spain see H. de Schepper & G. Parker, 'The formation of government policy in the Catholic Netherlands under the Archdukes, 1596–1621' in *EHR*, 91(1976), 241–54.

[90] Walsh, *Destruction by peace*, passim.

[91] Ibid., pp 164–7.

[92] Ibid., pp 29–30, 152–3.

[93] Ibid., pp 175–6, 179–80; B. Quinn, *Explorers and colonies: America, 1500–1625* (London and Ronceverte, 1990), pp 321–39.

[94] Walsh, *Destruction by peace*, p. 192. In her introduction to this important collection of documents, the editor tends to refer to this and other joint statements of O'Neill and O'Donnell as documents of O'Neill only. For its part this chapter is concerned with O'Donnell; it is not its aim to give a full account of the Flight of the Earls.

[95] *Cal. Pat. Rolls Ire., Eliz.*, pp 439–40.

[96] *Cal. S.P. Ire., 1603–6*, pp 74, 312–14, 418–20, 529–30, 536; 1606–6, pp 45, 111, 116, 134, 220, 522–3. Richard Nugent's father is also an interesting case. During 'the doubtful time of the siege of Kinsale' he had come under suspicion of collusion with O'Neill and having been arrested had died in Dublin castle in 1602 before his trial had taken place (Moryson, *Ireland from 1599 to 1603*, ii, p. 154).

[97] *Cal. S.P. Ire., 1606–8*, pp 320–1.

[98] Ibid., pp 254–6.

[99] Ibid., pp 259–62.

[100] The only formal evidence of the Brussels government's involvement so far available lies in the issuing of a license to go to Ireland to O'Brien, then in the Irish regiment there, on 16 August (B. Jennings (ed), *Wild geese in Spanish Flanders, 1582–1700* (Dublin, 1964), pp 91, 535). However, O'Brien appears to have been the Archdukes' emissary.

[101] Walsh, *Destruction by peace*, pp 50–55; *Cal. S.P. Ire., 1606–8*, pp 297–300.

[102] What would be sought on their behalf with James I was a pardon and an agreement 'to settle them in their countries in the same state that they were before the last rebellion, with liberty of conscience at least in their own countries'. Evidence that this was the intention comes, indirectly, from views expressed by the Franciscan Owen Groome Magrath. Magrath also asserted that in the event of war, the pope had undertaken to provide financial support to the extent of 50,000 crowns and also some soldiers, 'if he could conveniently bring it to pass' (ibid., p. 299).

[103] Walsh, *Destruction by peace*, pp 73–4, 231.

[104] *Cal. S.P. Ire., 1606–8*, p. 321 and also p. 299.

[105] On the efforts to enforce the reformation in the years after 1603 see Aidan Clarke in *N.H.I.*, 3, 188–92.

[106] Walsh, *Destruction by peace*, pp 189–95. The earls' view, as expressed here, would tend to suggest an earlier origin for the English civil war than is commonly now accepted. They may, however, have been referring to the anti-enclosure Midland Revolt of 1607. Undoubtedly, too, there were serious problems about taxation in England at this time, but on the other hand the burden of war taxation had been lifted given the peace with Spain.

[107] Rumours of thinking about an assault on England surfaced in the alleged remark of Owen Groome Magrath to the baron of Delvin that it was the earls' strategy to return with foreign forces to Munster and, 'when they had well settled there', that 'they would soon after attempt

England from thence' (*Cal. S.P. Ire., 1606–8*, p. 321). Also Cú Connacht Maguire is said to have told the people around Rathmullan on his departure with the earls 'that they should shortly hear of their being in England with a powerful army, from whence they would return into Ireland' (ibid., p. 275).

108 *Cal. S.P. Ire., 1606–8*, pp 311–13.

109 Jennings (ed.) *Wild geese*, pp 94, 97, 542.

110 C. Martin and G. Parker, *The Spanish armada* (London, 1988), pp 81–2, 96–8.

111 The reference was to Pope Adrian IV's bull *Laudabiliter*.

112 The document, which is undated, is published in *Archivium Hibernicum*, 3, 302–10 where a much later date is suggested. However, it may be the 'letter from Tyrone' which Cardinal Bentivoglio sent to Rome on 24 November 1607 or perhaps have been produced in 1608, though before O'Doherty's rising since it makes no reference to it. It referred again to the grander issue of Catholicism in the north of Europe. In May 1608 it was rumoured from Brussels that Tyrone sought from the pope 'the like allowance as he formerly gave for the maintenance of the war against the Turk' and that he should make a similar recommendation to Spain and that the earls sought only money and would themselves secure the soldiers (*Cal. S.P. Ire., 1606–8*, pp 660–1). It appears that Tyrone thought that no more than 12,000 men would he required 'to thrust all the English out of Ireland' (ibid., pp 664–5) and it looks likely that he hoped to have the use of the Irish regiment in Spanish Flanders to advance his purposes.

113 Jennings (ed), *Wild geese*, pp 538–9.

114 C. Giblin, 'Catalogue of material of Irish interest in the collection *Nunziatura di Fiandra*, Vatican archives' I, in *Collect. Hib.* 1 (1958), 556. Bentivoglio regretted the encouragement being offered to the earls by Archbishop Lombard in Rome.

115 Walsh, *Destruction by peace*, pp 197–200.

116 Jennings (ed.), *Wild geese*, p. 539; *Cal. S.P. Ire., 1606–8*, pp 641–3.

117 The petition of Cormac MacBaron O'Neill to Spain in 1596 to be granted the ownership of a substantial area of County Down, including old English land in Lecale, may be worth taking into account in this context (H. Morgan, *Tyrone's rebellion*, pp 233–5). Given the O'Neill aspiration to control north of the Boyne, the palesmen of Louth might well have felt uneasy. Cormac MacBaron was himself arrested after the Flight of the Earls and dispatched to the Tower of London.

118 *Cal. Pat. Rolls Ire., Jas I*, p. 134; *Cal. S.P. Ire., 1606–8*, p. 502.

119 *Cal. Pat. Rolls Ire., Jas I*, pp 197–8, 220–1, 238.

120 *Cal. S.P. Dom., 1611–18*, p. 65. He was also granted livery of his estate in succession to his father in December 1608 (*Cal. Pat. Rolls Ire., Jas I*, p. 139).

121 GEC, *Peerage*, VI, 607–8; V.J. McBrierty (ed.), *The Howth peninsula: its history, lore and legend* (Dublin, 1981), p. 26; L.J. Arnold, *The restoration land settlement in County Dublin, 1660–1688* (Dublin, 1993), pp 155, 158. The marriage took place in 1615 and St Lawrence died in 1619.

122 *Cal. Pat. Rolls Ire., Jas I*, p. 160.

124 *Cal. S.P. Ire., 1608–10*, pp 287, 305.

125 For an account of the rebellion, see B. Bonner, *That audacious traitor* (Dublin, 1975).

126 Walsh, *Destruction by peace*, pp 222–3, 226–8.

127 Ibid., p. 225. The very least that could, as a result, be achieved would he liberty of conscience.

128 Ibid., p. 226.

129 Ibid., pp 229–30.

130 Ibid., pp 234–6, where the Spanish ambassador summarises his discussion with the pope. For the conflict with Venice see W.J. Bouwsma, *Venice and the defense of republican liberty* (Berkeley and Los Angeles, 1968). An important study of the papal finances at this time is P. Partner, 'Papal financial policy in the renaissance and counterreformation' in *Past and Present* no. 88 (Aug. 1980), 17–62.

131 Walsh, *Destruction by peace*, p. 236.

132 Ibid., pp 237–40.

133 For Anglo-Spanish relations at this time see Quinn, *Explorers and colonies*, pp 321–39. Partner's study of the papal finances (p. 54) reveals that Pope Paul V spent 335,000 silver scudi on subsidies to Catholic powers and that he also allocated 1,000,000 silver scudi (4 per cent of income) to benefit members of his own family. See also W. Reinhard, 'Papal power and family strategy in the sixteenth and seventeenth centuries' in R.G. Asch and A.M. Birke (ed.), *Princes, patronage and the nobility* (Oxford, 1991), pp 329–56.

[134] G.R. Batho, 'Henry Ninth Earl of Northumberland and Syon House, Middlesex, 1594–1632' in *Ancient Monument Society Transactions*, New ser., 4 (1956), 102, 108.

[135] HMC, *Salisbury [=Cecil] MSS* 18, 140–41.

[136] *Cal. S.P. Ire., 1603–8*, pp 561, 564. For the acreage of the Assaroe abbey estate see Geraldine Carville, *Assaroe: 'Abbey of the morning star'* (Ballyshannon, n.d.), p: 15. The existence of the hill in question was confirmed by me on a field trip on 4 September 1993. On 18 September 1606 Donogh O'Connor Sligo was asserting that the castle of Bundrowes and twenty quarters of land associated with it should belong to him (HMC, *Salisbury [=Cecil] MSS* 18, 291–2).

[137] *Cal. S.P. Ire., 1606–8*, p. 35.

[138] Ibid., pp 95–6.

[139] Ibid., p. 308.

[140] *Cal. S.P. Ire., 1603–6*, pp 568–9. On this see p. 542.

[141] BL, Add MS 19,838, ff 35v–6.

[142] For a discussion of the use of recognizances by the monarchy in England a century earlier see G.W. Bernard, *The Tudor nobility* (Manchester, 1992), pp 57–65.

[143] For the earl's own account of this see *Cal. S.P. Ire., 1606–8*, p. 371. It is possible too that at this point a full freeholder settlement' might also have been attempted.

[144] *Cal. S.P. Ire., 1606–8*, pp 296, 398. One element in his debts was incurred through efforts to purchase the monastic estate of Kilmacrenan, thereby to establish a territorial footing in the north of Donegal.

[145] An informant in Brussels writing to London in January 1608 expressed the view that 'priests and friars are the doers of all' and said that those who had come with the earls had for the most part, a thousand times wished themselves safe hack again' (ibid., p. 643).

[146] On Randal MacDonnell, earl of Antrim see Jane H. Ohlmeyer, *Civil War and restoration in the three Stuart kingdoms; the career of Randal MacDonnell marquis of Antrim, 1609–1683* (Cambridge, 1993), pp 18–36.

[147] Ó Clerigh, *Aodh Ruadh Ó Domhnaill*, i, 345–7. The excellent paper by Michelle O'Riordan, 'The native Ulster *mentalite* as revealed in Gaelic sources, 1600–1650' in B. MacCuarta (ed.) *Ulster 1641: aspects of the rising* (Belfast, 1993), pp 61–91 was published just as this one, which is mainly concerned with government policy and the response it generated, was being written and should be read in conjunction with it.

[148] *Cal. S.P. Ire., 1606–8*, pp 508–11, 530–4.

[149] Niall Garbh had in fact asked for an interim custodiam of the lordship (ibid., p. 510).

[150] *Cal. S.P. Ire., 1606–8*, pp 511–14, 530–4.

[151] Ibid., pp 499–502, 524–7, 528–9, 547–9.

[152] Ibid., pp 580–1, 599–605.

[153] Ibid., pp 542, 599.

[154] Ibid., pp 573–4; Seán Ó Domhnaill, 'Sir Niall Garbh O'Donnell and the rebellion of Sir Cahir O'Doherty' in *IHS*, 3 (1942–3), 34–8.

[155] For the creation of the county see *Inq. Cancell. Hib. Repert.*, ii, 18–19.

[156] Michael Roberts, 'On aristocratic constitutionalism in Swedish history' in his *Essays in Swedish history* (London, 1967), pp 14–55.

[157] The title of Viceroy was used. Spain normally governed its dependencies through viceroys. Might the Earl of Essex (who himself had an Irish estate) have been in mind for this office?

[158] Lordly power would be safe within such a constitutional framework.

[159] *Cal. S.P. Ire., 1599–1600*, pp 279–80, 280–1 (a summary). This is the document which was endorsed by secretary of state Sir Robert Cecil with the word 'Ewtopia'. The alternative quest for a new Irish monarchy with O'Neill or a Spaniard as king, and how O'Donnell might be affected by it, cannot be dealt with here in any detail.

[160] This derives from comments made by Bartholemew Owen, a confidante of Hugh O'Neill's, in January 1606 (TNA, S.P. 63/218, no. 18 (1)). In this context it may be worth noting that Hugh O'Neill had his marriage to Mabel Bagnal in 1591 conducted by the Protestant bishop of Meath (S. Ó Faoláin, *The great O'Neill: a biography of Hugh O'Neill Earl of Tyrone 1550–1616* (London, 1942), pp 116–9).

[161] The phrase is J.G.A. Pocock's, from his *The ancient constitution and the feudal law* (Cambridge, 2nd ed., 1987), p. 16. In Sweden, Erik Sparre and other exponents of aristocratic constitutionalist ideas were executed in 1600 (M. Roberts, *Swedish history*, p. 23).

[162] R. Bonney, *Political change in France under Richelieu and Mazarin, 1624–1661* (Oxford, 1978), pp 384–400. To reduce local independence in France Henri IV destroyed a number of castles and forts after 1593, while over 100 fortresses were razed by Richelieu in the 1630s after a series of Huguenot and aristocratic rebellions (G. Parker, *The military revolution* (Cambridge, 1988), pp 41–2).

All dates are given in the old style except that the year is taken to begin on 1 January and not 25 March.

3

Plantation in Donegal

This chapter seeks to present a short survey of the plantation in Donegal against a background of the general plan of plantation in Ulster and to examine in more detail its impact in one area of Donegal. It will also consider the circumstances and effects of its establishment prior to 1641.

The plantation plan

The decision to carry out a plantation in Ulster was based on two considerations: fear and opportunism. If the earls returned, argued Lord Deputy Chichester, expressing his anxieties for security, 'they will assuredly land in Ulster', while to Sir Geoffrey Fenton, an old government official with many years of Irish experience, a 'door [was] opened' to the king now 'to pull down for ever these two proud houses of O'Neill and O'Donnell'. Through plantation, Chichester went on to show, revenue would accrue to the government equal to that from Munster or Connacht and, with the Ulster problem solved, the recurring burden of military expenditure would be lifted.[1] By the end of September 1607, following on such advice, the decision for plantation had been made in London in outline form.[2] The process of designing what turned out to be a complex and systematic plantation plan for the escheated counties, as well as the carrying out of the necessary preliminaries to its implementation, took some two years and it was not until 1610 that the new ownership arrangements could be brought into being. Once implemented, though, it was expected that the many norms and ways of law, order and obedience to government could be made to apply in Ulster too.

The scheme eventually adopted embraced six counties – Donegal with Armagh, Tyrone, Cavan, Fermanagh and the subsequent County Londonderry – and in five of these (excluding the Londoners' plantation) a relatively uniform plan was followed. The ownership arrangements provided for two types of new proprietor, undertakers and servitors – the first, English and Lowland Scottish (the latter arising from the linkage of Scotland with England incident on James I's succession to the English throne) in equal numbers, the second, as the name implies, mainly military officers – who received estates (called proportions) planned to range in size from 1,000 to 2,000 profitable acres. The other major group of owners comprised the Ulster Irish themselves. Although Dublin had not succeeded in redefining the larger lesser landholders as freeholders in the years before the flight (a policy so distasteful to the previous lords) and although now the patents of the departed were interpreted literally to allow a full-scale confiscation, Old Irish grantees, holding directly from the crown, formed an element in this plantation (as in most others), while pre-plantation grants to a small number of lesser Gaelic figures were also generally upheld where their patents had actually been, taken out.

In addition to those three main groups, land was allocated for other purposes. Church-owned land – collectively the monastic estates; the termon and erenach lands, though their owners were by now much more secular than ecclesiastical; episcopal property and various small areas appertaining to parish clergy and other ecclesiastical dignitaries – had constituted a multi-form separate category in the old order, accounting for perhaps close on 20 per cent of the total acreage. While some of this had been secularised already with the monastic dissolutions in the years before the flight, decisions concerning substantial parts of these lands were made at the time of plantation. Thus along with the previous episcopal lands, the now established reformation episcopate received the extensive termon and erenach lands, distributed, as they were, throughout the parishes.[3] In addition, the parish clergy (the link with the erenach lands being now broken) were newly endowed with small areas of glebe taken out of the confiscated secular property. To promote education, English-style, grammar schools, one to be established in each county, were provided with landed support and also the new university in Dublin received an Ulster estate.[4] In these ways, a financial basis for reform through religion and education was provided for. Finally, the scheme for plantation in Ulster contained urbanising proposals. In all twenty-five corporate towns were to be established – some to be based around the new forts (to the support of some of which land had already been allotted), many, to symbolise the changed order, to be centred on the focal points of the old regime – all of which were to receive an allocation of land to nurture them. Of the three main categories of grantee, the undertakers (with the Londoners) received over 40 per cent of the acreage, the servitors close on 15 per cent and the Irish about 20 percent.[5]

Plantation, of course, implies settling or colonising; however, only the undertakers, hence the name, themselves forming the largest grantee category, were formally required to colonise. Precise obligations were laid down. Thus for estates of 1,000 acres and with proportionate increases for the larger ones – all estates to be manors – the undertaker should settle himself on a demesne of 300 acres, and plant on the rest of it, in accordance with a prescribed social structure, nine other families, 'to be made up of two fee-farmers (or freeholders) each with 120 acres, three leaseholders for three lives or twenty-one years on 100 acres each, and on the remaining 160 acres four families 'or more' of husbandmen, artificers or cottagers. These ten families should constitute between them twenty-four adult males. The undertakers were also tied to two specific building obligations. Their construction programme should involve buildings for themselves and buildings for their tenantry. The undertaker of a great proportion (a 2,000 acre estate) should erect 'a stone house with a strong court or bawne about it', that of a middle proportion (1,500 acres) might build either a stone or brick house also with a bawn, while the grantee of a small proportion (1,000 acres) must build 'a strong court or bawne at least'. This obligation reflects the defensive element which the plantation was supposed to serve. The second commitment concerned the tenantry. The undertakers should 'draw their tenants to build houses for themselves and their families … near the principal house or bawne, as well for their mutual defence and strength, as for the making of villages and townships'. While this phrasing did not explicitly commit the undertakers to build the tenants' houses, elsewhere it was implied that they should 'erect habitations' for them.[6] Aside from that point, it is clear from this that the plantation planners were intent on ensuring that the settlement pattern on the undertakers' lands across the plantation should be one of village living protected by the landlords' bawns rather than one of dispersed settlement. The other categories of grantee (the servitors and native Irish), not being explicitly required to plant incoming tenantry, were tied only to build personal strongholds. The Irish grantees, for their part, however, must forgo the taking of 'Irish exactions' from those under them who must instead enjoy clearly defined tenancies with 'rents certaine'.[7] For all grantees, quit rents, a major source of government revenue, were set, which in the case of the undertakers were to be £5.6.8 per 1,000 acre estate. Faults in mensuration, however, subverted the government intention not to give out very large estates and had the effect, amongst others, that there were fewer grantees and less revenue gains than there might have been.

The original intention was that the estates should be allocated to their various grantees entirely by the haphazard mechanism of lottery. This, however, was not adhered to in the final plan. In 1609 a series of maps of the escheated counties, remarkable for their day, and given the speed of execution but not providing a means for the accurate calculation of acreages, on which the bounds of the estates were marked in, had been made. They were drawn by barony (the term normally used for the administrative sub-divisions of counties in Ireland), the Ulster counties having been divided into baronies in recent years. To satisfy the demands of the undertakers, many of whom had common local backgrounds in England or Scotland, that they might group together in Ulster for mutual support and to give them some re-assurance about their security, it was decided that estates should be allocated to 'consorts' of undertakers, English and Scottish, on a barony basis. This decision had implications for the other grantee categories as well: servitors and native Irish grantees grouped together were allocated other baronies. This pattern was duplicated across the five counties. This arrangement also had implications for the proposed treatment of all levels of the pre-existing Irish population. Those who were now to be restored to land would receive it only in the baronies allotted for servitors and Irish grantees. Also, and very significantly, since the undertakers must not 'alien', i.e. let, any land to Irish tenantry, the Irish occupiers on the estates in the baronies allocated to them (somewhat over 40 per cent of the acreage) must move entirely elsewhere and concentrate into the estates of any of the other grantee categories. Finally, and more generally, behind the plantation lay a broader ambition (though one perhaps both secondary and more long term) concerning the native population as a whole: that in the Ulster re-organised in this way – before the source of internationalised rebellion and now to be set on a new course of development, social and economic – they would be Protestantised through the concurrent advancement of the reformation, and integrated into an Ireland more unitary and more controlled.

Plantation in Donegal

The arrangements for the plantation in Donegal combined the elements of the general framework with some exceptional features. In accordance with the plan, estates were granted out on a barony or precinct basis in much of the county. Thus groups of Scottish undertakers were planted in two – Portlough and Boylagh joined with Banagh – English undertakers in just one – Lifford – while servitors and native Irish together got the barony of Kilmacrenan or Doe and Fanad. These were part of the general framework of the entire plantation, decided on in London with the assistance of the barony maps and the participation of officials from Ireland, and there is no conclusive evidence of what factors dictated the allocation. However, one factor which seems to have been influential in determining the allocation of Kilmacrenan to servitors and Irish grantees was the notion that servitors already in place at strategic locations, for example, Rathmullan, should not be moved. Hence, in places, the plantation built on grants or leases already made, whether of monastic property, or of lands reserved for forts and defences or indeed of grants previously made to some

49

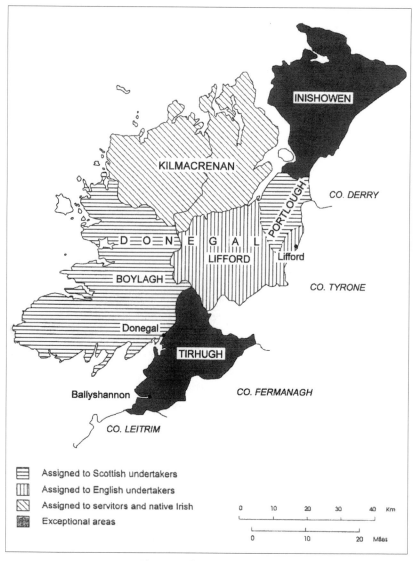

Plate 3.1 Plantation Donegal

individual Irish grantees. These may have been somewhat more numerous in Donegal than elsewhere.

The strategic consideration which had already entrenched Folliott as leaseholder at Ballyshannon with the lands reserved to it (the base from which he acquired the Assaroe monastic estate) in Tirhugh barony on the exposed south coast of County Donegal, may also account for the somewhat exceptional use to which yet more of that barony was put. Thus in November 1610, another military officer, Captain Basil Brooke, received a crown lease for twenty-one years of Donegal castle, O'Donnell's principal residence, its fishings, a small area of land nearby, which had supported it, and 'all customs and duties used and due to the said castle', at a rent of £1 Ir. per year.[8] Brooke, whose main estate was in Kilmacrenan, was later, in 1624, under a scheme for making economies in the forts, to be able to convert this title into one of outright ownership, on condition, however, that he should keep the castle under repair and permit the crown to place forces there in any 'time of rebellion or … general disturbance'.[9] A third such figure, Captain Paul Gore, a member of a prominent London merchant family (and with Folliott a grantee in Fermanagh as well), acquired, by a purchase from the grantee Richard Nugent, baron Delvin, mediated through the lord deputy's secretary, Henry Perse, the property of the two Third Order Regular Franciscan friaries of Magherabeg (close to Donegal) and Flannacharta, the latter a small MacSweeney Banagh foundation on St John's Point in the neighbouring barony.[10] Apart from this triumvirate, there, was one major Irish grantee. Contrary to the decision that such lands should go to the local Protestant episcopate, the lands of Termonmagrath with St Patrick's Purgatory and Termonomongan – a buffer zone inside and outside the county – were secured in December 1610 by James Magrath, son of archbishop Miler of Cashel and of the hereditary erenach family there. In the background to that lay a surrender and regrant ('for the purpose of reducing the lands to English tenure') involving Miler and his father in May 1596 and indeed the treatment of these termons fits in with the decisions concerning similar lands in Monaghan in 1591, including the obligation to build castles: James was required to build a 'capital house' within seven years.[11] The resulting structure – Castle Magrath – well underway in 1611, still stands.[12] In addition, a major beneficiary in Tirhugh, with about 25 per cent of the acreage, was the new university, Trinity College, Dublin. The college endowment (made up of lands in Armagh and Fermanagh too) came to include in Donegal, after complex post-war dealings in which Rory O'Donnell had been involved, the churchlands, originally Columban and latterly Franciscan, of Kilmacrenan as well.[13] Finally, the lands, assessed at 200 acres, allotted for the county grammar school (the 'royal school'), which it was proposed in 1609 to establish in the buildings of Donegal abbey, were located near Donegal in this barony.[14]

The treatment of the remaining barony, Inishowen, offers a striking contrast through its grant (church lands excluded)[15] to one man: Sir Arthur Chichester, the lord deputy. His entitling went through an evolution, reflected in instructions by 'king's letter' and one patent modified by another more careful in definition between June 1609 and July 1610 which amongst other things brought his grant to dovetail with that to the city of London of the future county of Londonderry, concerning which negotiations were finalised in January 1610. The principal difference related to Culmore and land adjacent. Initially intended to be granted to Chichester, who should receive the pay of a constable and gunner and the command of any warders maintained there, Culmore and this land was instead granted to the Londoners, they covenanting to maintain there 'at their own proper costs and charges' a ward of as many men and officers as should be necessary for its defence, without cost to the crown. This decision also had implications for the setting of the county boundary. Instead, however, and to increase coastal defences, Chichester was to receive the fees of a constable, gunner and ten warders to be kept at Greencastle castle. In his patents Inishowen was perceived as made up of four manors in each of which he might hold courts leet and courts baron before his seneschals, as well as markets and fairs. However, in his first – and this is missing from his second – he was given liberty (and by implication expected) to divide the territory into manors of 2,000 acres on each of which he should build a 'castle or capital messuage' within seven years, a reflection in the first instance of the estate-size norms of the plantation plan and in the second of the building prescriptions of earlier schemes. He was also given the quasi-medieval liberty to appoint four bailiffs 'to execute all writs and other processes ... no sheriff or bailiff of the crown to intermeddle'. He was not specifically required to colonise but he should institute 'free tenants' or freeholders, was allowed to hold in common soccage tenure and had his quit rent, set at £86.12.8 stg in his patent of February 1610, reduced to £30 in his second in July.[16]

We now turn to the urbanising proposals for Donegal. In the English order, society was seen as divided between countryside and town or county and borough, distinctions which had had less meaning in the prior Gaelic world where lords may anyhow have sought to accumulate power to themselves. Towns should be both centres of trades and commerce and lanterns of local civility – hosts of schooling, law, church and administration – which when incorporated returned, like the counties, members to parliaments to participate in central consultation and law-making. To support these settlements, areas of land were to be assigned to their corporations and to 'people' them there was to be 'a levy or press of tradesmen and artificers' from England. For Donegal eight places – generally of some significance, political or ecclesiastical, in the old order and now to be re-orientated as symbols of the new – were chosen for incorporation and urbanisation and listed in the 'project' of the plantation produced in January 1609.[17] One of them, Derry, located in another traditional buffer zone between the lordships, like Termonmagrath, though more complex in make-up and at this stage placed in County Donegal, to which 1,000 acres of escheated land was to be allocated, need not concern us here because shortly it was to be placed instead in County Londonderry.[18] Of the remaining seven places, Lifford, Ballyshannon and Donegal were to receive 300 'acres' apiece while Killybegs, Raphoe, Rathmullan and, apparently, Carndonagh were each to be allotted 200 'acres'.[19] Some of the allocations failed, however, to materialise. Thus Chichester's patents of Inishowen passed without reservation of corporation land for a town there, and Raphoe, seated within episcopal land, received no extra endowment. Also the crown did not pursue the proposed plan for town planting by impressment or coercion; rather it devolved the responsibility for urbanisation to individual planters. Accordingly, a local grantee received the lands on condition that he should build and settle townsmen.[20]

The grant to Basil Brooke for Donegal embraced a rudimentary planning aesthetic. In March 1612 he agreed 'to set apart a convenient place for the site of the said town to be built' and 'for the market place, church and church-yard'. The town should consist of twenty burgesses 'besides cottagers and other inferior inhabitants', to be accommodated with houses and lands within four years. In addition thirty acres should be set aside for common, to be called the burgess-field, and two acres for a school and exercise ground.[21] A year earlier, Sir Ralph Bingley had been tied to somewhat similar conditions for Rathmullan: he should plant within four years twenty Englishmen or Scots, 'chiefly artificers', to be burgesses and thereafter incorporated, each to receive two acres of ground, besides their houses and gardens, 'with the whole bog of Rathmullan for common of turf'.[22] Belatedly, in December 1615, Roger Jones, of Sligo (whose involvement highlights an old geographical link in a new, but reverse, form)[23] received the lands for Killybegs, again under similar conditions but with the variation that although he should build twenty houses, the burgesses should be twelve in number.[24] Even within this context of devolving responsibility to private men, the aspirations for Lifford, the county town, were grander. As early as October 1610 Sir Richard Hansard received a lease for twenty-one years at a rent of £2 Ir. of both the fort, 'commonly called Captain Brooke's fort', and of the lands (four quarters) which had already been reserved for Lifford by Chichester in 1605,[25] under specific urbanising conditions. Within five years he should allocate to sixty people sites for houses there, each with a 'curtilage or backside' and a garden plot 'adjoining', which they themselves should build, each to hold by rent from him for the remaining part of the twenty-one years. He should also assign and set out a specified area of land to be used by them as a common for meadow, pasture and turbary.[26] The final definitive plan for Lifford came in January 1612. At that point, Hansard received an outright grant of the four quarters of reserved land, with the exception of the fort, now to be called the king's fort, and the meadow of Stramore nearby (saving four acres of it granted to Hansard)[27] which the crown retained and which therefore now became a separate entity. Otherwise, he now became committed to a somewhat scaled-down colonising obligation. He was to settle within four years, thirty persons, English or Scots 'especially artificers or mechanics' to be burgesses and to be incorporated, fifteen of whom should receive two acres apiece and fifteen one acre apiece nearby, 'besides their several … sufficient places … for houses or messuages with backsides and gardens … within the said town to be erected', to hold for ever as freeholders. They should likewise receive the 'moor or bog' of Roughan for a common turbary and 100 acres for a common pasture.[28]

The process of incorporation followed quickly for a number of these places, its context being the meeting of the 1613–15 parliament. However, only some of the places originally designated received charters. Those which did receive them were Lifford and Donegal in February 1613 followed by Ballyshannon one month later, while Killybegs was incorporated in December 1615. In each, the corporate body established was made up of a chief officer (called guardian in the Lifford charter) and twelve burgesses.[29]

It is necessary to revert now to some brief comments on the areas where the plantation was applied in its normal form, beginning with Kilmacrenan barony (some 300,000 acres) which was allocated to servitors and Irish grantees. Here there were seventeen servitor grantees as well as a section of the estate granted to Trinity College. The servitors included men such as Sir Ralph Bingley and the Vaughans (John and Henry) who had been part of Sir Henry Docwra's Lough Foyle expedition, Captain Henry Harte, who had been at Culmore, and Captain William Stewart, a Scot who had been sent to Ulster with 200 foot to suppress O'Doherty's rising.[30] The Irish grantees between them received about 60 per cent of the barony which represented (excluding James Magrath's termon lands in Tirhugh) about 20 per cent of the county as a whole.

The Irish grantees, some fifty in all, divided into two groups. Thus six major figures received large estates within the framework of the plantation plan and there was also a second much more numerous category receiving smaller areas. The six included Donnell MacSweeney Fanad and Sir Mulmory MacSweeney a Doe, both from that area, and Donagh MacSweeney Banagh, the three heads of the MacSweeney sub-lord families, the latter transplanted from Banagh in south-west Donegal, and also a more minor figure, Walter McLoughlin MacSweeney. In addition, the young

Turlough O'Boyle, the other major sub-lord under the O'Donnells, from Boylagh, received an estate, while Hugh McHugh Duff O'Donnell, head of a branch of the former ruling family, retained just a life interest, in land based on Ramelton. For their part the lesser grantees may be taken to include many, though, of course, only a proportion of all, who would have been made freeholders had there been no plantation. One was Lughaidh O'Clery, 'chronicler', while another was a woman, Grainne ny Donnell. Two prominent widows received life interests – Ineen Dubh, Rory O'Donnell's Scottish mother and Honora Bourke (indicating a marriage alliance into old English Connacht), widow of the former O'Boyle.[31] In addition, the prior interests of the Dublin merchants with whom Rory O'Donnell had had dealings were compensated, and his own widow, Bridget, countess of Tyrconnell, was awarded a pension of £300 stg per annum in 1616.[32]

The locations of the grants of the Irish suggest that, a policy of interspersing them with the servitors was followed, though some of the latter were placed together from Letterkenny towards Ramelton (the 'lough shore' area). One factor, security-based, is also again clear. Only Hugh McHugh Duff retained his castle – for life at Ramelton. Though tied to build in accordance with plantation regulations, neither Sir Mulmory nor Donnell MacSweeney regained their castles at Doe or Rathmullan – the latter being retained by Sir Ralph Bingley and received their estates elsewhere, in Donnell's case further north and in Sir Mulmory's in the Dunfanaghy area. Nor did all these grantees, large or smaller, retain their lands up to 1641: varied pressures and problems of adjustment appear to have affected them. MacSweeney Banagh was one such casualty: he had lost much land by 1641. Another was Sir Mulmory Macsweeney a Doe, whose grandson was a captain in the rising of 1641. His entire estate had come into the hands of Sir Paul Davis, an exchequer and ward's official in Dublin since the mid-1620s and clerk of the privy council, by February 1640.[33] By contrast, MacSweeney Fanad had successfully retained his lands which were held in 1641, following an apparent practice of divided inheritance rather than primogeniture, by various members of his family.[34] Equally, the land granted to Walter McLaughlin MacSweeney, described in 1619 as 'a justice of the peace in the county and conformable to his Majesty's laws, serving the king and country upon all occasions', had by 1641 passed mainly to his son, Ervin, of Ray (then also a justice of the peace who wrote good English and an initial opponent of the rising in October of that year), though with provision for another son, Neale Mergagh and jointure for his widow Grainne Ni Gallogher.[35] Also a small number of MacSweeney proprietors in 1641, one of them the owner of a piece of land acquired from one of the servitor grantees, Henry Vaughan, had become converted to Protestantism.[36] Overall, however, there had been a clear decline in the holdings of the Irish grantees by 1641. Also, although the servitors were not specifically tied to colonise, some pockets of settler settlement had come into being in this barony. Generally, too, the major Irish grantees had shown a reluctance, at least up to 1619, to grant leases to the tenantry under them.[37]

In Boylagh and Banagh the plantation brought about the foundation of eight estates, each granted to a Scottish undertaker. However, early on, all the original grantees in the barony disengaged (including Sir Robert McClelland who became tenant of the Haberdashers' and Clothworkers' estates in the Londonderry plantation) and the estates came to be engrossed into the hands of one man, originally Sir Robert Gordon of Lochinvar, Kirkcudbrightshire and then John Murray, a relative of one of the original grantees and one of James I's Scottish courtiers in London – a groom of the bedchamber and keeper of the privy purse – whom the king created Viscount Annan in 1622 and earl of Annandale in 1624.[38] There is a suggestion that Murray and Gordon were linked and that pressure was brought to bear on some of the original grantees, especially the family of George Murray of Broughton, Wigtownshire (who had died at Lifford in 1613), to sell their estates. On the other hand, the plantation had been making only limited initial success in what was a geographically remote barony, and when the king, in October 1618, authorised the legitimisation of Murray's acquisitions through the issuing of a new patent, promise appeared to be held out of a new energy in the colonisation of the region, even to the extent that the groom of the bedchamber would 'be at great charge' in building Murraystown, a new town within it. Murray was in fact a 'rising' figure on the wider stage of all three kingdoms, and was to be, like his son (born in 1617), the second earl (he himself died in 1640), a royalist peer in the context of the Scottish covenanting rebellion which began in 1637. His presence in Donegal must, however, at best have been no more than occasional, though an agent, Herbert Maxwell, was quickly in place. Moreover, when he took out a patent of the eight estates in December 1620 (now re-organised into two manors), he agreed to a doubled quit rent into the Irish exchequer of £106.13.4 stg, a figure just in excess of half of what Rory O'Donnell had been tied to for his entire earldom in 1604.[39] His ownership, at any rate, brought a measure of continuity and stability: he renewed his patents, in accordance with the regulations then applying in both 1629 and 1639, the latter (in which the eight proportions were re-organised now into three manors) tying him to an increased quit rent of £146.16.8 and opening him as well, through the introduction of tenure *in capite*, to the scrutiny of the court of wards. He received also the fisheries, 'of salmon, herring and whale', and his last patent conferred the mountains (which initially in the plantation at large had been treated as a separate entity) of the area as well.[40]

Various expedients for the letting of the lands, often in large blocs, and sometimes proving to be of only a short-term nature, were adopted by Murray. Thus by 1619 the proportion, or estate, of the Rosses had been let to Captain Thomas Dutton, an Englishman, while in 1626 the whole eight estates were leased to Sir George Hamilton of Greenlaw, brother to the earl of Abercorn and an energetic planter in the Strabane area and himself a Scottish Catholic who married a daughter of the earl of Ormond, for eleven years at £1,000 per annum. This may not have endured, however, because in May 1632 one Alexander Cunningham appears as agent of the earl of Annandale.[41]

While full and precise detail on the tenanting of these estates is missing, it appears that colonisation was mainly confined to the southern part of the barony and especially to the area from Killybegs, or beyond, to Donegal town: that was certainly the case up to the 1620s. Also while the new town of Murraystown, intended 'to be the principal town of the ... barony' failed precisely to materialise, the growth of the 'new borough town' of Killybegs, over the development of which Murray appears to have gained control, limited though it was by the early 1620s to 'seventeen British and Irish inhabitants', took its place. Estimates for the settler population (mainly Scottish but including an English minority) of the entire barony, for the period up to 1630, given in adult males, mostly suggest a figure of some 150, though one in 1626, which stands out from the rest, gave 340 and offered 739 as the number of Irish.[42] While some of these may have held big tenancies, it is clear that in much of the barony the Irish, rather than having been removed in accordance with the requirement for undertakers' areas, continued in occupation. Also while many of the settler tenants were said to hold for twenty-one years, they held often by 'minutes' rather than regular leases and no freeholders had been created by 1622.[43] This, however, may have changed later on. The conditions under which some of the Irish occupied land emerge from an enquiry in 1632, designed to investigate what had prevailed since Annandale had taken out his patent in 1629. Some held relatively large areas, either from those such as Dutton to whom Murray had demised whole estates or as undertenants to his lesser settler assignees, but their actual conditions of occupation were commonly only of a short-term nature, often from six months to six months. Thus Coochogery O'Clery held a half quarter of land (perhaps about 300 acres) in this way at £8 stg per annum.[44] It also emerges from a report of a customs inspector in 1637 that, despite ownership change, a full ordered and disciplined society (a perennial obsession) had not been brought about. Referring to Killybegs, he saw a need for much more control.

> The place being wild and not inhabited with any men of power or quality and frequented especially in time of fishing by Redshanks and by divers of the Scotch Isles and other unruly and wild people that will do no right that is not enjoined on them by force.[45]

Thus both in terms of plantation and of social regulation, society in west Donegal remained transitional up to 1641.

By contrast the plantation in the barony of Raphoe (220,000 acres)[46] proceeded along much more orthodox lines. The forfeited land in this barony was divided into two precincts, Portlough and Lifford, the former, to the north-east of the barony, granted to Scottish undertakers, the latter (to its south-west) granted to English undertakers, with the churchlands of Raphoe forming one point of division between them. In Portlough, the land, considered to represent – in accordance with the estimations used by the plantation planners – 12,000 profitable acres, was allocated to nine Scottish grantees. The nine, which included Ludovic Stewart, duke of Lennox, a relative of the king's and both a privy councillor and lord high steward of the household in London and a one-time ambassador to France, as well as three others of that surname and also four Cunninghams from Ayrshire (a distinct sub-group) maintained, unlike their equivalents in Boylagh and Banagh, a reasonable level of continuity of ownership.[47] Many of the sites at which they built had previously been minor O'Donnell strongholds such as Dunboy or Coolmacitrain or Mongavlin, the latter Ineen Dubh's former place of residence.[48] This region came to be amongst the most effectively planted areas of the entire plantation in Ulster. By 1630 there were some 540 settler adult males in the area, about 180 of them on the estates of the absentee duke of Lennox and about 250 on the Cunningham group of estates. This figure represents close to double the minimum requirement of 288 adult males laid down in the conditions under which these undertakers had accepted their estates.[49]

After this overview, we can turn now to focus in more depth on the plantation in one area – the precinct of Lifford, granted to English undertakers.

The English plantation in Lifford precinct
What was called the precinct of Lifford (the south-west part of Raphoe barony) is comprised of the basin of the rivers Finn and Deele and the

southern half of the basin of the river Swilly. Where the Finn and Deele rivers merge with the Foyle is good fertile lowland. The Finn, Deele and Swilly rivers drain rolling countryside with potentially good farmland. Poor soils are scattered on the low hills throughout the area, but are largely confined to the mountainous fringe in the south-west and west of the precinct.

Those chosen to implement and benefit from the plantation in this area were a group of nine Englishmen selected in London in the spring of 1610 and assigned between them estates calculated to total in all 15,000 profitable acres.[50] Unlike most of the English undertakers elsewhere, they were not all people new to Ireland and simply with roots in English landed society. In fact they divided into two groups, of which the larger had already had Irish ex-military, or servitor, associations. Whether this latter arose from a need to grant patronage to those who had played a former military role, or because it was difficult to attract people to undertake in remoter west Ulster, or as a precaution against renewed sea-borne invasion, or through some combination of all, is difficult to determine.

One of this servitor group, Sir Henry Docwra, formerly governor of Lough Foyle and latterly one of the planners of the plantation, is already familiar. However, now building a career in Dublin, he immediately passed on his assignment to William Wilson, a lawyer and eldest son of deceased parents from Clare in Suffolk. Two others were captains: one the somewhat anonymous Ralph Mansfield, the other Edward Russell, then of London, who had served in Ireland (mainly at Newry) for two and a half years from 1595, and then returned to England claiming unpaid arrears of some £560, to be admitted to Gray's Inn in 1598, and who was probably a connection of former lord deputy, Sir William Russell. Another former captain had achieved more prominence with both a knighthood (in 1603) and a pension (in 1606) and also enjoyed Lord Deputy Chichester's favour in 1610. He, Sir Thomas Coach, had been sent to Ireland late in 1598 in charge of men levied in Leicestershire, as part of wider re-inforcements sent at that time. He had fought at the battle of the Curlews in 1599, was at Lifford in 1601 and had married, prior to 1607, Dorcas Sidney, widow of Alexander Cosby of Stradbally, thereby forging a link with the earlier plantation in Leix and Offaly. Sir Robert Remington, a man of Yorkshire origin, was another grantee who fits broadly into this category, though he was to die, late in 1610, before he could play any effective part in the plantation. His most spectacular wartime involvement had taken place not in Ireland but directly against Spain: he took part in the Anglo-Dutch assault on Cadiz and the Spanish navy in 1596 (the 'counter armada') and was knighted by the earl of Essex, commander of the soldiers in that expedition, off Cadiz, at that time. Through that expedition, too, he had formed a link with Lord Thomas Howard who played a part in it and who now, as earl of Suffolk and lord chamberlain, had a role in the choosing of the grantees for this area of the plantation. He had, however, a further claim to favour: he had been employed briefly in Ireland after the Nine Years' War as vice-president of Connacht – securing permission to return to England late in 1607 because of legal and financial difficulties there – during which time he had unearthed suggestive indications that the earl of Tyrconnell was seeking to re-engage Spanish interest in Ireland. Sir Henry Clare, another grantee, was again a person of somewhat similar career and circumstances. A man of Norfolk landed origin and a 'cousin' of Lord Deputy Burgh, he took part with him, perilously, in an engagement with O'Neill at the Blackwater in Ulster in July 1597 and hoped to benefit through him from land in the Byrnes' Country in Wicklow. His subsequent career in Ireland saw him as lieutenant-colonel of the regiment of Donogh O'Brien, earl of Thomond, briefly in Ulster again in 1600, and later garrisoned in Galway, where complaints were made against him by the townsmen, until he was discharged with army reductions at the end of 1602. Absence in Ireland could also bring its problems and, knighted in 1603, he had returned to England about then to confront financial difficulties affecting his wife at that time, and, later, now out of employment, became an advocate of a project concerned with corn. An articulate and ambitious military officer, he kept up a correspondence while in Ireland with Sir Robert Cecil who as Earl of Salisbury was James I's principal secretary of state at the time that the plantation in Ulster was being inaugurated.

The remaining three, Sir Maurice Berkeley, Sir William Barne and Sir Thomas Cornewall, conform perhaps a little more nearly to the character of the more usual English undertakers elsewhere. Sir Thomas Cornewall was one of a family group which had applied for this entire precinct. Son and heir of Thomas Cornewall, baron of Burford (d. 1615), a substantial Shropshire landowner, Sir Thomas (d. 1636), knighted on the king's accession in 1603 and known as the Great Baron, was a man active locally in county affairs and in favour centrally as a gentleman of the privy chamber of Prince Henry, James I's son. Of the others, Sir William Barnes (or Barne) although again a substantial property holder, was a man of entirely different origins. Of a London merchant background and son and grandson of two lord mayors, he had lived at Woolwich (eight miles from the capital) from at least the 1590s, was a justice of the peace of the county of Kent and had marriage connections with prominent Kentish men of affairs. Although his family had a well-established tradition of participation in numerous English long-distance mercantile enterprises, dating from the Muscovy company in the 1550s, Sir William (d. 1619) had however become drawn into the plantation through some connection with Sir Robert Remington. Finally, Sir Maurice Berkeley commands interest on many counts. A Somersetshire landowner, educated at Oxford and the Middle Temple, knighted at Cadiz in 1596, an active member of a number of parliaments and a leader in important negotiations about the royal finances just at this time, his family had already had Irish interests, both recent and medieval, and he was a relative of Sir Henry Folliott. He also played an active part in Virginia affairs, which appear to have taken precedence for him over the Ulster plantation. He died in 1617. Such were the people to whom the estates were assigned in 1610; not all of them retained a permanent association with them. While Berkeley and Barnes seem to be the only two with significant overseas connections, the military men as a whole will no doubt all have held anti-Spanish views and shared to some degree the religio-political sensibilities arising therefrom.[51]

Those assigned the estates were expected to meet the lord deputy and plantation commissioners from Dublin, who travelled through the escheated counties from August to mid-September, to receive possession. Only two in fact did so, Coach and Wilson, though Cornewall was to send over an agent, Edward Lyttleton, a likely relation of his wife's.[52] Indeed over the next few years there were to be a number of changes in ownership, with the effect that the plantation in the area got underway rather slowly.

By the end of the first year, when the first of a series of government inspections of it was carried out, by Sir George Carew, it was mainly some members of the servitor group, especially the two ex-captains, Mansfield and Russell, and also Sir Thomas Coach, all three of whom were already resident, along with the newcomer, Wilson, who were showing signs of activity, while the performance of the smaller civilian group of Berkeley, Barnes (who had already sold his estate), and even Cornewall (who at least, in common with Clare, had sent over an agent) was much less promising. Work on building and planting in accordance with regulation, which it was the main function of Carew's and subsequent government surveys to detail, was by this stage, on Carew's account, confined to just three estates. Wilson, through his agent Christopher Parmenter, a man from his home area in Suffolk, had begun the process of colonisation: there were 'some families of English resident who brought over good store of household stuff' and had as stock '21 cows and oxen, 9 mares, one service horse and some small cattle'. Russell's beginnings reveal another aspect of the plantation. He had imported a number of English labourers (but no tenants), presumably the builders of two timber-framed 'English houses' which had been erected, and his stock included six English cows. Finally, Sir Thomas Coach, who had four settler families on the land, none yet with leases, had made a start of another kind. He had chosen as site for his own residence the castle of Scarrifhollis, on the river Swilly, former residence of Caffar oge O'Donnell – who although destabilised (as has been seen) by Rory O'Donnell's behaviour towards him, had later gone into a 'kind of rebellion' capturing Doe castle and had been by 1608 lodged in Dublin Castle – and had already built a timber house adjoining it.[53]

The vacuum of absentee inactivity, evident now on most of the estates, was to be filled over the next few years, in some cases through people from neighbouring parts of the plantation acquiring some of them. One such was Sir Ralph Bingley – already holding land in Kilmacrenan – who by early 1613, when the next survey was carried out by Sir Josias Bodley, had acquired control of the estates granted to both Remington and Berkeley, thereby bringing two estates into the hands of one man. Another new owner by this stage was Peter Benson, a London craftsman-entrepreneur and to be the contractor for the building of the walls of Derry, who acquired Clare's estate based on Stranorlar. Some of these changes evolved through partnership agreements, possibly surviving for many years, involving some of the local former military officers, or others, the evidence for which does not always survive in full detail. Thus initially Benson, for example, had as associate Arthur Terry, later a customs official in Derry. In the case of the Barnes estate, which stretched south and westward from near Lifford, more evidence is forthcoming, showing that it simply got split up. By 1613 also it had been sold, for £50 stg, to Russell and Thomas Wilson (brother of William who had acquired Docwra's proportion) from whom Sir Richard Hansard of Lifford had in turn acquired an interest in a part (for £100), with the obligation that he should carry out the building requirement and also plant one-third of the households.[54] Another change in ownership, in September 1613, brought in a purchaser for the Cornewall estate from north Wales, Robert Davies of Gwysaney (near Mold and some ten miles from Chester) in Flintshire, whose home area and local links overlapped with those of Bingley and make it seem certain that it was through him that Davies was attracted to plantation Ulster. Of a self-anglicising Welsh family, Davies's career sprang from two roots: in Wales the family was consolidating an estate (1,750 acres) and engaging in coalmining, while through the act of union with Wales under Henry VIII a London connection was established – a grand-uncle had held military office at court. Robert (1581–1633), fresh from Oxford, had succeeded his father in 1603. His subsequent career suggests that, on the one hand, his presence in Donegal can have been no more than intermittent while, on the other, that he must have perceived his engagement there in some part in terms of advancing the Protestant cause. Certainly Davies and his brother Thomas, (who was acting for Robert in Donegal towards the end of the decade), both of whom appear to have received military training in London, came soon to be involved at the cutting edge of religious warfare in Europe. They were in Prague in 1620 prior to the defeat – with catastrophic consequences for Protestantism there – of the elector Frederick as king of Bohemia.[55]

Finally (as proof that so many of the original grantees lacked either the desire to stay or the financial resources to fulfil their plantation obligations), Russell's estate too passed to a new owner. By June 1614, Captain John Kingsmill (born 1579 and knighted in 1617), a younger son from Hampshire and one of a number of brothers who had had military careers in Ireland and himself (despite army reductions) recently placed in Glenfinn, Niall Garbh's former area of influence, in charge of some twenty-five horse, had acquired this estate.[56]

With these changes, a measure of stability in ownership of the estates had been achieved. Subsequent changes, down to 1641, including successions to heirs, were due mainly to family circumstances. In some cases, however, these brought new owners. In 1633 Robert Davies died, leaving an heir aged seventeen.[57] This ended the Gwysaney connection and the estate passed to Sir Paul Davis – not apparently a relation – a well-placed functionary in Dublin who held offices in the exchequer and the court of wards as well as being clerk of the privy council, and an absentee who, as has been seen, also acquired the lands of Sir Mulmory MacSweeney.[58] For his part, Sir Ralph Bingley, although an active enough planter, also maintained a London connection and was to seek a new military career in the context of a further English war with Spain and in France in the later 1620s. Living within an expansive mental world delineated by Anglo-Spanish conflict, he put forward at this time an elaborate plan, to he financed and manned from Ireland, for an intervention against Spain in the West Indies as a means of pre-empting a feared Spanish invasion of Ireland, which was before its time and came to nothing, but he was appointed instead a colonel in the English expedition to the Ile de Ré off La Rochelle (in support of a Huguenot rebellion) where he was killed in 1627.[59] Despite his death, the Bingley ownership of the estates continued for the time being, and following on the marriage of his widow to Robert Harrington, lessee of the Grocers' proportion in the Londonderry plantation, both took out a joint patent of them in May 1630, but they had passed by sale or possibly through a mortgage to Martin Basil of Essex and London by the end of the decade.[60] Of the original grantees, then, the families of William Wilson (replacing Docwra), whose son Sir John

(d. 1636) became a baronet and married a daughter of the old English Sir Thomas Butler of Clogrenan, County Carlow,[61] Sir Thomas Coach (d. 1621) and Captain Ralph Mansfield (d. 1633) remained in continuous ownership down to 1641, while on many of the estates there had been ownership change in the initial years, with change again affecting a few of them in the 1630s. This provides the background for assessing the plantation which came about under them, both in building and tenanting, and its implications for the previous landholders.

Collectively, the estates as granted out were held to constitute 15,000 profitable acres. To conform to requirement, the undertakers must introduce between them, incrementally but within a few years, a settler colony of 150 families or 360 adult males. While that number was, broadly, to be reached, the process of achieving it proved slower than was expected. Given the initial wave of ownership change, it is not surprising that Sir Josias Bodley who carried out the second government survey of the plantation early in 1613 found that although building operations were beginning on a number of estates, the number of tenants in place was still relatively small. Of the more active, William Wilson, who was resident, had 'planted some few tenants' (none of them yet made either freeholders or leaseholders) and his brother was in England 'to draw over others'. Similarly, Mansfield had 'some tenants, albeit not his full number nor estated as they ought to be ... engaged on the land', and was himself engaged in litigation about the extent of his estate, while Coach had five English tenants with formal tenancy agreements concluded. These were amongst the owners who were to endure. On the estates of many of those who departed, little or simply no settling had taken place, while some of the newcomer owners had made a varying impact. Thus Benson and Terry, themselves resident, had some of their tenants present with 'the rest to come speedily thither'. On Sir Maurice Berkeley's estate, held at this stage in partnership by Sir Ralph Bingley and Captain John Vaughan, Bingley had built seven tenements with chimneys and had tenants in them already, while Vaughan for his part stated that when he took over 'at Allhallowtide last' (1 November 1612) Irish tenants were in place and entitled to hold until Michaelmas (29 September) and now had their corn sown – an indication of the early impact of plantation on the Irish landholders – but that he had recruited 'one Clinton and nine Englishmen more' to settle there the following summer and also build their own houses.[62]

By the spring of 1619 with the completion of Captain Nicholas Pynnar's survey of the plantation, a dramatically different picture is revealed. Across the nine estates he recorded 193 settler tenant families, ranging from 13 on one to 32 on another, with in some cases undertenants as well, and presented a total figure of 536 adult males in place. These tenantry were presented in gradations both in type, freeholders, leaseholders, and in some cases cottagers, and in sizes of tenancies, the latter all expressed with acreage figures. In many cases with regard to the latter, for example tenants with 120 acres, his figures can perhaps be seen as representing the conventional acreages of the land divisions of the time (in Donegal, quarters, with their sub-divisions into trians or sessiaghs, which form the basis of the more numerous townland divisions of the present day), but in the cases of many of the smaller tenancies they have a precision (for example as between tenancies of 60 acres and 62 and 66 and 67, or 10 and 11) which could scarcely be attained at the time.[63] Hence while his account may have been broadly accurate, it has a superficial precision which perhaps should not be taken to be totally reliable in every detail.

From the final government survey of the series, carried out in 1622, a more conservative picture emerges. The inspector in 1622 found tenantry – the equivalents of Pynnar's tenant families – to the number of 135 on eight of the nine estates (including a few of Davies's who were then absent in Wales), having excluded Wilson's (where however they found 87 men present to Pynnar's 106, which had been made up, as Pynnar described them, of 20 tenant families with 50 more under them) on his admission that his conveyances did not follow due form. They also cast doubt on the status of some on a number of estates as 'reputed' freeholders or leaseholders for years or lives, which tends to suggest that some undertakers may not have given out such secure tenancies, particularly authentic freeholds, as the conditions of plantation laid down. Their total for 'British men present', in more striking contrast to Pynnar's, was no more than 263.[64] This discrepancy is a marked one. Apart from the likelihood of some errors, especially on Pynnar's part, in relatively quickly conducted surveys, it may possibly be accounted for in a number of ways. Some undertenants, who at any rate are not specifically mentioned, may have been omitted, while some building workers may now have moved away. However, it may also reflect an early plantation society, at Pynnar's time not fully settled down, in which some still moved elsewhere for better tenancies, or had decided (like some of the owners) not to stay, or were absentees, or held multiple tenancies. In the absence of estate papers, the surveys give the best impression available of the dimensions of the plantation they describe, though they may present an over-symmetrical picture of it.[65]

That also for some of the 1620s, when local tensions arising from renewed Anglo-Spanish conflict must have made Ulster at large less attractive to newcomers, there was no further major growth in settler numbers on these estates comes from the evidence of a muster in c. 1630 at which 248 men presented themselves from eight of the nine estates. If allowance is made for those from the estate, Coach's, which somehow got left out, perhaps 20 or so, and for a small delinquency in attendance overall, that total might creep towards 300.[66] There is no systematic evidence for the 1630s when some expansion may well have occurred, though it must be remembered that opening opportunities in the English new world across the Atlantic in the 1620s and 1630s also provided migrants (though probably more so English than Scottish) with alternative outlets. However, with regard to the essential feature of the tenanting of the land by the undertakers, the plantation had mainly come into existence in the reign of James I.

For their part, a core element amongst the tenantry would seem to be made up of people recruited by the undertakers from their home areas in England and Wales. Thus many Welsh tenantry appear on the Davies and Bingley estates. However many others must have been freelance arrivers aware, through the spread of news, that land was available. A very significant group of these – revealed by the names on the muster roll of *c.* 1630 – were Scots, arriving probably at Derry on Lough Foyle (though Lough Swilly may also have been used) and percolating through from the Scottish undertakers' area in Portlough or from the Strabane area which had also been granted to Scottish undertakers. Another element, since some of the undertakers here had had military backgrounds, was made up of former junior military officers and may even have included some former ordinary soldiers as well. Thus Lieutenants Edward Carter and John Dutton (d. 1629) are found as tenants on the Bingley estates. It is clear from a few names, Pitt and Babington for instance, that the plantation town of Londonderry, of which Peter Benson (d. 1642) became an alderman, was also a source of tenantry. Edward Torleton, who, as we will see, held a number of leases, himself lived in the new settler town of Lifford.[67] After all, Derry and Lifford were also the principal places giving access to seaborne trade through which purchases were acquired and surpluses exported.

In the plantation, in Donegal as elsewhere, the settlement pattern laid down to the undertakers, whereby their tenantry should all live together in village communities, was not to be followed. Rather, a mix of dispersed and nucleated settlement emerged. A number of factors would appear to account for this. With the estates in fact very much larger than planned, the pursuit of a farming life would have been impeded (often to the point of impracticability) by time spent in travel, requiring in some Donegal estates the fording of rivers. Also the defensive considerations which partly underlay the proposal in the first place – otherwise it sprang from, notions of the ordered society – were less imperative in the formative first decade of the plantation which was an interlude of international peace.

Furthermore many of the undertakers appear to have lacked the resources to engage on any substantial scale, without government subsidy, in building tenant villages (seeking sometimes, as we have seen Captain John Vaughan do, to pass on the building obligation to the tenantry), which was an all the more decisive consideration given that there was so much ownership change in the early plantation years. In some cases, indeed, a little group of cottagers may have formed the initial core of a plantation settlement, but since the process of tenanting was not all effected neatly in a short space of time the ordained pattern of exclusively village living could not bee easily imposed. Thus, as the settlement pattern stabilised, it came to be one of both small village and dispersed settlement.

Many who lived in the villages would appear to have held small acreages (with commons sometimes mentioned) with the adjacent land carved up to provide them, and must also have included workmen and artisans of various kinds amongst them. Sometimes, indeed, the houses varied in size and type, reflecting the differing sorts of people who lived in them. In some cases, the planter village beginnings of this period can be shown to form the basis of some present day towns, while the locations of others can only be tentatively identified. Thus Bingley on the estate acquired from Remington had erected by 1622 a village of twelve houses and cottages at Ballybofey, 'inhabited for the most part with British' and had an estate residence under construction on the opposite side of the River Finn, 'near unto the ford' (still an identifiable location) and so in Drumboe Lower townland, a settlement seen at the time as well placed since the ford was on 'the chiefest passage' into the Barnesmore mountains and 'where a bridge is very needful to be built'. Likewise and closeby, Peter Benson on his Stranorlar estate, had constructed his residence 'near' the Finn, and 'near' to it a village of ten houses and cottages.[68] Some four miles further west on the Davies estate two little hamlets, recorded in 1622, which can plausibly be identified as Welchtown and Gorey or Welchtown Upper respectively, both at the easterly entrance to the estate, one 'near' the planter's house (which may possibly therefore have been at Glenafton) the other 'about half a mile distant from it', suggest that again a centre had been chosen at a crossing (now bridged at Glenmore bridge) of the River Finn.[69] Likewise, eastwards along the Finn, on his Killygordon estate, Mansfield had built 'near' the river, and also had by 1622 two little villages of cottages nearby, one of which was by then 'decayed' and in decline.[70] For his part, Kingsmill had occupied and rebuilt Niall Garbh O'Donnell's castle of Castle Finn, also on that river, and had nearby a village of another kind – one of twenty-five thatched cottages, 'where his troop lies in garrison'.[71] Equally, planters chose sites on the other major rivers for their settlements. Thus on the Deele, the

Wilson site on a 'mount' in Killynure appears to be identifiable with the Killynure castle site in the townland of Killynure or Wilson's Fort and this would tend to suggest Convoy as the location of his little village.[72] On the divided Barnes estate the house and village settlement brought into existence by Sir Richard Hansard of Lifford can be identified with Ballindrait, also on the river Deele.[73] The remaining two estates were orientated towards Lough Swilly, in one case, that of Coach, involving a change from his original location. For his part, Sir Ralph Bingley established his own personal residence, on the estate acquired from Berkeley, at Farsetmore and had a little village nearly – 'within a mile' on Pynnar's account and 'in a place which is a continual passage' – the site of which may well be identifiable with one or other (probably Dromore Lower) of the little hamlets in the area.[74] Finally, the Coach estate was to undergo a change of centre and a consequent multiplication of minute concentrations of settler settlement. Sir Thomas abandoned Scarriffhollis, near which a little grouping of houses (perhaps Ardahee nowadays) had been erected, in favour of a new site and residence 'on Lough Swilly', which had four thatched houses near it – Pynnar found six – in 1622. The precise location of this 'mansion house' as it was called in the 1630s, when its location in Fycorranagh quarter was recorded, cannot easily be suggested because of the difficulty in establishing which group of modern townlands represents the quarter of that time; however a case can be made for a site in Coaghmill (erroneously gaelicised in spelling by the Ordnance Survey) townland, with the houses perhaps in Bunnagee, as may be suggested by the presence of some old lanes in the area which appear to interlink.[75]

Beyond the villages, the land on the estates was let out mainly in units comprised of the topographical entities of the time, either full quarters or their sub-denominations, to which Pynnar, for example, seeking to report in terms intelligible by reference to the plantation conditions, sought to ascribe acreage figures. Thus some tenancies were bigger than others. Those with the larger holdings constituted an emerging gentry class within the plantation society. However, with no collection of estate papers available for this area, it is not possible to establish, apart from the evidence of the government surveys, with certainty what the more common tenancies were, or even the amount of demesne land retained by the undertakers. Evidence, however, from a later period does reveal that commonly on each estate two or more freeholders had been created.[76]

Their building obligations constituted one of the principal demands for expenditure or investment which the undertakers had to meet. The residences that they built were not massive structures and were also completed slowly, mirroring the slow development of the plantation as a whole. Since none of these now survives substantially, it is necessary to rely on the contemporary descriptions of them, which are difficult to interpret and which can sometimes be inconsistent. The smallest and simplest, however, was on the Davies estate, described in 1622 as a stone house, thatched, and a bawn 40 feet square (rough, cast with lime, according to Pynnar) with two thatched flankers. The other bawns were larger, ranging, according to 1622 descriptions, from 60 feet square (Coach's, which was similar, therefore, to the surviving Brackfield bawn in the Londonderry plantation) to 100 or 120 feet square and, in the case of Bingley's at Farsetmore (described as a bawn of brick), 150 feet square, though not all planter buildings had bawns.

The houses were generally of stone construction and slated. The one exception was Coach's where a 36-foot long thatched timber house had been added to a 24-foot stone and slated one of one and a half storeys, thereby spanning the width of his bawn. None was longer than 60 feet, as was Mansfield's at Killygordon. Many featured a main house to which had been added two 'returns', which may possibly suggest that a common 'architectural' hand – perhaps even Benson's or Hansard's (the latter a military engineer) – had been involved in their construction. The relationship of these structures to the bawns is conjectural as is also the location of their entrances, but it is perhaps possible that some of these 'returns' were in fact advancing or projecting wings, with an entrance porch between them, as appears to have been the case with Goldsmith's Hall at New Buildings. Most were two storeys or one and a half high, with some in varying ways uncompleted by the early 1620s. Thus Mansfield's, described by Pynnar as three storeys and in 1622 as two, had then some of the 'partitions and floors' not finished, while the upper rooms of Wilson's house were then 'unfloored'. Bingley's Ballybofey house, described by Pynnar as a 'strong castle with four large towers' and three storeys high, but unfinished because of controversy between him and Remington's heirs, was still not fully completed by the early 1620s when it is described as two and a half storeys high and with returns. Kingsmill's activity at Castlefinn was of a different order, because he had occupied and re-edified Niall Garbh's former castle or tower-house there and made 'good additions' to it. Described in 1622 as 40 feet square and 43 feet high, constituting three and a half storeys and slated and battlemented, it now had adjoining a strong flankered bawn, to which he intended to make 'an outwork of fortification'.[77] To the crown the grantees' building obligations constituted an exercise in the privatisation of defence. It is in that light that Kingsmill's promise to build his 'outwork', an echo of the fortifications of the contemporary 'military revolution', can be seen. That this was ever constructed (through private finance) may be doubted, but by 1629 a long stone house, 15 feet high (itself reflected, though on a grander scale, in the elegant extension to Donegal castle), had been added to the castle.[78]

These building costs, to which have to be added some mills and the undertakers' part in village construction, may well have had to be met in some degree by borrowing. Through the absence of their own papers, the incomes the undertakers were able to generate only became known (and that roughly) at the end of our period because the rental incomes 'in time of peace' (c. 1640) of a few are given, 'to our best information', in the Civil Survey. Thus the Wilson estate yielded £430 per annum and the Benson one £109.[79] These may well represent increased rents negotiated in the mid-1630s when many early leases are likely to have expired. If we seek to go deeper, the economy of all lesser figures remains largely hidden.

The effects on the Irish population on these estates under the plantation is a question to which no precise and therefore entirely satisfactory answer can be given. Even though it meant the end of war and of the O'Donnell war taxation which had accompanied it and even though the plantation itself was a relatively thin one, plantation can scarcely have failed to be deeply traumatic for those who had held land in the previous society. In theory the native Irish population should move away entirely from the lands of the undertakers, in Donegal as elsewhere, to resettle on the lands of any of the other categories of grantee. That here, too, theory and practice diverged is well known, but how precisely is difficult to assess. That, in general terms no systematic and thorough government-conducted driving off of all of the native population from undertakers' lands was carried out to allow them free scope to plant on arrival, is clear. Equally, the government wished to see the regulation enforced (or at any rate to gain revenue through fines for its avoidance) and brought pressure to bear on the undertakers to do so, while they for their part, given the low intensity of the colonisation, actively sought modification of the rule.[80] Eventually in 1628 a compromise was reached, admitted in article 26 of the *Graces*. The grantees must take out new patents with a doubled quit rent and must covenant that three-quarters of each estate would be planted with settler tenants (with sound conveyances) or used as demesne. Apart from artificers holding small parcels of land who could remain on the three-quarters, Irish tenantry (who might also have leases) should be confined to the remaining quarter.[81] Since those refusing to comply with this compromise could be penalised, a large number of the undertakers were to take out new patents in the ensuing years. It is more difficult, however, to assess what actions may have been taken on the substantive point of Irish tenancies, though, in general, the one-quarter may have been approximating to reality as it then stood.

A mechanism of enforcement was, however, found when in July 1630 the committee for Irish affairs of the English privy council recommended that the income from lands held by Irish tenants in excess of the Irish quarter since the dates of the new patents should be sequestered, and applied to satisfy the arrears of two army captains, one of whom, Sir Henry Tichborne, was stationed at Lifford, who should hold such lands during the king's pleasure. Following on enquiries in the counties, a patent of the lands in question, valued in all at some £400, was granted to the two beneficiaries in December 1631.[82] This was also the final government initiative on the matter prior to 1641.

For the Lifford precinct estates, there is no source which links each denomination of land precisely to a tenant on all the estates from the time the plantation was reaching its full pre-1641 extent in the early 1620s. The impression is left, however, that much of the land on most estates had been let by then to settler tenantry, but within a framework of low-intensity colonisation, For what it is worth, inquisitions designating the one-quarter for Irish tenantry survive for Davies's Corlackey estate, Harrington's Ballybofey estate, Benson's at Stranorlar and Kingsmill's based on Castlefinn.[83] Furthermore, land Irish-held in excess of one quarter was sequestered from the undertakers to the benefit of the two captains and granted to them on four estates – Davies's Corlackey estate, Harrington's Ballybofey estate and also his Lough Swilly one and Wilson's, in the latter case involving only one tenancy.[84] What this evidence reveals is that the more westerly estates still offered greater opportunity to Irish tenantry and that also where two estates had come into single ownership – Bingley's, now held by his widow and Robert Harrington – plantation had been less effective. A further inquiry in 1632 revealed the same pattern.[85]

The evidence about Irish-held tenancies that emerges in these years (limited in extent though it be) shows that many of these tenancies were in fact sub-tenancies, indicating accordingly that many Irish land holders had undergone a marked descent in status to sub-tenants. Thus, for example, on the Davies estate, Owen ballagh O'Galchor held the trian of Cashel (183 acres) from Peter Payne, Davies's tenant, at a rent of £1 stg per annum, while the neighbouring trian of Altnapaste (nowadays 2,362 acres as triangulated by the Ordnance Survey) was held by Turlough ballagh McNulty and Donnagh McNulty at £2 stg per annum. An Irish tenancy on the Ballybofey estate was held from the widow, Owny, – the name perhaps suggesting an intermarriage – of Edward Carter. Sometimes quite longstanding and complex relationships were revealed. Thus, again on the Ballybofey estate, in 1632 Hugh Mergagh O'Donnell and his Irish undertenants held a half quarter of ground for £3.10.0 stg per annum, and had corn growing on it, originally by demise from Lieutenant John Dutton deceased, tenant to Sir Ralph Bingley, but now held from Edward Torleton, husband of Dutton's widow, under Robert Harrington who had married Lady Anne Bingley. In a further complex instance on the same estate, also involving Dutton and Torleton as upper tenants, poignant evidence is revealed of what must have been a disturbance arising in the context of the Anglo-Spanish war: Hughe oge O'Mulwoath, a blacksmith, held a half quarter of land, having been tenant to Owen McFerganan O'Gallogher who had been executed for high treason at the last assizes for County Donegal.[86] The disposition of Torleton's own holdings in the plantation, which comes to light a few years later, may well give a rough indication of the position of Irish landholders generally. One of those with multiple tenancies, he held somewhat over a quarter (here a multiple of modern townlands) on the Ballybofey estate, which was all held by Irish sub-tenants. In addition, he held three quarters of episcopal land in the parish of Leck. One of these, Trimragh (325 acres), was held from him by five settler sub-tenants, while the other two were held by Irish sub-tenants – Toole McHugh oge O'Gallogher, Shane O'Mullarkye and Cahir McArt O'Gallogher.[87] Irish tenants and sub-tenants were, of course, the elite of their type in this area, as were any from it who were restored to land in Kilmacrenan barony. The remainder of the Irish population remains as hidden as most of their sixteenth-century predecessors, for whom there is little clear impression of either their numbers or their social structure, especially the proportion of labourers and artisans. A more general point made by the commissioners in 1622 is also worth noting: that on all the estates in Donegal the number of Irish far exceeded the number of settlers, and that many engaged still in the practice of 'creting' and were also subject to woodkerne 'who take meat and whatsoever else they think fit from them'.

Ecclesiastically, the estates in Lifford precinct were comprehended mainly in five parishes – three, Leck, Stranorlar and Raphoe, in the diocese of Raphoe and two, Lifford or Clonleigh and Donaghmore, in the diocese of Derry. In accordance with the widely-held confessional principles of contemporary European governments, the reformation was being advanced in tandem with the plantation and hence both the churches and the sources of clerical income came into the hands of clergy of the Church of Ireland at this time. The state of the medieval church buildings and what was being done to them emerges from the ecclesiastical visitation in 1622. The cathedral at Raphoe was described by the bishop, Andrew Knox, as 'ruinated and all decayed saving the walls' but for it a roof had been 'these two years past preparing ... which, God willing, will be set up this summer at the bishop's and parishioner's charges'. Here Sir John Wilson was buried in 1636. The other two churches in Raphoe diocese were described just as 'decayed', but 'in repairing at the parishoners charges'. Since the cure of these parishes was linked to the deanery, both had by this stage curates who were graduates – James Scott, M.A. 'a qualified man in doctrine and conversation' for Leck and Robert Connell, M.A. at Stranorlar – paid respectively by the dean, Archibald Adair and like him probably Scots, £20 and £13.6.8 a year. Adair, successor to Phelim O'Doherty who had been presented by the crown in 1609, and himself an M.A. and an 'eloquent scholar and good preacher of God's word', held the position for about twenty years, to be succeeded by a fellow Scot, Alexander Cunningham, M.A., who had been in the diocese since 1611 and was linked by marriage to George Murray of Broughton, one of the original grantees in the plantation in Boylagh and Banagh. At this time the two parishes in Derry diocese, Clonleigh and Donaghmore, shared a common incumbent, Thomas Turpin, M.A., probably an Oxford graduate and prominent in the church system as a prebend, who lived himself at Lifford and who was described by Bishop George Downame as 'an honest man and a good preacher and given to hospitality'. He maintained a curate, however, at Donaghmore, also a graduate, these two, on Downame's account 'preaching either of them in the said parishes *alterius vicibus* every week'. Their churches, however, were still a different matter. Donaghmore was described in 1622 as 'much decayed having neither roof nor good walls saving that the inhabitants have covered one end of it and made it fit for divine service'. In Lifford, though, change was underway. Although the church of Clonleigh was 'ruined', it was soon to be abandoned. Within the town itself, the foundations of an entirely new church of the plantation, provided for in the will of Sir Richard Hansard (d. 1619), had already been laid. From the mid 1620s, the two parishes too had each their own incumbent, Richard Walker of Clonleigh and William Warren of Donaghmore, both of them young graduates of Trinity College, Dublin and the latter, at any rate, himself a product of the plantation.[88] The Protestant clergy in an English-granted barony had thus come to be both Scots and English, with Bishop Knox of Raphoe willing to condone Presbyterian-style ordinations by the laying on of hands as well. Clergy were clearly important as an intelligentsia in the plantation, forming its culture and ethos and linking it to its intellectual roots in England and Scotland. Equally, it might be wrong to assume that such a number of clergy could have had a profound pastoral effect on all members of a rural plantation community. Such English-speaking clergy were also scarcely likely, if so inclined, to provide a mission to the native Irish of the area at least until some measure of bilingualism had begun to arise amongst them as part of the plantation impact. A more effective, if more expensive, church would have been created had each estate been made a parish, as had formed part of the original plantation plan.

Conclusion

In the baronies granted to undertakers colonisation was most intensive in Portlough, less so in Lifford and less again in Boylagh and Banagh. While the Irish were not universally removed from the estates in these baronies, they underwent a descent in status which was, ultimately, conditioned by the degree of new settlement which took place in any specific area of them. Yet over much of this area, the plantation, prior to 1641, can be seen as of relatively low intensity in type. However, some of the other new owners beyond the undertakers' areas, although not specifically required to do so, leased land to new settler tenants as well. Thus the over-riding part of the episcopal lands was leased by the bishops of Raphoe and Derry, generally by the quarter or in longer multiples of quarters, to new settler tenantry, both English and Scots. At Raphoe itself a more intensive pattern emerged. Here, and on a small area of adjacent land, a group of a dozen people, essentially Scots, can be found by the mid 1630s. These, the poor of the plantation, formed the nucleus of the settler town of Raphoe, and were very small holders of land, none with more than eight 'acres' as computed in the Civil Survey of the 1650s. Thus one of them, George Buchanan, had a house and garden plot containing two acres, and four acres of land, and the grazing of four cows on the common of Raphoe. For this he paid £3.5.0 per annum with 'duties' of 6 capons and 6 hens and three days service of a man and a horse.[89] At Raphoe, too, Bishop John Leslie (appointed 1633), his predecessor, Knox, having lived mainly at Rathmullan and himself, like Knox, a Scot who was also formerly bishop of the Isles, built his palace, a symbol of his status and one of the architecturally-innovative glories of the plantation.[90] It is likely that some of these smallholders were artisans – one held a 'kilroome' – employed in the building of the bishop's castle or perhaps in the restoration of the cathedral. This little concentration relates, however, more to urbanisation than to the more normal settlement of the countryside, which must now be reverted to. In this regard, some of the servitors in Kilmacrenan also leased land to incomer tenantry, though the number of them was quite small. For his part Chichester, too, leased land in Inishowen to English and Scots but he also created a body of native Irish freeholders there.[91]

The new urban beginnings in County Donegal of this period can only be commented on briefly here more to note their scale than to seek to examine in detail (anyhow without adequate sources) their occupational structure. The borough and emerging county town of Lifford, approachable by boats from Lough Foyle, had 'about' 54 houses in it by 1622, 'some of stone and slated, the rest of timber thatched, inhabited for the most part with English'. It also remained a garrison centre at this stage, the king's fort, its walls now 'in most part decayed', having been reserved from the patent to Hansard. However, the fort itself and its land was granted away (for a rent of £2 Ir. per annum), as an economy measure, in 1627, though on condition that the crown might garrison it 'in time of rebellion or war'.[92] Of the original Lifford corporate body of thirteen, some had been soldiers. One of the corporators, Thomas Perkins was part of the pre-plantation settlement at Derry which arose under Docwra's tutelage, became lieutenant of Hansard's company and was an executor of his will, and so occupied a prominent position in the town. His descendant, Richard Perkins, came to hold the fort and its supply lands of Stramore. The town had been planned by Hansard to include freeholders and leaseholders or copyholders, fifty-four in all by the 1622 account. The authors of the Civil Survey recorded (anyhow after 1641) a smaller number, but confirmed that broad outline. They found twenty-five freeholders and fourteen copyholders each with a house and garden plot, two 'acres' of land nearby, and three cows grazing on Lifford common.[93] The occupations of the people remain elusive: some were probably artisans and there must have been a merchant or two amongst them. In November 1613, William Kney of Chester, merchant and his son (representing a place which was coming to have many links with Ulster) received a licence to keep a wine tavern in the town.[94] One who lived there was Edward Torleton, who, as has been seen, held a number of tenancies of land and may not have been an uncommon type of townsman: certainly a number of people who held land near Raphoe (in addition to the twelve smallholders) also had houses within it.[95] Lifford had many of the characteristics of a plantation town of the period, mainly English (though with some Welsh) in make up. Also, on the Hansard lands in the immediate neighbourhood, including the little out-village of Ballindrait, there were quite a number of settler tenantry, constituting a small concentration of settlement and with the likely implication that not only was the O'Donnell entourage of c. 1600 at Lifford dispersed, but that the immediately local occupiers of that time had been mainly dispersed too. Finally, Hansard's solicitude for the well-being of his new town and its future corporate identity was reflected in his will, providing for the building of the church and a school and for payments for the schoolmaster and his usher and members of the town's governing body.[96]

Although Lifford had a special status as county town and was distinctive given the freehold condition of many of its residents, a number of other of these settlements in Donegal were not dissimilar in size. Some were just the larger estate villages, their residents' occupations unknown, and not places designated for incorporation and urbanisation in the plantation plan. A number were in Portlough among the Scots, reflecting the degree of change there, and although there were none of this size in Lifford precinct, Letterkenny was just on its northern fringe. Thus the 'town' of St Johnstown (larger than Carrigans) 'erected' on the estate originally granted to the duke of Lennox 'which is intended to be made a borough town' and taking its name, we may safely assume, with deferential artifice, from that of Lord Deputy Sir Oliver St John, contained by 1622 some thirty thatched houses and cabins with a few more underway. Equally, by this time Newtowncunningham consisted of forty thatched houses and cabins 'with a stone cawsey in the middle thereof'. For its part, the 'market town' of Letterkenny consisted of fifty thatched houses and one watermill. Both Ramelton and Rathmullan in Kilmacrenan barony were similar in scale. At Ramelton under the aegis of Sir William Stewart there was a 'town' erected made up of forty thatched houses and cabins with a street 'well-paved from the castle to the foundations of a church'. Similarly, at Rathmullan held by Bishop Knox, who had married Bingley's daughter, there was a 'village' erected of fifteen stone houses and thirty timber houses and cabins. The three borough towns in south Donegal – Killybegs, Ballyshannon and Donegal – were somewhat smaller though they may have stood out more than those in Portlough precinct, being in a less colonised environment. Both Ballyshannon and Donegal (which contained the free school) each, by 1622, had some thirty households mainly English, though in the case of Ballyshannon where the English were mostly soldiers there were also some few Irish residents as well. In both cases, however, the townsmen (some of whom, especially at Ballyshannon, were probably involved with the fisheries) had no land given them in freehold and leasehold. The 'new borough town' of Killybegs was smaller, with seventeen British and Irish inhabitants, but here there was an area of common – thirty 'acres' – allotted to the town.[97] The size the towns attained related at least in some measure to the economic development of the resources that surrounded them,

Even with plantation, Donegal remained an agricultural economy (apart from the fisheries) based on arable and pasture, varying with its terrain, and with no decisive evidence available of how these components may have been altered prior to 1641. In the very sympathetic mid-seventeenth century description which accompanies the Down Survey map of the entire barony of Raphoe, the soil (which was 'finely watered' by the rivers 'gliding' through it and 'refreshing' it) was described as 'generally profitable consisting of arable and pasture chiefly ...'. While there was some 'woody land' and 'some bog', the first was 'advantageous ... for shelter, ornament and use' while the second was 'at some times of the year ... profitable and at all times fit for fuel'. The account in the Civil Survey, also of the 1650s, is, however, somewhat sharper and perhaps more informative: 'The soil is cold lying in patches intermixt with bog, heath, mountain and some parts towards Lough Foyle fens, most for oats, little for barley and less for wheat [and] reasonable pasturage for small cattle of all sorts'.[98] The effects which had been made, however, on the Donegal economy (subject anyhow to economic vagaries especially in the 1620s) in terms of its productivity, by the injection of new people quantifiable numerically (about 1,500 adult males)[99] though not in terms of the range of skills amongst them – and of the capital they brought to invest – scarcely quantifiable at all – is not easy to assess through lack of sources. But it would be wrong to assume that there had been none. One area of innovation in the methods of production can, at any rate, be found – the erection of new mills. Many of these were manor mills, powered by water, and used for the grinding of corn. In the Lifford precinct area, for example, these are referred to in 1622 on the Benson estate at Stranorlar, on Hansard's lands at Ballindrait, and on Bingley's Farsetmore estate. However, there is evidence also for the erection of a second type of mill: tuck mills, used in the making of cloth. One such 'tucking mill' which comes to light from the general sources had been erected by 1622 near St Johnstown, where there was also a watermill, on the estate granted originally to the Duke of Lennox. Two mills, a corn mill and a 'tuke' mill, on the Trinity College estate near Mulroy Bay, are mentioned in the Civil Survey, while the 'two mills' at Raphoe, noted in the same source, may possibly also have included a tuck mill.[100] Their existence testifies to the emergence of an otherwise concealed settler cloth industry in Donegal. The two descriptions already cited of the barony of Raphoe pointed to more general infrastructural changes which had come about there. In the first, that area was seen as 'neither ... a place uncouth or unfrequented' because there were on it 'many improvements as castles, churches, mills, houses and craghts with other conveniences namely bridges [and] highways', though in the second many of these, especially the planters buildings and also Convoy bridge, were described as 'ruinous', which reflected the impact of war in the previous decade.

Administratively, the plantation period saw the effective beginnings of the integration of Donegal, as a county, into the structures and legal framework of a centralised Ireland. Hence the judges of the assizes were now able to make their regular circuits into the county. The establishment of county, or local, government there meant the appointment of commissions of justices of the peace, their members drawn from the local society but selected by the central government in Dublin, charged with legal and administrative functions. Both their names and their operation are obscure for this period, but, since power was a function of property, the upper levels of the plantation society will have predominated in county government. However, the fact that, as has been seen, Walter McLoughlin MacSweeney had been a justice of the peace, as was his son, shows that the justices were not chosen to be an exclusively settler body. The office of county sheriff (appointed annually) requiring of its holder a familiarity with legal procedures and bearing numerous administrative duties, was a crucial one in county administration. Where names survive for Donegal in a few intermittent years before 1641, the sheriff was always drawn from the settler society.[101] In these ways, common and statute law procedures could now be extended into Donegal and Gaelic procedures discontinued.

The creation of the county and the incorporation of many of the proposed borough towns meant also that constituencies now existed for the return of members to parliaments, three of which were summoned in this period: 1613–15, 1634 and 1640. In the first two, the two county members of the house of commons were Sir John Vaughan and Sir William Stewart, representing a balancing of Scots and English, and both of them military men in origin and grantees in the county. This changed for the 1640 parliament, however, when two English people occupied the seats, Sir Ralph Gore (d. 1642) who was successor to Paul Gore in south Donegal, and Sir Paul Davis, himself now a Donegal landowner but also, as has been seen, prominent in official circles in Dublin. In Ireland, as in England, the influence of government, or of some prominent figure, on the borough or its patron could lead to members being returned for the incorporated towns who had no direct local connection. This was true for some of the Donegal borough seats in all of these parliaments. Thus the election of Thomas Tallis, who was a rent collector for Trinity College, Dublin in the 1630s, as an MP for Killybegs (which had been incorporated too late to send members to the 1613–15 parliament), both in 1634 and 1640, may well have been secured as a means of upholding the interests of the college. However, a number had local interests, and a few of them may be mentioned to convey a brief impression of who they were. Of the two members for Ballyshannon in the first parliament, Paul Gore is already familiar while Edward Cherry must have had some local connection, since a Patrick Cherry appears as a tenant on Peter Benson's estate in 1630. Andrew Wilson, an MP for Donegal in 1640, derives from the Wilson undertaker family. Edward Torleton, already much mentioned, who lived at Lifford and who had been sheriff in the early 1630s and was also Lady Coach's estate manager, was an MP for Killybegs in 1640.[102]

Obviously, then, the little plantation towns had not yet developed sufficient corporate identity and wealth to send members clearly their own to parliaments.

If thus 'one law' was beginning to be established, the achievement of 'one church' made little headway.[103] The effects of the extension of the reformation into Donegal at the same time as the plantation were much less profound. Some few, indeed, of the Irish population were drawn towards Protestantism, for example those MacSweeney proprietors in Kilmacrenan who have been already noted. Another was the master of the free school (the 'royal school'), Brian Morrison, M.A., 'an Irish native who is conformable in religion and is a very good humanist', the school itself being then (1622) at Donegal rather than Raphoe.[104] It is clear, though, that no movement of any significance towards religious uniformity was underway prior to 1641. Although Bishop Knox on his appointment promised an active policy of evangelisation and sought from the secular arm a rigorous policy of suppression, including the banishing of Catholic priests, both prongs of this necessary partnership appear not to have been brought into action, a fact which may have ameliorated somewhat the difficult relationships of settler and native laities in the new circumstances of plantation.[105] No strenuous mission of conversion of the Irish laity, backed by continuous coercive measures to ensure church attendance was systematically sustained.[106] Furthermore, the reconstruction of the Catholic church in Donegal, to which, as well, commitment may have been heightened by the crisis of the Nine Years' War, began to get under way with the appointment by the papacy of Dr John O'Cullenan, first as vicar-apostolic in 1621, and then as bishop in 1625. Himself of south Donegal origin and with strong Cistercian links, he had studied in the Irish College at Salamanca in Spain, had a doctorate in theology from Rheims and was, by 1618, tutor in the Spanish Netherlands to the young Hugh O'Donnell, son of Rory the first earl of Tyrconnell, who lived there (d. 1642) and was from 1632 to occupy a high military command.[107]

His appointment as bishop coincided with the deteriorating relationship between England and Spain which led to a naval war between them, again, until 1630. During this period, the Franciscan archbishop Florence Conry and Owen Roe O'Neill, a major in the Irish regiment in the Spanish army in the Spanish Netherlands, and both natural leaders of their type, ecclesiastical and aristocratic, were actively seeking to get Spanish backing for the launching of an invasion of Ireland through Killybegs and 'the port of Londonderry', under the leadership of Colonel John O'Neill, son of Hugh and the commander of the Irish regiment, and Hugh O'Donnell – the exile second-generation earls. Their aim, which embraced some of the broader thinking which lay behind the Nine Years' War project in its later stages, was to initiate a military *coup d'état* from there, with the hope of raising sympathetic insurrections, to be brought about by their own nobilities, in the other parts of Ireland, designed to the creation of a new form of government for Ireland, separated from England, which would have linked it and its lords to the protection of the Spanish monarchy, and made it a part of the wider 'Catholic international' in the Europe of the time. That new form of government for Ireland, which necessarily would override the sensibilities of many of the old English in Ireland, while conferring central power over Ireland as a whole, in some form, on the two northern 'earls' (each however concerned that the other would secure advantage), would presumably aim to do so in a way which would not disturb their pre-existing power-relationships in Ulster (prior to plantation) or their power over their 'followers' under them in their own lordships. It would, most likely then, reverse the innovations (which sought to curb the nobility) which had flowed from the drastic' 'growth of governance' which had accompanied the Tudor and Stuart new departure in Ireland in the century since direct rule. Thus both plantation and the elevation of the freeholders, the two principal innovations with regard to landownership in the outreach parts of Ireland, would probably be ended, and possibly also such centralising tendencies as the extension of county government (so that there would be a plurality of law in Ireland), and also the Catholic Church, holding the church property, would become, in a very prominent way, the official church in Ireland. In the preparatory thinking which underlay all this was a desire to see only militant Catholic ecclesiastics, important as opinion-formers on the spot, appointed to Irish sees. This whole proposition created a short-term emergency because of English uncertainties as to whether Spain was powerful enough to support it, because in the altered balance of power between England and Spain which would flow from it (making Ireland a Spanish dependency garrisoned by Spanish soldiers), English ambitions, especially in the new world, which challenged Spain's claim to sole empire there, and also its influence in Europe, would be checked. As it happened, the whole scheme foundered on its inherent implausibility, and so the plantation in Donegal, which would have been particularly vulnerable to it, remained unchallenged.[108] When, however, even in peacetime with Spain, in the later 1630s, but just as another English crisis – rebellion in Scotland which led to the English civil war – was unfolding, the Countess Bridget sought to negotiate the restoration (within the existing *status quo*) of her son Hugh, Lord Deputy Wentworth's opinion was that it would be too dangerous: it 'might render him little less than a Prince in Ulster'.[109]

These more general points have been necessary because they provide the context of Dr O'Cullenan's appointment. Against this background, his political stance came under suspicion when Lord Deputy Falkland received an information in 1625 suggesting that he had been endeavouring to induce Philip IV's court at Madrid to attempt an invasion of Ireland.[110] Whatever the truth of that, and what in fact also he did preach, which remains unknowable, except that his apparent distancing of himself from the exile earl O'Donnell is highly suggestive, he was arrested, and held prisoner for a time in Dublin, in January 1628.[111] His later career as bishop of Raphoe in peacetime (after 1630, the period of heightened tension in Ulster consequent on Anglo-Spanish uncertainties having probably been short-lived) was also not without its difficulties, because what, in effect, now existed in Donegal was an established Protestant Church and a disestablished Catholic one. The acute financial difficulties of a Catholic churchman within the plantation context are stressed in a letter he wrote to Rome in 1636 with the specific purpose of seeking to be transferred to the diocese of Derry instead.[112] In it he pointed out 'not without deep sadness of heart how thick [were] the weeds which the persistent heresy daily sows through the influx of the English and Scottish Protestants above all into [his] bishopric'. His poverty arose, because as a result, he said, there were scarcely more than 700 Catholic men of 'some note' (that is, of some economic substance) there, and also he had no more than sixteen priests. Nor was this his only problem: he alluded also to his arrest in 1628. Through 'the storms of various calamities and disasters' stirred up by 'false brothers and ecclesiastics' – the former presumably Franciscan friars (which might reveal Cistercian and Franciscan antagonisms or even, perhaps, reinforce the view that he was not, after all, strongly committed to their political thinking which would have involved the renewal of warfare), the latter Bishop Knox and his clergy – he had been detained in Dublin for three months, when he had been twice brought before the lord deputy. His letter perhaps best reveals what had happened in the plantation period – he, had been monitored but not expelled and he lacked the lands and revenues of his predecessors – and reveals too, more generally, that Donegal was emerging to be, in the main, in matters of religion a two-culture society.

A formidable exercise in government (though not without parallels in its time), the decision to have a plantation in Ulster was taken in an interlude in the European 'wars of religion' of the sixteenth and seventeenth centuries. Although itself still transitional in character up to 1641, for Donegal plantation had many consequences, not least the sweeping away of the O'Donnells as lords there and also of the landed base of medieval monasticism. Accompanying it, too, was the substitution of Protestantism (itself not fully orthodox) for Catholicism as the established church, though not to the exclusion of Catholicism which survived even within the plantation context. It also laid the foundations of a new culture there, English and Lowland Scottish, using the English language.[113] It survived through the 1620s, through the failure of Ulster Irish emigré schemes, just mentioned (themselves broader in conception), designed to achieve Spanish and papal backing for military intervention in Ireland. In the areas uncolonised, dues and revenues which had supported the old elite – henceforth taking mainly the form of rents, payable, in theory at any rate, in accordance with English property law conventions – now supported the beginnings of a new and more diffused replacement one of which some of the old owners formed a part. In the areas colonised the change, of course, meant much more than that. If the extent of economic expansion and re-orientation which resulted from plantation in its early decades is not fully apparent (in this context note must be taken of the 'improvements' and innovations and new urban beginnings mentioned above), and although the degree of concurrent religious change among the Donegal Irish was very slight, its political importance is clear: plantation saw the beginnings of the absorption of the former O'Donnell lordship into a centralised Ireland and therefore marked, in many ways, a decisive change from the past.

[1] *Cal. S.P. Ire., 1606–8*, pp 268–9, 275–7.
[2] Ibid., pp 289–90.
[3] There were some exceptions to this arising from prior grants of some of this land.
[4] Nothing came of a proposal to endow and establish a hospital' for 'diseased and maimed' soldiers.
[5] For more detailed figures see P. Robinson, *The plantation of Ulster* (Dublin, 1984), p. 86.
[6] *Conditions to be observed by the British undertakers of the escheated lands in Ulster* (London, 1610).
[7] Conditions to be observed by the servitors and natives (7 April 1610) in *Anal. Hib.* viii, 220–22.
[8] *Cal. Pat. Rolls Ire., Jas. I*, p. 182.
[9] Ibid., pp 195, 483, 561, 566, 572.
[10] Ibid., pp 197–8 (patent to Nugent). For architectural descriptions see B. Lacy et. al,, *Archaeological survey of county Donegal* (Lifford, 1983), pp 329–30, 340–41. Flannacharta was later acquired by Brooke and Gore built at Magherabeg,
[11] *Cal. Pat. Rolls Ire., Jas. I*, p. 187; *Cal. Pat. Rolls Ire., Eliz.*, pp 361–2; D. O'Connor, *St Patrick's purgatory, Lough Derg* (Dublin, 1931 ed.), pp 129–31; P. Ó Gallachair, 'The parish of Carn' in *Clogher Record*, 1975, pp 301–80; Lacy, *Archaeological Survey* pp 351–13. The conflicting claims of Bishop Montgomery and Archbishop Magrath came to a head in September 1609 (*Cal. S.P. Ire., 1608–10,* pp 288–9) and the decision to grant the land to Magrath was based on prior legal entitlement arising from the regrant of 1596. Magrath's patent (crown rent, £2 Ir.) also represented a defeat for Robert Leicester, whose general grant in 1604, procured by Lord Mountjoy, had included these territories. Uncertainty as to which county these lands were in – 'in the confines of the counties of Fermanagh, Tyrone and Donegal' in James Magrath's patent – permeates the official record.
[12] Two existing castles are, however, referred to in 1596.
[13] A. Gwynn and R.N. Hadcock, *Medieval religious houses: Ireland* (London, 1970), pp 39, 272.
[14] *Anal. Hib.*, viii, 291. It was thought that the bishop of Raphoe might also live there.
[15] There had been no recent late-wave monastic foundation in Inishowen by the O'Dohertys.

16 *Cal. Pat. Rolls Ire., Jas. I*, pp 149, 153, 161, 169, 173. A decision that Chichester should enter
    into a recognizance to surrender within three years 1,000 acres of land for the better maintenance
    of the Londoners' new city was silently omitted from his second patent. This decision hears
    relation to a similar one, actually carried out, that Sir Randal MacDonnell should surrender lands
    near Coleraine to the Londoners to enhance their second town there.

17 *Anal, Hib.*, viii, 288, 291.

18 This is the origin of the proposal that Chichester should surrender 1,000 acres from his
    Inishowen grant.

19 Carndonagh was probably intended by 'Dowagh in Enishowen', Another version of the 'project'
    does not include it (*Cal. Carew MSS*, 1603–24, p. 18).

20 I have set out the evolution of this policy below, ch. 14, pp 368–74.

21 *Cal. Pat. Rolls Ire., Jas. I*, pp 219–20.

22 Ibid., pp 224–5.

23 On Jones see M. O'Dowd, *Power, politics and land: early modern Sligo, 1588–1688* (Belfast,
    1991), passim.

24 *Cal. Pat. Rolls Ire., Jas. I*, p. 300.

25 Strictly, then, additional corporation land was not made available in all places.

26 *Cal. Pat. Rolls Ire., Jas. I*, p. 182. The area concerned was the Roughan, the Dorroghes and the
    remainder of the quarter of Liffer except the part called Stramore.

27 These 4 acres, to be measured at the rate of 21 foot to the perch, lay at the north-east of the
    meadow where the rivers of Deele and Finn joined.

28 *Cal. Pat. Rolls Ire., Jas. I*, pp 206–7. Amongst other rights that Hansard received were ferries over
    the Finn and Deele.

29 The incorporation of St Johnstown came later.

30 G. Hill, *An historical account of the plantation in Ulster at the commencement of the seventeenth
    century, 1608–1620* (Belfast, 1877), pp 322–7; M. Percevel-Maxwell, *The Scottish migration to
    Ulster in the reign of James I* (London, 1973), pp 360–61.

31 The most convenient list is in Hill, *Plantation in Ulster*, pp 327–30. I have generally tried to
    retain the spellings of names as they appear at the time in an effort to minimise confusion in
    identifications.

32 *Cal. Pat. Rolls Ire., Jas. I*, pp 248, 306, 309.

33 NAI, Lodge MSS, vi, 189.

34 *Cal. Pat. Rolls Ire., Jas. I*, pp 210–11; *Civil Survey* iii, 131–3.

35 *Cal. Pat. Rolls Ire., Jas. I*, p. 184; *Civil Survey*, iii, 129–30; *Cal. S.P. Ire., 1633–47*, p. 344.

36 *Cal. Pat. Rolls Ire., Jas. I*, p. 180; *Civil Survey*, iii, 106–7.

37 Hill, *Plantation in Ulster*, pp 526–7. MacSweeney Fanad's held 'from three years to three years'
    at that time.

38 M. Perceval-Maxwell, *Scottish migration*, passim; G. Donaldson, *Scotland: James V– James VII*
    (Edinburgh, 1971), p. 218; *Cal. Pat. Rolls Ire., Jas I*, pp 277, 483, 488.

39 BL, Add. MS 36,775, ff 104–5; *Cal. Pat. Rolls Ire., Jas. I*, p. 488.

40 NAI, Lodge MSS, v, 135–9; vi, 247, 490–501. Rory O'Donnell had claimed in 1607 that the
    duties of the fishing of Killybegs had been worth £500 per (quoted in C. Conaghan, *History and
    antiquities of Killybegs* (Ballyshannon, 1974), p. 88.

41 Hill, *Plantation in Ulster*, p. 501; *Inq. Cancell. Hib. Repert.*, ii, Donegal (32) Chas I.

42 BL, Sloane MS 3,827, f. 63.

43 This is based on Pynnar's survey of 1618–19 of the plantation in this area, printed in Hill,
    Plantation in Ulster pp 500–4 and on the survey of 1622 [henceforth cited as Treadwell (ed.),
    '1622 survey'], printed in V.W. Treadwell (ed.), 'The plantation in Donegal: a survey' in *Donegal
    Annual* 2 (1951–4), 513–5.

44 *Inq. Cancell. Hib. Repert.*, ii, Donegal (17) Chas I.

45 BL, Harleian MS 2138, ff 164–89.

46 This includes land drained and reclaimed prior to the mid-nineteenth century.

47 M. Percevel-Maxwell, *Scottish migration*, passim.

48 Coolmacitrain appears to be identifiable with Castle Forward.

49 M. Perceval-Maxwell, *Scottish migration*, p. 224.

50 *Anal. Hib.*, viii, 224–5.

[51] Since this section is a preliminary part of a study of the English in the plantation as a whole, I have deferred the detailed footnoting of it to that time.

[52] *Anal. Hib.,* viii, 209. In fact they met him outside Dublin late in September, and Lyttleton may not have come until 1611.

[53] *Cal. Carew MSS* 1603 –24, pp 221–22. On Caphar oge see *Cal. S.P. Ire., 1606–8*, pp 124–5, 129–30, 513; 1608–1 pp 29,87, 104, 112, 264.

[54] HMC, *Hastings MSS*, iv, 171–2; T.W. Moody, *Londonderry plantation*, p. 351. Arthur Terry, who was from Southwark, sold his half of what had been a joint purchase from Clare, to Benson, his partner, in October 1615 (*Inq. Cancell. Hib. Repert.*, ii, Donegal (10) Chas I).

[55] NAI, R.C. 9/1, p. 183; G.A. Usher, *Gwysaney and Owston.: a history of the family of Davies-Cooke of Gwysaney, Flintshire and Owston, West Riding of Yorkshire* (Denbigh, 1964), pp 7–50. (The author was unaware of the Ulster plantation connection).

[56] *Inq. Cancell. Hib. Repert.*, ii, Donegal (11) Chas I; *Cal. S.P. Ire., 1608–10*, p. 509; *Cal. Carew MSS*, 1603–24, pp 217–8, 385.

[57] Usher, *Gwysaney and Owston*, p. 47.

[58] NAI, Lodge MSS, vi, 304.

[59] See below, ch. 4, pp 86–101.

[60] NAI, Lodge MSS, v, 219–20; vi, 190–92; T.W. Moody, *Londonderry plantation*, p. 301, 314, 323–5, 337, 446.

[61] PRONI, T 1021, pp 116–28. Some time after 1641 a Scot, Andrew Hamilton, succeeded to the Wilson estate through marriage.

[62] HMC, *Hastings MSS*, iv, 171–2. Like Terry, Vaughan disengaged from Berkeley's estate, leaving it to be entirely owned by Bingley and with him probably went the arrangement with Clinton.

[63] Pynnar's survey of this area is printed in Hill, *Plantation in Ulster*, pp 514–22.

[64] For the text of the 1622 survey of this area see Treadwell (ed.), '1622 survey', pp 515–7.

[65] With regard to Pynnar's survey, while there are instances throughout it of conscientious endeavour to probe really dubious information, he may have presented his evidence (for example the acreage figures) – and also have had it presented to him – too readily in a form that would be intelligible in terms of the plantation conditions the performance of which he was sent to investigate.

[66] See below, ch. 5, pp 102–33.

[67] Ibid.; *Inq. Cancell. Hib. Repert.,* ii, Donegal (17) Chas I.

[68] Treadwell (ed.), '1622 survey', p. 515.

[69] Ibid.

[70] Ibid. Pynnar found just one village 'standing on a passage very commodious for the king's service …' (Hill, *Plantation in Ulster*, p. 517).

[71] Given the size of Kingsmill's command, the 1622 commissioners' number of 25 cottages is to be preferred to Pynnar's 30.

[72] Treadwell (ed.), '1622 survey', p. 516.

[73] The Ordnance Survey memoir also gives a hint to its location (RIA, OS memoirs, Box 21/111, p. 20).

[74] See ch. 4 above, pp 86–101.

[75] NAI, Lodge MSS, vi, 190. The site of the later manor house (now demolished) in Corravaddy has to be ruled out since Corravaddy was in a different quarter. I am indebted to Mr J. Harris of Coachmills for his assistance with the local topography.

[76] *Civil Survey*, iii, 24–37. More freeholds were created in the later seventeenth century.

[77] This section is based on the surveys of Pynnar and the 1622 commissioners.

[78] *Inq. Cancell. Hib. Repert.*, ii, Donegal (11) Chas I.

[79] *Civil Survey*, iii, 24, 34.

[80] T.W. Moody, 'The treatment of the native population under the scheme for the plantation in Ulster' in *IHS*, i, no. 1 (Mar. 1938), pp 59–63.

[81] *Cal. S.P. Ire., 1625–32*, pp 349–52.

[82] NAI, Lodge MSS, v, 526–7.

[83] *Inq. Cancell. Hib. Repert.*, ii, Donegal, (10), (11), (12) Chas I; NAI, R.C. 9/1. Only from the restoration do sources, especially the hearth money rolls, become available for Donegal that relate occupancy precisely to place names.

[84] NAI, Lodge MSS, v, 526–7.

[85] *Inq. Cancell. Hib. Repert.*, ii, Donegal (17) Chas I.

[86] Ibid., (14), (17) Chas I. Whether these were the original places of residence of these Irish tenants or whether they had moved from elsewhere is not clear.

[87] NAI, R.C. 9/1. These British sub-tenants are not a hidden sub-tier of the plantation; most are on the muster roll of 1630.

[88] TCD, MS 550, ff 193, 210; J. B. Leslie, *Derry clergy and parishes* (Enniskillen, 1937), pp 155–60, 195–200; Idem, *Raphoe clergy and parishes* (Enniskillen, 1940), pp 13–15, 102–3, 121–24. With regard to Lifford, the old Templebogan or Ballybogan church, of which parts still remain, some two miles from Lifford, may possibly have been used at first as an alternative to Clonleigh.

[89] *Civil Survey*, iii, 46.

[90] For the architectural genre see E. McParland, 'Rathfarnham castle, co. Dublin: a property of the Society of Jesus' in *Country Life*, 9 September 1982, 734–7.

[91] *Inq. Cancell. Hib. Repert.*, ii Donegal (11) Jas I.

[92] NAI, Lodge MSS, v, 52–3.

[93] *Civil Survey*, iii, 38.

[94] *Cal. Pat. Rolls Ire., Jas.* I, p. 261.

[95] *Civil Survey*, iii, 41–3.

[96] The inscription on his monument in Lifford Church of Ireland church gives the details.

[97] This section has been based mainly on Pynnar's survey and that made by the commissioners in 1622.

[98] NLI, Down Survey maps, terrier to Raphoe barony map; *Civil Survey* iii, 23.

[99] R.J. Hunter (ed.), 'The settler plantation of an Ulster plantation county' in *Donegal Annual* 10 (1971–3), 124–54.

[100] *Civil Survey*, iii, 45, 100.

[101] For a partial list of sheriffs see PRONI, D302, pp 55–6.

[102] For lists of the MPs see T.W. Moody, 'The Irish parliament under Elizabeth and James I: a general survey' in *Proc. RIA*, 45C (1939), 80; H.F. Kearney, *Strafford in Ireland, 1633–41* (Manchester, 1959), pp 255–6; *Commons' jn. Ire.*, i (Dublin, 1763), 217.

[103] The reference is to the French crown's ideal: 'one law, one church, one king'.

[104] TCD, MS 550, f, 220.

[105] For Bishop Knox's efforts in this respect in his early years, and for the support he sought from the government, see Alan Ford, *The protestant reformation in Ireland, 1590–1641* (Frankfurt am Main, 1985), pp 166–8.

[106] Even the churches themselves were in poor repair up to the early 1620s. There is little information available on the collection of recusants' fines in Ulster.

[107] On Bishop O'Cullenan see Donal F. Cregan, 'The social and cultural background of a counter-reformation episcopate, 1618–60' in A. Cosgrove and D. McCartney (eds), *Studies in Irish history presented to R. Dudley Edwards* (Dublin, 1979), pp 85–117. For Hugh O'Donnell see J.I. Casway, *Owen Roe O'Neill and the struggle for Catholic Ireland* (Philadelphia, 1984), pp 27, 29–33, 38.

[108] I hope to return to this later. For a short analysis of Owen Roe O'Neill, see Raymond Gillespie, 'Owen Roe O'Neill, *c.* 1582–1649: soldier and politician' in G. O'Brien and P. Roebuck (eds), *Nine Ulster lives* (Belfast, 1992), pp 149–68.

[109] W. Knowler (ed.), *The earl of Strafforde's letters and despatches* (London, 1739), ii, 269.

[110] *Cal. S.P. Ire., 1625–3* p. 5.

[111] Ibid., p. 304; Cregan, 'Counter-reformation episcopate', p. 94.

[112] F. Moran (ed.), *Spicilegium Ossoriense: being a collection of original letters and papers illustrative of the history of the Irish church from the reformation to the year 1800* (Dublin, 1874), pp 212–3. I am indebted to Robert Martindale and Joy Rutherford of Cambridge and to Frank D'Arcy for translations.

[113] A long-range reflection of that in the plantation society can be seen in the career (transcending Ireland) and writings (reflecting it) of William Allingham.

I am grateful to L.J. Arnold, Brian Lacy, Seán Connolly, Josephine Cowley, Laura Houghton, Henry Jefferies, Keith Lindley, John McCavitt, Michael McGuinness, Anne Moffett, Mary Monaghan, Winifred Montgomery and Hiram Morgan for their help in various ways, as well as to many people in Donegal who assisted with investigations on the ground and to the editors and publisher for their patience.

4

Sir Ralph Bingley, c. 1570–1627: Ulster Planter

The plan for plantation in the six escheated counties in Ulster devised between 1608 and 1610 provided, in its barest essentials, for the allocation of the forfeited land to individual grantees of three types, grouped together in precincts which corresponded in most cases with the baronies into which the counties had been divided. The prime responsibility for colonisation devolved to the undertakers, civilian grantees of either English or Lowland Scottish origin, themselves separately grouped by precinct and to whom the London companies in the Londonderry plantation are most nearly equivalent. Unlike the undertakers, the servitors, military officers and officials already in Ireland and mainly English were allowed to have Irish tenantry. In addition, Irish grantees selected from the forfeited area were restored to some of the land and were, with a consequent measure of transplantation, placed in the same precincts as the servitors. Provision was also made for land grants for proposed corporate towns, for a free school in each county and for the reformation parish clergy; and Trinity College, Dublin, received a substantial endowment. Exceptional features, however, distorted the symmetry here and there – the grant of the forfeited land in Inishowen to Lord Deputy Chichester was one such, the honouring of pre-plantation grants to a few prominent Irish owners was another. Termon and erenach land, disputed as to whether it had forfeited in accordance with the legal claims of the Crown to the temporal land or should be regarded as ecclesiastical, was finally granted to the bishops as a major addition to the traditional episcopal land.

Already since the end of the Nine Years' War and distinct from the plantation arrangements, grants of dissolved monastic land were being made mainly to the resident servitors, some of whom were also gaining possession of land reserved for the forts which had played an important part in the English wartime strategy. Hence a precinct or barony designed at plantation for a particular category or categories of new grantee would also contain some land the ownership of which was determined by considerations deriving either from the plantation plan itself or from other prior circumstances. The plantation plan, essentially to grant land to individuals of clearly defined type, was thus implemented in 1610 within a somewhat more complex framework. Also the principles of land measurement adopted meant that the intention to grant relatively small estates of three sizes, 1,000, 1,500 and 2,000 acres, was frustrated: estates granted under these conventions turned out to be many times larger while some accumulations by purchase also took place. Neither were the conventions themselves uniformly followed: many of the servitors received grants under the nominal 1,000 'acre' minimum, while in the case of the Irish grantees the principle was effectively abandoned and the majority received very small acreages. The number of grantees involved – some 120 undertakers, 60 servitors and 300 Irish – offers some impression of the scale of the operation.[1]

The career in Ulster of Ralph Bingley, a man tolerably representative of the servitor class, impinged on a number of the aspects of change in land ownership sketched above. Paid in Ireland as Captain of Foot from 8 August 1598, his appearance was part of a larger reinforcement of the English army intended, before plans were changed after the defeat at the Yellow Ford, to be shipped from Chester to Lough Foyle as a major tactical initiative in the conduct of the war. His immediate background was that of the professional soldier who had attended neither university nor inn of court. He had taken part in Drake and Hawkins's raiding voyage to Panama and Puerto Rico in 1595–6. In 1596 he was nominated to be joint mustermaster of the trained bands in Hampshire with responsibility for the defence of Portsmouth and in the following year was concerned with raising soldiers in Suffolk and especially with preparations for the Earl of Essex's Islands (or Azores) voyage.[2] This military apprenticeship was served in the context of the war, naval and privateering, with Spain; he must have approached his employment in Ireland very much in that light. The parentage and date of birth (*c.* 1570) of Ralph, the second of at least three brothers and probably a descendant of John Bingley, the Earl of Derby's bailiff of the manor of Hawarden in 1474, cannot be precisely established. Yet what evidence we have suggests that in the late sixteenth century his family, the Bingleys of Broughton – a place some five miles from Chester, where another branch of the family can be found, but in the parish of Hawarden in the Welsh county of Flint – were very minor landholders, hardly of gentry status but having some influential connections. The family seems to have been a fairly numerous one, some of whom were involved in Sir Ralph's enterprises, notably Richard, his younger brother, who was in Ireland initially as lieutenant of his company, and the older brother, William, who mortgaged his land in Flint to accompany him on the expedition, fatal to both, to the Isle of Rhé in 1627.[3]

A decisive moment in Bingley's career came when the proposed military expedition to Lough Foyle finally landed in May 1600. Sir Henry Docwra, commanding some 4,000 men, had as governor of Lough Foyle with his base at Derry a military jurisdiction over a region stretching to the Bann and Blackwater eastwards and taking in north Donegal. Docwra secured by diplomatic and military means the support of a number of prominent Irish figures including Niall Garbh O'Donnell, cousin of Hugh and an aspirant for the chieftainship, and in 1601 proceeded to install garrisons in strategic out-centres within his jurisdiction. Thus Bingley, commanding 150 foot, was lodged in Rathmullan priory in MacSweeny Fanad's country.[4] Even before the formal termination of hostilities in March 1603 he was building up a landed base within the area of Docwra's governorship. Hence in May 1602 he received a Crown lease of the monastic land of Rathmullan, of Inch island (3,069 acres), part of O'Doherty's country and of the entire fishing of Lough Swilly, the latter complementing Docwra's tenure of the fishing of Lough Foyle. A parallel grant of fishings in west Donegal in 1603 to John Bingley (probably a member of the Chester branch), who had held the influential post of deputy to the Treasurer at War in Dublin since c. 1599, indicates that both were co-operating at this early stage in a region appearing to be open to new English exploitation.[5]

Further, in May 1603 Ralph renewed his lease of the previous year, now greatly expanded to also include, principally, the monastic and erenach land on which Derry was based, the monastic land of Kilmacrenan near Letterkenny and lay lands at Carrigans some five miles from Derry, where an O'Donnell fort had been occupied 'with a little new dressing' by Docwra, the latter seemingly now, like Lifford, an arbitrary expropriation of lay land by the government.[6] Furthermore it can be safely inferred that he was able to convert much of this with additional Donegal monastic land into fee farm ownership by the notorious system of general grants, whereby a courtier or official authorised in London to receive a patent of land to a certain value had lands, usually very undervalued, included in his patent which he then disposed of to a local interested party.[7] The mechanism operated in Bingley's case through James Fullerton, a favourite of the new King and later one of the plantation planners, and Sir Henry Brouncker, president of Munster.[8] It may be superficially surprising then that many of these substantial takings were sold. Lands on the Foyle were disposed of to a fellow servitor, Edmund Leigh; Docwra came to own the land at Derry. By far his largest sale, of Kilmacrenan (some 29,000 acres) and other smaller areas of monastic land, for at least £1,200 and probably £1,600, was made to Rory O'Donnell, Earl of Tyrconnell. He thus retained, principally, the lands at Carrigans (possibly on lease) and Inch, footholds equidistant from

Derry, appointing his brother Richard, now holding a pension from the state, to let them in June 1604.[9]

A number of factors account for these sales. Although he had risen to be one of the colonels of the army, paid ten shillings per day apart from his captain's pay, and was knighted in Dublin in 1603, army reductions progressively eroded his income. His colonel's pay terminated in March 1604, his Irish foot were discharged in September when he was transferred to County Down and his English foot, reduced to fifty in June 1605, were entirely discharged in September of that year.[10] Thus, although he had been operating more successfully and somewhat independently of Docwra, the post-war reorganisation of Ulster must have been as discomfiting to Bingley as it was to the governor of Lough Foyle.[11] The restoration of Hugh O'Neill which frustrated Docwra's expectations and reversed the earlier strategy with which he had been intimately involved was paralleled by a somewhat similar settlement in Donegal. Although some provision was made for Niall Garbh, and O'Doherty's title to Inishowen was not disrupted, Rory O'Donnell who had only surrendered in December 1602 was created Earl of Tyrconnell.[12] Docwra's authority was limited to Derry, now developing as a settler settlement with Richard Bingley leaseholder of its customs and incorporated in 1604 with Ralph as an alderman.[13] Hence although Rory O'Donnell later catalogued his complaints against the local captains – extortions by their soldiers, partiality towards Niall Garbh who he claimed plotted with Bingley to murder him, and duplicity by Bingley, supported in Dublin, over the land sale whereby he 'lost both the lands and [the] money' amongst them – the captains for their part subject to army cuts and with their local contacts in disfavour could not predict the flight in 1607.[14] Many, like William Cole whose position in the Ballyshannon command was somewhat similar to Bingley's, sought military employment elsewhere. Those fortunate to retain command of a fort, like Caulfeild at Charlemont, would develop landed interests; others without a command, like Phillips at Coleraine, but temperamentally adapted to building up an estate, were fewer. Even Docwra disposed of his company and town in 1606.[15]

It need not be surprising in these circumstances that a man of Bingley's experience and energy became quickly involved in the renewed English interest in North American trade and colonisation. One such project, entirely independent of the Virginia Company chartered in April 1606, probably itself intended as a fishing expedition to Maine but which may have been linked either with a number of simultaneous schemes (precursors of Calvert's Maryland) to establish a Catholic colony or with two other venturers whose ships were at Drogheda in summer 1606, was that of a group of members of the London Fishmongers' Company negotiated in

March 1606. When the scheme was organised to the point where a passport was issued, in May, by the Lord High Admiral, Charles Howard, Bingley appears as captain of the ship *Triall* of London, owned by one group of Fishmongers and chartered to another, the master being Arthur Chambers, one of the charterers.[16] How Bingley came to be involved has not been explained. However he was already in London in the second half of 1605, engaged amongst other things in taking out a grant of arms, and could offer some investment derived from the previous five years in Ulster.[17] His most likely contact was with William Angell, fishmonger to the King, one of the owners of the ship. To Angell's numerous overseas interests must be added an Irish dimension, though it emerges only in 1607 when as a farmer of the impost on yarn he was negotiating with the Mayor of Chester on Irish yarn importation.[18] More plausibly the contact was made through John Bingley, whose profits in Ireland were considered to be exceeded only by those of his patron, Sir George Carey, who was in regular contact with London in his official capacity and about to move there as an exchequer official, and who appears to have been on the Irish fringe of a group of closely-linked speculators which included (with Angell) Arthur Ingram and Lionel Cranfield, all of whom had close contacts with high-ranking ministers of state, the Howards and the future Earl of Salisbury amongst them.[19]

Whatever its intended destination or broader affiliations, the *Triall* voyage, although afforced by Bingley who brought in at Chester a Welsh ship owner intent on a tobacco voyage to the West Indies, never got beyond European waters. There were delays, squabbles and unseemly incidents at Dublin, Waterford and Kinsale (where it was alleged Bingley was consorting with pirates) and Roger Bamford, the purser representing Angell (the other vessels had withdrawn), sought an order by Chichester to prohibit Bingley proceeding to sea. Eventually, when the charter period had expired in December, he went to sea with 100 men aboard. Although he apparently still claimed to be bound for Virginia – though he may perhaps have intended a privateering visit to the West Indies – the voyage degenerated into a piratical adventure to the Bay of Biscay and the Spanish coast before returning, six weeks later, to Baltimore, County Cork.

He later explained that his 'doings at sea' had been due to bad weather and loss of supplies, protesting that when he first 'intended' his voyage his 'thoughts did soar too high to stoop at [the] base and forbidden baits [of] pirates'. However in the altered circumstances of Anglo-Spanish relations after the Treaty of London (1604) his actions were to have diplomatic repercussions. The Spanish ambassador asserted he sold prizes in Irish ports with official connivance and Salisbury criticised him as having become a pirate while 'first insinuating his purpose to be an actor in that worthy action of enlarging trades and plantations'. Although he extricated himself after a short imprisonment from charges in the High Court of Admiralty, *Triall* having been recovered for her owners, the evidence for piracy is substantial though it does not prove this was Bingley's original intention.[20] Further, he continued to 'hover off and on' the Munster coast until July 1607 when he presented two boats for the admiral's use to a naval captain then attempting to deal with the ubiquitous problem of piracy there.[21] Also, though the evidence is not conclusive, he appears to have had dealings with Thomas Crooke of Baltimore, who had purchased land from Sir Fineen O'Driscoll, and was one of a group of English settlers (which included John Winthrop, uncle of the future governor of Massachusetts Bay) engaged in a post-war Munster plantation enterprise in that area of Cork.[22] Nevertheless for Bingley the *Triall* affair had been a disaster in spite of what limited and immediate profits it may have brought.

A combination of official support in Ireland and convenient circumstances led, however, to his complete rehabilitation. The urgent mobilisations required by O'Doherty's rising (April–July 1608), to the outbreak of which Bingley's lease of Inch had been a contributory factor, presented him with new scope and employment. Initially, promptly and at a time when Dublin feared invasion, his role was a naval one, successful in capturing O'Doherty's boats. Government accounts reveal payments to him for May and June as captain of two barques, almost certainly of the Wirral which he had pressed, hired, manned and victualled; for five months thereafter he was captain of foot, latterly garrisoned at Doe and Rathmullan and involved in the capture of Tory Island, a final place of resistance of O'Doherty's supporters.[23]

It is a measure both of their private expectations and official support that both brothers' attentions were now, as plantation planning proceeded, assiduously converging on Ulster. Captain Richard, dispatched with a royal galley from the Thames to the Scottish Isles in May 1608, was engaged in 1609 and 1610 in transporting Ulster swordsmen to Sweden and became Constable of Doe Castle in August 1610.[24] Sir Ralph, seeking to pre-empt any other grants that might be made under the plantation arrangements of the monastic land formerly sold to O'Donnell and now formally declared forfeit to the Crown by reason of his attainder, secured a Crown lease of some of this (including again a foothold at Rathmullan) in December 1609; the circumstances of this suggest that a mutually convenient accommodation had been arrived at with Lord Deputy Chichester, who had been successful in soliciting a grant of O'Doherty's country for himself and to whom Bingley surrendered his lease of Inch in the same month. In an explicit deal with Chichester in 1610 he re-secured title to the land, also formally forfeit, at Carrigans, the rents of which he had collected since 1608. There were, however, limits to what his Dublin influence could secure. The overall structure of plantation had been devised in London and as planning there was being completed in April 1610, Sir Ralph's expectations, despite Chichester's support and his claim that O'Donnell left £600 unpaid, of securing a regrant of the extensive Kilmacrenan monastic lands were frustrated. However, since in the allocation of land to servitors the Dublin government was to be given considerable initiative within the predetermined structure of precinct allotments, the English Privy Council recommended he receive 'an extraordinary proportion of land as a servitor in some other place as may best suit with the convenience of the plantation and the occasions of Sir Ralph Bingley'.[25]

Later in 1610 Chichester and the Dublin plantation commissioners travelled through the escheated counties to install the grantees or, technically, to issue warrants to the sheriffs to grant them possession. Bingley's assignment as a grantee in Doe and Fanad (otherwise the barony of Kilmacrenan, the allotment in Donegal for servitors and Irish) – a 1,000 'acre' estate (some 7,120 statute acres), with an extra 213 'acres', but also with the accompanying urbanising responsibility, to promote a settler town for the barony at Rathmullan as well as some additional privileges (ownership at their deaths of 999 'acres' assigned to two Irish widows and ferries over Lough Foyle and the Finn) – was that of a key though not over-endowed figure within the terms of the plantation plan. Further, the structure of grants in the barony conformed tolerably if not strictly with the local requirements of the plan that three-fifths of the forfeited land be guaranteed to Irish grantees. Also, with Richard Bingley granted land adjoining Doe Castle and Ralph's estate mainly in the Rosguill peninsula controlling Sheephaven and Mulroy Bay as well as overlooking the Swilly at Rathmullan, their local importance in the development of the plantation would be considerable. They not only held, the one as Constable of Doe and the other as grantee of Rathmullan, the two principal castles of the MacSweeney lords of Doe and Fanad but their lands were so located as to dominate those of a group of the Irish grantees.[26] Instead, with the residency requirement not enforced, Bingley embarked on a policy of expansion while his brother, an absentee, acquired the surveyorship of the navy in May 1611 and, knighted, sold his lands in 1613 to John Sandford, his successor in the constableship and an earlier associate in the transportations to Sweden.[27]

Sir Ralph's complex land dealings, a series of inter-related moves probably completed within a few years, by which he became owner of two undertakers' estates in Lifford precinct, are not precisely documented. However his ownership of Kilmacrenan land was greatly extended by two processes, one carrying a faint odour of corruption, the other suggesting an element of strong arm tactics. Additional monastic land conveniently adjacent to his plantation allotment and significant pieces of his 1609 leasehold – the monasteries at Rathmullan and Balleeghan, the latter close to Carrigans – were passed in a general patent in 1611, assigned immediately to Henry Perse the lord deputy's secretary and sold by him to Bingley in the following year. [28]Opportunity to acquire the lands of neighbouring Irish grantees presented itself to many servitors. Bingley's acquisitions, though some of the evidence derives only from the later patents of those to whom he sold land, appear to have amounted to as many as eleven of the Irish grantees' lands. Also, harsh methods may have been employed. Ten of these grantees took out their grants in a joint patent (to them an unfamiliar document) with Bingley in May 1611 which was probably held by him. Also we know that Bingley was himself 'the sheriff' against whom some of them complained in August that he 'detained' their land. Further, he had secured the temporary control of a group of horse from the garrison at Castlefin. At the same time, some Irish grantees – two O'Gallaghers and an O'Donnell have been detected – perhaps preferring not to transplant, may have opted for a mutually convenient if precarious alternative: year to year tenancies on his undertakers' estates.[29]

The sale of the land so accumulated in Kilmacrenan, probably some 26,420 acres,[30] much of it to former military associates and which may have made his purchases of undertakers' land self- financing, allowed him to pass over his building obligations. Thus Andrew Knox, the Scots Bishop of Raphoe, acquired, along with a Bingley marriage (Sir Ralph was childless), the Rathmullan lands (4,410 acres) and urbanising responsibility there, the discontinuity (since Knox was an energetic coloniser) probably accounting for its failure to be incorporated.[31]

Some of the less judiciously chosen English undertakers, reluctant to fulfill their obligations, opted instead to sell their assignments, creating in effect a minor land market in England from 1610 favourable to energetic purchasers. Two such in Lifford precinct were Sir Maurice Berkeley and the ageing Sir Robert Remington, a former Vice-President of Connacht rather than a conventional civil grantee. Their estates, both 2,000 'acre' proportions and one of them purchased on his behalf by Sir Richard in England, became Bingley's property, probably, in the light of other evidence, for no more than £200 or £300. These estates, the one based on Ballybofey (31,783 acres including mountain) the other (7,136 acres) stretching inland from the Swilly and bounding near Manorcunningham with the Scots in Portlough, linkable with Balleeghan and Carrigans and lying more closely within the hinterland of Derry with which his association (Mayor, 1624) continued under the Londoners as an alderman by the 1613 charter and where a relative was installed, had clear advantages over his Rosguill assignment.[32] They also became his final property. The lands at Balleeghan and at Carrigans where he had built houses and mills, deviously re-acquired in Ireland in 1610 and 1611, had, quite properly, been declared O'Donnell property by inquisition in 1608 and had on that basis formed parts of the estates allocated in England to various Scottish undertakers. Despite litigation with the new owners and persistent appeals, supported by Dublin, right up to 1627 to the English Privy Council, he failed to validate his title. London, with varying enthusiasm, would consider compensation – Bingley, demanding £800, turned down £500 in 1613; it would not, with similar claims being made, by recognising his title set a precedent for questioning the inquisitions of 1608 on which the plantation was based.[33]

It is then as an undertaker that Bingley's plantation performance must ultimately be judged. His building operations, since it has been possible to identify the sites, reveal indeed a measure of conformity to the plantation plan (which prescribed that the undertaker by 1614 at the outside should erect a residence on each estate surrounded by a bawn, 'near' which his tenantry should live in village fashion) but equally demonstrate that no fixed pattern was strictly followed. Thus on the Lough Swilly estate where he lived and also concentrated his initial efforts, with brick-making underway and seven houses for tenants already erected 'at his own charge' by 1613, his house and bawn, completed before 1619, had been built at Farsetmore overlooking the Swilly and 'well seated for service'; while the site chosen for the village placed it 'within a mile' away, probably at Dromany Little in a 'place of continual passage', the route from Derry via Letterkenny to west Donegal. On the Ballybofey estate building operations had not started by 1613 (an effect of ownership change) and, delayed by litigation – overruled by the English Privy Council in Bingley's favour in 1618 – with another claimant to ownership, had not been entirely completed by 1619. Here the landlord house, Drumboe, although having itself as described in 1622 some architectural similarity, in the use of returns, with that at Farsetmore (but without a bawn), had been built very much closer to Bingley's village of Ballybofey, where he was licensed in 1619 to hold fairs and markets, although it was separated from it by the unbridged River Finn. Both villages, typical of many throughout the plantation, were small: Ballybofey contained twelve thatched houses and cottages 'inhabited for the most part with British' in 1622; the other, a 'village of thatched houses' in 1622, contained six houses and a mill with 'more in building' in 1619.[34]

Any attempt to calculate the size attained by his colony, of course only partially village dwelling, runs into difficulties. It may well be however that the return in Pynnar's survey in 1619 for both estates of 50 tenantry recorded as families, making with undertenants 124 males, represents much the same group of people as that of the commissioners in 1622 who found 52 tenantry but only 55 British men 'present'. If his tenants were for the most part married, then a colony of some 50 at this time represented a tolerable if belated conformity with the requirement of 40 families, to constitute 96 adult males, of the plantation conditions. Against this has to be placed the list of 57 adult males, including only 2 of 8 named tenants deriving from 1611 and 1613, who mustered for the estate in *c.* 1630 shortly after Bingley had died.[35] Some account clearly has to be taken of a number of factors – imperfections of the sources, variations in family size, deaths and some betterment movement of tenantry as well. An example of the latter is found in the case of Thomas Lloyd who a source probably deriving from family tradition informs us moved to Leitrim after Bingley's death under the auspices of a fellow Welshman, Sir Maurice Griffith of Carrick-on-Shannon.[36] There is also, since the plantation estates cannot be seen as entirely self-contained entities, an element of localised absenteeism to be considered. One example of this is also strongly suggestive of the relationship between the region as a whole and the local towns. Thus Edward Tarleton, householder in Lifford and Derry, money lender and cattle dealer and recently Sheriff of Tyrone, emerges in 1633 not only holding land on the Ballybofey estate in right of his wife, widow of Lieutenant John Dutton, one of Bingley' tenants, which was sub-let to Irish occupiers, but holding, similarly, two areas of episcopal land as well.[37] Bingley's colony, more densely settled on the Farsetmore estate than on the other, was at any rate tolerably representative of the level of plantation prevailing on estates in this precinct as a whole.

His tenants divide in origins into a number of groups. Some 40 of the 57 on the muster roll were Scots, their presence, we may assume (unless recruited by Bishop Knox), due to the general participation of Scots in the plantation rather than to any direct recruitment by Bingley. However a small but significant element, some of them freeholders involved from an early stage, was made up of former army officers or their connections, some of Flint/Cheshire background, who like Bingley had had military careers in north-west Ulster but had not themselves succeeded in getting grants of lands. The presence of a larger group, probably part of a following of 'forty Englishmen' seeking land which Bingley had allegedly already 'drawn' to Ulster by 1609, some of whose surnames (Ridgate, Griffith, etc.) had firm Hawarden associations, taken with the fact that Thomas Lloyd, mentioned above, a recorded follower of Bingley's, came from Wrexham, Denbighshire, strongly suggests that he had recruited tenantry in his own home area.[38]

The stipulated removal of the Irish population from undertakers' estates as a whole was widely evaded. Government policy was obliged to take account of the undertakers' reliance on their rents and services; the resultant compromise, finalised as part of the *Graces* in 1628, permitted Irish tenants on one-quarter of each estate.[39] Although on Bingley's more densely settled Farsetmore estate much of the better land was in the hands of British tenants since the first recorded lettings in 1611, it is unlikely that on either estate the Irish share had been reduced to one-quarter by the time of his death. Many of his earlier Irish tenants had been men of sufficient local prominence to have been inserted into the pardons granted to Niall Garbh O'Donnell in 1601 or to Rory O'Donnell in 1603, or to appear in pardons granted after O'Doherty's rising. A few had acted as jurors in the taking of inquisitions concerned with plantation preliminaries, while a few also were, as we have seen, grantees in their own right. This continuity was, however, by no means an assured one. Irish tenants held on an annual or short-term basis, sometimes as sub-tenants to Bingley's British tenantry. Beyond this there are only the vaguest indicators of the relations of both elements: a trace of inter-marriage suggests a degree of co-operation but the execution at the assizes in 1631 of an Irish tenant from the Ballybofey estate for high treason suggests that prior to 1641 the framework of relationships, though they might deteriorate occasionally, was an effectively controlled one.[40]

Although no estate papers survive, material on estate finance is unusually forthcoming. In November 1637 Robert Harrington, farmer of the Grocers' lands in the Londonderry plantation who had married Bingley's widow, sold both estates for £5,850. If we think in terms of ten years' purchase and make allowance for intervening rent increases, it is possible to envisage an annual return of some £400 in the 1620s. This figure receives credence from some contemporary estimates: £400 or £500 by relatives, *c*. 1635; £500 by creditors in 1641. Against this, however, has to be placed the recoverable detail of debts and mortgages. His most substantial borrowings, a total of £1,050 – adequate to meet all his building costs – deriving from two merchants, one of London, one of Dublin, reveal a combination of military muscle and merchant finance in Ulster colonisation. Of this, £800 at 10 per cent interest had been borrowed on the security of the 'mill and lands' of Carrigans (hence Bingley's insistence, noted above, on £800 compensation) from Mathias Springham, London merchant tailor and a prominent member of the Irish Society. That Bingley had defaulted in his payments, probably after Springham's death in 1620, emerges from a chancery decree in 1624 in favour of Springham's heirs, the locally-installed George Costerdine of Coleraine amongst them, for the interest and arrears. More hazy details of further borrowing, about £80, and of an incompleted sale of a piece of land, involving John Ravenscroft (of Lifford in 1641), a Flint associate, come to light in damaged chancery pleadings in 1622 and 1624 in which Bingley admitted receipt of 'forty Barbary ducats and piratical stuffs and parcels of gold and silver lace and other trifles' which he denied were worth £100 and said had been anyhow recovered by Ravenscroft in rents. Later in 1630 and in 1641 two less substantiable claims were put forward. One, on behalf of Sir Richard's (d. 1625) widow, asserted that Sir Ralph had designated part of the estate as her jointure; the other, in a petition to the English House of Lords by two people, one, Richard Annyon, being probably a Chester merchant, was a claim for debts of £160 backed by a bond of November 1626. However when the estate was sold only one encumbrance – Springham's loan was, of course, secured on Carrigans – a 1620s mortgage for £100 to Sir Matthew de Renzi, collector of the impost on wine and midlands planter, comes to light.[41]

Part of the reason for this mid 1620s financial embarrassment may well be found in separate projects and more extravagant aspirations. While there is no suggestion that Bingley, with his estates a going concern, became a consistent absentee, he did make many 'journeys into England', clearly maintaining his contacts in north Wales and Chester. The debt to Richard Annyon suggests commercial connections with Chester; it was certainly a transit point, as in June 1620 when he and a tenant, John Nicholas, consigned to Derry baggage in quantity 'containing made apparel wearing linens and other household goods'. More significant, perhaps, were the contacts maintained in London, amongst them with William Ravenscroft, a Lincoln's Inn lawyer and early supporter, and, presumably through Ravenscroft, with the latter's powerful relative, the Cheshire-born Lord Chancellor Ellesmere, since Ellesmere's son appears as a trustee for Bingley's widow in 1628. It is almost certainly in an English context, where projects and projectors abounded, that we must see an abortive scheme, objected to by the monopolist in 1620, for the manufacture of looking glasses. Furthermore by 1621 he was a householder (or property owner) in the Charterhouse area of London, sufficiently established to be a local assessor of the subsidy.[42]

Bingley's failure, as we have seen, to get onto the reduced Irish military establishment in 1611 combined with the long peace of James's reign meant that continued military employment was denied him. However, to a soldier whose mind had been formed in the anti-Spanish warfare of Elizabeth's reign, the war with Spain from 1625 and with France from 1627 offered renewed prospects for a military career. In 1626 a scheme, addressed to the Duke of Buckingham, for victualling 6,000 soldiers in Ireland was his first attempt in this direction. In 1627, arguing from historical precedent for the dependability of Irish soldiers (whose military excellence was highly praised) in English service abroad if ably led, he put forward two schemes to employ them which would, he suggested, also improve the internal security of Ireland since 'it swarms with idle men that are more fit for the wars abroad than to disturb the peace … at home'. One, for which he sought Buckingham's approval, was a proposal to counter a likely Spanish invasion of Ireland with a privateering-style assault on Spanish treasure in the West Indies and Central America. This project, which would require only royal approval (for which the King should have 'the quinto of all the spoil') and the provision of arms to be paid for later, would involve soldiers raised by Bingley, their victualling by the adventure of each city and county of Ireland and the putting up of ships by merchants, all three parties to share in the takings of the expedition. It was assured of success, in his view, since the negroes in the Indies would act as guides in return for their freedom. It was however his other scheme which found favour; hence regiments of soldiers from Ireland, one led by Bingley, the other by Sir Pierce Crosby, were incorporated into an expedition led by Buckingham which was defeated, with Bingley's death, at the Isle of Rhé in October 1627.[43]

As an undertaker Bingley's performance in Ulster had been average or below. However his Ulster career as a whole, despite its greater complexity, had much in common with that of a number of other military captains who built up estates in a similar manner. He is therefore to some degree a representative figure. His lack of scruple seems to have been a family failing. Thus Sir John, after his downfall in the English Treasury scandal of 1619, was forced back in 1627 on a second Irish official career. Sir Richard, although suspended as Surveyor of the Navy in 1618, at a time when he was advocating with others an unsuccessful project to use Irish land for hemp growing, remained a naval captain (being later Vice-Admiral and Admiral of the Narrow Seas) with little further Irish connection. The early involvement in Ireland of all three had, however, laid the crucial foundations of their subsequent careers. Their participation also in wider English schemes of trade and colonisation – Sir Ralph as activist, Sir Richard and Sir John as prominent investors in the Virginia Company and the Africa (or Gynney and Bynney) Company – epitomises well the relationships between English enterprises in Ireland and further afield in the early seventeenth century.[44]

I am extremely grateful to Dr K.R. Andrews, Mr John Appleby, Mr Randal Bingley, Dr R. Loeber, Miss Joan Sinar of Derbyshire Record Office, Mr A.G. Veysey of Clwyd Record Office and Mr J. Grisenthwaite of Chester City Record Office for their advice and assistance.

[1] For a map see T.W. Moody, F.X. Martin, & F.J. Byrne, eds., *A New History of Ireland III, 1534–1691* (Oxford, 1976), pp 198–9. It may be noted that this plan did not apply at all to colonisation in Counties Antrim and Down.

[2] TNA, A.O. 1/287/1080, f. 66; S.P. 63/268, ff 63–4v; *Acts of the Privy Council of England* (hereafter *APCE*) XXVI (1596–7), 50–1, 79–80; XXVII (1597), 101–5, 160–4; XXVIII (1597–8), 250–4.

[3] R. Bingley, *Bingley: An English Family Notebook* (privately printed, Shenfield, Essex, 1978), pp 54–7, 82–5; TNA, S.P. 63/271, f. 4; Clwyd Record Office, Hawarden, D/BJ/C2; P/28/1/1, passim; National Library of Wales, Aberystwyth, Hawarden Peculiar, Probate Records, Inventory, O. Bingley [1567].

[4] H. Docwra, 'A Narration of the Services done by the Army ymployed to Lough–Foyle' in J. O'Donovan, ed., *Miscellany of the Celtic Society* (Dublin, 1849) (hereafter Docwra, *Narration),* p. 250; Chester City Record Office, M/MP/12/43.

[5] Fiants Ireland Elizabeth, no. 6653 in *18th Report of the Deputy Keeper of the Public Records in Ireland* (Dublin, 1886), p. 80; Docwra, *Narration,* p. 270; *Cal. Pat. Rolls Ire., Jas I,* p. 14.

[6] Docwra, *Narration,* p. 251; J.C. Erck, *A Repertory of the Inrolments on the Patent Rolls of Chancery in Ireland … James I* (Dublin, 1846) (hereafter Erck, *Repertory),* pp 64–5.

[7] For a discussion of how this system worked see T.O. Ranger, 'Richard Boyle and the Making of an Irish Fortune', *IHS,* X (1957), 288–9.

[8] Erck, *Repertory,* pp 22, 40–1, 112–14.

[9] *Cal. Pat. Rolls Ire., Jas I,* p. 46; *Cal. S.P. Ire. 1606–8,* pp 217, 370; *1608–10,* p. 172.

[10] TNA, A.O. 1/289/1085, ff 21, 44, 53v; *Cal. S.P. Ire. 1603–6,* p. 200. A crown lease in County Down *(Cal. S.P. Ire. 1606–8,* p. 67) appears to have had no long-term significance.

[11] Docwra decried the lease of Inch (dated one day before O'Doherty's pardon) as an affront to O'Doherty (Docwra, *Narration,* pp 271–2, 275, 277–9).

[12] N. Canny, 'The Treaty of Mellifont and the Re-Organisation of Ulster, 1603', *Irish Sword,* IX (1969–70), 249–62.

[13] RIA, Charters of Irish Towns, 7; Erck, *Repertory,* p. 61.

[14] *Cal. S.P. Ire. 1606–8,* pp 364–4. Chichester later said that Bingley had been 'in a sort compelled' to sell the land to O'Donnell *(Cal. S.P. Ire. 1608–0,* p. 172).

[15] T.W. Moody & J.G. Simms, eds., *The Bishopric of Derry and the Irish Society of London, 1602–1705,* I, *1602–70* (IMC, 1968), 40.

[16] D.B. Quinn, 'The Voyage of *Triall* 1606–1607: an Abortive Virginia Venture', *The American Neptune,* XXXI, No. 2 (1971), 85–103.

[17] BL, Add. MS 14, 295, ff 79v, 112. There is no evidence that he had commanded *Tremontana.*

[18] Chester City Record Office, M/L/2/201; 6/80. On Angell's position in the Fishmongers' Company see Guildhall Library, London, MS 5570/1, ff 56, 138.

[19] TNA, S.P. 63/217, f. 9; *Sackville (Knole) Manuscripts,* I (HMC, 1940), passim; *Salisbury [=Cecil] Manuscripts,* XXI (HMC 1970), 1; V. Treadwell, 'The Establishment of the Farm of the Irish Customs, 1603–13', *EHR,* XCIII (1978), 585–6; NAI, C.P./L, 1 indicates a later connection between John Bingley and John Halsey, another of the ship's owners.

[20] The treatment of the *Triall* voyage derives entirely from Professor Quinn's paper (see above, reference 16).

[21] *Cal. S.P. Ire. 1606–8,* pp 223–5. It was proposed to use one of these boats to patrol the north Irish and Scottish coasts to stifle opposition, allegedly supported from Donegal, to plans for a lowland plantation in the Scottish islands. Later, in August, during Bingley's imprisonment – in Dublin – Chichester, seeking authority to release him, stated that Bingley had agreed with the French merchant for the restoration of this ship and payment for its cargo (TNA, S.P. 63/222, ff 65–6v).

[22] TNA, S.P. 63/234, f. 162. Crooke, later a shipowner, was summoned to London in the summer of 1608 to answer general charges of abetting the local pirates; and was returned at the end of November, exonerated and approved and a partner in a scheme, supported by Salisbury and in which John Bingley was involved in 1609, with Dudley Norton and Thomas Wilson, two of Salisbury's secretaries, to produce local timber for the navy (TNA, S.P. 63/225, ff 222–4v; *Salisbury [=Cecil] Manuscripts,* XXI, 40). Yet also in November – and again two years later – the Lord High Admiral referred to the Munster presidency the hearing of a suit initiated by two Bayonne merchants against Crooke and an associate for the recovery of their ship, the *Mary* and

its cargo of pitch, allegedly taken by Bingley *piratico more* and received by them (TNA, H.C.A. 14/39, 61 and 149 (copies); 14/40, 48).

23 *Cal S. P. Ire. 1606–8,* pp 568, 594; TNA, A.O. 1/289/1087, f. 33v; 1/290/1088, ff 36v. 43, 43v; *Cal. S.P. Ire. 1608–10,* pp 27, 33, 97. Curiously O'Doherty's representations had led to the English Privy Council issuing orders to revoke Bingley's lease on the day his rising began *(Cal. S.P. Ire. 1606–8,* pp 475–6, 488–9).

24 *Cal. S.P. Ire. 1606–8,* pp 518–9; *1608–10,* pp 251, 264, 343, 387, 458–61, 496–7, 509.

25 *Cal. Pat. Rolls Ire., Jas I,* pp 159, 183; *Inquisitionum in Officio Rotulorum Cancellariae Hiberniae Asservatarum Repertorium,* II (Dublin, 1829), (hereafter *Inq. Cancell. Hib. Repert.),* Donegal (II) Jas I; *Cal. S.P. Ire. 1608–10,* pp 172, 441. The Kilmacrenan monastic land was granted to Trinity College but by 1614 Sir Ralph was tenant of a part of it (TCD, Muniment Room, D 71).

26 *Cal. Pat. Rolls Ire., Jas I,* pp 224–5; L.W. Lucas, *Mevagh down the Years* (2nd. ed., Portlaw, County Waterford, 1972), pp 47–58.

27 W.G. Perrin, ed., *The Autobiography of Phineas Pett* (Navy Records Society, 1918), pp 92–3; *Cal. Pat. Rolls Ire., Jas I,* p. 293

28 *Cal. Pat. Rolls Ire., Jas I,* pp 197–8, 292–3. It may be noted that a general grant to Sir John Davies in 1614 included Doe castle, itself excluded from Richard Bingley's patent, which he sold to Sandford in the same year *(*ibid., p. 268).

29 NAI, Lodge MS V, 498–9; VI, 343; *Cal. Pat. Rolls Ire., Jas I,* pp 224–5, 293; *Analecta Hibernica,* VIII (I.M.C. 1938), p. 253; *Cal. S.P. Ire. 1611–14,* pp 31, 262–3; *Salisbury [=Cecil] Manuscripts,* XXI, 302–3, 360; *Inq. Cancell. Hib. Repert.* Donegal (12) Chas I.

30 With the disappearance of the appropriate plantation maps of 1609, grants made in terms of the large Donegal quarters *(ceathrúna)* are not easily assimilable to modern townlands. Sir Richard's estate was some 4,627 acres in extent.

31 BL, Add. MS 4756, ff 115, 116–7; *Cal. Pat. Rolls Ire., Jas I,* pp 436, 508; *Andrew Knox, Bishop of Raphoe and His Descendants* (Derry, 1892), p. 18. Knox's efforts to secure a military command for Bingley, ostensibly to protect the bishop, were dismissed by Chichester in 1611 as a move on Knox's part to 'gratify' Bingley 'in respect of some private bargain betwixt them' *(Salisbury [=Cecil] Manuscripts,* XXI, 302–3).

32 *Hastings Manuscripts,* IV (HMC, 1947), 171–3; T.W. Moody, *The Londonderry Plantation* (Belfast, 1939), pp 132, 283, 448.

33 *Cal. S.P. Ire. 1611–14,* pp 214, 262–4, 322–4; TNA, S.P. 63/236, ff 121–24A; *Cal. S.P. Ire. 1625–32,* pp 131, 246; *APCE,* XXXIV (1615–16), 127–8, 418–9; XXXVI (1618–19), 78.

34 *Hastings Manuscripts,* IV, 171–2; G. Hill, *An Historical Account of the Plantation in Ulster at the Commencement of the Seventeenth Century* (Belfast, 1877), pp 519–21; BL, Add. MS 4756, ff 115, 116–7.

35 BL, Add. MS 4770, if. 192–2v; *Inq. Cancell. Hib. Repert.* Donegal (12) Chas I.

36 J. Burke, *A Genealogical and Heraldic History of the Commoners of Great Britain and Ireland,* IV (London, 1838), pp 89–91. (I owe this reference to Mr Randal Bingley). For a discussion of these problems as they arise in Tyrone see P. Robinson, 'British Settlement in County Tyrone, 1610–1666' *IESH,* V (1978), 5–26.

37 NAI, R.C. 9/1, pp 167–72. Bingley had himself become a tenant on a neighbouring estate in 1616 *(Inq. Cancell. Hib. Repert.* Donegal, (10) Chas I).

38 BL, Add. MS 4770, ff 192–2v; *Inq. Cancell. Hib. Repert.* Donegal (12, 14, 17) Chas I; Clwyd Record Office, Hawarden, P/28/1/1; sixteenth and seventeenth century deeds in F. Green, (ed.) *Calendar of Deeds and Documents,* III *The Hawarden Deeds* (Aberystwyth and Cardiff, 1931); W. Ravenscroft *&* R.B. Ravenscroft, *The Family of Ravenscroft* (London, 1915), pp 6–9, 14, 39–42; *Cal. S.P. Ire. 1608–10,* p. 172.

39 T.W. Moody, 'The Treatment of the Native Population under the Scheme for the Plantation in Ulster', *IHS,* I (1938–9), 59–63.

40 Fiants Ireland Elizabeth, nos 6483, 6761; *Cal. Pat. Rolls Ire., Jas I,* pp 136–9; T.W. Moody & J.G. Simms, (eds) op. cit. p. 28; *Cal. S.P. Ire. 1606–8,* pp 555–6; *Inq. Cancell. Hib. Repert.* Donegal, (12, 14, 17) Chas I.

41 TNA, C5/388/71; S.P. 63/271, f. 4; House of Lords Record Office, London, Main Paper, 20 January 1641; BL, Add. MS 19,840, f. 17; W.S. Ferguson, 'Mathias Springham, 1561–1620', *Transactions of the London and Middlesex Archaeological Society,* XXIII (1972), 194–203; NAI, R.C. 6/1, no. 304; C.P./AA, 109; /BB, 14; TCD, MS 839, ff 133–3v; Melbourne Hall, Derbyshire, Cowper (Coke) MSS, draft King's Letter 5 July 1630.

42 TNA, S.P. 63/271, f. 4; E190/1323/1, f. 24v; S.P. 14/113, no. 80; E179/142/279, [*m.* 16]; *Hastings Manuscripts,* IV, 1; NAI, Lodge MS, V, 95–6.

43 TNA, S.P. 63/243, ff 28–9v; /268, ff 63–4v; /244, ff 182–3v; *Cal. S.P. Dom. 1627–8,* pp 186, 197, 227, 324–5, 423, 443, 471, *535; APCE,* XLII (1627), 292–4, 297, 367, 472–3; XLIII (1627–8), 43.

44 *Cal. S.P. Ire., 1625–32,* p. 200; A.P. McGowan, (ed.) *The Jacobean Commissions of Enquiry 1608 and 1618* (Navy Records Society, 1971), pp xxv–xxvi; *APCE,* XXXVI (1618–19), 63; XXXIX (1623–5), 219, 221, 457; T.K. Rabb, *Enterprise and Empire* (Cambridge, Mass. 1967), p. 247. It may be noted that Angell, an unsuccessful applicant for Ulster land in his own right, and Halsey, two of the owners of *Triall,* held one-third each of the Fishmongers' lands in County Londonderry between 1619 and 1628 by lease from the Company's farmer (Guildhall Library, London, MS 5570/2, ff 684, 708).

5

Donegal: The Settler Population of an Ulster Plantation County

Introduction

One of the conditions binding on the undertakers in the plantation in Ulster was that they should 'haue ready in their houses at all times, a convenient store of Armes, wherewith they may furnish a competent number of men for their defence, which may be viewed and mustered euery halfe yeere, according to the maner of England'.[1] The servitor grantees, who were not obliged to introduce colonists, were also to 'haue a Convenient stoare of Armes in their howses'.[2] Not surprisingly, no such requirement was imposed on the native Irish grantees in the plantation.[3]

It would not be appropriate to attempt to generalise here about the extent to which the undertakers fulfilled their obligation to maintain arms. The muster book of *c.* 1630 is an important source in this respect. As in so many aspects of the plantation, there was considerable variation in performance amongst the grantees. The requirement that the undertakers should have arms 'in their houses' presupposed that their tenantry should live, in accordance with another condition, in villages close to the settlers' strongholds. However, in practice, the settlement pattern that emerged was one which involved both small village nuclei and dispersed settlement. Some grantees, like Sir Stephen Butler in Cavan who, on Pynnar's evidence, had 'very good' arms for two hundred men in his castle 'besides which are dispersed to his tenants for their safeguard'[4] recognised that the logic of such settlement was a measure of dispersal of arms as well. Other undertakers merely passed on the responsibility to their tenantry. Thus John Dillon in County Armagh stated in 1622 that his tenants were 'enioyned by lease to finde a musket, a pike, a sworde and dagger'.[5]

However although the government surveys of the plantation taken periodically from 1611 enquired into the amounts of arms, mustering, or the regular training of the tenantry in their use, which was a government responsibility, was for long neglected. It was not until 1618 that this was put in hand, for the country at large. The reason was not primarily due to the situation in Ireland, or Ulster which had in the previous years been disturbed. The outbreak of war on the continent had caused alarm in

England, and a mustering of the English forces was ordered in February of that year.[6] It seems reasonable to suggest that the decision for Ireland had the same background. On 8 May the king, on the advice of the Irish deputy, Oliver St John, decided to appoint two muster masters, Nicholas Pynnar, and Captain George Alleyne who became responsible for Ulster and Leinster.[7]

Alleyne's inspection was the first to be carried out in plantation Ulster.[8] He provided figures (not names) of those who attended for the nine counties of Ulster with a report on the difficulties he encountered. Calculating on the basis that the six escheated counties contained 197,000 acres and that 24 men were musterable for 1,000 acres, he computed that 4,728 men should appear (888 in Donegal), that is, he took the numbers of tenants required by the articles of plantation as being the norm also for muster purposes. In all he recorded that 1,966 men appeared or only some 40 per cent of his required total.[9] There is a nil return for County Donegal.

It emerges in 1624 at a time of crises in Anglo-Spanish relations which was having reverberations in Ulster that mustering there had not been continued. In that year, when it was decided to expand the regular army in Ireland,[10] a recommendation was also made for the revival of the muster in Ulster.[11] With the outbreak of war between England and Spain following on the accession of Charles I and lasting until 1630, the fear of insurrection, or internal disturbance, in Ulster, where the plantation was taking effect, received an added dimension with the possibility of invasion. By late in 1625 a substantial proportion of the standing army had been transferred to Ulster.[12] The appointment of provosts marshal, an already well-tried expedient for dealing with unrest, was also resorted to. The report[13] of the Donegal provost marshal, Robert Cartwright, printed below, is typical of many of the period. It consequently illustrates conditions in Donegal at the time when the more or less contemporary muster roll was being drawn up. It derives a special interest from the appended population abstract. It is clear from it that Cartwright lived in Donegal at this time, and it is likely that he was of a settler tenant family there.[14] As well as that he appears in 1617 as lieutenant of the horse troop under the command of Sir John Kingsmill,[15] who was an undertaker in the precinct of Lifford and had a military command as well.

A renewed concern with mustering and training the 'risings out' was manifest during these emergency years. Thus risings out were held in Antrim and Down in 1626.[16] In September 1628, following on royal instructions of the previous July to the lord deputy,[17] Lieutenant William Graham was appointed, for life, muster master for Ulster and Leinster with power to demand the same fees as his predecessor, Captain Alleyne, had received previously.[18] Graham, a native of Cumberland, had, earlier, in 1624 been responsible for the arrest and conveyance to England of 'two notorious malifactors' from Monaghan.[19] The muster roll, commonly dated as *c.* 1630[20] may then be ascribed to Graham.

The return, a somewhat slipshod undated transcript in a difficult hand apparently transcribed from field papers, is not for Graham's first mustering – a defaulter in Cavan is noted as having attended.[21] It thus cannot be prior to 1629, and Professor Moody has shown from a tenancy agreement in County Londonderry that it could not have been carried out after July 1631.[22] While the muster roll does not represent a census, it is the most exhaustive listing available. Not only is it a means of assessing the planting achievement of the individual grantees, but also a firm reference against which other sources providing names may be compared to assess, for example, settler mobility. The number mustered for the nine counties was 13,147.[23] The amount and quality of arms displayed was not re-assuring. There were some 7,000 swords and 3,000 pikes, but only 700 muskets. In addition there were 1,300 other weapons made up of calivers, snaphances, halberts, and lances.[24]

The accuracy or reliability of the muster book is probably variable. An analysis of its contents for Londonderry shows that its return for that county approximates very closely to the total of British males present.[25] It is my own view that this is also the case in County Cavan, but that the coverage for Armagh must be regarded as conservative. Apart from the brief comments below on the Donegal section no other county has been examined. While recalcitrance in mustering was characteristic of England at this time[26] and this could well have been reflected amongst the colonists in Ireland, Graham's return in comparison with Alleyne's is itself evidence of his greater thoroughness[27] and may indicate greater concern in this matter by the government in this period in comparison with 1618. It appears too that Graham continued to execute his functions for a long time. Wentworth who examined Graham's statistics early in 1634 was concerned by what they revealed, observing that the Ulster colony was but 'a company of naked men', underarmed or in many cases provided with arms of 'altogether unserviceable' types such as snaphances and 'birding peeces'.[28] His policy would be, he stated, to encourage Graham in every way. Graham still held the position in 1640, though then his function would appear to have been complicated by divergence of attitude amongst the colonists themselves.[29]

Only detailed research will enable us to make an informed assessment of the settler population in Donegal, at this time. However certain tentative points can be made. While Cartwright's totals, unsubstantiated by names, do not have to be accepted as the more accurate – indeed his Inishowen figures, 61 English and Scots are substantially lower than the 175 men named in the muster roll[30] – where they supplement Graham they seem to be reliable. Thus Graham notes that the servitors in Kilmacrenan and Tyrhugh did not cause their British tenantry to muster.[31] But Pynnar's survey of 1618–19 suggests a figure of about 190 British males for Kilmacrenan[32] (the barony which included the property of Cartwright's protagonist Marbury at Letterkenny) – the 1622 survey suggests well over 200[33] – as opposed to Cartwright's 128. The servitor-type owners in Tyrhugh are not discussed by Pynnar, however the 1622 survey indicates a settler population of at least some 65 British males,[34] and we know that there were, additionally, some British residents on the lands of Trinity College, Dublin in this barony,[35] so the 1626 figure of 78 does not seem excessive. The nil return in the muster roll for William Farrell, the occupier of the estate originally granted to Sir Thomas Coach, cannot be taken as implying the absence of British there – Pynnar found 56 men,[36] although the 1622 commissioners could only record 18.[37] The possibility, on the other hand, of dual appearances – Alleyne complained of this in 1618 – while not easily checked, must also not be ruled out.[38] Furthermore the occasional Irish name appears in the muster roll. The muster roll reveals beyond doubt that Scots predominated in the settlement of the county.[39] However Cartwright's division of colonists into English and Scots conceals the very interesting appearance of a body of Welsh on the estate of Captain Robert Davis,[40] and the occasional Welsh name elsewhere.[41]

More detailed criticism of these two documents will have to be based on an examination of other, primary sources, for example inquisitions printed and manuscript and any estate papers that may be located. In the meantime it can be suggested that a figure of 1,500 as the adult male British population of the county in 1630 is unlikely to be proved an over-estimate. It is sufficient to say in the context of this article that Cartwright's estimate of the numbers of Irish provides a lower ratio of the two populations than any of the few others that have come to hand for plantation Ulster.

Alleyne's nil return for Donegal has not been transcribed for publication. Cartwright's report has been printed without alteration of spelling or punctuation. In the context of neighbouring documents in the volume and contemporary usage it may be taken as dated in 1626. Individual totals of names and the county total in the muster roll have been checked. The county table contains two errors – Mr Cahoune's total should be 19, and Chichester's 175. The county total is thus 1,269. Other editorial problems are indicated in footnotes. I am very grateful to Mr K.W. Nicholls for his assistance in reading some difficult names, and to the Keeper of Manuscripts in the British Museum (now British Library) for permission to publish.

[1] T.W. Moody (ed.), 'The revised Articles of the Ulster Plantation, 1610' in *Bulletin of Institute of Historical Research*, xii (1935), pp 178–83. For a study of the English system see L. Boynton, *The Elizabethan Militia, 1558–1633* (London, 1967).

[2] 'Ulster Plantation Papers' No. 18 in *Analecta Hibernica*, viii.

[3] Ibid.

[4] G. Hill, *An historical account of the plantation in Ulster at the commencement of the seventeenth century, 1608–1620* (Belfast, 1877), p. 465.

[5] National Library of Ireland, MS 8014/8. Two fee-farm grants of land on the Taylor estate in Cavan in 1613 and 1815 were made in consideration of the 'bodily service' of the tenants and their successors to be at all 'time and times for ever done at the tyme of Muster being thereunto called' (NAI, M6956/4, 5).

[6] L. Boynton, *The Elizabethan Militia*, p. 237.

[7] Bodleian Library, Oxford, Carte MS 62, f. 481.

[8] His report, with transcripts of related documents is British Library, Add. MS 18,735 (*Cal. S.P. Ire., 1615–25*, pp 220–50).

[9] Ibid., f. 5. The calendared version has slight inaccuracies. Some detected faults of arithmetic have been corrected.

[10] See A. Clarke, 'The army and politics in Ireland, 1625–30', in *Studia Hibernica*, No. 4 (1964), pp 28–53.

[11] TNA, S.P. 63/238, Pt. 2, f. 55 (*Cal. S.P. Ire., 1615–25*, pp 510–11).

[12] *Cal. S.P. Ire., 1625–32*, pp 50–1.

[13] BL, Sloane, MS 3827, ff 62–3v.

[14] Both a George Cartwright and a Lieutenant Edward Cartwright held land in the precinct of Lifford (*Inq. Cancell. Hib. Repert.*, ii, Donegal (12, 14) Chas I).

[15] *Cal. S.P. Ire., 1615–25*, p. 176.

[16] BL, Sloane, MS 3827, ff 79–82.

[17] *Cal. Pat. Rolls Ire., Chas I*, pp 380–81; *Cal. S.P. Ire., 1625–32*, p. 367.

[18] *Cal. Pat. Rolls Ire., Chas I*, p. 365; NAI, Lodge MSS, Miscellaneous enrolments, p. 41.

[19] *Cal. Pat. Rolls Ire., Jas. I*, p. 552.

[20] BL, Add. MS 4770.

[21] Ibid., f. 9v.

[22] T.W. Moody, *Londonderry plantation* (Belfast, 1939), p. 278, footnote 3.

[23] BL, Add. MS 4770, f. 283. This is a corrected figure taking into account of in accuracies of arithmetic not only for Donegal but also Armagh and Cavan.

[24] Ibid.

[25] Moody, *Londonderry plantation*, pp 278–9, 319–22.

[26] L. Boynton, *The Elizabethan Militia*, pp 269–87.

[27] There is no evidence, for example, that he accepted Alleyne's convention that only 24 males were musterable per 1,000 acres. Leases of this period contained relevant stipulations. Thus a fee-farm grant of land in Cavan in November 1630 required the tenants to be 'allwayes furnished to ther power and abilitie w'th good sufficien armes and weapons both for the defence of themselves and the Country of the said plantation against the rebells and other his ma'ties enemyes' (NAI, M6956/8). Another Cavan, lease of *c.* 1635 required the tenant to appear at all musters and outrisings, and contribute, with the rest of the tenants, to a group of ten able men well armed with pike and musket for the King's service and the defence of the landlord when required (NAI, Deeds, wills and instruments … post mortem, vol. 25, pp 254–65).

[28] Sheffield City Library, Strafford MSS, vol. v, ff 37–48.

[29] E. Berwick (ed.), *The Rawdon papers* (London, 1819), p. 63.

[30] This, however, is roughly cancelled out by the Boylagh and Bannagh figures – muster book 143, Cartwright 340. The 1622 survey (V.W. Treadwell, 'The plantation of Donegal – a survey' in *Donegal Annual*, vol. 2, No. 3 (1953–4), pp 313–5 tends to confirm the former figure.

[31] BL, Add. MS 4770 f. 281.

[32] Hill, *Plantation in Ulster*, pp 522–27.

[33] Treadwell, 'The plantation of Donegal', in *Donegal Annual*, vol. 3, No. 1 (1954–5), pp 41–4.

[34] Ibid., *Donegal Annual*, vol. 2, No. 3 (1953–4), pp 512–13.

[35] TCD, Muniments.

36   Hill, *Plantation in Ulster*, pp 521–3.

37   Treadwell, 'The plantation of Donegal', in *Donegal Annual*, vol. 2, No. 3, p. 517.

38   Could the John Waus on f. 193v of the muster roll and the John Wause on f. 197 and indeed the John Vaux on f. 194 be one and the same person, and be the rector of Kilmacrenan and Mervagh at this time (J.B. Leslie, *Raphoe clergy and parishes* (Enniskillen, 1940), pp 97, 100) to boot?

39   On Scottish names see G.F. Black, *The surnames of Scotland* (New York, 1946).

40   BL, Add. MS 4770, f. 189v.

41   For example, ibid., f. 184v.

DOCUMENT I

The Muster Roll of the County of Donnagall
(BL, Add. MS 4770, ff 177–202v, 281)

Barony de Rapho
The Lord Duke of Lynox,
undertaker of 4000 acres,
his men and armes

Swords onely
Robert Leackye
James Wood
Andrew Wood
Mathew Lyndsey
William Douglas
Robert Lyndsay
Robert Buchanan
John Galbreath
Alexander Buchanan
Alexander Lawder
James Denniston elder
Andre Royare
William Laughlan
John Lowrye
John Ralston
William Cokeran
Hector Hinman
Robert Cocheran
John Buchanan
John mcConochy
Robert mcPeter
George Haldin
Robert Horner
Donell Galey
Robert mcKyndely
[f177v] Robert Glass
Archbell Campbell
ffyndley mcKindley
Andrew mcTyre
Alexander Galbreath

John mcKaine
John Thromble
John Smyth
Dunkan mcffarlen
Patrick mcNeron
Wm. McLentock
George Colmories
Robert mcffarlan
John mcffarlan
Patt. mcAndrew
Patt. mcArthur
Robert Denyston
Donnell mcBaxter
John Boyd
Humfrey Colquphone
William Gulilan
John Steward
John McIlman
John Scot
Robert Boyde
Thomas Lowrye

Swords and Snaphances
f178   John Wood
John Martin
John mcLenochan
John Cambell elder
Willam Deneston
John Buchanan
John Cambell
John mcffarlan
Donnell mcffarlan
Robert Michell
Costyme Ranckein
John Allen
Gilbert mcLyntock

John Brice
James Allan
Dunkan Speney
Thomas Ramsey
John Cock
James Cock
Andrew Cock
William Scot
John mcCawly
John mcGourden
Andrew Lackye
James mcKennye
James Hustone
Robert Lackye

Snaphance onely
James Dromond   f179
Archbald Gambell

Swords and Pikes
[f178v] Morrice mcConnell
John Cocheran
John Snodgarse
John Cambell younger
Owen mcNair
David Lyndsay
Alexander mcLentock
Robert Aickeene
Robert Morison
James Kilsoe
Donnell mcilchol
Dunkan Cambell
Donnell mcBaxter elder
Robert Barlaine
James Richye
John Swayne
John Valentyne
Dunkan Graham

Pikes onely
Robert Calmeris
Andrew Calmeris

Sword and halbert
Hugh Greire

Sword and Calleuer
John mcffarlan

No Armes
John Royer
Morrice Peacock
Walter Lowrye
William mcNevin
Robert Campbell
John mcKyndley
David mcKan
John mcIldonagh
Dunkan mcffarlan
John mcAdam
Alexander mcBoase
Patrick Gwin
Dunkan mcffarlan
John Crawfford
John Sempell
James Symison
William mcArthur
Robert Reroch
Thomas Crafford
Camack mcCole
Henry Cruse
John Barlone
Thomas Swaine
Patrick Porler
Randall mcAlexander
John Douglas
James Logan
Alexander Hamond
Mathew Gillrew
William Hewes
Robert Leman
Donnell mcCahey
Adam Quahone
Neece mcGilrouse
John mcffarlan

Walter Deneston
Anthony Steward
William Noble
John Parmenter
[f179v] Andrew Galbreath
William Wood
John Wood
John Steward
James Deneston
James Muthey
Walter Roger
John Brittein
Johh Young
Gawen mcConnell
John Watson
Walter Henry
Robert Cambell
Dunkan Crafford
George Allyson
John Pecock
Robert Craufourd
Archbald Ballintyne
Thomas mcKeeg
John Logan
Lamock mcColl
John Buchanan
David Gibb
John Pearce
John McGillione   166

f180   Barony de Rapho
Sr John Conningham
knight, undertaker of
4,000 acres, his men
and armes.

Swords onely
Robert Boyll
Gawen Michell
John Malfeild
John Wood
John fforret

James Lennox
Patrick Coningham
John Longpill
William Dunlap
Robert Young
David Coningham
Robert Wallas
John Blare
Robert Wernogh
Patrick Fould
Alexander Lawson

Swords and Snaphances
Thomas Hislat
William mcEask
William Saner[1]
Patrick mcCleland
Andrew Balmanner
Alexander Balmanner
Robert mcInteer
Walter de Jestame
Herbert Morison
James mcCreay
David Ramsay
James Young

Swords and Pikes
[f180v] James Patterson
Art mcCary
Donnell mcKee
Killetellon mcCury
James Robinson
John Frizell younger
Dunkan mcKinley
John Richee
John Cambell
Adam ffleming
Hugh Thomson
William Crafford
William Colwell
William Steauenson
Marcus Odoylson

William Marshall
Dunkan Lyone
Patrick Crafford
John Lyone
John Mathew
John Makee
Dunkan mcCostune
Hugh Barskemny
James Hutchison
Patrick Delap
Hugh Thomson
John Gylles
James Steill
f181   John Allason
William Wilson
John Hettels
John Hettels younger
Steaphen ffrag
George Scot
Henry Gaine
James Morrison
Killeollume mcKeynie
Wm. Dunlap younger

Swords and Muskets
Archbald ffleming
Robert Larges
James Hate

Swords and Calleuers
Robert Longpill
William Cutberson

No Armes
John ffleming
James Morrison
Gibert (sic) ffleming
Alexander Thompson
John Steavenson
James Steward
David Tullagh
William Young

John Watt
Patrick Wright
John Baytye
[f181v]   Christopher Walker
John Hunter
Archbald Hunter
Andrew Conningham
Donnell mcConnell
John Frizell
William ffrizell
William Iesack
Donnell mcIlman
John mcNevin
John Yoole[2]
Donnell mcKean
William Doone
Rober (sic) Roger
Robert Miller
Andrew Balmann'r
James Morison
William Young
John Bayly
John Steaphenson
James Cresball
John Lyone
John Crawfourd
Patrick Bright
John Wallas
John Morrison
f182   James Browne
William Snyp
Steaphen Cragg
James Knox
William Crag
Mathew Cuningham
Jame (sic) forsyth
William mcBaine
David Young
Patt ffleming
Barnard Cuningham
James Wilson
William Wighton

111

Hugh Sawer
Patt Adam
John Wallas   124

[f182v]   Barony de Raphoe
The Lady Conningham
Widdow of Sir James
Conningham, undertaker
of 2,000 acres, her men
and armes.

Swords and Pikes
William Conningham
James Calquahan
Andrew mcCorkill
John mcCorkill
Tobias Hood
James Davye
Peter Starret
John mcquchowne
James Knox
Adam Garvance

Swords and Snaphances
James mcAdowe
ffyndlay Ewing
Dunkan mcffarlan
Ninian ffoulton
James Scot
William Rankin
Daniell Ramsay
Martin Galbreath
Patrick Porter

Swords and Calleuers
William mclltherne
David Walker
John Barbor

Sword and halbert
James Makee

f183   **Swords Onely**
Andrew George
James mcIlman
Michaell Rot(h?)es
Patrick Miller
Robert Muntgomery
Alexander Conningham
Richard Leaky
Robert Staret
John mcIlhome
Sallomon Giffin
David Reed
Donnell mcDonnell
Alexander Carlell
William Gafeth

No Armes
Gilbert Highgate
Patrick Porter
Robert Hasta
William Gambell
John Hunter
John Crawfford
Robert Johnston
Henry Smyth
William Boyes
David Ramsay
William Steward
Robert Crafford
[f183v]   James Conningham
Andrew Conningham
John Crafford
John Hunter
John Wilson
James Bredyne
Mungo Davy
William Richey
John mcIlhome
Henry Hunter
John mcHutchon
James Rankin

William Killy
Robert Pots
William Gambell
John Lyone
James Knox 66

f184 Barony de Rapho
Sr John Kingsmell Knight,
undertaker of 2,270 acres,
his men and armes

Swords onely
Robert Hammilton
Andrew Hammilton
Robert Moderwell
George Stenson
James Symes
John Squiverell
Robert Warnog
John Speare
John Wilson
James Wilson
William Conningham
John Bordland
Thomas Coopson
William Coopson
Phillomy Huston
Hugh Carnog
William Carmighell
John Warke
William Euch³
James Crafford
James Henderson
David Bihit
Robert Wilson
[f184v] Rise Davis
John mcAlpinagh
Robert Wallice
John fflulton
George Young
John Patterson
John Smyth

Swords and Pikes
Gabrahill Morrison
Robert Marke
John Warnog
Walter Lewis
Michaell Lewis
Allyn mcCall
William Davis
Thomas Hoggard

Swords and Snaphances
Adam Moderwell
Alexander Browne
James Nealson

No Armes
Gilbert Moryson
William ffryer
Hugh Robinson
James Symes younger 45

[f185] Barony de Raphoe
Captain Ralph Mansfield,
undertaker of 1000 acres,
his men and armes

Swords onely
Thomas Ellis
James Benny
William White
William Wald
John Bell
Robert White
William Glen

Swords and Pikes
James mcTanlease
Thomas Dunlelly

Sword and Calleuer
William Gryffyn

No Armes

Robert Adam

Ralph Mansfield

Thomas Clarke

Thomas Gray

Thomas ffayrefax

Thomas ffayrefax
younger   16

[f185v] Barony de Rapho
Sr John Wilson Barronet,
undertaker of 2550 acres,
his men and armes

Swords onely

Robert Porter

William Makee

William Deasly

Gabraell Homes

John Homes

John mcCley

David Read

Alexander Cambell

Wenables Albones

Henry Roberts

John ffrizell

John ffulton

Robert Ray

Donnell Reth[4]

Thomas Cranston

Jathes Lassles

William Lassles

William Wilson

Richard Browne

John Kilpatrick[4a]

John mcClere

Anthony mcClere

Michaell mcCleare

William Moneyley

George Gray younger

John Michell

f186   John Waynes[5]

John Browne

John Hendry

David Hunter

Robert Read

John Weiton

James mcGumberry

Swords and Pikes

George Irwing

John Pitts

John Hendry

John Davis

John mcCowr

Richard mcCowr

Thomas Browne

Robert Bromside

John Kilpatrick

Pike onely

Alexander mcKee

Snaph: onely

James ffargison

John Willson

John Halbert

John Henderson

Thomas Henderson

Thomas Lassles

Swords and Snaphances

Alexander mcCowr

John Rowsell

John ffleming

Sword and Musket

James Hall

Swords and Calleuers

Walter Carr

William Dixon

No Armes

[f186v] Patrick Read
Robert Pitts
John Edger
Patrick mcMullaing
James Dunkin
Christopher Cale
James Nesbit
John mcClentock
Thomas Davis
Robert Robertson
Leonard Wisse
Robert Ray   66

f187 Barony de Rapho
Peter Benson Esqr.,
undertaker of 1,500 acres,
and his men and armes

Swords onely
James O[?]rines[6]
John mcCreary
James mcCreary
Wm. Kirkpatrick
Andrew Leapper
Jo: Kirkpatrick elder
Arch Mowberry
John Kirkpatrick
George Harkalls
Andrew mcKerry

Swords and Pikes
John Bree
Thomas Moraphie
Thomas ffarrell
Robert Kirkepatrick

Pike onely
Gilbert Hesee

Swords and halberts
William Kirkpatrick

John ffarrell
James Tath

Sword and Musket
Thomas Preston

Sword and Calleuer
Richard Gibson

Swords and Snaphances
Richard Roper
Patrick Cherry

Snaphance onely
John Davies

No Armes
[f187v] Edward Babbington
Robert Angleson
John Michell
Edward Smyth
Michaell Blanye
Jo: Kirkpatrick younger
Alexander Maxwell
Richard Babington
Edmond Jesopp
William Gibson
George Arkales
Mathew Browne
Andrew mcCheny[7]
John mcCheney[8]
David Key
Alexander Maxfeild   39

f188 Barony de Rapho
William Steward Esqr.
Lard of Dunduff,
undertaker of 1,000 acres,
his men and armes.

Swords onely
Archbald Thomson

Andrew Thompson
Robert Alexander
John mcKey
David Kenedye
Patrick Baruzathyn
Anthony Steward
John Steward
Archbald Steward
John Browne
Andrew Browne
Edward Roger
John Moore
John mcCullagh
John Moire
Patrick Conningham
John Allyson
John Smeally

Swords and Pikes
John Davidson
Archbald mcEmmory
Roary mcCleane
Patrick Thomson
Donnell Or
Mungo David
John Cambell
John mcLynienie
Archbald Hourd
William Houston   f189
James mcKee
Anthony Kenedy
George Steward
John mcClen
John Cambell
Hugh Gamill

Swords and Muskets
Robert Thomson
John ffife

Swords and Snaphances
[f188v] James Squire

John Conningham
Steaphen Marshell
John Smyth
Michaell Smith
Michaell mcCleary
Donnell Cambell
Archbald Bredene

No Armes
John Kelly
Humphrey Cooke
William Wan
ffynley mcKirdiy
Alexander mcClaney
John Conningham
John mcffay
Donnell mcNevin
alias mcNit
John mcKee younger
John mcWalker
James mcKergour
David Kenedy
Alexander mcWilliam
Patrick Steward
Donnell mcCarslaire
James Kenellye
John Campbell   61

Barony de Raphoe
Mr. Cahoune Lard of
Luce, undertaker of 1,000
acres, his men and armes

Swords and Snaphances
John Arrell
Patrick Boochanan
Humphrey Mountgomery
David Hume
Walter Barlowe
James Leach
James Creagh
John mcGillurne

116

Swords and Pikes
John Blare
John Watson
John Patterson
Thomas Allasonne

Swords onely
John ffoster
Arthur mcCurrin
Patrick Leach

Sword and halbert
Hugh Mure

No Armes
Patrick Morton
John Allison
John Okenhead   19

Barony de Rapho
Captain Robert Davis,
undertaker of 2,000 acres,   f190
his men and armes

Swords and Pikes
David Payne
Robert Grame
William Johnes
James Thompson
Richard Davis

Swords and Snaphances
John Newton
Peter Payne
Edward Euance

Snaphance onely
William Monely

Sword and Halbert
William Barr

Sword and Calleuer
John Parry

No Armes
Richard Prick
Evane Greefleth (sic)
David Edmond
John Apievin (?)
George Barret elder
George Barret younger
Ralph Loyd
Richard Lestor
John Price
Rice Evance
Evaine Peirce

Swords onely
Kinrick Thomas
Rice Williams
George Newson   25

Barony de Rapho
Robert Harrington Esqr.
undertaker of 4,000 acres,
his men and armes.

Swords onely
Edward Hill
Gabraell Griffyeth
Patrick Browne
William Michell
George Michell
John Arckly
Alexander Twig
William Boner
Archbald Hunter
John Walker
William Machan
William Sympson
James Gurskadyne
James Scot
Alexander Neesbit

Swords and Pikes
Robert Rowchester
Robert Wyne
Robert Makee
James Homes
John Nicholas   gorgets
Walter mcArthur   compleat
John Lang
Robert Grifeth   curasses
                       and gorgets
John Dealp   curasses
                       and gorgets
John Miller
William Miller
John mcManus
James Martin   f191
John mcGilwory
William Gambell
Arthur mcArthur
[f190v] Hugh Gwillin
John Pepells
George Russell
Thomas Haward

Pikes onely
William Ridgate
John Gursore

Swords and Muskets
James Ranag
George Miller
Robert Smelly
David Gillmore
Hugh Gambell

James ffleming
William Uprichard

Swords and Snaphances
Ralph Eorill
William Miller

Peter Steauenson
Gabraell Wilson
John Pepells
John ffisher
Alexander Teus
James Darson
Patrick mcLintog

Sword and Calleuer
John Awerd

Swords and targets
Andrew Steauens
Patrick mcArrell   57

Barony de Rapho
Mr. Alexander Steward,
undertaker of 1,000 acres,
his men and armes.

Swords and Pikes
John mcIlwane
Callum mcMuyre
James Cambell
Robert mcKenily
William Toyes[9]
William Conningham
WillIam Home
Neall mcCurid
Alexander Cambell

Swords and Snaphances
Alexander Cambell (sic)
John mcKenely
Robert Boyd

Robert Henedy
Storiment Carr

Sword and Musket
John Niweme younger

Sword and Target
Walter mcffarlen

Swords onely
John Kennan
Ninian Steward

No Armes
Andrew Cambell
Gilbert mcKenny
John Gillaspy
Robert Steward
John Steward
Archbald Steward
William Cambell
James ffyfe
Archbald Alexander
John Roger
John Boyill
William Boyill
John Cambell
Gilbert mcCan   32

[f191v] Barony de Rapho
James Conningham Esqr.,
undertaker of 1,000 acres,
his men and armes   f192

Swords onely
Andrew Crafford
John Gills
Hugh Lokehart
Arch ffynlagh
ffynlay mcCredy
John Browne

Swords and Pikes
John Alexander
George White
Joseph Browne
William Galbreath

Hugh Leag
Andrew Browne
John Harper
Thomas Stole
Patrick Robison
John Enery

Sn: only
Andrew Arnott
John Alexander
Adnarle[10] Hoomes
Robert Graham

Swords and Snaphances
John Smyth
William Gall
Andrew Smyth
James Gillmore
Robert Roger
Thomas Roger
Thomas Lars[11]
John Adam
Robert Davison
Michaell Beare

Swords and halberts
Robert mcKeene
Mathew Gieffe[12]

No Armes
James ffulloone
George Steavenson
Andrew Leag
John Hururence
John Hamilton
James ffulloone

Robert Patterson
John Cunningham
George Naught
Hugh Leag

James Browne
John mcEuan
George Speare
Mathew mcCadame
John Dyne
Andrew Dyne
Arch Boyle
John Calwell
Robert mcCamy
Robert mcCamy younger
Dunkan mcWrick
Thomas Richmoule
John mcJohn Keine
Mungo Willy
Andrew Cambell
Hugh Mure
Andrew Callhown   59

[f192v] Barony de Rapho
Mr. John Steward,
undertaker of 1,000 acres,
his men and armes.

Swords onely
Arch Steward
Andrew Cambell
William Cambell
Killime mcKaine
James ffife
John Steward

Pike onely
John Barkly

Sword and Snaphance
William Conningham

Sword and Pike
John Bullesine

No Armes
Robert Steward
John Boyle
John Roger
Arch Alexander[13]   13

Barony de Boylagh
and Bannagh
The Earle of Annadall,
undertaker of 10,000
acres, the names of his
men and armes.

Swords onely
Andrew Nesbit
Robert Rinkeny
James Read elder

Sword and Snaphance
David Greire

No Armes
David ffynley
Archbald Houet younger
George Molligan
David Jackson younger
John Reynold
John Kirkpatrick
John Hall
John Makye
George Miller
Andrew mcffarlan
Richard Murray
Gilbert Shaw
Walter Leaky
James Read younger
John William
Edward Griffeth
John mcClintog
John Menzes

Patrick Herron
John mcClanes
John mcCartney
John Chancellor
[f193v] Robert Walker
John Creighton
John mcKennet
Thomas Blane
John Blane
Sampson mcKee
James Blane
William Ellot
George Ellot
John Waus
John McKee
Hector Douglas
John Gourdon
Nichol Walker
Alexander Tyndy
Martin Shellan
Andrew Shellan
John mcKilvame
John Creighton
Robert Creighton
James Crafford
Andrew Dunne
David Kernes
Robert Kernes
David Jackson
John Creighton younger
Alexander mcMachan
Patrick Dunbar
Edward Houet
John ffynlay
Thomas Gressy
Andrew Keirs
Thomas Creighton
Robert mcKnaght
James mcKnaght younger
John Shane younger
John Scot younger

Gilbert Shankeland
John Milligan younger
John Vaux
John mcKilmain
James Shan younger
John Kirkpatrick
Alexander Shilan
John Walker
Robert Vaux
John Waker
Michaell mcKilwayne
Arch Horner
William Cocheran
John mcKlaughry
John Dunbar
Gilbert mcClelan
William mcClaughry
William mcConnell
John mcConnell
Dunkan mcKilmore
John Camell
[194v] Anthony Shaw
Patrick mcHutchin
John Bagster
Robert mcHutchen
John Harvye
Steaphen Price
James Hugones
David Barnes
John Smyth
James mcKnoe
Alexander Murry
James Murry
John Murry
Adam Makee
Robert Makee
James Frizsell
John Frizell
Thomas Carnes
Thomas Carnes younger
ffynlay mcCauley

Thomas Hutton
John Kirk
Peter Martin
Andrew Robinson
Patrick Davison
John mcClaughey elder
James mcClaughry
Alexander Scot
William Douglas

f195   Hugh Reed
Alexander mcCullogh
Thomas mcCullogh
George mcCullogh
Jo: Small younger
David Wilson
John Karnes
Robert Maxwell
Thomas Scot
George Scot
John Johnston
William Layser
William Kenedy
John mcKinley
John mcCormick
John Leis
William Leies
John mcKneilly
Patrick Dunbar
John Camell
John Dunbar
John Walker
Andrew Dunne
Andrew Leirs
John ffynlay
George Ellot
David Jackson
Robert Kernes
James Shaw
John Scot   143

[f195v]   Barony de Rapho
Mr. ffarrell undertaker

of 1500 acres w'ch he
houldeth by his wife lady
to Sr Thomas Cutch
deceased

f197   Barony de Rapho
(*sic*)   The Lo: Bpp of Rapho his
churchlands being 2,700
acres, his men and armes

Swords onely
Archbald Conningham
John Smyth
John ffulton
Matthew Patterson
Patrick mcMair
John Edward
Andrew Steaphenson
James Lang
William Kingham
John Key
George Wasson
Robert Boochanan
William Richie
Wm. Nickilvy
Thomas Elshintor
George Steaphenson
John Tocheran
Michaell Lyndsay
Richard Carson
Andrew mcIlvaine
William Lyne
Claud Donniell
John Walker
William Henry
John Wause
Hector Conne
Thomas mcArthur
Alexander Allen
John Harper

[f197v]   Archbald mcCalla
John Allan

Robert Wylly
William Pock
John Walker
John Kenedy
Robert ffleming
James Lard
John Morrison
Alexander Sterrep
Archbald Stenison
Robert Bachanan
John Graham
Thomas Cloughan
Dunkan Mountgomery
Alexander Gibson
Gabraell Maxwell
John Laird
Archbald Henderson
Symond Graham
John mcCalla
ffyndlay Huston
James Makeene
Wililam Atkin
James Davye
Alexander Johnston
William Makee
John Latay
James Hervy
John Heslet
John Carmouth
Thomas Kelson
John Calwell
Thomas Armor

Swords and Pikes

f198   John Wylly
James Dick
James Keare
John Steaphen
George Carmighell
John mcPeter
James Johnston
John Lyndsay

Ninian Thompson
John mcKinly elder
James Spreull
James Atterew
John Willson

Sword and musket
John White

Calleuer onely
Humphrey mcLeny

Swords and Snaphances
James Carmighell
Richard Horris
John Maxwell
Archbald Leaviston
James Mathey
William Lyndsay
Robert Barly
John Wylly
John Dunlap
Wm. Carmighell
Wm. Carssar'es
James Allen younger
Robert Lyone
John Deneston
William Home
[f198v] John Stenison
John Pirry

Snaphances onely
John Willy
John Wallice

No Armes
John Hammilton Esqr.
George Knox
Robert White
John Leige
Symon Elshinter
John Moore

Andrew Knox
John Leitch
Hugh Allan
Andrew Steaphen
Donnell mcPeter
John Snodgrass
Christopher Geat
Andrew Elshinter
Robert foulton
John Allason
John Steward
Dunkan mcGilmichill
Robert Deneston
John Roger
John mcKee
James Mathey
John Davy
f199 William Porter
Hugh Salsmond
John Henderson
Thomas Henderson
Michaell Henderson
Thomas Lassilles
Thomas Browne
Richard mcCuluer
Alexander mcCuluer
Thomas Parmenter
John Pitty
James Mathey
Robert Denton
ffrancis Lacillis
Wm. Lasillis
John Kirkpatrick
Michaell mcCleary
William Sterret
John Torrenc
David Prier
John Porter
Patrick Knox
John Hutchone

James Morison
William Boyd
Walter Lane
Robert Robinson
David Crassone
Edward Sill
William Rankin   150

[f199v] Barony de Rapho
The Deane of Rapho,
his churchlands being
300 acres, his men and
armes.

Swords onely
ffynlay mcClentock
Thomas mcKeag
Dunkan Cambell
John Braggat

Sword and Snaphance
William ffargison

No Armes
John Taylor
William Wallace   7

The Churchlands
of Tayboyne
The names of the
inhabitants and their
armes

Swords and pikes
John Denyn
John Strutter

Swords and snaphances
James Hammilton
George Morison

No Armes
Robert Carsby
Robert Callwell   6

f200   Barony de Eneshone
The Lo: Chichester, his
servitor's lands, his men
and arms

Swords onely
Robert mcKintire
James Kintire
William Douglas
William Maxwell
John Hammilton
Richard Pyn
Richard Benson
Andrew Cadwell
Nathaniell Couch
John Crosse
Archbalc Conningham
Henry Temple
Mungo Torents
Adam Rosbergh
Alexander Lacker
John Sampson
Paul ffaulse
James Henderson
James Porter
William Armone
Patrick Wallecs
Alexander Adams
John Cowbrone
John Lyone
James Neickill
Thomas Glyne
John mcKegge
(cancelled)[14]
[f200v] Donnell mcManus
John Bord
John Storret

John Nickollon[15]
Archbald Barnet
Robert Young
John Kirkwoode[16]
William Kirkowod
Abraham Houd
Henry Allicock
John Chamberlyne
Duke Chamberlyne
William Chamberlyne
Mathew Cadwell
John flyng
John Henderson
Aghey mcCorkey
Andrew Hud
Gilbert Woorke
Alexander Higat
Alexander Worke
Thomas Staret
John Clene
John Berry
Alexander Cadwell
Richard Sampson
John Koyne
Walter mcCowene
Thomas mcKeon
Robert Coweene
f201   John Staret
John Osborne
Adam Porter
John Richie
William Porter
James Porter
William Neely
Gabrahell fayrefax
Robert Cary
Wm. Cougheron
Mathew Alcorne
Donnell Denneston
Paul Elliot
John Knox

John Richy
Davye Worke
John Giffen elder
John Mountgomery
James mcgee
Alexander mcMathew
Gilbert mcNeal
Alexander Browne
Robert Browne
Hugh Browne
William Wallace
John Wallas
John Hall   f202
Robert mcLenaghan
John Elly
John Chambers
[f201v] Robert Whithill
William mcKeone
Willian Nelly
Richard Leister
Richard Leeth
John Bruse
John Greig
Owen Williams
James Heltch
John Hilbot
William Hibbots
James Sorerd
Peter Gibson
George Redgate
George Moorehead
James Young
Andrew Young
Patt Michell
George Cary Esq.

Swords and Pikes
Thomas Davenport
John Browne
Andrew Ramson
John Hogguyre
Nathaniell Willson

Swords and Muskets
Walter Illiner
Thomas Gutery
John Scot
Edward Parker
John Battes
Thomas Hodges

Sword and Corslet
George Hall

Swords and Snaphances
Robert Hammilton
Archbald Collaghan
John mcKegg
James mcKilveny
Mungo Barnet
John ffargusonne
Humphrey Turay
William Hunter

Swords and halberts
Thomas Moore
James Michell
John Bord
Water Salder

Halberts onely
William Fulton
George Burges
William Porter

[No Armes][17]
John Robinson
George Butler
Bryan Smelly
Walter Boy
John Lacker
Donnagh mcConoghy
William Crafford
John Glandoney
Bartholomew hog

William Newton
Edward Rudson
Thomas Bruma
William Mountgomery
Robert Smelly
Luke Lassels
John Cannall
Thomas Orr
[f202v] Robert ffals
Robert ffulton

Mungo Warden
John Warden
John Miller
Gilbert mcNeal
James Deniston
Richard Williams
Rich ffranncis

George Gawen
John Price
John Michell
William Richy
Robert Richy
Wm. Alcorne
David Richy
John Guy
John mcBy
Robert Browne
James Conningham
Donnell Scot
John Hunter
James Archbald
Henry English
John Wray
Peter Elder   175

---

1   Possibly Sauer.
2   Possibly Poole
3   Possibly Ench
4   Possibly Roth
4a 'Younger' after the name is erased.
5   Wagires.
6   Possibly C[?]rines. This name has been altered.
7   Possibly McClieney.
8   Possibly McClieney.
9   The 'y' has been struck out.
10 Possibly Aduarle or Aduarke.
11 Possibly Lard.
12 Possibly Giesse.
13 There is no reference to arms here in the manuscript.
14 This cancelled name is not included in the final count. It could possibly be McClagg.
15 The final '–on' has been corrected from '–yn.'
16 Possibly Kirkwooke.
17 There is some slight doubt about the arms of those listed on this page of the manuscript.
    The entry 'No armes' is made against the lower group of names on f.202. It has been assumed,
    although there is no entry: about arms on f.202v, that it applies to these names also.

Right honor'bill

According to your Lops: instructions annexed unto my commission for the
executing of marshall law in the county of Donagall, I bothe made
proclamation of my commission, and writt particuler letters, to the
byshoppes, and everye severall undertaker in the countye, to deliver me in
the names of all their tenants for whom they would be answearable at all
tymes requisitte, but no man would undertake for any of their Irish
tenantes, neither deliver me their names, until I went my self to booke them
(some fewe only xcepted) In consideration whearof I tooke pence a peece
of so manye as entred their names, and purposed to have sent your Lopp:
an exact book bothe of the Brittishes and Irishe inhabitants, whiche hitherto
I cannot compasse by reason of the late rumors of warre yet I have sent
your Lop: hear-inclosed a brieff abstract of the number of men in the whole
countye beseeching your Lop: to send me directions howe I shall proceed
against suche men of the Irishrye as no man will undertake for, for cutting
of mantles, and trowses I must confesse I have been sparing in hope of
reformation, only on daye I went into a markett towne of Sr. George
merburries and cutt about x'en or xii mantles, whearof he made a grievous
complaint to all the justices of peace, and threatned to indite me for it in
the Starre Chamber, saying morover that it was an yll business of your Lop:
to make a marshall in his countye, and it is very well knowne that willinglye
he will not suffer neither sheriff nor any other officer to exercise any
authoritye in that towne, and yet himself a man of so evill governient, and
given to drinking as makes himself a laughing stock and scorne to the
countreye, and although I have ever observed him (with too much
subiection) to hold frendshippe with him (being near neighbours) yet his
disarming firste on of my men, and then the other also, comanding the
constable to put him in the stockes without any occasion given, but only
to let his towne knowe that he had power to do any thing thear that pleased
him, and at my next meeting with him he told me that he was sending my
man to the stockes, I told him that I hoped he had some other better reason
then because he was my man, to which he answeared that if either my man
or myself came into his towne to do any thing he would thear disarme us,
and send us both to the jayle, which caused me to put my commission in
execution rather in that place then any other, partly in discharge of my
duty, that the countrey might take notice thearof in so frequent an sasembly,

and partly to remove an opinion that was roused, that I neither had power nor durst do any thing thear but by his consent, which appeared to be true, for having formerly aquainted him that divers lewd fellowes frequented his towne and used to playe thear for 4 or five daies togeather, whearof some of them had formerly broken the jayle, yet nothing was done, nor said against them, and when newes was brought me afterwards that they had been thear from fryday untill Tuesday playing all the clothes on their backs, I went thither and apprehended twoo of the gamsters but the twoo principall men that I looked for wear convaied away, the on throughe a windowe, and the other at a back dore, and the party that convaied them away, and the twoo other gamsters I delivered unto the constable with a mittimus to carrye them to the jayle, but Sr. George took them away from him and set them at liberty, saying that he would discharge as many as I should comitt [f.62v] Since the coming downe of my Lo: Blaney to Londonderry the gentlemen of our countye thinke it not convenient that I should be to forward in cutting either mantles or troweses, least I should give a great discontent unto the Irishe, I did apprehend twoo principall gent of our county and sent them to jayle for maintaining continually a company of yll people, and comon gamsters, and who are the comon receivers and entertainers of suche men as come from Rome, and other parts beyond the seas, for which, although some did approve of the fact, yet others wear of opinion that my comission and instructions tended only to apprehend idle-men and contempned me for it, and set them at liberty Thear be vi or viii Irish gentl. in our county that have nothing in the world to live uppon but their friends, and although hitherto they have done no act of hostility, yet are they dangerous and active men if any occasion should be offered, the priestes likewise are greatly encreased and growne so bold that they dare dayly frequent great townes and garrisons also to drinke in, and it is an easy matter to knowe whear the masse is said every daye, wheather I should entermedl with any of theise men or no, I humbl beseech your Lop: to advertise me, and [   ] the woodkerne that your Lop: gave lycence to depart the kingdome, are returned back before Christmas, and this daye I am going to prosecoute them with xii of Sr. Will'm Stuarts and xii of Sr. Henry Tychbirnes company, and sooner I would have gone, but that my Lo: Blaney could spare no men at his being in theise parts the comissary being thear-also, at that tyme, my twoo Irishe gwydes that I entertained by your Lo :ps instructions begin to grow out of harte for want of some recompense for their paines for I will not myself take any thing, nor suffer them to do it, and if any shall say your Lop: otherwise, and prove it, I will ask no favour, this much I have presumed to write unto your Lop: in regard that Sr. George Merbury is nowe in Dublin, who I double not but will excuse himself the best he can, because he knows I ever purposed to complain of him to your Lop: and would before this tyme have aquainted your Lop: withe other of his proceedings in the countrey, if by any meanes I could have procured money to have borne my charges, but I have written nothing to your Lop: but the truthe, whiche I will justefy upon my oathe, besydes other wittnesses sufficient, and thus beseeching your Lop: to excuse me for not writinge before this tyme (in regard of the great expectation wee had of some troubles in theise partes) I humblye take leave this xxviiith of January 1625

your Lops: to be commanded
in all services

Robt Cartwright

[f.63]

A brieff abstract of the number of the inhabitants
in the county of Donagall, both Brittish and Irish

In the baronye	English	....	147)	
of Raphoe	Scottes	....	1016)	2256
	Irishe	....	1093)	
In the baronye	English	....	0031)	
of Ineshowen	Scottes	....	0030)	1452
	Irishe	....	1391)	
In the baronye	English	....	0059)	
of Tyrewe	Scottes	....	0019)	1072
	Irishe	....	0994)	
In the baronye	English	....	0030)	
of Killmacrenon	Scottes	....	0098)	1112
	Irishe	....	0984)	
In the baronye	English	....	0024)	
of Boylagh	Scottes	....	0316)	1079
	Irishe	....	0739)	

The totall numbers

of the englishe	....	0291)	
of the Scottes	....	1479)	6971
of the Irishe	....	5201)	

Besydes the souldiers

[r.63v]
[Endorsed]

    To the Right Honor'bll the Lord Viscount ffalkeland
    Lo: Deputye of Ireland give theise

[In an other hand]   Cornett Cartewrighte concerning the executing
                of his comissn of Provost Marshall

f.281

The County of Donagall

fol 177	The Duke of Lennox out of his undertakers lands
fol 180	Sr. John Connigham out of his undertakers lands
fol 182	The Lady Conningham out of her undertakers land
fol 184	Sr. John Kingsmell out of his undertakers lands
fol 185	Captaine Mansfield out of his undertakers lands
fol 185	Sr. John Wilson out of his undertakers lands
fol 187	Mr. Benson out of his undertakers lands
fol 188	Mr. Stewart Lard of Dundug out of his undertakers lands
fol 189	Mr. Cahoune Lard of Luce out of his undertakers lands
fol 189	Captaine Davis out of his undertakers lands
fol 190	Mr. Harrington out of his undertakers lands
fol 191	Mr. Alexander Steward out of his undertakers lands
fol 191	Mr. James Conningham out of his undertakers lands
fol 192	Mr. John Steward out of his undertakers lands
fol 193	The Earl of Annadale out of his undertakers lands
fol 195	Mr. William Farrell out of his undertakers lands
fol 197	Servitors and Churchlands The Bishop of Rapho his Chur: L
fol 199	The Deane of Rapho his Church Lands
fol 199	The Churchlands of Taghboyne
fol 200	The Lo: Chichester his servitors lands in the barony of Eneshone All the rest of the Servitors in the County of Donagall who inhabit in the barony of Kilmacrenan and the barony of Terhew caused not their brittish to appeare at the general Muster at the tymes and places appoynted according to the warning geven them

Acres	Men	Swords	Pikes	Muskets	Call	Snaph	Halberts
4,000	166	100	14			25	
2,000	124	70	38	3	2	8	
2,000	66	33	10		1	8	1
2,270	45	40	8			1	
1,000	16	10	2		1		
2,550	66	52	9	1	2	5	
1,500	39	21	4	1		2	3
1,000	61	44	14	1		8	
1,000	9	6	4			8	1
2,000	25	13	5		1	3	
4,000	57	55	16	7	1	18	
1,000	32	17	9	1		5	
1,000	59	31	10			12	
1,000	13	8	1				
10,000	143	4				1	
1,500							
2,700	150	95	12	1	1	14	
300	7	5				1	
200	6	4				2	
	174	128	4	5		8	3
	1,258	746	162	20	9	119	8

6

Two Early Seventeenth-Century
Maps of Donegal

British colonisation in Ireland in the seventeenth century left many valuable historical by-products, not the least of which were the mapping achievements of Sir Josias Bodley and Sir William Petty. The division of Ulster into relatively small units for plantation purposes demanded an amount of detailed topographical knowledge, not previously available, which could only be of practical value if plotted on maps. Enquiries by inquisition in 1608 proved defective and inadequate,[1] so in 1609 a more thorough stocktaking was commissioned. This included a mapping project which was supervised by Sir Josias Bodley, an engineer of marked ability whose connection with the Irish administration was already well established.

Bodley's survey covered the northern counties, but the maps of Donegal and Derry have long disappeared.[2] However, this loss is in part repaired by two maps recently discovered in the Trinity College estate collection, preserved in the College Muniment Room. These would appear to be either fragments of the Donegal coverage or careful copies of the Bodley maps made for the College estate administration. The latter seems more probable as the maps lack the finished appearance and the bright and varied colouring of extant Bodley maps, but do at the same time display many of their unmistakeable characteristics. They use, for example, the same distinctive conventional symbols[3] and, in common with the rest of the collection, lake areas are dotted to differentiate them from the land while the scale (which is unmarked) is also comparable with the rest of the set, i.e., approximately one inch to the mile.

Besides their importance as an addition to cartographical material from the early seventeenth century, the precise provenance of the maps and their associations with the early history of the estates of Trinity College are of considerable interest. Both are maps of areas in County Donegal. The first map (plate 6.1), 10½ inches by 14½ inches, is bound in a large volume of Glebe maps dating mainly from the eighteenth and nineteenth centuries, and shows the lands of Kilmacrenan Abbey which became part of the College estates under the Plantation in Ulster settlement. The second, a single unbound sheet, 16 inches by 12 inches is dilapidated and consequently difficult to interpret. It shows the barony of Tirhugh (the 'Pullins' region on Donegal Bay) where the College also received an extensive grant in 1610 under the Plantation settlement.

As sources of historical geography the maps are of limited value. Like most maps of the period they were drawn primarily for the purpose of defining territorial boundaries and show little more than the locations and names of townlands. However, rivers and lakes are crudely indicated (the latter by ribbon-like symbols) and certain settlements are shown in a pictorial fashion including unroofed churches (e.g. Carrowkilunea) and fortified centres. As on most maps of the period no serious attempt is made at accurate representation of relief, the mountains being shown by elementary drawings of hills in profile. In this respect the maps are in marked contrast to most eighteenth-century estate maps with their elaborate hachuring, hill shading and frequent attempts to show the quality and utilisation of land. Indeed, the two maps are particularly interesting as being the first crude representatives of an important and increasingly refined series of surveys of the College estates, which, when taken together, provide an exceptionally complete record of the evolution of the Irish estate map.[4]

It is clear that the shapes of the townlands are very unrealistic, and although the orientation of Tirhugh barony is accurate, the orientation of the Kilmacrenan map is almost the reverse of the correct one. On both maps the internal orientation and relative location of townlands is confused. One example from Tirhugh can be given. Ballymunterhiggin now touches the southern boundary of the barony, but Bodley locates it some distance to the north. However, in many respects the geographical accuracy of the maps is difficult to assess, for where a discrepancy occurs between them and later maps, it may be owing to the deficiencies of the Bodley Survey or to real changes of townland structure. Hence transferring Bodley's information to an Ordnance Survey map demands ingenuity and persistence, and cannot be guaranteed to be correct. Notwithstanding these difficulties it is reasonably clear in Tirhugh barony that the townland pattern has changed substantially, owing both to the proliferation of townlands near urban centres and also to the expansion of settlement into hilly areas. The eastern boundary of the barony is very unsatisfactorily depicted largely because no information is shown for the Barnesmore mountains district. Although many of the townland names are recognisable, there are a number of names which do not appear on present day maps. For a large part of Ireland the Down Survey provided the first maps to give a relatively modern picture of townland boundaries and names, but for these areas of Donegal there are no Down Survey maps to act as a datum-line. Among the Trinity College estate records the next oldest maps of these areas

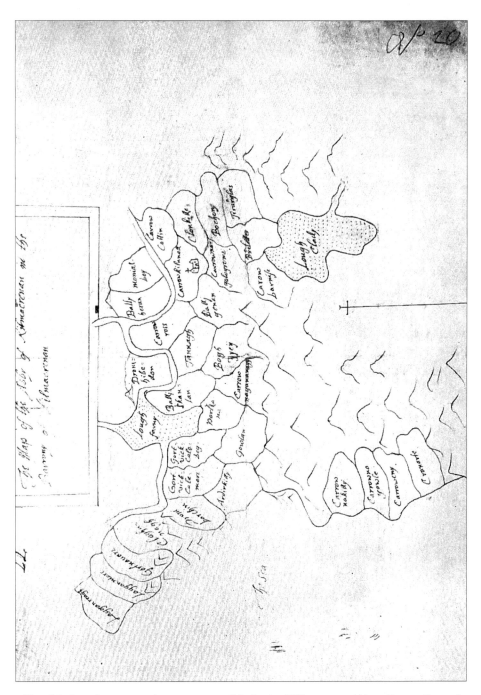

Plate 6.1 An early seventeenth-century map of the lands of Kilmacrenan Abbey, County Donegal

date from 1715. It is, of course, the absence of a Down Survey coverage which renders the Bodley maps of particular historical value.

The difficulties of Bodley's task should not be underestimated and must be borne in mind when criticising the results. Ulster was perhaps the least known of the four provinces and it had not been forgotten that a surveyor, Barkeley (Barthelet), sent to map Donegal under Mountjoy, had been beheaded by the inhabitants.[5] Moreover, the purpose of the maps dictated the urgency of their production, and inevitably the survey had to be based largely on oral evidence rather than strict admeasurement. The maps were produced on a barony basis. They differentiated the ownership of lay and clerical (i.e., generally, forfeited and unforfeited) lands as they stood on the eve of the Plantation, and often, in addition, showed the outlines of the old Gaelic territories onto which baronial divisions had been recently superimposed.

Finally, they divided the land into proportions in accordance with the government's policy for allotment to planters.[6] They do not reveal the parochial boundaries first plotted by the Down Survey in the 1650s.

When completed, the maps of the six counties were transported to England in February, 1610.[7] They were bound in six volumes, and at first sight they appeared not only attractive, but eminently thorough and painstaking.[8] However, their defects were quickly discovered. The relative location of places was often inadequate. The maps sometimes gave the estates of planters a much more coherent shape than in point of fact was justified. Moreover, it soon became apparent that a complete coverage of places then in existence had not been achieved. It could be speculated that full information was wilfully withheld by the native jurors in order to hamper the case of confiscation. In the early years of the colony the discovery of 'concealed' – or unplotted – lands was a widespread cause of litigation and ill-feeling between planters, and a special commission had to be set up to deal with this problem in 1612.[9] From papers in the Muniment Room it is evident that the map of Tirhugh was no less a source of difficulties than others. Not only were concealed townlands quickly found here, but it also became clear that the size of many areas had been under estimated.[10] The consequent loss of territory was an object of particular concern to the College authorities. Provost Temple (1609–27) was directly concerned with the Ulster lands, and the numbers which appear on certain townlands of the Tirhugh map would seem to have been inserted by his hand or one of his contemporaries.[11]

As previously stated it is unlikely that the two maps under consideration are from the original set which was sent to England in the early spring of 1610, or from a second set which was known to be in the possession of Sir

T. Ridgeway in London by 15 March 1610.[12] The first definite knowledge
that the College received of the extent and location of its grant in Ulster was
by a letter from Sir James Fullerton dated 28 April 1610.[13] However, it
seems beyond doubt that a further set of these maps, now completely lost,
was available for official purposes in Dublin because they are referred to in
subsequent disputes over ownership.[14] In view of the close connection
between the newly established college and the Dublin administration, it is
very likely that the two now recovered are careful copies of this set made
specifically for Trinity College estate administration.

[1] The returns of these are printed in *Analecta Hibernica*, 3, pp 151–218. A more detailed return for
     County Armagh only can be found in TCD, MS E.3.13, pp 177–195.
[2] The surviving maps are in The National Archives, London, MPF 35–64. These were published in
     1861 as *Maps of the Escheated counties of Ireland, 1609* (Ordnance Survey, Southampton).
[3] For a key to these see *Cal. S.P. Ire., 1608–10*, pp 402–3.
[4] F.H.A. Aalen and R.J. Hunter, 'The estate maps of Trinity College', *Hermathena* no. XCVIII,
     1964.
[5] *Cal. S.P. Ire., 1608–10*, p. 280.
[6] For the final version of the conditions of plantation for undertakers see the edition from British
     Library, Lansdowne MSS, vol. 159, pp 217–23 by T.W. Moody, *Bulletin of the Institute of
     Historical Research*, 12, pp 178–83.
[7] T.W. Moody, *The Londonderry Plantation* (Belfast, 1939), p. 36.
[8] *Cal. S.P. Ire., 1608–10*, p. 419.
[9] 'Ulster Plantation Papers' nos 55–7, (ed.) T.W. Moody in *Analecta Hibernica*, 8. For the report of
     this commission see TCD, MS F.1.20, ff 9–31.
[10] TCD, Muniment Room MS (Mahaffy Collection) E.23 'Concealment in Tirhugh. See also Box
     20, Bundle 1604–1702, 1, reference to 'concealments in Tirhugh.'
[11] Ibid, E.40; see also 'particular' of college Ulster lands in Box 2.
[12] *Cal. S.P. Ire., 1608–10*, pp 401–2.
[13] TCD, Muniment Room MS (Mahaffy Collection) C.19. For some study of the attendant
     circumstances of this grant see the histories of the college by Stubbs (1899) and Mahaffy (1903).
[14] *Cal. S.P. Ire., 1611–14*, p. 216; *Cal. Carew MSS 1603–24*, pp 247–8.

7

The Fishmongers' Company of London and the Londonderry Plantation, 1609–41

This chapter aims to throw light on the Londonderry plantation by an investigation of one of its estates. Firstly, it examines the evolving attitude of a great London company to the proposed plantation and shows how it came to be drawn into the plantation scheme for this county, which differed from that introduced elsewhere in plantation Ulster primarily by the fact that it was the city of London, rather than individuals (English or Scots), which received most of the forfeited land. In all the planted counties people from the upper levels of the old Irish society were restored to ownership of some of the land, forming a category amongst the grantees, but in this county they received very much less than elsewhere, just some 10.2 per cent of the acreage. The companies, who drew their titles from the city and who received some 57 per cent of the land, were, then, very important in the plantation.[1] Concentrating on just one estate, the chapter goes on to deal with the investment of the Fishmongers' Company in the plantation and how it came to lease the estate to a farmer or middleman. The process of plantation on that estate, with its core at Ballykelly, is then examined in so far as it can be recovered and some suggestions are made about how the native Irish of the area were affected by it. It seeks also to investigate the religious developments of the period and ends with some comments on the rising of 1641 in this area and the response to it. The topic is worthy of investigation since it provides the framework for life in the area for a long time to come.

The origins of the plantation and the Fishmongers' Company
In March and again in December 1610 the Fishmongers' Company of London, one of the twelve major organisations into which the city's business and mercantile community was organised (not exclusively by occupation), was informed by the lord mayor of a 'great mischief that was like to happen and come to this kingdom for want of sufficient means to plant Virginia', and its members were exhorted to contribute liberally to the financing of the plantation there.[2] In July 1609 they were drawn into the scheme for the plantation in Ulster.[3] Both enterprises had one common root: the

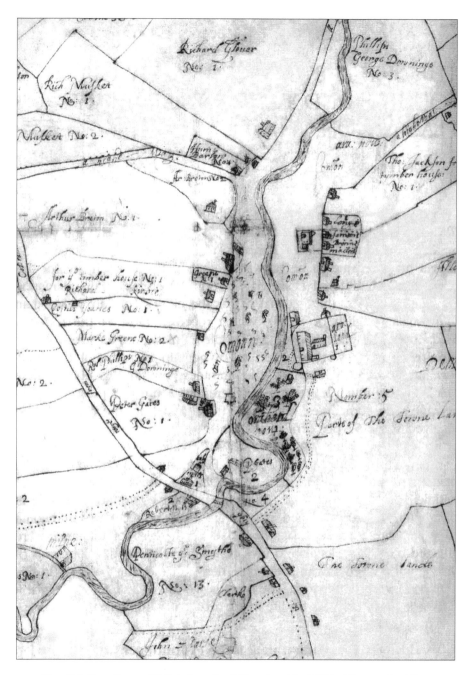

Plate 7.1 Part of map of Ballykelly and neighbourhood in 1623 by Thomas Croddin,
showing plantation village and land enclosure (Guildhall Library, London)

English ambition to encourage colonisation by the infant Virginia company was an expansionary attempt, still precarious, to challenge Spain's claim to sole imperial power in the Americas, while some part of the motivation for the scheme for plantation in Ulster lay in an English determination to ensure, by subordinating it, that Spain (then a great world power claiming also a divine mission to repress Protestantism), with whom the powerful Ulster Gaelic nobility sought alliance with the Flight of the Earls in 1607 as they had done in the warfare of the 1590s, should not gain a threatening footing in Ireland. That warfare – the Nine Years' War – itself, too, with a strong religious dimension, had arisen in the first place because of the crown's determination to absorb the lords of Ulster and their 'countries' (previously effectively ungoverned) in a rigorous manner, which would of necessity involve for them many changes and reductions in power, into a unitary and centralised Ireland, to be ruled in whole as an adjunctive kingdom by its government in Dublin.[4]

The initial response of the Fishmongers to these calls for investment as patriotic duty was a mixed one. By April 1609, forty-one members of the company including nine who adventured £62.10.0 each, had invested a total of £816 in the Virginia enterprise, but these were only part of the membership and there were a number – eighteen – who specifically refused to contribute anything.[5] A meeting of the company's governing body, the court of assistants, in December 1610, after the latest mayoral pressure, judging that the membership would not contribute further, agreed to put up instead £150 out of its own corporate funds.[6] When in July 1609, shortly after the city administration of London had been drawn by the crown to consider undertaking what became the Londonderry plantation as part of the larger confiscation and plantation in six counties (recently created out of the Gaelic lordships) in Ulster then being planned, and it in turn approached the companies for contributions towards the costs involved, the Fishmongers' response was also a mixed one.[7]

The first intimation of the proposal had been brought to a court of assistants on 3 July, which was told that the king wished to see two cities or towns built and planted there – at Derry and Coleraine – the financing of which was to be undertaken by the city, and that the mayor and aldermen had ordered that four from each company should meet as a committee to examine the matter in more detail and consider whether to accept or reject it.[8] A week later, when a precept (or mandate) arrived from the mayor requiring the four people chosen to attend a meeting at the Guildhall on the following Wednesday, the court had an opportunity to discuss the plantation proposal. Some thought it best not to 'intermeddle' at all in a project which could be 'exceeding chargeable' doubting that it could succeed unless a much more extensive area were to be planted, while others favoured involvement. All decided to accept the judgement of the committee.[9] By the end of the month, however, consideration of the matter had reached a more decisive state in the city's part. By 27 July the company had received a precept directing it to summon a meeting of the more prominent membership and to provide a list both of those who would contribute and their amounts and of those absent or refusing, 'to the intent his Majesty may be speedily informed of the readiness of this city in a matter of such great consequence'.[10] The response of the individual Fishmongers, like that of the other companies at this stage, was not an over-enthusiastic one. In their case, forty-three people offered to contribute between them £241.13.4, but this included one offering £100, while twenty-nine were absent and twenty three judged to be 'of good sufficiency' were listed as utterly refusing.[11] There was some overlap, indeed, between those offering to contribute and those who contributed to Virginia, though not an extremely pronounced one, while those who refused contained a number of Virginia investors. The London business community was clearly cautious enough about how it invested its money.

In January 1610, however, the city finalised its contract with the crown – ratified by its common council or governing body on 30 January – agreeing thereby to the plantation of the area embraced in the entire county of Londonderry (created formally in 1613) as well as to a specific town-building programme at Derry and Coleraine. It undertook to expend £20,000 on its activities, principally on building the towns, a figure which had been doubled to £40,000 by 1613 and which was, later, to reach a total of £62,000. At the same time, the body later to be familiarly known as the Honourable the Irish Society was brought into being, and it received a patent of the plantation territory finally in March 1613. The Irish Society was, in effect, a standing committee of the common council and included representatives of the principal companies of London and also bore a resemblance to the governing bodies of many early seventeenth century English joint-stock organisations such as the East India company or the Virginia company.[12]

In these circumstances the approach of the city to the companies to raise money was radically altered. On 15 January the Fishmongers dealt with a precept to assess £1,130[13] on their membership as their, proportion of the initial £20,000, the figure having been arrived at using the corn rate, a long-standing formula for dividing out on the companies the cost of purchases of corn in times of dearth, and the next day sessors appointed by the company apportioned this sum out over 206 people, eleven of them widows, to be paid by instalments. The managing of these contributions, some reluctantly paid, as between the company and individuals was much discussed at this time, leading to a decision in December 1610 that, for the most part, the company itself would make all the future payments out of the 'common purse'.[14]

What the companies were initially contributing to was the establishing of a plantation to be administered by the Irish Society from the income of which – principally the rents of the land, of the towns when built, and the fisheries – they might, like from the Virginia company, hope to receive a dividend. However, what was to be the definitive shape of the plantation in the county – one in which the twelve companies themselves became the owners of estates – began to emerge in 1611. The first intimation that the Fishmongers received of this possibility was when a court of assistants on 15 January 1611 considered a precept from the city as to whether they would accept a share of the land proportionable to their contribution, to build on it and plant it at their own cost in accordance with the regulations of the plantation as a whole (which had been set out in print), or whether they wished to leave its management wholly to the Irish Society. Their first response was in favour of the latter course, but on hearing that companies were favouring direct involvement and on the advice of Martin Freeman, a merchant with wide-ranging overseas interests who was both one of their senior officers, a warden, and also a member of the Irish Society, that the plantation might not otherwise succeed, they decided early in February after a number of discussions, to do likewise.[15]

It was to be over two years, however, before the estates were delineated. Much of the early endeavour of the Londoners' agents had been concentrated on building work at Coleraine and to a lesser extent up to this point at Derry. Now, in the summer of 1613, the city sent over two commissioners to assess how the money was being spent and, amongst other things, to divide the greater part of the land (57 per cent of it) beyond the towns and lands adjacent, which remained with the Irish Society, into twelve estates or proportions, reflecting the number of the principal livery companies of London. Afterwards in December, these estates were allocated by lottery to one or other of these twelve companies with each of which a number of the minor ones (whose contributions had been smaller) was linked.[16] As for the rest of the land, church land, excluding the monasteries and the estates which had been dissolved in recent years, was granted separately to the now official Protestant Church, and the remainder was allocated to both a group of the Irish elite who were restored (a smaller area than in the other plantation counties) and to one former military man, Sir Thomas Phillips of Limavady, while the Irish Society retained the two new towns and land close by them.

Linked with the Fishmongers were five lesser companies, on four of whom, the Plasterers, Glaziers, Basketmakers and Musicians, sums ranging from £30 to £60 were levied, while the fifth, the Leathersellers paid in £1,450 to the Fishmongers' £3,390.[17] The lesser companies generally disengaged – in the case of the Musicians in March 1614 when they sold their share to the Fishmongers.[18] The Leathersellers took a much more active interest in the estate at first, with the Fishmongers forming a committee with them in January 1615 to discuss common action after tensions between them had surfaced a year earlier about the appointment and fees of agents to go to Ireland, but in January 1617 they offered to sell their interest to the Fishmongers for a two-third part of their total investment, being willing to lose the other part. The detail of that agreement was completed at the end of April.[19]

The estate the Fishmongers received, formally conveyed to them by the Irish Society as the manor of Walworth in October 1618, took its name from Sir William Walworth (d. 1385), a former mayor of London and a Fishmonger who had played a major part in the suppression of Wat Tyler's rebellion (the Peasants' Revolt) in 1381, a figure of whom had been displayed in the mayoral pageant in 1616 and who was somewhat of a cult figure to the company.[20] Made up of some 24,000 statute acres, it stretched, roughly, in a line southwards which took in Ballykelly beside the Foyle on the north and Feeny on the south, though with some detached portions caused by the location of church lands. There were essentially three blocks of land; an area around Greysteel and one around Ballykelly (both villages nowadays), which formed the northern half of the estate and an area below Loughermore mountain, much of it in the Foreglen and taking in Feeny, which formed the southern half. Elongated, then, in form and constituted out of the Gaelic divisions called ballybetaghs which were multiples of ballyboes or townlands, it contained, as was intended, land of varying quality and accessibility, so that each company would receive an equitable allocation of both good and bad land (plate 7.2).[21] In the plans of plantation overall the companies were like to the 'undertakers' in the other counties, who received about 40 per cent of the land there, but the estates they got were much larger. Both, unlike the other categories of grantees, were formally tied to be colonisers. They must let the land only to British tenants – English and Lowland Scots (the latter to benefit because of the recent succession of James VI of Scotland to the English throne) – and in a structured manner embracing freeholders and leaseholders or copyholders. By implication at least, the previous Irish occupiers must move off these areas and concentrate elsewhere. They must also build a manor house surrounded by a 'strong court or. bawne', the novel feature of which, in the

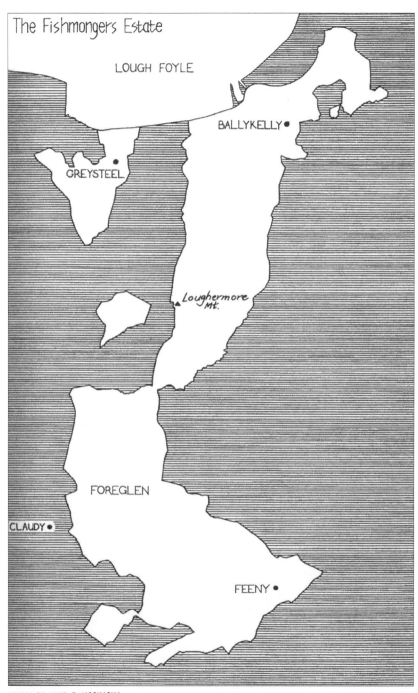

Plate 7.2 The Fishmongers' Company estate

history of fortification, lay in the flanker towers on its corners, with their gunloops, which allowed it to be defended with musket fire. Their tenants' houses must also be built nearby, both for their mutual defence and in order to create village settlements.[22]

How the Fishmongers' Company as an association in London would go about fulfilling these obligations needs now to be explored. Their first response, shortly after the allotment of the land in December 1613, was to dispatch agents. By the end of February when the Leathersellers, still involved, sought agreement on joint action, informal contact had been made with the Goldsmiths' agent, Andrew Bowdler, and now agreement was reached to send another on a formal basis. The person agreed on and already chosen by the Fishmongers, Alexander Fookes, had previously been an oast or buyer of fish at Rye on behalf of the company. His fee was to be 3s.4d, per day or £60.16.8 a year. Early in March at a court of assistants meeting he received his instructions (not now surviving) and also letters to deliver: one to Thomas Raven, the city's cartographer, one to Bowdler, letters to Edmund Hayward a brother of a company member who was then establishing himself as a merchant and timber contractor in Coleraine and one to Tristram Beresford, one of the Irish Society's two agents, and was given £10 of his wages in advance. On the question being raised that somebody should stand as surety for his 'good dealing and performance' in his duties and accounting for money, it was answered that John Halsey and William Angel, two prominent members of the company, had already done so.[23]

Alexander Fookes was to be one of a number of the company's agents in Ulster of whom some who followed him, such as Arthur Breton and Richard Kirby, became long-standing tenants on the estate. While his doings in detail unfortunately are unrecoverable, his remit was, clearly, to fulfil the company's obligations in building and planting, having inherited a situation where the lands had been let 'until Alhollantide next' (1 Nov.), presumably by the Irish Society and presumably still mainly to the original Irish occupiers, their rents to thus replace for them the more varied customary obligations or chiefries they had owed to their former O Cahan lord. At the end of January 1615 he was paid what remained due of his year's wages, but – it having been noted that he had been 'to and fro part of the time' – on condition that the year should not end until 'his next departing thence', and it was agreed that he should have £30 in advance for the following year. However, a year later, in early March 1616, at a court of assistants attended by some of the Leathersellers, all now interested in profit from the plantation, 'much suspicion' was 'conceived' of his 'untrue dealing' and neglect of responsibilities in Ireland, and it was decided to send over Robert Whitney, then the 'servant' of the company's clerk, Robert

Glover, to demand an account from Fookes. On his departure towards the end of the month, Whitney received £30 'towards his charges' and letters of credit for £20 in Ireland should he need it.[24] For his part, Whitney who claimed that he had 'well performed what he had in hand' had his payment made up to £60 in February 1617 after his return, he asserting that he had lost by his absence from London more than he received, 'besides the danger that he was in by his journey, escaping very hardly with his life'.[25]

Fookes's endeavours may nevertheless have been greater than had been feared. At any rate it is known that the company's 'great house newly built' had already been erected by April 1616 – at the beginning of Whitney's mission – and with it the decision to locate the estate headquarters and its village core at Ballykelly.[26] Now a village of mainly nineteenth-century build, it was located at a crossing of the Ballykelly river which meandered through slob land nearby, since reclaimed, into the Foyle and it was on the routeway from Derry, thirteen miles distant, to Coleraine, approachable through the ancient Caman wood (now partly replanted as Ballykelly forest) on higher ground nearby to the west. To the north of the road there were also some trees near the river, which had not been banked and straightened as it now is, and a wood upstream in the townlands of Oghill and Drumacony, and it was in the ballybetagh of Ballymacconagher. Going southwards were two other roads, both unhedged, on either side of the Ballykelly river: the one represented now by the Loughermore road (which went inland ultimately towards Claudy), the other known nowadays as the Glenhead road. Near the Foyle there was a small chapel with possibly a tiny holding of church land adjacent. While it seems extremely likely that there had not been a castle there to be taken over, especially with the O Cahan castle, or indeed castles, anyhow nearby in the Limavady area, some lesser family must have lived close by in what must have been a populous district, especially immediately eastwards on good land stretching towards Limavady. It is also uncertain how life there may have been affected by recent devastations in the Nine Years' War, which in the absence of large towns to besiege had been fought in great measure by simply ravaging the countryside.[27] Here at any rate, by 1616 the company had built its 'great house', the architect-contractor for which is unknown, and some other tenant houses near the chapel, which it was understood the 'bishop of Armagh' (Christopher Hampton), then in London, was willing to make a parish church, and a group of the wardens was asked to speak to him on that matter.[28] Fookes was now, also, being viewed more sympathetically by the company. When, anyhow, in July of that year his wife sought £10 to cover her expenses 'into Ireland, being going thither to her husband', it was agreed, upon debate, to give it to her.[29] Later, now back in England, at an assembly of the company's committee for the plantation in October 1617, she made 'pitiful complaint' of her husband's 'want and misery' setting out, as he had apparently done in many letters, reasons why he was 'utterly undone and impoverished'. She referred to his 'losses and hindrances' in 'not, getting in of any rents', and through the costs of entertaining people coming to view the estate with a view to renting it, and also in attending assizes and quarter sessions, these the outcome of the extension from Dublin of a unitary system of law just at this time into an area formerly ruled under Gaelic law and custom. Although the committee took the view that his 'want and poverty' had come by his 'own means and negligence', it was thought good 'in charity' to make them a gift of £10.[30] The plantation, however, continued to be very costly for the company up into the 1620s. With the buying out of the Leathersellers, their contributions towards the general plantation fund exceeded £4,000 while the expenditure they outlaid on what was now their own estate may well have reached to about £3,000.[31] It is not surprising therefore that further appeals in the years 1612–14 for investment in Virginia evoked a limited response. The company having been 'at great charges for plantation in Ireland', took a cold approach to Sir Thomas Smith's Virginia lottery scheme, offering £25 which he 'scornfully refused', though eventually £89.15.0 was collected for it.[32]

No sooner had the company been allocated the estate in December 1613, than it began to receive intermittent overtures from a range of people to lease it. The first to appear, at a court of assistants on 31 January 1614, was 'one' Captain [Edward] Panton, who was in fact the trainer of the London militia company and who had played some part in the company of commissioners from London, the previous autumn, in the designing of the new city of Londonderry. He sought 'for a friend of his, as he saith', to take the whole estate in fee farm (i.e. in freehold for ever), to build and perform in accordance with the plantation requirements, and offered a rent of 13s.4d. per ballyboe. His offer was, however, premature and unaccepted; his entrepreneurial drive to be later, instead, put into the development of Panton St in London.[33] In May Thomas Raven, the cartographer, approached the company for a conveyance in fee farm of some of the land in the Ballykelly area, or the entire estate, for which he offered 4½d. an acre and to discharge all the company's plantation obligations and to pay the crown rent – a land tax. However he was told that since the company had as yet no 'intelligence or information of the value of those things', it could not 'conclude with any man for anything'.[34] In November 1615 they were approached by a 'gentleman of Scotland' seeking on behalf of his father, a bishop, a sixty-one year lease at a rent of £100 per annum with a down-payment or entry fine of £200 and an undertaking to pay both the crown rent and 'perform the rest of the plantation not yet performed', but he was told that the company had already expended more money in plantation than his offer would recompense.[35] In 1616 applications became more numerous and the company's approach more considered: it was moving towards the idea of leasing the estate en bloc to one man. To an approach in January by a Mr Lawley, a London merchant, 'and another' on behalf of Sir Thomas Phillips, in what may well have been an attempt to form a consortium by Phillips, it expressed a willingness to lease but not to sell, and in that regard a preference to deal with him rather than any other. He was to be informed, however, that they had already been offered £160 rent and an entry fine of £400 for a thirty-one year lease 'and to be freed of all plantation'.[36] If nothing more was heard from Phillips, there were to be a number of other applications. In April Edward Rone, who had taken over the Grocers' estate and who died shortly thereafter, sought the use of the company's 'great house' until Michaelmas, while in July Raven sought a freehold of two townlands and a lease of two others, offering to measure the whole estate and make the company 'such a plot of it as that they may know every particular parcel of land being here as if they were upon the ground'.[37] Competition increased in the autumn. 'One' Mr Vaughan, a member of a military family which had been at Derry since the Nine Years' War, sought a lease for years offering £200 per annum, to be told that if they did lease it, they would not exceed a term of forty one years. They would consider further of his offer which he persisted with, though later seeking instead to be made a freeholder on the estate and tenant of the 'great house' – while pointing out that the rent he offered would not be sufficient recompense for their outlay.[38] Finally there is evidence of a more broad-based consortium seeking the estate. At meetings of the court of assistants in November a Mr Bowland accompanied first Sir James Craig, a Scottish grantee in the plantation in County Cavan and a man with extensive ambitions in Ireland, and secondly a Mr Gore, one of a prominent London merchant family whose relative Captain (later Sir) Paul Gore had fought in the Nine Years' War, and sought, first a lease of 100 or 99 years and then offered £200 per annum for a sixty-year lease, they to have the right to designate all freeholders and copyholders. Negotiations with them, however, 'brake off' quickly when the company, on 18 November, insisted on a forty-year lease and an entry fine of £1,000.[39]

A week later William Angel, a warden of the company and very prominent in its affairs, urged the need for decision, and in January, when Angel brought news of the Leathersellers' interest in selling their share to the company, a committee was appointed made up of the four 'upper' wardens and nine other prominent members, including John Halsey, to 'conclude' on all 'Irish affairs', though they should refer back to the company, 'before they absolutely go through withal'.[40] The 'committees' in which Angel took a leading part opted to let the land wholly to one farmer (or middleman) and furthermore entered into immediate negotiations with James Higgons a fellow London merchant with a small export trade and himself a member of the Grocers' company, who lived on London Bridge, close to the Fishmongers' Hall. In their bargaining with him the committee's opening demand was either for a £500 entry fine and £160 per annum rent for a sixty-year lease or else a fine of £1,200 and £100 yearly, 'he to Perform the rest of the plantation', while he in turn offered a fine of £600 and £100 yearly. Eventually he was given two options: either £400 fine and £150 per year (returns respectively of about 10 per cent to 15 per cent and about 4 per cent or 5 per cent on their outlay on the estate) or £800 fine and £100 yearly and to pay the crown rent (a tax in this case of £17 per annum), and given some days – until the next meeting of the court of assistants – for consideration, At the ensuing court of assistants these options were again put to him and on his promise to give his decision at the next meeting one week later, agreement was reached with him then (10 February 1617) on the first option, he to 'undergo all charges of plantation from this day'.[41]

From the company's point of view, the adoption of a farmer for an ultramarine estate, and with plantation requirements to boot, is perhaps not surprising. Already various problems, notably suspicion of Fookes's behaviour, and financial irritants were presenting themselves. Edmund Hayward was making demands for payment for timber for the building operations and a bill of exchange for £50 taken up by Hayward from John Hatton, a Coleraine merchant, 'for the works at Walworth town now in land' was being presented for payment.[42] Part of the reason why a London-based rather than an Irish-based farmer had been chosen may well have been in the hope that his rent payments would be made regularly and such difficulties avoided, though, as will be seen, the links that Higgons himself came to have at any rate by 1619 with Angel and Halsey may perhaps provide another reason for choosing him. Efforts were now made to ensure that Higgons (who disputed responsibility for commitments he claimed he had not entered into) should shoulder such costs.[43] But the most pressing matter now coming to bear on the company is also that with most human interest to investigate: the advancement of the plantation itself on the estate.

In May 1617 the Irish Society, itself under pressure from the king and the English privy council, sought answers from the company – the first in a series of demands for information which recurred up to 1631 – about the progress of the plantation.[44] In the background had been a minor conspiracy to overthrow it, detected in early 1615, in which some of the

O Cahans, including Rory O Cahan, son of the last lord now in the Tower of London, had been involved, which was suppressed by trials and six executions at Derry at the end of July, and in response to which the company, in May, had sent from its armoury, by order, some armour and weapons, notably four corslets and eighteen calivers, to be kept at Derry and Coleraine.[45] The conspiracy therefore resulted in government pressure on the planter grantees to advance the plantation as it should be according to the rules. When this came to bear on the Fishmongers in 1617, their first response was that Higgons should be spoken to 'very effectually' and they parried by informing the Irish Society that Higgons had dispatched a 'messenger' – probably George Downing on whom see below – and that they would acquaint them with what had been done on its return.[46]

If there is uncertainty about the full impact of the plantation on the estate up to this point (beyond the building work), it is mainly from now that that impact can begin to be assessed. Yet the absence of records kept by Higgons the farmer, especially a rental which would link occupier to place, leaves the attempt to do so somewhat tentative. Although by early 1614, the time the companies were taking over the estates from the Irish Society, those in the immediate vicinity of Derry and probably Coleraine already had some settler tenants, the two infant towns of the Londoners (both of which had been little outposts of settlement anyhow since after 1600) probably proving the initial dispersants of settler tenantry onto the land,[47] the process of colonising estates further afield appears to have been slower to start and a more gradual one. That was certainly the impression given by Sir Josias Bodley who was employed by the crown to report on the progress of the plantation in the county in 1614. In his view the Irish Society (concentrating on town-building) had tended to neglect the county lands, and the companies, having only belatedly taken over their estates 'with promises thereupon to plant and to strengthen with castles and bawns', had only that summer sent over agents, caustically described as 'but meanly qualified to undertake that charge'. With the exception of the Salters little had yet been done, while many companies were seeking to devolve over their responsibilities to farmers or middlemen.[48]

In the case of the Fishmongers this was soon to change. In September 1616 the company made a lease – its only one, just a few months prior to its demise of the entire estate to Higgons – of two townlands, Carrickhugh and Tullamaine, to a Coleraine-based merchant, and innkeeper, Lawrence Rathborne (himself, as will be seen, with links to Phillips) for twenty one years at a rent of £8 per annum.[49] Both the location of the land as leased and the attendant circumstances of the making of the lease are significant. Both places then include the western part of the Caman wood and stretched down into it to a little stream, still to be found, which had been designated the boundary between two baronies, or administrative sub-divisions, of the county. Usually such boundaries were of some antiquity. This meant, then, that the area from the stream, now Walworth (Keenaght) townland, down to the Ballykelly river beyond which the 'great house' with some few other tenant houses nearby had by now been built, close to the chapel had already been occupied and planned to be the core of the estate to be divided up, as will be seen, into fields to provide small holdings for the settler villagers there.[50] The attendant circumstances are also significant: Rathborne should compensate 'one Eustace [Jones]' for a small dwelling house he had on part of the leased land or allow him to remove it, Hayward and Fookes to be the arbitrators in this matter.[51] Eustace Jones (d. 1633), as it happens, can be identified as a likely follower of Sir Thomas Phillips: in November 1612 he had been nominated to be a burgess of Phillips's new town, some few miles distant, of Limavady.[52] Phillips, then, (though this can only be conjectural) in expectation of a lease from the Fishmongers – in which he was to be disappointed – may well have over-awed the residents of this area sufficiently for the process of tenurial changeover, on a small scale and in favour of some of his own followers, to have first begun. Other settler tenantry and workmen must have come under Fookes.

James Higgons, George Downing and the plantation

Higgons took over a plantation, then, in 1617 which had already begun in stages but which was still small and largely concentrated on its Ballykelly core. He and, at first, his associate George Downing were to be actively engaged with it, coming and going with supplies, over the next few years. He paid the company £200 (half his entry fine) on 31 March 1617, his tenancy having begun from Lady Day (the week before) and since the company was cautious about giving him the lease until his own title was conveyed (in late October 1618), he sought a letter of attorney empowering him to negotiate leases and such like.[53] His lease from the company, which he had requested in November 1618, made out on 14 December, was only formally sealed in London on 4 January 1619, when he made some further payments, and provision was then made by letter of attorney for Fookes and Robert Goodwin, a London lawyer now living in Derry, to take and deliver possession on the ground.[54] It is an indication of the speed of action at that time, though also of its thoroughness, that Higgons's copy of the lease was delivered by Fookes to Downing on Higgons's behalf on 18 March following, 'as the very act and deed' of the Fishmongers 'in the castle or capital mansion house situate in Ballykelly'. This formal solemnity was carried out in the presence of a group of sixteen witnesses, who included

Goodwin and the Rev. Luke Astry, the latter having therefore already arrived to be parish minister by this time. The other fourteen were made up of four Irish and ten English. The Irish, two of whom signed by mark and one of whose final names is now illegible, can be taken to be prominent local residents and now tenants of the estate. One, Patrick O Mullan, signed in a precise English hand. The others were Orpe (?) (or perhaps Quhi [*Cú Maighe*]) Ballagh McKnogh[e]r and Hugh O Curran. Most of the English witnesses may be taken as residents on the estate also, including David Bramson who came in 1615 and died in 1621, some of them to remain there for long and one, John Carter (who signed by mark), to have been allegedly killed in the rising in 1641.[55] Three of the twelve English who signed and two of the four Irish, signed by mark, which gives a literacy rate, if the sample has any value, of 75 per-cent for the English and of 50 per cent for the Irish. The presence of the Irish may also say something of the early, and peacetime, relations of the English and Irish.

The first matter to be addressed by the company with Higgons, its farmer, concerned the organisation of the estate: the matter of freeholders. Freeholders, after all, were the omnicompetent men of English-style society. They played a role, unpaid, both in local government and law administration and should a parliament be summoned they were amongst those who constituted the electorate. Where land had not been forfeited, as in the composition of Connacht and the 'settlement' of Monaghan in 1591 and indeed elsewhere in Ireland at this very time, attempts were made to re-design the society by turning the major landholders under the lords into freeholders so that one system of law would operate across the whole island. In the government blueprint for the plantation it had therefore been laid down that each undertaker's estate of 1,000 'acres' must have two freeholders. Since the Fishmongers' estate was held to be just over 3,000 acres, it must have six settler freeholders. This was now a matter of some urgency, because before the estate could be itself transferred by the Irish Society to the company, the question of freeholders on it had to be resolved.[56] At an assembly of the company's 'committees' for the plantation, with Higgons brought into attendance, in October 1617 a list of six possible names was brought forward: Hayward, Captain Vaughan (either Henry or John, brothers of the Mr Vaughan already' mentioned), Thomas Raven, Alexander Fookes, George Downing and a certain John Wells, who never took up a freehold allocated to him ('he came not thereupon'), the view being that the company should have the nomination of three and the farmer of the rest.[57]

The names put forward, though some were to be changed, are significant because they represented various strands of the plantation up to then, for example Vaughan, the pre-existing military officer, or Hayward (also spelt Haward), the merchant who claimed money from the company: many of them were unlikely to become primarily residents on the land allotted to them. The company, too, questioned the actual land proposed for them. 'Being looked at in the plot', it was found that most were being placed near the company's 'principal house' and on the 'best ground in the whole proportion', and it was thought fit by the committee to place them in 'some remote part' of the estate near the Skinners' lands – i.e. inland and to the south in the Feeny area – where they might build together 'for their own strength'. This was laid down, though Higgons argued that they would not accept freeholders in that location.[58]

The issue of the freeholders was not to be resolved for some time and in the longer term (up to the 1630s), the freehold lands were to be passed from one person to another, making it unlikely that the company's plan for a settlement of freeholders to the south of the estate would be brought into being in our period. Meanwhile some decisions were taken, as in May 1618 when it was considered that 13s.4d. should be a sufficient rent for a freeholder (per townland) given their building obligations and their administrative services.[59] By this stage also however objections to two of the names had raised by the Irish Society – to Hayward's son (who had been substituted for him) presumably on grounds of age and to Captain Vaughan (an exemplification of a tension between the military and the mercantile) because it was thought he had made criticisms to government of the Londoners' plantation performance.[60] The first formal grant of a freehold was made in October 1618 not in fact by the Fishmongers themselves, but by the Irish Society on the eve of the transfer of the estate to the company. Downing was the beneficiary, and the lands, based on Altinure and Ballytemple, were in the southern section of the estate.[61]

If, then, the freeholds were indeed located in this area, the decision went not without protest from one beneficiary: the cartographer Thomas Raven. His relations with Higgons, who would prefer these low-rent freeholds not to absorb too much land and who for his part insisted that 'whatsoever Mr Raven shall have it will never content him', were not good, and by June 1619 Raven had complained to the company 'disliking his freehold … in regard of the badness thereof.[62] By late 1620, however, the company was able to state that five freeholds (including Downing's) had been created, though it was obliged to note about the beneficiaries, as it had to again later on, that 'whether they do as yet inhabit upon the same they know not', and in early March 1624 Robert Goodwin, then in London, who, once again, had acted for the company in conveyancing, was paid £4 by it for his work in addition to £2.2.0 that he had received earlier.[63]

The names of the freeholders survive and the lands they received can be reasonably well re-constructed. What happened, however, presents a pattern of substitution, with many of the actual freeholders not being exclusively linked to the estate but rather mainly being people who lived in or near Derry and having also other interests. Thus although Captain Vaughan was indeed denied a freehold, his relative James received one – at Ballyrory – but immediately in 1619 he sold it to Thomas Skipton who, himself a building contractor it would seem, was at this point establishing himself with many areas of land on both the Goldsmiths' and Grocers' estates a few miles opposite Derry and who, a persistent tradition has it, had been killed by some of the Irish in the early 1620s. Certainly he was dead by 1624, leaving a son, also Thomas, a child under age who in the 1630s was to attend Sidney Sussex College, Cambridge and then follow the law at Gray's Inn in London.[64] These were not the conditions for establishing a subplantation of settler tenant farmers in the southern part of the estate and it looks likely that the former owners, the O Harrons, were in occupation as rent payers of some kind up to 1641. While the Skiptons may have had their special circumstances, the others who came to hold these freeholds by purchase from those originally selected were from a somewhat similar emerging elite within the plantation class. Amongst them was Robert Goodwin, already mentioned, town clerk and chamberlain of Londonderry, one of the intelligentsia of the plantation town and living there, who bought Raven's freehold of Teredreen, while for his part Downing passed on his freehold to Robert Thornton who again lived in Derry.[65] Similarly Alexander Fookes, who it seems returned to London and may even have been dead by 1629 when at any rate we find reference to the 'widow' Fookes (though possibly also his mother) as the company's leaseholder of a house in George Alley in Aldgate, disposed of his freehold to Edward Warren, a member of the new merchant class in Derry.[66] The sixth freehold, embracing Feeny townland and conveyed at first to one John Wells who never took it up, was finally granted to James Higgons, to be for his son, in 1633.[67]

The principal impact of the plantation up to the 1630s was in fact on the accessible northern half of the estate which also contained much land. Pressure by government on the planter grantees to ensure that their obligations were met resulted in a series of reports on each estate being produced up to 1622 and these, taken with company responses to demands for information from the Irish Society up to the years later, give a good impression of its scale, though the absence of estate papers held by Higgons (probably destroyed in 1641) indicating tenancies and rents leaves gaps in precision which just cannot now be filled .[68]

As early as August 1618 Higgons insisted in an answer to the company that there were already 38 Britons placed and dwelling on the estate, and that more should be placed as soon as he could procure them.[69] Pynnar's government survey conducted some months later offers some corroboration: he recorded 34 families of settler tenants (including six freeholders), some with undertenants, making up in all 40 men. The survey in 1622 was more exacting, if perhaps too critical. There were four freeholders but only one (probably Downing) resident, the latter crucial point being one which would seem to conform to the facts.[70] Otherwise there were 14 people holding leases for terms of years and 10 tenants at will, but for reasons which must include taking account of absentee tenants or people holding on more than one estate, only 23 settler males were found to be present at this stage.[71] Lists of people on the estate (apart from the freeholders) provided by the company in the 1620s did not fully reach to thirty names. When, later, in *c.* 1630 a muster was carried out for the purpose of militia organisation the names of 42 people who were present were recorded.[72] That list is, however, somewhat deceptive because by then the estate had been split between two chief tenants, Higgons and Christopher Freeman, and these were the names of those who mustered under Freeman though not necessarily all exclusively from his part of the estate. A list drawn up by the company in March 1631 in answer to an anxious precept from the Irish Society contained a total of 69 names but this was probably somewhat generous towards itself.[73] Overlaps between these various lists, especially the latter two, are by no means complete, though a hard core of settlers, except where mortality had intervened, runs through them from an early stage up to the 1630s. It is possible to suggest that a settler male population, including in some cases more than one person of the same surname, of possibly close to 100 was, by the 1630s, beginning to stabilise itself on the estate. Most were English, though many who mustered under Freemen were Scots. Many were likely to have been sub-tenants or smallholders: the undertenant poor. Some, also, were tradesmen of various kinds. Amongst the latter were 'Penticost the smith' and 'Peter the cooper', both, as well, holding small areas of land at Ballykelly, while the names of both a weaver (indicating a settler cloth industry) and a merchant of Ballykelly village also come to light.[74] The lists go however without occupation being provided, thereby leaving the range of skills present impossible to detect.

It was at the estate core at Ballykelly that the main effects of the company's financial investment were to be seen: the building of their manor house and bawn, the renovation and extension of a pre-existing chapel to be the parish church, the building of a rather diffused village, the construction of a mill and mill house and a lengthy water course to power

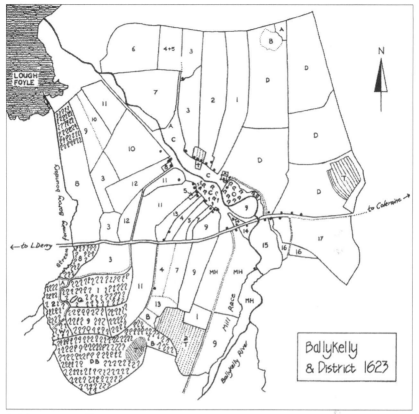

DRAWN AND INTERPRETED BY DAVID J. McCONAGHY

Plate 7.3 This map of Ballykelly and district, drawn by David McConaghy of Portstewart, is based on an estate map of 1623 by Thomas Croddin. Buildings, apart from the church (marked with a cross) and the bawn, are represented by black dots. The tree-like symbol adopted by the cartographer for woodland has been re-used. Letters to represent information given by Croddin have been used as follows: A = Arable, B = Bog, C = Common, D = Demesne, MH = Mill holms, O = Orchard, Q = Stone quarry, W = Waste. The letter T has been placed on areas represented by Croddin by dotted lines, which may well have been employed to show some kind of tilled ground. Numbers have been used to represent the tenants' names and the fields they held as follows: 1 = Alexander Fookes, 2 = Mary Bramson (or Brabson), widow, 3 = Thomas Jackson, 4 = Eustace Jones, 5 = Mark Greene, 6 = Thomas Long, 7 = Ralph Phillips and George Downing, 8 = Humphrey Barlow, 9 = Peter Gates, 10 = Richard Glover, 11= Arthur Breton, 12 = Richard Muskett, 13 = Richard Kirby, 14 = Robert Myles, 15 = Pentecost the smith, 16 = John Clarke, 17 = Peter the cooper. Four small plots allotted to three houses opposite the church, one of which had two tenants, have not been numbered. The tenant of one of these was, however, Thomas Long (no. 6). The other tenants' names were Samson and, of one house, Browne and Madock. A further small plot with a house, held by one Oaky (?), next to that of Robert Myles (no. 14) is also unnumbered. It will be seen from the map that there were also a few houses, without land, facing onto the common, while a few on the main road were depicted without land too.

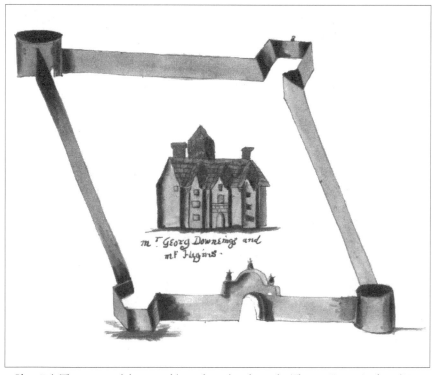

Plate 7.4 The company's bawn and 'great house' as drawn by Thomas Raven in the 1620s
(PRONI, T510, f. 29)

it, and the laying-out and enclosure of a substantial area of land. All this can
be described mainly from a map made by Thomas Croddin, an English
cartographer, in 1623 (plate 7.3).[75]

At that time the river at Ballykelly followed a more meandering course
than nowadays and the village as constructed was on both sides of it with
just a few houses built on either side of the 'high way' (the present main
road), giving it a double T-type form. The houses were dispersed in plan,
related generally to areas of land allotted to their occupants. Thus while
routeway and river were the natural features which gave it its form, its form
did not arise from an aesthetic impulse to create a compact symmetrical
mini-town. In addition, a few houses were built further out from this
central core. The defensive disadvantage of this lay-out was commented on
in 1622: the houses were 'so dispersed that they were 'unfit to relieve one
another'.[76] Yet the village was clearly not without plan. Previously trees had
grown beside the river in part of an area now made to form a common
between river and houses on the south-west side, while others, or perhaps
newly planted ones, on its north-east (immediately south-east of the bawn)

were now enclosed as an orchard, with a small building within it. The bawn and house was approached by a curving entrance which came in on high ground from the main 'high way' passing two houses in its route (plate 7.4). Two other 'high ways' (as they were called) led out of the village south-west of the river, one joining the pre-existing main road, the other 'a high way to the strand', while on the other side beyond the bawn and church, where there was another area of common, a third short route way (or lane) had been constructed.

That the lord of a manor had the right to provide a mill at which all those under him should have their corn ground was a familiar feature of manorial society. The mill and mill house (stone-built) were erected at what is still a definable location slightly upstream from the village, the present Milltown House, which probably incorporates much of the original building (making it, if so, one of the oldest dateable structures in the area), stands. The construction of the water course to power the mill, which was diverted from the river at a point, almost a mile away, where there is a waterfall and now a footbridge, was a difficult and labour-intensive feat of engineering. Some of the water course, which drew also from a short stream coming down from near to Caman wood, can still be followed on the ground through an area of land, itself bisected by the Loughermore road, which was called the 'mill holmes' and the miller was called Peter Lussher (plate 7.5).[77]

The bawn, with its curving avenue approach passing the orchard below it on the left and land converted to demesne on the right, and itself close to a bend in the Ballykelly river, was the most prominent building on its Limavady side, while beyond it was the church, with a distinct group of three houses beside it. Otherwise there were only a few tenant houses on this side of the river, between the bawn and the Foyle: the tenant houses, then, were mainly on the other side. With an arched entrance facing the river, the bawn was a 'strong' and large one some 125 feet square, complete, unlike some, with four corner flankers – 'two square and two round' – of differing and elaborate construction.[78] A quarry in the Caman wood which is marked on Croddin's map of 1623 must have been the source of the stone. Behind the bawn was a kitchen garden enclosure of somewhat similar size. While much of the bawn remains, the manor house, free-standing within and also built, does not, and somewhat conflicting descriptions of it survive. Drawings reveal it as having a mid-centred back return, such back wings being a feature common to many plantation estate houses. One description made it 40 feet long and 26 feet, broad slated and two storeyed – though it was two and a half – with the return 23 feet square, while another had it 'a good house ... fifty feet square'. Architectural features

Plate 7.5 A surviving section of the mill race near Ballykelly

which stand out on Raven's drawing of it in the 1620s (Raven's drawing) are its brick chimneys, its gabled windows on the top and an arched doorway, curving rather than pointed with possibly an inscription above.[79] The company described it as having sixteen rooms.[80] However, though strikingly new *in situ*, a frontage of 50 feet or even of about 140 to take in bawn wall and flankers left the building as a whole somewhat small in comparison with the large mansion houses of the time in England.

Since the plantation was to be Protestant in identity (and indeed in general a transfer of contemporary English culture), a question regularly put to the companies concerned the state of their church buildings. When the chapel (the location of which may well have contributed to the decision to build where they did) was first discussed by the company in 1616 it decided, just as the estate should be called Walworth so it should be made the parish church and called – after the patron saint of fishermen – St Peter's church (plate 7.6).[81] This church, a chapel of the parish of Tamlaght Finlagan of which the principal church lay, two miles away, outside the estate, had been 'neatly made up' by the time of Pynnar's survey in 1618–19.[82] Shortly afterwards it was extended by the addition of a chancel and as it stood, slated, in 1622 it was described as 44 feet long and 27 feet broad (measurements which are remarkably accurate since the ruin survives to offer confirmation) with the chancel being 21 feet square and somewhat lower than the rest.[83] The chancel had both a theological and an architectural importance. It was entered through a large round arch. A departure from the normal

Plate 7.6 Ballykelly church as drawn by Thomas Raven in the 1620s
(PRONI, T510, f. 29)

conservative Gothic tradition in church building (as seen locally in the surviving window of the much larger new church built by the Grocers' company at Eglinton), this arch has remote rural tones of the classicism which was becoming influential, through Inigo Jones, at the court of James I. It thus, it may be argued, conveyed an assurance of royal power and symbolised the creation of a new order. Theologically, the chancel may well have held the communion table lengthwise, enabling communicants to partake of the sacraments sitting on either side (plate 7.7).

Some credence is lent to this suggestion of a puritan order by what is known of the incumbent, described as 'a good preacher to teach the people'. Born in Bedfordshire in 1586, the Rev. Luke Astry was a graduate (B.A. 1607, M.A. 1610) of what was at any rate then a moderately puritan college, Queens' College, Cambridge, where he had been a sizar – the lowest social rank amongst the students – people who augmented their scholarships by carrying out various menial tasks. Most likely he took his theological temper from that of the college in which he was brought up or may even have come to share the more firmly puritan views of the subsequently famous intellectual the Rev. John Preston, with whom he will have overlapped for a time at Queens'.[84] In one of its many answers to queries about its plantation performance, the company stated, in November 1620, that it had 'a convenient church with a chancel and seats therein of joiner's work fit for divine service'.[85] To another in March 1631, which

Plate 7.7 Arch leading into chancel, Ballykelly church

required more detail, they responded (somewhat grandly) that they had a 'church with a chancel of lime and stone, slated and ceil and in good repair, having pulpit, seats, books, a communion cup silver and gilt and ornaments complete'.[86] In one point the response was not strictly true, but it may have stirred them to action. In 1622 the company had agreed that a 'small standing gilt cup' it owned, valuable enough, appropriately engraved, should be sent to Walworth to be used as a communion cup, its cover to be altered suitably to be used for the communion bread,[87] but almost ten years of inertia had intervened. In October 1631 it was agreed to dispatch it to Ireland with James Higgons and he brought in a certificate one year later testifying to its receipt.[88] That a bell, worth about £5, should be bought and sent over was discussed the following year, in a gesture, perhaps, to the high church Anglicanism now favoured at court, but nothing further is heard of it.[89]

As for the village, it grew considerably in the years from 1619, when we get a first description of it, to 1623, when it is represented on Croddin's map. Pynnar, reporting to the government in 1618–19, found fifteen houses, while drawn on Croddin's map were, excluding the bawn, church and mill, forty-one structures of various kinds and sizes, some possibly even sheds or outhouses. The houses have the further interest that in some cases at any rate they represent the transfer to Ulster of English rural housing types – to be subsequently influential as designs – which had been, especially those of the rising 'middling sort of people', undergoing considerable architectural change in the post-medieval period. This was most notable in the division of open spaces into rooms and in the insertion of chimneys to facilitate the creation of upper storeys. This modernisation can be seen in the obligations to which the freeholders were tied in their agreements with the company. Thus in his indenture of 1618, Downing undertook to build within three years a 'house of timber, stone or brick containing six or four rooms fit and convenient for habitation' – not, of course, particularly large – while Higgons covenanted in his grant of Feeny townland in January 1633 to erect there a similar 'sufficient and substantial house' of six or four rooms 'at the least' by Michaelmas 1636.[90] These houses and the accompanying obligation to live in them were hardly built since both lived at Ballykelly, where, also, Higgons died in 1634. Some version of the building convenants required of Lawrence Rathborne was built; he moved to live there where he died in 1630, though did not transmit the lease to a successor. These embodied a farm house and farm yard organisation: he undertook to build a 'strong substantial and convenient dwelling house with walls all of stone' and spend on it £100 stg 'at the least' and also to spend £50 on building 'some convenient housing

Plate 7.8 Arthur Breton's house as drawn by Thomas Raven in the 1620s
(PRONI, T510, f. 29)

for stable room, barn room or such like near adjoining …'[91] The company indeed claimed in 1631 that there were forty settler dwelling houses on the estate as a whole.[92] In short, not all the settler tenantry continued to live in the village.

Descriptions and drawings of the houses which actually were built in Ballykelly village show, in fact, a number of types. These ranged from cabins or cottages which were thatched (the dwellings of the poorer settlers) to larger houses made both of stone and of timber ('rough cast with lime'), all slated and described as one and a half storeys (plate 7.8). The dimensions of some of the larger houses were given in the government-commissioned survey of 1622: three stone houses were 53 feet long by 24 feet broad while four timber ones were 38 feet broad length not being given. The company normally described these larger houses in terms of room numbers, six in each case. Some had chimneys centrally positioned, some at both gable ends. While the chimneys were brick-built, brick otherwise is not mentioned as a construction material. Croddin's map also shows a narrow, probably wooden, bridge crossing the river. What is perhaps most notably absent from the village is a school house. Although the cultural infrastructure of the plantation had been provided for with the building of a grammar school at Derry as early as 1617, no village school building had, as yet, been erected there. Astry, who in 1622 the bishop of Derry, Dr George Downame praised especially as 'a very good scholar and a good preacher' may possibly, have taken some pupils himself. He also had a curate who was 'a preacher and schoolmaster', but he was 'otherwise employed perhaps – speculatively – in the household of Sir Thomas Philips.[93]

Associated with the building of the village had also been a programme of land enclosure in its vicinity. While little is known about it in Ireland at this time, the land enclosure movement was one of the more controversial social changes taking place in post-medieval England. Some advocates of it there saw it as beneficial to both landlord and tenant, with the surveyor John Norden, writing in 1607, arguing that one acre enclosed was worth one and a half in common fields, but to the poor some enclosure represented the abolition of old customary common rights.[94] Behind the harshness of the plantation lay the normal obsession of the reformer be he governor or opponent, to bring about change and standardisation in many areas of life, for example in housing and in agriculture. The latter was expressed initially in terms of implanting the husbandry of the Pale in Ulster. One of the questions commonly put to the companies by the Irish Society concerned what houses they had built and also what enclosures they had carried out and the Fishmongers' reply in 1624 conveyed accurately enough what had been done:

> The several houses before mentioned have several homestalls, gardens and backsides and divers of them have orchards and divers meadows and pastures enclosed with ditches, quicksetts and rails.[95]

The area which can be shown to have been enclosed (see plate 7.3) because Croddin's map of the 'inclosures' survives to reveal it, embraced essentially five townlands: Drummond, Ballykelly, Walworth, (Keenaght), Glasvey and Drumacony, an area of just over 1,000 statute acres. However in part of it some fields were extremely large and are not ascribed to tenants, while some others were designated demesne land. The enclosures on Walworth and Ballykelly, on the other hand, had been designed to provide holdings for householders, all exclusively settler in origin and some of whom became tenants of other land as well. The arrangement of fields between them – seventeen tenancies in all – is represented on plate 7.3. A few of the householders received no land beyond little plots behind them and one house two occupants. In addition, a few houses were built on the common, probably because they had been put up after the allocation of the land had taken place, and were probably occupied by labourers. Clearly, considerable labour both in quicksetting and railing (at one point Downing brought 50,000 lathe nails with him), had been put into work, part of which had involved assarting into the Caman wood. The value of Croddin's map is that it gives a special insight into how a plantation estate had been organised at its village core.

It is impossible to know if further enclosure was carried out, because no other estate maps survive. However, payments by the company to its various agents tail off in the 1620s and this tends to confirm the view expressed by some at the time that if the crown wanted major change in Ulster, it would not be sufficient to leave its implementation to private enterprise. The process whereby the countryside got its present face was, therefore, a protracted one. Indeed after the lease was made to Higgons he was expected to bear all future charges.[96] What he was tied to do was to effect a possessive perimeter bounding of the entire estate: he should 'cause the land to he measured over, butted, bounded, doled or staked out' from all other lands within four years and thereupon deliver 'a true survey in writing' to the company. The convenants into which the freeholders entered in townland grants required them to 'sever and part' these lands for those adjoining with 'good and sufficient fences, hedges and ditches' within a defined time span, leaving adequate passages and rights of way for neighbours.[97] Something of that order was probably built into the tenancy agreements, none of which has been located, made by Higgons and his associate, George Downing, after he had become the company's chief tenant, to the tenants under him.

Who the settler tenantry were might seem an impossible work of detection, yet some impression of them and their backgrounds can be conveyed. Apart from the freeholders, already discussed, some rough categorisations may be suggested. Lawrence Rathborne sprang from a group of civilian traders who had followed the garrisons established at Coleraine and Derry in the later stages of the Nine Years' War. Of a name with a strong Lancashire provenance appearing as merchants and shipowners in the ports of Liverpool and Chester, Lawrence seems to have had links to Coleraine and Sir Thomas Phillips since early in the century. With the spread of the law in early seventeen-century Ireland, legal proceedings, especially in the court of chancery, can be used to cast an albeit wry glance on aspects of people's careers which would otherwise be hidden. Rathborne was a man whose various entrepreneurial activities outstripped his capacity to finance them and perhaps also his probity, though the evidence on that is somewhat one-sided and anyhow such people always had cash-flow difficulties. Some of his early activities are revealed in litigation with William Knee, a Chester merchant: a dispute about an alleged joint adventure in a fishing voyage with two tons of herrings from Killybegs to 'South' Spain and also over the supply of 60,000 slates to Sir Thomas Phillips 'in lieu of a proportion' of pipestaves, i.e. timber cut for the making of containers. Knee also accused him that on hearing of the 'surprisal of the Derry' (by O Doherty in 1608) and 'hearing that the inhabitants thereof were all put to fire and sword', he had sought deviously to acquire possession of a ship and goods of his which were there at the time, while he argued that the ship had been valued at £35, a sum taken account of in his dealings in varied commodities with Knee. Anyhow, he held, he had been obliged later to sell the ship, 'being old and decayed and not fitting, unrepaired, for men to adventure their lives and goods in'. He was, therefore, a businessman of the early plantation, now acquiring the tenancy of land. He may even have used Carrickhugh boat harbour for the bringing in and out of ships and been the originator of a little industrial settlement nearby, the remains of a much later phase of which can be seen on the ground. Such a person as he, furthermore, was unlikely ever to have become a mere full-time tenant farmer. He was likely to have had sub-tenants. When we first get a full glimpse of who actually lived on the land, admittedly as late as 1659, there were seven English and Scots and six Irish in occupation. The land, too, at the start appears to have been used as security to raise money. In later chancery proceedings (about 1632 and thereafter) after Rathborne's death, in which his widow as executrix was involved as complainant, it was argued that he had mortgaged the land to George Downing for £60, which mortgage then came to be passed to Higgons in dealings between them, who in turn passed it to his wife's son John Dransfield. Yet while Higgons and his connection may have viewed Rathborne's separate lease from the company with distaste, the relations between Rathborne and Downing were not permanently strained ones. When in a suit of the 1620s about a debt owed by Rathborne to the Irish agent of John Taylor of Chester, ironmonger, indicating other commercial links, which was at one stage heard before the lord deputy at the council table and which resulted in him being incarcerated in the marshalsea in Dublin, Rathborne persuaded Downing, now 'son-in-law to the lord bishop of Londonderry' (his second wife was a daughter of Dr George Downame) to mediate for his release.[98] A few others who came to live on the estate, such as Eustace Jones, may have sprung also from this pre-plantation stream.

Amongst those who came with the plantation were some who had connections to the Fishmongers' Company or members of it, while others, more tentatively, may have shared the backgrounds in England of those prominent in the management of the estate, such as that in East Anglia of George Downing, Higgons's factor and relative. It is tempting to see Samson Couch or Crouch as a relative of the widow. Crouch living in the parish of St Magnus the Martyr near the Fishmongers' hall, who was receiving a pension from the company in the early 1640s, she having been a 'servant to this company ... in scouring the vessels and pewter and washing and cleansing the rooms at the hall and garden' for more than twenty years. Arthur Breton, a much more prominent figure who was for a time the company's agent, may well have had links to William Angel and may well also have shared the latter's Northamptonshire background, where at any rate the surname was not then uncommon. Richard Glover, a small tenant and villager, was probably a relative to Robert Glover, clerk of the company, though, like Fookes, he probably did not intend to stay permanently. George Askew, present by 1630, had a Leatherseller as well as a Fishmonger connection.[99] However, it must also be remembered that while the Fishmongers' plantation was mainly an English one, a considerable number of Scots moved onto the land as well. Most likely, most of the tenantry were of rural background in both England and Scotland, poorish and engaging in energetic betterment migration, with some probably to be more innovative than others in their new environment.

It is at this point necessary to turn to the two crucial figures in the management of the plantation: James Higgons, the company's farmer and his brother-in-law and factor, George Downing. As has been seen, Higgons was a minor London merchant, living on London Bridge and so close to the Fishmongers' Hall. His background indicates the attractive power of a London growing dramatically in population: he was 'descended of the Higgons in Shropshire near Shrewsbury', where the name was a well-established one. After 1614 he married Thomasine, the widow of Avery Dransfield, a London merchant of only moderate wealth and Yorkshire birth who had been an investor in the Virginia company. George Downing comes to light as a witness to Dransfield's will in 1614 and as his brother-in-law: his two children, Anne and Thomasine Downing each received bequests of £5. Downing's own background, like that of his wife and her sister, was in Norfolk, both being of families with members who had also been drawn to London. He has been taken, it seems correctly, to have been of the family of Downing of Lexham (between King's Lynn and Norwich) which intermarried with the neighbouring family of Calybute and which had a connection with Hackney in London, where the famous divine and author the Rev. Dr Calybute Downing was to be vicar from the 1630s, since at least *c.* 1600. It seems likely that George was a cousin of Dr Calybute Downing. It was in Hackney that he married his wife Jane Ruckwood (or Rockwood) in 1610. Her father, Edmund Rockwood of Weston-Longville, also in Norfolk but nearer to Norwich, had married a Londoner (also Thomasine) in 1577. George Downing has been taken also to have been the son of John Downing who came to Ireland as an army lieutenant during the Nine Years' War. Closer links than appear justified between these Norfolk Downings and the Suffolk family of the same name, who were, however, in some way related since they bore somewhat similar coats of arms, have been claimed by family historians writing one hundred years ago. One of those had Emmanuel Downing (father of Downing of Downing St), associate and brother-in-law of John Winthrop in establishing the Massachusetts Bay colony in America from 1629, and Calybute Downing as brothers. The connection, however, is not as close as that. Yet some of these Suffolk Downings (and indeed the Winthrops too) had also been in Ireland in the early seventeenth century, where Emmanuel, later a lawyer in London and well connected with a brother Joshua (d. 1630) a naval administrator, had found his first wife, a daughter of a Dublin government official, Sir James Ware. A fuller link between them is possible but conjectural: Richard Kirby who was prominent in the Ballykelly colony from the 1620s may well have been a relative of Francis Kirby (d. 1661), a London merchant and trading partner with the Downings and Winthrops in America in the 1630s and husband of Emmanuel's sister, Susan.[100]

If these connections are correct ones, they evoke neatly the interlocking paths along which English expansion, itself belatedly catching up on Spanish imperial precedent and so much a feature of this period, was progressing. It also tended to have a religious dimension. Many of these people were of a puritan cast of mind. The mentality of such people led them to the view that English Protestantism, which they genuinely thought was under renewed threat of repression especially with the outbreak of the Thirty Years War, was best protected by expanding it: into Ireland and into America. Thus their own individual economic self-advancement could be endowed with a cloak of religious principle.

However, if, as suggested earlier, the company may have chosen Higgons as farmer in preference to other suiters because he was based nearby in London and so could be got to pay his rent, this turned out not to be the full explanation. The rent fell into arrears. Gradually the company became aware that William Angel and John Halsey, two of its leading members, had formed an arrangement with Higgons for running of the estate. This came to light first in 1622 when the company was pressed by the Irish Society to provide arms to be used in the training of the tenantry as a militia (or just for their defence) or to be deposited in Ballykelly. Although Higgons was tied in his lease to bear such expenditure, Angel and Halsey sought to persuade the company, in November, to provide 'twenty serviceable armours furnished and twenty muskets, bastard muskets and calivers furnished and ... one barrel of powder'.[101] One year later the wardens brought before a meeting of the court of assistants the fact that the rent was one and a half years in arrears and while both Angel and Halsey protested that they had been to considerable personal expense, the company requested to see the assignments that had been made by Higgons. A fortnight later the matter came up for fuller discussion at a meeting which became in part acrimonious with one member accusing Angel in particular of procuring the lease for Higgons in an irregular fashion, but eventually a resolution was reached, though it proved, however, to be only a temporary one. The company agreed that in present circumstances the matter lay 'too heavy' on Angel and Halsey, and it was agreed that if the arrears were paid in instalments, the rent would be reduced by £50 a year.[102] In truth, it may well have been difficult for tenants in so early a stage of a plantation to pay rents.

Problems and difficulties

For a time the rent was paid, but the matter came to a crisis again in 1627 and 1628. The possibility that the company might 're-enter' on Higgons's lease and forfeit it was considered at a meeting in June 1627 and a thorough investigation began when a special committee of the company, with Angel and Halsey in attendance, was assembled at the end of January. Bargaining ensued. Angel and Halsey protested that the reason for the arrears (two and a half years) lay with the 'ill dealing' with them of their tenants in Ireland. If the company would evict Higgons and make them a new lease at £100 per year, then they would, in turn, pay the arrears due. The committee insisted, however, on the company's behalf that although it would give them its support in Higgons's eviction, it would bear none of the costs of the suit, and that it would only agree to the recently modified rent of £117.[103] Eventually, after many debates at meetings of the court of assistants in the spring and early summer, with on one occasion the suggestion being made that legal action should be taken against Angel and Halsey too, agreement was reached. Since now – in June – both were willing to 'settle and compose this business in peace' to 'preserve the unity of the house' and since a lawsuit against them 'being ancients and eminent members of this company' would 'occasion much heart burning and discontent' within it, arrangements were made, on which legal advice was taken, whereby they surrendered all their interest in the estate and all documents surrounding it.[104]

Angel, who died in 1629, and Halsey were both by now prosperous London merchants. Born in Northamptonshire and therefore a new London merchant, Angel, sometimes in association with Halsey, had been involved in numerous overseas shipping and trading ventures since about the turn of the century as well as being an investor in a number of the new English overseas companies. He had been able to purchase the office of sergeant of the accatory to the king – he was the king's fishmonger – for £1,500, as well as the gentleman portership of Windsor Castle and he had his house in the parish of St Thomas the Apostle.[105] Halsey, of the parish of St Mary Magdalen in Old Fish St, (near St Paul's), who died in 1633, had had a similar career.[106] Their involvement with James Higgons both as backers and hopeful beneficiaries was formalised in deeds of 10 March 1619: Higgons conveyed to each one-third of the lease, they to pay one-third of the rent to the company and, in return for bearing one-third of all necessary expenses, to receive one-third of the rents.[107] Further conveyances had been made by Angel and Halsey to Henry Rockwood of London in 1621.[108] Then in 1626, their arrangement with Higgons having become unrewarding, Angel and Halsey had found a new person with whom to do business in Ireland: Christopher Freeman. A relation of John Freeman from Essex who was farmer of the Goldsmiths' estate centred on New Buildings and who may well have been a relative of some of the major London merchants of the same surname, and himself at this time living in Derry, Christopher Freeman took on leases from both, for thirty years, of their third parts, to pay each an annual rent of £80 stg.[109] It was all these arrangements which were surrendered to the company by Angel and Halsey in June 1628.[110]

These financial problems were not, however, entirely surprising because the 1620s were, growingly, a time of economic difficulty. The latter part of the decade was also a time of serious military uncertainty occasioned by the new Anglo-Spanish war of 1625–30. During the course of it, Owen Roe O Neill, nephew of Hugh O Neill, earl of Tyrone and the Franciscan archbishop and intellectual, Florence Conry who had played a major part in formulating the thinking of the Ulster Gaelic nobility since the Nine Years' War in their relations with Spain, and both now in the Spanish Netherlands, sought Spanish backing for an invasion plan for Ireland. Their aim initially was to land at Killybegs and Derry, where they thought the new town built by the Londoners was sufficiently large and strong to be occupied as a base. Although they had doubts about how the old English of Ireland might respond they hoped that their actions would initiate a more widespread *coup d'état* to be led by the native nobility and gentry elsewhere in Ireland. Had it succeeded, a new form of government for Ireland would have arisen which would have made Ireland a Spanish protectorate rather than a kingdom of the English crown.[111]

Their scheme, if successful, would also have effectively ended the plantation in Ulster as well as, more broadly, probably making Ireland a base from which English trans-Atlantic ambitions could be impeded. It would seem to be an indication, however, of how much the balance of power in the world between England and Spain had been altering since the days of the Armada and Kinsale that, unfortunately for them, the Spaniards did not now back their proposal. The Dublin government also sought to take pre-emptive action. The exercise of authority in Ulster which in civilian terms had rested with the justices of the peace (mainly, though not exclusively, of settler composition) and the sheriffs of the counties and also with the judges of assize, was greatly enhanced by the increase of garrison troops. The Fishmongers' Company was informed by Robert Goodwin, then in London, in July 1627 that, 'fearing an invasion in the north parts of Ireland', order had been taken for the increasing of the garrison at Londonderry from 50 foot and 25 horse to double that number. For supplying them, he said the lord deputy was demanding a loan to be imposed on the city's plantation, and were it not to be paid he would 'lay' some soldiers on each estate 'to eat it out upon the land', and he told them that there were soldiers at that time on the company's manor of Walworth.[112] The Londoners' performance in the entire Londonderry plantation came more under scrutiny too in these years and thereafter, leading eventually to the confiscation of the plantation from them by the crown in the later 1630s.

However, having brought Angel and Halsey to surrender their leases the company, which had decided also to repay the contributions made by members at an early stage to the plantation fund,[113] was determined to evict James Higgons and there were now those amongst its membership, more so than at the beginning of the plantation, who were willing to take part in this and offer alternatives. Two proposals were in fact brought forward in June and July 1628, the one by Hamlet Clarke, now a warden of the company and a longstanding member, and the other by Robert Charleton, now moving up in its affairs as an 'assistant'. Along with his other business interests, Charleton, who lived in Mincing Lane and was on his way to considerable wealth, was a trader in French wines who just at this time was engaged with others in a scheme, later abortive, for trade and perhaps colonisation in Canada.[114] Clarke suggested that his son-in-law William Lathum, a lawyer then living in Derry and one of those new professionals which the plantation had come to include, be employed to conduct the suit against Higgons, for which he thought £100 or more should be set aside by the company, on the expectation that he, with Clarke as his backer, should then receive a lease of the land. Charleton offered to bear legal costs himself in hope that he be considered for the new lease. The company having decided to make no lease until Higgons was evicted and not wishing to be detained from its customary summer break from meetings, agreed, it having been 'put to counters' – they took a vote – to entrust the conduct of the litigation to Charleton.[115]

Yet Higgons was to extricate himself partly from his predicament: he eventually received a new lease of one-third of the estate. While he initiated litigation in chancery in England and, seemingly, in Ireland too, the company, through Charleton's agency, appointed George Cary, recorder of Derry, another lawyer of the plantation, to collect the rents and conduct the legal proceedings in Ireland, both in chancery and at the assizes. The detail of all this runs through the company's minutes, as well as of numerous appearances made by Higgons before it, in the ensuing years. Gradually, since Christopher Freeman was also pressing his case to be confirmed as tenant of the two-thirds he had held under Angel and Halsey, the company came to accept the status quo, to the manifest distaste of Charleton whose aim may well have been to use a footing in north-west Ireland not only as a source of personal profit but as a staging post in his Canada project. A court of assistants on 19 November 1630, 'called chiefly to confer about the Irish business', discussed the matter and another, a few days later, decided to appoint a committee to negotiate with Higgons. It was calculated that he owed £278.6.8 (or five years rent) of which Cary had stated that he had received £117.6.4. If all arrears were paid within six months, they would grant him a new lease for forty-one years (or less than the forty-six which were to come on the old) at £55.13.4, one-third of the original £167, per annum.[116] It was to be some time, however, and only after many further appearances by him before the company, on one of which in September 1631 he formally withdrew his lawsuit and all complaints against it,[117] before the lease was actually granted to Higgons. Although in the meantime (in January 1633) he was given the freehold grant of Feeny townland, always called Neffeene ('in the ballibettoe ... called Ballimullan') in the documentation, on the persuasion of John Halsey, which was intended for his son, also James, Halsey's godson then under age,[118] he had to wait until July of that year before the lease was finally issued, when he was given four years to pay in instalments arrears of £80 then due.[119] For his part, Christopher Freeman, protesting that he had paid two-third parts of £200 levied for the upkeep of the soldiers while they had been in place and being only £50 in arrears, was granted a new lease by the company in January 1631 to run for thirty-one years at the same rent, £160 stg, which had been in his agreement with Angel and Halsey.[120]

From the company's point of view those new leases might seem to herald a new departure. Yet soon for it too, as will be seen, a new crisis loomed: the mid 1630s were to be in many ways a turning in the plantation. On paper, however, it had increased its rent from the original £167 (to which should be added Rathborne's £8, though it had been paid to Higgons) which had been reduced to £117, to now £215.13.4. They had also found a mechanism (though it was not to be exclusively followed) for the transmission of these sums to England. The rents were to be paid by bills of exchange through those, Abraham Chamberlain and his agent Mansfield

Tucker, both themselves members of London mercantile families with widespread interests, who were renters of the fisheries from the Irish Society.[121] Briefly too the company had got a dividend, drawn from the profits of those fisheries on the large sums of money it had put, at the beginning, into the Irish Society. It received dividends of £80 in 1624 and at the end of 1626; and it emerged later that the quit rent or government tax of £17 per annum was being paid from that source.[122] Its expenses, however, had also been considerable. In 1632 it paid £100 to Robert Charleton to defray his costs in the litigation, he protesting that he would have preferred a lease of the land, and it allowed Carey a fee of £40.[123] In addition, Edward Waterhouse, a member of the company who lived in Dublin, claimed that he, on the soliciting of Charleton, had overseen the conduct of the suit against Higgons there, and after much discussion, in October 1633, it was decided to give him £20.[124] Earlier, the clerk of the company had been given a gratuity of £5 for his extra writing obligations.[125] The company also made a contribution, on demand from the treasurer of the Irish Society, William Spurstow, in 1632 towards lead and glass for the cathedral then being built in Derry on which it was told £3,000 had already been spent, and again in 1635 for that and for the legal expenses of the Irish Society at that time.[126]

Not surprisingly, the relations of Freeman, the newcomer who moved to live at Ballykelly, and Higgons were not good and the company was plied with complaints by one against the other.[127] Both also were tending to fall into arrears, while Freeman applied to the company for a supply of arms (which he did not get), arising from the fact that a muster had been ordered for the training of a militia at which only half of his followers, 20 out of 42, had appeared with arms of any kind.[128] The essence of the dispute between Higgons and Freeman concerned the division of the land between them and characteristically of an age in which disputes were increasingly solved by litigation and in which the legal profession was growing, litigation arose between them. The burden of Freeman's complaint, which he brought before chancery, was that in proceedings under a writ of partition,[129] unfair influence had been exercised by Higgons through his connection – Downing, Richard Kirby who was sheriff, and others: Ralph Mattocks, Ralph Phillips and Mark Greene. He sought to be awarded the rents of some lands near Ballykelly and he argued to the company, in March 1634, that while Higgons's portion had been allotted near the town (Ballykelly), his had been 'on the mountains'.[130] It is clear that the settlers, then, were not some harmonious, cooperating community. In December (1634) when the company received a letter of 28 October from Freeman enclosing a bill of exchange of £60 and the promise of another £60 payment later, it sought to reconcile their differences: if Higgons and Freeman would come to London in the springtime 'the house' would 'endeavour to make an end thereof between them'.[131]

But unknown to the company, Higgons had died at Ballykelly one month earlier, though not without heirs, while Freeman was to die sometime afterwards, drowned, it was said later by his descendants, on a voyage from England.[132] Higgons, who was buried, next to his wife, within the church in Ballykelly – a symbol of his status – had not died a rich man. His will throws light on his circumstances and connections. The land he held was to be divided, following London practice, between his son and executor James then in England,[133] who should get half, and his two daughters Frances and Jane (the eldest, also Thomasine, being now dead) who should receive the other half in equal shares. He appointed a large group of eleven 'very good friends' to be overseers, which included Downing and the Rev. Luke Astry, Robert Goodwin, Jerome Alexander (who was a lawyer), Richard Kirby, Peter Gates and Arthur Breton, who were three long-standing residents on the estate, and Henry Rockwood and his cousin Reginold Stevens, who were probably in London. To his four Dransfield step-children, one of whom, John, had already come over and was establishing himself as Higgons's assistant and otherwise, he left £25 stg each 'in token of my love to them … in memory of' their mother and for the 'preservation of quietness, peace and mutual amity' between his own children and them. Dransfield and William Downes (who was Rathborne's successor) were to receive all rents and have custody of his goods and cattle to the use of his son and have £5 each for their pains. All his other bequests, some £14 in total, were small ones ranging from 6s.8d. (apart from 1s. to a nephew) to £2 and including 10s. to his servant Joan and £2 to Ballykelly church. Amongst them were bequests of 6s.8d. to each of the overseers and two of their wives to buy them a ring with a 'death's head', which was a mortality symbol expressive of the 'melancholy' of the age. Links and friendships were also revealed with some of the mercantile element in Derry (where Downing had a house): two of the witnesses of his will were Thomas Ince and Toby Smith, both merchants there.[134]

Crown confiscation

In an action which reveals something of the 'personal rule' of Charles I and the financial exigencies of his regime, the city of London authorities and the Irish Society were brought for trial before the star chamber court in London early in 1635 accused of grave failings in the promotion of the plantation.[135] Their entire title to the land of Londonderry plantation was forfeited to the crown and they were severely fined. For the Fishmongers, as for the other companies, this meant the forfeiture of the land. The company, earlier called upon for money to defend the suit, was ordered by the attorney general in March to surrender the estate.[136] It received a promise of payment of £80 from Christopher Freeman the younger in 1636, but otherwise the rents now remained in abeyance while a major government discussion took place as to how the plantation should in future be conducted, and in late 1638 the company, on a precept from the mayor to do so, paid £496 to the city authorities as its part of the £12,000 to which the original fine of £70,000 in the star chamber had been reduced.[137]

Eventually in 1639 a body of commissioners was appointed in London to release the lands.[138] At about the same time a group of seven surveyors or cartographers, one of whom, Nicholas Lane, was an accomplished mapmaker from near London,[139] was appointed 'surveyors of Londonderry' and were later to receive a payment of over £1,000 for their work.[140] The outcome was that the lands were re-leased for twenty-one years at greatly increased rents, which in the case of the freeholds meant a trebling of the existing figure. While there may possibly have been some new tenants, generally what happened was that the estates were divided between the farmers (in the case of the Fishmongers' estate, Higgons's and Freeman's successors) and their previous principal undertenants, now also holding their leases directly from the crown.[141]

It is possible to reconstruct, reasonably completely, who these tenants were for the former Fishmongers' estate from the accounts of the receivers of the rents in *c.* 1640.[142] This is therefore the first rental of the land to become available. Equally, it is not possible to establish fully from such a source who actually lived on the land, as their sub-tenants or in other capacities. The total rent now payable contrasts dramatically with the company's previous rent of £215.13.4: it was £565.6.4. But since it was now directly rented by the crown, for it the change would be a major one, since this figure replaced the old quit rent of £17. James Higgons the younger, who retained the 'capital messuage', i.e. the bawn and manor house, retained also 1,596 acres and 3 roods of land, which shows that the surveyors had been at work in that area, at a rent of £46 and, with his wife Mary, a daughter of George Downing's, jointly, the Feeny freehold. For his part, Christopher Freeman became the largest tenant, retaining twelve townlands as well as the right (at £4 a year) to hold the manor courts. The holdings of George Downing, the third of these principal figures, were more complex. They included a house (a possible ancestor of Rush Hall or one still in Ballykelly village) and two rather rich townlands north of the road from Ballykelly to Limavady now leased at a rent which can be calculated to have been as high as 2s. per statute acre; a house and small area held in partnership with Henry Finch, a Derry merchant; and also an area of land measured then to 560 acres held jointly with the Rev. Luke Astry and Arthur Breton.

The twenty-nine tenants listed were those who had paid rent and since they did not include the entire group of six freeholders, there were in fact close to thirty-five now in all. For the core settlement around Ballykelly, there were now just ten tenancies accounted for, or less than those recorded by Croddin in 1623, which shows that some of those, for example Fookes's which had been transient or nominal, had been acquired by some of the greater men, their occupants paying rent to them. The two bigger holders in this area now were Richard Kirby and Arthur Breton, both longstanding associates of Higgons and Downing. But Breton also held land further out, which shows that some tenants on the estate continued to live in the original village. One such had extended his grasp yet further: Peter Gates had also acquired a lease of land about seven miles away on the Haberdashers' Company estate.[143] Some in the village just held houses or cottages and small areas including gardens as direct tenants, such as John Carter, who went back a long time, and John Dowdale, who may even have been palesman, who first comes to light at this time. The remaining tenants who included seven Irish tenantry who will be discussed below, generally now held groups of townlands and were therefore very substantial figures. They were mainly English, but a few were Scots.

The principal historical value of this information lies in the light it throws on how the estate had been disposed of up to now, because all was to be disrupted shortly by the rising of 1641. The immediate precipitant of that rising had been the growing challenges to the king's regime both in Scotland and in England. When, as a result of these pressures, the long parliament in England had been summoned and met on 3 November 1640, the treatment of the Londoners over the plantation came to be one of the matters raised there. Indeed as early as 12 November, Isaac Pennington, MP, who was to become a leading opponent of the king during the English civil war and was a warden of the Fishmongers' Company, urged the company to consider what actions it should take.[144] Also the recent drastic increases in rents under the crown now as landlord may have had the effect of alienating some of the settlers on the ground from the monarchy, to predispose them towards its opponents as the issues in the English civil war came to impact on the settlers in Ireland. However, it was only after the defeat and execution of the king in England in 1649 and then the defeat of the attempted Irish counter-revolution of the 1640s by the republican regime which succeeded the king, that the Irish Society and the companies under it were restored and the plantation on the ground was revived to enter a new phase. They were restored formally by patent by that regime in March 1657 and again, with the restoration of the monarchy, by Charles II's regime in April 1662, thereby cancelling the experiment in direct management of the later 1630s.

The native Irish, the plantation and religion: the Fishmongers' estate

It may not be amiss to say at the outset that the plantation was not in the interest of the native Irish population, even though the king promoted it as something that would end the internecine strife of the chieftains and bring about a new ordered, transformed and prosperous society. Ulster was not some empty new found land on which the rural, and indeed urban, order first of the English Pale and then of southern England itself was to be superimposed. Although not the plantation in Irish history, the plantation in Ulster had been decided on in the aftermath of the Flight of the Earls, out of a mix of considerations: fear that the earls would be returned with a consequent new Spanish intervention in Ireland which would threaten England, combined with a determination to take full advantage of their departure. Not only was it to be, in effect, a security measure, it was also to be an economy measure: the new settlers would pay taxes and would also be the means whereby the English system of local administration – county government – would be extended into Ulster. In short, it was also a centralising measure, unifying Ulster with the rest of Ireland under one system of law and administration to the exclusion of the 'independent' power there of the former Gaelic lords.

In the theory of the plantation the lands held by the companies in this county, equivalent to those granted to the undertaker category in the other five (though taking up a higher proportion of the land) were to be settled exclusively with British tenantry (English or Lowland Scots), the Irish occupiers who lived there to move and resettle under any of the other types of grantee including the Irish ones. In practice this did not prove practicable and it is how that had worked out on this estate prior to 1641 that must now be investigated. What in fact happened is that the company and then the settlers became a kind of layer superimposed in varying ways (sometimes from a distance like the freeholders in the southern part of the estate) for the most part on top of the native Irish.

For a time government persisted with threats to the companies that the Irish must be removed. Thus in April 1620, only a short time after Higgons's lease had been made, John Halsey brought to the company's attention information he had got 'by letters sent him out of Ireland', that a warrant had been received from the lord deputy in Dublin for removing the Irish from the companies' estates. Were this to happen, he said, 'the tenants cannot pay their rents' which would 'redound to all companies' general hurt and loss', and he urged it to join with the others in an approach to the Irish Society to have the warrant lifted.[145] What did happen was that fines were imposed for the Irish to remain on. When in November 1623 Angel and Halsey were questioned by the company about the arrears that had been run up, amongst the points they made in extenuation was one referring to 'the yearly great imposition laid upon them for continuance of the Irish'.[146] The company in its response to a questionnaire from the Irish Society in early 1631, which is part of the background to the star chamber trial, claimed that over five years 'near' to £265 had been paid in these fines.[147] Otherwise its normal response was that whatever tenancies the Irish had, derived, not from it, but from its farmer or chief tenant.[148] It is the principal ones of these tenancies that come to light when the crown took the land into its own hands in 1639 and carried out the releasing of it. However from a yet later source, otherwise beyond the scope of this chapter, it will be possible to give a brief more over-all picture of the position of the Irish on the estate.

The group of Irish leaseholders, some seven in all, revealed c. 1640, derived from great landed families at the upper levels of the previous Gaelic society: two O Harrans, three O Mullans, one O Cahan and one MacCloskey. A principal location of the O Mullans as landholders in the O Cahan lordship, itself claimed by the O Neills as a vassal lordship, was in the ballybetagh of Ballymullan, a region south-west of Feeny, part of which was restored to two O Mullans under the plantation and part of which was given to the Fishmongers' Company, but another branch would seem to have been located further north in the Greysteel area, reflected perhaps in the place name recorded as Glasse Mullin, also in the company's holding. Edmund Duffe O Mullan, the only Irish landholder to now hold a lease directly under the crown in the northern part of the estate – a townland in the Greysteel area – may well have been a son of the Patrick O Mullan who had been a witness to the formal transfer of possession on 18 March 1618.[149] The other Mullans, Shane Rowe and Murtagh, the latter jointly with an Edmund O Cahan, held townlands, presumably in the general area where they had always lived, in the southern part of the estate. Arthur' MacCloskey also held one townland.

The other leading family to hold land on a parity with the principal settler leaseholders was the O Harrans. Their area of influence in the former Gaelic order, reflected in such place names as Straidarron and Ballyrory, neighboured on that of the O Mullans. Two of them, Aughy O Harran and Rory O Harran, were leaseholders of a substantial area of land – between Claudy and Feeny – in this general area. Some years earlier, before the crown confiscation and while the company still had its two farmers or chief tenants, Higgons and Freeman, Rory O Harran and, probably, the O Mullan chieftain became involved in the controversy between them about which land each should hold. Freeman, whose share had then included much of this area, resented the fact that the company had made the freehold grant of Feeny townland to Higgons in January 1633 and Higgons in a letter to the company in March 1634 protested about what he considered the ill-dealing about land and land boundaries, to his disadvantage, in this area by Freeman. He argued that Freeman with the help of Rory O Harran, who had been undertenant of Feeny, was seeking to absorb some of the land involved, and, with regard to a bigger area of land nearby (including Drumcovett) had also entered into collusion with 'an old Irish chief formerly owner of this land and others adjoining' (who was therefore probably an O Mullan), to make statements about boundaries which disadvantaged him.[150] Rory O Harran proved in fact to be a great survivor. He was stated to be living in the late 1650s on Ballyrory, which was Skipton's freehold, and made a statement before the mayor of Londonderry in, 1669 confirming Skipton's title to it.[151] In the early 1640s, during the rising, he had, according to a Franciscan account, operated as a 'plunderer', a freelance figure acting arbitrarily in acts of destruction and depredation in opposition to the leadership of the rising.[152] He became a figure of legend in his own area and John O'Donovan, the Gaelic scholar who worked for the Ordnance Survey in the 1830s, recorded stories about him, which he thought, 'wild' though they were, might contain a 'great deal of truth'. One concerned the 'tribute' – rent in kind, in methers of butter – which he took from those under him. This had been stored in a house in a known location which had been set fire to by those who deemed his exactions too high. One held, plausibly enough, that he may have been a justice of the peace. Another concerning his death might well throw light on the conflicts that arose between neighbouring gentry in the old Gaelic order. When, it was told, in old age his horse got bogged down as he travelled, he was rescued by a young man who was at hand. However, when he told his rescuer, who was an O Mullan, that in the past he had hanged many of his family on a tree nearby, the rescuer killed him 'in the very slough out of which he had saved his horse'.[153]

The fate of the Irish under the plantation on the estate overall can be established in very general terms, but only at c. 1659 when the so-called *Census* enumerated either occupants of the land or those subject to a tax, distinguishing between English and Scots on the one hand and Irish on the other, but by then settlers were more numerous than prior to 1641. On the northern sections of the estate, above Loughermore, which was approximately half of it, these two categories now existed in roughly equal numbers. Even at Ballykelly, which then represented the village and the area towards Caman wood (much of the original plantation core), both categories were found: 42 English and Scots and 30 Irish are recorded. On the southern half of the estate the situation then was the reverse. All the land there was in Irish occupation except for four English and Scots who, with four Irish, lived in Drumcovett.[154] This re-inforces the view of the 1622 commissioners that the estate had only been partially planted. They had found 23 settlers and 243 Irish and argued that it were 'fit there were another plantation into the land ... for the better defence of the inhabitants thereof who are daily spoiled'.[155] As a result of the confiscation, then, the Irish on the accessible northern part, which had been planted, had been reduced in circumstances, while those on the remoter southern part had remained in occupation, but subject to rents, which Freeman was to plead in the early 1630s they were reluctant to pay.[156] The precise tenurial circumstances of any of these Irish are not revealed by this c. 1659 'census'. However, since the estate was restored to the company in these years and it in turn leased it again, in the 1660s, to one farmer or middleman a pattern of descending tenancies, under him, somewhat similar to which the leases of 1639 throw some light on, was probably recreated. Thus the farmer will most likely have had a relatively small body of large undertenants forming, with the freeholders, a gentry class which, probably still included a small element of upper-level Irish (such a Rory O Harran), under whom again the various farmers and occupiers of the land, many of them Irish, will have held sub-tenancies, sometimes possibly only on a year to year basis. How all that worked out for the future is for a historian of the ensuing period, when sources, too, become more numerous, to investigate.

If the severity of the plantation was then mitigated in its practice, so also its effects in matters of religion diverged from what may have been expected. By 1600 or so the religio-political climate in Europe had become one in which it was increasingly felt by rulers, themselves engaged in many ways in tightening their control, that conformity to their preferred version of Christianity was a necessary test of loyalty and identity: the era of the confessional state. The maxim of the French monarchy, now Catholic in the outcome of the French wars of religion – one king, one law, one church – encapsulated it. Rulers strove to ensure conformity or to penalise, often very harshly, those refusing to conform, and religious toleration, or liberty of conscience, was only grudgingly conceded. It was unfortunate for the great majority in Ireland, where the reformation had made little headway, that a disjunction had arisen between a Protestant king and a largely Catholic population. Only with plantation was a Protestant episcopate

Plate 7.9 A flanker of Walworth bawn as of 1996

effectively established in Ulster: in Derry diocese Protestant clergy often, like Luke Astry, nominated by the Londoners, arrived with it. Yet even in Ulster, Protestantism failed to gain a monopoly of religion. While some few indeed of the native Irish there adopted it (an increment of what remains to this day, a native Irish element among Ulster Protestants),[157] the most striking fact to emerge in the plantation period was the continuity of Catholicism amongst the native Irish population. In 1632, as the star chamber case against the Londoners was beginning, Sir Thomas Phillips (d. 1636) brought forward a list of priests living in Derry diocese, some of them tenants of land. Their presence would be objectionable to him on religious grounds because he, too, would want only one church, and also on political ones. He would see them also, just in the aftermath of the most recent Anglo-Spanish war, rightly or wrongly, as opinion-formers on the ground, pro-Spain and alteration, occupying key positions just at the place where religion and politics interacted. He even argued that they were a *de facto* toleration from the secular authorities, suggesting that the sheriff of the county, Richard Kirby, had allowed suits involving priests to be heard in his sheriff's court.[158] On these grounds, then, the plantation had not brought about the religious change that was thought might follow from it. Rather, in religion, a two-culture society – to be (despite numerous other acculturations) one of the great determinants of the ensuing course of Ulster history – was emerging from it.

Phillips recorded the names of the priests in the four parishes within which parts of the estate lay. Vicar O Lynne of Tamlaght Finlagan (of an errenach family) was probably Fr Dermot O Lynn, who, then of Tamlaghtard, had been described just after the end of the Nine Years' War as 'speaking Irish, Latin and English' and 'guileless and able'. Owen O Cosseglen, priest of Faughanvale, an apparent scrivener's error, was most likely Eugene or Eoghan McCloskey, a similar figure of continuity, vicar there at the end of the Nine Years' War.[159] On the southern part of the estate there were Fr Neice O Devenny of Bannagher and Fr Donnoghie (or Donnogh) O Cahan of Cumber. Phillips also stated that nine 'mass houses' had been erected on the companies lands: one on the Fishmongers' and another on the Grocers', 'near one another'. Where these were or what they looked like can only be guessed at. It would be a symbol of the continuity of Catholicism in one place, if that on the estate could be shown to have been on the site occupied by the present 'Hollow Church' (St Finlogh's), on the outskirts of Ballykelly. However, since the Grocers' estate was to the west, a site elsewhere has to be found, possibly on the land – Gortgarr – held by Edmund Duffe O Mullan.

The Fishmongers' estate and the outbreak of the rising in 1641

While little is known about the outbreak of the rising in this area, the most crucial fact surrounding it is that its leaders failed to capture Derry. It would seem, though, that with the rising, here, as elsewhere, many of the settlers fled, some were killed and some – of the men – were recruited into new army companies under royal commission. The bawn and settlement at Ballykelly was probably abandoned, at an early stage with many seeking refuge in other places or escaping to England and Scotland. Only one statement or deposition by any of the settlers on this estate, setting out his version of events in 1641, that of Peter Gates of Drumgavenny, seven miles from Ballykelly, made in Dublin in 1643, survives. He claimed that his house on Drumgavenny had been burned late in November and that at the same time 'one James Farrell' [*Recte* Farren?] of Ballykelly and his associates had killed a group of five English who had remained there and in some cases members of their families. Most, at any rate, had names recognisable from other sources. He also particularised Shane Rowe O Mullan, leaseholder in Foreglen, as amongst those supporting the rising.[160]

For its part, the Fishmongers' Company on an approach from London's mayor seeking 'a cheerful and ready contribution towards the relief and succour of the distressed Protestants of Londonderry in Ireland' agreed on 31 January 1642 to contribute 100 quarters of wheat or £150 in money. When, later, in March, the company was requested, again by the mayor, to enlarge its contribution for the relief of Londonderry 'by providing one or more pieces of artillery for the said city', it agreed to make available a demi-culverin.[161]

When the commanders of some of the forces that had been assembled, notably those in Derry and Culmore and in Donegal, mounted a counter-offensive in 1642, one of their actions was to march early in May to Coleraine, which was then close to surrender. On their way, they relieved the Phillips stronghold near Limavady and the castle at Ballycastle near Aghanloo, in which many refugees were hemmed up.[162] But no mention is made of Ballykelly, where the house within the bawn may well have been damaged, fired or occupied much before this time (plate 7.9). Although for a time in 1645 a section of Major General Robert Munro's army, which had arrived in east Ulster from Scotland in April 1642, was placed at Ballykelly,[163] in the main the principal engagements in the decade of warfare after 1641 were elsewhere. Yet the effects of this first year of war – of rebellion and response – on the area (the inevitable consequence of warfare) were to be noted much later on: there was 'little of eminency or note' to be seen in the countryside, 'it being totally destroyed and laid waste in the first year of the wars'.[164] What happened, however, in this locality in the long period between 1642 and when Owen Roe O Neill made Ballykelly his base in the summer of 1649 and then up to the Cromwellian re-conquest which followed and which re-instated the plantation, may never be recoverable in full detail.[165]

What it is more certain is the fate of some of the principal settlers on the estate. A number of these died within Derry, where conditions due to over-crowding, food shortages or plague must have been deplorable, between May and July 1642. Christopher Freeman of Ballykelly was buried on 18 May while the Rev. Luke Astry and his wife Anne were both buried on 24 May. James Higgons was buried on 5 July, one of his daughters, Jane having died in June. Arthur Breton was buried there on 12 July. Edward Warren, freeholder, died, later, in February 1643 but his wife died in the previous May, while Robert Goodwin's wife had died in October.[166] On the other hand, Robert Thornton (d. 1662), also a freeholder and Henry Finch, Downing's merchant associate, became captains of two of the new companies which had been assembled to counter the rising.[167] George Downing, however, was long lived. As a secondary figure, he must content himself to be a tenant under the new middleman, Randal Beresford, to whom the company leased the estate in the early 1660s.[168] In fact he died about that time and his widow turned up in London in May 1664 to ask the company to intercede with Beresford on her behalf, since she and her late husband had dwelt in Ireland for fifty years.[169] They had both, then, been figures of continuity in a plantation which was now proving to have been one of the most momentous happenings in Ulster history. The cultural evolution of that plantation, with an intelligentsia – clergy, teachers, lawyers, architects – was still, however, only at an infant stage, while its impact on the native population, in for example, the spread of the English language and its literature[170] or of housing types, had only just begun.

Acknowledgement

I am very grateful to Joanne Taggart for her kindness and skill in producing the typescript of this chapter and to the Deputy Keeper of PRONI and to the Fishmongers' Company of London for permission to reproduce illustration in their possession.

---

[1] T.W. Moody, *The London plantation 1609–42: the city of London and the plantation in Ulster* (Belfast, 1939), p. 445.

[2] Guildhall Library, London MS 5570/1, p. 547; /2, p. 5. These manuscripts will hereafter be cited by volume number and page only.

[3] /1, p. 558.

[4] On the Nine Years' War, War see Hiram Morgan, *Tyrone's rebellion: the outbreak of the Nine Years' War in Tudor Ireland* (Dublin, 1993). For some account of what O Neill and O Donnell sought from Spain and the papacy after the Flight of the Earls see ch. 2, pp 11–45.

[5] /1, pp 547, 549–50.

[6] /2, pp 5–6.

[7] For a full account see Moody, *Londonderry plantation*, passim.

[8] /1, pp 558.

[9] Ibid., p. 559.

[10] Ibid., p. 560.

[11] Ibid., pp 561–2.

[12] Moody, *Londonderry plantation*, pp 75–83, 122–38, 270.

[13] /1, pp 573, 606–11. The total amount assessed seems in fact to have been £1,086.

[14] /2, pp 2–5.

[15] Ibid., pp 6–8, 10–11.

[16] Moody, *Londonderry plantation*, pp 143–56.

[17] Ibid., pp 442–5.

[18] /2, p. 102.

[19] Ibid., pp 100–1, 132, 207, 208–10, 215, 226, 227.

[20] Walworth's tomb was in the parish church of St Michael, Crooked Lane in London close to the Fishmongers' Hall and in April 1609 they appointed a committee to consider whether it needed any 'amendment' (/1, p. 549). In 1636 they decided to have it 'trimmed and artificially painted' by Henry Lilly, rouge-dragon pursuivant, the distinguished armorial artist (/3, p. 278). The church was destroyed in the fire of 1666.

[21] Plate 7.2 is based mainly on an estate map of 1717 (PRONI, T2499: I am grateful to William Roulston and Anne Creighton for their help with this and estate maps of 1807 (Guildhall Library, London, Fishmongers' Co., Plans and drawings, Folio 1). Foreglen is a neat bilingualism, incorporating the Gaelic ballybetagh name of Fohor.

[22] For the text of the conditions binding on undertakers see T.W. Moody (ed.), 'The revised articles of the Ulster plantation, 1610' in *Bulletin of the Institute of Historical Research*, xii (1935), 178–83.

[23] /1, p. 597; /2, pp 100–2. The Goldsmiths' in fact sent two agents: Bowdler and Robert Glynn.

[24] /2, pp 101, 134, 157, 159–61.

[25] Ibid., p. 214.

[26] Ibid., p. 163.

[27] Unfortunately the barony maps made in 1609 for this county do not survive. One name in the Ballykelly area may have been Farren.

[28] /2, p. 178.

[29] Ibid., p. 179.

[30] Ibid., p. 249.

[31] There are a number of somewhat different sums in the company's minutes, but Moody thought that the company may have spent up to £3,333 on the estate (Moody, *Londonderry plantation*, p. 335).

[32] /2, pp 52, 105–6.

[33] Ibid., p. 98; GA. Raikes, *The history of the honourable artillery company* (London, 1878), 1, 39–56.

[34] /2, p. 106.

[35] Ibid., pp 148–9.

[36] Ibid., pp 153–4.

[37] Ibid., pp 163, 177–8. The map was thought 'a very necessary thing to he done'.

[38] Ibid., pp 189, 193, 212, 216.

[39] Ibid., pp 195–7.

[40] Ibid., pp 200, 207.

[41] Ibid., pp 207–8, 210, 212.

[42] Ibid., pp 220, 248–9, 271, 281–2.

[43] Ibid., p. 249. The company eventually made a payment to Hayward of 100 marks (ibid., pp 281–2).

[44] Ibid., pp 227, 230.

[45] Moody, *Londonderry plantation*, pp 165–7; R. Gillespie, *Conspiracy: Ulster plots and plotters in 1615* (Belfast, 1987); /2, p. 139.

46 /2, pp 227, 242.
47 This seems to be true anyhow for the Goldsmiths' estate.
48 Goldsmiths' Hall, London, B 393/1645, Henry Carter's collection, 1609–19, pp 452–3, 458–9. I am grateful to Fr P. Arkinson for this reference.
49 Guildhall Library, London, MS 7270, no. 3.
50 See plate 7.3. The original names of Walworth (Keenaght) would seem to have been Maghere Carr and Turner, Walworth (Tirkeeran) was formed later out of the western part of Caman wood, thereby restricting the sizes of Carrickhugh and Tullamaine. Caman was the name of a ballybetagh.
51 /2, p. 186.
52 Bodleian Library, Oxford, Carte MS 62, f. 214.
53 /2, p. 222. A copy of the formal conveyance of the estate as a manor by the Irish Society to the company in late October 1618 is in Guildhall Library, London MS 7270, no. 5.
54 /2, pp 309, 315.
55 This derives from a faded and damaged endorsement on the back of Higgons's lease (Guildhall Library, London MS 7270, Indenture 14 December 1618 between Fishmongers' Co. and James Higgons (unnumbered)). On Carter see TCD, MS 839, ff 107–7v.
56 For a discussion of this stage of the proceedings with regard to the Londonderry plantation as a whole see Moody, *Londonderry plantation*, pp 179–83.
57 /2, p. 248.
58 Ibid.
59 Ibid., p. 284. Ten shillings should be the fine at every change of tenant.
60 Ibid.
61 Guildhall Library, London MS 7270, no. 74.
62 Ibid.
63 Ibid., pp 397, 509–10.
64 *Civil Survey* III, 225, 227, 234; G. Mawhinney (ed), *John O'Donovan's letters from county Londonderry (1834)* (Draperstown, 1992), p. 115.
65 /2, pp 619; 887; *Civil Survey* III, 237.
66 /2, p. 736; *Civil Survey* III, 236. Hayward's son, Francis, acquired a freehold circuitously as assignee of one Robert Bonner and may well have continued to live in Coleraine.
67 /2, p. 885.
68 The appropriate sections of the two relevant government surveys, by Nicholas Pynnar in 1618–19 and by commissioners in 1622, appear in G. Hill, *An historical account of the plantation in Ulster at the commencement of the seventeenth century 1608–1620* (Belfast, 1877), pp 578–9 and in BL, Add. MS 4756, f. 120. A report from the company to the Irish Society in 1631 is in /2, pp 885–9.
69 /2, p. 299.
70 If it were Downing who were meant, he lived at Ballykelly rather than on his freehold and he also came to have a house in Derry.
71 BL, Add. MS 4756, f. 120.
72 BL, Add. MS 4770, ff 123–3v.
73 /2, pp 886–7.
74 The locations of their tenancies are recorded on a map made by an English cartographer Thomas Croddin in 1623 (Guildhall Library, London, Fishmongers' Co. Plans and drawings, Folio 2, no. 8).
75 What follows is mainly based on an analysis of Croddin's map combined with intensive fieldwork. The reason for the commissioning of the map in the year 1623 may have been to answer possible government complaints arising from the survey of 1622 or simply a desire on the part of the company to be more informed at a time when, Higgons being in arrears, it had appointed two receivers (Robert Glover and Robert Whitney) to collect rent from him (PRONI, D3029). Alternatively, Higgons himself might have got it made.
76 BL, Add MS 4756, f. 120.
77 I am very indebted to Mr Gabriel O Kane of Milltown House for his help with the local topography.
78 I am very grateful to Mr and Mrs Brian Brown for allowing me to visit on a number of occasions.
79 Drawings are on Croddin's map and in D.A. Chart (ed.) *Londonderry and the London companies* (Belfast, 1928), plate 10. The descriptions are by Pynnar and the commissioners in 1622.

80 /2 p. 517. For a fuller architectural account see J.S. Curl, *The Londonderry plantation* (Chichester, 1986), pp 232–8.

81 /2, pp 178, 184. Reformed Anglicanism had not dispensed with saints and in fact the old name, St Finlogh's, was retained, but the common usage became Tamlaghtfinlagan Parish Church or, as in Higgons's will, simply 'the church at Ballykelly'. Saints, in short, were less emphasised.

82 Hill; *Plantation*, p. 579.

83 BL, Add. MS 4756, f. 120. Lead and glass to the value of about £20 was purchased in London at about this time (/2, p. 299). The present-existing ruined chancel, built in 1719 after the depredations of the Williamite/Jacobite war, is much larger. The present Church of Ireland church, which replaced this one, was built, on a new site, in the 1790s.

84 For Queens' at this time, see John Twigg, *A history of Queens' College, Cambridge 1448–1968* (Woodbridge, 1987). I am indebted to Dr John Morrill for this reference.

85 /2, p. 396.

86 Ibid., p. 886.

87 Ibid., p. 452.

88 Ibid., p. 926; /3, p. 48. Shortly after the restoration, when, after previous devastations, the damaged church was being restored at 'great cost' by the inhabitants of Ballykelly, the company made a grant of £40 towards these repairs and to buy another communion cup (/4, pp 1136, 1141). It may well have fallen victim to the Jacobite/Williamite war.

89 /3, p. 104.

90 Hill, *Plantation in Ulster*, p. 579; BL, Add. MS 4756, f. 120; /2, pp 396, 517, 886.

91 Guildhall Library, London, MS 7270, nos 5 and 22.

92 Ibid., no. 2. A house on Carrickhugh is shown on Raven's map of the estate. Seeking an extension of his lease from the company, in London, in October 1629, Rathborne claimed that he had been 'at great cost to the great value' of £300 in building and other expenses on it (/2, p. 757). The tenancy did not remain with his family after his death. A fragment of tin-glazed earthen ware, of a mug or jug 4" in diameter, found by Mr A. Hepburn in 1995, throws a little light on the contents of one of the Ballykelly houses.

93 TCD, MS 550, f. 196.

94 Norden's views are cited in the discussion in D.M. Palliser, *The age of Elizabeth: England under the later Tudors 1547–1603* (London, 1983), p. 179.

95 /2, p. 519.

96 In one of the company's returns on the settlers present on the estate made in 1627 (/2, p. 619), Croddin was listed as living there, but this was probably in an effort to boost their numbers.

97 Guildhall Library, London MS 7270.

98 NAI, C.P./U40; /P118; /R121 (Some of these documents are extremely damaged); *Census Ire.* 1659, p. 126.

99 This is based on the company's minutes, for example /3, p. 503 on widow Crouch, and on an accumulation of pieces of genealogical information too numerous to list here.

100 Genealogical Office, Dublin, Funeral Entries VI, 213; TNA, Prob 11/123 ff 302v–3v; W.C. Downing and R. Wilberforce, *Genealogy of the Downing family and immediate collateral relations with biographical and historical reference and notes 1509 to 1901* (Philadelphia, 1901), passim; J.J. Muskett, *Suffolk manorial families* (London, 1900) I, 96–9; TNA, Prob 11/157, ff 180v–82v; /306, ff 182–3.

101 /2, pp 446–7, 464, 465. Arms were expensive and in short supply and what the company agreed to (p. 465) was somewhat less than that. In April 1624 these arms had still not been made available (p. 518) and they may never have been provided. The commissioners in 1622 said that the twenty-three men they found present were 'meanly armed' and that there were arms in the manor house 'for as many more'. Of those who mustered in *c.* 1630, only 20 out of 42 had arms of any kind (BL, Add. MS 4770, ff 123–3v).

102 /2, pp 491, 492, 493–4.

103 Ibid., pp 632, 659–60.

104 Ibid., pp 663, 665, 667, 677, 680, 681, 682, 684–5, 694, 708.

105 TNA, Prob 11/156, ff 193v–4v. For a short account of his early career See D.B. Quinn, *Explorers and colonies: America 1500–1625* (London, 1990), pp 365–6.

106 His will is TNA, Prob 11/164, ff 441–4.

107 Guildhall Library, London, MS 7270, nos 13 and 14.

[108] Ibid., no. 15.

[109] Ibid., nos 17 and 18.

[110] Ibid., nos 19 and 20.

[111] For a short account of this see W. Nolan, L. Ronayne and M. Dunlevy. (eds) *Donegal: history and society* (Dublin, 1995), pp 317–8.

[112] /2, p. 632. Many of the soldiers were probably based at Culmore fort.

[113] Ibid., pp 631, 635.

[114] R. Brenner, *Merchants and revolution: commercial change, political conflict, and London's overseas traders, 1550–1653* (Cambridge, 1993), pp 123–4. I am grateful to Dr K. Lindley for detailed information on Charleton.

[115] /2, pp 677, 680–81, 685, 694–5.

[116] Ibid., pp 854, 858, 860–61, 862.

[117] Ibid., p. 925.

[118] Guildhall Library, London, MS 7270, no. 23; /2, p. 885; /3, pp 52, 59–60, 67.

[119] Guildhall Library, London, MS 7270, no. 22; /2, p. 923; /3, pp 98, 102–3, 104.

[120] Guildhall Library, London, MS 7270, no. 21, /2, pp 869, 871–2.

[121] /2, pp 834, 874, 893, 931; /3, p. 16.

[122] /2, pp 518, 608, 872.

[123] Ibid., pp 927, 931.

[124] /3, pp 18–19, /3, pp 106–7.

[125] /2, p. 821.

[126] /3, pp 15, 21, 196–7.

[127] See especially /3, pp 142–3, 152.

[128] /3, pp 48, 77, 103–4; BL, Add. MS 4770, ff 123–3v. It was agreed in July 1633 that he should have ten corslets furnished and ten muskets furnished.

[129] Higgons brought in to the company in London in March 1631 a 'note of the division of the land (/2, p. 889) and Freeman submitted a copy of it in 163 (/3, p. 104).

[130] /3, p. 142; NAI, C.P./H153. How the land had been divided can be established from the *Civil Survey*.

[131] /3, p. 194. The first payment was to be made by Mr Ferrers and Mr Briggs of London, the second through one Mr Browne, a Bristol merchant. Other London merchants involved in bills of exchange at this time were Rowland Wilson, George Thimbleby and a Mr Foster.

[132] /3, p. 279; /4, pp 905–6.

[133] He proved the will in London in 1635.

[134] TNA, Prob 11/168, ff 30v–32. The will contains one of those lengthy introductions which sought to convey a devout Protestantism, but which may have become stylised by now. However, the Rev. Thomas Higgons, D.D., of Shrewsbury may have been a relative.

[135] The suit and the background of enquiries and sequestrations in the later 1620s which led up to it is examined in T.W. Moody, *Londonderry plantation* (Belfast, 1939).

[136] /3, pp 196–7, 208.

[137] /3, pp 279, 341, 343.

[138] Moody, *Londonderry plantation*, pp 385, 399. The Fishmongers' Company was instructed to hand over its deeds and writings, but, carefully, it only gave copies (/3, pp 357, 359).

[139] There were two Nicholas Lanes, father and son, who were surveyors. On them see D. Gunasena, 'Nicholas Lane, seventeenth-century land surveyor and cartographer' in *The Wandsworth Historian* 34 (1982), 1–8. The younger Nicholas was later to marry the widow of James Higgons the younger and establish himself in Ulster.

[140] TNA, 5/7, warrant to exchequer, 22 July 1640.

[141] Moody, *Londonderry plantation*, pp 399–400.

[142] TNA, S.P.63/259, ff 19–23.

[143] TCD, MS 839, ff 107–7v.

[144] /3, p. 481.

[145] /2, pp 373–4.

[146] Ibid., p. 493.

[147] Ibid., p. 889.

[148] Ibid., p. 887.

[149] The townland he held, Carrigar or Cargar (at £9.10.0 per annum), became merged with Gortnaleck to form the modern townland Gortgarr, which is an amalgam of elements from both names.

[150] /3, pp 142–3.

[151] *Census Ire. 1659*, p. 127; Guildhall Library, London MS 7270, certificate dated 20 January 1669 (unnumbered).

[152] L.P. Murray (ed.), 'An Irish diary of the confederate wars' in *County Louth Archaeological Journal*, 5 (1921–4), 239, 241. A 'plunderer' or camp-follower seeking loot was a recognised type: 'an ill race of people and very hurtful to an army' (D. Stevenson, *Scottish covenanters and Irish confederates* (Belfast, 1981), p. 119).

[153] G. Mawhinney (ed.), *John O'Donovan's letters from county Londonderry* (1834) Draperstown, 1992), pp 113–5.

[154] *Census Ire.* 1659, pp 126–9, 132.

[155] BL, Add. MS 4756, f. 120.

[156] NAI, C.P./H153.

[157] The disappearance of parish records makes any precision on this point impossible.

[158] W.P. Burke, 'The diocese of Derry in 1631' in *Archivium Hibernicum*, V (1916), 1–6; It was primarily monasticism which did not survive. The monasteries were dissolved in west Ulster, for example those at Derry and Macosquin, at the beginning of the seventeenth century and their estates were granted to new owners. Bishop Redmond O Gallagher had been killed towards the end of the Nine Years' War and he was now replaced by a Vicar Apostolic.

[159] A.F. O'D. Alexander (ed.), 'The O'Kane papers' in *Anal. Hib.*, 12 (1943), 93–102.

[160] TCD, MS 839, ff 107–7v.

[161] /3, pp 570, 578. This was Roaring Meg.

[162] HMC, *Cowper (Coke) MSS*, II, 299–300.

[163] D. Stevenson, *Scottish covenanters and Irish confederates* (Belfast, 1981), pp 228–9.

[164] *Civil Survey* III, p. 220.

[165] At one point (a demonstration of the settler recovery) some of the companies formed in Derry were located at New Buildings and at Eglinton. A. Hogan (ed.) *Letters and papers relating to the Irish rebellion between 1642–46* (Dublin, IMC, 1936), p. 183. On Owen Roe O Neill and Ballykelly see J.I. Casway, *Owen Roe O'Neill and the struggle for Catholic Ireland* (Philadelphia, 1984), pp 251–6.

[166] R. Hayes (ed.), *The register of Derry cathedral (St Columb's) parish of Templemore, Londonderry, 1642–1703* (Dublin, 1910), pp 3–7.

[167] BL, Thomason Tracts, 669 f. 10.

[168] The agreement with him was that he should hold for forty-one years at a rent of £200 per annum and with an entry fine or down payment of £1,125.

[169] /4, p. 1141.

[170] It is a quite remarkable fact that George Farquhar, a prominent figure in that literature at the end of the seventeenth century, was himself a product of Foyle College.

8

Sir William Cole, the Town of Enniskillen and Plantation County Fermanagh

Introduction

Important historical events with long-term social and cultural consequences deserve a full treatment, and so it seemed better that rather than seeking to produce within short space what could only be a cursory survey of the entire plantation in this county, to concentrate instead on the activities of one man who himself played a big part within it. Since Sir William Cole was one of the category of military men who received land in Plantation Ulster in 1610, a servitor in the terminology of the time, his career – in Ireland since *c.* 1600, prior to the Plantation – leads also to some background consideration (with the many flaws that brevity entails), of Maguire's country before and at the ending of the Nine Years' War. Moreover, since he was to be long-lived (to die as late as 1653), some attention must be given to his place in the warfare of the 1640s thereby extending the treatment beyond the normal cut-off point for the Plantation era at 1641. If examined carefully, an account of his activities as an Ulster planter can yield an insight into the Plantation in this county overall. What is attempted here, therefore, is essentially a case study of a military man in the Plantation, who not only acquired land in County Fermanagh, but was also charged with the development of the town of Enniskillen.

Background, connections and early military career

Cole was baptised on 7 October 1576 in the parish church of St Mary Woolnoth in the city of London, a child of a London mercantile and business family with roots in the gentry family of Cole of Slade in Devonshire. His father, Emmanuel Cole, a member of the Goldsmith's Company of London who had married Margaret Ingram, aunt of the subsequently famous financier Sir Arthur Ingram, in the neighbouring church of St Mary Woolchurch Haw on 23 November 1574. William's sister Margaret was baptised in St Mary Woolnoth on 1 August 1578 and her mother was buried on the eighteenth of that month.[1] When Emmanuel himself died in late 1592 or just at the beginning of 1593, probably of one of those epidemic illnesses which had afflicted London in the 1590s, he

191

had moved to the parish of St Botolph without Aldersgate (where the Goldsmith's Company themselves had their own property), and had also remarried, leaving a relict Marie Cole as his widow on his death.[2]

Emmanuel, born about 1542, was a son, perhaps the third, from the family of nine sons and two daughters of Thomas Cole, a London merchant 'who descended from a second son of Cole of Slade in County Devon', all except two, including, tantalisingly, himself, having been baptised in the parish church of All Hallows, Honey Lane, between 1540 and 1554. Thomas Cole, a merchant of the Grocer's Company and who may well have been second generation in London, had married the daughter of another merchant, Thomas Hargrave, mercer (possibly of Yorkshire roots) and was buried, on his death, in this church in April 1571. When his elder son William (born 1540 and the uncle after whom our subject was no doubt named), a merchant of the prestigious Mercer's Company, died early in 1601, he had a house and garden in Mill Alley in Coleman Street (less grand than on the main street), where it was said his father had lived, in the parish of St Margaret's in Lothbury, and he was buried – an indication of at least some prominence – in the choir of the church, there. These parishes were in wards close to the Guildhall, with the exception of St Botolph without Aldersgate which was further west in the city and north of St Paul's. While William Cole, mercer, was certainly well established, none of these sixteenth-century figures emerges, however, as a major London merchant of his time. This was also true of Emmanuel Cole. The careers of most of his brothers and sisters remain – and can be left – somewhat obscure. One, Solomon (b. 1547), married an heiress in Hampshire. Another Thomas (b. 1543), in what was to be a family trait, may well have become a lawyer. He is likely to have been, as he has been tentatively identified elsewhere, the lawyer of that name who died in 1597, whose practice was at Barnard's Inn in Holborn 'in the suburbs of London', and who was not only the holder of minor office as keeper of ponds at Westminster and Hampton Court but also MP for the former in 1593 and 1597.[3]

This was not the only branch of the family, attracted by the opportunities available to the energetic in the capital and its hinterland, to have migrated eastward. A branch in business at Sudbury, Suffolk, by the early sixteenth century produced, along with a military captain, two Elizabethan members of parliament. Yet another branch, at Heston in Middlesex and then at Petersham in Surrey (all now in the greater London area), was successful in the practice of the law. In matters of religion, the Coles seem to have fitted themselves well to the tone of the parish Protestantism practised in the 'church of Elizabeth and James' of this era in England. The Devonshire Coles of the main line, styled as, esquires, were themselves of above average wealth amongst the landowners of that county as a whole. Cole's own sister, Margaret, married firstly a member of the Scriveners' Company of London and secondly a man from a legal family with Lincolnshire links. Some members of these Cole families and their connections may have been attracted to Dublin in the early seventeenth century on account of Sir William's success in Ireland.[4]

The Devon of the sixteenth century from which the Coles originally sprang was, in the eyes of the late sixteenth-century antiquary John Hooker of Exeter, greatly improved by contrast to the 'former ages when men lived as salvages without any nurture or civility, when the ground was not manured or tilled, when there was no stayed rule of government and when all was in intestine broils and wars and overlaid with foreign enemies and daily under … new conquerors and oppressors'. Since then (when it just had been inhabited with 'a few salvages and barbarous miscreants'), there had been a 'marvellous metamorphosis', so that now Devon had 'a populose and a great multitude of such as do fear and serve God in true religion and according to his love … leading a civil life'. The people of Devon, he insisted, were 'in matters of knowledge, learning and wisdom … of a deep judgment, in matters civil and for the commonwealth they be wise, pregnant and polytuyque', while 'in matters martial they be very valiant and prudent'. With its land 'most part … enclosed' and 'bettered', both 'public wealth and private profits' now accrued from its produce of 'corn and cattle, … cloth and wool … tin and metals and … fish and sea commodities', all which have 'passaged into all nations', furnishing 'no small number of ships'. Its cloth in particular, he pointed out, was dispatched to London as well as abroad.[5] Since, conventionally, much the same analysis of contemporary Ireland was made by English commentators as Hooker claimed had characterised the now distant Devonian past, Cole, later, in seeking land in County Fermanagh, thereby to advance his fortune, may also have seen himself as the agent through which similar change would now be brought about there. He might aim to be an improver too.

William Cole himself no doubt attended one of the many schools in contemporary London, but there is no indication that he had been to either of the universities or to an inn of court. Some combination of factors – of personal circumstances (with his father now dead), of perhaps the impact of the economic difficulties of the 1590s and even of martial-patriotic feeling – must have motivated him to seek the employment which was at once offered, and, in a manner, necessitated by the warfare of the time. Growing up in London especially, he may have been in some measure conscious that he lived in an age of altering European thinking and action, in which government power was now to be strengthened and more effectively exercised, and one also in which religion was giving an ideological dimension to contemporary warfare. After all (from his own English perspective), ever since the papal excommunication of Queen Elizabeth in 1570, efforts to prevent the establishment of reformed religion in England – and Ireland – had been playing some part in the motivation of England's foreign enemies, while in turn, through supporting, since 1585, the Protestant Dutch in revolt against Spanish rule, English foreign policy was coming itself to have a Protestant dimension to it.

Cole's military career began in Holland, but, given his age, can only have been of short duration there. Then, about 1600, at a crucial stage in the Nine Years' War, he was sent to Ireland, where efforts to govern the entire island in a much more centralised fashion had been afoot, and where the advancement of the reformation, to secure uniformity with England, had proved difficult. That war had opened as a revolt in Ulster to oppose the growing and multi-dimensional expansion there of the power of London's direct-rule Dublin government over formerly effectively ungoverned Gaelic lords.[6] By this stage of it, indeed, its aristocratic leadership was seeking – in effect – to take over that newly redesigned Dublin government for themselves (in what can now be seen as a form of Home Rule), and was insisting also that people in Ireland should be exclusively Catholic. They had also been actively courting the support of both Spain and the papacy and, alternatively, offering that Ireland might become a kingdom of the Spanish monarchy. There were others yet again who advocated the setting up of a new Catholic monarchy for Ireland as a whole in the person of Hugh O'Neill, its authority to be conferred on him externally by the Pope. In retrospect it may indeed be argued that the firm identification of Irishness with Catholicism dates from this time. Accordingly, to meet these challenges (which with Spain involved could threaten England too), a substantial build up of English military forces in Ireland became necessary. As it turned out, this great revolt was largely defeated at Kinsale, where Spanish forces had landed, in December 1601, by an army which included old English-led companies (since many of the old English of Ireland had not joined in the revolt) as well as new English, under the command of Lord Deputy Lord Mountjoy, himself appointed to Ireland in 1600.[7] It is at this point that Cole's presence in Ireland first comes to light.

Despatched from the camp near Kinsale as the bearer of letters to secretary of state Sir Robert Cecil on 13 December 1601, Cole was personally recommended by Sir George Carew, president of Munster, as a lieutenant who had served under Captain Hansard for two years. If given a command in new reinforcements, he would give a good account of it.[8] Richard Hansard (b. 1562), from Lincolnshire and a man very skilled in fortification who must also have had previous experience of continental warfare, can be found in Ireland in late 1599 with control of the ordnance. As lieutenant of the ordnance, he accompanied the old English Earl of Ormond who campaigned against Hugh O'Neill in Munster in early 1600. He was one of twenty captains given command of conscripted soldiers despatched to Ireland in July 1600, his own company having been levied in Lincolnshire. In early summer of 1601 his company was allocated amongst 'the forces northwards', to Moyry, 'to stop the Ulster rebels from coming into Leinster'. When, also in 1601, further recruits were levied in England, Hansard, accorded special praise for his military ability was given command of a second company. Then, 'during the whole time of the siege before Kinsale', he was lieutenant-colonel to the regiment of foot commanded by the Earl of Thomond and also lieutenant of the ordnance.[9] Cole's precise movements as Hansard's lieutenant at this time are unclear; what is clear is that he had gained much experience of warfare in Ireland in a short time. When he can be picked up again in October 1603, Cole was in Ulster, and eventually in Fermanagh. The County Fermanagh into which Cole was to come had formerly been a Gaelic lordship in Ulster – Maguire's country – and it was also the place in which the Nine Years' War had broken out.

Fermanagh in transition
He who was Maguire was, by the sixteenth century, a man of some substance and power. He was ruler of a lordship made up of some 450,000 (or almost half a million) acres. It was a land of much beauty and variety too. His own personal estate or demesne lands, approximating to a ballybetagh (about 2,500 acres or so), was in the vicinity of his Enniskillen Castle, and he also had various entitlements, which maintained his status, from the other landholders under his rule (sometimes called freeholders in English terminology), who held their land in gavelkind.[10] One estimate of the army that Maguire maintained, in peace time, put it at 120 horse and 600 foot.[11] Above all, perhaps, a lord was expected to have military skills. By the fifteenth century a Maguire too might also be a bishop, such as Rosa Mág Uidhir (bishop of Clogher, 1448–83) who was son of a ruling chieftain, while some became high-ranking churchmen in the diocese of Clogher, such as Cathal óg MacMaghnusa (d. 1498), whose name was an offshoot from that of Mág Uidhir, and who played alike a major part the running of the diocese on the death of Bishop Rosa Mág Uidhir, his maternal uncle, in 1483 and in the compiling of the *Annals of Ulster*.[12] A Maguire might also be abbot of Lisgoole (a few miles from Enniskillen Castle and also on the Erne), the only monastic foundation within the lordship to enjoy an anyway substantial estate, which was reorganised along

Franciscan lines – an important conjunction – during the time when Cuchonnacht Maguire was chieftain and probably in the early 1580s.[13]

However, within the power structure of contemporary Gaelic Ulster (west of the Bann) Maguire was not just like his counterpart MacMahon of Monaghan for example, an entirely independent ruler, but was subject to the influence of one or other, most commonly the former, of the two greater Ulster lords, O'Neill or O'Donnell, in relation to whom he had acquired and must accept the lesser status of an *uirrí*, or underlord. The place-name Boith O'Neill, in the vicinity of Enniskillen and known in the seventeenth century, may well give a hint at the exercise of O'Neill control over Maguire's country. Nor were conditions always peaceful. The succession to the chieftainship in Maguire's country as elsewhere was sometimes accompanied by violent engagements between the factional supporters of contendants drawn from different branches of the ruling dynasty. Hence when Cuchonnacht Maguire of Enniskillen died in 1589, his son Hugh, whose mother, Nuala, his father's first wife, had been a daughter of Manus O'Donnell, succeeded him against the aspiration of Conor Roe Maguire (of the Lisnaskea branch) through securing the intervention of Donnell O'Donnell (Manus's grandson and himself to be killed in the following year in an attempt to seize power from his father) on his behalf.[14] Bitterness between these two branches was to reverberate over the next twenty years. As to landownership, churchland in the lordship was mainly of the termon and erenach variety from the families of whose owners (thereby giving them some economic status) parish clergy often derived. These lands were distributed across the parishes, with the parish churches normally located within them. The largest area of episcopal land was at Clogher and not in Fermanagh itself. More of the land of Fermanagh was wooded in the sixteenth century than nowadays, but it would be rash to attempt any guess at the size of its population.

The Maguire lord when he gained power had not only, then, to take some account of the O Neill claim to overlordship and to operate within the complex dynastic power politics of Ulster, but by the second half of the sixteenth century was also confronted by the aims of the lord deputies of London's direct-rule Dublin government to absorb all Ulster under their control, to be ruled in a uniform fashion within the framework of a centralised united Ireland. With this growth of governance in view, these aims were expressed in terminology which emerges also in the convulsions which surfaced with the growth of state power elsewhere in early-modern Europe; the lords must be 'bridled' and their local 'greatness' brought down. Ulster resistance to all this came to a climax in the early 1590s in the Nine Years' War. In the 1580 Lord Deputy Sir John Perrot had devised schemes for Ulster which would have brought a firm element of control, for example for the building of bridges and new towns (none of them in Fermanagh), the costliness of which prohibited their implementation. However, he initiated surrender and regrant proceedings with Cuchonnacht Maguire (also knighted) in 1585–86, who should receive a title to the lordship, wish obligations of taxation.[15] In addition, Fermanagh was defined as a county with its constituent baronies itemised in 1585.[16]

Cuchonnacht Maguire died in June 1589 before any real permanence could be given to these important developments, which would have brought the entire area within Dublin government control. In the *Annals of the Four Masters,* he is given succinct praise by way of obituary: he had been, it was said, 'a lord in his munificence towards churches, ollaves, soldiers and servants; and a learned and studious adept in Latin and Irish'.[17] That for such a regional lord life could be lived at different levels emerges from the *duanaire,* or book of poems, which was assembled under his patronage, because in these poems he was told that he indeed could be king of all Ireland. In them, firstly, his rule in his own lordship was praised: the trees there had 'become languid through weight of fruit', while Enniskillen was 'the castle of a warrior who does not permit its fame to be injured'. Even stern justice through capital punishment was enforced there: 'your gallows are bent through all the guilty men you have hanged'. His generosity to poets was – even obsequiously – proclaimed, and his wife was also complimented. But that was not all; he was also presented as the ruler of all Ulster, and above all it was his martial virtues which were extolled. Playing on his name, he was compared back to Cuchullain: he was a 'hound with warrior's arts'. He was 'Cú Chonnacht of the land of Ulster', and, it was insisted, 'from Loch Foyle to the land of the Boyne there is no land whose tribute you do not levy. He was 'acknowledged as supreme ruler of the land of Ulster' – on their recognition – 'by the poets'. But that was not even all; some of the poems then moved to Ireland as a whole. While these poems can not only be verbose but somewhat impenetrable in places, their argument here seems simple enough. 'Ireland', it was asserted, 'belongs to Ulster' and 'Ulster is the same thing as Ireland'. Then, shifting from territory to lord (without any significant reference to the consent of its people), it was claimed that 'the Maguires are the same thing as Ireland' and indeed (though on another line it was said that 'nobody in Ireland is against him'), that 'Ireland' – again – 'is not against them'. It seems probable then that it was the notion of the old pre-Anglo-Norman high kingship of Ireland that was being kept in mind here. Certainly – although verse can only be an oblique and contracted medium to convey ideas about political structures – the kind of kingship involved was of a somewhat old-fashioned character (scarcely a government in any sense of this time elsewhere), with battles in fords, hostages in fetters and the receipt of tributes. To achieve his ends he would not desist from raiding ('there is fated to be a dearth of cattle after him') but when 'everyone' was 'under tribute' then they would have 'a king's rule over them' and the Maguires would abstain from raiding. Indeed one poet insisted that 'a country' [i.e. a lordship] 'is' – somehow – 'better from the oppression of the Maguires'. As it was, Maguire was already powerful: 'so many were his burnings that no stream was gripped by frost at the beginning of winter', and anyhow 'the five roads lead to his house, the destination of the five provinces; every road leads to the Rome of generosity' – a reference to old imperial power – so 'it is natural for everyone to approach it'. Now the 'hosts of the five provinces ... abide by the judgement you give'. He was now a good king who 'has remembered that he should love good ordinances'. He was indeed a new Alexander of Greece, than whom 'there was found no prince in Europe to compare with him'. Now that he had achieved power, he ruled 'quietly and without any desire for contest', but there had been a time 'when the smooth fair plain of Bregia trembled at your vigorous raids'. Given all this, it is perhaps possible that these poems were no more than a time-locked exposition of old conventions of power and its quest, requiring little new thinking. In that case, at any rate, they show that the cult of royal power still had its Irish rehearsers. Nonetheless there was also a seeming darker ethnic mentality to the programme, in effect, set out before him. 'White castles', it was said, were black again when he had burned a foreign city (*Gallchathoir*) and 'a raiding band has come to the fair land of Meath, into the depths of a foreign town (*Gallbhaile*)'. And again, 'your frequent raids are sufficient title to the Liffeyside ...; it is your doing that there are so many trees growing through the roofs of houses in the fair plain of Meath'. On this reading, it seems, a new monarchy which would be all-comprehending and inclusivist, to embrace the old English of the Pale too, was not being set forth by the Ulster poetic intelligentsia of the later sixteenth century as an ideal to which Maguire should aspire. His 'claim to the land of the Boyne', on the other hand, seems to place him in an old pre-Anglo-Norman context.[18] In reality, of course, any Gaelic 'king' seeking now to establish a monarchy over Ireland would encounter not only the unease of the old English (apart entirely from the opposition of the English government) but, most likely, the opposition of others of his fellows, as was revealed in Ulster alone, in the jealousies of O'Neill and O'Donnell in the Nine Years' War and thereafter. However, although the bardic poets could ascribe to him amazing potentials, what must be most obvious of all from any consideration of these poems is how much, in all the circumstances of the later sixteenth century, for a lesser Ulster ruler such as Maguire, reality and prognostic encomium were apart. Reality was to change even more for his successor.

Fermanagh during the Nine Years' War

Hugh (*Aoidh*) Maguire's career (1589–1600) proved to be largely carried out in the military field. The capture of his castle at Enniskillen in 1594 was an important early event in the Nine Years' War, while he was himself to be killed, famously along with his opponent Sir Warham St Leger, in Munster where he had accompanied Hugh O'Neill's army, in March 1600. Before 1594 he can be found in various engagements; after it he emerged as a member of that confederation of the Ulster nobility (the *ccommbaid coccaidh na ngaoidel* as the Four Masters called it), which was the essential driving force behind the Nine Years' War. Thus in 1595 he and Brian MacHugh Oge MacMahon led an army into County Cavan, just recently re-ordered through surrenders and regrants agreed with the O'Reilly lords in the 1580s, which (to overturn this) they 'plundered and ravaged' on the account of the Four Masters, leaving not 'a cabin in which two or three might be sheltered in all Cavan which they did not burn'. Some months later he and Hugh O'Donnell were in action in County Longford. In 1597 he can be seen engaged with O'Donnell in the defence of Ballyshannon Castle, and in action with his relative Cormac MacBaron O'Neill at Mullingar. In 1598 he was at the battle of the Yellow Ford and in 1599 in action with O'Donnell again in Thomond.[19] The recovery of Enniskillen Castle, precariously held in between, in 1595 had the effect that Fermanagh itself was not to be a major theatre of warfare. Picture views of the taking of the castle, one immortalised by being re-used somewhat freely on Speed's map of Ulster in 1610, provide evidence (to be described below) of what a Gaelic lord's stronghold in Ulster looked like at the end of the sixteenth century.[20]

Although his brother Cuchonnacht ('Tyrone's Maguire' as he was to be called) succeeded him, it was not without a hotly-contested succession struggle between himself and Conor Roe Maguire. Conor Roe initially had been backed by Hugh O'Neill, but Cuchonnacht got powerful support from Hugh's brother, Cormac MacBaron O'Neill, father of his wife. Such were the 'intestinal broils' in the Gaelic lordships. After much 'murdering and killing' (as it was said), the outcome was that Conor Roe now joined himself to Mountjoy, and later was encouraged by the crown to present himself in a role which might be mutually beneficial. Initially, as 'chief of his name', he received a 'reward' of £50 'for divers services performed by him', and, having gone to Dublin, for the 'charges of himself, his son and some of his men' there, where he was kept at first 'the better to retain him in his duty'. He took part in Mountjoy's northern campaign of September–October 1600. Now taken into the army, Conor Roe accepted payment of £468.15.0 for the wages of twenty-five horse and 150 foot 'under his leading' between 1 October 1600 and 31 March 1601. These payments continued to him, though with reductions in line with army reductions, down to March 1606, and after that he received no further military payments.[21] Also, following on royal instructions of 31 December 1600, Conor Roe proceeded immediately to engage in a surrender and regrant. He received a regrant of Fermanagh on 20 February 1601 under conditions similar to Cuchonnacht's in 1586, but was unable to make it effective.[22]

However in 1602, following on Kinsale, Lord Deputy Lord Mountjoy carried out a devastating campaign in parts of Ulster (to which Hugh O'Neill and some of his associates had returned), in order to bring the entire war to an end. Urgency to do this was given by fear and rumour that the Spaniards might send another expeditionary force to Ireland, to prevent which in Ireland a hasty programme of fortification was embarked on at ports in Munster and Connacht. Eventually Hugh O'Neill was brought to submit, in March 1603, and under terms which allowed for his conditional restoration. In 1604 Spain and England also made peace, but it remained a shaky one for some years, since uncertain negotiations with the Dutch dragged on until the Twelve Years' Truce was agreed in April 1609, and also given the tensions caused by the establishment of the English Virginia Company's settlement at Jamestown, Virginia. In Ireland too some hopes of a Spanish return, which would allow resumption of warfare and break the peace with England, were around in the years before and after the Flight of the Earls, though over-optimistic ones, although the Spanish government did decide to give pensions to O'Neill and O'Donnell in 1606 on the grounds that 'should war break out again they could be of great use and so it is well to keep them well disposed'.[23]

But what is more immediately relevant to Fermanagh in 1602 must now be returned to. Having put a new garrison at Monaghan, Mountjoy then placed Conor Roe Maguire in a MacMahon chieftain's house close to Fermanagh 'so that he might from thence easily plant and settle himself in his own country' and be able to do 'good services in those parts'. Another important initiative was the capture of Ballyshannon Castle, to the west, and the placing of soldiers there under the command of Sir Henry Foliott. Foliott was instructed to give a protection to Cuchonnacht Maguire, who had now deserted Hugh O'Neill, but he must be content to have Fermanagh divided between Conor Roe and himself and must also surrender – and rebuild – the castle of Enniskillen which, to make it unusable, he had himself 'lately brake down'. However, Cuchonnacht soon proved to be discontent under these conditions and reverting to opposition, was, in turn, 'exposed to prosecution' by the lord deputy who, by the autumn, had instructed Captain Edward Blayney – at Monaghan – to give Conor Roe his 'best assistance' and, as for 'the other Maguire in rebellion', not to accept any submission from him 'except he undertake some extraordinary good service, because he had lately abused the favour offered him' by Foliott.[24] When the lord deputy went to Galway for Christmas to receive the submissions of the Connacht lords (and to order the completion of fortifications there as precaution against foreign invasion) the only one there of them remaining in arms was Brian O'Rourke, who had 'drawn unto him Tyrone's Maguire' and some few others, and a further prosecution followed. But by then anyhow Enniskillen had been entered by men – further breaking the castle – under Niall Garbh O'Donnell (who himself sought possession of Donegal instead of Rory O'Donnell who had been appointed as his successor by his brother Hugh) combined with English soldiers and proceeding in boats on Lough Erne. They also occupied the monasteries of Devenish and Lisgoole, and in them left warders. In this way then, very tentative steps of gaining control along the Erne had been taken. Cuchonnacht Maguire, however, also survived, and submitted, to receive a pardon in December 1603, and it is likely that Conor Roe had by now also, tentatively, re-established himself in south-east Fermanagh.[25]

The aftermath of the Nine Years' War in Fermanagh

The matter of Fermanagh was taken up again in 1603 and 1604 by the interim administration in Dublin of Sir George Carey (appointed as Mountjoy's successor on the latter's return to England in May 1603) on foot of instructions from England in September 1603. 'Maguire country' should be granted to the chieftains by letters patent (according to decisions recently reached by the council in Ireland) and commissioners were to be appointed to do this and a range of other matters.[26] These instructions came just after the restoration of Hugh O'Neill – without underlords or *uirrí* – had been confirmed in England. Already Fermanagh, one of these lesser lordships, was being looked into in Ireland.

To begin with commissioners were appointed in Dublin at the end of June to investigate landownership there. They should record all monastic and church lands and any lands forfeitable by attainder, with their yearly values; the names of all parishes with the parochial income of their clergy; and also the names and possessions of all 'freeholders' in the county. The resulting survey of the 'county of Fermanagh, called Maguire's country' was put down in an inquisition taken on the evidence of local jurors at Devenish on 7 July. While working by barony, it noted ecclesiastical land competently enough (and found no attainted land), the treatment of the freeholders was significantly incomplete. They were recorded mainly by group, or 'slought' (such as Sleught McMulroony in Clankelly barony or Sleught Brian Maguire in Magheraboy), or even by sept (such as O'Flanagan's sept in Magheraboy barony) or clan (such as Clan Gaffrey in Magherastephana barony) and with the areas of land they held not specified at all. With, in this regard, 'their particular portions of land unknown to the jury', the inquiry only had a preliminary character. A number of further steps were, however, taken. Cuchonnacht Maguire received a pardon on 7 December 1603 and Conor Roe on 7 March (each defined as esquire), along with in both cases a long list of followers – each over 100 – who between them must have included most of the principal men of the lordship. Finally, on 14 January 1604 a division between them was made of the 'county' by the lord deputy and privy council in Dublin with each, and separate interpreters, in attendance, whereby each was allocated certain baronies and with Cuchonnacht to retain Enniskillen. Two days later Conor Roe made a surrender of his grant of 20 February 1601. For legalistic completion an inquisition had been taken at Devenish on 17 July before the judge Sir Edward Pelham chief baron of the exchequer, then riding one of the first assizes whereby, for uniformity, English law (replacing Irish law and the lord's power to administer it) was extended into these now new counties in Ulster, which found that Hugh Maguire had died in rebellion with the consequence that his country had then escheated to the crown.[27]

This remained merely an outline arrangement until new energy was given to the conduct of affairs in Ireland when Sir Arthur Chichester took up office as lord deputy in 1605, and of whose government Sir John Davies, as principal law officer, formed a part. In 1606 Chichester sought to make rule a reality not only in County Fermanagh but in the other two smaller lordships of south Ulster; Cavan and Monaghan. And it should be done along the extremely radical lines already devised in the 'settlement' of County Monaghan in 1591. What had been done there represented an attempt at the entire re-modelling of society The essential element of the settlement had been the division of the land amongst a number of the heads of the MacMahon dynasty, each to hold their own demesne estate and under each of whom was placed, in manorial fashion a number (some forty or so each) of the lesser landowners, now – a proto-gentry – to become their freeholders, and to owe them no further obligations than just a fixed annual money rent. Some loss of land, though not on a very grand scale, had also been involved in it: principally, the demesne of the chieftainship (around Monaghan) were allocated to an English figure, a seneschal, to supervise the entire new departure. Also, all would become subject to the then current rules of taxation and law emanating from the Dublin government. For good measure, and to ensure compliance, the existing chieftain had also been executed.

Much of objective of the lord deputy's expedition in 1606 was to revive this settlement in County Monaghan and to impose a similar arrangement in the other two counties. As Sir John Davies reported it to his superior in England, Chichester had 'made stay' of the granting of the patents to Conor Roe and Cuchonnacht until he had established a 'competent number' of freeholders under them, which would be less easy to achieve if patents already had been granted. An inquiry into who the freeholders should be, done barony by barony and described in some detail by Davies, was accordingly carried out. When this diffusion of ownership should be implemented, Davies felt assured, the lord deputy would 'cut off' for ever 'three heads of that hydra of the north, namely MacMahon, Maguire and O'Reilly', deprived of 'their Irish duties and exactions'. With such stability of ownership once accomplished this, Davies, back in Dublin, wrote enthusiastically would bring about a social and economic transformation: 'Thence will arise villages and towns which will draw tradesmen and artificers' and 'these countries' would not only become 'quiet neighbours to the Pale, but be made as rich and civil as the Pale itself'. The freeholders, some 200 with none to hold less than two tates or townlands, would also provide the jurors through whom English law would be introduced, while an annual revenue of £250 or £500 would be raised for the exchequer from the country.[28] Chichester himself, reporting in September, was of the view that to make change effective a few English owners would also need to be put in place in these counties. In the Fermanagh countryside as they observed it he said they had found 'no manner of town … and the people very poor in goods and understanding', although it could be brought to 'equal most parts of England in pleasure and profit'. Although reluctant to advocate substantial government expenditure (since the Irish revenues were still heavily dependent on payments from England), he thought that a bridge should be built at Lisgoole (as a mechanism of control) and the beginnings to a town made there, to be the county town. He had already asked Sir Henry Foliott to move the little group of warders then at Devenish to Lisgoole instead.[29] Davies thought that a school should also be established there.

Some other changes were already proceeding. In October 1605, in accordance with existing policy for the dissolution of the monasteries, a twenty-one year lease had been made of the estates of the abbey of Lisgoole and Devenish, the former relatively substantial, to William Bradley of Dublin, himself soon to be appointed as clerk of the Irish house of commons and probably a follower of Sir John Davies. These lands were granted outright in November 1606 to Sir Henry Brouncker, Lord President of Munster, one of a small group of people authorised from London to receive grants of forfeited land in Ireland.[30] The 'priors' of these foundations in 1603 had been Shane McAnAbbot [Maguire] (of Lisgoole) and Prior O'Flanagan. That change of another kind would in addition be attempted was also by now forecasted. The appointment of Rev. George Montgomery to be bishop of Derry, Clogher and Raphoe indicated that (in accordance with the 'one king, one church, one law' principles of the age), for the laity Protestantism should be substituted for Catholicism in their religious practice. He, and his successors as bishops, would also thereby become possessed of the episcopal estates. It had already been decreed that the two Maguires should not be granted any rights to nominate parish clergymen. It was against this background that the Flight of the Earls and Cuchonnacht Maguire took place in 1607. However strong indeed the push factors, this proved an ill-judged departure because they were never returned with either Spanish or Papal armies to contest the disempowerment which lay behind the changes all now being introduced. Fear that they would be, however, formed part of the motivation for the change of gear in government policy made after it with the decision to carry out a plantation.

Cole in Ulster, 1603–10

The second stage in Cole's Irish career, when he appeared in Ulster, fits with his pattern of events. By April 1602 Hansard (under whom he had been lieutenant) had been placed with one hundred foot amongst 'the forces lying northward upon Leinster' (which included Moyry, Kells and Dundalk) but was soon moved to Augher, to become part of the Lough Foyle army by 1603 and to be eventually placed at Lifford in County Donegal.[31] For his part, Cole re-emerged in Ulster in 1603 as part of the Ballyshannon command controlled by Sir Henry Foliott. From October 1603 he was captain of boats and barks at Ballyshannon. These as now established were intended to operate on Lough Erne and also to go by sea to Donegal. At first he had wages for himself at four shillings per day and for twenty-two sailors at one shilling each per day, but the sailors were reduced to twenty from 1 October 1604. He received payments for the building and repair of these vessels and for 'ropes, sails, ankers and other necessaries' for them over the period 1 October 1603 to 30 March 1606 and for his costs in 1604 for a 'pinnace or barge' of twelve tons 'by him newly built' at Foliott's direction and for repairs to three other barges, all totalling some £245. From 1 April 1605 however, his men were reduced to ten and at ten pence per day. He was now indeed a captain, but, with reductions, it was not proving to be a very lucrative employment nor necessarily a permanent one. Soon too further financial exigencies were to have their effect: from April 1606 his own entertainment became 3s. 4d. per day, with his ten boatmen correspondingly reduced to eight pence. Hence from 1 July 1606 to 30 September 1607 he was paid at this rate (3s. 4d. for himself and 8d.) and received £228.10.0.[32] Also unlike Foliott at Ballyshannon (who was set to receive a lease of land there already excepted, for security reasons, from Rory O'Donnell's patent), and with the Lisgoole monastic estate coming to the hands of a Dublin-based figure, he could not benefit from any grant of land. He did not have command of any separate fort. In all these circumstances, and as Ireland was 'now in good obedience', he sought military employment entirely outside of Ireland, and approached Sir George Cary, then in London, to seek to procure it for him. On 21 January 1607 the latter requested the Earl of Salisbury (formerly Sir Robert Cecil and now principal Secretary of State in England) to recommend him to the Dutch authorities for the command of a foot company there.[33] What happened was different; it left him remaining in Ireland but with some security of employment. In May 1607 instructions were issued from London that he should be continued ('during good behaviour') in his 'place' – at 3s. 4d. per day and eight pence each for ten men – and a patent to him of the 'office' of captain of the long boats and barges at Ballyshannon and Lough Erne ensued on 10 September.[34] A limited hold on Ulster was thus to be maintained, though as cheaply as possible. Cole had earlier, familiar with London, received a payment of 13s. 4d. for carrying a packet of letters (presumably different from the Kinsale ones of 1601) to the privy council there.

With the Flight of the Earls Cole's prospects somewhat improved, though not immediately. After the flight, too, a new phase in the history of Enniskillen (as of County Fermanagh as a whole) began, because Edmond Ellis, who must, have been part of the larger west Ulster command based either at Lough Foyle or Ballyshannon, was placed there as constable in late November 1607 with ten warders under him, and Cole succeeded him as constable of Enniskillen on 1 April 1609. For this he received a wage of three shillings per day, with the warders to each have a daily pay of eight pence, and he was concurrently paid as captain of the boats at Ballyshannon. He also secured an agreement (which ran into 1610) for payments to him, in advance, from 1 April 1608, of £26.13.4 per annum for 'keeping and repairing in serviceable manner' these boats. In terms of useful services, he was paid £13.6.8 in December 1608 for taking up two brass pieces of ordnance 'hidden and sunk under water' ten miles from Enniskillen, and for bringing them there, now, as it was, under new control.[35] When, therefore, in 1608, in the atmosphere of anxiety as to what might be the outcome of the Flight of the Earls, Sir Josias Bodley, appointed as, overseer of fortifications in Ireland, was dispatched to Ulster to report on the state of the forts and garrisons there, Enniskillen could now come within his scrutiny. He saw 'the broken castle' there, now warded, as the 'fittest' place 'for service' in the whole area, since it stood 'in the heart of Fermanagh', though as it was, he thought, with the ward small and the passage by water difficult, little use could be made of it. He recommended therefore that it be 'enlarged', as it could be for £500 or £600, so as to contain greater numbers 'upon occasion and yet to be defended by a small number as the time should require'. He felt that it would prove, on its own, 'a sufficient bridle upon that country', provided that some small sconces were erected at Belturbet, Belleek and elsewhere for the safety of the boats.[36] This work – and the building of a new town there as well – was indeed to be done under Cole's agency, but only after and as, Plantation was introduced.

Plantation in County Fermanagh

The Plantation in this county, initiated in 1610, followed the plan devised over the previous two years for the six escheated counties as a whole, though with some local variation. Using the barony as the unit of aggregation, most of the land was distributed in estates allotted to individual owners drawn from three broad categories. Thus, undertakers (so called from the conditions they must fulfil), both English and Lowland Scottish, were granted lands in some baronies. This came to give the Plantation both its Anglo-Scottish and its regional character. Servitors, generally military men though also including some government officers of state, were another category, while the third was made up of Irish owners who were restored to land. Both of these latter were usually placed in the same baronies. Smaller areas were devoted to other purposes. To promote a policy of urbanisation, it was decided that a number of new towns should be established in every county, each to have its own governing body through charters of incorporation and to receive an area of land nearby for the use of its townspeople and to provide for its development. Where new forts had recently been established (none in County Fermanagh), pieces of adjacent land had already been designated for their support. Also, importantly for cultural transmission to those who would attend, land was set aside to endow the foundation and maintenance of a grammar school in each county. At a higher education level a similar cultural purpose lay behind the decision to grant an Ulster estate – in counties Donegal, Fermanagh and Armagh – to Trinity College, Dublin. For the individual owners, estate sizes were to be in the range of 1,000, 1,500 and 2,000 acres (of profitable land), but through defective mensuration (in which full scientific accuracy for large areas was not to be achieved before the Ordnance Survey) they proved to be much larger. It was the undertakers above all who were required to be the planters. Although this was to prove a far from fully attainable goal for many, they were tied by the conditions in their grants to introduce English and 'inland' or Lowland Scots (not Islesmen) onto their estates, to the complete exclusion of Irish tenantry. Separately from the Plantation, which was concerned with the confiscated secular land, though concurrently with it and in accordance with the contemporary norm of 'one church', the new Protestant bishops, in succession, were granted the church land, mainly of the termon and erenach variety, spread as it was in each county throughout its various parishes. To provide income for parish clergy, small areas of glebe, taken out of the confiscated secular land, were also allocated. In this way, the clerical wing of the Protestantism now introduced into the Plantation counties was provided for. On the other hand, a plan to redesign the parish boundaries so that they would overlap with the Plantation estates was not proceeded with. All owners (though with those of churchland, principally, exempted) were required to be a source of revenue to the exchequer in Dublin through the payment of annual land taxes and in other ways. From this, then, something of both the magnitude of ownership change inherent in plantation and of the expectations for the emergence of a new complex society, compliant to the rule of the king's Dublin government deriving from it, becomes apparent. To indicate the context of Sir William Cole's place within it, a brief outline of the Plantation in this county as a whole is now necessary.

At the core of the Plantation in County Fermanagh lay the estates granted to the undertakers. The forfeited land in almost four of the county's seven baronies was distributed to them. Scottish undertakers were placed in the baronies of (to use the names by which they finally came to be known) Magheraboy and Knockninny (which included Coole). English undertakers were placed in Lurg and much of Clankelly, where the Fermanagh estate of Trinity College, embracing the area know as Slutmulrooney, was also located. Servitors and Irish grantees, placed in the same baronies, were put in the baronies of Clanawley, where also were the school lands, and Tyrkennedy where the Enniskillen town grant was mainly located. The entire barony of Magherastephana was granted to one Irishman and one Scot, and one Irishman, Brian MacMulrooney, was restored to a small portion in Clankelly.

The thirteen Scottish undertakers who were selected had origins in eastern and southern Scotland. The two principal ones amongst them, Sir

John Home (in Magheraboy), and Michael Balfour, Lord Burley (in Knockninny), were prominent in Scottish life with court and government connections; the former from North Berwick in East Lothian, was one of the king's servants, the latter, with lands in Fife and Kinross, had been ennobled in 1607 and was made a member of the Scottish privy council in 1610. Three of the Knockninny group, for example Thomas Moneypenny from Fife were east Scottish lairds. James Gibb (later to be advanced in England) was probably of Carribber – close to Linlithgow – and a servant to the king. A few had mercantile and administrative links to Edinburgh and Mid Lothian. One was from Lanarkshire. Of the eleven English undertakers to receive estates, a significant proportion had East Anglian origins. Amongst these were Sir Edward and Thomas Blennerhasset and Thomas Flowerdew from Norfolk, and Robert Bogas and Henry Huning from Suffolk. John Archdale, with property in Suffolk, had a London mercantile family connection. In addition, Sir Hugh Wirrall had a Yorkshire background, while Robert Calvert may well have shared the Yorkshire roots of his more famous namesake, George Calvert, then being advanced in position to become the clerk of the privy council in England. In County Fermanagh there were seven servitor grantees. Apart from Captain William Cole, two, Sir Henry Foliott (whose lands took in Ballinamallard) and Captain Paul Gore, sprang from the County Donegal command, where they also obtained property. Roger Atkinson, a former captain, was placed near Enniskillen. Two lesser people, Samuel Harrison and the Welshman Peter Mostin (the former at Belcoo) received just small areas. Different was Sir John Davies, a figure from the central administration, who was granted an estate in Clanawley barony, which included the Lisgoole monastic lands acquired by him from Brunckar. The Irish grantees must now receive brief attention.

These divide into two groups: a small number who received – within the constraints of the Plantation – sizeable personal estates, and a much larger one who each received just small areas. Conor Roe Maguire (d. 1625), who had not gone on the Flight of the Earls, got a substantial proportion of the barony of Magherastephana (and a pension), where, however, Balfour also received land: it was not thought 'prudent' that he should receive any more. The same concern for future security meant that he did not retain his tower house at Lisnaskea. His son Brian was later ennobled, English-style, as Baron of Enniskillen. However, if Conor Roe was constricted, some attempt at balance was achieved though the grant, situated around Tempo, made to Brian McCuchonnacht Maguire, brother to Cuconnacht who had fled. On the other hand, the amount of land available for local restoration was reduced when Conn McShane O'Neill (d. 1630), also from the upper levels of Ulster Gaelic society, was transplanted to County Fermanagh, to receive an estate (which included Clabby) mainly in Tyrkennedy barony. The lesser Irish grantees, some sixty in all, were from amongst those who would otherwise have been made freeholders under the two Maguire lords, had the plans – following the County Monaghan model – which were being considered before the flight had been acted on. Many were Maguires; some were from other septs. Amongst them were Oghy O'Hossy (as he was spelled) and Brian O'Corcoran, drawn from the poetic caste, while Shane McEnabb, whose son succeeded him in 1630, may well have been the last abbot of the dissolved monastery of Lisgoole. The Irish grantees, who between them may have been restored to about 25 per cent of the statute acreage, will receive more detailed treatment in a fuller work, now in progress, on the Plantation as a whole.

The effects of the Plantation, down to 1641, can only receive brief and tentative treatment here. In the first place, not all the estates remained in the hands of their original grantees. When Sir Stephen Butler, an English undertaker in neighbouring County Cavan, acquired an estate in Coole and Knockninny (hence Newtownbutler), a process of estate accumulation, of which there are other Ulster examples, was underway. This also broke down somewhat the symmetry of the division between areas of English ownership and areas of Scottish which was inherent in the plan. Equally, when the Rev. James Heygate, a churchman in the diocese, acquired an estate – for the benefit of his children – in Clankelly, this brought Scottish ownership into an English area. Again, when Sir Gerard Lowther, an English judge in Dublin, purchased an estate in Lurg, this not only brought in a measure of absenteeism in ownership, but it was also to be one of a number of links between Plantation Ulster and a growing new English element in Dublin which was also bringing about that city's expansion and transformation. For their part, the numbers of the lesser Irish grantees had diminished somewhat by 1641. Some parts of the county too, appear to have become areas of greater settler concentration than others, and so the condition of the Irish as tenantry on the estates (apart, that is from those that were owners) varied greatly in accordance with the number of settler tenantry. At first some undertaker's lands were very thinly planted, while others were much more so. However, many of the servitors also introduced some settler tenants. Also, the episcopal lands were, on the whole, leased by the bishops in big blocks to a small number of tenants, who tended to have settler sub-tenants under them on at least some of that land.[37] On one count, in *c.* 1630, not likely to be just a fully complete one, there were then 971 British adult male settlers in the entire county. With the growth of the new town of Enniskillen taken into account, the area controlled by Cole became one of those areas of settler concentration, already mentioned, accounting for 133 males or some 14 per cent of the county total.[38]

Sir William Cole and the town of Enniskillen

With the Plantation, Cole was granted an estate as a servitor close to Enniskillen, and he was also made patron of the new town to be established there, itself the only one to be so established in the county. Within a short time he purchased from its Scottish grantee a neighbouring undertaker's estate (which came to be know as Portora) in the barony of Magheraboy, in an example of an English owner acquiring property in a Scottish-designated area. Now, too, he was gradually civilianised. His pay for warders at Enniskillen was reduced to six by 1616 and to four by 1618. He retained his employment as constable of Enniskillen (with four warders) down, anyhow, to 1623, and indeed produced a supply of arms and munitions (valued at £33.15.11) during a period of tension around this time, but the fort itself at Enniskillen was privatised, as will be seen, in 1623.[39] He was knighted as Sir William in Dublin in 1617.[40]

During the two-year period ending in September 1611 Cole received a payment of £266.13.4 for 'building and finishing of the castle and bawn of Enniskillen, utterly defaced in the late rebellion'.[41] Plans for the main island of Enniskillen, and the role that Cole should play in them, emerged in a series of grants made to him in 1611 and 1612. By the first of these, in June 1611, he received a lease for twenty-one years or life of the castle and two-thirds of the island (notionally forty acres), and two small islets at a small rent. By implication this military zone could be garrisoned at any time and Cole was probably tied – to save government expenditure – to maintain the site in good repair. He did, however, receive one further government payment, at or before 30 September 1613. For 'finishing and perfecting' the works begun by him upon the 'bawn and castle' of Enniskillen, but remaining defective and 'lying open both to ruin and decay and also to the hazard of surprise or assault if it should be attempted', he was made a second payment of £133.6.8.[42] This £400 was fairly close to what Bodley had recommended, and with it a fair amount could be done. The other sector of the island was designated to be the site of the new town.

How to actually establish the new Plantation towns became a problem, with consequent delays; the eventual solution was to grant the land designed for their support to a neighbouring planter, under conditions, and devolve responsibility to him.[43] For Enniskillen interim arrangements were made in January 1611: the lands were to be rented for one year under the direction of Foliott and Cole, and the corporation, when established (and presumably intended to be the beneficiary of the land), should consist of forty-three members 'all English, Scotish and Civill Natives'.[44] These lands, after some adjustments of location, were granted to Cole in May 1612.[45] They consisted of five tares, each by the estimation of the time sixty 'acres', and the remaining one-third of the island (twenty 'acres') – in all 320 'acres' – the castle site and the remaining two-thirds being 'reserved' to the crown. They should also be revenue-bearing: he must pay a quit rent of £1 (IR). In statute measure, there were some 700 acres in all. At this point a pause may allow some tentative assessment of what had been there on the island before. For this the plans drawn in 1594 remain the principal source.[46] Apart from the castle site, rendered with some differences on both plans and to be discussed later, a number of other structures were indicated. Maguire's gallows (already mentioned) if that it were, is shown on high ground above, roughly along Darling Street near the churches nowadays. Two houses, some distance apart, are shown nearby, both single-storied. One other house is drawn on the north point of the island, later the site of the Old Militia Barracks, and protected then by a 'ditch cut' which separated it from the rest of the main island. Yet another small building was immediately outside the castle wall. A group of houses (three on one plan and four on the other) along with trees is shown on Piper's Island. Trees also grew beside the Erne on the south side of the island. Such anyhow was how it appeared to the eyes of the surveyor. It had no bridges and the parish church was on another small island some distance away. Other elements which might go towards the make-up of a Medieval town, such as a monastery or a bishop's residence, were entirely missing at Enniskillen: both were at other, and separate, locations.

Cole was tied in 1612 to a number of basic initial planning responsibilities. On the twenty 'acres' site, though not, in fact, to be confined to it, the new town should arise. To there he must 'bring or cause to be brought' within four years 'twenty persons being English or Scotch and chiefly artificers and mechanics to make, erect and construct a town in a convenient place' there, they to be burgesses of the town of Enniskillen, which should be incorporated within the same time. He should also mark out and set aside sites for a church and cemetery, for a market house, for a jail or prison for the county, and for a public school with a court and garden adjoining – the latter two to reflect the county status of the intended town. At another point, it was stipulated in more general terms that he should 'build and erect edifices and buildings ... in streets and squares, in such manner and form as shall best suit with [its] site and situation, and for the defence and decency of the said town'. For the townspeople, in addition to the town site, Cole should allocate in an adjacent area two acres of land each for ten of the 'principal' burgages and one acre each for ten other burgages 'of inferior place and condition', these lands to be assigned together in an area to be known as the 'burgage field', the burgages and lands to be held for ever by the tenants in fee farm. He must also allot a further thirty acres as a common for the inhabitants' cattle, this to be conveyed to the corporation for ever without rent, though each person using this land should pay Cole four pence (English) per annum. If the burgesses' houses were built by Cole they should pay him an annual rent at the rate of 10 per cent of the sum expended, if built by the burgesses they should pay, for the greater burgages and their lands, five shillings (English) per annum, and for the lesser, 2s. 6d. Cole and his heirs were also empowered to hold a Thursday market and a Lammas fair there.

Incorporation proceeded quickly, the issuing of the charter of Enniskillen on 27 February 1613, by which it would return two members to parliaments, being part of a large scheme designed to give the new English a place in that institution.[47] Cole was made first provost, and amongst the fourteen first burgesses were a number of planter landowners in the county. It may be that they were expected to participate in the development of the town; something similar took place at Belturbet. Certainly Roger Atkinson, whose lands were near Enniskillen, held two 'burgess acres', presumably appropriated to houses there.[48] The first provost should hold office until the ensuing Michaelmas, the burgesses during life. All the inhabitants of the town and such as the provost and burgesses might at any time admit to its freedom, were constituted the commons. The provost should be elected annually by the provost and burgesses. When a vacancy should occur amongst the burgesses, the others might elect a replacement. The provost, burgesses and commons might assemble from time to time to make bye-laws. The corporation might establish a guild merchant, and could appoint two sergeants-at-mace and other municipal officers.

The principal components of the new Enniskillen now require attention. Perhaps its central feature may first be referred to: the Diamond. Diamonds of varying size – with streets entering them at mid point on each of their four sides – gave a very distinctive aesthetic to much Ulster Plantation town planning. That at Enniskillen bears comparison in size to another at Belturbet, also a new Plantation town. The town itself mainly followed the line of one main street. By the 1740s when the first map (plate 8.1) to survive was published,[49] there was an intersection not only, necessarily, at the Diamond, but also (nearer the church) at Middleton Street and Paget Street but the pre-1641 settlement can scarcely have exceeded fifty houses, many probably of one storey with attic accommodation lit by dormer windows above a second floor which would make them one and half storeys. The detail of one house survives, building

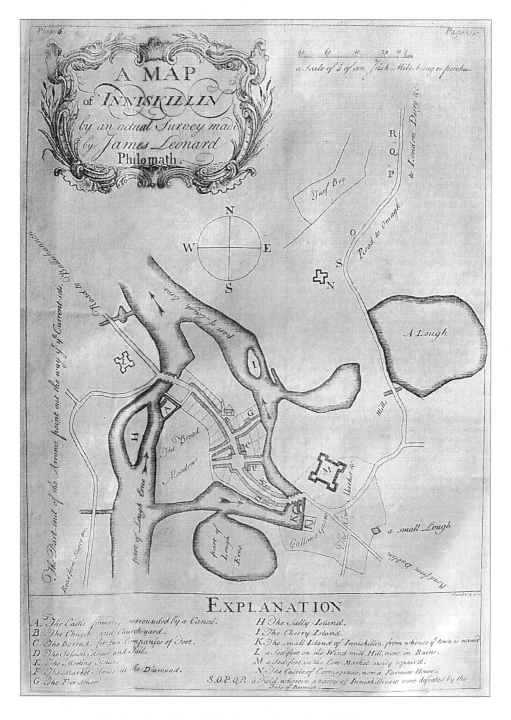

Plate 8.1 Map of Enniskillen by James Leonard published in W. Harris,
Life and reign of William Henry in 1749

having proceeded apace. On 1 May 1613 Cole leased to one John Hickes, yeoman, 'one house then new built and the ground whereupon the said house now standeth and four score foot of ground at the backside of the said house, as it is now measured by the rule and eight foot of ground at the end of the said house', to be held for one hundred years or five lives, paying yearly ten shillings (English) rent, with two 'good fat hens' each Christmas.[50] Another house, probably one of many (in accordance with the plan), had a strip of ground leading 'front the town street to the lough'.[51]

That Cole himself had been active in many ways at Enniskillen is clear from the comments of Bodley, now back as inspector of the Plantation, early in 1613.[52] He had already been occupied in 1611 and 1612, Bodley reported, in 'building up' the castle and bawn (works described earlier, in their then state, in Carew's 1611 Plantation survey), and in constructing two bridges 'over the lough'. Now, as for the town, he had taken bonds from twelve burgesses to build their houses this next summer, while 'divers carpenters and other artificers that purpose to settle there' were about the works then in hand. He had himself provided for the making of 300,000 bricks and 'tile proportionable', with 'good store' of timber for the works of the corporation. For all this work in fact, quite a number of craftsmen – possibly even from London – must have been engaged by Cole; Irish labourers may also have been employed there. Some hint as to who might have had a part in laying out the town comes from a witness to an Enniskillen deed of April 1616: one John Widdowes. Widdowes, or Woodhouse, now in Ireland, was a man with the new scientific training of the age with some link to Gresham College, London, and may have been at this stage in some way in Cole's employ.[53]

The erection of the other important buildings proceeded more slowly. The church, placed, like the Diamond, on a little hill, was complete by 1627, with its tower (if a date stone be in its original location) finished in 1637. It had a large east window with intersecting tracery, a porch to the south-west, and a transept on its north side with a vault beneath. The importance as a Plantation centre with which Enniskillen was viewed by the authorities can be seen in a clerical appointment made, when a vacancy occurred, in 1633. Like Bishop Bramhall at Derry (and a fellow Yorkshire man), the Rev. John Smith, now appointed, followed the theological emphases, more sacramental and more ceremonial, of the Anglicanism which then had the king's support.[54] The *Agnus Dei* on the date stone of 1637, in this case a lamb with a cross and a crown of thorns symbolising the resurrection (plate 8.2), was obviously a symbol congenial to the church of the 1630s. Church monuments within, surviving from the seventeenth century, follow English styles now being introduced to Ireland too. The

Plate 8.2 Agnus Dei of 1637 on tower of St Macartin's, Enniskillen
(Photograph: Walter Baumann)

first building of a sessions house (and jail), now in East Bridge Street, is less certain, though Cole had collected '£500 or £600' towards it by 1622. A small jail at any rate (perhaps beneath it) was in existence in the 1620s. A precise date for the first market house or town hall (now in the Diamond), although likely to have had its place in the original plan, is also elusive. For its part, the royal school was initially established at Lisnaskea, though it may have been removed to Enniskillen prior to 1641.[55]

What now of the people there? The names of some fifty to sixty adult males survive from the 1630s suggesting, in all, about 200 men, women and children.[56] Of the English amongst them, some may well have been 'western men': names such as Browning, Nicholls, Pearse, Ford, Hayes, Grible and even Elliot then had a Devonian provenance. Others may have come from many parts of England, including the north. Common Scottish names amongst them were Johnston, Buchanan, Armstrong, Caldwell and Maxwell. The balance between the two may well not have been particularly uneven, though it may have favoured those of English birth. That there was some coming and going, especially in the early years, is also apparent. Thus, in April 1616, John Hickes sold the lease of the house acquired from Cole in 1613 to James Johnston, yeoman, from 'Moanee' in Magheraboy, who in turn assigned it in April 1618 to Andrew Farelye, a merchant. In April 1623 Farelye assigned it to David Greer, another Enniskillen merchant, who had acted as his surety in a debt of £17 to a Drogheda merchant, George Fleming, and Greer in 1631 transferred it to his son-in-law Edmund Coghlan.[57] The existence of this new merchant and shopkeeping class within the town, of which John Caldwell – from Ayrshire – was another member, testifies to its emerging importance as a centre of internal trade. Enniskillen was becoming, as it was to be later described, 'the only place of consequence upon Lough Erne'.[58] Some sense of pride of achievement now may also have passed the minds of its citizens: the term Enniskilliners (though it then referred to the larger army there) was in use by the 1640s. Although it was, as it was intended to be (for their security and to preserve against cultural dilution) essentially a planter settlement, some few Irish may also have lived about it. Certainly Cole's Irish associate and employee John Carmick had a 'chamber' in the castle, while, after the restoration, his descendant William McCormick was an apothecary in the town. In *c.* 1659, thirty four out of 210 'persons' recorded as living there were Irish.[59] In this way, Enniskillen's eventual modern expanded composition was forecasted, and modern (or 'early modern') urbanisation in Ulster was underway.

Cole's building activities at Enniskillen

Cole's first building works, those on the castle site, have been left for consideration to the last. How thoroughly the tower had been demolished – perhaps to leave a stump (Bodley's 'broken castle' of 1608) at one end – cannot be stated with certainty; what is clear is that its present base was of Maguire construction, since its dimensions, fifty-six feet by thirty-eight feet, conform precisely to the measurements made by John Thomas in 1594. Its height then, as he gave it, was fifty-six feet. Its 'barbican wall', shown as somewhat curving on one plan and, more stylised, as rectangular on the other, was, he stated fourteen feet high, being distant from the castle (by which he cannot have meant on all sides) by forty-five feet. The dimensions of Maguire's keep were thus almost identical to those of O'Donnell's castle at Donegal, but the bawn of the latter was somewhat larger. Defended by water as well, it all stood on ground then cut off from the rest of the island by a 'double ditch' with 'deep water', which was thirty-six foot wide at a point – to the north and below Wellington Place

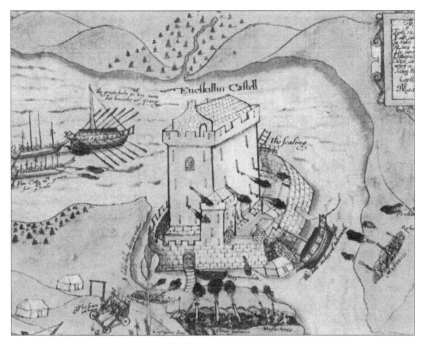

Plate 8.3 A version of Maguire's Castle, Enniskillen, in 1594
(British Library, Cotton MS Augustus I ii 39)

Plate 8.4 A version of Maguire's Castle, Enniskillen, in 1594 (TNA, MPF 1/80)

nowadays – where a gate ('the bridge gate' as Thomas called it), through the wall, was approached by a bridge, possibly constructed of planks. Within, and to its side, this gate was protected by a small barbican tower. Facing the front door of the castle (on its north-west side), there was a second gate ('the water gate'), also entering through the wall. Within, here, the plans of 1594 (plates 8.3 and 8.4) had indicated two buildings one on either side of it, both of them (having been set alight by the defenders during the assault) shown with their roofs on fire on one of the plans. A breach nearby made then by the assailants is also shown. What might appear from one of these plans to have been a third building, unroofed and touching the barbican tower, was probably, however, a simple misinterpretation of other features indicated on the other plan. On these drawings, the castle blinds out anything that may have been behind it to its south, but no buildings other than those shown were mentioned in the account of the assault.[60]

The only description of Cole's building works here comes from Sir George Carew's survey of the Plantation in 1611, made, as it was, before his operations had been completed.[61] An associated plan (plate 8.5) may perhaps show what was intended rather than what was then completed; it can only be adequately verified or disproved now by archaeological investigation in places where that would be possible.[62] Carew's description is in itself of great value. In the first place it sets out Cole's works on the south side, close to the river. These had included the Watergate (plate 8.6.). As Carew described these works, Cole had 'newly erected' with the money allocated to him a 'fair and strong wall' which was twenty-six foot high (the height of the Watergate), with flankers, parapet and a walkway on its top. In fact he would seem to have erected two buildings here, thirty-two feet apart on the river side, since much of the second, probably of the same date, still remains within the present wall. These buildings, though projecting beyond it (and so enlarging, as Bodley had recommended, what had been a relatively small site), were probably linked into surviving portions of Maguire's original wall. The Watergate was in fact more, than, a 'wall' with walkway, since (then or when completed) a building (with a brick chimney), in alignment with the keep, extended backwards behind it, and it had a well within it also. Indeed a range of building here with dormer windows (somewhat similar – if perhaps less grand – to the larger Jacobean residence which was built as an extension to Donegal Castle) might well have extended to the gable of the keep (which has no windows in it), as a water colour view of the town in 1787 may perhaps suggest. The flankers that Carew referred to must, then, be the two turrets on the Watergate. Although striking, architecturally, in construction, the design of the Watergate was defensive; militarily, its two stylish corbelled turrets projected

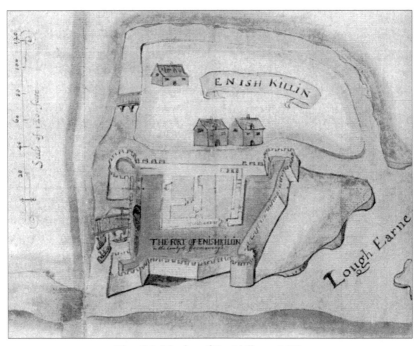

Plate 8.5 The fort of Enniskillen, *c.* 1611.
Probably not fully executed (TCD, MS 1209/29)

in such a way as to protect the wall on two sides. The Watergate was not itself a ceremonial entrance construction in any way akin, for example, to the magnificent Duke of Buckingham's water gate in London erected in 1626 by Nicholas Stone; a new entrance, however, directly from the river, might even have been created between these two buildings. That this had all been of Cole's construction receives conformation from the Irish writer, Dolan, in the early eighteenth century: the 'stately part next the water', he said, had been built by the Coles.[63] In addition, Cole had also 'begun' by 1611 a 'fair house' upon the 'foundation' of the old castle, fourteen foot high (presumably above the vaulting) which he is likely to have brought to the height of three storeys (revealed in the eighteenth century and nowadays just over thirty feet) with dormers at the top above a fourth floor, with windows for domestication instead of the original 'spike holes', and with a brick chimney.[64] Also, 'other convenient houses' for 'store and munition' (which may have included the second building already discussed or even, possibly, houses shown outside the bawn on the plan of *c.* 1611) had by now been erected. The bawn Carew described as ditched about with a 'fair large ditch' with the river on one side, and it now had a 'good' drawbridge. There were also three 'good boats' there, 'ready to attend all services'. Finally, on a 'large piece of ground near adjoining' the 'fort' Cole had built

Plate 8.6 The Watergate, Enniskillen (Photograph: R.J. Hunter)

a 'good timber house after the English fashion' as his own residence and had established a 'fair garden' for it 'all upon his own expense'. The best view of what the castle site may have looked like in the seventeenth century comes from a painting of Enniskillen made in the eighteenth century.[65] A section of it (plate 8.7) has been reproduced here.[66] Unlike Coleraine or Derry where much more initial outlay of money had been possible, the town as a whole (apart from being smaller in numbers of residents), 'having

220

no other walls save the water', had no further protection by means of walls or other fortification at this stage.

In more general terms, the town itself had become a place of occasional ceremonial; as when the judges of assize arrived to conduct their sessions, or the muster master to exercise those who appeared before him, or at meetings of the town corporation. The school made it, in a manner, a cultural centre.

Cole's estates

The principal source of Cole's income came from the lands he acquired. To his initial servitor's grant of a notionally 1,000 'acre' estate called Cornagrade he added by purchase, also close to Enniskillen, an undertaker's one of similar notional size, later called Portora. By the 1630s, he had increased his holdings through the acquisition of the lands originally granted to about six of the native Irish owners. He had also taken over the lands, relatively small in extent, originally granted to the servitor, Peter Mostin.[67] In 1623 he acquired the castle site at Enniskillen (originally held by lease), outright and by purchase, in a cost-saving exercise by the government, though under conditions of maintenance.[68]

Development work on both estates was slowed by Cole's works at Enniskillen; soon, however, he had erected defensive dwellings on each, one, at Portora (much of which is still preserved), being a particularly good examplar of the genre, the other long since demolished. Placed in one – Cornagrade – as his tenant was Clinton Ogle, a former lieutenant from Lincolnshire now out of pay, while Bishop James Spottiswood,

Plate 8.7 Eighteenth-century painting of Enniskillen Castle site (Florencecourt)

Montgomery's successor, lived in the other. Modern mills – one a windmill – were erected on both estates, on sites still identifiable. By the early 1620s his undertaker's estate (where he was held to be a model landlord) was thoroughly planted; inspectors in 1622 stated that they could not 'learn' of any Irish tenants on the land there, not even as sub-tenants holding grazing rights.[69] Regulation, for an undertaker's estate, was therefore being adhered to, and this had apparently become one of those areas, already referred to, of settler concentration in the county. Yet Cole too took advantage of a compromise reached with the undertakers in 1628 whereby Irish might occupy one-quarter of each estate; in 1629 such a one-quarter of this one was duly set out by inquisition.[70] However, in the absence of that certainty on this matter which only estate records could provide, caution requires that the earlier statement be taken fully at face value.

On his servitor's estate, where this regulation did not apply, the situation was different. There, on the evidence of the same source, he did indeed have a few British tenants, but the 'rest' of the land was held by Irish 'in fee farm or to lease'. By contrast, on other estates in the county many Irish tenants held only from year to year. Amongst the Irish more generally (apart from these Irish tenants and probably some employees), Cole built up an association with John Carmick, who himself acquired land, Flartagh McHugh, successor to an original Irish grantee under the Plantation, and some others.

Cole in county affairs and in politics

Many consequences flowed from the shiring of Maguire's country, once it had been made effective. While the records of the new county administration do not survive, Cole will have been made one of its justices of the peace and on occasion sheriff of the county. He was also made the first provost – equivalent to mayor – of Enniskillen. As a justice of the peace, he became involved with a great settler dispute in the county in the later 1620s, the detail of which indicates that the settler society initially contained elements of the violence which had also characterised the old.[71] He had a part as well in curbing native Irish plots and disturbances which arose in the fraught years of the mid-1620s when there was some expectation of a further Spanish intervention in Ireland.[72] Cole was also to be one of the first new Ulster members of parliament, though not in that of 1613. He sat as a county member in the parliaments of 1634 and 1640, both summoned by Lord Deputy Wentworth, whose policies of 'thorough', especially in financial matters, had considerable effects on landowners in Ireland. In the latter parliament he was a member of a number of committees including one concerning the commons's petition of remonstrance of 7 November 1640 and was on the committee sent later to the king in England to present the grievances of the house against the conduct of government.[73] He could also have been a little ill at ease with the theological leanings of the new clergyman at Enniskillen, over whose appointment he might well have had no influence.

Cole in warfare, 1641–c. 1650

But if Cole were a critic of Wentworth's administration, all changed, inevitably, with the outbreak of the rising in 1641. In the attempt at repossession which formed part of it, many of the settlers in the county were expelled from houses and lands, some were killed, and some – of the men – went on to join armies of defence. Given the powerful religious impulse which lay behind the rising, it seems that Protestant clergy and churches (if it be safe to generalise from some known instances) were particular targets. Spottiswood escaped to London, to be buried on his death in March 1645 in Westminster Abbey.[74] However, neither Cole nor Enniskillen – like Derry – was captured, and it became, for some, a centre of refuge. But ultimately now (if the existing order were to be preserved) support and protection had to be sought from England. Cole was one of those British colonels in Ulster who were granted commissions by the king in November to raise troops to combat the rebellion. However, as the king's deteriorating relations with his parliament in England and with the Scots (which had provided the circumstances for the outbreak of the rising in Ireland) soon broke down into civil war and a lengthy war of all three kingdoms, and with the king's capacity to raise money greatly reduced, it was to the parliament of England that he must apply for support. He received payments for the supply of his forces from the English parliamentary authorities in 1642 and 1643.[75]

Cole's own military actions at this time are less well known, but it is likely that men of Enniskillen took part in the crucial battle of Clones in June 1643, when Owen Roe O'Neill's army was defeated and so an extremely important event for the planter recovery (already underway) in this part of Ulster. Immediately thereafter he campaigned, alongside the forces of the Laggan army, into County Tyrone, and he took Crevenish Castle later that year.[76] But Cole also had his critic. In December 1644 the ambitious Scotsman Sir Fredrick Hamilton of Manorhamilton levelled a range of charges against him including one of partiality towards some of the Irish of the county, but Cole responded that the protection he had given Brian MacCuchonnacht Maguire (d. 1655) had saved the lives of many Protestants. He also insisted that he had been one of the first colonels of the British regiments in Ulster to take the oath of the Solemn League and Covenant, the objective of which had been to seek to secure the establishment of a Presbyterian system of church government.[77] In February 1645 Cole was in London (along with John Carmick) for the trial of Conor, Lord Maguire, who had been arrested following on the failure of the *coup d'état* against Dublin Castle which had formed part of the plan of the rising in 1641. Then in October 1645 Enniskilleners with others took part in a successful engagement in County Sligo. However, in November a detachment of Owen Roe O'Neill's army carried out an attack on Cole's winter quarters on Boa Island in Lower Lough Erne which, though the force was probably afterwards pursued by Cole's men, may have deterred him from taking part then in another intervention on Connacht. No attempt, however, was made on Enniskillen itself at this time.[78] In July 1646 (after the battle of Benburb) Cole sought substantial supplies from the Committee of Both Houses for Irish Affairs, and received a lesser amount in that and the following year.[79] Early in 1649 the fort at Enniskillen was seized from Cole by some of his own officers, in an instance of the royalist reaction to the English revolution, when (after the Second Civil War) the king had been executed and when a Commonwealth or Republic had been instituted by those who carried it out. Enniskillen was back in Commonwealth control by 1650, and the lengthy (and intermittent) war in Ireland was soon thereafter brought to an end. Sir William died in Dublin in October 1653, at an advanced age.[80]

Cole's family and will

Cole got married in Ireland, but exactly when is not known. His wife was Susan or Susanna, a daughter of John Croft of Lancashire and widow of Stephen Seagar who had been keeper of Dublin Castle. They had two sons and two daughters. His eldest son, Michael (who died or might have been killed during the Confederate War), married Katherine, daughter of the well-connected Sir Laurence Parsons of King's County, in 1640.[81] His second son, John (who held property in County Dublin), married Elizabeth, daughter of John Chichester of Dungannon. In a mingling of Scots and English in Ulster, his daughter Mary married the Rev. Robert Barclay, the Scottish-born dean of Clogher, who was to be Cole's agent in London in 1642 and 1643. His eldest daughter Margaret (bearing her aunt's name) married Sir James Montgomery, son of the Scottish settler Sir Hugh Montgomery in County Down.

Cole's will, made in October 1653, began with a common religious formula. He bequeathed his 'soul to Almighty God assuring myself, through the merits, death and passion of Jesus Christ my only saviour and redeemer, to have remission of all my sins, and life everlasting with his angels in heaven for ever …'. In accordance with a marriage settlement made in July 1640 (when his deceased son Michael married Katherine Parsons), he provided that his grandson, also Michael, should inherit his property. Following a proviso in that marriage settlement, Cole now also bequeathed a sum of £1,500 (to be taken out of the rents and profits of the lands) to his second son, John Cole, who should be executor of the will and have charge of the estate until his nephew should come of age. In default of male heirs, the estate should descend to John Cole and his heirs, and in default there, to Cole's 'kinsman' Richard Cole, who was son of Thomas Cole (grandson of Sir William's uncle, William) who had been a lawyer in London and an official in the court of wards there.

For his education and maintenance, the grandson (who entered Trinity College, Dublin in 1659) should receive a yearly allowance of £36 stg until the age of fifteen years, to increase to £60 until eighteen and to £80 until he were twenty one, these sums to be paid to his guardians at Strongbow's tomb in Dublin. Perhaps aware that in the circumstances of the time the sum of £1,500 might not be raised quickly, Cole also laid down that John Cole should receive the income from the lettings (£52 stg in all) of some of his demesne lands at Enniskillen and nearby. Hence a group of parks there (very English in conception) come to light, the miller's park, the pigeon house park, the horse park and the 'Connyberry' park being amongst them. The hop ground was rented at £2 per annum, and the profits of his two boats brought in £10 per year. Omonery alias Paget's land returned £10 a year, and provides also the surname from which Paget Square in Enniskillen derives.

A number of bequests were made to those with family connection. His daughter Mary Barclay should receive £26 stg per annum during the life of her husband and should he die before her, £400 after his death. An annuity of £36 left to John Warnett, probably himself now living in Dublin, brings to light a member of a legal family, the Warnetts of Sussex and London, one of whom, Katherine Warnett, had married Thomas Cole the lawyer, whose son Richard was (as has been seen) a remainder man in Sir William's will. In addition, a nephew and niece were to receive £80 and £30 respectively. Of two beneficiaries who probably were not relatives, one, Henry Gillett who was left £30, may well have been Cole's agent from his estate. Cole ended his will with (for him) an expression of hopefulness. Since, 'by reason of crosses which have happened unto me in this time of rebellion and war', he had not been able to leave some 'better token' of his 'love and affection' both to those people and to 'other of my poor friends', he enjoined his executor, 'that as God shall bless him with means and estate hereafter' he should 'contribute what help he may unto them'.[82]

Conclusion

Although he was buried in Dublin rather than in Enniskillen, when he died – after fifty years in Ulster affairs – Cole knew by then that the Plantation would continue. In these fifty years and in all these ways, for good or ill, the foundations of a two-culture society had been laid.

Appendix 1:
The castle site in Enniskillen in the seventeenth century

It seemed to me, on a visit to Florencecourt, that the best indication of what this site looked like in the seventeenth century, and, indeed, probably as a result of the works carried out there by Cole in his own time, can be found on a painting of Enniskillen, made in the eighteenth century, which is kept there and of which the appropriate part is reproduced here (plate 8.7). The drawings (plates 8.8–8.10) by David McConaghy (who made a number of journeys with me to Enniskillen to take measurements) are based on that painting along with other sources, including Clarke's watercolour of the town in 1787.

The suggestion made here in the light of it, is that a substantial portion of Maguire's original wall (which was fourteen feet high) was retained by Cole, and McConaghy has plotted it, at the distance of forty-five feet from the castle measured by John Thomas in 1594, onto a modern map. He has, convincingly, indicated the location of Maguire's water gate entrance, since it also can be observed on the painting in the correct location. Whether that wall had had a walkway on the top, as exists on surviving portions of O'Donnell's wall at Donegal, is a little uncertain, He has drawn the two new buildings constructed by Cole – the Watergate and the building beside it, which were thirty-two feet apart on the river side – and shown how they projected beyond the line of the original wall. The castle with its brick chimney, as shown on the painting, was probably also Cole's reconstruction (lower than Maguire's had been) rather than a later rebuild.

Although the stone bridge shown on the painting is in the same location as both Maguire's bridge and Cole's drawbridge had been, it is not suggested that the painting at this point is a good indicator of what had prevailed in Cole's time, since by now much of the ditch seems to have been filled in. After all, Leonard, in drawing the castle site on his map, had noted that it had been 'formerly surrounded by a canal'. Some remnants of this waterway to the south can, however, still be seen on the painting. Those buildings shown on the painting which were extensions of the castle northwards, both inside and outside the wall, were probably, therefore, later constructions. Maguire's small barbican tower (demolished probably when the keep was),

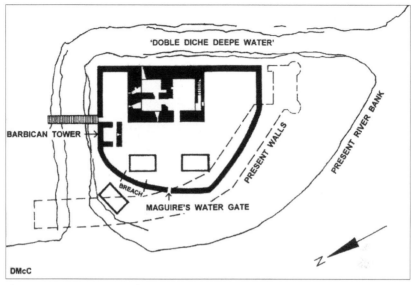

Plate 8.8 Conjectural plan of Maguire's Castle site, Enniskillen, in 1594 (D. McConaghy)

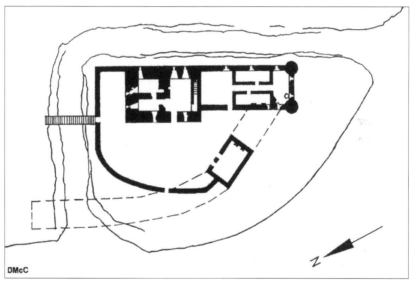

Plate 8.9 Conjectural plan of Cole's Castle site, Enniskillen (D. McConaghy)

which was beside the bridge, had not, it would seem, been rebuilt since it
does not appear on the painting. Cole might perhaps also have re-orientated
the entry by boat directly from the river, if there were indeed an entrance,
well protected, between the Watergate and the other new building beside
it. He might even also, or otherwise, have had an arched gate as part of the
new building between the keep and the Watergate. These, however, are only
conjectures, with the latter less likely.

Plate 8.10 Conjectural reconstruction of Watergate building, Enniskillen
(D. McConaghy)

This interpretation of Cole's works, based as it is on visual evidence, is
probably to be preferred to another, based on the plan of *c.* 1611 (plate
8.5), which has been given elsewhere.[83] That plan may well have been
designed to show what was intended rather than what was completed, since
Cole was soon now to move towards building on his estates. Three new
houses shown on this plan (two of them two-storeyed and dormered, one
single-storeyed) outside the castle complex on the Broad Meadow (which
is somewhat misdrawn it would seem in relation to the river) have not been
drawn, since their precise locations can only be somewhat conjectural. No
attempt also has been made to show the site of Cole's own new timber
house, mentioned by Carew in 1611 (which would probably not have been
long-lasting), and garden, since its exact location is probably also still
somewhat uncertain. Although it might well have been one of those three
houses, the suggestion made by W.C. Trimble that it could even have been

to the north, under the street which ran from the new West Bridge, may perhaps be worth some consideration. Hints of what might once have been a walled garden there could also be taken from the painting.

Appendix 2:
One account of the assault on Boa Island in November 1645

The following account of the military action on Boa Island has been taken from the *Commentarius Rinuccinianus*.[84] I am very grateful to F.J. D'Arcy, sometime of Magee University College, for making the translation.

On November 23 William Cole, a cavalry commander and heretic enemy in that area, received a letter from Sir Charles Coote, also a heretic enemy. In this he was requested to bring his cavalry force from Ulster into the Sligo area on November 27, and thus he and Charles with their united forces would attack deep into Connacht, and there they would carry our some plan which doubtlessly would be unknown to the Catholics. The greater part of William's cavalry squadron was then based with their horses on the island of Boa in Lough Erne – about sixteen miles north from the camp at Enniskillen. When they received the letter they set out on the journey on November 24 accompanied by two companies of infantry from the same Williams's regiment who were in winter quarters on the island. They were followed on November 25 by about twenty horsemen from the Enniskillen garrison. Their plan was to camp that night about fifteen miles from Sligo.

Owen O'Neill meanwhile divided his force which amounted to scarcely 3,000 men into two sections. He sent 500 under the command of Rory Maguire to seize the island of Boa mentioned earlier, while he himself as evening fell on November 25 made an appearance with about 2,000 foot and 200 horse on the brow of a hill a mile away from Enniskillen. He did this to deter the Enniskillen garrison, whom he saw as more of a danger to Rory, from moving against Rory when they heard of his raid. For Rory indeed on the morning of that same day, the 26th, following his orders, crossed over with his 550 men to the southern part of that island (of Boa), having been provided with two boats by Brian O'Hara and other Irishmen who lived there under the yoke of the enemy. These boats actually belonged to the enemy.

The herds supplying the enemy troops were kept on this island, as also were oxen, weapons, clothing, provisions and the wives of the Enniskilliners, as it was deemed a very secure place against attack. Rory and his troops captured all this material, as many of the enemy's troops were then absent (as we said above), and then Rory arranged that what could be

Plate 8.11 Three grave monuments, 1675–1707, in St Macartin's, Enniskillen
(Photograph: Walter Baumann)

transported was to be carried away, with the herds driven to the south of the island. He also saw to it that even the clothes of the women were seized leaving barely enough to cover them, and that a number of soldiers in garrison were made prisoner, and other material burned. This was for the great good of the Catholic cause, as Nicholas O'Byrne in the passage already cited tells us that the enemy had previously placed there military provisions and livestock for the invasion of Connacht but now their projected expedition against the Connachtmen was not possible because they lacked the means to carry it out.

While this was going on and while the Enniskilliners, as I have said, were hindered by Owen O'Neill from going out to do harm to Rory, that body of enemy foot and horse whom we have described as moving off towards Sligo heard on the way the news that to them was so distressful. They abandoned their Connacht expedition (which was a kind of second victory for the Catholics), and returned at a great pace, with even the infantry making speed by mounting the horses. But through their bad luck, they made their way to the northern part of the island, three English miles away from the southern part by which Rory had entered and departed with his men. This did not stop William Cole from writing to England and the English Parliament ordering it to be printed in London, that Cole's men had then pursued Rory as he was making off with his booty and at daybreak on November 27 they had caught up with him and after a stubborn struggle they had put our men to flight. Cole added that a nephew of Terence O'Neill, Henry's son, together with a colonel and two subordinate officers, had been killed, that some of our men were captured, that a major part of the booty was recovered and the men whom we had seen made captive in Boa had been liberated. The heretic squadrons and companies had then returned to Enniskillen at the northern part of Lough Erne on November 30.

The Nuncio who had just come to Ireland in the month of October tells the story in his diary of how far from reality(?) was this victory of theirs, as he does the account of Nicholas O'Byrne in the place already cited, and the latter adds that Owen's forces took much booty in that expedition and that many islands in Lough Erne close to Enniskillen and inhabited by the enemy were destroyed by fire. When this military episode was completed, Owen then went with his troops into the county of Monaghan ...

Appendix 3:
An after-look: a two-culture society, *c.* 1700

A number of little pointers to the bi-cultural society that had arisen in County Fermanagh by the beginning of the eighteenth century, and to the thought processes that existed within it, are brought together here. All need – very obviously – much fuller exploration and refining.

In the first place one may note the contents of a large group of manuscripts transcribed under the patronage of a Maguire landholder in the county in the early eighteenth century.[85] Brian Maguire of Knockninny who commissioned them was a very able man who now held the tenancy of a substantial area of land. The materials collected on his behalf included Maguire pedigrees and historical tracts and legends and also lives of saints and a range of devotional literature. These were obviously of great importance to him as, no doubt, they would have been also to other Irish landholders and to Catholic clergy. Full studies of other such collections, or of collections of Gaelic poetry from the county in this period, should also be carried out.

Little pointers to characteristics of some in the planter society at this time can also be detected. In a small way the influence of the scientific revolution then underway in contemporary England can be seen in the fact that a sundial had been attached to the tower of the church in Enniskillen some time before 1674.[86] The same scientific mentality can be observed at work in the map of the town made by James Leonard, 'philomath', in the early eighteenth century. Again, the influence of contemporary English rationalist thought (as well as the limitations which still lay upon it) may be found at one point in the account of the Williamite/Jacobite war in

County Fermanagh published by the Rev. Andrew Hamilton, rector of Kilskeery, in 1690. Although he was, he said, not 'very *superstitious* to lay great stress' on such things, he mentioned in it pillars of light said to have been seen over Newtownbutler and elsewhere, while leaving it to the reader to form 'his own conjectures of them'.[87] Innovation can also be seen in visual terms. Three grave monuments in St Macartin's, Enniskillen (plate 8.11) dating from 1675 to 1707 were exercises, albeit unlearned ones, in an architectural classicism – the 'new way of building' – later to flourish in some of the great houses of the county including the Cole's Florencecourt.[88] All these little indicators point in general to a culture shared in common (though perhaps with some small time-lag) with people in England.

One medium of convergence between both societies was coming to be the use of the English language. Hence, for example, Dolan wrote his account of the county in very good English in 1718.[89] Needless to say, by the early eighteenth century the Gaelic society in County Fermanagh was also a much diminished one.

Acknowledgements

I am very grateful to Helen Lanigan Wood of Fermanagh County Museum, to the staff of Enniskillen Library, and to the Rev. Precentor Courtney and Norman Hilliard of St Macartin's, Enniskillen, for allowing me access to resources under their control. I have to thank Mrs Joanna McVey of the *Impartial Reporter*, descendant of W.C. Trimble, author of the compendious *History of Enniskillen*, for permission to see Clarke's water colour of Enniskillen in 1787. I also have to thank James Chesnutt and Charles Bennett of the National Trust at Florencecourt. For permission to reproduce illustrations used here. I am grateful to the British Library, the Public Record Office, Kew (for Crown copyright material), the Board of Trinity College, Dublin, and to the National Trust. I would also like to pay tribute to the memory of Fr P. O Gallachair, historian and a friend of former years. I have to thank David McConaghy for the drawings that he has produced and Vernon Hood for information about Devonshire. I am most grateful, once again, to Joanne Taggart of the University of Ulster for her kindness and skill and preparing the typescript.

[1] J.M.S. Brooke and A.W.C. Hallen (eds), *The transcript of the registers of the united parishes of St Mary Woolnoth and St Mary Woolchurch Haw, in the city of London … 1538 to 1760* (London, 1886), pp 16, 193.

[2] This, and what follows, is based on J. Edwin-Cole, *The genealogy of the family of Cole* (London, 1867), passim and *The genealogie or pedigree of … Sir William Cole …* (?London, 1870), passim.

[3] W.B. Bannerman (ed.), *The registers of St Mary le Bowe, Cheapside, All Hallows, Honey Lane, and*

of St Pancras, Soper Lane, London (London, 1914), pp 99–101, 260; P.W. Hasler, *The history of parliament: the house of commons, 1558–1603*, i (London, 1981), pp 628–9.

4   Edwin-Cole, *Genealogy*, pp 9–41.

5   W.J. Blake (ed.), 'Hooker's Synopsis Chorographical of Devonshire' in *Transactions of the Devonshire Association*, 47 (1915), pp 334–48.

6   On the war in general see H. Morgan, *Tyrone's rebellion: the outbreak of the Nine Years' War in Tudor Ireland* (Dublin, 1993).

7   For the Spanish intervention see J.J. Silke, *Kinsale: The Spanish intervention in Ireland at the end of the Elizabethan wars* (Liverpool, 1970), and on armies J. McGurk, *The Elizabethan conquest of Ireland: the 1590s crisis* (Manchester, 1997).

8   *Cal. S.P. Ire.*, 1601–3, p. 218.

9   TNA, AO1/287/1081–/288/1082; *Acts of the privy council of England* (hereafter *APC*), 30 (1599–1600), pp 444–45, 467–68; *APC*, 32 (1601–4), pp 102–3, 107, 120–21; *Cal. Carew MSS*, 1601–3, p. 93; *Cal. S.P. Ire.*, 1600–01, p. 447.

10   For Sir John Davies's comments on this see H. Morley, *Ireland under Elizabeth and James I* (London, 1890), pp 362–71.

11   E. Hogan (ed.), *The description of Ireland, and the state thereof as it is at this present in anno 1598* (Dublin and London, 1878), p. 25.

12   N. O Muraile (ed.), *Cathal og MacMaghnusa and the annals of Ulster* (Enniskillen, 1998), passim.

13   A. Gwynn and R.N. Hadcock, *Medieval religious houses: Ireland* (London, 1970), p. 254.

14   *AFM*, vi, pp 1875–77, 1889–93.

15   *Fiants Ire., Eliz.*, nos 4682, 4809–10.

16   *Inq. Ult.*, p. xviii.

17   *AFM*, vi, p. 1875.

18   D. Greene (ed.), *Duanaire Mhéig Uidhir: the poembook of Cú Chonnacht Mág Uidhir, Lord of Fermanagh 1566–1589* (Dublin, 1972), passim.

19   *AFM*, vi, pp 1959, 1965–67, 2000, 2039, 2099.

20   BL, Cotton MS Augustus I ii, 39; TNA, MPF 1/80.

21   *Cal. S.P. Ire.*, 1600, pp 126, 282; TNA, AO1/287/1081–/289/1085.

22   *CPR, Eliz.*, pp 584–85.

23   M.K. Walsh, *Destruction by peace: Hugh O Neill after Kinsale* (Armagh, 1986), p. 176.

24   F. Moryson, *An itinerary*, iii (Glasgow, 1908), pp 180, 182–3, 206–7, 224.

25   Ibid., p. 237; *AFM*, vi, p. 2329.

26   J.C. Erck (ed.), *A repertory of the inrolments on the patent rolls of chancery in Ireland commencing with the reign of James I*, I, pt i (Dublin, 1846), pp 11–14.

27   *Inq. Ult.*, pp xxxi–xl; *CPR, Jas I*, pp 32–3, 34–5; HMC, *Hastings MSS*, iv, 153.

28   H. Morley, *Ireland under Elizabeth and James I*, pp 348, 372–73, 379.

29   *Cal. S.P. Ire.*, 1603–6, pp 562–63.

30   *CPR, Jas I*, pp 83, 91, 122, 135.

31   Moryson, *Itinerary*, iii, p. 148; *Cal. S.P. Ire.*, 1601–3, pp 526, 555.

32   TNA, AO1/289/1085–1087.

33   HMC, *Salisbury [=Cecil] MSS*, xix (1607), p. 17.

34   *CPR, Jas I*, pp 113, 115.

35   TNA, AO1/290/1088.

36   J. Buckley (ed.), 'Report of Sir Josias Bodley on some Ulster fortresses in 1608', in *Ulster Journal of Archaeology*, 2nd series, 16 (1910), p. 64.

37   This is based on a larger study of Plantation Ulster on which I am at work. For useful studies of plantation in County Fermanagh already published see J.D. Johnston, 'Scottish settlement in county Fermanagh, 1610–1630' in *Clogher Record*, ix (1976–78), pp 367–73; idem, 'English settlement in county Fermanagh, 1610–1640' in *Clogher Record*, x (1979–81), pp 137–43; and idem, 'Settlement patterns in county Fermanagh, 1610–1660' in *Clogher Record*, x (1979–81), pp 199–214.

38   BL, Add. MS 4770, ff 48–9, 64–64v, 66 (I am engaged on an edition and study of this entire document).

39   TNA, AO1/291/1091–1092.

40   W.A. Shaw, *The knights of England* (London, 1906), ii, p. 166.

41   TNA, AO1/290/1089, f. 30v.

42 *CPR, Jas I*, p. 215; TNA, AO1/290/1090, f. 34.

43 For this in general see ch. 14, pp 368–74.

44 *Analecta Hibernica*, viii (1938), p. 244. For the detail on this and the eventual choice of Enniskillen as against Lisgoole, see ch. 9, pp 236–50.

45 *CPR, Jas I*, p. 232. A translation of the patent in full appears in W.C. Trimble, *The history of Enniskillen* (3 vols, Enniskillen, 1919–21), i, pp 166–70.

46 See footnote 20 above.

47 *CPR, Jas I*, p. 243. An English translation is in Trimble, *History of Enniskillen*, i, pp 171–78.

48 Earl of Belmore, *The history of two Ulster manors* (2nd edition, London and Dublin, 1903), p. 93.

49 W. Harris, *The history of the life and reign of William-Henry, prince of Nassau and Orange, stadholder of the United Provinces, King of England Scotland, France and Ireland etc. in which the affairs of Ireland are more particularly handled, than in any other history* (Dublin, 1749), facing p. 213.

50 NAI, D1028.

51 NAI, D1040.

52 HMC, *Hastings MSS*, iv, pp 167–68.

53 NAI, D1028; C.R. Elrington (ed.), *The whole works of the most reverend James Ussher*, xv (Dublin, 1864), pp 89–90.

54 W.H. Dundas, *Enniskillen: parish and town* (Dundalk and Enniskillen, 1913), pp 68–70.

55 For more detail see Hunter, 'Cole and Enniskillen' (see above footnote 44).

56 BL, Add. MS 4770, ff 64–4v.

57 NAI, D1041.

58 A. Hamilton, *The actions of the Enniskillen-men from their first taking up arms in 1688 … to the landing of Duke Schomberg in Ireland* (London, 1690, reprinted Belfast, 1813, and Dalbeattie, 2001), p. 2.

59 S. Pender (ed.), *A census of Ireland, circa 1659* (Dublin, 1939), p. 119. In the 1660s, there were some sixty-six householders in the town (including one Huguenot family) who paid hearth tax, of whom five had houses with two fireplaces with all the rest having one. Cole's residence is not included in this list (PRONI, T808/15068, p. 7). There was a friary within the town by 1688.

60 TNA, SP63/173, ff 99v–104v. Those features which might be misinterpreted as indicators of a third building came then, it would appear, to be further misinterpreted as turrets on Speed's map (I am indebted to David McConaghy for his help with this).

61 Lambeth Palace Library, Carew MS 630, f. 53v.

62 TCD, MS 1209/29.

63 P. O Maolagain (ed.), 'An early history of Fermanagh' in *Clogher Record*, ii (1957–59), p. 292.

64 The *c.* 1611 plan shows the base only.

65 The painting is in Florence Court. A photograph of a small part of it is published here by permission of the National Trust.

66 Apart from the castle complex the town had no further defensive fortifications and was unwalled. Some additional works of fortification were, however, carried out by the defenders in 1688–89. If these had included something in *bastion* form on the other side of the island, then an origin for the street name Boston might be forthcoming. At one point, however, both bridges onto the main island were defensible. The west one (repaired or reconstructed, *c.* 1698, having been 'newly' rebuilt by the 1680s) had a 'square tower with a gateway and a guard room in the midst' while the east bridge had once been a drawbridge (W. Harris, *Life and reign of William-Henry* (Dublin, 1749), p. 213).

67 NAI, Lodge MSS, vi, pp 111–18.

68 *CPR, Jas I*, p. 566.

69 BL, Add MS 4756, ff 106v–7.

70 *Inq. Ult.*, Fermanagh (4) Chas I.

71 R. Gillespie, 'The trials of Bishop Spottiswood, 1620–40' in *Clogher Record*, xii (1985–87), pp 320–33.

72 *Cal. S.P. Ire.*, *1625–32*, pp 35–7.

73 M. Perceval-Maxwell, *The outbreak of the Irish rebellion of 1641* (Dublin, 1994), pp 74, 88, 90, 131, 216.

74 J.L. Chester (ed.), *The register of Westminster abbey* (London, 1876), p. 139.

[75] TNA, SP28/139, pt 12.

[76] C. Dillon and H.A. Jefferies (eds), *Tyrone: history and society* (Dublin, 2000), pp 351–52, 356; J.T. Gilbert (ed.), *A contemporary history of affairs in Ireland from 1641 to 1652*, i, pt 2 (Dublin, 1879), pp 564–5.

[77] *The information of Sir Frederick Hamilton, Knight and Colonel, given to the committee of both kingdoms concerning Sir William Cole, Knight and Colonel, with the scandalous answer of the said Sir William Cole, knight, together with the replication of Sir Frederick Hamilton ...* (London, 1645); *The answer and vindication of Sir William Cole ...* (London, 1645).

[78] J.T. Gilbert (ed.), *A contemporary history of affairs in Ireland from 1641 to 1652*, i, pt 2 (Dublin, 1879), pp 626–30; *Good news from Ireland, being an exact relation of the late good success at Sliggo against the Irish rebels ... performed by Sir Charles Coot, Sir William Cole and Sir Francis Hamilton, with the particulars thereof* (London, 1646); B. O'Ferrall and D. O'Connell, *Commentarius Rinuccinianus*, i (Dublin, 1932), pp 577–9. For Cole's account of the raid on Boa Island, see below footnote 84.

[79] *Cal. S.P. Ire., 1633–47*, pp 483–4.

[80] He was buried 'in St. Michan's over the water' there (GO, Funeral Entries, Vol. 4, p. 7). For another study of plantation in County Fermanagh see ch. 18, pp 461–79.

[81] This corrects the error made in Edwin-Cole and elsewhere which has Katherine Parsons as Sir William's second wife.

[82] PRONI, D1702/1/27/1. In addition to Henry Gillett, the other beneficiary was Sarah Cosby, relict of Captain Arnold Cosby, who should receive £60. Cole also laid down in his will that any daughter or daughters of his grandson, Michael Cole ('if any such shall be'), should receive £2,000 stg out of the estate for her or their portions 'and full claim as heirs general' to the estate, and should have half of its annual rents and value until that sum should be satisfied.

[83] E. Halpin, 'Excavations at Enniskillen castle, County Fermanagh' in *Ulster Journal of Archaeology*, 3rd series, 57 (1994), p. 122. The outline architectural interpretation given by H. Dixon some years ago is close to what is now suggested in this appendix (A. Rowan, *The buildings of Ireland: North West Ulster* (Harmondsworth, 1979), p. 280.

[84] O'Ferrall and O'Connell, *Commentarius Rinuccinianus*, i, pp 577–79. Cole's account is *A true and fuller relation from Ireland of the service performed by the men of Iniskillen of Sir William Cole's regiment and troop at Lowtherstowne upon Thursday Novemb. 27. 1645 about one of the clock in the night; wherein they did not only (by God's providence) rescue their prey, but having there routed a party of four or five hundred men of the rebels, did likewise put the whole army of Owen MacArte O Neale to flight* (London, 1646).

[85] B. Cunningham and R. Gillespie, 'The purposes of patronage: Brian Maguire of Knockninny and his manuscripts' in *Clogher Record*, xiii (1988), pp 38–49.

[86] Dundas, *Enniskillen: parish and town*, p. 33.

[87] Hamilton, *Actions of the Enniskillen-men*, pp 49–51. For attitudes to 'superstition' (mainly now in its non-theological sense) in English thought at this time, see R. Porter, *Enlightenment: Britain and the creation of the modern world* (London, 2000), pp 149–51.

[88] Dundas, *Enniskillen: parish and town*, pp 91–3. I am indebted to Dr E. McParland for his advice on this point.

[89] O Maolagain, 'An early history of Fermanagh', *Clogher Record*, i–iv (1953–62).

9

Sir William Cole and Plantation Enniskillen, 1607–41

I

William Cole, a Londoner born perhaps in 1575, derived from a branch of the family of Cole of Slade in Devonshire, his grandfather or perhaps great-grandfather having migrated to London. His grandfather was established in the parish of All Hallows, Honey Lane by 1540 and died there as a grocer in 1571.[1] His father, Emanuel Cole, a third son, was married to Margaret Ingram, a member of a family who had also moved to London – in this case from Yorkshire.[2] At least two MPs in the reign of Elizabeth belonged to branches of the larger Cole family and another London and Surrey branch had military and legal members in the early seventeenth century.[3] A Cole relative had been mother of Sir Richard Grenville who had had Irish interests in the 1560s and 1580s,[4] and William's cousin, Sir Arthur Ingram, began an involvement with Ireland when he was appointed to investigate the customs in 1607.[5] Although an only son,[6] Cole's immediate economic circumstances as he grew up are not clear. However he had inherited from both parents a tradition of mobility and he opted for a military career. There is no evidence that he attended either of the universities or an inn of court.

After what must have been a short military career in Holland, Cole turned to Ireland. In December 1603 from the 'camp before Kinsale' he was recommended to Cecil for promotion to captain by Sir George Carew, lord president of Munster, as a lieutenant who had served under Captain Hansard (later to be a planter at Lifford) for two years.[7] He next comes to light, in post-war Ulster, as Captain Cole, overseer of the barges at Ballyshannon, in 1605.[8] During the Nine Years' War the governor of Ballyshannon had had a military jurisdiction over south Donegal and Fermanagh first established in 1600 in the hands of Sir Matthew Morgan, similar to that granted to Sir Henry Docwra to the north as governor of Lough Foyle.[9] This governorship was now held by Sir Henry Foliot of Ballyshannon, Cole clearly occupying a subordinate position to him.[10] Cole's appointment brought him payment by concordatum for building the barges, and later a small fixed fee,[11] but he was not constable or commander of a fort and Foliot's acquisition of dissolved monastic lands in Donegal combined with Sir John Davies's (the attorney-general) determination to acquire the lands of Lisgoole abbey in Fermanagh cut off for him opportunities for pre-plantation land acquisition such as fellow captains established in other areas of Ulster were enjoying.[12]

In these circumstances Cole thought of leaving Ireland. In January 1607, Sir George Cary, lord deputy in 1603, referring to his good services at Kinsale and Ballyshannon urged Salisbury to recommend him to 'the States of the Low Countries' for appointment to a foot company.[13] Instead Lord Deputy Chichester was instructed, in May, to formalise his position by patent as captain of the King's long-boats and barges at Ballyshannon and Lough Erne, and he received his patent in September.[14] Early in 1609 he became constable of Enniskillen castle in succession to Edmond Ellis.[15]

Enniskillen, an island in Lough Erne long fortified by the Maguires, had not been permanently garrisoned by English forces during the latter years of the war. Thus while in the post-war arrangements for the earldoms of Tyrone and Tyrconnell, certain forts with areas of land attached to them were reserved for the crown and then leased to the incumbent commanders,[16] the post-war arrangements for Fermanagh, concluded in 1604 (though never formalised by patent) and involving a division of the county between Cuchonnacht Maguire and Conor Roe Maguire, did not exclude any fortified centre or land appertaining.[17] Cuchonnacht Maguire received 'Inishekellin', and it could not have been until after the Flight of the Earls that a constable was appointed. Cole did not get his lease of the castle and a very small area of appertaining land until June 1611,[18] but by then he had been assigned land as a servitor in the plantation in Fermanagh. Indeed in May 1610 the English privy council wrote specially in his favour to Chichester. However, after his position had been regularised in 1607, just before the flight of Cuchonnacht Maguire, Cole was well positioned in the run up to plantation.

Now in transition from soldier to landowner, Ireland seems to have been his exclusive interest. Although a number of Coles, some of whom may have been relatives, were involved in English overseas ventures,[19] Cole himself was essentially a professional soldier who had looked to Europe and Ireland for advancement and had married, presumably in Ireland, the widow of the lieutenant of Dublin castle.[20] The composite William Cole of Professor Rabb's computer – Ulster landowner, member of the Spanish Company and investor in Virginia – has, regrettably, to be unravelled into three.[21] He received land as a servitor in the baronies of Clanawley and Tyrkennedy, two 'precincts' which formed a central zone in Fermanagh divided by the Erne and pivoting on Enniskillen which were allocated to servitors and Irish grantees under the plantation scheme, and became patron of the town of Enniskillen as well. After 1610 he built up an estate of substantial proportions in Fermanagh making him one of the larger landowners in plantation Ulster before 1641. He played an active part in the rising, filling, albeit on the side of parliament, the military role of the servitor in the plantation. He lived until 1653.[22] This paper, however, is concerned only with the growth of the town of Enniskillen up to 1641.

II

The 'project' of plantation in January 1609 envisaged the establishment of three incorporated towns in Fermanagh as that county's share in twenty-five proposed corporations in the six planted counties. However although land was to be allocated to the corporations of these planned urban settlements in the plantation, the two fundamental problems of recruiting residents and building houses, for all of them except Derry and Coleraine in the Londoners plantation, remained unresolved until after the land in the counties had been allocated to the new owners in the summer of 1610. The proposed 'leavy or presse of trades men and artificers out of England' had not materialised. It was not until December that an expedient suggested by Chichester and agreed to by the English privy council in 1611 provided a means of breaking the deadlock. Responsibility for establishing the towns should be devolved to a local undertaker or servitor as patron or superintendent and the lands intended for the corporation should be granted to him. Also by the autumn of 1611 the number of proposed corporations had been scaled down to eighteen. By 1613 fourteen places in the six escheated counties, subsequently increased to sixteen, had received charters. The processes followed a standard form, but with a degree of local variation.[23]

Thirty tates of land estimated at thirty acres each were allocated in the 'project' for three towns in Fermanagh – at Lisgoole, Lisnaskea and at a site to be chosen mid-way between Lisgoole and Ballyshannon.[24] The revision of 1611 reduced this to one town for the county, to be developed at Enniskillen.[25] This reduction was already pre-determined at the time of allocating the land to grantees in 1610 by the erosion of the reserved 30 tates or some 900 acres to a mere 5½ tates, though now after an intervening general revised valuation of the tate at 60 acres estimated at 330 acres.[26]

In January 1611, while the quest for a means to get the towns in general underway was afoot, interim arrangements for the lands (the 330 acres) allocated 'for a town at Lisgoole or Inishkillen' were made. The lands were to

238

be rented for one year under the direction of Foliot, the governor, and Cole, and the corporation when established was to consist of 43 members 'all English, Scotish and Civill Natives'.[27] Most important was that underneath these arrangements a planning muddle was revealed. Not only had the endowment for two towns gone entirely by default through the allocation of the reserved land to private individuals, but the remaining allocation, which was in the barony of Clanawley and mainly in Ordnance Survey sheets 27, 13 and 14 was inconvenient to either Lisgoole or Enniskillen. The originally proposed site at Lisgoole was on abbey land held independently of the plantation by Sir John Davies. However, Davies, one of those who drew up the 'project' of plantation in 1609, as one of the commissioners for the allocation of land to grantees in 1610 could have ensured that escheated lands comparatively close to the monastic were allocated to the town and surrendered the site (by an appropriate exchange of land), as the plan then envisaged, to the proposed corporation, rather chose to consolidate his own holdings in the area by receiving his lands as a servitor grantee nearby.[28] Enniskillen, an alternative with its castle in government hands comparable to other places in the plantation designated for urban development, also presented difficulties. Contiguous lands to the north-west in the barony of Magheraboy had all been allocated to Scottish undertakers. Contiguous church lands to the south and some nearby to the north must be granted to the bishopric of Clogher (whose incumbent, George Montgomery, had also been one of those who drew up the 'project') by the terms of a general arrangement for the disposal of church lands. A privy council directive of May 1610 instructing that Cole should receive his servitor's grant 'as near as may be' to the castle of Enniskillen[29] ensured that remaining contiguous escheated land, mainly to the east in the barony of Tyrkennedy, must be granted to him. Given these factors, and with no firm arrangements worked out in advance of the allocation of land in 1610 for the actual establishment of the Ulster towns (except those in the Londoners plantation) to the corporations of which the land should be granted, it was not perhaps surprising that the plantation commissioners, under no immediate pressure to grapple with the local problem, allocated it where they did.

However, Enniskillen island (with its castle) remained in crown hands, uniquely unassigned to any grantee by the plantation commissioners in 1610. As the superintendency idea, whereby town lands would now be granted not to the corporations, but to a local landowner admittedly under conditions, began to emerge at the end of 1610, Enniskillen could present itself as an alternative to Lisgoole if a suitable arrangement could be reached with Cole which the more highly placed Davies would not seek to pre-empt for himself. The interim arrangement of January 1611, although it did not embody the necessary explicit decision in favour of Enniskillen, stated that Cole had agreed to exchange some of his servitor's grant for the town lands.[30] From this the final arrangement emerged. Hence Cole exchanged some of his servitor's lands in Tyrkennedy near to Enniskillen, later granted to him under the superintendency system to establish the town as part of, in fact, a tripartite re-arrangement involving some of the lands allotted for the Fermanagh royal school, also originally proposed to be established at Lisgoole[31] and now to be located, explicitly, at Enniskillen, as well, and hence his servitor's grant came to be in two substantial detached portions, one in Tyrkennedy barony and one in Clanawley.[32] Thus the flexibility and thrust of the locally resident Cole, unopposed by Davies, necessarily absentee as a member of government and who as well had received other plantation lands in Tyrone, must have contributed powerfully to the decision to locate the town at Enniskillen. The strategic position of Enniskillen island, where government money had recently been expended in rebuilding the castle, and its trading potential on the Erne at the conjunction of three baronies must also have weighed heavily as deciding factors.[33] Urbanisation had been an important element in the plantation plan, yet it had been neglected in its implementation. In this case initial faulty planning had been overcome.[34]

The working out of the plan for the town itself was implicit in a series of grants to Cole in 1611 and 1612, its elements formalised in the first of these, a lease of 19 June 1611.[35] The island of Enniskillen, viewed as one tate or 60 acres, was divided into two sections.[36] In June the castle and two-thirds of the island (40 acres) to be associated with it (and two small islets) was leased to Cole for twenty-one years or life.[37] This military zone could be garrisoned at any time and would be independent of the urban settlement. The exchange of lands for the town had taken place by the time of his patent of his re-organised servitor's grant on 16 November 1611.[38] The patent of the town lands to Cole finalised the arrangements on 28 May 1612, included the remaining and easterly one-third of the island on which the town was to be built, and contained stipulations similar to those in other grants under the superintendency arrangement being made at this time.[39]

The principal conditions in this grant may be outlined. First Cole should pay an annual quit rent on the property of IR£1. In return he should within four years 'bring or cause to be brought' to the designated third part of the island 'twenty persons being English or Scotch, and chiefly artificers and mechanics to make, erect and construct a town in a convenient place' there to be decided on by Cole, to be burgesses of the town of Enniskillen, which should be incorporated within the same time.[40] He should also mark out and set apart sites for a church and cemetery, for a market house, for a gaol or prison for the county, and for a public school with a court and garden adjoining, the latter two to reflect the county status of the intended town. He should 'build or cause to be built in a decent or uniform manner, twenty burgages or houses of stone or framed timber according to the form of building usual in England', five annually over the ensuing four years.[41] In addition to the 20-acre town site, Cole should also allocate from the town grant 60 acres of land[42] adjacent to the town, as follows – two acres each for 10 of the 'principal' burgages and one acre for each of 10 other burgages 'of inferior place and condition', these lands to be assigned together in an area to be known as the 'burgage field', the burgages and lands to be held for ever by the tenants in the farm; and a further 30 acres as a common for the cattle of its inhabitants (implying the burgesses) to be conveyed to the corporation for ever without rent, except that each person using this land should pay Cole four pence stg per annum. If the burgesses' houses were built by Cole they should pay him an annual rent at the rate of 10 per cent of the sum expended, if built by the burgesses themselves then they should pay, for the greater burgages and their lands 5/- stg per annum and for the lesser 2/6. Cole and his heirs were empowered to hold a Thursday market and an annual fair in August, together with a court of pie powder and all appropriate tolls, and might keep a toll booth and be clerks of the market.[43] No person might sell goods by retail within a three-mile radius of the town except its own inhabitants.[44]

Much of the intended character of the town and the role of the patron can thus be inferred, and the plan provided also for the erection of civic and county facilities to be built by the appropriate authorities and for a new relocated church for the parish of Iniskeene. It might be incorporated when the 20 burgesses were housed there, within four years, though 'cottagers and other inferior inhabitants' were also envisaged. A notional 110 acres out of the notional 320 acres of the town grant was thus to be allocated by the patron (under regulated rents and conditions) to the stipulated uses of the town. The real size of the entire town grant was in fact some 730 statute acres.

Incorporation, however, proceeded quickly, probably in advance of the arrival of the full stipulated population. Already there had been a scaling down from the 13 of January 1611 to the 20 in the common form of the superintendency grants. Now, concurrently with the issuing of these patents, as preparations for a parliament were being made, the privy council in London despatched regulations to Dublin on 26 September 1612 governing the nature and privileges of forty 'new boroughs' which were to be created. The corporations were to consist of just thirteen members, each to return two members to parliament. Thus urban planning in plantation

Ulster was merged with a scheme of borough-making throughout Ireland which was in part a tactic of parliamentary management.[45]

The processes of incorporation for the new boroughs, already underway by September 1612, culminated in the case of Enniskillen in the charter of 27 February 1613,[46] which followed fairly closely the standard form of 26 September 1612. The first provost and burgesses, nominated in the charter and numbering 15 rather than the now prescribed and generally common 13, derive from a list[47] in Chichester's hands by 20 October 1612 when the lord deputy issued the warrant for the fiant for the charter. This list, unsigned and undated, corresponds approximately to the 'petition' in the contemporary process of granting charters to English boroughs,[48] and does not normally survive for the Irish incorporations at this time. Its survival suggests that the first corporations were nominated locally presumably as a result of a request from Dublin. It is not in Cole's hand, but probably in that of a secretary and may well have been supplied by Foliot in his capacity of governor. Foliot's name is listed first, presumably implying that he should be provost, and Cole's was not included. The list appended to the warrant, in a secretary's hand and similar to other warrants of the time, included Cole for the first time, excluded Foliot, but otherwise made no change. Chichester himself designated Cole to be provost.[49]

Apart from this larger corporate body (with peculiar features discussed below), the charter in other respects generally complied with regulation, but with the noteworthy feature that the incorporated area was the entire island, except the 'castle or fort', rather than the planned urban site of the earlier patents. The provost and 14 burgesses were nominated in the charter 'to the intent that it may appear in future times that this new incorporation is now first composed of worthy and honest men'. The first provost should hold office until the ensuing Michaelmas, the burgesses during life unless removed under exceptional circumstances. All the inhabitants of the town, and such as the provost and burgesses might at any time admit to its freedom, were constituted the commons. The provost should take the oath of supremacy before the justices of assize at the next general sessions for the county, as well as an oath to fulfil his duties of office. The provost should be elected annually by the provost and burgesses, meeting on the feast of St John the Baptist, from amongst the burgesses themselves. He should hold office from the ensuing Michaelmas for one year, but before admitted should take the oath in the presence of the preceding chief officer. Should he die or vacate the office during his term a successor might be elected from amongst the burgesses to complete the term. When a vacancy occurred amongst the burgesses, either by death or removal from office, the others might assemble and elect 'one or as many more as are deficient … from the better or more worthy inhabitants of the borough' to take the vacant place. The corporation was granted a weekly court of record, to be held before the provost each Thursday, to hear civil actions not exceeding the sum of five marks. The provost, burgesses and commons might assemble from time to time to make bye-laws, and impose penalties for the breach of them, provided these were reasonable and not repugnant to statute. The corporation might establish a guild merchant, and could appoint two sergeants-at-mace and other necessary municipal officers.

The essential feature of the charter is that civic government was vested in a small self-electing and, in the first instance, entirely settler group. Granted neither land (precluded by the superintendency arrangement) nor fairs and markets, the corporate income would be very limited. Also, it is probably significant of the scale of development envisaged that no provision was made for the organisation of specialist craft guilds.

The first corporate body of fifteen listed in the charter and nominated possibly by Foliot rather than Cole, or perhaps by both, contained a unique element. Presumably to promote its status as county town and sole corporation in Fermanagh, many of the burgesses were planter landowners, most of them English. Chichester disapproved of this component, in October 1612, but the membership was not recast.[50] Robert Calvert was an English undertaker in Clankelly barony; Henry Hunyng and Thomas Barton were English undertakers in Lurg, with whom may be grouped Edmund Sibthorpe (presumably a relative of the judge) who was then 'joined … with' Hunyng in planting his estates.[51] Roger Atkinson was a fellow servitor living close by. Sir John Wishart was a Scottish undertaker in Knockninny, while Alexander Dunbar was probably another Scottish undertaker, but from Donegal.[52] It is not clear that all of the remaining seven were residents in the town, but one at least, Thomas Shawe, was when in July 1613 he became a tenant on Cole's estate nearby.[53] Most of them seem to have become established on land in the vicinity, if they had not already done so.[54] Two, however, Ferdinando Burfield and Joseph Waiters, perhaps two of Cole's warders, disappear entirely from Fermanagh. While the estate-owning element would be non-resident from the start, only one of the other group seems to have maintained a strong connection with the town. Gerard Wiggen, who lived in the town and mustered in 1630,[55] and was provost in 1634,[56] was apparently the son of Alexander Wigham, corporator in 1613. But the other few surviving provosts' names – William Roscrow (1618),[57] Francis Bird (1630),[58] Richard Gutridge (1638, who lived at Lisgoole in 1626 and mustered for the Hastings, formerly Sir John Davies, estate in 1630)[59] – do not suggest a closely-knit corporate body rotating the office amongst its members, such as may have prevailed elsewhere.

Yet the corporate body had some cohesion. In May 1618, following on an order of the privy council which cannot be recovered, Cole conveyed to the corporation, if a supposed nineteenth-century copy of the document be authentic,[60] the tolls of the fairs and markets of Enniskillen, for ever at an annual rent of £7.10.0, and, possibly linked to this and included in the same rent payment, the corporation also held prior to 1641 a small townland, Kilnaloo (123 statute acres), presumably a piece of concealed land, touching an estate Cole had purchased in Magheraboy.[61] The documentation of these tenancies presents a minor historical problem which is little clearer now than when it was argued over at various times in the eighteenth and nineteenth centuries.[62] But it is likely that these arrangements arose from a spirit of assertiveness in the corporation which was paralleled at this time in Belturbet and Strabane.

The initial building of the town nucleus was, seemingly, a joint operation between patron and residents. Bodley in his survey of the plantation in the spring of 1613 indicated that although Cole had himself been engaged in 'building up' the castle and bawn and erecting two bridges, he had taken good bonds from 12 burgesses 'to build their habitation this next summer' along with 'divers carpenters and other artificers' then employed there who intended to settle, and had provided at his own cost materials for 300,000 bricks, tiles and timber.[63] Part of the explanation for involving local landowners in the corporation of the town would seem to have been to engage them in building it by the mechanism of the building lease, though our limited surviving evidence – the fact that Roger Atkinson held two houses in Enniskillen[64] – makes this largely a conjecture. Building seems to have proceeded quickly. On 1 May 1613 Cole leased to one John Hickes, yeoman, who was not a burgess, 'one house then new built and the ground whereupon the said house now standeth and fowre scoore foote of ground at the backside of the said house as it is now measured by the rule and eight foote of ground at the end [of] the said house' for one hundred years or five lives, paying yearly 10s. stg rent with two 'good fatt henns' each Christmas.[65] This may well have been a typical non-burgess house, whether built by Cole or by the tenant is not clear. Whatever his precise role in house building, Cole did fulfil the principal conditions of the grant of the town lands in May 1612: burgage and non-burgage houses were built and burgess acres and a common were allocated.[66]

The erection of those public buildings, a church with cemetery, a market house, a gaol and a public school, for which Cole should assign sites and the embodiment architecturally of fundamental political change, made varying progress. The building of the church – a recognition that the new settlement was the appropriate location for a new church[67] – paid for probably by parochial applottment or with the recusants' fines,[68] had begun by 1622 when it went 'slow forward as all works of that nature' and was complete, with its shingled roof and probably steepled, by 1637 or earlier.[69] The first building of a gaol and of a market house is less readily dated. Cole himself may possibly have erected some kind of structure at the market place on the Town Hall site in the Diamond area, where a succession of market houses have been built.[70] A gaol, which would incorporate a sessions house, its building a county responsibility, on the site of the present Court House in East Bridge Street, may not have been built before the second half of the seventeenth century, but there is some evidence to suggest a pre-1641 structure. By 1622 Cole had collected '£500 or £600' to build a sessions house, and a constable or keeper of the gaol at Enniskillen was appointed in 1619.[71] The school, however, by a characteristic early modern lapse in supervision, went for a time to Lisnaskea and may not have reached its site in Enniskillen before 1641.[72]

Surviving evidence, in the absence of all standard sources, gives only hazardous impressions rather than a general picture of the town, its residents, and their occupations. As it grew it seems to have been a centre of dispersal into the countryside with which it was linked. Thomas McCartny, a witness to an Enniskillen deed in 1623,[73] was living in the Fermanagh countryside in 1641 and claimed that with the rising, at the outbreak of which he was travelling between Newry and Carrickfergus, he had lost two houses in Enniskillen and two acres of land (presumably burgess houses) which had cost him £80 and might have been sold for £100.[74] One house, that of John Hickes, already mentioned, for which almost unique – and reliable – evidence survives, changed hands a number of times between May 1613 when it was first leased by Cole and 1631 and its documentation, for want of any better, sheds light on occupations in the town. In April 1616 Hickes (who disappears from Fermanagh) sold the lease to James Johnston, yeoman, a Scot from Mo[a]nee in the barony of Magheraboy who in turn in April 1618 assigned it to one Andrew ffarelye, a merchant. In April 1623 ffarelye assigned it to David Greer another Enniskillen merchant who had acted as his surety in a debt of £17 to a Drogheda merchant, George Fleming, and Greer in 1631 transferred it to his son-in-law Edmond Coghlan.[75] Probably, by contrast, the most stable and successful of the merchant group in the town was John Caldwell, born in Preston, Ayrshire, who was there by 1630. In 1634 he leased from Gerard Wiggen provost of the town a house, originally 'allotted' by Cole to Alexander Wiggen (the burgess) and recently held by a tanner, John Hayes, to which was attached a strip of ground (excepted in the lease) leading 'from the Town Streete to the Lough'. Caldwell's son, Sir James, received forfeited property after the rising and purchased undertakers land in the barony of Lurg.[76]

Enniskillen had clear advantages as a growth centre for internal trade: urban density in this area of Ulster was low and the inland navigation potential of the Erne could be exploited.[77] We have already seen a connection with Drogheda. Caldwell died in Dublin in 1640, which suggests trading links there. It is likely also that there were contacts with Ballyshannon.[78] Essential skills were also represented in the town – 'carpenters and other artificers' were there in 1613, a tailor appears in 1623.[79] Its merchants and artisans, while their operations may have been on a small scale, had the opportunities of pioneers in forfeited territory. But there were also hazards: if there were no poor law contributions there were also no benefits, there was no almshouse, and Ireland offered no exemption from ubiquitous urban disasters – Enniskillen 'suffered much by fire' in 1618.[80]

Although the detail is indistinct, the fundamental features of the town can be established. Fifty-two townsmen, a high proportion of them Scots, mustered in 1630,[81] and to these a few more names can be added making perhaps 60 in all,[82] and suggesting if two-thirds were married (using a multiplier of four) some 180 men, women and children, and it is likely that this had increased somewhat by 1641. This was indeed very much smaller than the Londoners' Derry and Coleraine, both of them effectively coastal towns which had been actively developed with 500 and 300 adult males respectively in 1630, and after them in the six escheated counties came Strabane with 200 adult males and Armagh with 100. A few other towns, for example, Belturbet, had about the same population as Enniskillen. The evidence does not suggest, however, an entirely stable population. Also, although John Carmicke, an agent of Sir William Cole, had a 'chamber' in the castle, we can assume that the town was exclusively settler. Certainly that was the intention: Provost Wiggen when leasing the house to Caldwell in 1634 stipulated that he should not 'alien sett or lett the aforesaid p'misses or any p'te or p'cell thereof unto any of the Meere Irish nac'on or to any other p'son … refusinge to conforme … in … religion according to the now established orders in the Church of Englande'.[83]

Although we have no map prior to the eighteenth century, the topography of the emerging town seems clear. It was built essentially as one 'towne streete' in the easterly one-third of the island, running from the new East Bridge to the church, represented nowadays by Church Street, High Street (formerly the Hollow), Townhall Street and East Bridge Street though not necessarily a completed streetscape by 1641, with likely breaks or intersections at the Diamond and in the Hollow, and with the sites for the various public buildings, some of which had been erected prior to the rising, interspersed with this development.[84] It is unlikely that on this site, distant as it was from the Maguire fortifications, any building of significance had taken place prior to plantation. On the western two-thirds, Cole leasehold from June 1611 and where the expropriated Maguire stronghold was located, Cole had already by 1611 built 'a good timber house after the English fashion' where he then lived and had proceeded substantially with an elaborate re-construction of the castle, financed from government funds, which was viewed by Carew on 25 August, described in his survey and represented on an associated plan hitherto mis-dated as *c.* 1550.[85] These building operations on behalf of the crown, which most likely included the Water Gate, were effectively completed by 1613.[86] Thereafter Cole probably lived in the castle itself, and in September 1623, as part of a general arrangement for the inland forts of Ulster and Connacht, he became by purchase the outright owner of the castle and associated two-thirds subject to conditions of maintenance and other regulations.[87] From now on the two zones were formally integrated under Cole ownership. Small though it was, Enniskillen had thus emerged by 1641 as residential settlement, county town, and fortified centre and was already by then, as it was to be described in 1690, 'the only place of consequence upon Lough Erne',[88] and an ideal exemplar of an Ulster plantation town.[89]

---

[1] J. Edwin-Cole, *The Genealogy of the Family of Cole of the County of Devon and of those of its Branches which Settled in Suffolk, Hampshire, Surrey, Lincolnshire, and Ireland* (London, printed for private circulation, 1867), pp 22–3; Genealogical Office, Dublin, MS 174, pp 222–55, MS 292, ff 191–229; W. Bruce Bannerman (ed.), *The Registers of St. Mary le Bowe, Cheapside, All Hallows, Honey Lane, and of St. Pancras, Soper Lane, London* (London, 1914), I, 99, 260. The family history, while not accurate with regard to Sir William Cole's children, is probably reliable on his immediate ancestry because it is based on a certified pedigree Cole had drawn up in 1630. The parish register indicates the trade, omitted in the family history.

[2] Edwin-Cole, op. cit., pp 41. The parish register, however, does not record Emanuel Cole's baptism.

[3] Edwin-Cole, op. cit., pp 9, 11, 14–16.

[4] Ibid., p. 13; D.B. Quinn, *The Elizabethans and the Irish* (Ithaca, New York, 1966), pp 109, 112–5.

[5] A.F. Upton, *Sir Arthur Ingram, c. 1565–1642* (Oxford, 1961), p. 14.

[6] The evidence is his own statement in the heading to the pedigree he had drawn up in 1630.

[7] *Cal. S.P. Ire., 1601–3*, p. 218.

[8] *Cal. S.P. Ire., 1603–6*, p. 280.

[9] J. O'Donovan (ed.), *Miscellany of the Celtic Society* (Dublin, 1849), pp 287–95.

[10] Hugh O'Neill described him as vice-governor of Ballyshannon in 1607 (*Cal. S.P. Ire., 1606–8*, p. 368).

[11] *Cal. S.P. Ire., 1603–6*, p. 280; ibid., *1608–10*, p. 227.

[12] *Cal. Pat. Rolls Ire., Jas I*, pp 83, 91, 95, 101, 129.

[13] *Salisbury [=Cecil] MSS, XIX (1607)* (Historical Manuscripts Commission, 1965), p. 17.

[14] *Cal. S.P. Ire., 1608–10*, pp 148–9; *Cal. Pat. Rolls Ire., Jas I*, p. 113. He received an allowance for himself and 10 men.

[15] The historian of Enniskillen states that he was appointed in 1607, but this was probably a reversionary grant (W.C. Trimble, *History of Enniskillen* (Enniskillen, 1919), I, p. 163.

[16] Foliot, for example, received a lease of the Castle of Ballyshannon and associated lands in July 1607 (*Cal. Pat. Rolls Ire., Jas I*, pp 101–2).

[17] *Hastings MSS* IV (Historical Manuscripts Commission, 1947), p. 153.

[18] *Cal. Pat. Rolls Ire., Jas I*, p. 215.

[19] T.K. Rabb, *Enterprise and Empire* (Cambridge, Mass., 1967), pp 267–8.

[20] Edwin-Cole, op. cit., p. 45.

[21] Rabb, op. cit., p. 268. Two William Coles, both of Bristol, appear in the 1605 charter of the Spanish Company (Pauline Croft, *The Spanish Company* (London Record Society, IX, 1973), par. 642) when our William Cole was at Ballyshannon. The William Cole who subscribed to the Virginia Company in 1609 was a London merchant tailor (A. Brown, *The Genesis of the United States* (reprinted New York, 1964), I, p. 305.

[22] I am engaged on a detailed study of Cole.

[23] For a general treatment see R.J. Hunter, 'Towns in the Ulster plantation', *Studia Hibernica*, II (1971), pp 40–79.

[24] T.W. Moody (ed.) 'Ulster Plantation Papers' in *Analecta Hibernica*, 8 (IMC, 1938) (hereafter *Anal. Hib.* 8) p. 293.

[25] *Cal. Carew MSS, 1603–24*, p. 136.

[26] *Anal. Hib.* 8, p. 244. The archive of the surveyor-general does not survive so these decisions can only be inferred. The figure of 30 acres to the tate derives from the survey of 1608 (*Anal. Hib.* 8, pp 192–204). A figure of 60 acres to the tate was common in the Fermanagh patents. Surviving figures for the lands of servitors and Irish grantees which relate to the period of allocating the land in 1610 indicate calculations on the basis of 50 acres to the tate (*Anal. Hib.* 8, pp 206–7), while a later, though undated, schedule of grantees (*Cal. Carew MSS, 1603–24*, pp 239–41) which relates to the patents, suggests that 60 acres was then the working yard stick.

[27] *Anal. Hib.* 8, p. 244.

[28] *Cal. Pat. Rolls Ire., Jas I*, p. 189.

[29] *Cal. S.P. Ire., 1608–10*, p. 450.

[30] *Anal. Hib.* 8, p. 244.

[31] Ibid., p. 293. However the school lands remained largely unchanged from where they were assigned.

[32] *Cal. Pat. Rolls Ire., Jas I*, p. 215.

[33] It may be noted that Chichester in September–October 1608 suggested Enniskillen 'now altogether waste and desolate' as the fittest place for the shire town (*Cal. S.P. Ire., 1608–10*, p. 57), though earlier, in March, he mentioned both Lisgoole and Enniskillen as places to be 'reserved for his Mat'es service' (*Anal. Hib.* 8, p. 283). Davies may have been responsible for inserting Lisgoole into the 'project'.

[34] Somewhat similar problems concerning town land arose elsewhere, but in those cases there does not appear to be any evidence of negotiations of the kind with Cole.

[35] *Cal. Pat. Rolls Ire., Jas I*, p. 215.

[36] It may perhaps have been in this decision that Sir Ralph Bingley and Captain Basil Brooke, two Donegal servitors, who are referred to in secondary sources (e.g. Edwin-Cole, op. cit., p. 42) as having an unspecified planning role, were involved.

[37] *Cal. Pat. Rolls Ire., Jas I*, p. 215.

[38] Ibid.

[39] Ibid., p. 232. A translation appears in Trimble, *Enniskillen*, I, pp 165–70. The lands granted were estimated at 320 acres.

[40] Elsewhere it refers to the 'English, Welsh, or Scottish nation'.

[41] Each should have 'a convenient quantity of land for a mansion-house, courtyard, and garden'. At another point it is stated in more general terms that he should 'build and erect edifices and buildings ... in streets and squares, in such manner and form as shall best suit with [its] site and situation, and for the defence and decency of the said town'.

[42] At 21 feet to the perch. These lands were to be laid out by the surveyor-general and commissioners. It may have been with this that Bingley and Brooke were involved.

[43] For these associated privileges he should pay an annual quit-rent of 13/14 IR.

[44] Saving the rights of the bishopric of Clogher in Devenish and elsewhere.

45 R.J. Hunter, op. cit., pp 46–7.
46 English translation in Trimble, *Enniskillen*, I, pp 171–8.
47 Bodleian Library, Oxford, Carte MS 62, f. 203.
48 S. Bond and N. Evans, 'The process of granting charters to English boroughs 1547–1649', *English Historical Review*, XCI (1976), pp 102–20.
49 Carte MS 62, f. 201. A copy of this warrant, acquired from the Bodleian Library, was presented by Mr John Kerr of Enniskillen to Enniskillen Urban District Council in 1949. At the same time he presented another copy to the Public Record Office of Northern Ireland. Its reference there is T1036. I am grateful to Mr Kerr for clarifying this point for me. It is this copy and not the original fiant which is stated to be in Enniskillen in P. Livingstone, *The Fermanagh Story* (Enniskillen, 1969), p. 393. Fr Livingstone's book contains a valuable chapter on Enniskillen.
50 He commented: 'These cannot well stand for those he should name must be of the towne, these are undertakers, etc' (Carte MS 62, f. 201). There was some slight similarity in the first governing body of Belturbet. Perhaps another reason was lack of townsmen.
51 *Hastings MSS*, IV, p. 167.
52 Or possibly a connection of Sir John Dunbar through whom Cole had purchased an undertaker's estate nearby in Magheraboy.
53 Trimble, *Enniskillen*, I, p. 182.
54 Their dispersal may probably be indicated in the appearance of their names or surnames subsequently on a number of Fermanagh estates, including Cole's, as follows: a) Nicholas Ozenbrooke: Cole and Gore estates; b) Alexander Wigham: Cole estate and church lands; c) William Hall: Davies/Hastings estate and Robert Hamilton estate; d) Edward Moore: Atkinson and Wyrrall estates and church lands. The principal source is the muster of *c*. 1630 (BL, Add. MSS 4770, ff 46–71v).
55 BL, Add. MSS 4770, f. 64. He was also there in 1626 (Trimble, *Enniskillen*, I, p. 225).
56 NAI, D1040.
57 Trimble, *Enniskillen*, I, p. 188.
58 BL, Add. MSS 4770, f. 64.
59 Ibid., f. 67v; Trimble, *Enniskillen*, I, pp 188, 223, 225.
60 Printed in Trimble, *Enniskillen*, III, pp 728–9.
61 NAI, Book of Survey and Distribution, Co. Fermanagh; Trimble, *Enniskillen*, I, p. 179.
62 PRONI, D1702/1/26/1, 2; Trimble, *Enniskillen*, III, pp 721–6. The supposed copy of the deed Cole to the corporation, has ambiguities, including its date, but 1618 is to be preferred. Kilnaloo does not appear in any patent to Cole, but it must have been held from him by the corporation, and an eighteenth-century map of an adjacent estate describes it as Cole property (PRONI, D496/1).
63 *Hastings MSS,* IV, 169. The town is not commented on in later government surveys of the plantation.
64 Earl of Belmore, *The History of Two Ulster Manors* (London and Dublin, 2nd. ed. 1903), p. 93. Trimble stated that a burgess house, although altered, survived in East Bridge Street (Trimble, *Enniskillen*, III, p. 755).
65 As recited in deed of 11 April 1616, NAI, D1028.
66 Two 'burgesse acres', presumably appropriated to his houses in Enniskillen, were leased by Roger Atkinson in 1627 (Belmore, *History of Two Ulster Manors*, p. 93), but a date for the commons is not available. The lands so allocated, however (Trimble, *Enniskillen*, I, p. 197), were on part of Cole's servitor lands rather than on part of the town lands.
67 The plantation plan had proposed a general restructuring of the parishes in the plantation counties to conform to the boundaries of the plantation estates, but little was done to implement it.
68 The recusants' fines were used at Lisnaskea.
69 W.H. Bradshaw, *Enniskillen long ago* (Dublin, 1878), pp 33–43, incorporating architectural description by Wakeman; W.H. Dundas, *Enniskillen Parish and Town* (Dundalk and Enniskillen, 1913), pp 31–3; H. Dixon, *List of Historic Buildings ... in the town of Enniskillen* (Belfast, after 1973), pp 16–19.
70 Dixon, op. cit., p. 13; Trimble, *Enniskillen*, III, p. 1,059 second addendum, a and b.
71 Dixon, op. cit., p. 22; Trimble, *Enniskillen*, III, p. 868; *Cal. Pat. Rolls Ire., Jas I*, p. 430.
72 Trimble, *Enniskillen*, III, pp 793–801.
73 NAI, D1041.

74 TCD, MS F. 3. 6, f. 194.

75 NAI, D1028, D1041.

76 Genealogical Office, Funeral Entries, vol. 8, p. 325; BL, Add. MS 4770, f. 64v; NAI, D1040; Trimble, *Enniskillen*, II, pp 409–10.

77 Hence probably the importance of the passage 'from the Towne Streete to the Lough' referred to above.

78 Supplies for Cole's forces were sent in by parliament in 1643 through County Donegal (C. McNeill (ed.), *Tanner Letters* (IMC, 1943), pp 165–9).

79 NAI, D1041.

80 Trimble, *Enniskillen*, I, p. 194. The Pockrich tomb in the church with its skull and crossbones (one of the few surviving from the plantation period and an example of the standard of its craftsmanship) illustrates the transplanted spiritual insecurity of an English settler.

81 BL, Add. MS 4770, ff 64–4v.

82 Trimble, *Enniskillen*, I, p. 225; NAI, D1028, D1040, D1041.

83 NAI, D1040.

84 Trimble, *Enniskillen*, I, pp 179–80, II, pp 335–42. There is no firm evidence for the size and construction of the houses.

85 *Cal. Carew MSS, 1603–24*, pp 218–9, 222. The map, TCD, MS 1290/29, is reproduced in Trimble and Dixon, op. cit., I am grateful to Mr W. O'Sullivan for helpful advice on the map. It is my opinion that the map corresponds with Carew's description.

86 *Hastings MSS*, IV, 167. For an alternative view see E.M. Jope 'Scottish influences in the north of Ireland: castles with Scottish features, 1580–1640', *Ulster Journal of Archaeology*, 3rd series 13 (1950), p. 41.

87 *Cal. Pat. Rolls Ire., Jas I*, p. 566.

88 Andrew Hamilton, *The Actions of the Enniskillen-men from … 1688 … to the Landing of Duke Schomberg in Ireland* (London, 1680, reprinted Belfast 1813), p. 2.

89 The contrast with Derry, however, in carefulness of initial planning and scale of development remains striking. For a valuable and thorough discussion see T.W. Moody, *The Londonderry Plantation* (Belfast, 1939), passim.

10

The English Undertakers
in the Plantation of Ulster:
A Cavan Case Study, 1610–41

When in the second half of 1610 settlers were arriving from England and Scotland as grantees of land in the plantation in Ulster then being inaugurated, they were fitted into a regional scheme of colonisation, the planning of the previous two years, with specific obligations and responsibilities. The basic territorial arrangement was one by which groups of owners with a common background were settled in a more or less uniform way throughout the confiscated counties – or five of them, Derry becoming the colonising responsibility of the city of London – in the baronies, administrative sub-divisions, into which the counties had been divided.

There were three different categories of grantees, English and Lowland Scottish undertakers (civilian groups, so called because of the conditions they undertook to fulfill), servitors (military officers and government officials who had been employed in Ireland), and Irish from the confiscated counties who were restored to some of the land. The servitors, who were allowed to have Irish tenantry, were placed in the same baronies as the Irish grantees, it being considered that their military experience could be of value in such a juxtaposition. The necessary land measuring and cartographic work, essential to such a scheme, was carried out, though defectively, on government tours in Ulster in 1608 and 1609. The main weight of colonisation was made the responsibility of the undertakers, English and Scottish. Also an attempt was made to allocate the land across the five counties on a definite proportionate basis to these groups. English and Scottish undertakers were to be granted equal amounts of land, and their combined share was to be one and a half to the proportion jointly allocated to servitors and native Irish, The proportion of the Irish was to be one and a half to that of the servitors.[1]

In addition to the individual grantees, within each county much smaller areas of land were designated for the support of corporate towns and schools. Trinity College, Dublin received an extensive endowment in Donegal, Armagh, and Fermanagh. Furthermore, land was allocated to provide glebe for each parish which should be co-extensive with each proportion or estate. In this way the temporal or non-ecclesiastical land was to be disposed of. Small portions of land already allotted for the support of forts were not re-designated. Grants made to a small number of prominent old Irish figures, in Armagh and Tyrone, immediately before the plantation, if they had a definite legal basis in patents, were not disturbed. Some old English and indeed new English acquisitions in Cavan because of its position as a county more open to such influences, also continued after 1610. Indeed it was only in County Derry that prior interests were systematically bought out to allow the Londoners unhampered initiative. The remaining, ecclesiastical, land was broadly of two types – land the property of or claimed by the bishops which was all granted after much debate to the bishops in the Protestant succession, and land the property of other ecclesiastical figures; and, secondly, former monastic property, which just before or at the time of plantation (but independently of the plantation scheme) was granted to lay proprietors who were in almost all instances of new English origin though County Cavan was again somewhat exceptional here. Thus a barony (or precinct) allocated, at the plantation to a particular category or categories of new grantees, might well also accommodate some or many of the above types of landowners as well. The value of a barony study is that it can bring to light in detail these local variations. In Cavan the English undertakers with which this paper is concerned were allocated the barony of Loughtee.

The final conditions of plantation binding on the various grantees had been evolved by the spring of 1610. Three sizes of estates, or proportions as they were called, for undertakers and servitors, were decided on – 2,000 acres, 1,500 acres, and 1,000 acres, as then calculated (great, middle, and small proportions), though these should include in addition such bog and wood as lay within them without that being assessed for rent payment to the crown. The estates granted to the Irish in the planted counties, with about some twenty-five exceptions, were generally very much smaller though a more numerous body of grantees was involved.

The conditions of acceptance were most onerous for the undertakers. The main burden of colonisation in each county fell to them; they were forbidden to let any of their lands to the native Irish. The estates of undertakers in baronies so allocated were to become coherent areas completely devoid of old Irish occupants who must move to the lands held by the other types of owners. A time limit of three years was prescribed to each undertaker for the installation of a minimum replacement British population of twenty-four adult males to represent at least ten families per 1,000 acre, or small, proportion; to be proportionately larger on the larger estates. Each undertaker should also erect a stronghold on his estate. At the minimum the grantee of a small proportion should erect a bawn or courtyard. Undertakers of the larger units should also erect a stone or brick house within their defensive bawns. The settlement pattern should be one of villages protected by these structures. Also, for defence, the undertakers should have arms in their houses, in the use of which their tenants should be trained and mustered according to English practice. Undertakers and tenants should take the oath of supremacy. To ensure that the scheme got vigorously underway the undertakers should be resident in person upon their estates for the first five years, or have an accredited agent, and also for this period they should not sell their estates. Finally, a definite social organisation for each estate was laid down. Thus on a 1,000 acre proportion the undertaker himself should have a demesne of 300 acres. The remaining land should be allocated, as follows – 120 acres each to two fee-farmers, 100 acres each to three leaseholders for three lives or twenty-one years, and upon the residual 160 acres four families or more of 'husbandmen, artificers or cottagers'.[2] The activities of the English undertakers in Loughtee can be examined in terms of these conditions.

The state of landownership in Loughtee just before the plantation, as in Cavan at large, was less homogeneous than in the other planted counties. Mulmory O'Reilly who was killed on the English side at the battle of the Yellow Ford in 1598 was found by an inquisition in 1601 to have had extensive lands there as well as the castle and town of Cavan,[3] the seat of chieftainship and described by another source of this period as a 'market town wherein are two strong castles'.[4] The second of these was that of Walter, Patrick and Thomas Brady, members of a somewhat anglicised merchant family,[5] who also had a water mill there.[6] In addition, as Lord Deputy Chichester pointed out in 1608, there were 'many freeholders (as they pr'tend) in the barrony ... namely the McBradies, McCabes and others'.[7] However this traditional pattern had already been somewhat indented. Thus monastic land, that of Loughowter and Drumlahen, (some 4,150 acres) had, as early as 1571, been leased to Hugh Connelagh O'Reilly, then chieftain,[8] and around 1610 was in the old English hands of James Dillon, earl of Roscosmmon.[9] The abbey at Cavan was being transferred at about this time from Theobald Bourke, baron Castleconnell,[10] to Sir Thomas Ashe,[11] a new English landowner at Trim,[12] who strengthened a number of tentative connexions with Cavan landownership at the time of plantation.[13] Through grants of attainted land, ownership of lay property was also changing prior to the plantation. Thus Richard Nugent, baron Delvin and subsequently earl of Westmeath, had acquired land in Loughtee as part of a substantial acquisition in the county,[14] and the new English

Roger Downeton, a clerk of the pipe in the exchequer,[15] received a patent in August 1611[16] of some 1,200 acres of attainted land, earlier, in 1606, granted to Sir John Kinge, the muster master general.[17] These latter grants arose from the Nine Years' War which had torn up an earlier English division of the county of Cavan amongst the O'Reillys in the 1580s arranged by Lord Deputy Perrot (whereby Sir John O'Reilly had received the baronies of Loughtee and Tullaghgarvy),[18] just as the Flight of the Earls in 1607 put paid to arrangements then being worked out by the Dublin government whereby the county would be divided amongst a numerous body of local Irish landowners holding from the Crown, along the lines of the settlement of Monaghan in 1591, with only a minority of British grantees.[19]

When the plantation of English undertakers in the barony was inaugurated, at the beginning of August 1610 by Chichester yet further areas did not fall to undertakers. These, however, are in large part accountable for within the framework of plantation planning. Thus while the incorporation of Cavan in November 1610 and its endowment with some 683 acres was somewhat unique,[20] it was part of the plan of plantation to establish corporate towns in each county. Provision had also been made to endow a school in each county, and, as it happened, the Cavan 'Royal' school received its lands in Loughtee. Episcopal and glebe land could also be expected. The servitor, Hugh Culme, holding the lands assigned to Cloughowter fort[21] had many equivalents elsewhere. More interesting, then, is the appearance of five old Irish grantees in the barony. This was a unique feature of a barony allotted for undertakers – the plan of plantation envisaged, we may recollect, that Irish grantees should share baronies with servitors. The Brady's anglicised character, already noted, may have saved them from such transplantation. As far as Mulmory McHugh Connelagh O'Reilly, the chieftain in Irish eyes, was concerned it was noted in 1611 that he had received his 'owne lande' back at the plantation.[22] Our main concern, however, is with the undertakers.

For plantation purposes the forfeited land in the barony was divided into eleven proportions, eight small and three middle, making 12,500 acres as then calculated.[23] It was allocated to seven grantees. That the acreages in statute measure were very much more enormous emerges from Table 1. The shares of different groups in the barony can also be seen from it – undertakers 54,014 acres, native Irish 10,367 acres, smaller British grantees who were not undertakers[24] 2,852 acres, old English 4,948 acres, school and town land 1,600 acres, ecclesiastical land 16,075 acres, and a small area of unidentified ownership as well as 67 acres the property of Sir Claud Hamilton, a Scottish undertaker in Tullyhunco, which crosses the modern barony boundary. The table seeks to indicate ownership after various initial problems and disputes, discussed below, had been resolved. The modern barony boundaries of Loughtee Lower and Upper have been used, and the acreage figures have been computed from the Ordnance Survey areas of townlands. The acreages must, however, be treated with some caution. They derive from a laborious exercise in identifying the modern equivalents of the seventeenth century place names, and allowance must be made for error through mistaken identifications. It may be added that the share of the English undertakers in the land of the county at large was some 12 per cent.

TABLE 1
Landowners, *c.* 1610–20

Acreages are in statute measure. The accompanying figures, given for the undertakers, indicate the size of proportions as granted.

John Taylor	6,842	1,500
John Fishe	8,868	2,000
Sir Hugh Wirrall	6,606	1,500
Stephen Butler	13,552[1]	2,000[2]
Richard Waldron	7,093	2,000
Sir Nicholas Lusher	6,619	2,000
William Lusher	5,754	1,500
Walter, Thomas and Patrick Brady	2,265	
Hugh McGlasney [O'Reilly]	371	
Mulmory oge O'Reilly	893	
Tirlagh McDonnell O'Reilly of Killagh	5,834	
Mulmory McHugh Connelagh O'Reilly	782	
Shane Bane O'Moeltully	222	
Hugh Culme	1,215	
Roger Downeton	1,195	
William Binde	292	
Sir Thomas Rotherham	141	
Sir Thomas Ashe	9	
Sir Claud Hamilton	67[3]	
Richard Nugent, Baron Delvin	299	
James Dillon, Earl of Roscommon	4,150	
Edward Nugent	499	

School lands	917
Town of Cavan	683
Bishopric of Kilmore	14,116
Glebe	1,959
Unidentified ownership	1,585

1. This includes 1,320 acres in modern Tullaghgarvy barony.
2. 284 acres as then calculated granted to establish the town of Belturbet should be added.
3. A small portion of a Scottish undertaker's estate in Tullyhunco barony, which crosses the modern barony boundary.

The undertaker' names given in Tables 1 and 2 are those who actually took out patents. Three of the seven originally selected, Sir John Davies, the attorney-general in Dublin and more properly a servitor, Reynold Horne and William Snow had almost immediately disposed of their lands, Davies who also received lands in Fermanagh and Tyrone,[25] transferred his interest in Loughtee to a fellow undertaker there, Richard Waldron, who in turn disposed of his own allotment to Reynold Horne.[26] Horne received a warrant of possession on 4 September 1610 but by 24 September had passed the lands to Sir Nicholas Lusher.[27] Snow did not come to Ulster but disposed of his land to Lusher's son William.[28] Of the seven after these initial rearrangements, two, the Lushers, came from Surrey.[29] Sir Nicholas Lusher and Sir Hugh Wirrall from Enfield in Middlesex seem to have been associates in minor public office.[30] They may then form a distinct section of our group, receiving their grants through government connexion. Richard Waldron was from Leicestershire.[31] Two of the others, John Fishe and Stephen Butler (the latter probably the most well-off amongst a group who were not people of special substance by the standards of contemporary England[32]) came from Bedfordshire, while the remaining grantee, John Taylor, was from Cambridgeshire,[33] a contiguous county. The south-east of England was home for most of them. All were present to receive possession in August and September 1610.[34] Chichester in October commended the earl of Northampton – he had got the consort together apart from the Lushers[35] – on his selection, if 'their resolution be as good to abide a storme when it happens, there is no doubt but they will doe well and will finde commoditie by it.'[36]

Yet his appraisal of the English undertakers in general – plain country gentlemen some of whom had already changed or sold their proportions[37] – would also, to a great extent, have fitted the Loughtee group. Certainly little was done by them before spring 1611. John Taylor remained for most of the winter, and Stephen Butler had a deputy and some 'twelve or sixteen men'[38] present, but, more typically, most of them had sought permission to appoint deputies,[39] and it is not surprising that with such circumstances applying generally in the plantation the government had extended the time during which native Irish might remain on undertakers lands to May 1611.[40] Personal predicaments also impinged. Thus Richard Waldron applied for permission to be an absentee for five years,[41] and in February 1611 the English privy council allowed him, because of pressing litigation in England, to appoint an agent, Clement Cottrell.[42] Hugh Wirrall, also detained in England by a lawsuit, was in April 1611 allowed to substitute another deputy for one who had died.[43] From the autumn of 1611 intermittently to 1622 a series of government surveys illustrate the development of the plantation. Collections of estate papers, leases and the like, which could fill out the picture, are all too rare.

Carew's survey in 1611[44] is the first to allow such a systematic picture. He found only two proprietors, Butler[45] and Fishe resident, though Sir Hugh Wirrall's family were in occupation. The Lushers made a belated arrival at the end of September with some 'artificers and servants'. Taylor's estate, like Waldron's, was in charge of a deputy. The preparing of bricks and stones and the processing of timber was in hand on the five occupied estates. Fishe had carpenters felling trees in Fermanagh with two 'English teemes of horses' and English carts drawing materials to his buildings, had made some 140,000 bricks, had burnt 200 barrels of lime, and had his lime-kiln still going. Butler, who was equally energetic, and Wirrall had each built houses at Belturbet, and had jointly built five boats. In all seventeen houses had been built, some of them 'Irish walled houses' others built 'after the English fashion', most for tenants, and preparations were in hand for two manor houses and a bawn. On Waldron's own estate an Irish house had been restored and equipped. There was a blacksmith's forge, and two mills, one, on Butler's estate, a 'fayre water myle with a framed house buylte and finished.'

This predominantly constructional preoccupation, not surprising at this stage in the colony, is reflected in the occupations of the British population. Carew states that Stephen Butler had 'bricklayers, carpenters, smiths and mylewrights, and a shipwright'. When an attempt is made to quantify Carew's somewhat inexact information, about 130, perhaps a few more, adult British males', excluding the landowners appear to have been associated with the plantation at this stage[46] (though eight had returned to England for their families). A very high proportion of these are defined as artificers and servants, the 'tenant' class amongst them being smaller.[47] Carew found arms for about eighty men. The settler distribution across estates was unequal, an indication of that considerable variation in endeavour by the grantees, obvious in other respects too, which was already and was to remain characteristic of the plantation.

Bodley's survey[48] conducted in the spring of 1613 closer to the deadline for building and planting of the articles of plantation allows us to assess the undertakers performance in terms of the conditions of their grants. Ownership had remained stable, and five of the seven undertakers were resident and active, but the Lushers, though represented by a 'factor' had no British tenants, and only a minimal achievement in building. Bodley provides evidence for over ninety tenants of various kinds, though some were absentee. There were in addition about eighty-three servants of various types, including Waldron's personal entourage of about fifty, some of whom must have been women, but excluding 'divers masons, carpenters, and labourers' on his estate. There must thus have been a male colony of approaching 170 an increase of about forty since 1611, but not fully 60 per cent of the norm of 300. The tenant class, however, had been strengthened.

All estates, except these of the Lushers, provided evidence of diversified building. Work in hand, described in detail, must be assessed by the evidence of later surveys. Taylor and Butler had erected substantial bawns, the latter's being 'square', stone built, 88' by 144', with four flanker towers. Fishe had a brick house 'thoroughly finished' and seated in a 'rath or Danish fort', old and new in the landscape being here brought together. Taylor was actively building a castle at a site, prescribed earlier to him by the lord deputy,[49] 'to the best advantage of service being near to a common passage or ford of the river of Owenmore', but it was raised as yet only to the second storey. Waldron, lately arrived and at work with 'diligence', had built a 'thatched house with an upper loft … nightly well watched by his people'. Wirrall still lived in his 'English thatched house' in Belturbet, 'til the accomplishment of his greater work'. Waldron was, notably, causing his tenants to build in 'two several places, together, for their better safety'. Taylor had built three or four houses of 'English frames'. There were now three mills and a fourth in construction, and Fishe also had boats, one of ten tons and one of six 'on the river of Belturbet', a further response to the potentialities of inland navigation. The villages, the houses and bawns, and the settler population of the articles of plantation were thus only slowly appearing. Nevertheless Bodley's statement of Stephen Butler that he had 'laid the ground work of a good plantation' applied, though to a lesser degree, to five of the seven grantees.[50]

By the time of Pynnar's survey in 1618–19,[51] three of the seven estates had changed hands. Sir Nicholas Lusher had sold, in March 1616, to Sir George Mainwaring from Shropshire,[52] and his son William had disposed of his land to Peter Ameas, who appears as collector of the subsidy for the county in June 1618.[53] Sir Hugh Wirrall's estate had been mortgaged or sold twice by this stage – in 1614 it was held by Thomas Mountford,[54] an unsuccessful candidate for land at the time of allocation,[55] and now by a Mr Adwick. Otherwise the original owners remained actively in occupation; only Mainwaring appears to have been absentee.

There was by now a fairly general compliance with building obligations. On all estates except Adwick's and Waldron's bawns and 'castles' are described as 'long since finished' or of 'great strength'. Waldron's stone house was completed and occupied, but his bawn was of sods 'much of it … fallen down'. Adwick's house had remained unfinished for two years, and no bawn had been constructed. The settler population had also risen considerably to some 439 males (excluding Belturbet and Cavan), a substantial increase since 1613, and almost one and a half times the required figure. A fairly general pattern of settlement also emerges. It was one which applied more or less generally across the planted counties – one of village and dispersed settlement. Thus we find built on the Waldron estate 'a town consisting of thirty-one houses, all inhabited with English'. Fishe had two villages, one of them possibly Stradone, of ten houses each. It would seem that these villages were, for the most part, occupied by a cottager class which Pynnar normally records. Thus the thirty-one cottagers 'each having a house and two acres of land, and commons for twelve cattle a-piece' on Waldron's estate seem the most likely residents in his thirty-one house village.[56] The numbers do not always match so equally; indeed Taylor had a group of seven freeholders, seven lessees for years, and ten cottagers on his estate, who lived, 'most of them', in a village of fourteen houses – Ballyhaise. It is not surprising when estates were much larger than intended that tenants of land should live on their holdings in dispersed fashion. This represented, however, an important deviation, security-wise, from the scheme laid down. That the logic of such a compromise pattern of settlement involved the dispersal of arm's amongst the tenantry for defence had been grasped by Sir Stephen Butler who was 'able to arm 200 men with very good arms which are within his castle, besides others which are dispersed to his tenants for their safeguard'. Not all the undertakers were, however, so provident in this respect. In all there were six villages on five estates. These were essentially small dwelling settlements, but in two, which stood upon a 'road way', there 'was a 'good innholder', in another a windmill. There were in all five mills at this stage, one, on Butler's estate, being a fulling mill.

The 1622 survey,[57] the last in the series, is considered more critical than Pynnar's. The Wirrall estate had again changed hands, being now owned by

Edward Bagshaw, clerk of the court of wards,[58] an administrator who lived at Finglas outside Dublin.[59] Three of the remaining six proprietors, Taylor, Butler and Fishe, were resident, Waldron was in England but 'daily expected', Ameas's family was present, and Mainwaring was represented by an agent. Bawns and houses existed on all estates but presented diverse images – the Bagshaw house being not yet complete. Fishe's bawn was the most elaborate, being 'a strong round bawne of lyme and stone 8 foot high and 415 foote compasse built upon a rath with a chamber over the gate and a draw bridge'. However others had marked deficiencies, some being merely of sods and 'going to decay'. Houses or castles were equally individualistic. Fishe's was 'strong and handsome', thirty-four feet square and four storey's high. But they were not all so large some being only two or two and a half storeys.

The settlement pattern of village groups and dispersed dwelling, revealed in 1618–19, receives confirmation. Only on the estate of Bagshaw and Ameas were clusters of houses absent. Waldron's village may have been at modern Farnham where there is now a large house but no village. Mainwaring had a 'smale' village of seven houses not all tenanted. This was subsequently known as Moyneshall, after Mainwaring's successor as owner, and in 1629 contained '24 English like howses and more, all inhabited with Englishe and Britishe families.'[60]

The colony was around the size it had attained by the time of Pynnar's survey, but there are problems in assessing the evidence of the survey. Butler, who was absent as sheriff on the day of visitation, made no return for his tenantry. Elsewhere it would seem that there were probably about 370 males resident, including 34 families in Belturbet which we have taken as making 60 males. This assumption of almost two adult mates per family (although the term family, is not used, but 'lease holder', 'cottager', etc.), made in arriving at this figure, may have produced a very slight inflation. Pynnar's figure for Butler's estate, 139 men, may be taken to supply the deficiency. Thus a figure of about 510 adult male residents emerges, or 450 excluding Belturbet, the latter figure being very close to the corresponding 439 of Pynnar's survey. No figure for the British population of Cavan town can be adduced from the survey.

It is evident, however, that the colony had unstable features. Thus on almost every estate tenants were noted who were absentee or had previously disposed of their lands. Six of seventeen fee-farmers and four of eleven leaseholders on Taylor's estate were non-resident. A man who had acquired fee-farm grants on Ameas's estate lived in Dublin and sub-let 'wholy' to Irishmen, As to Fishe's estate it was reported that many of the first leases have been passed over from one party to another and ... the tenants have not performed their covenants of buildings and planting with their landlord as by their deeds they are tyed to doe, but some of them have and continue Irish upon the lands, whereof Sir John Fish complaines, and others doe place poor undertenants upon it at rack'd rents.

Complaints came also from the tenants. Some of Bagshaw's had 'no deeds to be seen'. Butler's protested that they 'could get 'noe reasonable bargaine till the Irish be removed'. It was, indeed, generally true that the Irish were willing to pay higher rents and accept shorter terms, than the British tenantry.

We may perhaps outline here the criticisms of the undertakers at large which are appended to this 1622 survey.[61] Many were absentee, employing agents to collect their rents. They retained 'great store' of Irish on their lands to the prejudice of their British tenants. They made few bona fide freeholders, some being their own children, many freeholders and leaseholders not having legally valid instruments and so being liable for eviction. Those that were validly made had small quantities of land, paid high rents, and found difficulties in meeting the demands of jury service, which were consequently imposed on leaseholders and undertenants. Few of the undertakers had performed their building obligations within the specified time, and many of the bawns built were unserviceable, some having no gates, or houses within 'and therefore of no use when nobody dwells in them'. Few had settled their tenants in villages near their strongholds, but rather allowed them to live in dispersed fashion 'subject to the malice of any kerne to rob, kill and burne them and their house'. Many undertakers did not have adequate arms in their houses as required. Some exacted duties and services or only let their lands from year to year contrary to the articles of plantation. Finally, estates had been sold without license whereby some proprietors had accumulated properties 'which is a principall cause that the conditions are not performed and chiefe freeholders are extinguished'.

It is clear indeed that the undertakers in Loughtee as elsewhere had been slow to get the plantation under way, but before assessing the Loughtee group more closely in terms of these criticisms, we should, perhaps, note some of the initial difficulties and problems the undertakers, here, and elsewhere, encountered which were not of their own making. There were numerous cases of dispute between grantees about ownership and boundaries, arising from faults in the maps of 1609 and other administrative failings by the government at the time of allocation of the

TABLE 2

Proportions	Patentees, 1610–11	1611	1613
AGHTEEDUFF	John Taylor	John Taylor	John Taylor
DROMHILL AND DROMELLAN	Richard Waldron	Richard Waldron	Richard Waldron
DROMANY	John Fishe	John Fishe	John Fishe
MONAGHAN	Sir Hugh Wirrall	Sir Hugh Wirrall	Sir Hugh Wirrall
CLONOSE	Stephen Butler	Stephen Butler	Stephen Butler
LISREAGH	Sir Nicholas Lusher	Sir Nicholas Lusher	Sir Nicholas Lusher
TONNAGH	William Lusher	William Lusher	William Lusher

1618–19	1622	*c.* 1630	1641
John Taylor	Brockhill Taylor	Brockhill Taylor	Elizabeth and Mary Taylor
Thomas Waldron	Sir Thomas Waldron	Thomas Waldron (a minor)	Sir Thomas Waldron
John Fishe	Sir John Fishe	Sir Edward Fishe	Arthur Culme Benjamin Culme Thomas Burrows Richard Burrows Edward Phillpot John Baker John Sugden
Thomas Mountford (1613–14) Mr Adwick	Edward Bagshaw	Sir Edward Bagshaw	Sir Edward Bagshaw
Sir Stephen Butler	Sir Stephen Butler	Sir Stephen Butler	Stephen Butler
Sir George Mainwaring	Sir George Mainwaring	Roger Moynes	Roger Moynes
Peter Ameas	Peter Ameas	John Greenham	Thomas Greenham

land. A few examples may be given. Captain Hugh Culme claimed a townland in Fishe's proportion as being included in his lease of the fort and lands of Cloughowter.[62] The matter came before the English privy council and Fishe arrived in Dublin in May 1611 bearing a letter instructing Chichester to guarantee possession to him, to grant it to the servitor Culme being considered 'expressly contrary to the articles of plantation'.[63] Fishe's patent was issued in July 1610,[64] Culme's lease dated from November, the difficulty having arisen from a failure to corelate the two documents.[65] Difficulties involving pre-plantation grantees were, as we might expect, most common in Cavan.[66] The 1609 barony maps did not record the recent grant of attainted land's made to Richard Nugent, baron Delvin, and the plantation commissioners in allocating lands to the new grantees took inadequate care of his prior claims. Contention about some of these lands in Loughtee involving Waldron's and Snow's (i.e. William Lusher's) grants led to a sequestration by the lord deputy and plantation commissioners in May 1611.[67] Delvin eventually solved his problems by recourse to the king, and returned bearing a king's letter of 11 July 1612 authorising Chichester to grant him so much of the lands of the dissolved abbey of Fore, which he had in lease, as should amount to the value of the twenty-four polls in Cavan which he had consented to surrender, 'for the benefit of the plantation'.[68] Not so many of the cases were so significant however, but by the summer of 1612 they had become so numerous and so complex that it was found necessary to appoint special commissioners to go to Ulster and carry out a local investigation of the problems.[69] County Cavan provided them with their most numerous body of cases. Such disputes deflected energy into highly unproductive channels. Concealed – that is to say un-mapped and so ungranted – land also caused problems. Indeed in the years after 1628 concealed lands in Cavan were still being investigated.[70] Also, if the undertakers military preparedness could be questioned, the government seems to have been somewhat heedless of the dangers of insurrection. A muster master to train the tenantry, as the articles of plantation said they should, was not appointed until 1618, and continuous mustering was not enforced until after ten years later.[71] Similarly although some of the Cavan undertakers including Butler and Wirrall were empowered to administer the oath of supremacy there for a time,[72] there is no evidence of any special general provision being made for its administration, yet the fact that the oath had not been widely taken by the settlers was a point of criticism of the plantation in the late 1620s.

Some of the 1622 criticisms applied more fully than others in Loughtee. Also, although our source materials are more scant after that period, it would seem that patterns then defined were not to be substantially altered prior to 1641. We may therefore assess the development of the plantation up to 1641 in terms of these criticisms.

Our survey of ownership up to 1622 has indicated a considerable number of changes. No Loughtee undertaker had accumulated estates in the barony, though Sir Stephen Butler as early as 1617 purchased an estate in Fermanagh.[73] By the late 1620s two estates of previous unstable ownership had again changed hands. Sir George Mainwaring had sold his estate to the bishop of Kilmore and Ardagh in October 1627 and on his death in the following January it passed to his son Roger Moynes.[74] Ameas had disposed of his before July 1629[75] to John Greenham (a brother-in-law of Bishop Moynes, a graduate of Emmanuel College, Cambridge and a Dublin lawyer[76]). In the 1630s the estate of Fishe became fragmented, being in part held in 1641 by relatives of Sir Hugh Culme,[77] in part by five British owners, most of whom had been his tenants.[78] The most substantial of those was Thomas Burrows of Stradone. Thus we discount the numerous initial re-arrangement, and survey of ownership as from Carew's survey in 1611, during the succeeding thirty years only three estates out of seven had remained in the hands of the families of the original patentees. The vicissitudes of ownership are set out in Table 2.

Any analysis of the structure of the settler communities should be related to the pattern laid down by the articles of plantation. The requirement of a total of twenty five freeholders (two per 1,000 acres) within three years on the seven estates might be said to have been more or less met by the twenty-eight recorded by Bodley on five of them, but it was not until Pynnar's time, 1618–19, that freeholders were found on all estates and the 1622 commissioners found some of them absentee.[79] Also, some hardly conformed to the planners intentions. Thus Sir Hugh Wirrall was a freeholder to his fellow undertaker, Fishe.[80] Leases for lives and terms of years seem to have been generally made, though doubtless there were irregularities. On the Waldron estate twenty-one year leases were common,[81] whereas most of the recorded leases made by Sir George Mainwaring were for periods of forty-one years.[82] The balance of advantages between landlords and tenants, as well as the rules of plantation, is probably reflected in the lengths of leases.

The pattern of village and dispersed settlement was at variance with a fundamental part of the plan of plantation. This clearly had implications for the security of the colony. Government surveyors generally had pronounced themselves satisfied with the arms the Loughtee undertakers had in their strongholds.[83] However a muster conducted about 1630,[84] which can also be used as a guide to population, produced disquieting evidence about the military preparedness of the colonists at large, Wentworth observing later that the Ulster colony was but 'a company of naked men'.[85] The total of arms mustered on the estate was 71 swords, 32 pikes, 21 snaphances, 7 muskets, 3 callevers and 1 halbert. The militia on Taylor's estate also had a drum. In addition the townsmen of Cavan produced three swords, one musket, and a pike.[86]

Though it did indeed deviate in some important ways from the plan of plantation, the colony in Loughtee was not inconsiderable. The 1630 muster roll records 420 names for the undertakers' estates. It is possible to add a few more to this from other contemporary sources. This figure does not include the settlement at Cavan town,[87] although Belturbet is probably included. Small numbers of British on churchlands should also be considered. A total of almost 500 British adult males for the barony is unlikely to be exaggerated; the minimum of 300 on undertakers' estates had been substantially overtaken.

In the last resort the most striking divergence from plan in the plantation concerned the Irish population. The scheme of settlement necessitated their removal completely from lands allocated to undertakers. However the Dublin government took no effective steps in this direction when the plantation was being initiated, and because the British population grew slowly in the crucial initial years on estates which furthermore were much larger than the planners had intended, a series of temporary dispensations from the order for removal followed. The undertakers developed a strong economic interest in the retention of a population which would not require costly importation and which would pay higher rents. Finally, in 1628 as part of the *Graces*, a compromise was reached whereby the undertakers might receive new patents, to secure them against dispossession by the state for breach of conditions, though doubling their rents and paying a fine, on the agreement that Irish tenantry might be retained on one-quarter of each estate.[88]

How thoroughly this was implemented remains in doubt – but it may even be that a reason why this compromise proved acceptable to the undertakers – it was initially proposed by them in 1620 though on a half and half basis[89] – was that if construed narrowly as referring to *direct* tenants to the undertakers, a restriction of Irish to one-quarter of each estate would approximate in quite a number of cases to the position then pertaining, and that many Irish were already in the position of being sub-tenants, holding under the British tenantry.

The regranting took effect between 1628 and 1633, the regrant of an estate being normally preceded by a commission of inquiry. The inquisition, among other things, set forth that one-quarter of the estate considered most appropriate for Irish occupation.[90] Little is known of what steps the undertakers took to give effect to the new arrangement.[91] The new government, however, in 1630 decided on punitive measures whereby the income from lands illegally held by Irish could be diverted to satisfy the arrears of two Ulster captains, themselves owning undertakers' lands, Sir William Stewart and Sir Henry Tichborne.[92] Inquisitions were held in all five counties and in December 1631 the lands thus discovered, a townland or so on most estates, were granted to the two beneficiaries. The patent recited that the lands had reverted to the king for such term as they were granted to or occupied by the Irish.[93] The completeness of the inquiry cannot readily be checked. It would seem, however, that it took little account of Irish sub-tenancies.[94] But without collections of estate papers conclusive statements cannot be attempted. It would seem that the Irish, increasingly confined to the lower rungs of the ladder anyhow, were able to hide there effectively enough. We can speculate that further change was not great in the 1630s since there does not appear to have been any substantial English population in coming which would put pressure on the already diminished Irish share.

The predicament of the Irish in Loughtee[95] is not entirely obscure. Thus while Bodley, in 1613, was given to understand that Stephen Butler 'hath not any Irish upon his proportion', when treating of Taylor's estate he made the more general statement that 'divers of the Irish are yet remaining both on this proportion and others, without whose assistance for a while they pretend impossibility of proceeding in their undertakings.'[96] Pynnar, who saw economics and security precariously balanced in the position of the Irish in general on undertaker's estates,[97] passes over the Irish unmentioned in Loughtee, but on almost all estates the presence of Irish in quantity was noted in 1622. They either held directly from the undertakers or subsidiarly from their British tenants. On the estates of Bagshaw, Ameas, and Mainwaring, which had been subject to ownership changes, the 'greater part' or 'much' or 'most' of the land was in Irish occupation.[98]

Although inquisitions taken in connexion with the granting of new patents at the end of the decade survive for four of the seven estates,[99] they pose problems in interpretation, one, for Waldron's lands, being a defective transcript. That for the estate of Sir John Fishe (who had been himself involved in negotiating the arrangement) is susceptible to analysis. Of the estate, made up of 44¾ polls, 37¼ were leased, leaving 7½ or 17 per cent of the total, as presumably in demesne. 27¼ polls were demised to British, being 61 per cent of the total estate. Thus just under one-quarter was held by Irish tenants, generally with one townland each, all of them except one holding on a yearly basis.[100] On the Waldron proportion there appear to have been few Irish holding directly from the landlord, and they also seem to have held smaller areas – thus in 1617 he had granted one townland unto 'Cnogher O'Reilly, James Brady, Patric McEdmond Brady and Laghlin O'Sherridane for a term of years.'[101] It is not surprising that the Irish, because they were holding under the undertakers in breach of the articles of plantation, should not have been given long leases.[102] The inquisition for Cavan in 1631, taken to implement the Stuart-Tichborne grant, revealed unsegregated Irish tenantry on four polls of land in Moynes's proportion and on three in Fishe's.[103] Whatever may have been the exact position in Loughtee, it is fair to say that the plan to make the undertakers' areas all-British enclaves had not been successful there. At the same time opportunity for the Irish was very greatly restricted.

The relations of settler and native in Loughtee remains obscure. Irish and old English predominated in the corporation of Cavan and these and new English co-existed there throughout our period. On the other hand, Belturbet, the other incorporated settlement in Loughtee, had an exclusively settler corporation and appears to have been very much more new English in character.[104] There were some native Irish Protestant clergy in the barony in 1622.[105] In 1636 a certain Daniel O'Leary, a tenant on the Fishe estate, in 1616,[106] had as wife a certain 'Susanne Leary als. Partridge' who must surely have been of settler origin.[107] Others periodically opted for or plotted the military solution. In an insurrection scare in 1624 Rev. William Andrews, who lived at Belturbet, urged Charles Waterhouse, a prominent settler there, to return and bring gunpowder, there being very little available in the town 'and that which is the Irish send to buy it up.'[108] The plantation was hardly in the interest of the Irish collectively however variously they reacted to it.

A collection of leases in the Public Record Office [NAI][109] for the Taylor estate allows us to probe in this instance more deeply than the government surveys. The first, a fee-farm grant of 26 July 1612 illustrates the response of an undertaker at an early stage to the problems of organising his estate. The grantee was Robert Reader, English but from Carrickfergus and so obviously not imported by Taylor, and his grant was a large one, five and a half polls. Reader covenanted to within 'seven months dwell and remaine upon some part or parcel' of the land. He would also before 20 February 1613 procure 'two sufficient men' with their families to live on 'some part or parcel' of the lands, 'and thereon to build up and place their dwelling houses.'[110] We have here then a case of the landlord passing on his obligations to bring in tenantry to a substantial tenant figure, and there is no reference to building in a village settlement. A fee-farm grant of November 1613 (as well as two others in 1614 and 1615)[111] does, however, imply that houses were to be built together and the tenant, moreover, bound himself to very precise building stipulations, to within eighteen months erect buylde sett upp and fynishe a good and sufficient dwelling house to containe twenty and four feet by the rule at least and twelve feet in wydenes by the rule at the least with a chymne.[112]

That the tenant should do service at muster featured in grants of 1613[113] and 1615;[114] and in two of 1630[115] and 1636[116] when the training of the militia was being insisted on by the government, the having of arms and weapons was required. Tenants in 1612 and 1621 insisted on a precaution against the interruption of their efforts – no rent was to be payable for any period when the lessee could not quietly enjoy the lands by reason of war.[117] The leases normally provided also that the tenant should take the oath of supremacy and not sublet any of the land to Irish,[118] one made in 1630 when the latter was very much an issue expressly forbade any letting of the land 'either by way of pasturage, herbage, grasseing or any agistmente of cattle to the mere Irish.'[119] In addition to rents – Reader for his grant of 5½ polls in 1612 undertook to pay £4 for the first year, £8 per annum thereafter during Taylor's life, and after his death £3.10.0 per annum – tenants normally undertook to do service and suit of court at the landlord's manor court to be held twice a year and to pay fees. They also undertook to pay duties. Thus John Melton who received a fee-farm grant in November 1613 of thirty acres and one acre to build on undertook to pay Taylor 'two good fatt sweete lyving henns and twenty good swete henn eggs' per annum, and every second year 'one good fatt sweet lyving shepe or mutton of the age of two yeares or upwards'.[120] Tenants in 1630 undertook to grind all their corn and grain at the landlord's mill in Ballyhaise.[121] Rights of re-entry for the landlord for non payment of rent as well as defined heriot and relief payments to him were included. The landlord retained rights of 'hawking, hunting, fowling and fishing' as well as rights of way, and in Reader's grant of 1612 right of way was provided for another tenant 'unto the Highe waye leading from Belturbett towards the Cavan not doing any hurt or destruction to anie of the corn then growing near the said waye on the said lands'.[122]

These deeds also throw some light on Robert Reader's fortunes which may indicate how justifiable as a colonising expedient Taylor's original grant in 1612 to him was. By 1621 three of the five and a half polls had been in the hands of a certain Richard Clough who had died, and who may have been installed by Reader, had then passed to John Greenham the Dublin lawyer, whose interest must have been that of a speculative absentee and with whom Reader had been engaged in litigation in chancery, before being passed on to a certain Robert Nicholson, also of Dublin, who was not tied to live there.[123] Thus not only amongst the owners of the estates, but amongst the tenantry, Dublin interests (facilitated no doubt by the location of the county) were intruding. By 1630, Reader who had lived at Ballyhaise was dead and one and a half polls were renewed by Brockhill Taylor, John's son, to Thomas Reader, who lived there, and his widowed mother.[124] In December 1639 Thomas Reader mortgaged this holding to Sir William Ryves of Dublin, a prominent judge.[125] The remaining poll in the original fee-farm grant to Robert Reader had been sold by him as early as June 1615 for £23 but to a settler who lived within the barony.[125a]

Nor was it only through the Readers that Dublin interests were gaining a footing on the estate. In June 1636 Thomas Taylor of Belturbet (probably a relative of the landlord) leased one and a half polls for ninety-five years to Matthew Mainwaring who had been a customs official for Derry and Coleraine in 1619, held office in the court of wards in 1622, and was now constable of Dublin Castle.[126] He undertook to build 'one sufficient English house' on the land, but implicit in the further undertaking that he should 'have always resident and dwelling upon the p'misses one able man that shall be of the British race and discent' was that he would be himself absentee.[127] Mainwaring, who later extended his position on this estate,[128] was since 1621 a tenant also to Sir Stephen Butler,[129] and further, in 1637, became leaseholder of the landed endowment, also in Loughtee, of the Cavan 'royal' school.[130]

We have thus been able to give some impression of an estate which had received favourable comment in government surveys and which was one where ownership remained with the family of the original grantee right up to 1641.[131] The 1630 muster roll recorded a settler population of eighty-five males[132] (including Robert Reader though not his son Thomas and to which a few further names could be added from these estate papers) which was the second largest colony in the barony. Dr Faithful Teate, a famous ecclesiastic, had been rector there since 1626 and had personally a freehold in Ballyhaise[133] – the first minister was appointed in 1615 – holding Castleterra parish pluralistically along with Drung.[134] The 1622 Protestant ecclesiastical visitation stated that the old parish church was 'ruinous' which was not uncommon in Loughtee and indeed throughout the plantation. They recommend that it was 'not fitt to be repaired, but one to be built de novo at Bellahayes'.[135] Here, as in many other places, the new concentrations of settlement made the old churches, taken into the possession of the new dispensation, inconvenient for use. However, by 1639 a church had indeed been erected, and an acre of land assigned for building a 'vicar's house'.[136]

The economic impact of the colony remains for attention. Government surveyors, not writing for posterity, recorded little of the agricultural pursuits of the settlers. However there is evidence for the importation of livestock. By 1613 Waldron had 'stocked his ground with English and Irish cattle'.[137] In 1622 he and Fishe had 'a great store of English cattle'.[138] As early as 1611 both of them had two teams of English horses with English carts.[139] Although, as we have seen, mills were erected, reference to tillage is less common. Pynnar found 'no great store of tillage' on Taylor's lands, though there was 'a little' on the Waldron estate.[140] Furthermore one of his general conclusions was that the Scots in Ulster were more prone to engage in tillage than the English.[141] None of the leases examined for this area required land enclosure.

If evidence of occupation derived from the depositions of 1641 can be accepted there was then a strong skilled element amongst the colony. There were, at least, in Belturbet five merchants, two carriers, one baker, one gunsmith, one feltmaker, one shoemaker, and one innkeeper who also had a tannhouse.[142] A clothier on the Butler estate, where there was a fulling mill by 1619, claimed that he had lost the profits of his tuck mill, worth £20 per annum.[143] Fresh and salt eels were commercialised in this area.[144] The right to hold fairs and markets was granted to John Taylor in 1618, and was also included in the charters incorporating Cavan and Belturbet.[145] A dispute which came to a head in the 1620s between the corporation of Cavan and a private claimant deriving from a pre-plantation patent of 1603 about market rights indicates how control of such facilities was valued.[146] The inquiries held in County Cavan (and elsewhere) in 1629 as a result of the scheme for the regranting of undertakers' estates made recommendations in some cases about fairs and markets. Although the recommendation for the Moynes estate in Loughtee, that

> it will be very fytt and convenyent for the inhabitants to have 2 fayres kept within the … towne of Oughall al' Moynehall, every yeare, one upon the 1st of may, and the second upon the 8th of september being lady-day in harvist, there not being any fayers kept, upon any of those dayes, at any towne or place within 7 myles of the said towne.[147]

was typical of these, it was not in fact carried out. Such institutions, however, were clearly recognised as important.

Although many Loughtee estates changed hands the sales values are not recorded. However surviving leases suggest an upward movement of rents as the plantation developed. Thus for example a fee-farm grant in March 1613 of two townlands by Richard Waldron to Clement Cottrell (who had been his agent) was at a rent of 10/- per annum,[148] and Taylor's fee-farm grant of five and a half polls to Reader in 1612 was at £4 for the first year,

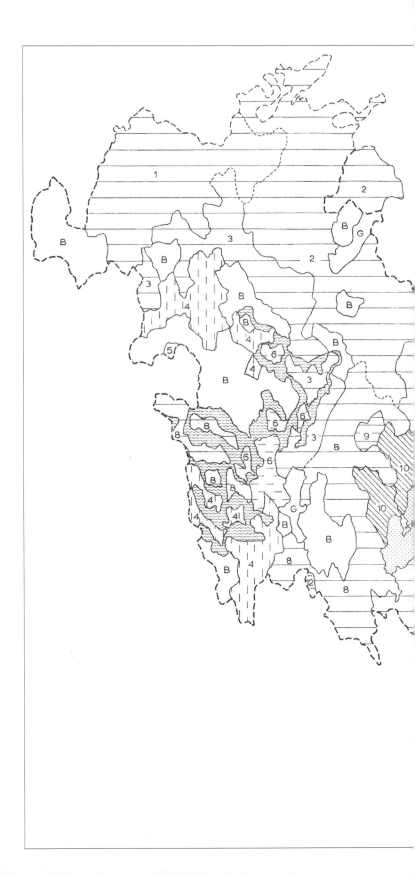

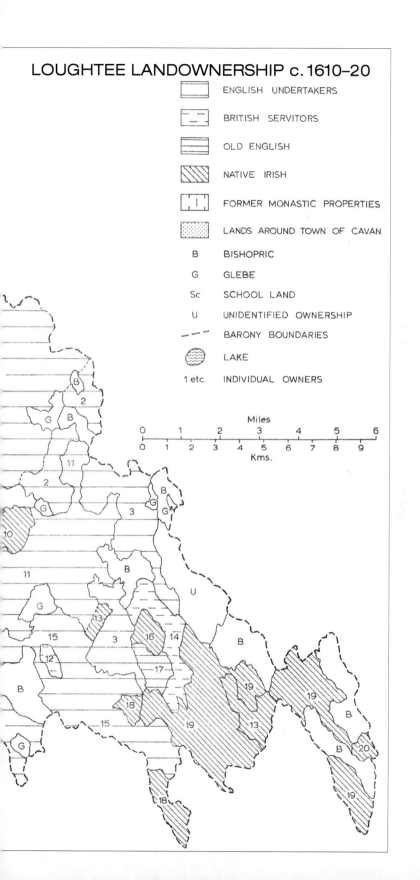

LOUGHTEE LANDOWNERSHIP c. 1610–20

	ENGLISH UNDERTAKERS
	BRITISH SERVITORS
	OLD ENGLISH
	NATIVE IRISH
	FORMER MONASTIC PROPERTIES
	LANDS AROUND TOWN OF CAVAN
B	BISHOPRIC
G	GLEBE
Sc	SCHOOL LAND
U	UNIDENTIFIED OWNERSHIP
– – –	BARONY BOUNDARIES
	LAKE
1 etc.	INDIVIDUAL OWNERS

Miles
0   1   2   3   4   5   6
0   1   2   3   4   5   6   7   8   9
Kms.

thereafter during Taylor's life £8, and after his death £3.10.0.[149] By the 1630s much higher rents are evident. Thus a fee-farm grant by Brockhill Taylor in 1630 of the two polls was at £9 per annum,[150] and one and a half polls on the same estate were leased in 1636 for 95 years at £7.3.0 per annum.[151] However the significance of all these figures could be affected by unrecorded entry fines.

The sums that could be raised from the sale of leases are also instructive. Thus Clement Cottrell sold his two polls in September 1618 for £100.[152] Four townlands and a water mill near Belturbet were sold to Butler for £400 in 1622.[153] Thomas Reader mortgaged his one and a half polls for £100 at 10 per cent in 1639.[154] Undertakers' incomes are not easily determined. The expansionist Stephen Butler was able in 1617 to pay £550, while values were low, for the middle proportion of Kilspinan in Fermanagh which he bought from Michael Balfour,[155] thus inserting himself into the ownership of a Scottish-allocated barony, and from a partial transcript of his will which survives it emerges that he was able to envisage bequests of £800 and £600 to his sons and daughters.[156] On the other hand something of the position of Peter Ameas can be inferred from the answer of Butler, who had acted as his guarantor, to a bill of Sir Hugh Culme in a chancery suit concerning debts of the estate. Butler stated that the estate was worth £80 per annum, and it appears that Ameas owned no more than seven horses, four cows, six young heifers, and twenty sheep.[157]

This paper has tried to give some impression of the colonising activities of the undertakers in Loughtee in terms of the articles of plantation. There is much that is strictly outside its scope. The lands of the Irish and old English and the smaller British landowners, and the lands of the church, the town of Cavan and the royal school, some 37,500 acres approximately as opposed to the undertakers 54,000, had no prohibition against Irish occupation, but how these were used and how their owners fared must be left aside. There is much of interest too that remains obscure. Stephen Allen, probably the person of that name who had been appointed king's attorney in Ulster in 1617,[158] and who was sovereign of the town of Cavan and lived in the abbey there, claimed in 1642 that he had been seneschal of four manors – those of Butler, Taylor, Greenham and Moynes,[159] but no manor court records survive. The role of settler – and native – in the county administration is for the same reason irretrievable – Fishe was sheriff in 1616 and Butler in 1622.[160] We know nothing of the cultural proclivities of the settlers beyond that Sir Stephen Butler bequeathed books in his will.[161] However that they had installed a fairly substantial colony in Loughtee is evident. If we take the settler adult male population as about 450 on some 54,000 acres this represents a much greater density of settlement than the 900 men installed by the London companies (undertaker equivalents) on some 291,000 acres in County Derry.[162] It was nonetheless a very thin spread and it was unevenly distributed. In the absence of reliable comparative population statistics, we may end with the impression left by bishop Bedell's son of Cavan during his father's episcopate. It was

> meetly well planted with English, but scatteringly here and there which facilitated their ruine ... [and] the Irish were more than five times their number and all of them obstinate papists.[163]

NOTE ON THE MAP

The numbers represent the estates of individual owners as follows:

1   Sir Hugh Wirrall
2   Sir Stephen Butler
3   John Fishe
4   James Dillon, Earl of Roscommon
5   Sir Claud Hamilton
6   Hugh Culme
7   John Taylor
8   Sir Richard Waldron
9   Richard Nugent, Baron Delvin
10 Walter, Thomas and Patrick Brady
11 Nicholas Lusher
12 William Binde
13 Mulmory oge O'Reilly
14 Roger Downeton
15 William Lusher
16 Hugh McGlasney [O'Reilly]
17 Edward Nugent
18 Mulmory McHugh Connelagh O'Reilly
19 Tirlagh McDonnell O'Reilly of Killagh
20 Shane Bane O'Moeltully

The delimitation of ownership in a small area surrounding the town of Cavan proved difficult. It was therefore decided not to attempt to indicate boundaries on the map. The area has been given a separate shading. In this way it is hoped that this area will not appear to represent an individual holding or to constitute corporation property. The boundary line merely indicates that this is the smallest area within which ownership could not be accurately plotted, especially on a map of 1" scale. It was, however, possible, by various means, to arrive at a reasonably accurate impression of the amount of the land so indicated which was held by each owner, and so possible to incorporate these acreage figures into Table 1. The breakdown of the area (904 acres) may be presented here:

Cavan corporation	683	acres
Sir Thomas Ashe (abbey land)	9	acres
Sir Thomas Rotherham (castle land)	141	acres
Glebe	71	acres

The land of Sir Claud Hamilton, a Scottish undertaker in Tullyhunco barony, 67 acres, a very small area across the modern barony boundary and no. 5 on the map, is left unshaded. The introduction of a new category on the map for this small piece of land would not be justified.

Serious doubt about boundaries is indicated by dotted lines. The possibility of other errors must not be ruled out.

I am indebted to Mr C.J.W. Edwards, Lecturer in Geography, and to Miss Shirley Keeley, Cartographer, New University of Ulster, whose draftsmanship has given my map its highly professional appearance.

---

[1] *Cal. S.P. Ire., 1608–10*, pp 404–6; 'Ulster plantation papers' no. 22, in *Analecta Hibernica*, viii. These planning decisions, however, were based on estimates of the acreages of the counties which were faulty in many respects.

[2] T.W. Moody 'The revised articles of, the Ulster plantation, 1610' in *Bulletin of Institute of Historical Research*, xii (1935), 178–83.

[3] NAI, R.C. 9/1, 168–75.

[4] E. Hogan (ed.), *The Description of Ireland ... in anno* 1598 (Dublin, 1878), p. 121.

[5] *Cal. Fiants Ire., Eliz.*, no. 4547; *Cal. S.P. Ire., 1600*, pp 418–20; TCD, Muniments, Mahaffy collection, C.12a; *Cal. Pat. Rolls Ire., Eliz.*, p. 277.

[6] NAI, R.C. 9/1, p. 168.

[7] 'Ulster plantation papers' no. 73, in *Analecta Hibernica*, viii; *Cal. S.P. Ire., 1608–10*, p. 55.

[8] *Cal. Fiants Ire., Eliz.*, no. 1681; see also *Cal. S.P. Ire., 1509–73*, pp 399–400. For subsequent developments see *Cal. Pat. Rolls Ire., Jas I*, pp 2–3; Ibid., *Eliz.*, p. 456; NAI, C.P., D.54; Hill, *Plantation in Ulster*, p. 113.

[9] TCD, MS E.3.7, f. 312.

[10] *Cal. Pat. Rolls Ire., Jas I*, pp 53–5, See also ibid., *Eliz.*, p. 219; *Cal. S.P. Ire., 1588–92*, p. 462, ibid., *1592–96*, pp 529–30.

[11] *Cal. Pat. Rolls Ire., Jas I*, p. 199; TCD, MS E.3.7, f. 312.

[12] Hill, *Plantation in Ulster*, p. 348.

[13] He had received a lease of one piece of termon and errenach land in Cavan in 1603 (*Cal. Pat. Rolls Ire., Jas I*, p. 10). The termon and errenach lands in the plantation counties in general were granted to the Protestant bishops at the time of the plantation.

[14] *Cal. Pat. Rolls Ire., Jas I*, p. 145. Some 500 acres, confirmed by patent in June 1611 (ibid., p. 211) to Edward Nugent, also old English, may have represented a previous purchase.

[15] J.L.J. Hughes (ed.), *Patentee officers in Ireland, 1173–1826* (Dublin, 1960), p. 43.

[16] *Cal. Pat. Rolls Ire., Jas I*, p. 212. See *Inq. Cancell. Hib. Repert.*, ii, Cavan, (64) Chas I.

[17] *Cal. Pat. Rolls Ire., Jas I*, pp 80–2.

[18] *Cal. Carew MSS, 1575–88*, pp 391–2; *Cal. S.P. Ire., 1574–85*, pp 522, 539; *Cal. Fiants Ire., Eliz.*, nos 4541–2; H. Morley (ed.), *Ireland under Elizabeth and James the First* (London, 1890), pp 348–50.

[19] The theoretical assumptions about landownership in Gaelic Ireland upon which this was being based were altered with the plantation, a point which did not go unnoticed by those affected. They failed, however, to upset the plantation in the county by legal argument (see G.A. Hayes-McCoy, 'Sir John Davies in Cavan in 1606 and 1610' in *Breifne*, vol. 1, no. 3 (1960), pp 177–91).

[20] R.J. Hunter, 'Towns in the Ulster plantation' in *Studia Hibernica*, xi (1971), pp 40–2, 68–75.

[21] *Cal. Pat. Rolls Ire., Jas I*, pp 182, 586–7; *Cal. S.P. Ire., 1611–14*, p. 33.

[22] Lambeth Palace Library, London, Carew MSS, Vol. 630, f. 70.

[23] *Cal. S.P. Ire., 1608–10*, p. 404; 'Ulster Plantation Papers' no. 22, in *Analecta Hibernica*, viii.

[24] Two of these have not so far been discussed. Sir Thomas Rotherham, surveyor-general of buildings from 1618, received a lease of Cavan castle and associated lands in 1616 (*Cal. Pat. Rolls Ire., Jas I*, p. 313). For earlier plans for this property see 'Ulster Plantation Papers' no. 27, in *Analecta Hibernica*, viii, see also *Cal. S.P. Ire., 1611–14*, p. 39. It was owned by Lord Lambert in 1641. The dating of William Binde's patent, 21 March 1617 (*Cal. Pat. Rolls Ire., Jas I*, p. 317) suggests that he had received a small grant of concealed land.

[25] He may not have considered it convenient, in view of the role he had just played in arguing the case for confiscating Cavan land (see G.A. Hayes-McCoy, supra) to benefit from the plantation in that county.

[26] 'Ulster Plantation Papers' no. 21, in *Analecta Hibernica*, viii.

[27] Ibid., no. 11.

[28] Ibid.

[29] Hill, *Plantation in Ulster*, 282.

[30] Ibid.

[31] 'Ulster Plantation Papers' no. 37, in *Analecta Hibernica*, viii. Hill may have been incorrect in stating (p. 280) that he was the son of an Elizabethan adventurer in Ireland. He was in error in the number of grantees in the barony, omitting William Lusher.

[32] The incomes they claimed when they applied for land can be given. Fishe claimed an income of £300 per annum, Butler represented himself as having an estate of £1,500 (*Cal. S.P. Ire., 1608–10*, p. 549). It is not easy to find comparative figures for England at this time, but a study of the Kent gentry between 1640 and 1660 shows that the average income of 135 families with well-documented fortunes was £656 per annum, though the author states that hundreds had an income of under £250 a year (A. Everitt, *The community of Kent and the great rebellion, 1640–60* (Leicester, 1966), pp 41, 329).

[33] Hill, *Plantation in Ulster*, p. 283. He submitted his income as 200 marks (*Cal. S.P. Ire., 1608–10*, p. 550).

[34] 'Ulster Plantation Papers' no. 11, in *Analecta Hibernica*, viii. John Taylor was the first undertaker in the plantation at large to be assigned his lands, on 4 August 1610 (ibid.).

[35] Ibid., no. 21.

[36] *Cal. S.P. Ire., 1608–10*, p. 521.

[37] Ibid., pp 525–7. See also ibid., *1611–14*, p. 178.

[38] Lambeth Palace Library, London, Carew MSS, vol. 630, ff 61v–62v.

[39] 'Ulster Plantation Papers' no. 11, in *Analecta Hibernica*, viii.

[40] Ibid., no. 5; *Cal. Carew MSS, 1603–24*, p. 63.

[41] *Cal. S.P. Ire., 1608–10*, p. 477. He suggested two agents, George Sharpe and Clement Cottrell.

[42] 'Ulster Plantation Papers' no. 37, in *Analecta Hibernica*, viii.

[43] *Cal. S.P. Ire 1611–14*, p. 34.

[44] The Loughtee coverage is in Carew MSS, vol. 630, ff 61–3.

[45] He was involved with some initial problems at the beginning of May ('Ulster Plantation Papers' no. 36).

[46] In the few cases where families are referred to in the report, the number of adult males has been taken as one – families emigrating were probably young.

[47] This balance would appear to reflect a 'national' characteristic of the plantation at large at this stage – the English undertakers were concerned with construction, the Scots more with farming.

48 The Loughtee coverage is HMC, *Hastings MSS*, iv, 161–3.

49 *Cal. S.P. Ire., 1611–14*, pp 140–41; *Cal; Carew MSS, 1603–24*, pp 23–4.

50 In February 1614 in a letter to Lord [Northampton] Sir Robert Jacob wrote from his circuit in Cavan and described the settlement. 'Those gentlemen you recommended to be undertakers in the barony of Loughtye, in Cavan, viz., Mr. Waldron, Mr. Butler, Mr. Fisher, Mr. Cragge and Mr. Claude Hamilton [the latter two were in fact Scots undertakers in Co. Cavan], have built and planted very well. I lay last night at Mr. Waldron's house, who has built a very fair house of stone for himself and 27 houses for English tenants and has made a very handsome village where there was not one stone laid these twelve months, and intends to enlarge his own house a great deal more' (HMC, *Hastings MSS*, iv, 14).

51 The Loughtee coverage is in Hill, *Plantation in Ulster* pp 460–67.

52 *Inq. Cancell. Hib. Repert.*, ii, Cavan (23) Chas I.

53 NAI, Ferguson MSS, xi, 271.

54 *Inq. Cancell. Hib. Repert.*, i, Cavan (16) Chas I.

55 Hill, *Plantation in Ulster*, p. 149, Mountford was Wirrall's father-in-law (*Cal. Pat Rolls Ire., Jas I*, pp 252–53).

56 Indeed a transcript of an inquisition on the Waldron estate in 1631, refers to the 'cotegers of the town of [   ]' (NAI, Calendar to the exchequer inquisition of the counties of Ulster, Cavan, (3) Chas I).

57 The Loughtee coverage is in BL, Add. MS 4756, ff 101v–3. The survey for the county has been edited by P. O'Gallachair in *Breifne*, vol. 1, no. 1 (1958), pp 60–75.

58 *Cal. Pat. Rolls Ire., Jas I*, p. 327.

59 *Inq. Cancell. Hib. Repert.*, ii, Cavan, (1) Chas II. Bagshaw also developed landed interest elsewhere in Ireland. He became a leaseholder to the earl of Ormond in December 1631 (NLI, Ormond deeds, D 3835).

60 Ibid., (23) Chas, I.

61 BL, Add. MS 4756, ff 118–18v.

62 *Cal. Pat. Rolls Ire., Jas I*, p. 182.

63 *Cal. S.P. Ire., 1611–14*, p. 33.

64 *Inq. Cancell. Hib. Repert.*, ii, Cavan (26) Chas I.

65 For statements of some of these problems throughout planted counties see *Cal. Carew MSS, 1603–24*, pp 244–51.

66 For some Armagh examples see ibid., p. 251.

67 'Ulster Plantation Papers' no. 35, in *Analecta Hibernica*, viii. See also no. 53. Sir Francis Rushe who had a prior claim over the castle and lands at Belturbet was bought out (ibid., no. 34).

68 *Cal. S.P. Ire., 1611–14* p. 275; *Cal. Pat. Rolls Ire., Jas I*, p. 249. He received a patent accordingly in January 1613 (ibid., p. 238). Waldron, one of the planters benefitting most from Delvin's surrender, received a king's letter for the surrender and regrant of 'the lord of Delvin's and other lands' in August 1614 (ibid., p. 300. For a further king's letter of December 1616 see ibid., p. 326 and BL, Add. MS 4794, pp 359–60). A bond, accompanying a lease of the same date, entered into by Waldron to a tenant, Clement Cottrell, on 18 March 1613 contained the undertaking that he would enjoy the land free 'from all and all manner tytles … and demands' of Delvin (NLI, Farnham Papers, D20409–20475). In June 1613 Waldron was in dispute with an Englishman who claimed he had broken an agreement to convey to him one-third of the estate (*Cal. S.P. Ire., 1611–14*, pp 370–72). See also ibid., p. 500.

69 'Ulster Plantation Papers' nos 55–7, in *Analecta Hibernica*, viii, Their report is in TCD, MS F. 1 20, pp 9–31.

70 See for example *Inq Cancell. Hib. Repert.*, ii, Cavan (23) Chas I. The undertakers sometimes took out new patents, or at least secured king's letters authorising these as did Sir Stephen Butler in 1817 (BL, Add. MS 4794, ff 358v–59), to record more fully or more accurately the details of their properties.

71 For the development of government policy on this see R.J. Hunter, 'The settler population of an Ulster plantation county' in *Donegal Annual* (1972), pp 124–29.

72 'Ulster Plantation Papers' nos 36, 68, 69 in *Analecta Hibernica,* viii.

73 NLI, Butler Deeds, D8896–8926, Indenture 2 March 1617 between Michael Balfour … and Sir Stephen Butler. Indeed by the time of Pynnar's survey Adwick (who held Wirrall's lands in Loughtee), Butler, and Wirrall all had lands in Fermanagh (Hill, *Plantation in Ulster*, pp 477,

578–80, 484). John Waldron, a relative of the Loughtee family acquired land in Armagh in 1629 and afterwards, and also land in Leitrim (NAI, Lodge MSS, Records of the rolls, v, 293–95; *Cal. S.P. Ire., 1625–32*, p. 621).

[74] *Inq. Cancell. Hib. Repert.*, ii, Cavan (23) Chas I.

[75] NAI, Lodge MSS, Records of the rolls, v, 147–9.

[76] E.S. Shuckburgh (ed.), *Two biographies of ... William Bedell* (Cambridge, 1902), pp 302, 341; TCD, College muniments. Greenham also acquired land in Fermanagh (*Cal. Pat. Rolls Ire., Chas I*, p. 573; NAI, Lodge MSS, v, 250–51), and had interests in houses in Dublin (ibid., p. 359).

[77] He died in 1630 (A. Vicars, *Index to the prerogative wills of Ireland, 1536–1810* (Dublin, 1897), p. 116). He had been a tenant there in 1617 (*Inq. Cancell. Hib. Repert.*, ii, Cavan (26) Chas I).

[78] For their names see Table 2. They appear on the muster roll of *c.* 1630 (BL, Add. MS 4770. f. 20). The patents taken out under the commission for defective titles have been helpful in identifying their holdings (NAI, Lodge MSS, v, 486, 487; vi, 45–6, 134–35), and supplement the Book of Survey and Distribution. Difficulties were found in making townland identifications, and allowance must be made for possible errors.

[79] Some inquisitions taken at the end of the 1620s, while they may be somewhat unreliable, throw light on the dates when some of these freeholds were created (*Inq. Cancell. Hib. Repert.*, ii, Cavan (23, 26) Chas, I; NAI, Cal. exchequer inquisitions, Ulster Cavan (3) Chas I).

[80] *Inq. Cancell. Hib. Repert.*, ii, Cavan (26) Chas I. Sir Hugh Culme purchased a freehold created by Sir George Mainwaring (ibid., (23) Chas I).

[81] NAI, Cal. exchequer inquisitions, Ulster Cavan (3) Chas I.

[82] *Inq. Cancell. Hib. Repert.*, ii, Cavan (23) Chas I.

[83] However Pynnar criticised Adwick for having no arms, nor 'any place to keep them in' and only Stephen Butler, as we have seen, appears to have dispersed arms amongst his dispersed tenantry.

[84] BL, Add. MS 4770, ff 3–23 (Cavan section).

[85] Sheffield City Library, Strafford MSS, Vol. V, ff 37–48.

[86] BL, Add MS 4770, ff 3–6v, 12–16v, 20–20v, 22v. Butler's men only showed 30 swords and 7 pikes. It is possible though that arms in landlords' houses were not recorded at all. In his will, of which a partial transcript survives, Butler bequeathed to his eldest son 'all my armes and [   ] pikes, halberts, bells, etc.' (NAI, deeds, wills and instruments ... post mortem, vol. 25, pp 265–70).

[87] See my 'Towns in the Ulster plantation' in *Studia Hibernica*, xi (1971), 72–3.

[88] For developments up to this see T.W. Moody, 'The treatment of the native population under the scheme for the plantations in Ulster' in *Irish Historical Studies* I, 69–63.

[89] TNA, S.P. 63/236, ff 19–19v (*Cal. S.P. Ire., 1615–25*, pp 322–23) Sir John Fishe of Loughtee appears to have been one of the proponents. The petition has not survived, but it was probably the same as that submitted to the commissioners of inquiry in 1622 (NLI, Rich papers, MS 8014/3; Plantations, 11 May 1622).

[90] Many of these are in *Inq. Cancell. Hib. Repert.*, ii.

[91] It could conceivably have involved the breaking of leases held by British of land now earmarked for Irish.

[92] *Cal. Pat, Rolls Ire., Chas I*, p. 588.

[93] NAI, Lodge MSS, v, 526–27.

[94] An inquisition, subsequently, in November 1632, on the Perse estate in Clankee barony, County Cavan, revealed that one of his freeholders had demised two polls of land in the British area to native Irish tenants (*Inq. Cancell. Hib. Repert.*, ii, Cavan, (41) Chas I).

[95] There must also have been a small old English non-landowning element, including, for example, some residents in Cavan town.

[96] HMC, *Hastings MSS*, iv, 162–63.

[97] 'If the Irish be put away with their cattle the British must either forsake their dwellings or endure great distress on the suddain. Yet the combination of the Irish is dangerous to them by robbing them and otherwise' (Hill, *Plantation in Ulster*, pp 589–90).

[98] BL, Add. MS 4756, ff 102–3.

[99] *Inq. Cancell. Hib. Repert.*, ii, Cavan, (16, 23, 26) Chas I; NAI, Cal. exchequer inquisitions, Ulster, Cavan, (3) Chas I. For the Butler estate see Marsh's Library, Dublin, MS Z4. 2. 6, no. 96.

[100] *Inq. Cancell. Hib. Repert.*, ii, Cavan, (26) Chas I.

[101] NAI, Cal. exchequer inquisitions, Ulster, Cavan, (3) Chas I.

[102] In August 1616 a certain John Reley was demised a half poll by Sir George Mainwaring for forty-one years (*Inq. Cancell. Hib. Repert.*, ii, Cavan, (23) Chas I).

[103] Ibid. (38) Chas I.

[104] See my 'Towns in the Ulster Plantation' in *Studia Hibernica*, 11 (1971) pp 68–75.

[105] Armagh Archiepiscopal Registry, Ulster visitation book, 1622, diocese of Kilmore.

[106] *Inq. Cancell. Hib. Repert.*, ii, Cavan (26) Chas I.

[107] NLI, Butler deeds (unclassified).

[108] *Cal. S.P. Ire., 1615–25*, pp 479–80. Waterhouse was one of the first burgesses of the town (ibid., *1611–14*, p. 299). He later acquired land in Fermanagh (*Inq. Cancell. Hib. Repert.*, ii, Fermanagh (8, 39) Chas I). Also, the 1613 elections had been disputed.

[109] NAI, Newburgh Papers, M6956. Other very much smaller collections are the Farnham papers and Butler deeds already referred to. Some individual abstracts of leases and deeds are in NAI, Lodge MSS V, 524; VI: 20, 434–35. For some legal problems of Loughtee landowners see *Cal. S.P. Ire., 1625–32*, p. 360. Two further Butler deeds are NAI, D1038 and 2325. For abstracts of other Taylor deeds see *Cal. Pat. Rolls Ire., Jas I*, pp 276, 83.

[110] NAI, M6956/3. Reader does not appear to have been prominent in Carrickfergus (S. M'Skimin, *The history and antiquities of … Carrickfergus* (Belfast, 1829, passim).

[111] NAI, M6956/5, 6.

[112] NAI, M8956/4.

[113] Ibid., /4.

[114] Ibid., /5.

[115] Ibid., /8.

[116] Ibid., /9.

[117] Ibid., /3, 7.

[118] Ibid., /3, 4, 5, 8, 9.

[119] Ibid., /8.

[120] Ibid., /4.

[121] Ibid., /8.

[122] Ibid., /3.

[123] Ibid., /7; NAI, Repertories to the decrees of chancery, 1,320.

[124] Ibid., /8.

[125] Ibid., /13.

[125a] *Cal. Pat. Rolls Ire., Jas I*, p. 285.

[126] Hughes, *Patentee officers*, pp 86, 89.

[127] NAI, M6956/9, a (original), b (copy).

[128] In October 1636 he purchased a lease of a smaller area of the estate from a tenant, John Whisson of Drumgolyn (ibid., /11), who had himself recently acquired it from relatives of an earlier tenant, the Rev. William Andrews, M.A., of Belturbet, ibid., /12; Andrews had been appointed rector of Annagh (modern Belturbet) in 1617 (NLI, MS 2685, p. 50).

[129] NAI, Lodge MSS, vi, 434–35.

[130] Ibid., v, 532.

[131] In April 1639 a new patent was granted to co-heiresses, Elizabeth and Mary Taylor under the commission for defective titles. (ibid., vi. 192–93; see also *Inq. Cancell. Hib. Repert.*, ii, Cavan (63) Chas I).

[132] BL, Add, MS 4770, ff 14–15v.

[133] NAI, M69561/15.

[134] NLI, MS 2685, pp 95, 165.

[135] Armagh Archiepiscopal Registry, Ulster visitation book, 1622, pp 144–45.

[136] NAI, Lodge MSS, vi, 192–93. For the Moynes estate in this respect see *Inq. Cancell. Hib. Repert.*, ii, Cavan (23) Chas I.

[137] HMC, *Hastings MSS*, iv, 162.

[138] BL, Add. MS 4756. ff 101v–2.

[139] Lambeth Palace Library, Carew MSS, vol. 630, ff 61v–3.

[140] Hill, *Plantation in Ulster*, pp 461–62, The 1622 survey, otherwise unhelpful, found 'very good' tillage and 'inclosures' upon his land (ff 101v–2).

[141] Hill, *Plantation in Ulster*, p. 589.

[142] TCD, MS F. 3. 3, 4 passim. A carrying trade of agricultural produce to Dublin of some sort appears to have existed (TCD, MS F. 3. 3, ff 125–5v, 135; F. 3. 4, f. 144).

[143] TCD, MS F. 3. 4, f. 272.

[144] TCD, MS F. 3. 3, ff 111–12v; F. 3. 4, f. 188.

[145] NAI, Lodge MSS, Records of the rolls, xiv, 18–21.

[146] *Cal. Pat. Rolls Ire., Jas I*, p. 12; NAI, Chancery salvage AA. 96; *Inq. Cancell. Hib. Repert.*, ii, Cavan (68) Chas I.

[147] *Inq. Cancell. Hib. Repert.*, ii, Cavan (23) Chas I.

[148] NLI, Farnham papers, D20409–20475 in bundle '41 deeds re town and county of Cavan, 1612–1805'.

[149] NAI, M6956/3.

[150] Ibid., /10.

[151] Ibid., /9. A townland, at Butler's Bridge, with a corn mill, was leased by Sir Stephen Butler for £26 per annum some time before 1626 (NAI, Chancery salvage, V, 61), and another townland on this estate was declared in 1637 to be held for £8 a year (NAI, Ferguson MSS, xii, 329).

[152] NLI, Farnham papers, D20409–20475, in bundle '41 deeds …'

[153] NLI, Deed of sale between Charles Waterhouse and Etheldred his wife, and Sir Stephen Butler, 4 May 1622 (uncatalogued).

[154] NAI, M6956/13.

[155] NLI, Butler deeds, D8896–8926, Indenture, 2 March 1617, between Michael Balfour … and Sir Stephen Butler.

[156] NAI, Deeds wills and instruments post-mortem, 25, 265–70.

[157] NAI, Chancery salvage, Q.9.

[158] Hughes, *Patentee officers*, p, 2.

[159] TCD, MS F. 3. 3, ff 173–4, 175–7.

[160] RIA, Upton MSS, 19a.

[161] NAI, Deeds, wills and instruments post-mortem, 25, 265–70.

[162] T.W. Moody, *Londonderry plantation*, pp 321, 455.

[163] T.J. Jones (ed.), *Life and death of William Bedell* (London, 1872), p. 62.

11

'Plantation' society:
Antrim and Down, 1603–41[1]

Unlike in the escheated counties, there was no general or total forfeiture in Antrim and Down. Nevertheless the ownership there came to be subject to processes of change from the beginning of the seventeenth century which, unlike most of their sixteenth-century counterparts (notably the attempted plantation of the 1570s) proved to be definitive and enduring, and resulted in a very substantial colonisation of significant parts of both counties. Like the other counties, Antrim and Down had a post-war reorganisation; but unlike in them, this did not lead on to the second stage of formal general confiscation and plantation.

What had made plantation possible in West Ulster was the Flight of the Earls in 1607. No East Ulster Gaelic Lord did fly, but anyhow East Ulster was much more politically complex, divided as it was into a number of zones, for a general confiscation to be justifiable on the basis of actions by any individual lord. Furthermore – and perhaps more to the point – changes and neat arrangements in landownership were so sufficiently advanced in Antrim and Down before the Flight of the Earls as to open up substantial areas of it to a no less major because less formalised colonisation, already underway by 1610, than that which took place in the escheated counties planted after 1610. The effects, however, were two-fold: the new owners' estates for the most part were very much larger than in the regulated plantation to the west and, secondly, the colonisation which arose was very heavily – though by no means exclusively – Scottish in character. But since these changes did not result from the application of a single government policy, but rather arose from a number of processes which we have to examine in turn, Antrim and Down were left with a social and cultural diversity in landownership and society which gives the area as a whole a special interest.

The term unofficial plantation is sometimes applied to what happened here, but it is too imprecise. Some of the ownership change that took place was far from unofficial, because it resulted from the application of a government policy which justified confiscation (this applies to North Clandeboy in particular), but the very substantial colonisation that ensued from it there was not exactly plantation because the new owners were not precisely tied to obligations governing how many tenants they should introduce. Equally, to apply this term to the two whole counties is misleading because some of the constituent segments of the counties were much less affected by either ownership change or colonisation than others. The term applies best to the areas where ownership change by the sale of land, notably in MacCartan's country, took place in another major area, the Magennis territory of Iveagh; change was indeed brought about by government action, but it followed the lines laid down in the later sixteenth century and exemplified in Ulster in the settlement of Monaghan in 1591 – here a freeholder settlement was brought into being. Change (but not confiscation) along these same lines which was being tentatively initiated in North Clandeboy at the same time as the settlement of Monaghan was, however, now to be significantly overturned. Again the old English remnant in south-east Down was very little affected by government action in this period. Some zones then were affected by change c. 1603–41 more than others. The most helpful approach may well be to examine the processes of change as they affected these various zones, one by one.

Sixteenth-century Antrim and Down, on which changes now came to be superimposed, had itself become an area of quite diverse constituents. Much of south and west Down was made up of small Gaelic lordships on the coastal south-east Down area (Lecale, the Little Ards and the Dufferin – which was on the west side of Strangford Lough). A number of Anglo-Irish landowning families survived from the dissolution of the Norman earldom – Whites,[2] Savages and others – gaelicised no doubt in part from the exigencies and indeed influences of living just north of the Pale in frontier conditions, but retaining contacts with the Pale as well and supporting little towns such as Downpatrick, Ardglass and Strangford. In north Down and south Antrim was the very large O'Neill and Clandeboy lordship which had however been splitting into two – North/Lower and South/Upper Clandeboy – since about the middle of the century. The north of Antrim was made up of essentially two main divisions – the Glynns and the Route – the earlier populations of both of them (some deriving from the Norman conquest) living increasingly under the control of the Scottish MacDonnells. In the Glynns the ancient followers of the country had come to accept MacDonnell overlordship, 'because they do better defend them and less spend them than the Irish lord doth'. In the Route, MacDonnell rule was bitterly, and increasingly unsuccessfully, contested by the MacQuillans. By the mid 1580s 'the Scot' had 'well nigh expulsed him from the whole and driven him to a small corner near the Bann, which he defendeth,' it was said by Bagnal, 'rather by the maintenance of

Turlough [Luineach] O'Neill[3] than his own forces.' The principal smaller 'ancient' families there, the O'Hares and the O'Quins, continued to live on their land and yielded 'rent and service to the Scot'.[4]

Out of all this, the Crown had retained Carrickfergus, aspired to control the Bann fishery, and concentrated much of its earlier sixteenth-century effort on south-east Down. Its most enduring 'successes' later were the Bagnal grant of Newry and surrounding area, in the extreme south of County Down at mid-century, and its use of Carrickfergus in Antrim as a base. There were limits to that success too, however: its grander schemes of colonisation – the 'conquest' patents to Smith, Essex, Malby, etc. in 'the enterprise of Ulster' – in the 1570s had not succeeded. However, all of Antrim and Down, it is probably fair to say, had seen a greater level of government interference, with varying effects[5] in the second half of the sixteenth century than had been possible in north-west Ulster. Then with the Nine Years' War, Carrickfergus and Newry and such places as Carlingford to the south became immensely important bases and there was a massive build-up of military power around those points.

Victory in the war ensured that things would not remain as they were. A series of new departures ensued which both introduced new owners and confirmed some older ones.[6] The character of a significant element in the changes that did follow arose from another influential development – the succession of the Scottish king as James I to the throne of England at the same time. Another factor determining ownership was the aggressive acquisitiveness of some of the English military commanders that the war had deposited in both counties, one of whom, Sir Arthur Chichester, becoming lord deputy in Dublin in late 1604. The new situation also allowed another development – the dissolution of the monasteries. Crown action here in the sixteenth century had been largely confined to County Down with Bagnal the most well-known beneficiary.

The MacDonnells
We must now examine the processes of change in turn. Perhaps the most important confirmation of the old was that concerning the MacDonnells in Antrim. This was done under Lord Deputy Mountjoy in May 1603.[7] It therefore followed hard on the submission of Hugh O'Neill having been accepted at the end of March, but took place a little while (a few days) before O'Neill departed for England with Mountjoy on 30 May to negotiate the terms of his own restoration. The regrant to Randal MacDonnell, who was knighted, arranged under Mountjoy rather than Chichester on the instruction of the new Scottish king James I, would seem to be the first actual regrant in the reorganisation of Ulster in the aftermath

of the Nine Years' War. Randal MacDonnell had accompanied O'Neill to Kinsale and was intermarried with him. However, we must be careful not to conceive too firmly of some monolith of 'the Irish of Ulster' with the MacDonnells linked to them, standing in opposition to the Crown. What we have are dynastic links and confederations of lords, not unified ethnic blocs. At times the MacDonnells were seen as the enemies of the O'Neills; Shane certainly wished to subordinate them in order to vindicate his claim to be provincial king. The MacDonnells themselves put down the MacQuillans whose lands they were taking over. It is not surprising, therefore, that if the king were willing to legitimate Randal's position in Ulster, he would be willing to accept. After all, sixteenth-century governments had been trying to expel them.

In return for his patent, it would seem that Sir Randal MacDonnell was happy to concur with and facilitate changes which could be to his advantage anyhow. He was to divide his massive estate into manors of 2,000 acres each (which, Michael Perceval-Maxwell notes, forecast the division of land into small estates in the later plantation[8]) so that an English-style estate organisation could prevail in Antrim; but, as Raymond Gillespie points out,[9] the lord of the manor always got the revenue which arose from manor courts. He undertook to build castles, but he could live in them himself. He undertook to encourage new tenants to come from Lowland Scotland (i.e. to facilitate colonisation with the right kind of Scots), but he could do well from them – they would replace the hostile McQuillans – with good rent prospects. Thus through the security of his patent he could become a very big landlord indeed: he would no longer need to be a warlord. Now he had secure title under the Crown to about one third of a million acres. By 1608 he was described as 'a gentleman his majesty employed and trusted in those dangerous times in Ireland'[10] – i.e. he now had associations with the court of James I. By 1611 he had carried out his building operations. He had estate managers from the Lowlands. By 1618 he had been made first Viscount Dunluce and then Earl of Antrim in 1620. In giving order that he be elevated to the peerage, the king said that he 'hath behaved himself as well for the setting of the general peace in that our kingdom as in reducing to civility the barbarous people of those parts where he doth reside'.[11] Sir Arthur Chichester, Irish lord deputy, was a little suspicious of him; he thought the king had granted him too much. However, by politicking in London he had pulled a fast one on lord deputies: if he enjoyed the king's favour it did not matter too much that he was seen with some suspicion as a potential over-mighty subject by the king's Irish lord deputies. He even tried (as did his son later) to regain little areas in Scotland. Remote from Dublin he was not subjected to the heavy pressures of the Reformation – he did not have to be a model of civility. He had succeeded by pragmatism where Hugh O'Neill had failed.

O'Neills of Clandeboy

Account now must be taken of another major block of land – that of the O'Neill's of Clandeboy. This lordship had divided essentially into two branches – that of the O'Neills of North (or Lower or Nether) Clandeboy,[12] the County Antrim part and that of the O'Neills of South (or Upper) Clandeboy in County Down – and constituted about half a million acres. The importance of studying this area is because in both regions of it there was a substantial change in the ownership in the early seventeenth century (in fact between 1603 and 1606), and this change of ownership led to very major colonisation. How this change came about at this time needs to be accounted for, because it was exceptional to the pattern of restoration being laid down in those years for the rest of Gaelic Ulster.

Drastic change in ownership took place in both sections of Clandeboy through two sets of circumstances which, though inter-related, had best be taken in turn. The change in South Clandeboy has been discussed often enough.[13] What follows on North Clandeboy is an attempt really for the first time to explain these changes. The first stage came in 1603 when instructions from London were transmitted to Dublin by king's letter to issue patents of areas of land in North Clandeboy to two men, both of them English military men employed in the garrison at Carrickfergus – John Dalway and Arthur Chichester. The grant to Dalway, then constable of 'the king's palace' at Carrickfergus, was authorised by king's letter of 4 September 1603.[14] He received his grant on 8 October 1603, following on a surrender of some ten days earlier to hold for ever in free and common soccage. The legal basis of the title to him was 'founded upon an act of parliament passed Dublin, 23 Feb. 11 Elizabeth, confirming to the Crown the whole country of Clanneboy, in which the premises lay.'[15] The act in question was that of 1569, forfeiting the land of Shane O'Neill and his adherents which had provided the legal basis for the forfeiture and attempted plantation of Clandeboy in the early 1570s.

The resurrection of this act at this time was immensely important because all the land of Clandeboy, North and South, could be forfeited and all negotiations with the Gaelic lords of Clandeboy in the interval since the failure of the plantation schemes of the 1570s could be overturned. Specifically, it silently overturned a freeholder settlement, similar to that for Monaghan, being worked out for the Irish of North Clandeboy in the early 1590s and in which Dalway had found a place as a freeholder, but which had not been fully finalised at that time by the issuing of patents. The area of land Dalway, who had apparently come to Carrickfergus with the Earl of Essex in 1573, now received by patent was one 'teugh' called Braidisland (near Carrickfergus) and this was precisely the piece of land he had received as a freeholder under the lord Shane MacBrian O'Neill (d. 1617) in 1592 on the grounds that he was married to Shane MacBrian's aunt, Jane Ní Brian O'Neill, a sister of Sir Brian MacPhelim's.[16]

The other important patent at this time was passed to a more recent arrival, Sir Arthur Chichester, who also held the office of governor of Carrickfergus – the key man in the local garrison during the latter stages of the Nine Years' War. He had gone to London in 1603 to advance his prospects and had secured a king's letter to Antrim on 8 August 1603 with instructions that he be continued in that office for life and that he should receive a grant of the castle of Belfast 'with lands thereunto annexed'.[17]

The importance of these grants is twofold. In the first place a thirty-year-old Crown title had been revived. What they show secondly is not only the ambition for land of two local servitor figures, but that they were seeking to secure it on the best possible terms against the Crown. They were seeking to secure patents for ever (outright grants) with quit-rents to the Crown, which therefore could never be altered, and with the least onerous tenures.[18] The implications of the first were disadvantageous to the native Irish. The implications of the second were disadvantageous to the finances of Dublin government.

In both respects, these two grants ran contrary to the general spirit of home (i.e. London) government policy at that time. The general thrust of this policy at this stage was both conciliatory towards the Ulster Irish lords (as Mellifont and the subsequent restoration of Hugh O'Neill and Rory O'Donnell reveals), and also informed by a concern to eliminate the deleterious effects of corruption or smart moves on Crown finances in Ireland. There had been complaints from the Ulster lords about grants of land being made to Englishmen in the immediate run-up to the Nine Years' War and these, as we saw (though their extent may have been exaggerated), were portrayed as a major source of discontent in the localities. Secondly, the way in which many of the grants in Ireland as a whole were being engineered (especially in the conversion of Crown leases to outright grants) had benefitted the grantees rather than the government in terms of revenue from the land.[19] Accordingly, and to address this latter matter perhaps in particular, inhibitions were sent to Dublin at this time (in September and in October 1603 and again in April 1605)[20] forbidding it to make grants of any land save by special warrant from the king. Chichester himself reveals that the validity of this title was itself being questioned, presumably on these latter grounds. Indeed in this context it is worth noting that what

Chichester had been trying to achieve with his grant, since Belfast and its associated lands had been conferred on a temporary basis on Sir Ralph Lane (who had since died) in 1598, was the conversion of a short-term grant, the rent on which to the Crown could be improved with the passage of time, to an outright one for ever with therefore a static quit-rent.[21]

In the next stage a number of factors, personal and governmental, came together leading to the final outcome for Clandeboy North and South. In July 1605 the government in London finally made up its mind about the conditions under which the Irish in Ulster were to be restored and a commission was issued to Sir Arthur Chichester, who had by now become lord deputy, and others to bring this about. What must in some measure account for the fact that Clandeboy, quite exceptionally, did not follow the course which prevailed elsewhere was the revival of the title, founded on the act of 1569, which allowed much of it to be expropriated and granted to new men. Who those new men came to be has a lot to do with personal circumstances or opportunism. Two men in particular, both Scots, have to be considered – Hugh Montgomery and James Hamilton.

In 1601 Conn O'Neill of South Clandeboy had entered into a minor rebellion and was held prisoner in Carrickfergus. His wife got Montgomery to snatch him from prison. Montgomery was one of the numerous group of Scots who felt that the new king, James I, was under obligation to him and when he brought O'Neill to London, he secured the king's agreement to a bargain whereby O'Neill would be pardoned and restored to half of South Clandeboy while he, Montgomery, would get the other half. At this stage James Hamilton emerged on the scene arguing that the king was under obligation to him because he had acted as a supporter of James's candidature for the throne in Dublin.

The result was a carve-up of both Clandeboys. Eventually in 1606 the leading former O'Neill owners were restored to about one-third of the land in both areas and the rest was granted by patent to the new. What finally happened in South Clandeboy was decided by the king. Hamilton and Montgomery were awarded one third each on one condition that they should introduce colonists to their estates. Conn O'Neill was restored to the remaining third.

The outcome in North Clandeboy was more complex. Here Chichester, as lord deputy during the course of a tour in Ulster in the summer in 1605, in which he was carrying out its administrative re-organisation, 'reserved' (to use his own word) in an arbitrary kind of way, to the use of the government about a half, or perhaps two-thirds, of the land and that being the part nearest to the coast and nearest to Carrickfergus and Belfast. He argued on the grounds of government interest that in the interest of security or contract that land should be granted out to new owners. At this same time Hamilton secured from London instructions to Dublin that he should be granted patents for a considerable amount of forfeited land in Ireland. These followed also in 1605 and 1606. However, Hamilton transferred the land in North Clandeboy, which was included in these patents, in return for sums of money paid to other owners who were mainly Chichester himself and a group of fellow English military men such as Sir Hugh Clotworthy. The outcome was that about two-thirds of North Clandeboy came to be owned by a group of English ex-military men, while about two-thirds of South Clandeboy went to the two new Scots. The leading local O'Neills were restored to the rest. In both areas the new owners secured the former monastic land as well. In both areas also the new owners made a very considerable 'developmental' impact – building new houses, villages, etc. Both areas also saw substantial colonisation under them.

Magennis

Another zone where significant change was brought about in the early seventeenth century was in the Magennis territories in County Down. These lands are represented by the modern baronies of Iveagh which are made up of some 275,000 acres. The diocese of Dromore also overlaps reasonably well with the bounds of the Magennis territories[22] while also taking in the land of the MacCartans.[23] These lands derived from the old *Uí Echach Cobo* kingdom.[24] They survived reasonably well the Anglo-Norman conquest, though one of its two principal military bases, Dundrum castle (the other was Carrickfergus), in Lecale, was just on the fringes of the Magennis lands.[25] With the decline of the Earldom of Ulster, the Magennises came to occupy Dundrum castle which they held in the 1540s as tenants of the Crown (as successor of the Earldom of Ulster), though in practice they paid no rent.[26] This is an example of the way the balance between Gaelic and Anglo-Norman in East Ulster had altered by the end of the middle ages.

But if they survived well in that regard, the Magennises were in turn subject to the pressures of the O'Neills. The *Ceart Uí Néill* sets out the obligations imposed on the Magennises by right of the O'Neill claim to overlordship.

> The right of O'Neill from the *Uí Eachach Uladh*: that they come in full muster, and if they should not come, O'Neill shall have from them what his own judge shall award. Three hundred beeves from them or six ounces of (of gold) and 200 marks instead. Provision for 200 men as normal billeting from them: provision for 50 of them

in one from the *Uí Eachach* themselves, namely MacAonghusa, and
provision for a hundred from the three chieftains MacShuileachain,
MacDuibheanna and O'Haidheidh.

There was also an O'Neill claim for a fee when a lord took the name: 'every
lord and chieftain that is appointed in the province of Ulster namely [the
list includes Magennis] is bound to pay [to O'Neill] a hundred cows, each
one who is made lord, in addition to the intercession fee for the high
stewards.'[27] They were therefore in effect claimed by the O'Neills as *uirrí*.

When we encounter the Magennis lordship in the sixteenth century, it
had divided into two branches, the Magennises of Iveagh (the main branch
with the lord at Rathfriland) and the Magennises of Kilwarlin, with in
addition a sub-branch or more minor family, the Magennises of
Clanconnell (represented *c.* 1600 by Glasney McAghooly Magennis)
existing within the Iveagh territory. The division took place *c.* 1400, when
Cathbarr Magennis, third son of the Art na Madhmann Magennis, who
had died at Trim in 1383 as prisoner of Lord Thomas Mortimer, then
deputy to Roger Mortimer, Earl of March, chief governor of Ireland and
also Earl of Ulster, killed his elder brother Rory, leaving a second brother,
Hugh (d. 1424), to be ancestor of the Iveagh line, with him becoming the
founder of the Kilwarlin one. [28]

What follows now is a summary account (of necessity very short) by
way of background, which aims to set out the conflicting pressures which
came to bear on the Magennis lord in the later sixteenth century and up to
1602. It may be taken as a tentative exploration of the options and
responses of a lesser lord and more particularly an East Ulster one, during
that period. It focuses more on the main branch than the smaller ones –
though the latter are mentioned – and centres mainly on two of their
leaders, Sir Hugh and Sir Arthur. Against this background it will be possible
to examine the new arrangements brought into being from *c.* 1608.

Before proceeding to ascribe the composition that was now carried out,
some background account of the relations between the Crown and the
Magennises is required. In the early 1540s there was some negotiation with
the Magennises, but no full surrender and regrant was worked out then.
The Magennises appear to have been affected – seemingly drawn into a
kind of dependence by the Bagnals being established at Newry. It also
appears to be clear that Shane O'Neill was able to assert the O'Neill claim
of overlordship over them. In the act of attainder of Shane O'Neill in 1569
the Magennis 'country' of Iveagh was amongst those thereby declared forfeit
to the Crown.[29] It was not, however, to be granted out to any planter in the
subsequent plantation in East Ulster of the early 1570s. Also from the mid

1570s Sir Hugh Magennis – he had been knighted – was showing a willingness to sue out a patent under the Crown. Thus we find him in October 1575 writing to Lord Deputy Sidney from Carrickfergus asserting that 'ever since his revolt from Shane O'Neill, he had showed assured testimony of his fidelity' to the queen. He offered a yearly rent of 100 marks and a rising out for Iveagh[30]. There were plans to make a grant to him at this time.[31]

This was all at the beginning of Sir Henry Sidney's final spell in office as lord deputy[32] (1575–78) when surrender and regrant with composition and freeholders became what gave coherence to his policy for the outlying areas.[33] He was clearly showing a willingness to conform and place himself within the protection of the 'state' in what appeared to be a new direction in policy after a few recent years when the plantation policy in East Ulster – now itself coming to be a failure – must have caused him considerable anxiety. In fact Essex had drawn Magennis into an intermediate relationship with Crown government. In March 1575, Magennis as 'chief of his nation' was granted (in effect recognised as) the office of 'captain of the whole country of Eveaghe' at the nomination of Essex, to hold for life with all rightful benefits.[34]

This new application for title under the Crown on Sir Hugh Magennis's part in October also took place, of course, in the context of an agreement Essex had negotiated some months earlier (at the end of June) with Turlough Luineach O'Neill whereby the latter, amongst other things, had undertaken to claim no authority east of the Bann. The initial response of the privy council in London to what was now becoming a phase, or initiative, in native reconstruction (rather than plantation) came on 23 January 1576 in a letter from it to the lord deputy. He was thanked for his energetic behaviour generally – 'for his travail in establishing the North and South and West of Ireland'. But they confessed that 'weighty affairs prevent[ed] their spending much time about Ireland'. However, they confirmed the general drift of Ulster policy: Chatterton and Malby to be 'treated with', i.e. allowed to opt out of their failing plantation obligation; Magennis to be made a baron and (amongst other things) they noted Turlough Luineach's request to be made an earl for life.[35] A month later Sidney was promising 'to bring Ireland in three years to that state that it shall cost nothing to England'.[36] For whatever reason – perhaps because Sidney now wanted to work out an arrangement whereby freeholders would be created – the formal process of making the regrant to Magennis now faltered.[37] It awaited completion to the period between October 1583 when Sir Hugh surrendered his 'country'[38] and March 1584 when the grant was proceeded with.[39] The primary cause of the delay was no doubt that the energies of the Dublin government had been diverted to dealing with the Desmond rebellion in Munster (which had had its reverberations in Ulster) between 1579 and 1583.

The grant to Magennis, initiated and perfected just before Perrott took up office can be seen as an early instance of confirming the loyalty of a lord who was in effect an *uirrí*. On the other hand it procured revenue for the Crown from Iveagh. The conditions built into Sir Hugh Magennis's grant were as follows. He was to hold with remainders to Arthur, Phelim and Hugh, his sons. He was to hold *in capite* by the service of one knight's fee. His rent was to be 120 fat cows of three years old, payable at Newry and for every 'town' beyond 80 'which he shall inhabit' one fat cow or 13s. 4d. sterling. He should attend, when required, all hosting in the province with 12 horsemen and 24 footmen; should supply one labourer one day in each year; should supply as many beeves as might be required for the queen's army when within the country, receiving 12 shillings Irish for each; and he should aid the sheriff (i.e. the principal county government officer) in the execution of processes it required. Should he 'combine with traitors or rebels' the grant should be forfeited. Whether these rent cows were paid regularly or not, the records will not allow us to say. It has to be added that as part of Perrott's composition scheme Hugh Magennis was also to be required to maintain 40 foot.[40] His involvement within 'the system' was to be such that he was one of the Irish who attended Perrott's parliament in Dublin in 1585.[41]

That he should not 'combine with traitors or rebels' raises the crucial question of Magennis's relations with the other Irish lords. The crucial point here is the relations between the Magennises and the O'Neills and also Magennis's position in relation to Bagnal's desire to be a great power in Ulster. Space here will only allow a few brief suggestions. Clearly Magennis was resentful of Turlough Luineach O'Neill's attempt to impose his authority on him because we have a letter of complaint from Magennis, dated 29 August 1580, to Lord Deputy Grey. Turlough Luineach had 'prised him of 400 kine, 60 mares, 200 swine, 300 sheep and killed 16 of his followers'.[42] There were also 'contentions' between the baron of Dungannon (i.e. Hugh O'Neill) and Magennis in 1583.[43] Indeed that Magennis was generally reformed emerges from the account of Ulster drawn up in 1586:

> Evaghe, otherwise called McGynis country is governed by Sir Hugh McEnys, the civilest of the Irishry in those parts. He was brought by Sir N.B. from the *bonaght* of the Onels to contribute to the Q. to whom he payeth as annual rent for his lands, which he hath taken by letters patent, to hold after the English manner for him and his heirs males, so in this place only of Ulster is the rude custom of Tanestship

> put away. Magennis is able to make custom of Tanestship put away.
> Maginis is able to make above 60 horsemen and near 80 footmen;
> he liveth very civilly and English-like in his house and every festival
> day weareth English garments amongst his own followers.[44]

The question of combining with 'traitors or rebels' only became a real issue
after the other lords had in fact gone into rebellion. Thus while obviously
subject to conflicting pressures, this issue arose not so much for Sir Hugh,
who died in the mid-1590s, but for his son Arthur.[45] Arthur, whose wife
was Sara O'Neill, daughter of Hugh O'Neill, became a formal adherent of
O'Neill's in the Nine Years' War. It is not important for our present
purposes to explore his part in it, nor do the circumstances of his eventual
submission need to be gone into. It is also worth pointing out that it is
likely that tensions in Iveagh between himself and other leading Magennis
landholders came to the surface in those years.

The turning point for Magennis as a member of the confederation came
more generally with the expansion of the forces on the Crown's side under
Sir Arthur Chichester at Carrickfergus in 1601 and in particular with a
campaign by Mountjoy in June of that year. Their effectiveness in East
Ulster was such that Mountjoy and members of the privy council could
report at the end of June that 'Magennis, for all his nearness to Tyrone hath
made very great means ... to be accepted to mercy ...'[46] By August a
relative, Glasney Magennis, the head of the sub-branch of the Magennises
(the Magennises of Clanconnell), had become one of the group of Ulster
Irish who had been taken into Crown pay as captains of horse and foot.[47]
By this time too, many of the local castles had been occupied – 'taken in' –
certainly those in Lecale.[48]

What precisely had brought Magennis to submit was a decision in May[49]
by the lord deputy to go to Dundalk for a campaign in south-east Ulster.
The highlights of this June-onwards campaign included the building of the
Moyry fort – the Dutch engineer Levan de Rose was involved in designing
it[50] – and the placing of a garrison in Lecale. In addition Mountjoy
proceeded upwards and inwards to make a brief assault on O'Neill which
the Gaelic annalists were to describe as significant:

> It was an exaltation of the name and renown of the Lord Justice to
> have gone that length and distance with Tyrone on this occasion
> such as his predecessors had not been able to do so for the three or
> four years before.[51]

Mountjoy's actions in Lecale and Iveagh brought pressure on Magennis and
resulted in the surrender of a number of castles, e.g. at Dundrum (held by

Phelim McEver [Magennis]) and at Ardglass. The holder of another castle, at Ardglass, one 'Jordane' – clearly an examplar of the English loyalist attitude and obviously a man of the old medieval colony of Down – who had held it 'for the Queen all the time of the rebellion … never coming out of the same for three years past' – was relieved.[52] As a result Arthur Magennis, 'chief of his name', and Edmund Boy Magennis his uncle made overture to surrender and for pardon. He and others were given 'protection' for nine days on 3 June and on 3 July Sir Francis Stafford, governor of Newry, brought him to Dundalk where he 'made his submission to her Majesty, kneeling before the lord deputy [who had returned there the previous day] and Council'. He was granted his pardon and a promise of the land granted to his father by letters patent with the exception of the lands of Glasney Magennis.[53] On 8 August Mountjoy, as Moryson describes, it 'gave warrant for the passing of her Majesty's pardon for land, life and goods to Arthur Magennis, chief of his sept, with some 170 followers'.[54] He received his formal pardon the following year on 3 May 1602.[55] This examination of the means whereby Magennis was brought to submit can be taken as an example of the process whereby the Crown secured the submissions of the local lords and so fragmented the confederation.

With the surrender of Magennis, real authority and power in the area lay, effectively, with the commanders of the military garrison there. One of them in a famous account of their doings in Lecale after Christmas 1602 talks of a visit to Magennis's house – 'the island of Magennis' – where they 'drank ale and usquebaugh with the Lady Sara … a truly beautiful woman …', whom they kissed at their departure.[56] The presence of the garrison in Ulster was also to bring into play another pressure – the ambition of some of its officers to acquire land.

Thus we find in May 1601 an initiative by Sir Geoffrey Fenton in Dublin to London on behalf of Captain Edward Fisher, supported by Stafford requesting that Fisher be given a grant of Narrow Water Castle and associated land, 'fallen to her majesty by the treason of Magennis' and which Stafford claimed he had been the first to 'take … in, on the death of old Magennis'.[57] In fact Fisher's suit was not acted upon – as we saw Magennis was to be brought within a matter of weeks to surrender, on promise of pardon for life and land, thereby serving the broader war aim of weakening the confederation.

It was to take some time, however, before Magennis was formally restored and when this did happen, an elaborate arrangement for land tenure in the whole area was devised, embracing not only Iveagh, but Kilwarlin also, and dealing with church land as well. It was indeed to be one which essentially restored the Irish, but in a carefully restructured way. It was clearly, in fact, a variant on the settlement of Monaghan in 1591 and it was to be one within which one of the local military men was to benefit as well. The working out of the new arrangements for the whole area must now be turned to.

The Magennis territory of Iveagh, which must have accounted for almost one third of County Down, did not receive close attention in the lord deputy's northern journey of 1605. However, shortly thereafter, and in a process which took a number of years to finalise, a freeholder settlement was brought into existence there. Its origins go back to about February 1607,[58] but the main work of bringing the practical arrangements of it into effect was given over by the lord deputy and council to Sir Robert Jacob who went on the assizes into Ulster at the end of February 1609 and sat first at Newry.[59] Jacob was suspicious of the people there – they were 'false in their hearts, though they make a fair outward show of obedience.' But Sir Arthur Magennis 'was very busy ... about the dividing of his country and seeking to get more land to himself – as if he meant nothing but peace and to set up his rest upon that portion which was left to him ...'. Such a freeholder settlement had clear merits in Jacob's eyes:

> ... the dividing of so large a territory into several men's lands where he himself had been heretofore the sole proprietor will so weaken him and raise up so many opponents against him, that he will never be able to make any strong party if the freeholders' patents shall once be made and the country continue quiet but two or three years.[60]

Sir Arthur Magennis had been regarded with great suspicion at the time of O'Doherty's rising in 1608. One correspondent of Salisbury's, Sir Henry Dillon, at that time said that there had not been hitherto 'sufficient caution taken of the great men of the north' and expressed his concern about Sir Arthur, amongst others: he was, he pointed out, married to Sara, daughter of Hugh O'Neill, and was 'a malicious man in his heart to the English ... This man is not unlike to deal with the Newry as the Grecians did with Troy.' Dillon recommended that the state should 'countenance' Glasney McAghooly Magennis who was against Sir Arthur 'in faction' – if the state should 'grace' him, 'he will surely keep Sir Arthur Magennis in order'.[61] O'Doherty's rising, then, seems to have been the precipitant for introducing the freeholder settlement. Dillon in fact offered advice on a number of the Ulster lords and urged that for the 'full settling' of the province, the king should establish a president and council there: 'for now there are so many petty governors and some of them so desirous to enrich themselves they oppress the country much and withdraw the hearts of the people from the love of civility.'[62]

In fact the Iveagh settlement proceeded rather slowly, becoming just one of the government's Ulster concerns of which the big new one was implementing the decision to carry out the plantation in the escheated counties. Early in June 1610 Chichester wrote to London asking for confirmation of the settlement, however, which 'he had long laboured in and first effected'. It would keep 'Sir Arthur and his dependents within the rule of justice and obedience hereafter' and increase Crown revenue to boot.[63]

The final arrangements for the Magennis land were authorised by a king's letter from London to Antrim of 26 June 1610. This provided for a comprehensive settlement by way of surrender and regrant involving Sir Arthur Magennis of Iveagh 'or Magennis's country' and Brian Oge Magennis of Kilwarlin and it provided for a grant of title of the bishop's lands in the area as well.[64] Thus authorised from London, an elaborate settlement was now brought about. A full accord of these new ownership arrangements appears in an order of the lord deputy and council dated 20 January 1608[65] and it was essentially the arrangements provided for in that document which were now implemented. Basically what it embodied was a variant on the settlement of Monaghan of 1591 – it continued a freeholder element – and it is obvious that the thinking behind it followed the principles for the remodelling of a Gaelic lordship which that had embraced. It was now to be embodied – indeed enforced – in a series of patents taken out, mainly early in 1611. Like that settlement of Monaghan, it was basically a reconstruction rather than a confiscation, but like that settlement also it contained an element of endowment of new owners. The reconstruction process, therefore, involved an element of loss for the old occupiers.

The arrangement for Kilwarlin can be dismissed quickly. It was also the first to be completed. The 'entire' area was regranted to Brian oge McRory Magennis 'esquire' on 10 December 1610 following on a surrender of 20 November under a quit rent of Ir£20.[66] In Kilwarlin, then, no structure of freeholder was created. It was to be in Iveagh that the most drastic change was brought about. Here the lordship was in reality split up. This was in marked contrast to the situation which had prevailed after March 1584 when the entire country of Iveagh had been regranted to Sir Hugh Magennis. Hence, while his son Sir Arthur was indeed restored to a very substantial estate and so became a very large landowner,[67] quite a number of others received estates as well, to hold directly under the Crown. Some twelve other Irish in fact received individual grants.[68] Two other grantees of the estate were new English: Edward Trevor (of Narrow Water), a military captain who appears as assignee to an Irishman,[69] and Arthur Bagnal of Newry.[70] The twelve included some other prominent Magennises – Glasney

McAghooly Magennis of Clanconnell (already mentioned) and Ever McPhelimy Magennis of Castlewellan amongst them. Then there was the freeholder element. To compensate him for the loss of his rights of lordship, Gaelic-style, over Iveagh, eleven men – one of them new English, William Worseley of Hallam in Nottinghamshire[71] – were constituted freeholders (each of quite big areas) under Sir Arthur Magennis, each to pay him fixed annual money rents. They also received patents defining their obligations[72] The total annual income accruing to Sir Arthur Magennis from the freeholders was £139.6.8.[73] The rent the Crown received from those who held by patent under it was in the same order. In making the grants, the Crown also provided itself with the rights accruing from tenure.

All the grants under the Crown – with the exception of Brian oge McRory – held their land by knight's service *in capite* and were thus open to the Crown's fiscal feudal taxation demands of livery, wardship, etc.[74] These demands, when they arose could be quite arduous. On the other hand they were not tied to other obligations – no castle-building requirement was built into the Magennis patents and of course, there was no colonising obligation. Tenure under the Crown meant also that they could not be subordinate to any other Irish lord, i.e. Magennis could not be claimed as an *uirrí* by an O'Neill. A few of the grantees also had local powers conferred on them in their patents. Thus Glasney McAghooly received power to hold a court baron on Mondays every three weeks,[75] while Sir Arthur Magennis received wider powers: a court leet and view of frankpledge and a court baron at Rathfriland and at Narrow Water to Omeath; fairs and markets at Rathfriland; half of all waifs and strays; a ferry over the river at Narrow Water to be rent free; and the advowsons of one rectory and three vicarages.[76] These were all standard local powers that a large landowner under the Crown could enjoy.

Nor was the reconstruction of this whole area confined to the lay landowners: church land also came within its scope. Hence the bishop of Down, Connor and Dromore received a grant of the episcopal land of the see of Dromore, and other rights, at this time also, in February 1611.[77] This grant followed the order of the lord deputy and council of January 1608 which also recorded a small area of land in the area as the property of the archbishopric of Armagh. The bishop's patent recorded the episcopal land of the diocese of Dromore and also its tenants' names and what should be their conditions. Twenty people, all Gaelic Irish with one exception – Jasper Keyres[78] – became freeholders to the bishopric of areas of one townland and above to pay rents of Ir£2 per townland. These include such local names as O'Sheale, O'Rownie and Magin. Two larger blocs – one much bigger than the other – went to newcomers. The tenant of the larger of these, William Worseley, with a rent to the bishop defined at Ir£40, was tied to important obligations. He must build for the bishop of Dromore a mansion-house at or near Dromore and also a castle within five years and he must also allocate to the incumbents of three parishes 60 acres each adjoining the churches, to be their glebe land. In return he received a freehold of the land. The tenant of the smaller area was once again Edward Trevor. Glebe land was also provided for in the patent for six other parishes.[79] When it is noted that one of the grantees of 20 February 1611, Art oge McBrian oge McBrian McEdmond Boy Magennis of Loughbrickland, half a townland adjoining the church of Aghaderg to its rector for glebe,[80] then it seems likely that this concern to endow the parishes with glebe land as part of the general reorganisation of the territory was taken over from the escheated counties plan. In his patent also, the bishop received the advowsons of a large number of benefices within the diocese.[81] The episcopal land was itself constituted a manor – the manor of Dromore – and the bishop, who now held it from the Crown 'in pure and perpetual alms' was granted the usual powers of courts and fairs and markets. Built into his patent was a provision – which also embodied a restriction empowering him to make leases to English, Welsh or Scots for 60 years at not less than £8 a year per townland.[82]

McCartan's Country

Another partition of a small Gaelic lordship in Down through the process of sale was that of McCartan's country in the Ballynahinch area and east of Iveagh. Here the beneficiary was the English military man (servitor) Sir Edward Cromwell. Cromwell had been stationed at Dundalk in 1599.[83] After the war, in September 1605, he received a grant of the office of governor of Lecale, McCartan's country, Dundrum and of the 'borders and limits thereof'.[84] This was part of that framework of seneschals, governors, etc. for outlying areas – quasi-military local government – which was being brought into existence in the second half of the sixteenth century. The sale negotiations were taking place at this time. They took place in two stages. Initially, by deed of 12 September (it survives because it is enrolled in the patent rolls) Phelomy McCartan and Donell oge McCartan (the latter perhaps associated as the tanist) are recorded as conveying 'the third part of all his country' to Cromwell to be 'allotted in each part as Lord Crumwell shall deem most convenient, the chief seat or house of McCartan and the demesnes thereto adjoining only excepted'. Cromwell was to hold it for ever, i.e. it was a sale not a lease, in 'consideration of a certain sum of money' (the purchase sum is not specified). There was also the further consideration: 'that lord Crumwell had taken into his keeping and bringing

Patrick McCartan, the eldest son of the said Phelomy and hath undertaken to educate, instruct, apparel and provide all other necessities for his education in gentlemanlike manner'.[85] The definitive arrangement took place a few weeks later. Thus we have on 28 September 1605 a formal surrender by Edward Cromwell and Phelim McCartan 'chief of his name, in Down county, esq.' being made 'of the territory and or Lordship of Killenarten, commonly called McCartan's country ... on condition of a regrant thereof being made to them, half to each.'[86] The regrants to both were recorded in formal patents issued a few days later, on 4 October. Each got a patent of the moiety (i.e. half) of the territory: to hold, for ever, in fee farm, by the service of a knight's fee; each was to pay to the Crown a quit-rent of £2 stg per annum; all monastic land, church land, appropriate rectories and advowsons were secured to the Crown.[87] Thus not only had the division of the land taken place, bringing in the new owner, but it had all been regulated by the process of regrant. Both seller and purchaser now held their parts securely under the Crown and the Crown gained in turn the quit-rent (and other incidents) from both.[88]

This was not the only sale of land to be recorded by either McCartan or others in south Down. In July 1617 we have a deed whereby Phelim McCartan of Ballynahinch sold some six townlands or some 500 acres to Sir Francis Annesley of Dublin.[89] Nor is it only old Irish that we find selling land in south Down to new English. A further example may be given. Thus in 13 James I (1615–16: we do not have the exact date) Roger Chamberlain of Nizelrath, County Louth – an old Englishman of the Pale – can be found selling land he owned in County Down also to Sir Francis Annesley.[90] Mainly in this way, it would seem, by commercial transaction, a small, but not inconsiderable, penetration of new English owners (Trevor of Rostrevor may be noted) into south Down had taken place by 1641.

So there were a number of processes which affected the landownership of Antrim and Down in the early seventeenth century – the confirmation of the MacDonnells in Antrim; the reconstruction, with freeholders, of the large Magennis territory of Iveagh; private sales such as that by McCartan in Down and the arrangements in both North and South Clandeboy which brought in major new owners into significant parts of these two O'Neill territories. Some of the processes facilitated colonisation, some not. Generally speaking it was only where ownership change had taken place, that substantial colonisation followed. Hence because Antrim and Down were not formally confiscated, they were not systematically planted. Rather they came to be unevenly planted. However, because they were close to Scotland, the planting, where it took place, was very dense. Equally many of the old owners went on without being interfered with, for example, much of the old Anglo-Norman remnant in Lecale, County Down, while Bagnal's new mid-sixteenth-century colony at Newry grew and remained important. The application of one single policy, however – to resume it all on the basis of the resurrection of ancient title, the old Norman earldom of Ulster with which it overlapped having reverted to the Crown in 1333 – and then to start from scratch with a systematic plantation, was an option which was not pursued: it was not apparently even considered.

The evidence of the 1630 muster roll

As previously noted, where ownership changes took place the most heavy colonisation followed. To chart the detail and chronology of both building operations and colonisation in Antrim and Down is more difficult than for formal plantation counties because we do not have for Antrim and Down the regular series of government-commissioned surveys or reports (1611–22) conducted in those counties to assess the progress of grantees bound by formal obligation to the Crown. However, we do have two reasonably systematic guides which are useful, one towards the beginning of the period and one towards the end. Lord Carew, who carried out the first of the surveys in the escheated counties in 1611, travelled through all the Ulster counties and leaves us a report on the 'voluntary works',[91] carried out beyond the area of the formal plantation. Then in *c.* 1630 we have the Ulster muster roll which is the fullest listing of the tenant settler population.[92] This is not entirely complete – some estates are missing, for example, the Chichester estate in Antrim. There is also no return for the Bagnal estate at Newry. And there is no return for the town of Carrickfergus. Its totals must therefore be treated as minimums. On the other hand not all the people on it for all estates may have been new arrivals, or their sons, in the period since 1603. This seems certainly to apply to the estate of the earl of Antrim. Nevertheless it is an extremely useful guide indicating the adult male population of arms-bearing age. The grand total for Antrim is 1,618 men and for Down 4,045. The total for all nine Ulster counties (because Monaghan was included in it with 93 men of whom many were of Irish 'rising-out' of the large McMahon estate, was 13,092. So Antrim and Down taken together were more densely settled than on average the six escheated counties were.

The book[93] throws convenient light on the colonisation as the structure of ownership in the counties. In County Antrim, the dominating figure is the earl of Antrim mustering 947 men for his lands, 'being half that county'. Of a group of English owners in North Clandeboy, Sir John Clotworthy mustered 229. Four others there had smaller numbers to show – Dalway 38, Upton 92. The two Scots who had acquired land in the area – Adair and

Edmonston – mustered 135 and 151. Here were for the most part a small number of large estates controlled by a small number of landowners.

The return for County Down demonstrates again the predominance of a small number of new owners and the their effectiveness as colonisers. Thus: Lord Cromwell 480 men; the Lord Viscount Ards (i.e. Montgomery) 1,317 men; the Lord Viscount Clandeboy (i.e. Hamilton) 1,778 men. These were the dominating figures. Also in Down, the Earl of Kildare had survived as an owner of land going back to the early sixteenth century and mustered 125 men most of whom may well have been old English. It is clear that the structure of estates in Antrim and Down with great local power in a limited number of landowners' hands was very different from what had been brought into being in the escheated counties. Only rarely on the smaller estates in the escheated counties did a man muster over 150; only a few mustered *c.* 100 and the figure was generally under 50.

Conclusion

Antrim and Down ended up as curious mélange, very different from the six escheated counties, where a plantation had been imposed and different also from Monaghan where the freeholder settlement had survived. The dominating figure in the landownership of County Antrim, was the earl of Antrim, the legitimated descendant of the Hiberno-Scots of the sixteenth century and earlier, an aristocrat partially transformed – since they had abandoned the O'Neill confederation, except, crucially, in religion, who got on better at court than he did with the lord deputy. The dominating newcomers in south Antrim and north Down (Clandeboy) were a small group of owners, some English and some Lowland Scots, each with an estate of very substantial size. Principal of these, in North Clandeboy, were Chichester and Clotworthy and in South Clandeboy Hamilton (now Lord Viscount Clandeboy) and Montgomery (now Lord Viscount Ards). But in both Clandeboys some Irish owners had retained land as well. Further south we have, through a sale of land, the emergence of Cromwell, also to become a viscount. However, ownership change was less pronounced in south Down. What we have there, especially with the Magennis freeholder settlement, is a change in the conditions of ownership – from Gaelic lordship to tenure under the Crown. In south Down also the old English in Lecale (the remnant of the medieval colony) appear to have been little affected by the early seventeenth-century change. Finally, the Bagnal lands at Newry and nearby continued in Bagnal ownership.

The arrangements about ownership that emerged in the two counties in the early seventeenth century were to be definitive and to survive reasonably intact up to 1641, leaving Antrim and Down an amalgam of zones of differing character. Nonetheless another trend can be detected in between: some penetration of new English by private process or commercial transaction into the Gaelic areas. Although the most striking impact was made by the new owners there were subtle changes affecting the surviving elements of the old. As they came to hold by patent under the Crown, they, along with the newcomers came to be subject to its regulation – they must pay its quit–rents and be subject to the court of wards. The impact of government on them needs further study, subject to the very limited surviving sources.

[1] This essay was left in manuscript amongst Bob Hunter's papers. It is much more complete than other draft essays, but it was not finished. The manuscript had been fair-copied from earlier drafts and then significant changes indicated. On one occasion about 200 words were crossed out, on several occasions new sentences added in the margins. At two points Bob had indicated an intention to add more (by a note to himself and blank pieces of paper added). Although most of the citations are complete, many were in short form and many lacked precise page numbers. I have tried to bring those footnotes up to full professional standard but have occasionally been defeated. The destination of this paper is not clear – at 9,645 words of text (plus 2,000 in footnotes) it was clearly not a lecture.

[2] The Whites of the Dufferin (from whom came the famous Rowland White in the sixteenth century with his tracts on reform) had bits of land just outside Dublin, at Kilmainham and Chapelizod (*Cal. Pat. Rolls Ire., Jas I*, p. 75).

[3] This shows that Turlough Luineach could still be influential east of the Bann; his power must otherwise have declined there since the early 1570s.

[4] This treatment is partly based on H.F. Hore (ed.), 'Marshal Bagnal's description of Ulster, *anno* 1586', *Ulster Journal of Archaeology*, 1st series 2 (1854).

[5] Seneschals, some surrender and regrant agreements, etc.

[6] The summary phrase derives from Hunter and Gillespie, above ch. 1, pp 4–6.

[7] M. Perceval-Maxwell, *Scottish Migration to Ulster in the reign of James I* (Belfast, 1973), pp 47–9.

[8] Ibid., pp 48–9.

[9] R. Gillespie, *Colonial Ulster: the settlement of East Ulster 1600–1641* (Cork, 1985), pp 130–31.

[10] Chester City Record Office, [Mayors' Letterbooks] M/L/2/218.

[11] BL, Add. MS 36,775.

[12] Killultagh was sometimes considered not to be part of North Clandeboy, but to be a separate lordship. Hill defined it in relation to the modern baronies (George Hill, *An historical account of the MacDonnells of Antrim: including notices of some other septs, Irish and Scottish* (Belfast, 1873), p. 133) and so it is possible to calculate its modern acreage, using the *Townland Index*, as some 375,000 acres. This excludes what may have been Killultagh (some 70,000 acres). By Hill's definition (which equated to the baronies of Castlereagh Lower and Upper), South Clandeboy was about 107,000 statute acres.

[13] For a good short discussion, see Perceval-Maxwell, *Scottish Migration to Ulster*, pp 49–60.

[14] *Cal. Pat. Rolls Ire., Jas I*, p. 5.

[15] Ibid., p. 7.

[16] J. O'Laverty, *An historical account of the Diocese of Down and Connor, ancient and modern* (Dublin, 1878–84), iii, pp 88–9.

[17] Belfast Castle was reputedly where the Anderson and McAuley building now stands. [It was at the corner of Donegall Place and Castle Street and closed in 1994 – added by ed.]

[18] Dalway's quit rent in his patent was IR£4 or £3 stg per annum.

[19] On all this, see T. Ranger, 'Richard Boyle and the making of an Irish fortune 1588–1614', *Irish Historical Studies*, x (1956–7), pp 257–97.

[20] TNA, SP63/217, fo. 116.

21 There is much discussion of all the latter grants and dealings in this area in this context of self-betterment in T.M. Healy, *Stolen Waters: a page in the conquest of Ulster* (London, 1913).

22 E.D. Atkinson, 'The Magennises of Clanconnell', *Ulster Journal of Archaeology*, 2nd series 1 (1894), pp 30–2.

23 A. Cosgrove (ed.), *A New History of Ireland*: 2 *Medieval Ireland 1169–1534* (Oxford, 1987), pp 17–18.

24 Ibid.

25 T.E. McNeill, *Anglo-Norman Ulster* (Edinburgh, 1980), pp 6–9.

26 D.B. Quinn, 'Anglo-Irish Ulster in the early sixteenth century', *Proceedings & Reports of the Belfast Natural History & Philosophical Society* (1935 for 1933–4), pp 56–78.

27 M. Dillon (ed.), 'Ceart Uí Néill', *Studia Celtica*, 1 (1966), pp 1–18.

28 Henry S. Guinness, 'Magennis of Iveagh', *Journal of the Royal Society of Antiquaries of Ireland*, 62 (1932), pp 91, 102. For fuller information on the Magennises at this period, see Cosgrove, *New History of Ireland*, pp 343, 559, 574.

29 *The Statutes at Large passed in the Parliament of Ireland ... 1310–1761*, I, pp 335–6.

30 *Cal. S.P. Ire., 1574–85*, p. 82 (no. 46).

31 'Articles to be inserted in the grant to be passed to Sir H. Magennis of the county of Evagh in Ulster' [heading only] (TNA, SP63/53, no. 47).

32 He was reappointed 5 August 1575 and sworn in on 18 September (T.W. Moody, F.X. Martin, F.J. Byrne (eds), *A New History of Ireland, IX: Maps, Genealogies, Lists* (Oxford, 1989), p. 487).

33 For one of Edmund Tremayne's letters on this policy of 23 January 1576 see *Cal. S.P. Ire., 1574–85*, p. 88.

34 *Cal. Fiants Ire., Eliz. I*, no. 2565.

35 *Cal. S.P. Ire., 1574–85*, p. 88 (TNA, SP63/55 no. 5). Earlier, in about December 1575, there was a 'note' from Sir Lucas Dillon, chief baron of the Exchequer 1570–93, to the effect that 'the warrant for taking surrenders and passing grants may extend to the lands in Ulster given to Her Majesty by parliament' (*Cal. S.P. Ire., 1574–85*, p. 86).

36 *Cal. S.P. Ire., 1574–85*, p. 90.

37 Recriminations over the delay surfaced between London and Dublin in July (ibid., p. 97). An example of the slowness of early modern governments?

38 *Cal. Fiants Ire, Eliz. I*, no. 4218 (surrender of Sir Hugh Magennis of County Down, 18 October 1583).

39 Ibid., no. 4327, 3 March 1584. This is a fiant for a patent which most likely was taken out. (It does not survive in the Patent Rolls, but then they do not survive very well).

40 TNA, SP63/112, no. 23. Kilwarlin, a separate lordship, was to maintain ten. These agreements were erected at Newry early in October 1584 (*Cal. S.P. Ire., 1574–85*, p. 534). In May 1585 a surrender and regrant was negotiated with Ewer McRorire of Kilwarlin (*Cal. Fiants Ire, Eliz. I*, nos 4649 and 4650).

41 *AFM* sub. 1585. For more on that, see *Cal. S.P. Ire., 1574–85*, p. 570.

42 *Cal. S.P. Ire., 1574–85* p. 246.

43 Ibid., pp 459, 468.

44 Hore, 'Marshal Bagnal's Description of Ulster, *anno* 1586', p. 152.

45 Sir Hugh is said to have died in 1596 by Henry S. Guinness in his article already cited. The annals record the death of 'Magennis' (i.e. implying that he was lord), Hugh, son of Hugh, son of Donnell Oge, in 1595. Their year may have run to March. He must be our 'Sir Hugh'. But if he was son of Hugh, son of Donnell Oge, then he was grandson rather than son of Donnell Oge who had met Henry VIII.

46 *Cal. Carew MSS, 1601–3*, p. 86. On O'Neill's attempts to confront those who submitted later that year see J.J. Silke, *Kinsale: the Spanish intervention in Ireland at the end of the Elizabethan wars* (Liverpool, 1970 (and Dublin 2000)), p. 120 and *Cal. S.P. Ire., 1601–3*, pp 116–18 where these vacillations are discussed. They had submitted and been pardoned. Sir Francis Stafford described them as 'people of Ireland, perfidious, ungrateful, and apt to wind with every innovation.' He had, however, some hope of O'Hanlon and Magennis (ibid., 117–18).

47 *Cal. S.P. Ire., 1601–3*, p. 19.

48 *Cal. Carew MSS 1601–3*, p. 86. Compare the campaigns of Dowcra of the surrenders and dates of them, in west Ulster.

[49] Fynes Morrison, *An itinerary, containing his ten yeeres travell through the twelve dominions of Germany, Bohmerland, weitzerland, Netherland, Denmarke, Poland, Italy, Turky, France, England, Scotland & Ireland* (4 vols, Glasgow, 1907), II, pp 234–5.

[50] G.A. Hayes-McCoy, *Ulster and other Irish Maps* c. *1600* (IMC, 1964), p. 2 and n. 15.

[51] *AFM*, VII, p. 2,259.

[52] For an account of the campaign, see Moryson, *An itinerary*, II, pp 234–96.

[53] Ibid., pp 258–9. This contains Magennis's requests at this time. One of his requests was that 'he might enjoy the corn he had sowed in Lecale, which being sowed on other men's lands could not be granted, only favourable respect to him was promised' (p. 259). This, taken with the relief of Jordan in his castle, throws a bit of light on the old English remnant in Lecale during the Nine Years' War, suggesting that these people had remained loyal to the Crown and he had had their lands occupied. Mountjoy's campaign in Ulster had ended by 29 August when he had returned as far as Trim, p. 296. Apart from securing Magennis's submission, its most spectacular achievement lay in going as far as Benburb and to the Blackwater. He returned, of course, to strong rumours that the Spaniards were on their way.

[54] Ibid., pp 273, 294.

[55] *Cal. Fiants Ire., Eliz.*, no. 6616. Brian Oge McRory Oge Magennis of Kilwarlin and a number of others, all of Kilwarlin, were pardoned in December 1603 (*Cal. Pat. Rolls Ire., Jas I.,* p. 31).

[56] C. Litton Falkiner, *Illustrations of Irish History and Topography* (London, 1904), pp 331–2. The Lady Sara, Magennis's wife, was Hugh O'Neill's daughter – something well-known to the author of this account. This hospitality episode throws light on the lifestyle of a Gaelic Lord.

[57] *Cal. S.P. Ire., 1600–1*, pp 314–15, 328. Stafford said that the castle had been given by Sir Henry Sidney to a gentleman of Offaly who had afterwards sold it to Magennis for £100 or thereabouts. For more detail on Captain (later Sir) Edward Fisher, see *Cal. S.P. Ire., 1601–3*, pp 26, 200, 350, 488, 525; *Cal. Carew MSS, 1601–3*, passim.

[58] *Cal. Pat. Rolls Ire., Jas I*, p. 195. This is a 'submission' by Sir Arthur Magennis to the order of the lord deputy and council for making freeholders in Iveagh, dated 4 February 1607.

[59] *Cal. S.P. Ire., 1606–8*, pp 193–4.

[60] Ibid.

[61] Ibid., pp 485–7, 25 April 1608.

[62] Ibid.

[63] Ibid., *1608–10*, p. 457.

[64] *Cal. Pat. Rolls Ire., Jas I*, p. 182.

[65] Ibid., pp 38–6.

[66] Ibid., p. 181.

[67] Ibid., pp 188–9, 395.

[68] Ibid., pp 190–93. These patents were taken out on 2 and 22 February 1611.

[69] Ibid., pp 190, 395.

[70] Ibid., p.190. The Magennises appear also to have lost Dundrum Castle.

[71] Worseley may have bought this land from a previous Irish occupier.

[72] *Cal. Pat. Rolls Ire., Jas I*, pp 190, 235, 395.

[73] This is calculated from the patents (ibid, pp 190, 235) and is in Irish currency.

[74] On what these were, see J. Hurstfield, *The Queen's Wards: wardship and marriage under Elizabeth I* (2nd ed., London, 1973) which deals with England. For the court of wards in Ireland, see V. Treadwell, 'The Irish Court of Wards under James I', *Irish Historical Studies*, xii (1960–1), pp 1–27 and H.F. Kearney, 'The Court of Wards and Liveries in Ireland, 1622–41', *Proceedings of the Royal Irish Academy*, section C, 57 (1955), pp 29–68.

[75] *Cal. Pat. Rolls Ire., Jas I*, p. 193.

[76] Ibid., pp 188–9, 235.

[77] Ibid., pp 190–1.

[78] Ibid., pp 394–6.

[79] Ibid., pp 180–91. Worseley was later to forfeit the land granted to him. For non-performance of conditions and they were thereupon granted to the bishop in October 1616 (ibid., p. 309).

[80] Ibid., p. 190. Half a townland was probably construed as 60 acres.

[81] The only layman, then, to receive a grant of advowsons appears to be Sir Arthur Magennis.

[82] Ibid., pp 180–81. [Editor: at this point the author left a blank page with a note to whoever was to type up his manuscript indicating that 'I intend to add something next year'].

83 *Cal. S.P. Ire., 1599–1600*, p. 32.
84 *Cal Pat. Rolls Ire., Jas I*, p. 72, 30 September 1605.
85 Ibid. It appears undeniably to have been a sale rather than a mortgage because no right of redemption is built in. Before the division of the land took place – on the feast of St John the Baptist – Cromwell might 'cut timber on any of the lands and make castles of the same.' There was no protection built in for any of the ancient followers (freeholders) of McCartan who might actually live on it.
86 *Cal. Pat. Rolls Ire., Jas I*, p. 74.
87 Ibid.
88 [Editor: at this point in the MS, the author left a gap and wrote in the margin: 'additional regrants to Cromwell'.]
89 *Inq. Cancell. Hib. Repert.*, II, Down (50) Chas I.
90 Ibid., (49) Chas I.
91 The section on Antrim and Down is printed in G. Benn, *History of Belfast* (London, 1877), pp 85–8, 674–78.
92 British Library, Add. MS 4770.
93 A summary of it appears in J.T. Gilbert, *A contemporary history of affairs in Ireland from 1641 to 1652* (Dublin, 1879), vol. 1, part i, pp 332–7.

12

County Armagh:
A map of plantation, c. 1610

The county

In July 1591 the bounds of the newly-created County Tyrone, defined by a body of commissioners, were ratified by Lord Deputy Sir William Fitzwilliam.[1] By implication, the defining of County Armagh, with the Blackwater between them, could follow suit. At first sight it might seem odd that this could contribute to the outbreak of warfare in Ulster. However counties were governmental units of a greater whole, and, in this second phase of county creation in Ireland, they were portals through which might enter the enlarging control of London's Dublin government as it sought, under Tudor direct rule, to expand beyond the untidy limits of the middle ages so as to rule all Ireland in a centralised manner. This process could not but threaten the power and rulership of the great lords of outreach Ireland, in this case that of the O Neills, previously effectively ungoverned in mid-Ulster, who had been fashioning their power as regional potentates since the mid-fourteenth century.

Designed, as it had to be, to bring down the 'greatness' of the lords in their localities, it had also had an underlying severity in its application, recently in Connacht and just now in Monaghan in Ulster. Essentially what was entailed was the redesigning of the relationship between lord and lesser landowner, the latter to be elevated to the status of a rent-paying freeholder and the former to be reduced merely to a landowner and landlord. Moreover, where embarked on thus systematically, some loss of land, and, importantly, of strategic castellation, was also involved: newcomers from England, or, sometimes Palesmen, gained a small share. A tier of management above them with military powers of enforcement – in Connacht the presidency and council, in Monaghan a seneschal – could now also be made effective. The circulation of judges in these counties, and indeed the nomination of justices of the peace, might also become normal, with significant implications for the authority of lords, while taxation to government in the varied forms of the period, could now also be expected to accrue. Religious change, to bring uniformity with England through the substitution of Protestantism for Catholicism in the practice of the laity, might also be advanced.

The creation of counties at this time in Ulster clearly, then presaged that a programme of very significant change was underway, and the rebellion or war which soon followed from its attempted implementation there did not remain, like rebellions in Tudor England, merely a local Ulster affair. Before long its confederate Ulster leaders, of whom Hugh O Neill, recently created earl of Tyrone, was the most important, sought, in turn, to expand their actions as widely as possible in Ireland, as a whole, arguing that they were fighting in defence of faith and fatherland, an important conjunction which must, in retrospect, have made the Nine Years' War the defining landmark in the identification of Irishness with Catholicism in opposition to the reformation. From it soon also sprang radical ideas for the future of Ireland as a whole. The militant Catholic theorist, Cornelius O'Mulrian, bishop of Killaloe (d. 1616), sought to petition the Pope requesting that he be the fount of authority to appoint the northern potentate as a new king over all Ireland (and to give his support in other ways including the excommunication of opponents); in practice the leadership of the revolt offered the kingship of Ireland to Spain, then both the great imperial power and the champion of Catholicism and at war with England, in return for the expectation of military intervention. Either outcome would threaten English rule – and also caused anxiety amongst the old English of Ireland, however uneasy they might have become through recent trends in government policy – while the latter would threaten England itself.[2] Later, in 1599, when Spanish intervention was uncertain and before it in fact took place, proposals for a comprehensive re-organisation of the government of Ireland, still (sharing a common crown) in connection with England but whereby its own nobility would gain power and with Catholicism only to be practised, were advanced to the government in London.[3] If Ireland was being fashioned – and severely – into a unity, now counter-proposals for the government of that unity had emerged. These, a form of aristocratic reaction, would not make O Neill king, but would guarantee him a prominent place in a conciliar government. A range of ideas, then, came out of the Nine Years' War.

When, however, in conditions of mutual exhaustion, the revolt had been largely suppressed and Spanish intervention defeated, the English government engaged in a pacification. For his part, rather than face eventually, the fate – execution – endured by the English nobleman the earl of Essex after his rebellion in London in 1601, Hugh O Neill was drawn to submit under the 'articles' (later to become known in Ireland as the treaty) of Mellifont, in County Louth, of 30 March 1603 on promise, though not unconditional, of restoration both as earl of Tyrone and to massive landownership in counties Armagh, Tyrone and what is now County Londonderry. One astute effect of this was that with O Neill disengaged, the government of James I could conclude a peace – however uneasy it remained for some years – with Spain in 1604, thereby defusing, it was hoped, an external threat to his security to rule all his three kingdoms, and allowing, shortly thereafter, English entrepreneurship to break in on the Spanish claim to imperial monopoly in America by establishing, as it proved, enduringly the Virginia colony. If, however, Hugh O Neill hoped, as a result for him, to recreate that complex of regional power and rulership, within the lordship over the different O Neill branches and others, and beyond it, over subordinate rulers (his *uirrí*) – an O'Neilldom once again or to be 'a prince' in Ulster – which he who was O Neill had sought and held (sometimes with instances of the brutality which characterised the age) in the past, he was to be disappointed.[4] In France the Protestant Huguenot nobility and urban elite had secured exemptions in 'clemency' from central rule – and religious freedom too – to end the wars of religion in 1598, but these were gradually reduced there before the centralising and uniformitising tendencies of the 'state'.[5] In the special circumstances of Ireland, as it may seem equally unjustly, O Neill was, decidedly, not to achieve territorial exemption from Dublin rule. What follows attempts, at the risk of briefest summary, to deal with the extension of the government system into the *county* of Armagh and also, more generally, with the question of O Neill's landownership, in the years after 1603. In these years a number of important changes were implemented, thereby reverting to the programme for extending rule over Ulster which had begun before the war, the detail of which for Armagh may be outlined here.

Firstly with regard to local government, the administrative structures of a county were now laid down. In an important expedition into Ulster in 1605, Sir Arthur Chichester, newly-appointed lord deputy, and his entourage divided the county into five baronies, or administrative sub-divisions, by order made on 3 August. Three coroners for the county were appointed, John Fleming, Daniel McCasy of Tynan and Patrick Oge Macgillran of the Fews. As constables for each barony substantial members of local families were chosen. Thus Rory O Hanlon was constable of Orior, Neill McCoddan for Armagh barony, Patrick McCuls Carrach McArdill for the Fews, Donell O Hugh for Tiranny and Neill O Quin for the barony of Oneilland. The amalgamation of the older Irish territories into baronies and the appointments of officers were 'published in open assizes'.[6] The names of the sheriffs of the county, mostly new English, can be recovered reasonably well from 1606.[7] As to the assizes, held thereafter with regularity, two judges from Dublin, Sir Edmond Pelham and John Elliot had been the initiators of these circuits in Ulster at large, when they held courts in a number of counties there: Cavan, Monaghan and Fermanagh and also Armagh along with Antrim and Down in the period between 23 July and 14 September 1603.[8] With this a uniform system of law and local government, administered from Dublin, was now being introduced to the exclusion of difference through Gaelic law and custom which had previously been maintained under O Neill rulership. To initiate ecclesiastical change and seek to advance the reformation, the lord deputy instructed Archbishop Henry Ussher in 1605 to install a minister forthwith at Armagh, where he had found clergy practicing under papal authority, and to reside and preach there himself every 'summer season'.[9] With these steps the foundations for the government of this area (directly under Dublin because no provincial presidency and council was established), aspired to only in the sixteenth century, and with their many implications including taxation, to follow, ideally, the 'one law, one church' principles of the age, had now at any rate been laid.

Some change in landownership was brought about too, most notably in regard to the estates of the monasteries, which could now be dissolved, In particular the extensive estate of the abbey of St Peter and St Paul in Armagh, which extended beyond the county, was granted on lease from the crown for twenty-one years to Sir Toby Caulfeild, commander at Charlemont, in June 1607.[10] In addition, the monastery of Kilsleve had been leased for the same period in July 1606 to Marmaduke Whitechurch who had been based at Carlingford and who held the office of sheriff of the county in this year.[11] Both were enabled later, in 1610 and 1612, to convert these leases into outright grants, though Caulfeild was to be obliged to surrender that part of it which lay within the territory granted to the city of London in County Londonderry.[12]

The provision of portions of land for the upkeep and supply of three army forts was also arranged. These had been just recently established during the Nine Years' War, with commanders holding military jurisdictions, though now, however, due to post-war financial retrenchment, only small numbers of troops were retained in them. An area of land, reserved out of the earl of Tyrone's patent for Charlemont fort (like a similar area for Mountjoy fort in County Tyrone), defined during the visit of the lord deputy and council in 1605, was eventually leased to Sir Toby Caulfeild in June 1607.[13] Also in 1605 land was allocated to Mountnorris fort with the concurrence of Patrick O Hanlon, who held land 'in tanistry' nearby, whose father had been killed on the Queen's side in the previous war, who

Plate 12.1 A map of the Plantation in County Armagh, *c.* 1622.
Original in NLI, Rich Papers, MSS 8013–4. This copy is reproduced
from a plate in *Ulster Journal of Archaeology* 3rd series, xxiii (1960)

held a pension from the crown and who had been the captain of a king's
ship probably previously engaged in coastal trade (which indicates that
people from this area, not far distant the sea, could have naval occupations),
and who in turn received a patent of his own lands (over 2,000 acres) in
1609.[14] Similarly, a Redmond O Hanlon was granted title to land (nearly
4,000 acres), 'in consideration of his faithful services', at the same time.[15]
In this context, then, two O Hanlons in Orior had received individual title
to land, prior to plantation. Mountnorris fort and lands were leased to the
resident commander, Captain Henry Atherton, who was 'now a good help
… for execution and administration of justice in those parts', for twenty-
one years in February 1606.[16] Similarly, Captain Anthony Smith received
the fort and lands of Moyry in June.[17] These leases were a form of money-
saving privatisation, because they contained covenants to keep the buildings
in repair. Atherton was appointed sheriff of the county in 1608, while
Smith held that office in the previous and succeeding years.[18]

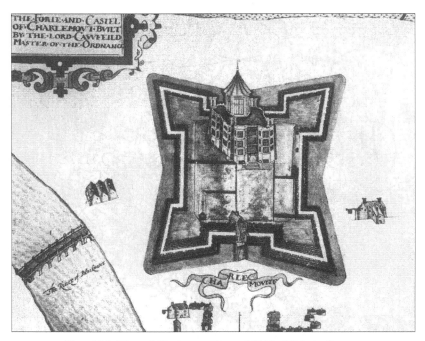

Plate 12.2 View of Charlemont Fort *c.* 1624 by Nicholas Pynnar.
Original in BL, Add. MS 24,2000. This copy has been prepared by Gillian Coward,
from a plate in *Ulster Journal of Archaeology* 3rd series, xxiii (1960)

The great issue of O Neill's, landownership in Ulster, and also the constraints placed on him in matters of wider affairs following his restoration in the post war settlement, must now be turned to. As well as the existence of the forts, he was obliged to accept that two lesser O Neills should have independent ownership of the areas they controlled because they had been promised that on their submission. Thus Turlough McHenry O Neill (knighted as Sir Turlough), who lived at Glasdrumman (plate 12.3) and who died in 1640 leaving as heir his elder son, Henry, received title by patent in September 1603 to lands in the Fews which amounted to over 33,000 acres.[19] Secondly, Sir Henry og O Neill, who had submitted in July 1602, took out a patent of his 'country or territory', partly in Armagh partly in Tyrone, in June 1605 which, on his being killed along with his son in repressing O Doherty's rising leaving his grandson Phelim O Neill a minor, was divided in 1613 amongst his descendants, seven of them in County Armagh.[20]

These independent titles were not unresented by O Neill himself. On the other hand, he had been granted ownership of all the secular land ruled by O Cahan, his principal *uirrí*, itself the core of modern County Londonderry, but otherwise could exercise no sway over formerly

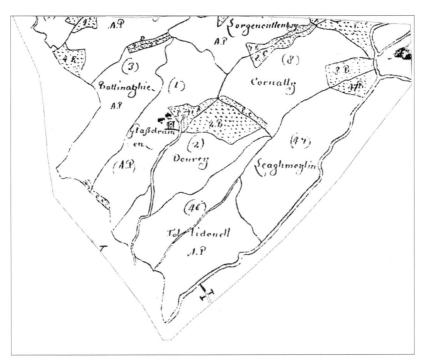

Plate 12.3 O'Neill's tower house at Glasdrumman and part of his estate from
the Down Survey map of Orior barony

dependent lordships elsewhere in Ulster. Again, his title to what he received,
itself also not recorded in detail because no survey of it by townland had yet
been made, was not unconditional: he must confer freehold status on
numerous landholders, great and smaller, within it, thereby bringing about
its manorialisation and the substantial restriction of his own power. O Neill
sought to evade this when attempts were made to secure its implementation
by Lord Deputy Sir Arthur Chichester. Another important restriction on
him concerned his relations with foreign powers. He, and O Donnell, must
sever their contact with Spain, and he must withdraw from there his son
Henry. This was not done. Rather his son came to have a military command
in the Spanish army in the Spanish Netherlands and Spain agreed to make
payments to both O Neill and O Donnell in November 1606, on grounds
both of sympathy for their decline, and because 'should war break out again
they could be of great use and so it is well to keep them well disposed'.[21]
Later, rumour arose of a plot, allegedly masterminded by Rory O Donnell,
to attempt a coup d'état by the seizure of Dublin Castle, the centre of
government, and of other forts, and, with some expectation of Spanish
backing, to thereupon demand of James I both a new political settlement

for Ireland, to embrace, most likely, a prominent governmental role for O Neill, and also an untrammelled, landownership and regional powers for the great northern lords in what, plausibly, would become a much less centralised Ireland with greater influence for its own nobility.

The crisis for O Neill came in the context of a suit against him in 1607, upon which members of the newly-established settlement at Derry (also a fort site since the Nine Years' War), alike precarious in their security and anxious to extend their sway, interacted, by Donnell O Cahan (now knighted as Sir Donnell), the last Gaelic lord of O Cahan's country. O Cahan sought independence from O Neill; O Neill asserted that there was no such thing as O Cahan's country. When it was decided that the case should be finally determined in London before the king, later in the year, attorney-general Sir John Davies visualised an outcome which would reduce the landownership of both. Relying on the act of attainder of Shane O Neill in 1569, he advised starkly that present titles could be questioned, so that ownership could be dispersed not only amongst lesser Irish figures, but also, crucially, amongst a body of new English proprietors as well. Were this opportunity not taken, and O Neill in particular not reduced to the 'moderate condition of other lords in Ireland and England at this day', then there would be 'no commonwealth in Ulster'.[22] Lord Deputy Chichester would have been of the same view. It cannot but be noted that there were now in Ireland, much more so than in the 1580s, a body of English army officers, many unemployed since their wartime victory, who were anxious to secure their rewards in grants of land. The most likely outcome, then, for O Neill, and his successors for the future, would be that a substantial curtailment in his landownership, not easily undone, would have been decreed, to retain perhaps some 20,000 acres or his own demesne lands. Had he gone to London, he might also have been detained, like his somewhat equivalent north of England counterpart Northumberland, even his execution might have been considered.

The plantation in County Armagh

All this provides the background against which the Flight of the Earls took place. Certainly they and their principal adviser, Fr Florence Conry, had expectation that they would be returned with the military and financial backing of both Spain and the Papacy for renewed warfare.[23] If in this they were to be disappointed, the overhanging threat of it accelerated the thinking of policymakers in both London and Dublin, and led quickly to the decision for plantation in Ulster. In that way 'two heads of that hydra of the north' would he cut off, while settlers on the ground would be a source of defence, taxation, and many other changes.[24] Even the reformation would be advanced. Somewhere in the mix of aims that underlay the formidable decision can be found the contemporary English ideal of 'improvement': land would be used better, society would be more ordered, domestic dwelling would be transformed. 'Civility' would ensue, renewed rebellion in Ulster would be entirely pre-empted and English culture extended into the formerly Gaelic north.

Planning the plantation, which came to take in the secular land in six counties – Armagh, with Cavan, Fermanagh, Donegal, Londonderry and Tyrone – and which was implemented in 1610, proceeded along many lines. Maps, made by barony in 1609, were an essential prerequisite, but they were not, given the time available, measured surveys; rather the townlands were given notional acreages of profitable land, with the effect that the estates, as granted out, were larger than intended. The suppression of O Doherty's rising in 1608 both delayed and gave impetus to the plantation. Begun as an attempt to expel the new and irksome settler community in pre-plantation Derry and to seize Culmore fort nearby, it may well have grown in the belief that it was laying the groundwork for further Spanish intervention in Ireland, since the expectation had been spread that O Neill would be returned that year.[25] In Armagh, it also had reverberations. Here, Oghy oge O Hanlon, who was married to O Doherty's sister, took part in it. When he finally submitted, late in 1609, he was dispatched, with a contingent of swordsmen, to the Swedish military service.[26] His father, moreover, the more pacific Sir Oghy, who could claim title to Orior – O Hanlon's – country separately from O Neill going back to 1587, was induced to surrender it in October 1608 in return for an annuity of £80 for life, with a promise to pay his debts to the extent of £300. In this Sir Arthur Chichester felt that he had made a good bargain for the king and a fair way for the plantation.[27] Orior became the barony allocated to servitors and Irish grantees generally under the plantation in this county, and twelve O Hanlons were finally to retain land as owners there, ten (or nine) under the plantation and two by prior grant.[28]

The plantation as finally planned was systematic. First, estates were to be of moderate size, to encourage effort and lest their new owners in turn should become overmighty: 1,000, 1,500 and 2,000 'acre', estates were to be granted, though a few might hold 3,000 acres. Second, there were to be three categories of grantee. Of these, the undertakers with the greatest obligations to fulfill, should be both English and Lowland Scottish, the latter to benefit because of the union of Scotland with England through the succession of James I. Servitors, that is to say military men with recent careers in Ireland, were to be another category, while those Irish who should be chosen for restoration to ownership were the third. The undertakers must carry out a building programme, both of defensible residences for themselves and of houses in villages for their tenantry, who should be exclusively, British – English or Lowland Scots – and whom they must plant at the rate of ten families, notionally twenty-four adult males, per 1,000 'acres'. The exclusion of the Irish from undertakers' estates was, it may be noted, not to be achieved, though clearly their circumstances there were very much diminished ones indeed, because planting of settler tenantry was not as dense as it might have been, especially given that the estates turned out to be so much larger than intended, though in County Armagh, despite variations from one estate to another, it came to be more intensive than in some other places. Partly due to pressure from undertaker applicants who knew each other and who wished to plan together for their greater security, it was decided that the grantees should be grouped by barony. Hence English undertakers were allotted specific baronies to plant in, Scots others, while the servitors, who need not have settler tenantry but must build, and the Irish grantees, were to be placed together in yet other baronies. This gave the plantation in Ulster its regional character. In addition, a programme of urbanisation was envisaged, with the foundations to be laid for the development of a number of new towns in each county by the allocation of areas of land to support them. The plantation also had a cultural and educational dimension: land was set apart to endow the new university, Trinity College, in Dublin, and to support a grammar school to be established in each planted county. This all concerned the forfeited secular land. Church land, itself now, since the monasteries had already been dissolved, mainly episcopal, which had either been owned by the bishops of the past or was land over which they could claim some rights, was conferred on the bishops, some just recently appointed, and their successors, to be their source of income to sustain the new Protestant religious dispensation. Also, though this was taken out of the secular land, glebe was made available to provide income for the Protestant parish clergy in succession, similarly now newly being appointed in Ulster. Revenue, in the form of an ownership tax, or quit rent, was payable to the government in Dublin by the new lay landowners: £5.6.8 per thousand 'acres' by the undertakers, £8 by the servitors (reduced if they planted), and £10.13.4 by the Irish. Other forms of tax would also arise.

Although the arrangements for the plantation in all of the six escheated counties followed a common framework, each had its own variations and distinctiveness, of which the agreement with the city of London for the Londonderry plantation was the most distinct.[29] In County Armagh the acquisitions of the English undertakers, placed in Oneilland barony in the north of the county, were much greater than those of the Scottish undertakers, placed in the Fews barony, part of which had been granted to Sir Turlough McHenry O Neill prior to the plantation and who was not curtailed: some 21 per cent as opposed to 5 per cent of the county's total acreage. The share granted to servitors (which here includes the land previously designated for the upkeep of the forts) reached just on 9 per cent though since some were the beneficiaries of pre-plantation grants of the former estates of the dissolved monasteries, also about 9 per cent of the acreage of the county, their acquisitions, combining secular land with ex-monastic, amounted to some 18 per cent.[30] One fact which made the grants in the county distinctive was that part of the estate allocated to endow university education in Ireland was here: along with other land in Fermanagh and Donegal, Trinity College, Dublin received some 7 per cent of the land of Armagh, in Armagh barony. The area restored to Irish grantees in this county, which includes the grants made prior to plantation, amounted to just over 25 per cent, a proportion which, incidentally, had become reduced to 19 per cent by 1641. Those Irish restored to ownership as a category amongst the plantation grantees were placed in Orior barony where the servitors were also placed. Church land, apart from the monastic properties, may well have been slightly more extensive in Armagh than in some other Ulster counties. All former episcopal land along with the quasi-ecclesiastical errenach lands, from whose owners parish clergy had regularly derived in the past, now conferred on the archbishopric, concurrently with the plantation, made up together, in a patchwork throughout the county, some 15 per cent of the acreage. Glebe, to provide a landed income for the new parish clergy in succession, was as a result allocated out of the secular land and made up about 2 per cent. The parish boundaries were not however, redrawn, as had been intended, to coincide with the plantation estates. The old lands of the deanship (about 7,000 acres) now went to the dean in the new order, while the lands of the Culdees were designed to support a body of Vicars Choral which should be established around the cathedral, which was now being restored. No land in this county was specifically allocated to lay the groundwork for town development. However Armagh, to be the county capital and within the episcopal lands, Charlemont and Mountnorris, two of the fort sites, were intended to become centres of urbanisation, to be incorporated too (as happened for Armagh and Charlemont in 1613) and so, along with the county, each to return two members to parliaments in Dublin. An entire new phase of town development began at Armagh under Christopher Hampton and James Ussher as archbishops.[31] As a new endowment for grammar school education in the county, some 1,500 acres, in Orior, were bestowed, therein lie the origins of Armagh Royal School. (All this is expressed in summary in Table 1, opposite).

Allowance must be made for some element of error since the calculations derive from an arduous attempt, by me, now of many years past, to construct a map of the plantation (reproduced here) in the entire county. As the places granted to each owner were identified they were mapped using the one inch sheets of the Townland Index Maps of the Ordnance Survey and the acreages of the estate were calculated using an 'adding machine' of the time (late 1960s), from the Townland Index. The map itself is easily understood. The owners were each given a number or letter by which their names can be found in the appended list. The reader is asked to accept, however, that while the map conveys a very good impression of owners and locations, it may not be entirely error free.[32] The ownership of a small area centred on Armagh could not be readily disentangled, and so is represented by an asterisk (*) on the map. The following is its approximate breakdown: Archbishopric, *c.* 900 acres; Dean of Armagh, *c.* 100 acres; Vicars Choral, *c.* 15 acres; Sir Toby Caulfeild (monastic property), *c.* 72 acres; Francis Annesley (assignee of Francis Edgeworth, monastic property), *c.* 5 acres.[33] It remains now to be seen who the principal new owners were at the beginning of the plantation. Some proved to be more enduring than others.

TABLE 1

Landownership, County Armagh, *c.* 1610 (see map set inside back cover)

Proprietor Groups	Percentages of total acreage
English undertakers	21.33
Scottish undertakers	5.05
Servitors	8.97
Irish	25.21
Archbishopric	15.44
Trinity College, Dublin	7.36
Ex-monastic	9.57
Glebe	2.11
Other ecclesiastical proprietors	2.77
School	0.50
Mountain	0.32
Unidentified ownership	1.37

Estates in the barony of Oneilland were allotted to ten English undertakers in 1610. One of these was Sir Richard Fiennes, Lord Say and Seale, an English nobleman given 3,000 'acres' in order to exercise a leadership role

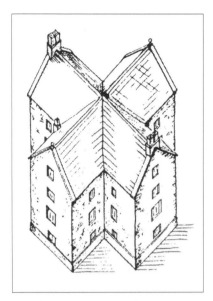

Plate 12.4 Conjectural isometric reconstruction of Anthony Cope's house, Castleraw by E.M. Jope.

in that barony's plantation. With his own estate at Broughton in Oxfordshire and with a house in London which gave him access to decision-makers, he had promised more than he was wealthy enough to fulfill. He would build along with others, he had said in his application, a new town, to be rented to tenants, which should be named, to induce favour, after Sir Robert Cecil, then principal minister in the English government. Now anyhow ageing, having died by 1613, although he took out his patent in June 1610, the estate was to be passed on to Sir Anthony Cope by the following year. Cope, an old Elizabethan, who died in 1615 and who acquired it for Anthony, one of his sons, was himself a substantial Oxfordshire landowner at Hanwell near to Broughton. He is most famous in English history as the member of parliament who, during the religious controversies of the 1580s, had sought to introduce legislation, against official opposition (the 'bill and book' affair), designed to furtherly advance religious reform in lay practice by establishing the Genevan *Forme of Prayers* as the official liturgy of the Church of England.[34] His younger brother Walter (d. 1614), London-based and at the centre with his house, Cope Castle, in Kensington, held office in the financial administration becoming master of the court of wards, was a loyal Cecil supporter, and had invested in the Virginia Company.

The rest may well have been of lesser landed background. Two estates were granted to a father and his son: John and William Brownlow. Of Derbyshire origin, the family was a rising one in Lincolnshire, with a Nottingham branch from which they may have sprung. What may well have been decisive for their selection was the presence in London at this time of a namesake, Richard Brownlow, himself acquiring Lincolnshire land, who was an official in the courts there as protonotary of the common pleas. Unusually, William, the son was to marry Eleanor, the daughter of Sir Cahir O Doherty and her old English mother, whom he had probably met in the Pale. Another grantee had a more direct legal connection and also a Lincolnshire link. John Heron, Lincolnshire born in

1584 was third son of a judge in London and Lincolnshire landowner who had just died in July 1609. Two others had immediate East Anglian origins: both William Stanhawe and James Matchett, a parish clergyman, were from Norfolk. Another, Francis Sacheverell, a man with financial and legal problems at home, was from Leicestershire. The remaining three had Staffordshire links. One, Richard Rolleston, a recent Cambridge graduate and an inventor – he devised a power-driven sawmill – who was ordained, which was probably customary for graduates of the time, but not necessarily beneficed, may well have come from a landed family who were tenants within the 'honour' of Tutbury there, which was part of the royal estate. Another, John Dillon (d. 1637), had some kind of holding there also at the time of his selection, but that does not mean, necessarily, that he had been born there; there is a possibility – no more than that – that he had

Plate 12.5 Surviving masonry of Cope's house, Castleraw (photo by W. Roulston)

Devonshire roots and a Chichester connection. The final grantee owed his selection to his position as a royal servant or minor courtier; he quickly disposed of his grant. William Powell was one of the thirteen equerries of the king's stable and overseer of the king's 'race' and stud of horses at Tutbury.[35] Such were the initial grantees of the estate in Oneilland barony, some of which were passed on to others. Some may have seen principle behind their potentially perilous advancement: through it they would advance the English Protestant cause and English civilisation generally into dangerously hispanised Ulster. All would at any rate have been familiar with the type of English society that was expected to be introduced.

The Scots undertakers had a lesser share in the plantation of this county than in others: five of them received grants in the Fews barony. Sir James Douglas from Haddingtonshire, now called East Lothian and east of Edinburgh in the Lowlands, was one of those Scots whose advancement to positions in England by the king – he became a gentleman of the privy chamber – was, not surprisingly, resented by those there who might otherwise have gained them. A son of the earl of Morton, he had died by 1641. Later his Ulster estate came into the hands of Sir Archibald Acheson, brother of Henry Acheson, another grantee, and originally from Gosford, Haddingtonshire, but then in Edinburgh (plate 12.6.) and a leading Scottish public official. Sir James Craig who had also, like Douglas, accompanied the king to England, where he held positions in the Wardrobe from 1603, was another to receive an estate and came to be a man of many ambitions in Ireland. The other two grantees were William Lauder of Belhaven (near Dunbar) in East Lothian and Claud Hamilton who also came from Haddingtonshire, now East Lothian.[36] All the undertakers, Scottish and English, or those who took over from them, in this county, were to be, in their varying ways active builders and planters, but the Scots as a group were to be initially somewhat more energetic planters than the English. Although the architecture of the plantation is outside the scope of this chapter, it may be noted that the origins of many of the plantation estate villages of the county can be traced to this period: Brownlow's at Lurgan, Obyns's (in succession to Powell) at Portadown, Sacheverell's at Richill, and Acheson's at Markethill amongst them.

The servitors must now be turned to. Some can be shown to have been engaged as military men in many theatres of the Anglo-Spanish war before being transferred to Ireland; a few were more minor figures. Sir Toby Caulfeild, whose grant pre-dated the plantation, fits the former category. Born in Oxfordshire in 1565, as a career professional he had served in the 1590s in naval expeditions against Spain and on land in the Low Countries in support of Dutch independence. In Ireland he had been a captain at the

Plate 12.6 Edinburgh Canongate, Acheson House from Bakehouse Close, 1633

battle of Kinsale and when Lord Deputy Mountjoy built Charlemont fort in 1602, he was left there to command it. He died in the later 1620s. Sir Oliver St John, a second son from Lydiard Tregoze in Wiltshire, had a similar career. He had been colonel at the time of Kinsale, was sent to England with dispatches and was viewed by Sir Robert Cecil as 'very discrete'. By 1622 he had built on his grant in Orior, which took in Tandragee, a castle in a 'pleasant park' paled around, a 'handsome' church, and a village of twenty-seven houses 'well built of the English fashion, making a fair large street'. He was also to add to his holdings as a servitor by acquiring the undertaker's estate granted to Matchett in Oneilland. Another grantee George, Lord Audley was a minor nobleman from Staffordshire who had also opted for a military career. Again in Holland in the 1580s and one of the colonels in command at Kinsale, his aims for land were held to outrun his capacity to bring into being a developed and ordered plantation on the ground. He got, however, a small area in Orior and estates along with members of his family in Omagh barony, County Tyrone, but did not come to be resident in either place and died, probably in London, in 1617. Sir Garret Moore (1566–1627), whose grant included Drumbanagher, was of a somewhat different type. Of Kentish roots and now a privy councillor and lately a captain in the Nine Years' War and to be ennobled as a viscount in 1621, he was second generation in Ireland, his father having been seated on a dissolved monastic estate at Mellifont in Louth 'on the borders of Ulster', and he was now enabled to extend his holdings further north in County Armagh. Different again was Charles Poyntz. From Gloucestershire, probably younger and merely a lieutenant, he was to be active and resident on the ground, where he built, at Acton or Poyntzpass, introduced settlers, and added to his initially small grant by acquiring some of the lands granted to Irish grantees.[37] Two others, not strictly servitor grantees, had penetrated inwards from Newry and south Down. When

Arthur Bagnal, whose father had perished at the Blackwater, took out a new patent in 1613, he was renewing a grant of the dissolved monastic estate of the abbey of the Blessed Virgin and St Patrick in Newry, where his family had been seated since the mid sixteenth century, and where they had built a town on the basis of it, some of which land had stretched into Armagh.[38] When Edward Trevor, Down-based and related to the Bagnals, took out a patent in 1615, it contained miscellaneous small areas in Armagh which had been omitted from the earlier grants.[39]

And there is a further point to be made. In the new Ireland under creation in the early seventeenth century, some of these servitor grantees came also to hold positions in the government in Dublin, or places under it, probably with houses there too, having links with London also through their official positions which brought them over and back, and probably owning some property in England as well. Sir Toby Caulfeild as master of the ordnance was one such member of the Dublin government. Sir Oliver St John, ennobled as Viscount Tregoze, came to be the head of it as lord deputy. One can see with his grant (and subsequent acquisitions), an early stage in the career of Francis Annesley, subsequently Lord Mountnorris. Through their persons, then, their lands and tenants in County Armagh were at the top of a triangle political and cultural too, of which one foot was in Dublin and the other in London.

The Irish grantees now remain for mention. Those who received patents prior to the plantation have already been discussed, as have been the O Hanlons. Although, now, some fifty Irish were to be restored to some land and obliged, on the whole, to relocate in Orior barony, most received small acreages and only two of those now granted land under the plantation received estates similar in size to those of the undertakers.[40] Hence Art McBaron O Neill, the earl's brother, and his wife received a 2,000 'acre' estate (some 7,000 statute acres) which included Forkhill, but this was to be for their lives only; on their deaths it should pass to Lord Audley. It was this estate which had come into the ownership of Rory O Moore by 1641. Henry McShane O Neill, a son of Shane's and an opponent of Earl Hugh's, received a similar estate. Owing to his poverty he was exempted from building on it. He was in fact to sell it and, now 'lately dead', by 1619 it had, with the exception of one-third which was his widow's jointure, come into the possession of Sir Toby Caulfeild.

Those who received the smaller grants were all people of varying prominence. Two were sons of Oghy oge O Hanlon. Some are more easily identified than others. Six McCanns from Oneilland, including Carbery, 'chief of his name', were grantees. Carbery McCann was not however, to take up his grant at all but sold it, presumably to Poyntz whose family owned it in 1641, and moved to Clandeboy, where he took lands from Conn O Neill. Seven recipients of land were members of the McDonnell gallowglass family, two, Calvagh and Colla McArt, being the sons of Art McDonnell, chief of the gallowglass, from Clancarney in the Fews barony. There were three O Hagans and two O Quins, families originally from Tyrone, one O Mulchrewe, one McMurphy, one McGilleduffe, one O Mellan, one O Donnelly and one O Donnell (probably also an O Donnelly) among the beneficiaries.

The remaining grantees were all O Neills. Owen McHugh [McNeill Mor] O Neill was an enemy of Sir Turlough McHenry and a claimant to the lands in the Fews.[41] He was of Toaghy in 1609,[42] the land for the most part granted to Trinity College. Felim McTurlough Brassilogh, Turlough oge McTurlough Brassilogh, Cormac McTurlough Brassilogh and Neill McTurlough were all recognizable members of a branch of the O Neill nobility. They were sons of Turlough Brassilogh O Neill, a grandson of Conn, the first earl of Tyrone. Art McTurlough, Henry McTurlough, and Hugh McTurlough were sons of Sir Turlough McHenry O Neill of the Fews, and Brian McDonnell McPhelim Roe was his cousin, while Hugh McCarbery O Neill was a distant member of the Fews sept. Donnell McHenry and his cousin Eugene Vally represented the sept of Murtagh O Neill (d. 1471) of Clanconaghy. Conn McTurlough O Neill was a nephew of Sir Henry Oge, and Shane McTurlough may have been Conn's brother.[43]

Conclusion

This chapter has aimed to do no more than examine the organisation of the plantation in County Armagh and indicate the magnitude of the ownership change which it entailed. This was done against a background which brought in, generally, some brief discussion of the Nine Years' War, and which, more specifically, examined the establishment of the county organisation in Armagh. Its statistical basis arises from the construction of a map of the plantation in the county which cannot but have some errors in it, and for which some allowance must be made. Despite the fact that it has not sought to discuss the development of the plantation in any of its aspects or the multi-cultural society that arose from it, it may still have been of some value.[44]

APPENDIX 1 (See Table 1 on page 317)

Landowners, County Armagh, *c.* 1610
O = Oneilland, F= Fews, Or. = Orior, A = Armagh, T = Tiranny

No. on Map	Barony	Owner	O.S. Acreage	Acreage as granted
		English undertakers:		
1	O	John Brownlow	4,817	1,500
2	O	William Brownlow	8,062	1,000
10	O	William Powell	8,676	2,000
6	O	John Heron	5,316	2,000
9	O	Rev. James Matchett	3,455	1,000
13	O	Rev. Richard Rolleston	3,430	1,000
7	O	Sir Anthony Cope	8,365	3,000
12	O	John Dillon	4,897	1,500
11	O	Francis Sacheverell	7,499	2,000
4	O	William Stanhowe	11,747	1,500
		Scottish undertakers:		
30	F, Or.	Sir James Douglas	7,083	2,000
29	F	Henry Acheson	1,962	1,000
26	F	James Craig	2,634	1,000
27	F	William Lawder	2,292	1,000
28	F	Claud Hamilton	1,727	500
		Servitors:		
33	Or.	Sir Oliver St John	4,806	1,500
58	Or.	Sir Garret Moore	2,681	1,000
64	Or.	Sir Thomas Williams	2,760	1,000
14	Or., O	Sir John Bourchier	3,685	1,000
34	Or	Francis Cooke	2,877	1,000
38	Or.	Charles Poyntz	674	200
63	Or.	George, Lord Audley	1,654	500
15	O	Richard Atherton	105	
3	O	Edward Trevor	1,773	
5	A	Sir Toby Caulfeild: Charlemont fort land	500 approx.	
79	Or.	Captain Anthony Smith: Moyry fort land	4,447	
69	Or.	Henry Atherton: Mountnorris fort land	1,134	300
70	Or.	Francis Annesley	778	
73	Or.	Marmaduke Whitechurch	713	

Holders of former monastic property:

5, in*	F, A, T, O	Sir Toby Caulfeild	20,168	
73	Or.	Marmaduke Whitechurch	3,276	
8	O, Or.	Arthur Bagnal	5,575	
In*	A	Francis Edgeworth	5 approx	
B, in*	All bars	Archbishopric	47,986	
G	A, F, O, Or.	Glebe	6,561	

Other ecclesiastical proprietors:

24, in*	A, F, T	Dean	7,162	
17	A	Chancellor	9	
18 in*	A	Vicars Choral	1,426	
Sc	Or.	Armagh school land	1,552	
16	A	Trinity College, Dublin	22,875	4,700
Mountain	Or.	John Sandford (Mountain)	987	

Irish:
[The spellings follow that used at the time]

21	T	Turlogh oge O'Neill	561	
22	T	Brian O'Neill	3,293	
25	T	Neill O'Neill	332	
23	T	Henry and Charles O'Neill	344	
19	T	Conn boy O'Neill	1,278	
20	T	Catherine O'Neill	4,531	
76	Or.	Art McBaron O'Neill: life interest only	7,082	2,000
68	Or.	Henry McShane O'Neill	4,910	1,500
48	Or.	Turlogh groom O'Hanlon	801	140
47	Or.	Shane McShane O'Hanlon	295	100
74	Or.	Rory McPatrick McCann	688	120
36	Or.	Rory McFerdoragh O'Hanlon	250	120
35	Or.	Patrick Moder [O'Donnell?]	198	120
81	Or.	Laughlin O'Hagan	242	120
59	Or.	Felim McOwen oge McDonnell	203	100
49	Or.	Shane oge McShane roe O'Hanlon	219	120
57	Or.	Conn McTurlogh [O'Neill]	1,008	360
75	Or.	Owen McHugh McNeill Mor O'Neill	1,352	240
53	Or.	Patrick O'Hanlon	2,150	
72	Or.	Redmond O'Hanlon	3,841	
32	Or.	Cormac McTurlogh Brassilogh O'Neill	168	120

42	Or.	Redmond McFerdoragh O'Hanlon	140	60
43	Or.	Turlogh oge McTurlogh Brassilogh O'Neill	141	60
67	Or.	{ Mulmory O'Donnell Art McTurlogh O'Neill Neill McTurlogh O'Neill	754	240
37	Or.	Neece Quin	181	120
46	Or.	Phelim and Brian O'Hanlon	584	240
45	Or.	Patrick McManus O'Hanlon and Ardell Moore O'Mulchrewe	293	120
80	Or.	{ Donnell McHenry O'Neill Felim McTurlogh Brassilogh O'Neill Eugene Vally O'Neill Edmond oge O'Donnelly	2,708	540
55	Or.	Shane McOghy O'Hanlon	213	100
54	Or.	Donell McCann	167	80
39	Or.	Carbery McCann	815	360
56	Or.	{ Brian McDonnell McFelim roe O'Neill Hugh McCarbery O'Neill Shane McTurlogh O'Neill	480	240
62	Or.	Donogh Reogh O'Hagan	325	100
60	Or.	Colla McArt McDonnell	145	120
77	Or.	Donogh oge McMurphy	728	180
78	Or.	{ Hugh McTurlogh O'Neill Art McTurlogh O'Neill Henry McTurlogh O'Neill	962	240
40	Or.	Hugh McGilleduffe	117	120
52	Or.	Cahir O'Mellan	123	100
51	Or.	Hugh McBrian McCann	362	80
61	Or.	Brian McMelaghlin McArt O'Neill	118	60
41	Or.	Felim O'Quin	293	100
44	Or.	{ Carbery oge McCann Toole McFelim McCann	59	160
66	Or.	Edmond Groome McDonnell	56	80
65	Or.	Alexander oge McDonnell	112	83
71	Or.	Brian oge O'Hagan	694	100
50	Or.	Ferdoragh O'Hanlon (in 1637)	43	(20)
31	F	Sir Turlogh McHenry O'Neill	33,704	
	Or.	Collo McEever McDonnell	unidentified	80
U.	Or.	Unidentified ownership	4,247	

APPENDIX 2

Richhill House and Lurgan estate village

Richhill House was a sophisticated architectural achievement built by the Richardsons who succeeded to the ownership of Sacheverell's estate. Although it cannot be dated with precision, it may have been built some time in the later seventeenth century, when the plantation had been restored in the aftermath of the failed Irish attempted counter-revolution of the 1640s. Lurgan was an estate village, one of many in the county, built on the Brownlow estate, of which a map has been constructed, as of 1667, by W.H. Crawford, based on a leasebook of that year. Both throw light on the second phase of the plantation. Crawford's map (plate 12.9) is reproduced here from R. Gillespie (ed.), *Settlement and survival on an Ulster estate: the Brownlow leasebook, 1667–1711* (Belfast, 1988), p. xliii. It indicates a plan which took in a church, a market house, and the landlord's residence. The following is the account of Richhill House written by the late Professor E.M. Jope, and reproduced from his seminal paper 'Moyry, Charlemont, Castleraw and Richhill: Fortification to architecture in the north of Ireland, 1570–1700', in *Ulster Journal of Archaeology*, 3rd series xxiii (1960), pp 97–123.

There is no certain *dating* evidence for the building of Richhill. Edward Richardson paid Poll-Tax on the property in 1660, and though no Hearth Tax was paid in 1664, a house must have been built here soon after. The more distinctive features of Richhill (plate 12.7) – shaped gables, parallel brick chimneys, symmetrical layout with centrally placed stair-projection at the back – were current in England through the seventeenth century, and it is possible that the existing house is that built *c.* 1670, though some features – the ground plan with wings in echelon (which do not seem additions as are the corner projections at Waringstown), and the door surround – are more appropriate to the eighteenth century. The house has been little changed architecturally since it was built.

Richhill (plate 12.10) is a two-storey house with attics and dormers with shaped heads. It is an oblong block, with shaped-gabled wings broken forward in échelon at the front corners. The entrance is symmetrically placed in the front, and a square projection carrying a scale-and-platt stair lies opposite to it centrally placed at the back. This layout has its roots in the medieval hall-and-cross-passage house type and is persistent in the sixteenth and seventeenth centuries. The hall lay to the left of the entrance, the kitchen (by the size of its fireplace) being to the right. The wings must have contained private dining and withdrawing rooms. The upper floors would have contained sleeping chambers, with perhaps a further large public room over the ground floor hall, as indicated by the extra fireplace with corbelled-out chimney stack at the back.

The walls are of local rubble harled over, with brick chimney-stack having recessed panels with semicircular heads and imposts.

The *Ground-plan* with wings set forward in échelon, has its roots in the European or English sixteenth century house-designs with corner towers or partitions, a layout seen also on Scottish towers. Wings thus set are rarer, plain cross-wings being the usual in England – in the early seventeenth century they are indeed considered 'unique to Bramshill' (Hants, 1605–12) – but they may be quoted for the early eighteenth century at Boughton, Northants (1736).

The basic layout of the main oblong block has its roots in medieval hall-and-cross-passage house type, which was very persistent through the seventeenth century because it was convenient. At Richhill the entrance hall has been partitioned into a vestibule by light screen walls, perhaps not original. Square stair-projections are most usual in the sixteenth and early seventeenth centuries, but in England such stair projections can be found unobtrusively in the builders' usage through the later seventeenth and much of the eighteenth centuries.

The general appearance of Richhill however, with shaped gables scantily-windowed, can be seen in English smaller houses of the mid-seventeenth century, as at Glinton Manor, Northants, and beyond this in Holland and Denmark. The type is rare though not unknown in Scotland, but the English origin of the Richhill design is indicated by the panelled brick chimneys and the pedimented gables. The latter – a 'Holborn gable' – though Flemish in ultimate origin, was brought to England about 1610 and soon became fully naturalised. These may be compared with the

FRONT   BACK

Plate 12.7 Isometric views of Richill House from front and back

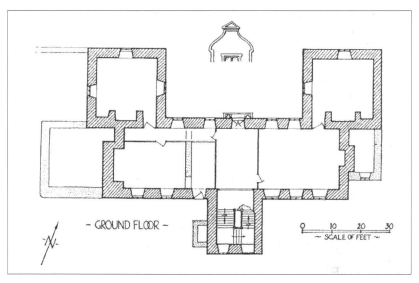

Plate 12.8 Ground-plan of Richill House ('castle')

pedimented shaped gables over the dormers at Waringstown (probably *c.* 1666), and Thomas Raven showed similar gables (though not pedimented) when he drew the Drapers' strong house at Moneymore. An engraving of *c.* 1746 of Rubane house, on the Ards, County Down shows a series of similar pedimented gables on a house with cross wings projecting forward from the front.

Chimneys with recessed semicircular-headed panels were mainly current in England during the middle decades of the seventeenth century, but the style had a long history. It may be seen in the brick-style buildings of Francis I (1515–45) round Paris, and earlier in the Loire (Chateaudun, on a wing begun 1502), while Blois itself has a wing finished in 1503, with Gothic tracery in the chimney panels. Though it seems to have a French origin, in Britain it is English and not Scottish, perhaps because French brick styles did not find much favour among the stone-building Scottish patrons and their masons. The style was thus already time-honoured when used at Swakeleys (1629–38), Scole (1655), Moyles Court (Hants, 1660), and in Ireland it must be considered an English style, seen at Brazeel House near Dublin (probably 1650) as well as at Richhill. In England a few examples are later seventeenth century, and one (without imposts on the panels) occurs on an early eighteenth century building (*c.* 1715) at Bourton-on-the Hill, Glos. The close comparison between Richhill and Brazeel, and the English mid-seventeenth century group – Swakeleys, Scole, Moyles Court – are the strongest reason for considering Richhill a house of the later seventeenth century, and it is to this period that the datable examples in the

New World belong – Bond Castle or Holly Hill (Anne Arundle County *c.* 1667), though even there Mount Clare, Baltimore, is a house of 1750 with stacks having recessed panels (with imposts) of this style.

The fine wrought iron gates of Richhill were probably the work of brothers named Thornberry from Falmouth who settled in County Armagh. The gates were probably put up for William Richardson in 1745. They were removed to their present position on the governor's house at Hillsborough in 1936.

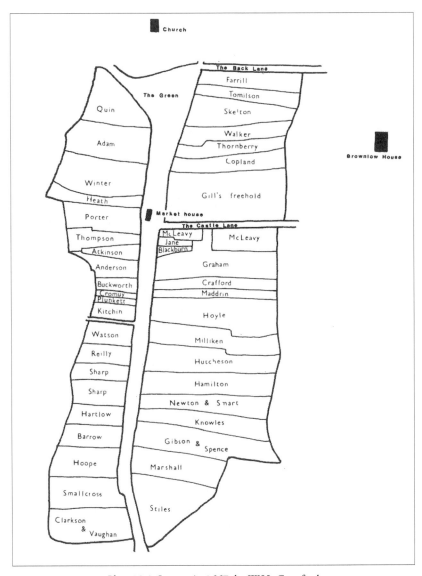

Plate 12.9 Lurgan in 1667, by W.H. Crawford

330

Plate 12.10
Richill House from front and towards the stair projection at the back, showing
the shaped gables and panelled chimneys of brick

Acknowledgements

I am much indebted once again, to Joanne Taggart, School of History, Philosophy and Politics, University of Ulster, Coleraine for her skill and kindness in preparing the typescript of this chapter. I would also like to thank C.J.W. Edwards, then of the Geography Department, Magee University College for drawing my original map. A longstanding debt of gratitude to W.H. Crawford must also be acknowledged. Gillian Coward prepared the plates.

[1] *Inquisitionum in officio rotulorum cancellariae Hiberniae asservatarum repertorium*, II (Dublin, 1829), xix–xx.

[2] The definitive study of the origins and early development of the Nine Years' War is Hiram Morgan, *Tyrone's rebellion: the outbreak of the Nine Years' War in Tudor Ireland* (Dublin, 1993).

[3] The content of this blueprint for government had much in common with the 'aristocratic constitutionalism' which surfaced within Sweden at this time.

[4] Under government this would be the equivalent of that palatinate jurisdiction which he had sought earlier.

[5] Mark Greengrass, *France in the age of Henry IV* (Harlow, Essex, 1995), pp 89–116.

[6] *Cal. S.P. Ire., 1603–6,* pp 317–23; Armagh Public Library, Armagh Papers, pp 427–9.

[7] PRONI, T808/14926.

[8] TNA, AO1/289/1085, ff 71–lv.

[9] *Cal. S.P. Ire., 1603–6*, p. 317.

[10] *Cal. Pat. Rolls Ire., Jas I*, p. 102.

[11] Ibid., p. 97.

[12] Ibid., pp 159, 229.

[13] Ibid., p. 102.

[14] *Cal. S.P. Ire., 1603–6*, p. 129; *1608–10*, p. 338; *Cal. Pat. Rolls Ire., Jas I*, pp 5, 156.

[15] Ibid., p. 156.

[16] *Cal. S.P. Ire., 1603–6*, p. 318; *Cal. Pat. Rolls Ire., Jas I*, p. 78.

[17] Ibid., p. 96.

[18] PRONI, T808/14926.

[19] *Cal. Pat. Rolls Ire., Jas I*, p. 67; *Inq. Cancell. Hib. Repert.*, II, Armagh (36) Chas I.

[20] *Cal. Pat. Rolls Ire., Jas I,* pp 262–31.

[21] M.K. Walsh (ed.), *Destruction by peace: Hugh O Neill after Kinsale* (Armagh, 1986), p. 176.

[22] *Cal. S.P. Ire., 1606–8,* pp 212–13. For a brief account of O Cahan's career and ultimate fate see R.J. Hunter, 'Sir Donnell Ballagh O Cahan' in *Oxford DNB*.

[23] For what they sought see Walsh, *Destruction by peace,* pp 189–95.

[24] *Cal. S.P. Ire., 1606–8,* pp 268–9.

[25] *Cal. S.P. Ire., 1606–8,* p. 321.

[26] *Cal. S.P. Ire., 1608–10,* p. 287.

[27] Ibid., p. 67.

[28] See the list of names in appendix 1.

[29] For the Londonderry plantation as a whole see T.W. Moody, *The Londonderry plantation, 1609–41: the city of London and the plantation in Ulster* (Belfast, 1939) and for a case study see ch. 7, pp 139–90. A summary examination of another county is in R.J. Hunter, 'Plantation in Donegal' in W. Nolan, L. Ronayne and M. Dunlevy (eds), *Donegal: history and society* (Dublin, 1995), pp 283–324.

[30] In making the map, the extent of the monastic land may have been slightly inflated at the expense of the fort land in the Charlemont area.

[31] See below, ch. 15, pp 393–427.

[32] It has to be explained here that in the making of the map, the area granted as mountain was taken just to be Slieve Gullion. The areas granted as glebe land may also have been slightly inflated. The allocations of glebe were not made until the late 1620s and clergy were sometimes involved in disputes with neighbouring owners.

[33] The area taken as about five acres here represents the property of the 'house of monks' in Armagh called Templefartagh, who also had acquired entitlements to tithes, and the 'house of monks' of Templebreda (*Cal. Pat. Rolls Ire., Jas I*, pp 354–6). Its disposition provides an example of how areas of forfeited land in Ireland changed hands, *independently of plantations*, in the early seventeenth century. These, along with other lands, had been bestowed in patronage on Sir John Eyres, a gentleman of the king's privy chamber in England. He then disposed of them to Francis Edgeworth who in turn passed them on to Francis Annesley, who thereby built up his estate.

[34] P. Collinson, *The Elizabethan puritan movement* (London and New York, 1967), pp 306–16.

[35] This information all derives from work for my book, in preparation, on the English in plantation Ulster.

[36] The biographical information derives from M. Perceval-Maxwell, *The Scottish migration to Ulster in the reign of James I* (London, 1973), pp 323–58.

[37] This again derives from my research on the English in the plantation in Ulster

[38] *Cal. Pat. Rolls Ire., Jas I*, pp 246–7.

[39] Ibid., pp 299–300.

[40] The grants all derive from *Cal. Pat. Rolls Ire., Jas I*, passim.

[41] *Cal. S.P. Ire., 1600*, pp 312–14.

[42] *Cal. Pat. Rolls Ire., Jas I*, p. 158.

[43] I wish to record here my thanks to K.W. Nicholls of University College, Cork for his help, some years ago, with the making of many of these identifications.

[44] I hope to expand on all this, in due course, in a book on the English in plantation Ulster.

13

Style and Form in Gravestone and Monumental Sculpture in County Tyrone in the seventeenth and eighteenth centuries

The graveyards and churches of countryside and town form everywhere a museum in which the curious and the observant may readily gain an insight into thinking of the past, since styles and terms of carving and construction in gravestone and monumental art reflect in a visual way the undercurrents of thought and the mental framework prevalent in the society of the time. Where the craftsmanship is likely to be that of country carvers, as in the case of gravestones, then light is also thrown on the standards of skill available in a specific area, while work of more elaborate quality – as in church monuments which would appear to have been brought in from outside – illustrates the taste and cultivation of those in that area who commissioned it. A properly thorough study would reveal a chronology for the penetration and duration of specific forms and styles in the area concerned. By taking just a few examples, this short essay aims to do no more than to give an outline indication of the possibilities which an exploration of this subject in County Tyrone would disclose.[1]

EARLY BRITISH MONUMENTS
Robert Granger and his wife: an early plantation gravestone
Seventeenth century gravestones or any sculptures of pre-1641 vintage are rare, but two pieces of work, though not akin in purpose, one of 1625 and one, much damaged, of *c.* 1630, both in the vicinity of Strabane, throw light on early seventeenth-century society there and its contrasting theologies. Robert Granger, whose memorial (plate 13.1) in Grange graveyard is the first to be discussed, was a Scot given a lease of land on the estate called Dunnalong granted at plantation in 1610 to the earl of Abercorn. Having a namesake Andrew in the new plantation town of Strabane, the family linked both town and countryside in the emerging plantation society of Tyrone in that area, which here was one of Scottish rather than English colonisation.[2]

Plate 13.1 Recumbent gravestone to Robert Granger and wife, Grange graveyard

The significance of the Granger stone, in memory of himself and his wife Kathren Hill, also of another new settler family there, lies both in its inscription and in its design. It is a recumbent grave slab (i.e. flat at ground level), 32½ in. wide and some 74½ in. long, but it is now compressed length-wise through having been broken. The inscription is marginal (or carved continuously around the edges), an old form later abandoned in favour of inscriptions in lines, but is not in what had been the common Gothic or 'black letter' script of the past, but in Roman, and is in English rather than in Latin. The spelling 'heir' for 'here', which is Lowland Scots, a dialect of middle English native to most of the Scots settlers of this time, gives clue to who the carver was. He was probably one of those Scottish masons who had been employed in the building works on the plantation estates in recent years. Indeed the name of one such, James Miller, is actually known. A common Scottish practice, the inscribing of the wife's maiden name, also stands out.[3]

Both design and inscription, it can be argued, also show a percolation downwards of some important pre-occupations of early Protestantism. Hence 'Heir lyet[h the bo] dyes of', which was to remain a common form, hints at a religious practice which had discarded the notion of purgatory. If the fate of the soul were to be now more in the hands of God, to await Resurrection and final Judgement Day, then imprecations to the lay bystander in inscriptions in the past incorporating 'Pray for the soul of" (*orate pro anima*) the deceased, sometimes with references also to indulgences, could be discontinued. The absence of religious imagery from the Granger memorial may again reflect early Protestant theorising, transferred now into the Tyrone countryside, because many of the leaders of the reformed churches had embarked on a major re-appraisal (later modified as will be seen) of images or, in effect, of religious art, seeing as latent in its many forms the 'peril' of idolatry for the laity. Indeed were these views to be followed, the arts – of sculpture and painting – would re-orientate into more secular directions.[4]

This is apparent here even in Granger's quite ordinary gravestone, where the artistic element is clearly confined to armorial carving: three stags couped in relief within a shield. The Granger stone then, it can be seen, primarily commemorated the individual deceased and his family buried together. This essentially familial conception of a memorial emerges from another stone, somewhat earlier and again a rare specimen, in a graveyard nearby – which, interestingly, has a small cross as well as an armorial element – though with a different initial form of words, also marginally inscribed. To 'here is the burial place of the deceased is added 'and his family'.[5] As a gentry class in settler society achieved clearer definition – the poor after all leave no memorials – the armorial element (which is held, in a perspective, to be the replacement of the effigy common in medieval monuments to much larger landholders) came to be more developed in many such memorials. Many can be found in Tyrone, especially, Clogher, from the early eighteenth century onwards. The person might be dead, but the stone placed there to commemorate him demonstrated with its arms the continuity of the family (or 'house') while with its text it carved out the deceased's place and status in local history for posterity.

Robert Algeo's crucifixion plaque: the Catholicism of a Scottish settler

The next stone to be discussed has also to be placed in its religious and artistic context, because it is a crucifixion plaque of 1625 and it highlights the Catholicism of a Scottish planter. It is located now beside the footing of the bridge at Artigarvan, deeply below the ground level above, where, according to a brief nineteenth-century notice of it, it had been placed by a man, compelled to do so by spirit visitations having first removed it from some church ruin to his home.[6] Dating within the era of the counter-reformation, the crucifix was by now supremely a Catholic image, and the appearance of this sculpted one at this time in the neighbourhood of Strabane points to a highly exceptional feature in the plantation there, the presence of a small but significant Catholic element, mainly Scots, possibly some English and even some Irish of old English extraction, within the settler population of this region. Although at home these Scots could indeed be under pressure to conform, there were obvious pull factors for them too, to occupy, like their Protestant equivalents, land and place at the expense of fellow Catholics in Ulster.

One of these was Robert Algeo. Of a surname commonly found then only in Renfrewshire, Algeo had thus come from the home area in Scotland of James Hamilton, earl of Abercorn, who had his base at Paisley, just south-west of Glasgow, and who, with others of his family having associations, eastwards towards Edinburgh, with Lanarkshire and Linlithgowshire, now West Lothian, had received grants of estates in the plantation barony of Strabane, and was himself a Hamilton retainer.[7] Algeo was, in fact, a prominent figure in the plantation: he was one of a number of agents or estate managers, obviously men of considerable ability, employed by these Hamilton grantees. He first appears in an administrative role in 1614 on the estate granted to Sir Claud Hamilton of Schawfield, Lanarkshire, a brother of the earl's. With the death of Sir Claud in that year, that estate came thereafter under the management of another brother, Sir George Hamilton of Greenlaw, himself also the grantee of an estate in his own right. Algeo emerges in 1622 as linked to Sir George Hamilton, having then himself the oversight of both estates on Sir George's behalf. He was also a leaseholder of land on Sir George's own estate – called Cloghogenall and including Artigarvan – on which he had built a stone house. Further indication of the special position accorded to him in settler society is found when he is seen in 1630 as the bearer of the colours in the settler militia mustered for Strabane.[8]

On the death in 1618 of the first earl of Abercorn, who had been Protestant and had indeed begun building a church at Strabane, Sir George, who came to be guardian of the earl's children, and generally very influential in Strabane barony, and the earl's son, Claud, known as the Master of Abercorn (d. 1638), who inherited the Strabane lands when he came of age, as his brother, James, the second earl, did the lands in Scotland, were both Catholic. Sir George, moreover, was to gain a wider Irish connection with a lease of land and a residence at Roscrea, County Tipperary, finalised in 1631, through an aristocratic marriage to a daughter of the old English Walter, earl of Ormond, negotiated in 1629.[9]

It was under Sir George's and the Master's patronage that a significant, if small, element of lay Catholic settlers had grown up around Strabane. Not only that, but the Catholic vicar-apostolic of the diocese of Derry, Turlough O'Kelly, lived there since November 1629, 'amongst the Scots in and about Strabane', supported by these landlords, as his predecessor, Eugene MacSwiney, had done prior to his promotion to the bishopric of Kilmore just at this time, and himself a figure, albeit a lesser one, of that Catholic revival in Ireland, after its nadir of the later sixteenth century, which was promoted by the counter-reformation papacy. What brings this group of people at Strabane to our attention as a perceived threat to the established Protestant order lies in the circumstances of the 1620s. First, the attempt by James I to negotiate a Spanish match for his son Charles, and then the renewal of war, 1625–30, between England, to which Scotland was linked, like Ireland, since 1603 through a common monarchy and established religious system, and Spain, still the principal champion of Catholicism in Europe, generated amongst Catholics the expectation of some beneficial modification of the status quo, if not necessarily now of the reversal in toto of the reformation. In Paisley too, even in an area of Scotland ('the radical south-west') coming to be known for the commitment of its people to Protestantism, there were incidents of Catholic opposition, given aristocratic leadership by Dame Marion Boyd, widow of the earl of Abercorn. In north-west Ulster O'Kelly was feared, in an intersection of religion and politics, because of his putative connection to the Irish regiment in Spanish Flanders, from within which Owen Roe O'Neill in these years was seeking Spanish backing for an invasion plan for

Ireland, designed to bring about a whole new political order there. Had that come about and been successful, its implications for the survival of the plantation in Ulster would have been stark, and O'Kelly would have been put in an invidious position because of his connection with those Ulster planters. The date of Algeo's crucifixion stone, 1625, coincides with this period and gains its significance from it.[10]

If Granger's gravestone may show some of the influence of the reformation, Algeo's plaque fits into the era of the great Catholic counter-reformation and gains meaning from it. Spearheaded in the decrees of the council of Trent and the work of the popes of the time it was both a renewal within the Catholic Church as well as a response to the challenge of Protestantism. The religious value of images was reaffirmed but with clarification: 'not that any divinity or virtue believed to be in them on account of which they are to be worshipped or that anything is to be asked of them; or … trust reposed in' them 'because the honour which is shown them is referred to the prototypes which' they 'represent'. Constraints, indeed, were placed on religious artists to eliminate superstition, heresy and renaissance exuberance from their work; in the longer term emerged a Catholic religious art of intense emotionalism.[11] Belief in purgatory was reasserted, but reforms of the Mass were produced designed to eliminate local 'superstitious' practices in lay religion.[12] Even the design of the crucifix came in for re-appraisal. More generally, amongst the laity to whom it penetrated, the counter-reformation generated a strong spirit of conviction. It was to the glory of a Catholic God that Algeo linked himself, as the prominence of his name on the inscription makes clear.

The slab itself (plate 13.2) is some 53½ in. long, its width about 22 in. while the length of the cross is just very slightly less than 22 in. It is carved in raised relief within a moulded border, the latter lost along the top edge. The Latin inscription I.N.R.I. appears above the figure, which is flanked by AD DEI GLORIAM (to the glory of God), with below it Robert Algeo's name and, below again, the date 2 May 1625, the panel beneath being left blank. The semi-circular ornament at the foot of the cross is either a rendering of the hill of Golgotha or perhaps of the skulls, legendarily found there, or just simply some decoration.[13] Christ's arms are somewhat drawn up, especially on the left, though not pronouncedly so, and his head tilts slightly. He is wearing a short and flowing perizonium, a feature characteristic of the renaissance, rather than one of knee-length. Its other notable feature is that Christ is nailed to the cross with three nails, one foot being placed over the other, as opposed to four nails with his feet placed on a suppedaneum.

It has been shown that the design of the crucifix had gone through an evolution with three nails long common by the fifteenth century.[14] It was

Plate 13.2 Algeo crucifixion stone, Artigarvan bridge

this feature in particular which engaged some of the leading writers of the counter reformation, though no authoritative instruction was issued as to which form should be followed.[15] Accordingly, this feature in the design of the Algeo slab cannot be given any special significance. The intended destination of the slab cannot now be determined, unless it had been proposed to erect it within the church in Strabane, previously unfinished, and planned originally for Protestant worship. Since Robert Algeo was alive in 1630, it was not a grave monument. It derives its very special interest from the circumstances of its creation combined with its present highly impenetrable location.

Death and destruction: the Montgomery tomb in Newtownstewart

Large tombs or monuments surviving within churches in Ulster are rare for indeed most of the seventeenth century. Just as the effects of war and change in later sixteenth-century Ulster and the monastic dissolutions which followed, leave now little intact by which to assess the funerary creations for Gaelic lords or ecclesiastics, so also Protestant churches fell victim in some instances to insurgent damaging in the 1641 era or to depredation by the armies of James II later in the century. In Tyrone, Newtownstewart is a case in point. There the present Church of Ireland church dates from 1724. It replaced however, a seemingly new church of the plantation for the parish of Ardstraw, built some time after 1622 on an eminence facing Sir William Stewart's castle some 0.15 miles distant, each defining the end of the plantation village's main street. Stewart's daughter, Katherine, who died in February 1634[–?5] had been married to Sir James Montgomery second son of Hugh Montgomery, first viscount Ards, of County Down. Within the church, there is a small plaque in black marble which refers to a grander monument which no longer survives, but of which it had been clearly a component. It reads in part

> S'r Ia Montgomerie Kt. Gentleman of His Ma'tie's/Honno'ble Privie
> Chamber and sone to the Lo. Visc/Montgo. of the Airds erected
> this Monument/in memory of his most vertuous and beloved/wife
> Katherine Lady Montgomerie daughter to/S'r Will'm Stevart Kt.
> and Bart. and of the Honno'ble/Privie Chamber who departed this
> life/the 15th Feb'y 1634 leaving issue one sonne.

The other evidence for this lost monument and indeed for the circumstances of its destruction, may not be fully reliable, dating as it does from 1690s, but it is worth recording. Katherine, so it was stated, had on her death been 'embalmed and kept two months' and then 'was put in a black marble coffin and laid five foot above ground in the middle of her monument ... '. This was 'curious and sumptuous, of divers colours, all polish'd marble, inscribed with motto's and verses of his own composure and gilded in every fit place', but 'standing in Newtownstewart church was with it burned and demolished by the Irish' in 1641.[16]

Since Montgomery was a man of some education and travel (as well of martial experience) and with a place at the king's court in London, where he had acted as agent for his father's affairs in the 1620s[17] (in effect, an anglicised and royalist Scot), the monument, itself of a recognisable type, had probably been commissioned from some London workshop and brought across for erection in Newtownstewart. Akin (if not alike) to the earlier monument of *c.* 1611, still surviving, to the first earl of Dunbar in Dunbar in Scotland by Maximilian Colt, it would point to the radiation of contemporary London metropolitan taste to Ulster at this time, as it had also done in the Dunbar instance to Scotland.[18]

Of a type with larger tombs of both pre- and post-reformation vintage, its construction, as well as giving an example of embalming in an Irish context, demonstrates another point, that of consciousness of status, itself now displayed all the more perhaps because newly acquired. Although Sir James was a second son and the defunct merely the daughter of a knight, his father had been made a nobleman as Viscount Ards and had divested an estate at Greyabbey to him in April 1629.[19] The 'mottoes and verses', characteristic of an age of many literary creations, no doubt extolled the virtues of the defunct, joined together with the very ideas and ideals current in contemporary English thinking, as proper and fitting for the populace of church attenders to recognise and emulate. For them too, importantly, the monument was to reflect glory onto their own landlord, the father of the deceased, showing how well-connected he was.

Yet, while this monument's destruction in 1641 seems confirmed, it is unlikely that its recovery now hints at a numerous corpus of lost glories of pre-1641 plantation artistic patronage, which had fallen victim to the destruction of the period. After all, the Montgomerys had acquired greater landed wealth, which could be drawn on for such projects, than the average first-generation owner of a plantation estate in County Tyrone. One is on surer ground from the end of the seventeenth century, in the aftermath of the seventeenth-century wars deciding as they did property ownership and so artistic patronage for a long time to come. Some of the stonework of that period must now be turned to.

AFTER THE WILLIAMITE WAR
Wall monuments and inscriptions
There are a number of wall monuments in the county, both on the inside and outside walls of churches. Dating as they do from the end of the seventeenth century, they conform to a trend, apparent now in England too, towards a smaller monumental sculpture. The two chosen for illustration here, both within churches, one to a prominent layman and one to a churchman, show the continuing use of Latin as a literary language amongst the elite of the period. Apart from the symbols on them, to be discussed below, they spring from the age of laudatory epitaphs and

inscriptions, themselves the equivalents, in a later period of newspaper obituaries. However, their other principal characteristic lies in their architectural element: the classicism of their carving. Both are aedicules, literally little buildings, designed with the classical orders on display.

The monument (plate 13.3) to Gilbert Eccles (d. 1694), commissioned by his son Charles, is on the south wall near the east end of the ruined Church of Ireland parish church of Donaghcavey parish in the Castletown area of Fintona. Eccles, a man of Lancashire birth and established at Shanock in County Fermanagh, had acquired the plantation estate, originally English-granted, based on Fintona, in c. 1659.[20] In 1703, as a surviving date stone demonstrates and in the aftermath of the decisive Williamite war, his son Charles had erected at Fintona his own personal residence, later either expanded or rebuilt to be the larger but now demolished Ecclesville house. The old church in which the monument is located (to which the tower was added 1818), which was replaced by the present one in 1840, and itself a substitute for the medieval one some 2 miles away in the countryside, has been described, somewhat implausibly, in the only, and brief recent account of it as mid seventeenth century, and noted for its east window, since badly vandalised, and itself possibly even taken from the old church, as made of a 'row of fine round-headed lancets surmounted by intersecting Y-tracery'.[21] It is possible, though the evidence is not conclusive, that its date of erection may have been somewhat later, and that church, monument and landlord residence were all put up at much the same time. The residence, then, might be seen as an example, in this area, of the transition from fortification to architecture in early modern Ulster, and the one craftsman's hand may possibly be found in the entire project, with church and landlord linked in a common order. For the church, much depends on how the statement in the diocesan visitation of 1693 that the parish church was 'not repaired' should be interpreted.[22] If that refers to the old – and distant – church rather than meaning that this new one had been damaged in the recent war, then a date of construction for it after 1693 is not implausible. While it could be dated to after the Restoration, which had re-instated episcopalian Protestantism, the fact that a local man, Nicholas Browne (b. 1661), who had gone to school in Enniskillen and then to Trinity College, Dublin, was incumbent there from 1696 to 1704 (until promoted upwards in the diocese) may give added weight to the point.[23] Indeed, a church monument in Enniskillen to a Fermanagh Eccles, Daniel (b. 1646), who had died (perhaps in warfare) in March 1688–9, which was made in 1707, may well point to a larger Eccles family engaged in various works of construction and patronage just at the beginning of the eighteenth century. That Charles's son Daniel was sent to

Plate 13.3 Monument to Gilbert Eccles, Castletown church, Fintona

Trinity College for education in 1710 shows a Dublin orientation,[24] albeit a little later, which might allow of the speculation that some Dublin workshop had been the source of both monuments.

The placing of the Fintona monument near the communion table in the theologically-privileged east end of the church, built itself without chancel, shows his son commandeering a special place for the memorial, favoured as it had been throughout Europe for such purposes in the past. In another respect, however, there was a break with past tradition of burial within the church, to have the living with the dead during services, itself an issue much debated in the sixteenth and seventeenth centuries. Here this is not the case, since a cenotaph (Gr. *keinos taphos*) is an empty tomb; graveyard burial for the great, as of course, it had always been for the poor, was coming to be practiced. The essence of the monument lies in its Corinthian columns, which is the order most associated with rule and authority. Between is the Eccles coat of arms above their motto, *Nec animus deficit*, which can be translated as 'Let not the spirit fail' or, simply, 'do not lose heart'. The inscription is essentially biographical (showing too that the father had continued to live in Fermanagh until his death in 1694), with just succinct adulation at the end. What it stated can be given in translation:

> This cenotaph Charles/Eccles of Fintonagh in Co/unty Tyrone esquire,/caused to be made in memory/of his father Gilbert Eccles/ of Shanock in County/Fermanagh, esquire who/honourably lived and piously died/on the 6th of the Kalends of August in the year of our Lord/1694, in the 92nd year of his age.

To this was added a cautionary note in the use of the skull and crossed bones between *memento mori* (remember death) at its base.

The second mural monument (plate 13.4), to the Rev. John Sinclair and in Leckpatrick Church of Ireland church, is a much more elaborate aedicule and is one of two to members of that family in the church. Sinclair, a Scot, had not long after the Restoration been appointed rector of Leckpatrick, which he held until his death early in 1702–3. From 1669 he also held Camus-juxta-Mourne (the parish of Strabane) and kept a curate, and himself served Camus 'in the morning and Leckpatrick in the afternoon'. To both cures was added later, pluralistically, a parish in Raphoe diocese as well. By background, he sprang from some branch of a prominent landholding family in Caithness in north-east Scotland with earlier links to Roslyn in the Lothian lowlands, and he married, as a second wife, a member of another Scottish family, the Galbraiths, now acquiring property as settlers in Ulster. These origins were proclaimed too by integrating the family arms and motto (in English) – 'Commit thy work to God' – into the monument above the aedicule. He had also acquired property in own right in the neighbourhood when, in the early 1680s, he came into possession, by purchase from its previous occupant, of a number of townlands of freehold land, centred on Hollyhill, and part of the plantation manor of Cloghogenall, a Hamilton-owned estate.[25] Because his income and background had set him somewhat apart from the common run of clergy of the time, it is not surprising that clerical monuments such as this are not readily found.

The inscription claims for him many of the virtues of the age: hospitality; charity to the poor; good counsel to the family; status through both parentage and education; not being extravagant. A translation from the conciseness of the Latin can he given as follows:[26]

> In sacred memory of the Reverend John Sinclair lately rector of this church, Anna his widow sprung from the house of Galbraith dedicates this.
>
> Pause reader look and weep at the remains laid below of a man who himself caused no tears. He was born of no lowly parentage, well educated and of outstanding virtue. Where shall be found an equal in integrity and unbreakable trust, in judgement and prudence long developed, in piety towards God, good will towards men and a more than fraternal love towards his friends, in charity to the poor, in counsel within his household, in humanity and hospitality and finally in devotion in spreading the orthodox Christian faith and zeal in suppressing schismaticks of all kinds?
>
> (Let no one speak enviously against him)
>
> For almost forty years he served in the camps of Christ and continued most zealously caring for his flock as much by example as by instruction even in face of the threatening danger to his life and the ever-growing rage of his enemies. Neither seeking the riches of any other nor extravagant with his own, and richer in kindness than in lands, he departed from the living, leaving his friends sorrowing, his children in greater sorrow and his wife most sorrowing of all in the 62nd(?) year of his age and in March 1702 of the Christian era. Buried here are his children Elizabeth, Ezechial, John William, Anne(?), Elizabeth, Andrew and Rebecca.

His devotion to the 'orthodox Christian faith' defines him as a churchman of that episcopalian Protestantism which had been re-established for Ireland at the Restoration. But another point is also made clear from the inscription. His 'zeal in suppressing schismaticks' reveals that the fixation with the ideal of uniformity ('one church'), still a characteristic of the age, had not been achieved amongst Ulster Protestants. There especially, Presbyterianism was emerging as a denomination, but subject to disabilities which continued into the eighteenth century, because unlike the 'glorious revolution' in England, which provided for the toleration of Protestant dissenters, its Irish counterpart had had no equivalent legislation. The 'threatening danger to his life' may well allude to his predicament during

Plate 13.4 Monument to Rev. John Sinclair, Leckpatrick Church of Ireland church

the recent Jacobite war. That his widow, a second wife, had the monument erected suggests a date for it in the early part of the eighteenth century.

While the symbols on both monuments will be turned to later – though the prominence of the angel, after all an image, on the Sinclair one must just be noted now – the principal significance of these monuments at the end of the seventeenth century in Ireland must lie in their classical features and their interpretation. This, it can be argued, sought to convey a sense of British order and decorum. The origins of British neo-classicism it has been shown, lie in the influence of Inigo Jones at the beginning of the century. Jones, who worked as architect for the government of James I, first joint monarch of England and Scotland as well as of Ireland, had himself engraved in Rome, while on a study tour of Italy in 1614 as *Architector Magnae-Britaniae*. In short, classicism was from now to be made the British architectural style.[27] Now, at the end of the century, and afterwards, in Tyrone the heirs of the deceased, Ulster settlers, including Sinclair's, a man of Scottish birth, had chosen artists to commission to frame their memory and to instruct the beholder in the third kingdom, Ireland, within the aedicular form of a neo-classical but, crucially, now a British elite style, designed to convey visually the proclaimed perfection of a culture common to all three kingdoms.

A more developed classicism is to be found in a monument (plate 13.5), undated and uninscribed, now fully complete with a pediment and winged cherub within, in Leckpatrick old graveyard. Certain similarities in the columns to the Sinclair one might even suggest that it was made by the same craftsman. Sometimes claimed locally as an Abercorn memorial, and deserving of fuller study, it is upright against the east wall of a free-standing mausoleum-type structure, unroofed and so open to heaven, built just of undressed stone with elements of brick, and with, for the beholder on the ground, a very elementary pediment design over its entrance, which is separated, unlike its medieval predecessors, from the church itself. In its way a miniature of civility, it shows the Anglicisation of a patron of Scottish background, as Sinclair had been, which is a subtlety not sufficiently recognised by those who posit an exclusively Scottish-derivative culture for Ulster plantation society.

The mortality symbols

One form of carving which recurs both on monuments and gravestones involved the use of the mortality symbols. The mortality symbols particularly skulls, or death's heads, and crossed bones are held to be the successors, now further reduced, of those large cadaver carvings on tombs which take their origin from the Black Death in fourteenth-century

Europe.[28] But if the crisis of the Black Death gave currency to the genre, the recurrence of warfare and other disasters everywhere in the early modern world which succeeded, can account for its continuation. Reflecting, therefore, a contemporary mood, skulls and crossed bones appeared across Europe, to be found alike on the tomb of Anne of Cleves of *c.* 1607 in Westminster Abbey as on that of Rory O'Donnell and Hugh, son of Hugh O'Neill, in the church of S. Pietro in Montorio in Rome, who had died after the Flight of the Earls. When carved alone, then, at this time they had gained no specific denominational significance. They survive in quantity in Scotland, and from England they were transferred across the Atlantic to America. Their appearance in seventeenth century Ulster probably derives

Plate 13.5 Abercorn(?) monument, Old Leckpatrick graveyard

Plate 13.6 Part of gravestone to Rev. John Hamilton(?), Old Donagheady graveyard

from Scotland and England, but they had a currency in other parts of Ireland also. It would not be easy to say whether they had appeared in Ulster before the end of the sixteenth century. They can be found carved in Tyrone along with many other additional symbols in the later seventeenth and early eighteenth centuries.

In complete form on gravestones, along with the inscription, the symbols were accompanied by a motto or short pithy phrase, of which the Latin *Memento Mori* (Remember that thou must die) was the most common, the effect deriving from both elements. Comparison can be drawn, in the medium of print, with emblem books, popular in England from the 1580s (and in which the theme of death also makes its appearance), where on the unity of each page there was motto, engraving and then verse containing various exhortatory sentiments. Sometimes, however, this motto phrase was omitted on gravestones. The purpose of the motto was clear, inculcating preparedness for death in an age of its particular ever-presence, and even for that 'good death' which was a contemporary pre-occupation. The symbols themselves may even have a superstitious quality, the product of circumstance, surviving long past the era of religious reform and oblivious to the calls of its leaders, Protestant and Catholic alike, to that transcendent 'true religion' which should be shorn of 'superstition'. That their appearance might even be more tightly connected to times of specific crisis may perhaps be the case; one group in County Tyrone, mainly discussed here, seems so to cluster, perhaps not entirely accidentally, to the aftermath of the Jacobite war.

The stones in County Tyrone illustrated here with mortality and other symbols fall into two groups: flat slabs, though including one table stone, most of them outside churches, and those attached upright to graveyard walls. The former are the more numerous and come from five sites: Ardstraw, Old Donaghcavey, Old Donagheady, Old Drumragh and Grange. If attempts to recover dates from these recumbent ones (plates 13.6–12), with their enormously weathered inscriptions, were any way successful, then they may range in construction from after 1689 to perhaps about 1710. In appearance they vary from the compact elegance of the symbols, overwritten by *Memento Mori* on the stone at Donagheady (plate 13.6), which records a death some year in the 1680s, to the essential primitivism of the prominently placed symbols of 1701 (if not 1761) in high relief, without *Memento Mori* at Ardstraw (plate 13.7). Those at Grange (plates 13.8–10), all perhaps a little later and one of which may read 1706 or 1708, have a somewhat different appearance. These, all aligned, too, on correct east-west axis (befitting a 'civil' graveyard), are at once a little lighter, plainer and less sculpted and with the symbols more diffused, but also a little less frightening and less spiritual or superstitious.

Most of the inscriptions on these stones, generally now done in lines rather than marginally, defy full reading. On one at Grange a date in 1741 stands out clearly in an inscription, with probably the name Hill or perhaps Hamilton going with it, but this is deceptive for dating the stone itself, because it has been added later and refers to a later interment. Close inspection shows that originally the stone had been inscribed marginally, though that inscription is now largely illegible. But if weathering leaves these stones at Grange as now largely anonymous memorials, they can probably be taken, like that at Ardstraw from which the name of John Craford can be extracted in slanting sunlight, as memorials to those who had emerged as a gentry tenant class – which could afford them – on the plantation estates. It is worth noting too, because these are in areas of Scottish plantation, that the standardised English spelling 'here' has replaced the Scots 'heir' of 1630 by the end of the seventeenth century. The prominence of the symbols on these stones might well be an indicator of the traumatic effect of the recent Jacobite war.

The 1680s stone at Old Donagheady (plate 13.6) deserves individual comment. From it the surname Hamilton may have been detected in the correct light, and if the last number in the date were 9, then this could be a stone to the Rev. John Hamilton, who had died in Derry towards the end

Plate 13.7 Gravestone to John(?) Craford, 1701 or 1761, Ardstraw graveyard

of the siege.[29] A Presbyterian, he had been arrested for non-conformity as minister of Donagheady in 1663 after the Restoration had brought back Episcopalianism, to be ejected and replaced shortly thereafter by an Episcopalian conformist of the same surname and to whom the stone might also refer, though he had been promoted elsewhere.[30] The position of the stone indicates burial outside the church, which was a practice the leaders of the reformation in Scotland had from the start, re-affirmed by decree of the General Assembly there in 1688, particularly sought to inculcate.[31] Here the stone is placed, however, as near as possible to the east gable of the church so as to touch it, but on the outside. It is also placed on east-west

Plate 13.8 Gravestone with mortality symbols, Grange graveyard

axis, though with the lettering of inscription and *memento mori* facing westwards towards the church gable, not only was the visual effect impaired for the observer, but unless the body had been buried in reverse order to the inscription, he would not rise up, as this practice intended, to face the returning Christ at the Second Coming. In all, there is much that suggests a clergyman attuned to Scotland here, and the Rev. John Hamilton's will, made on 1 June 1689, in which he sought to provide for the education of his son and daughter there, at either Glasgow or Hamilton, shows his own close cultural links to the Scottish lowlands.[32] The symbols on this stone dominate its west end. Although one is weathered to the point of

Plate 13.9 Gravestone with mortality symbols, Grange graveyard

uncertainty, most can still be read clearly enough: the open Bible with foliage on either side, a bell with clapper over-written with *Memento Mori*, a key, a skull and crossed bones, an hour glass, and possibly a crook.

Unlike this one, the symbols on the Grange and Ardstraw stones are more towards the tops. None has the open Bible, which may have been reserved for clergy or members of their families. However at Grange a religious bell with handle appears on all three, with the handle curving on one as if in motion. Skulls, one reversed, and crossed bones are on all three also, as are coffins. In addition a spade and an hourglass are both on two, while one has a grave-like hollow cut out on it.

Plate 13.10 Mortality symbols on gravestone, Grange graveyard

The Old Drumragh stone, outside Omagh, here just with skull and crossed bones and *Memento Mory* (sic), now lowered, too, to its east end which is placed within the church but at the back of it, reading eastwards, provides an example of church burial. The inscription on the part illustrated here (plate 13.11), in reverse orientation (to a person Stewart, a probable descendant, who died in 1818), does not refer to the original interment, but the right one is now hard to read. Depending on its date, the stone had either been placed in the church before a new one had been built in Omagh itself some time in the earlier eighteenth century,[33] or soon after the church had been replaced. The former is more likely.

Plate 13.11 Mortality symbols, memento mori and later inscription
on part of gravestone, Old Drumragh church

In the Fintona region, an area of English-owned plantation, early
seventeenth-century colonisation had been much less intense than
elsewhere, leaving the Gaelic Irish in occupation of a good deal of land.[34]
Coinciding roughly with the building works carried out at Fintona by the
Eccles family, the parish priest had a new 'Masshouse' erected for his own
parish sometime before 1714. This was the direct ancestor of the present
Catholic church. A Presbyterian meeting-house must also have been in
existence by this time. The memorial at Old Donaghcavey, outside Fintona
(plate 13.12), all the more impressive because it is a very striking tablestone,
elevated on six well-worked supports and outside the east end of the
church, commemorates that parish priest. It demonstrates that the basic
core of mortality symbols crossed the ethnic divide. It also demonstrates a
capacity to expend money on a monument more lavishly than that involved
in the others discussed in this section. On this tablestone the carved
decoration is centrally placed. The inscription, in English, contemporary
to it is above and is now entirely illegible to the eye, while below another
is added, in a poorer hand, to a 'Hew' or Henry O'Neill who had died

either in 1763 or 1703. It is an indication of the weathering process in action that Fr P. Ó Gallachair had been able to read it clearly in the late 1960s, as a memorial to Fr Laughlin O'Neill 'priest of this parish, who departed this life 3rd January Anno Domini 1719, aged 70 years'. He had been ordained by Archbishop Oliver Plunkett in 1674 and he may well have derived from that O'Neill segment which, prior to plantation, had established their power in this area by about 1450. The ornament shows clearly a skull, crossed bones and coffin, to which are added circling hands raised up either in prayer (a posture, that of 'lifting up holy hands' to pray, for which there is New Testament Pauline injunction) with an hour glass between them or, if between them a chalice were intended, which is very much less likely, than raised to elevate it. It is above all those hands raised in prayer and the fact that it is a priest's tomb and a tablestone which give this memorial, an example of early eighteenth century workmanship, its very special quality.[35]

Finally, a group of memorials (plates 13.13–14) placed upright on a graveyard wall in Old Leckpatrick derive their positioning from Scottish precedent. Beginning with one of 1671 and all to members of the Sinclair clerical family, they are enclosed by a later low wall and railing. Here is, then, an Edinburgh Greyfriars cemetery in the making, begun by that family but not followed by others, or merely just in scale with Ulster rural proportions. With a Scottish appearance to boot, the symbols here must derive also from Scottish practice; for example, the bell, or dead bell, though found all over Scotland is most frequent in the north-east, where the Sinclairs originated.[36] Along with the basic core of symbols, the open Bible and the tree of knowledge with a serpent can be seen on these stones. One, also, has a framing architectural element, now lost on one side. Perhaps these pillars were simply intended to convey that the Sinclairs were building anew in Ulster, or – as intimators of immortality – that they had gone to mansions in heaven.

By mid-eighteenth century the skulls and crossed bones, as at Clogher, no longer in high relief and now generally alone, akin to those of contemporary England, tend, if they appear at all, to have a more restrained place on gravestones. Although skulls and crossed bones can survive, outside the county, to the middle of the nineteenth century, in Tyrone itself the cautionary phrases alone (without the symbols), sometimes in Latin and sometimes in English, can be found to recur towards the end of the century.[37] The growth of literacy, as well as refinement, probably meant that the symbols could disappear, but the sentiments may possibly have gained renewed currency from the return once again of troubled times. However, *Memento Mori* alone (with a cross and no symbols) appears in

Plate 13.12 Ornament on tablestone to Fr Laughlin O'Neill, Old Donaghcavey graveyard

Plate 13.13 Part of a Sinclair monument, Old Leckpatrick graveyard

Plate 13.14 Part of a Sinclair monument, 1671, Old Leckpatrick graveyard

Old Leckpatrick in the 1720s and as 'Remember death' (in translation) in the same place as late as 1806.[38]

These mortality symbols also appeared on the two large mural church monuments discussed earlier. On the Sinclair one, however, an angel (or angel head), which is an immortality symbol, denoting the soul in flight, is poised spectacularly on the family arms on top, with another angel head in the aedicule beneath the arms. Since an angel is an image, forbidden in the sixteenth century, it is clear that by now, at least in the Episcopalian tradition, art had overcome theology, and that the strict early-Protestant prohibition of images – here to avoid angelolatry – was simply overlooked. Thus the angel had flown back into Anglican art here in Tyrone at the end of the seventeenth century. A winged cherub, or angel of lesser rank, on its own graces the pediment on the Abercorn(?) memorial erect in its mausoleum in Old Leckpatrick, where the structure itself was left unroofed perhaps as a conceit of openness to heaven. Another angel head of oriental appearance, surrounded by the moon and the stars, forms part of the Kyle monument of 1759 at Castlederg.

Angels, cherubs and crosses: the later eighteenth century

Somewhat of a transition in carving can begin to be detected from about the middle of the eighteenth century, though it must be remembered that many stones at all times had merely verbal inscriptions. Another important point seems to be that memorials to Catholics are also by now much more numerous, and with elements of differentiation on them which distinguish them from Protestant ones. Cherubs or angel heads, sometimes with

Plate 13.15 Headstone to Bryan McCauell (d. 1741), Old Drumragh graveyard

crosses, sometimes without them, can now be seen in many places. Suns also appear. Crosses, sometimes linked with I.H.S., are a noteworthy feature of Catholic memorials, while their absence from Protestant ones shows that Protestant unease with the cross had become conventionalised, the 'thing itself' to be preferred to the 'sign' of it. Headstones, which are no more than recumbent gravestones in erect posture, also become more common from now, allowing, in special instances, of ornamentation on both sides.

Plate 13.16 Headstone to John McGirr, younger (d. 1770), Clogher Cathedral graveyard

Just a few are illustrated here, because the graveyard sculpture of the later eighteenth century deserves a full study.

A 1741 headstone (plate 13.15) piously hugging the outside of the east end of the old medieval Drumragh church, itself by now probably disused and, it may be added, some 69 ft. by 28 ft. in external dimensions, seems to be a good example to take for the beginning of these transitions. To Bryan McCauell, and erected after his death, aged twenty-two, on 21 April 1741,

Plate 13.17 Headstone to Francis Kane (d. 1792), Ardstraw graveyard

its inscription, in English (possibly in itself a landmark of some kind in the process whereby the Irish had learned English from the English and Scottish settlers), reads at the end, where it says 'John McCauell caused me to be medd', as if it had been translated from the old Latin phrase of the past, *me fieri fecit*, by which the patron's name had been for so long inscribed into the memorial. But it is the carving on it, coming as it does from the time of 'great frost' and famine of 1740–41,[39] that gives it its importance. Here is an old mortality symbol, the hour glass, alongside a cross – purely religious – (though not a crucifix), onto which, above, an I.H.S. is joined.

Just two more examples, both Catholic, may be taken to mark a change in mood in the later eighteenth century: one from Clogher and one from Ardstraw. The first (plate 13.16), by a carver of great skill and lightness, of whose work other examples can be found in this cathedral graveyard, is of very special quality. It is to John McGirr the younger who died in 1770. On the inscription side and above it, are two angel heads with a tree between, above which are two kneeling figures with hands raised in prayer, with beside one an I.H.S. joined with a cross. On each side of the inscription are birds bearing branches, representing the dove which brought back the sprig of olive to Noah's ark, and a symbol of the making of God's peace with man. There are figures on the edges and across the top, and on the reverse of the stone, below an armorial element, stand Adam and Eve on either side of the tree in the Garden of Eden. Workmanship of more common appearance at this time can be seen in the 1792 headstone (plate 13.17) to Francis Kane at Ardstraw.

Conclusion

These memorials deserve study for many reasons. In terms of cultural and intellectual history, they indicate the flow of ideas in the society of their time. Also, although untended decay as well as destruction warn against using what survives, without qualification, as a means of assessing the standards of taste and skill in that society, best done anyhow along with all other indicators, a full study of what does remain is essential, so that an effort to do just that can be attempted.[40] Some policy of curation and protection for monuments for this period, and for old churches, should also be worked out.

Acknowledgements

I am particularly grateful to Walter Baumann whose very fine photographs (with the exception of that of the Algeo plaque which is by Brian Lacey) are reproduced here. What value this chapter has may lie more in the photographs than in the text of which they are the source. The photographs were printed by Gillian Coward of the University of Ulster and Brian Hobson of Warminster, Wilts. I would like to thank all those who over many years went with me on search expeditions, to discover that graveyards enjoy no sanctuary against rainfall. I am most grateful to Joanne Taggart for producing the typescript and to the editor and publisher for some little indulgence in the matter of the deadline. I also want to thank Frank D'Arcy for three or four hours of his superb Latin.

[1]   My interest in this began about twenty years ago, but then the aim was to assess workmanship and mentality just down to 1641.

[2]   County of Huntingdon and Peterborough Record Office, certificate on Abercorn estates, 1622; *Cal. Pat. Rolls Jas I*, p. 307; BL, Add. MS 4770, ff 90v, 95v.

[3]   D. Love, *Scottish kirkyards* (London, 1989), p. 52.

[4]   C. Daniell, *Death and burial in medieval England. 1066–1550* (London, 1997), pp 196–202; S. Michalski, *The Reformation and the visual arts* (London, 1993), passim.

[5]   Old Leckpatrick graveyard, Macgee gravestone, 1618.

[6]   E. Buchanan, 'Note', in *Ulster Journal of Archaeology*, 1st series 4 (1856), pp 272–3.

[7]   M. Perceval-Maxwell, *The Scottish migration to Ulster in the reign of James I* (London, 1973), pp 325–7, 344–6.

[8]   PRONI, T 544; NLI, MS 8014/ix; BL, Add. MS 4770, f. 94v.

[9]   NLI, Ormond deeds, D 3753 and D 3793.

[10] *Cal. S.P. Ire., 1625–32*, pp 509–13. For more detail see R.J. Hunter (ed.), *The plantation in Ulster in Strabane barony Co. Tyrone* c. *1600–41* (NUU, Derry, 1982). I would like to thank Louise Yeoman for her advice on Scotland.

[11] Anthony Blunt, *Artistic Theory in Italy, 1450–1600* (Oxford, 1978), pp 103–36.

[12] For a discussion of the impact of those liturgical changes in Madrid see Carlos M.N. Eire, *From Madrid to purgatory: the art and craft of dying in sixteenth century Spain* (Cambridge, 1995).

[13] I would like to thank Dr Nigel Llewellyn of the University of Sussex for providing me, in correspondence in 1987, with this part of the description. Ian Fisher told me about another Scottish crucifixion of about the same date which is in the painted gallery in Provost Skene's House in Aberdeen.

[14] P. Thoby, *Le crucifix des origines au concile de Trente* (Nantes, 1959), passim.

[15] Emile Male, *L'art religieux après le concile de Trente* (Paris, 1932), pp 270–2. Cardinal Bellarmine (d. 1621) argued for four nails on the grounds of returning to former practice since he had seen the four-nail version in manuscripts in the royal library in Paris, while Toletus went back further to argue that the four soldiers who divided Christ's garments amongst them at the crucifixion had themselves driven in four nails. On the other hand, Francisco Suarez (d. 1617) thought the problem insoluble and Molanus felt that artists should be allowed their liberty on this point.

[16] *The antient and present state of the county of Down* (Dublin, 1744), pp 50–1.

[17] G. Hill (ed.), *The Montgomery manuscripts, 1603–1706* (Belfast, 1869), pp 77, 346–7.

[18] On the Dunbar monument see G. Donaldson, 'The Dunbar monument in its historical setting' in *Dunbar parish church, 1342–1987* (Dunbar, 1987), pp 1–16.

[19] NAI, Lodge MS V, 302–3.

[20] PRONI, D 1048/1.

[21] A. Rowan, *The buildings of Ireland: North west Ulster* (Harmondsworth, Middlesex, 1979), p. 295.

[22] RCB, Library, Dublin, MS GS 2/7/3/33.

[23] J.B. Leslie, *Clogher clergy and parishes* (Enniskillen, 1929), pp 67, 169, 272.

[24] G.D. Burtchaell and T.U. Sadlier (eds), *Alumni Dublinenses* (Dublin, 1935), p. 256.

[25] On Sinclair see J.B. Leslie, *Derry Clergy and Parishes* (Enniskillen, 1937), pp 133, 136, 254; on Sinclair and Hollyhill see J. Dooher, 'Hollyhill' in W.H. Crawford and R.H. Foy (eds), *Townlands in Ulster* (Belfast, 1998), pp 194–5.

[26] I wish to thank Frank D'Arcy, sometime of the University of Ulster, for this fine translation of my transcript of the text.

[27] D. Howarth, *Images of rule; art and politics in the English renaissance, 1485–1649* (London, 1997), pp 29–34.

[28] C. Platt, *King death: the black death and its aftermath in late-medieval England* (London, 1996), is a wide ranging discussion. Finbar McCormick, 'The symbols of death and the tomb of John Forster in Tydavnet, Co. Monaghan' in *Clogher Record* 11 (1983), pp 273–86, is the seminal article in the Ulster context.

[29] C.D. Milligan, *History of the siege of Londonderry* (Belfast, 1951), p. 320.

[30] Richard L. Greaves, *God's other children: Protestant nonconformists and the emergence of denominational churches in Ireland, 1660–1700* (Stanford, California, 1997), pp 86, 143, 196; J.B. Leslie, *Derry clergy and parishes* (Enniskillen, 1937), p. 191.

[31] D. Love, *Scottish Kirkyards* (London, 1989), p. 37.

32   PRONI, T808/6461. There was however a view that a clergyman should rise up facing his congregation.

33   Leslie, *Derry clergy and parishes*, p. 212.

34   This emerges from the 1666 hearth money roll (PRONI, T307A, pp 225, 256–7).

35   P. O Gallachair, *Old Fintona: a history of the Catholic parish of Donaghcavey in County Tyrone* (Monaghan, 1974), pp 68–72, 87–9, 99. The tablestone need not necessarily have been made just immediately after the priest's death. It does not bear an I.H.S. The N.T. reference, which I owe to Trevor Temple, is to I Tim. 2, 8.

36   D. Love. *Scottish Kirkyards* (London, 1989), p. 72.

37   S. and D. Todd, *Register of gravestone inscriptions in Grange burial ground, Strabane* (privately printed L'derry, 1993), pp 22, 31–2, 47, 58, 59, 71, 76–7. I have benefited greatly from this erudite listing when discussing the gravestones at Grange.

38   S. and D. Todd, *Register of gravestone inscriptions in Leckpatrick old Burial ground, Artigarvan, Strbane*. (L'derry, 1991), pp 8, 56.

39   On this, and on the fire in Omagh in May 1741, see D. Dickson, *Arctic Ireland: The extraordinary story of the great frost and forgotten famine of 1740–41* (Belfast, 1997) The measurements of the Old Drumragh church are from a survey done by myself and Aine Howard in May 1991. This parish church, substantial, not very large, built without a chancel, may well have been erected under O'Neill patronage. With the extension of the reformation to Ulster at the time of plantation, these churches came into Protestant use, although the plan had been that a new church should be built at each plantation centre. That happened, indeed, in a few cases of which Newtownstewart may well have been one. New Church of Ireland churches, perhaps just a little larger than the medieval ones, for example at Castletown, Fintona, were in some cases built within the towns as they grew from about the early eighteenth century. For the Catholics, the 'Masshouse' outside Fintona, also of this period, is an early one (although some were built in Ulster in the earlier seventeenth century) in the history of the building of Catholic 'chapels'. Presbyterian 'meeting houses' began from the later seventeenth and early eighteenth centuries. The spelling 'medd' in the inscription is North of England and Scots dialect.

40   Studies are underway by Finbar McCormick and Amy Harris. William Roulston has published a list of inscriptions in *Familia*, 14 (1998). For a general overview see Brian P. Kennedy and Raymond Gillespie (eds), *Ireland: Art into history* (Dublin and Colorado, 1994), pp 155–68.

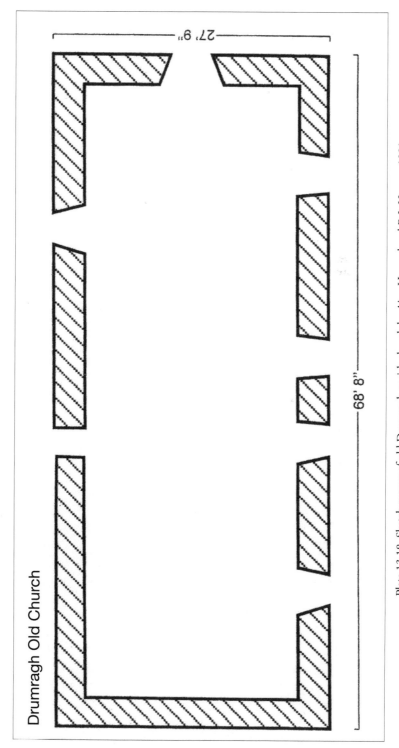

Plate 13.18 Sketch survey of old Drumragh parish church by Áine Howard and R.J. Hunter, 1991. This substantial late medieval church c. 1400–1500 was built without tower or chancel

14

Ulster Plantation Towns, 1609–41

Although there were urban aspects to various colonising schemes in Ireland in the second half of the sixteenth century, the plantation in Ulster in the six escheated counties of Cavan, Fermanagh, Donegal, Derry, Tyrone and Armagh was the first with proposals. The plan in 1609 stated that twenty-five incorporated towns should be established, to the corporations of which, quantities of land should be assigned, townsmen of unspecified number to be recruited by 'levy or press' in England. Most of the locations proposed were places of longstanding political importance where in many instances castles had recently been occupied or small fortifications established. Many of these were also monastic centres. A smaller group, Armagh, Raphoe and Clogher, were based on surrounding areas of episcopal land. The significance of a further three, indicated by their names, Mountjoy, Mountnorris and Charlemont, derived from the forts recently established there. Indeed entirely new foundations were to be few – essentially two, a town midway between Kells and Cavan to provide an extra link with Dublin and one midway between Lisgoole and Ballyshannon presumably to take advantage of the Erne.[1]

The choice of predominantly traditional sites, not surprisingly in view of their changed circumstances, was, however, to present problems. Many were based on small contiguous areas of monastic termon and erenagh or episcopal land, all land which did not form part of the forfeited temporal land, and which was coming into the hands of local army officers independently of the plantation conditions or which was to be granted to the bishops simultaneously with the plantation.[2] In addition, a few of these and the newly established forts had already had areas of land allocated to them in support of the forts.[3] It would only be if additional land were granted (and it was not) or if these new owners were bought out that urbanising arrangements could be made, and it was really only at Derry, based on ecclesiastical land that had come into the hands of Sir Henry Docwra, military governor of Lough Foyle and incorporated in 1604 as a place 'fit to be made both a town of war and a town of merchandize', that new English urban beginnings of any scale had been made.[4]

The compensation of prior interests was an essential implication of the arrangement made with the city of London by the English privy council for the colonisation of the entire county of Londonderry in January 1610. Accordingly, the city was granted a notional 4,000 acres at Derry and 3,000 at Coleraine and was required to build at the former place 200 houses and leave space for a further 300 with corresponding figures of 100 and 200 for Coleraine.[5] But these were special arrangements made some months before final plans for the plantation as a whole were concluded. More interesting from the point of view of the plantation in the remaining five counties, which was to be based on grants of land to individuals, was the last minute arrangement made in July, when it had already been decided that tradesmen would not be 'pressed out of England to inhabit the towns',[6] for building and settling the town of Belturbet in the English undertakers' barony of Loughtee in County Cavan.[7] This, although the details cannot be precisely recovered owing to, the destruction of the relevant London privy council records, was an attempt to forge a device for joint operations by the individual landowners in that barony. Essentially, the town land was granted to a neighbouring undertaker, Stephen Butler, but the other undertakers were to build and live there, or procure freeholders, on sites to be allocated, presumably, by Butler. They should also build a church. Related to this was a privy council order whereby Sir Francis Rushe and his wife should be compensated for their rights in the castle of Belturbet and lands and fishings.[8] This imaginative effort to insert a co-operative element into a colony based on individual planters may have been intended as a model but there is no evidence of its being attempted with any other group of undertakers, English or Scots. Instead London's instructions to Dublin on 1 August merely transferred responsibility: the lord deputy and council should arrange for 'peopling' the towns 'so far as the means of the country will yield' and when forty houses and families were attained they should be incorporated.[9]

Thereafter matters proceeded more slowly The lord deputy and plantation commissioners distributed the forfeited land to its grantees in an Ulster tour in August and September, but land was allocated to only one town, Cavan, a small established Irish town incorporated in November and the only town corporation to actually receive the town lands.[10] Indeed some corporation land was silently allotted to other owners – notably in Fermanagh where endowments for three proposed towns were reduced to sufficient for only one – or allocated in inconvenient places.[11] However by the end of the year the Dublin government had come up with an expedient (already adopted in a lease made in October of the town lands for Lifford to the local military commander, Sir Richard Hansard, on condition that he should assign plots for houses to sixty people[12]) agreed to by London in the spring of 1611: the lands intended for the corporations should be granted to a local undertaker or with conditions for urban development.[13]

Later in 1611 the number of proposed incorporations was reduced to eighteen.[14]

Land grants to patrons or superintendents were ultimately made, mainly in 1612, for only eight places – Dungannon and Augher in Tyrone, Lifford, Donegal, Rathmullan and Killybegs in Donegal, Enniskillen in Fermanagh and Virginia in Cavan.[15] Thus only in these places, along with Derry, Coleraine and Belturbet, were formal urbanising conditions laid down. The minimum size of settlement now prescribed in these grants was also a reduced one: the grantee should procure within four years twenty persons 'English and Scotch and chiefly artificers and mechanics' who should be burgesses of the town when incorporated, though 'cottagers and other inferior inhabitants' were also envisaged.[16] The town should be built 'in streets and squares, in such manner and form as shall best suit with [its] site and situation, and for the defence and decency of the said town'.[17] He should 'build or cause to be built ... twenty burgages or houses of stone or framed timber according to the form of building usual in England',[18] and allocate two acres each to ten of these and one acre each to the remainder in an area to be known as the 'burgage field', houses and lands to be held forever in fee farm. If the houses were built by the landlord he should charge rent at the rate of 10 per cent of the sum expended; if built by the tenant (this option was available) then the ten with two acres should pay 5s, the others 2s 6d per annum.[19] Normally he should allocate sites for a church and churchyard, a marketplace and a public school and, occasionally, for a gaol or prison. The amount of land to be employed to the uses of the town, its site, the burgesses acres and a common, did not generally exceed one-quarter or one-third of the notional acreage allocated to the patron.

The process of incorporation, followed speedily, so that by 1613 fourteen places, excluding two, Virginia and Rathmullan, for which land grants had been made and including Strabane, not originally proposed for incorporation, had received charters, later to be extended, with Killybegs and Clogher, to sixteen. However these incorporations were part of a wider move to create forty 'new boroughs', whose charters should follow regulations sent from London in September 1612, hence urban planning in plantation Ulster was merged with a scheme of borough-making throughout Ireland which was in part a tactic of parliamentary management. The corporations were generally made up of thirteen members, were empowered to fill their own vacancies and had a limited income, since they did not receive grants of the town lands.[20]

Any attempt to view the corporate towns as a whole in this period is severely restricted by problems of sources. Municipal records (apart from a few deeds) and subsidy rolls do not survive; landlord's accounts are scant.

Furthermore the superficial completeness of the principal sources used for the study of the plantation as a whole, the series of government surveys between 1611 and 1622 and the muster of 1630, is in fact deceptive. The depositions of 1641, while they offer little on towns which did not surrender in 1641 such as Derry and Enniskillen, are not sufficiently numerous to provide more than valuable supplementary material on other towns. In the absence of standard sources a number of oblique (and somewhat discontinuous) approaches have been adopted.

The upper limits of urbanisation can be seen in the four towns of Derry, Coleraine, Strabane and Armagh. At Derry within the walls some 215 stone and slated houses (though considered inadequate in size) had, by 1616, been built by the Irish Society, the body appointed by the city of London to manage its Ulster affairs, about, 25 more being built by private individuals.[21] A rental in 1628 indicates 265 houses apart from suburban growth outside the walls which was already underway by 1616.[22] The location of this and an indication that its scale was not inconsiderable emerges from partially surviving agreements for leases in 1639.[23] At Coleraine 116 houses had been built by the Irish Society by 1616. However some were built of timber, others of 'loam and lime' and were decaying 'by reason of the bleakness of the weather' so that already remedial slating was necessary. By 1622, 80 additional privately built houses had been erected, some in response to a premium of £20 per house and favourable rents offered by the Londoners.[24] At Strabane, on a site somewhat removed from Turlogh Luineach O'Neill's former castle, the town built by 1619 'about' the castle of its Scottish undertaker landlord, James, Earl of Abercorn, consisted of some 80 houses, 'a great many of them ... of lime and stone' others of timber and had 'above' 100 by 1622. It seems almost certain that at least some 30 of these houses, held by freeholders, had been built by the earl.[25] This descending scale is reflected in the muster returns of adult male residents in 1630, some 500, 300 and 208 respectively.[26] Two factors would seem to account for the growth of these larger settlements – energetic landlord sponsorship especially in house building and favourable geographical location for sea-borne trade. In sharp distinction to these three towns Armagh, like Cavan but perhaps twice as large and having an English corporation and episcopal landlord, initially retained its essential Irish character. Of 123 houses held from the archbishop in 1618, four fifths, described in 1622 as 'cottages ... let yearly to the natives' were in Irish occupation. An elaborate building lease scheme initiated by the archbishop in 1615 for the 'replanting and re-edifying of the decayed city' whereby the tenant would undertake to erect a two-storeyed house, of specified dimensions, to be built of brick or stone and timber 'according to the form of English houses and buildings' did not generate wide interest. Yet here, as also in Cavan, a settler element grew which could muster ninety males for the town and surrounds in 1630.[27]

Urban growth at the other places rarely exceeded some thirty to forty houses, while in a few cases it did not reach the minimum of twenty stipulated in the patronage grants. Lifford, at the upper end of this scale, developed around a royal fort on land held by the English servitor Sir Richard Hansard, had at least 54 houses by 1622 (of which 21 had been built by Hansard as early as 1611) and so presumably a male population of about 100.[28] Enniskillen with some 60 adult males in *c*. 1630 and where a careful town building plan in relation to the royal fort had been worked out, may probably be taken as the typical inland plantation town.[29] Town growth was in fact vulnerable to the fortunes of the town patrons. This is obvious at the lower end of the scale. Virginia underwent a number of changes of ownership, eluded incorporation and only had about 19 male inhabitants by the 1630s.[30] The 'new town' of Killybegs had only some 17 'British and Irish inhabitants' in 1622. Here the patron Roger Jones was constable of Sligo, his right to the town lands was disputed by the bishop of Raphoe and the town was later disposed of to a local Scottish undertaker, the Earl of Annandale.[31] For the most of the period the bishops did not live at Clogher.[32] It is tempting to suggest that too many of the towns were granted to servitors who did not have an immediate English or Scottish background from which to draw settlers. Certainly, at some towns set in servitors' areas (for example Virginia), where the landlords generally were not required to introduce settlers, growth was smallest. This applies to some extent to Ballyshannon, a servitor town (like Donegal) essentially of 'Irish houses' lived in by 'soldiers for the most part and some few Irish' and set in an exceptional area of the plantation, the barony of Tirhugh, where the settler colony achieved was a sparse one.[33] An important consideration was whether the landlord built houses or availed of the option of the building lease. At Augher the latter took place and growth there was relatively small.[34] Also, it would be wrong to suggest that the towns had entirely stable populations: there seems to have been both movement out of the towns and between towns.[35]

Population figures cited so far refer only to British adult males. Plantation regulation only expressly forbad the leasing of town land to Irish, though a clause in a lease of a house in Enniskillen made in 1634 by the then provost, Gerald Wiggen, stipulating that the tenant should not 'alien set or let the aforesaid premises … unto any of the mere Irish nation' suggests that a wider exclusion was intended.[36] There was, however, a small Irish element in the population of many of the towns, not just in Armagh and Cavan where up to 1641 settlers were probably a minority. Irish residents in Dungannon were a significant minority; the name of Farrell O'Reilly, tobacco merchant, of Belturbet survives.[37] At Derry there were two priests in the parish in 1631 and the prior of the Dominicans there had a silver chalice made in 1640.[38] Not only were there some Irish householders within the walls, but the suburbs housed a settler and seemingly also an Irish population of considerable size. Roger Markham who was ironmaster to Sir Thomas Staples of Lissan, who had been leaseholder of the bishop's land in the immediate vicinity of the city, stated in his deposition in February 1642: 'It had been often desired by my master and others that they would put the Irish out of Derry which we heard they did, 300 men in one day and pulled down the suburbs'.[39]

Urban growth of this scale need not be surprising. The plantation plan had set a realistic target of some 5,000 adult males for the plantation as a whole.[40] This was in fact well surpassed and towns had grown proportionally. However the plan also militated against substantial concentrated urban growth by prescribing a settlement pattern to be based on landlord villages on each undertaker's estate. The kind of settlement, pattern that did emerge was in fact a compromise varying from estate to estate between dispersed and village settlement. While many villages were smaller than ten houses, some, for example Lurgan, Lisnaskea, Letterkenny, Ramelton and Rathmullan, were of forty and above.[41] Only if the Belturbet arrangement had been somehow adapted, after the model agreed with the Londoners for Derry and Coleraine, perhaps to promote one town per county, might comparable systematic urban development have taken place in the other counties. Also the quantities of land granted to the town patrons (for example 730 statute acres to Captain William Cole for Enniskillen, some 1,297 acres to Captain John Ridgeway for Virginia) were minute in comparison to the amount of land (29,900 acres) held by the Irish Society in relation to Derry and Coleraine, and were in fact no larger than the allocations (for example 1,552 acres in County Armagh, 917 in Cavan) made available for the county schools.[42] The income from land of that quantity (some £60 per annum from the Augher lands)[43] was not sufficient to encourage a town patron to expend money in house building (twenty houses built by Sir Arthur Chichester at Dungannon may well have cost close to £100 each)[44] or in promoting immigration. Nevertheless, although the circumstances were very different, urban growth in the Ulster plantation compared favourably with its counterpart in colonial Virginia where what initial town growth there had been declined, and in the later colony of Maryland where by the 1670s the capital, St Mary's City, contained at most, eighteen buildings.[45] The most fruitful comparison (religious matters aside) is probably between the two ports of Derry and Boston both with populations of between 1,000 and 2,000 by 1640 and some similarities in structure.[46] However, although the term town was applied to them by contemporaries, by English seventeenth-century standards most of the plantation towns were no larger than the average village with a population of less than 200. Comparison with the average English market town, with a population of about 1,000, should be restricted to the few larger towns. Even Derry must be regarded as 'micro-urban' in terms of one recent definition which would limit the term town in early modern England and Wales to settlements of 5,000 and above.[47]

The county towns fulfilled functions entirely independent of their size. After the plantation got underway, the assizes which had begun tentatively in Ulster a few years earlier, were held in the six county towns of Cavan, Enniskillen, Derry, Lifford, Dungannon and Armagh.[48] Also in Tyrone we have evidence that quarter sessions were held at Strabane (where a sessions house and prison, under the market cross, for the temporary custody of prisoners prior to their transfer to the king's gaol at Dungannon, had been erected), Augher and Dungannon; the arrangement which limited quarter sessions to Derry in the neighbouring county being probably exceptional.[49] Such county functions required public buildings. The allocation of sites for sessions houses and gaols was the responsibility of the town landlords, while their building was seen as a county responsibility. In August 1619 royal directions were issued for the erection of a sessions house and gaol in Armagh.[50] In moves not confined to Ulster counties the assize judges in 1619 and 1621 imposed fines on the county of Londonderry for failure to build a sessions house at Derry.[51] These pressures were not without effect. By 1622, £500 or £600 collected in Fermanagh and received by Sir William Cole had been expended in building a sessions house in Enniskillen and money had similarly been collected in County Cavan.[52] In Derry on the other hand a town hall costing at least £500 was erected by the Irish Society.[53] The sessions house in Dungannon erected between 1619 and 1622 at the charge of the county was of a crudely classical design. Timber-built, of 'extraordinary strong and curious cage work', supported by a 'rank of fair large turned pillars', it incorporated a market house on the ground floor. The gaol was a separate building, made of stone, battlemented, and with 'strong vaults' – though not escape-proof – while the sessions house and gaol in Armagh were both in the same building.[54] Such building within the towns was the visual representation of fundamental political change in the six escheated counties. But there were limits to institutional building. No Ulster plantation town had a privately endowed almshouse or a county sponsored house of correction such as were, at least, receiving active consideration in County Cork, at Bandon and Mallow respectively, in 1634.[55]

The most common ancillary building operations were of bridges, churches and mills. Thus the ford of 1613 at Belturbet had been replaced by the bridge of 1641. Cole built two bridges at Enniskillen prior to 1613, demolished, incidentally, by him in 1641. The building of a new bridge at Charlemont was, after debate in the privy council in 1627, made an inter-county responsibility; it had been erected by 1634.[56] But here too there were limits to achievement. Thus at the Tyrone assizes in 1636 Sir Arthur Leigh of Omagh was fined £15 because at the previous assizes he had been paid for building a bridge at Omagh which he had not done.[57] Although there was a bridge beside the mill at Strabane, river crossings at Lifford, Derry and Coleraine were served by ferries.[58] Road maintenance between the towns fell to the appropriate parishes, whose inhabitants were often fined for their remissness.[59] Church building, or rebuilding, proceeded, often slowly 'as in all works of that nature' by means which included landlord building (conspicuous at Derry where the crown provided bells) and the application of the recusants' fines.[60] The principal constraint on public works was inadequate urban income. Apart from Cavan, the corporations had not received grants of land by charter and such income as they had, for example from fairs and markets (themselves important but ill-documented urban functions), could not provide finance in any way appropriate to major operations. Thus when it was proposed to build a new quay at Derry in 1639, the building lease was the devise adopted. A consortium of leading townsmen undertook to expend £300 on the project.[61] Hence also only Derry and Coleraine were walled and so the defensive value of the towns was limited. Attempts were made to rectify this in later plantations, for example in Wexford where landholders were to pay by annual levy or cotization for the walling of Newborough (Gorey).[62] Nevertheless, the government, for reasons of economy, disposed of the inland forts in Ulster (and Connacht) around which a number of the towns were based, to the resident commanders, though under conditions of maintenance, in the early 1620s.[63]

Although it may be true of some of the smaller incorporated settlements that no 'course of corporation [was] observed' as Bishop Spottiswood, a hostile witness, asserted in the case of Augher, there is evidence, in the absence of all corporation books, that many of the town corporations did function with some continuity.[64] Thus what can be assembled of the succession of provosts of Strabane indicates that the members of the first nominated corporation of 1613 held the chief office in rotation amongst themselves as a closely-knit body.[65] The corporations of Enniskillen and

Belturbet obtained privy council orders in their favour in disputes with the town patrons, and Belturbet had a silver mace.[66] Sir Richard Hansard made financial provision for the corporation of Lifford by will.[67] The provosts, like those of Strabane, were normally justices of the peace and can sometimes be found like Sir John Vaughan, mayor of Derry, in 1627, engaged in routine matters of legal administration.[68] Yet when in 1629 Bishop Downham of Derry wished the provost of Strabane to take action likely to be unpopular with the landlord of the town he wrote also to the landlord ordering him not to obstruct the provost.[69] Internal order seems to have been the function of the constable – Letterkenny, for example, had a constable and stocks.[70] Townsmen were also subject to the control of the clerk of the market, an official concerned with the regulation of prices, weights and measures and standards, whose functions were given a new impetus in Ireland, as in England, at this time.[71] A record survives of fines inflicted by the deputy clerk of the market for County Tyrone at his sessions held at Stewartstown, Augher, Clogher and Omagh in January and February 1618.[72]

As centres for professional services – doctors, schoolmasters and lawyers – many of the towns played important roles. Medical practitioners can be, found at least in Derry and Strabane and possibly in Coleraine and Charlemont. In Derry two can be identified, a 'chirurgeon' and, almost certainly, a physician as householders in 1628. Four occur in the 1630s, three of them surgeons or 'barber chirurgeons'.[73] A prominent Chester apothecary, Robert Blease, appears as supplier: he despatched 'drugs', five boxes and one trunk of them, to Derry in January 1632.[74] By far the most distinguished of these Derry doctors was the physician Paul de Laune. Born in London, graduate of Cambridge, doctor of medicine in Padua in 1614, and Fellow of the College of Physicians of London in 1618, he was later in the 1640s professor of physic at Gresham College and appears to have died acting as physician general to the Cromwellian fleet at the taking of Jamaica in 1654.[75]

De Laune's period in Derry may have been relatively short, but James Miller, chirurgeon, died in Derry in 1655 which suggests he had practised there for some twenty years.[76] If some of these Derry practitioners may have come there as army surgeons – one of them, William Walter, re-appears in that capacity in 1642[77] – Strabane was ungarrisoned yet in 1629 it had its physician, Dr Berkeley, 'an apostate from the true religion', in the words of Bishop Downham: 'having masses and meetings of priests in his house … [and] seeking to pervert whom he can especially on their deathbeds'.[78] As early as July 1614 William Wiggs, 'chirurgion', travelled with 'apothecary drugs and waters for his use' on a ship bound for Coleraine from Chester.[79] Dr Hodges, conscripted, unsuccessfully to make gunpowder at Charlemont by Sir Philim O'Neill after the outbreak of the 1641 rising, must also have been a medical doctor.[80] A succession of schoolmasters served the county grammar schools located mainly in the county towns, each, except that in Derry, endowed with land as part of the plantation scheme, and there is evidence that buildings had been erected for these schools in at least a few towns. There is also evidence that schooling was not restricted to these centres. A schoolmaster at Stewartstown is recorded in 1622 and plans, at any rate, were being made to establish schools elsewhere, notably at Clogher and Lifford.[81] Lawyers may have been sparser: recorders (and a chamberlain) in Derry, Coleraine and Cavan are most conspicuous. However they carried out more functions than those purely of their office and may well have acted for litigants in the courts. Thus, Robert Goodwin, chamberlain of Derry, was also clerk of the peace for the county. Stephen Allen, king's attorney in Ulster, who lived in Cavan abbey, was not only recorder of the town and sovereign in 1641 but was also seneschal of thirteen manors in Counties Cavan, Fermanagh' and Armagh.[82]

When we seek to examine the hinterlands and trade of the towns as a whole, an element of guarded speculation must intrude. The hinterland, of Derry as a port can be shown, from identifiable destinations of imports, to have extended as far into Tyrone as Dungannon and to north-west Fermanagh. Strabane and presumably Lifford traded through it and there is ample evidence linking it with much of north Donegal. Its links in County Londonderry included Limavady and Desertmartin, yet the trade of Coleraine and its outports was also considerable.[83] Armagh (some what like Strabane in relation to Derry) was considered to be linked with Newry through Mountnorris and significantly some Drogheda merchants were amongst the first to build houses there.[84] Killybegs (and the west Donegal ports) had a seaborne trade of small proportions but was not a wide distributing centre. Thus while trade statistics in 1626 attribute some 12 per cent of Irish herring exports to Killybegs, its share in land-based exports, butter and tallow, was negligible.[85] Furthermore such traces of this off-shore fishing industry as have been located in English port books reveal no participation of local vessels, English or Scottish shipping being involved. Many of the cargoes are noted as having been 'taken and killed' with the master's 'own nets and boats at his own proper costs'. Imports from England were minute.[86] Statistics for the 1630s and 1640–41 reveal very small exports of hogshead staves and pipe staves, hides and linen yarn.[87] Customs returns, for what they are worth, were, in the 1630s, amongst the smallest for the country as a whole, about ¼ – ½ per cent of total returns.[88] Yet one local ship, the *Arthur* of Ballyshannon, which carried wine from Bordeaux in 1614–15 for Sir Henry Foliot, has come to light.[89] The three towns of Enniskillen, Belturbet and Cavan were, arguably, considerable centres of inland trade with boats in use at Enniskillen and Belturbet to avail of the navigational potential of the Erne.[90] Not only was there a carrying trade from County Cavan to Dublin and cattle were driven there from south Fermanagh,[91] but there is an accumulation of small pieces of evidence to link the trade of these three towns to Dublin also. Thus, for example, as early as 1612 a Belturbet merchant can be found importing goods from Liverpool through Dublin and the names of two Belturbet carriers in 1641 are recorded.[92] David Greer, one of a known group of Enniskillen merchants, exported yarn from Dublin to Liverpool in 1618.[93] In the 1630s a Dublin merchant and freeman of Cavan, John Gibson, became a major property owner in Cavan.[94] This attempt to set the towns in a regional context must, however, remain somewhat tentative.

The materials for occupational analysis are extremely restricted. The plantation surveys, when they reported on towns at all, referred only occasionally to occupations and then in very general terms. Scarcely more helpful is the pejorative description of the townsmen of Dungannon as 'shoemakers, saddlers and rascals' attributed to Patrick moder O'Donnelly in 1641.[95] Deeds and depositions provide occupations for only a minority of townsmen in the case of Lurgan, a large village on an English estate in Armagh, however, a uniquely complete list of 47 householders in 1622 (holding 59 houses) with their occupations, can be analysed. Apart from a large agricultural group of 27, 4 gentlemen, 14 yeomen and 9 husbandmen, representing 57.4 per cent of the names, 12 occupations are recorded, with coopers, joiners, turners and shoemakers represented more than once. Building trades, 1 carpenter and 1 mason, occupied only 4.3 per cent; the largest group, 16 or 34 per cent, being engaged in a number of simple manufacturing processes. Here 3 coopers, 4 joiners and 3 turners worked with wood, 2 shoemakers and 1 tanner with leather and in leather making, 1 weaver and 1 tailor in textiles, and there was 1 smith but no baker. Merchants and shopkeepers were represented by only 1 butcher (2.1 per cent); there was only 1 labourer (2.1 per cent), though perhaps more were sub-tenants. A miller can be inferred. The townsmen include two Irish names, a yeoman and a cooper. The tradesmen held areas of land also and were engaged in agriculture as well as providing services for the neighbourhood.[96] Other lists (surviving for Armagh and Tyrone) are less complete and concern smaller settlements. Of 30 leaseholders, 'indwellers of my town and certain land annexed to it dwelling about the church', listed by a Scot, Lord Ochiltree, also in 1622, for Stewartstown, 3 were gentlemen, 3 appear without occupation and 8 simply as tradesmen. Of the remaining 10 occupations, there were 3 butchers and 3 tailors, 2 weavers and 2 carpenters and 1 each of shoemakers, maltmakers, smiths, ditchers and quarriers as well as a schoolmaster.[97] A petition in 1622 'of the poor tradesmen' of Clogher for relief from payment of 'trades money' to the dean originated from 9 individuals, probably the leading townsmen: 2 merchants, a cordwainer, a weaver, a tailor, a cooper, a carpenter, a sadler and a butcher.[98] Trades at Benburb included a pointmaker and a cloth-maker.[99] Such a range of occupations is likely to represent the common core of pursuits in most of the small inland towns. Some more specialist crafts emerge by 1641, mainly from depositions: metal-workers (a brazier in Virginia, a gunsmith in Belturbet, a snapmaker in Strabane),[100] and others such as a feltmaker, a buttonmaker and a heel maker.[101] Such occupations may well have been more common. Innkeepers appear not only in county towns such as Armagh and Cavan, but also elsewhere.[102] Keepers of alehouses and winetaverns ('tap-houses' in Derry) were widespread.[103] While it is obvious that considerable allowance must be made for deficiency of sources, the wide range of manufactured goods which was imported tends to support the view that most towns must have had a fairly simple occupational structure.

The formation of a settler merchant and shopkeeping element in many of the towns, some of whom also held land on neighbouring estates, was a development of especial significance. Although merchants are not specifically mentioned in the landlord villages already examined, these were probably served, apart from pedlars and stalls at fairs and markets, by out-shops kept by merchants, such as that of John Gowrly, merchant of Armagh, at Loughgall.[104] The treatment which follows of the merchant class in Belturbet and Strabane, the one English the other Scottish, and of that in the port town of Derry, throws some light on the minimum size of the merchant community in three towns of average, large and largest population. It is not suggested that these provincial merchants had an exclusive control of trade – landowners sometimes traded in their own right; English and Scottish merchants operated through the ports; the role of merchants from the ports of Drogheda and Dundalk, while obscure, must have been considerable; old Irish merchants were important in Cavan and Armagh – but their presence represents a significant change in post-plantation society.

In Belturbet at the time of its occupation in 1641 there were, on the evidence of a deposition of February 1643–4, four principal merchants specified by name whose 'houses, shops and goods' were, it was alleged, after a division of 'all the merchants shops there' occupied by individual members of the O'Reilly leadership including Phillip McHugh, 'the rest of the shops (being all very rich)' having been shared amongst his followers.[105] The depositions of four Belturbet merchants (two from the suggested more substantial group and two others) taken earlier, on separate dates in 1642 offer some corroboration: the larger merchants claimed losses in 'wares' much higher than the others. Also one of the smaller merchants specified the commodities: 'wares in the shop vizt broadcloth, kersies, frizes, hops, iron, steel, stockings, tobacco' – goods similar though perhaps more limited in range to those being imported by other Ulster merchants of this period – which he valued at £300. The degree of exaggeration in claims is hard to determine – two of the larger merchants claimed for £500 and £900, but in the latter case his son-in-law gave a figure of £700. In all, the names of eight merchants from a town with thirty-four houses in 1622 but probably larger by 1641 have been recovered from these sources.[106]

At Strabane evidence of a different kind throws light on a larger group of merchants, Scottish in origin. Here seven of the twelve first burgesses of the town are also to be found trading in the surviving port books of Derry for 1612–15, along with at least one other Strabane townsman, David Morrison.[107] The names of four more Strabane merchants of this period, though nothing of their trading context, can also be recovered.[108] The commodities imported demonstrate that the merchants dealt in a wide range of goods, domestic, agricultural and industrial. Thus, for example, David Morrison imported on the *John* of Dumbarton in January 1615 goods as varied as soap, fat madder (used for dyeing), iron and wrought iron, brass pans, iron pots, lead, woollen and course linen cloth and aniseeds. Salt, including French salt (for the preparation of hides), was a significant import for industrial use, nets and ropes also appear 'for the fishings' The activities in the year 1614–15 of William Hamilton, who became a freeholder in the town in 1616 and later held one townland on the earl of Abercorn's estate as well,[109] illustrate the nature of the export trade. His total exports, in three consignments, were made up of 13½ dickers (135) of hides, 3 barrels and 2 hogsheads (i.e. 7 barrels) of beef, 1½ cwt of tallow, 6 barrels of oatmeal and 100 goat skins valued in total at £87.13.4. The destination of these goods, carried in Scottish ships, was Scotland, especially Glasgow and Renfrew. His imports were slighter: 3 half barrels of onions, 8 yards of grey cloth and ½ ton of salt. The career of Hugh Hamilton illustrates best that of the successful merchant with a considerable rural base. Born a third son in Lanarkshire, he was apprenticed in Edinburgh in 1603.[110] During the two years 3 October 1612 to 5 September 1614 he exported 'goods' valued at £215.10.0 to France and to Ayr in Scotland. His imports in the same period were made up of 79 tuns of French wines and 'goods' valued at £33.3.4. In 1615, when he was already living outside the town, he became a freeholder on the earl of Abercorn s estate, empowered to pay his rent (£6 stg per annum) either in money or merchandize – wine, pepper, loaf sugar and marmalade. He was also a freeholder on another estate in the Strabane barony. He was provost of Strabane in 1625.[111] By the time of his death in 1637 he had acquired interests in abbey land nearby, bequeathed, along with 'houses in Strabane', in his will.[112]

The investigation of the Strabane merchant community over a more extended period is hindered by intractable problems of sources. Some reconstruction can be made from English port books. Linen yarn was the principal commodity exported by two merchants, John Patterson and Hugh Kneeland, identified as Strabane townsmen in 1630,[113] to Chester in 1632.[114] The commodities imported in return illuminate the trade of the non-specialist merchant. Thus John Patterson's imports, in July, valued at over £40, included hardware (240 sickles and 12 lanthornes) and drapery.[115] James Gibb, provost of Strabane in 1630, brother-in-law of Hugh Hamilton and one of the executors of his will,[116] emerges in the 1630s as a merchant trading with both Chester and Bristol. From Chester he imported commodities such as Sheffield knives and nails along with cloth of varied type – northern kersey, cottons, broad cloth and northern dozens singles – and kersey stockings. His imports from Bristol, to which he (probably) exported, in 1618, tallow, beef, wool, skins, butter, salt, hides and white herrings, were apparently more specialised: 'parcels of wares', i.e. pottery, appear in 1637, conveyed in a Derry ship, the *Margaret*, which traded regularly with Bristol.[117] Clearly no broad conclusions can be based on such minutiae; without them, in the absence of all other sources, a sizeable Strabane merchant community would remain entirely obscure.

Against this general background, the unique scale of development at Derry becomes readily apparent.[118] Here an allocation of land to the townsmen, carried out in 1616 by commissioners appointed by the city of London, contrasting sharply with the potential of the superintendancy grants elsewhere, forms an element in a coherent town plan. The householder normally received in leasehold, for thirty-one years, two distinct pieces of land: an area of perches 'for gardens and orchards' in the immediate surrounds of the town outside the walls, and, separated by episcopal land,[119] an area of acres, usually six to twelve, in the liberties to the north.[120] These allocations came to 45 and 1,142 acres in nominal Irish measure.[121] Earlier, by 1614, the corporation as a body had been assigned a notional 1,500 acres (some 3,482 statute) to the south-west of the city which was successfully claimed as episcopal by the bishop in the 1630s but continued to be held under him in lease by the corporation.[122] The remainder of the notional 4,000 acres held by the Irish Society in the Derry liberties was leased in larger areas, some to pre-plantation servitors such as Sir John Vaughan, or allocated to the keeper of Culmore fort.[123]

This grander scale of urban organisation is reflected in the trade and occupational structure of the town. Although it had been disrupted by O'Doherty's rising in 1608, the Londoners not only inherited from Docwra's pre-plantation settlement a nucleus of townsmen including some who were to be amongst its most dynamic as merchants and shipmasters, but also its embryonic trade links with Scotland and with at least the English ports of Liverpool and Chester.[124] The port books of 1612 to 1615 reveal an established pattern of trade. It divides into three sections – Scottish, English and foreign European. In the year 1614–15 these three sectors appear to be represented by 44 per cent, 31 per cent and 25 per cent respectively of exported goods valued in total at £9,935. The port books show a growth in the total volume of Derry's trade, itself double that of Coleraine, over these three years.[125] They also indicate the size and character of the town's merchant class. Out of more than 100 people (excluding shipmasters), mostly English and Scottish merchants but also some local landowners, trading, some twenty Derry merchants can be identified.[126] Amongst them were the three most active merchants, themselves representative of important strands in the town's population – Jesse Smith, probably freeman of Chester in 1585, a pre-plantation settler in Derry who was made a member of the town corporation in 1613 and mayor in 1620.[127] George Hammond, of a family with London connections, who settled under the Londoners;[128] and John Power (or Poore) a Scot.[129] Smith and Hammond traded almost exclusively with Chester; Power added trade with Scotland to an extensive and largely export European trade with Bordeaux (whence he imported wine, sugar, whale bone and prunes), Dieppe, Bilbao and Rouen.[130] The merchant class in Derry was complemented by its ships and shipmasters, who usually traded in their own right. Seven ships (one a 'small boat of Lough Foyle') were already engaged actively in the trade of the town. In the year 1614–15 Derry shipping (including also *The Gift of God* of Strabane and the *Jannet* of Mongavlin) carried 18.5 per cent of total exports. The largest Derry vessel, the *Peter*, burthen 70 tons, of which the master Wybrand Olpherts, a Dutchman, later became a Donegal landowner,[131] was mainly engaged in importing timber ('meiborough deal') from Norway.

Mounting criticism of the County Londonderry plantation as a whole culminated in the forfeiture of the Londoners' patent and the appointment of commissioners in 1639 to make new leases on behalf of the crown.[132] Although severely damaged by fire, a substantial section of a book of entries of these agreements survives for Derry which, when taken in conjunction with other sources, indicates a much greater diversity of occupations than has been found elsewhere.[133] The following 25 trades, divided among 47 people, only some 10 per cent of the settler population, are recorded: tailors (5), bakers (4), butchers,[134] smiths and vintners (3 each), sadlers, joiners, coopers, feltmakers, chandlers, shoemakers and weavers (2 each) and one each of buttonmakers, tanners, winecoopers, victuallers, masons, fellmongers, brewers, beerbrewers, cutlers, glovers, glasiers, pewterers and slaters.

A merchant element of some twenty members which also emerges may well represent not much more than half their total numbers.[135] Some of these merchants, along with other townsmen, also held land. Thus Henry Finch, mayor in 1640[136] and a wine importer from France, not only released his house, 'near unto the market place', with other holdings in the town and liberties and acquired business interests which included a share in the operation of the ferry in 1639, but also held land on the Fishmongers' estate near Ballykelly.[137] Luke Ashe, a merchant prominent in the trade with Chester and an alderman, also owned a small area of land in County Donegal.[138] Both, while leading Derry townsmen with appropriate territorial ambitions, were representative figures in its trade. The existence in this period of a merchant fleet of at least eight ships, commonly of thirty tons burthen, has been established mainly from English port books.[139] These ships are likely to have employed some forty Derry seamen.[140] The trade of the town generated work for carmen, found in the 1630s, and labourers of various kinds, including porters who appear as mainly Irish in the parish register in the 1650s.[141] A tanhouse, held by Edward Rowley of Castle Roe, is the only specifically industrial premises to emerge in 1639.[142] Professional men included medical practitioners and civic officials, already noted, as well as clergy and a schoolmaster with whom may be linked a land surveyor (probably a by-employment) and various customs officials.[143] In sum, a wide range of some thirty-five occupations can be established. It is also worth noting that where evidence of literacy can be recovered sixty-four signed by name and twenty-three by mark in 1639.

In contrast to imports of extraordinary variety, the essential components in the export trade of Derry were basic agricultural products along with fish and, at least in the 1630s, timber.[144] Livestock products, hides, sheepskins, wool, beef and tallow; grain, especially oats and barley; linen yarn and salmon predominate in the early port books. With all port books before 1644 missing, trends in the nature and direction of the town's trade are difficult to establish. If Scottish trade declined until the late 1620s, all recorded exports (only three cargoes) in the period 25 March–29 September 1644 were to Scotland.[145] English port books suggest that the pattern established by 1615 in trade with England, principally with Chester, was sustained, and it also seems certain that the earlier European contacts were continued.[146] Imports in 1644 included, wine, vinegar and salt from France and timber (deal) from Norway.[147] In October 1637 Charles Moncke, surveyor-general of the customs, found at Derry 'more ships from foreign parts and England than in all the northern ports besides'.[148] A cargo of tobacco ('4,000 wt.' i.e. 2 tons), entered in September 1644 from Barbados, possibly a wartime stray, may provide a glimpse of a recent transatlantic dimension in trade.[149] If so, then the possibility of such trade, put forward in 1609 with reference to Newfoundland as an inducement to the Londoners,[150] had come to some fruition. Exports of at least linen yarn and wool appear to have expanded considerably by the 1630s.[151] To the more important question of the share of Derry in Irish trade as a whole the answer can only be approximate. Calculations based on customs returns for various half years between 1632 and 1635 and in 1641 place it in the range of from 3 per cent to just over 5 per cent.[152] In the light of these estimates, the document printed as Table II would seem to fit Derry tolerably enough within the over-all framework.

Though the degree of urbanisation achieved was limited, in fulfilling the various functions they did, Ulster plantation towns in this period underwent developments of very great significance.

TABLE I

Proposed towns 1609	Proposed Towns 1611	Towns Incorporated
Dungannon	Dungannon	Dungannon 27 Nov. 1612
Clogher		Clogher c. 1629–34
Omagh	Omagh	
Loughinsholin		
Mountjoy	Mountjoy	
	Strabane	Strabane 18 Mar. 1613 Augher 15 April 1613
Limavady	Limavady	Limavady 30 Mar. 1613
Dungiven		
	Coleraine	Coleraine 28 June 1613

Derry	*Derry*	Londonderry 29 Mar. 1613
Lifford	Lifford	Lifford 27 Feb. 1613
Ballyshannon	Ballyshannon	Ballyshannon 23 Mar. 1613
Killybegs		Killybegs 14 Dec. 1615
Donegal	Donegal	Donegal 27 Feb. 1613
Raphoe		
Rathmullan	Rathmullan	
Dowagh in Innishowen		
Lisgoole		
Castleskeagh		
middle way between		
Lisgoole and		
Ballyshannon		
	Enniskillen	Enniskillen 27 Feb. 1613
Cavan	*Cavan*	Cavan 15 Nov. 1610
Belturbet	Belturbet	Belturbet 30 March 1613
midway between Kells and Cavan	Lough Ramor	
Armagh	Armagh	Armagh 26 Mar. 1613
Mountnorris	Mountnorris	
Charlemont	Charlemont	Charlemont 28 April 1613
Tandragee		

Italicisation indicates that incorporation had taken place by this time. (I am very grateful to the editor of *Studia Hibernica* for permission to reprint this from no. 11 (1971), p. 79).

TABLE II

A Contemporary Synopsis of Irish Customs Returns, Probably Late 1630s

Rates of Magnitudes	*Ports*	*Proportion per cent*
I	Dublin	41
II	Cork	10
III	Waterford	7
	Galway	7
IV	Limerick	5
	Kinsale	5
	Youghal	5
V	Drogheda	3
	Londonderry	3
	Carrickfergus	3
VI	Ross 1½	1
	Wexford	1
	Dundalk	1
	Baltimore	1
	Sligo	1
Under Rate or Minute	Killybegs	½
	Dungarvan	½
	Donnaghadee	½
	Strangford	⅓
	Coleraine	⅓
	Dingle	⅓

This table (TNA, S.P. 63/276, ff 30–30v) which is undated requires more critical attention than is appropriate here. It is headed as follows:

Comparing together the proceed of the duty for six years of this last farm received from the several ports of Ireland. They may be thus ranked in classes according to their worth respectively and will at a medium be found to bear each to other very near these proportions expressed in whole numbers without fractions for more clearness of apprehension.

It is endorsed 'Dr Woods remarques concerning the exports and imports Ireland', and, in a later hand, P. 12, F. 337.5.

A transcript of this Crown-copyright record in the Public Record Office [TNA] appears by permission of the Controller of H.M. Stationery Office. I am grateful to Professor M. Perceval-Maxwell for bringing it to my attention.

---

[1] See below, ch. 15, pp 393–427; 'Ulster plantation papers, 1608–13', (ed.) T.W Moody, in *Analecta Hibernica*, no. 8 (1938), pp 286–96; James Buckley (ed.), 'Report of Sir Josias Bodley on some Ulster fortresses in 1608' in *Ulster Journal of Archaeology*, 2nd series, xvi, nos 1 and 2 (Feb. and May 1910), pp 61–4; *Analecta Hibernica*, no. 3 (1931), pp 151–218. For a list of the proposed towns see Table I.

[2] This sentence derives from the cartographic identification of land grants.

[3] See below, ch. 15, p. 397–9.

[4] Moody, *Londonderry plantation*, pp 55, 58; T.W. Moody and J.G. Simms (eds), *The bishopric of Derry and the Irish Society of London* (IMC, Dublin, 1968), i, 27–8, 29–31, 40–2; *Cal. Pat. Rolls Ire., Jas I*, pp 10, 15, 65, 131; RIA, Charters of Irish towns, 7, charter of Derry, 11 July 1604.

[5] Moody, *Londonderry plantation*, p. 78; *Cal. Carew MSS, 1603–24*, p. 36.

[6] *Cal. S.P. Ire., 1608–10*, pp 415–16.

[7] The essential framework of the plantation as far as settler landowners was concerned was one whereby groups of baronies or precincts were allocated to undertakers, English and Scottish whose estates should be settled with a British population only and servitors, military officers whose estates were in the same precincts as lands restored to some Irish grantees, who might have Irish tenants. For a map and discussion see T.W. Moody, F.X. Martin and F.J. Byrne (eds), *A new history of Ireland* (Oxford, 1976), iii, 198–9.

[8] Hill, *Plantation in Ulster*, pp 282–2, 465–6; *Hastings MSS*, iv, 163; NAI, Lodge MSS, vi, 169; BL, Add. MS 11, 402, f. 159; *Analecta Hibernica*, no. 8 (1938), pp 237, 246–7.

[9] *Cal. Carew MSS, 1603–24*, pp 56–7. It seems very likely, however, that when the patron of nearby Enniskillen, Captain William Cole nominated six County Fermanagh landowners to be burgesses of the town in 1612 he was himself seeking to imitate the Belturbet arrangement (above, ch. 9, pp 242–4).

[10] RIA, Charters of Irish towns, 4; 130–52; above, ch. 15 pp 394–5, 414–15.

[11] Above, ch. 9, p. 236–9. The town lands for Augher were located close to the town of Clogher.

[12] *Cal. Pat. Rolls Ire., Jas I*, p. 182.

[13] Lambeth, Carew MS 629, ff 68–72; *Cal. Carew MSS, 1603–24*, pp 141–2; *Cal. S.P. Ire., 1611–14*, pp 36–7.

[14] Below, ch. 15, pp 396–7. See Table 1.

[15] *Cal. Pat. Rolls Ire., Jas I*, pp 206–7, 217, 219–20, 224–5, 232, 236, 256, 300.

[16] These extracts are taken from an uncalendared translation of the patent made to Captain William Cole for Enniskillen (*Cal. Pat. Rolls Ire., Jas I*, p. 232) published in W.C. Trimble, *History of Enniskillen* (Enniskillen, 1919), i, 165–70.

[17] Very similar language was used in the Virginia Council's orders in 1609 to Sir Thomas Gates, governor of Virginia, who was told that in building his towns he should 'prepare for ornament

and safety at once' (S.M. Bemiss (ed.), *The three charters of the Virginia company of London with seven related documents, 1606–1621* (Williamsburg, Virginia, 1957), p. 61).

[18] It may be noted that in London at this time the use of timber in constructing the outer walls of houses was forbidden by proclamation as a fire precaution and to conserve timber (J.F. Larkin and P.L. Hughes (eds), *Stuart royal proclamations, i; royal proclamations of King James I, 1603–1625* (Oxford, 1973), nos 51, 78, 87, 120, 175, 186).

[19] These stipulations as to rent and otherwise are referred to and embodied in a surviving building lease for the town of Augher of 1 April 1615 (NAI, D 4859). It required that the house be built of 'stone, brick or timber with chimneys'.

[20] Hunter 'Towns' pp 48–54; transcripts of many of the charters are to be found in RIA, Charters of Irish towns, 1, 4, 5, 7 and in NAI, R.C. 3/2, 4, 5, 7, 8. For a detailed discussion of the charters of Londonderry and Coleraine see Moody, *Londonderry plantation*, pp 122–42.

[21] Moody, *Londonderry plantation*, pp 81–3, 274–6; Corporation of London Records Office (hereafter CLRO), Jor. 30, f. 136v.

[22] R.G.S. King (ed.), *A particular of the howses and famylyes in Londonderry, May 15, 1628* (Londonderry, 1936), pp 6–23; CLRO, Jor. 30, f. 138; Moody, *Londonderry plantation*, pp 243–4.

[23] CLRO, Irish Society MSS, Great Parchment Book, ff A1–A26.

[24] Moody, *Londonderry plantation*, pp 274–5; CLRO, Jor. 30, f. 136v.

[25] Hill, Plantation, pp 527–8; BL, Add. MS 4756, f. 110; County of Huntingdon and Peterborough Record Office, Kimbolton MS ddM70/35; A.A. Campbell, *Notes on the literary history of Strabane* (Omagh 1902), pp 4–5.

[26] Moody, *Londonderry plantation*, p. 279; BL, Add. MS 4770, ff 94v–8.

[27] For a more detailed discussion see below, ch. 15, pp 405–12 (Armagh), pp 414–17 (Cavan).

[28] BL, Add. MS 4756, f. 115v; *Cal. Carew MSS, 1603–24*, p. 221. Its size has been concealed by the absence of a muster return in 1630.

[29] Above, pp 239–47. However for a number of towns which were based on forts without land grants to patrons and therefore technically outside of the formal plantation, e.g. Charlemont, there is no adequate documentation.

[30] Below, ch. 16, pp 428–35.

[31] BL, Add. MS 4756, f. 114v; NAI, C.P., W/65; TCD, MS 550, pp 224–5; *Cal Pat. Rolls Ire., Jas I*, p. 300.

[32] Perceval-Maxwell, *The Scottish migration to Ulster in the reign of James I* (London, 1973), p. 262.

[33] BL, Add. MS 4756, f. 113v.

[34] NAI, D 4859; BL, Add. MS 4756. f. 111 v; Hill. *Plantation*, p. 540; Emanuel Ley's certificate, 1622 (NLI, MS 8014/ viii); notes by commissioners in 1622 on Clogher barony (ibid.).

[35] Above, ch. 9, pp 244–5.

[36] NAI, D 1040. Towns in undertakers' baronies were probably considered to be covered by the general exclusion of Irish intended in those areas.

[37] Certificate by provost of Dungannon and others, 1622 (NLI, MS 8014/viii); TCD, MS 832, ff 166, 166v, MS 833, f. 36

[38] W.P. Burke (ed.), 'The diocese of Derry in 1631' in *Archivium Hibernicum*, v (1916), p. 3; [W. Doherty], *Derry Columbkille, souvenir of the centenary celebrations … of St Columba in Derry, 1897–9* (Dublin, 1899), pp 103–7.

[39] CLRO, Irish Society MSS, Great Parchment Book, f. A10; TCD, MS 839, f. 22.

[40] *Cal. S.P. Ire., 1615–25*, p. 224.

[41] Hill. *Plantation*, pp 477, 523, 524–5, 557; BL, Add. MS 4756, f. 116v.

[42] Above, ch. 9, p. 240–41; Moody, *Londonderry plantation*, p. 454; cartographic identification of land grants.

[43] TCD, MS 550, p. 175. In 1620 an arrangement was made whereby for five years £40 per annum out of the rents of the corporation lands should be expended 'on 'the building, enlarging and strengthening of Spur-Royal castle [the landlord's castle at Augher], and … building fit and necessary houses edifices or buildings for and near or adjoining to the said castle' (NAI, D 4862).

[44] Certificate concerning manor of Dungannon, 1622 (NLI, MS 8014/ix). For house building costs in Derry see Moody, *Londonderry plantation*, pp 249, 254 and in Armagh below ch. 15, pp 407–8.

45 W.E. Washburn, *Virginia under Charles I and Cromwell, 1625–60* (Williamsburg, Virginia, 1957), p. 2; L.G. Carr, 'The metropolis of Maryland: a comment on town development along the tobacco coast' in *Maryland Historical Magazine*, 69, no. 2 (Summer 1974), pp 124–45.

46 For a valuable discussion of Boston at this time see D.B. Rutman, *Winthrop's Boston: portrait of a puritan town, 1630–49* (Chapel Hill, North Carolina, 1965) There may have even been some contemporary connections. Thus, Owen Roe of London, who exported tobacco to Derry (or possibly Coleraine) via Chester in 1634 (TNA, E190/1335/1, f. 53) can probably be identified with that Owen Roe of London who acquired a house and land in Boston in 1635 to which he dispatched servants and cattle and which he rented out as an absentee (Rutman, *Winthrop's Boston*, pp 83, 158).

47 Peter Clark and Paul Slack, *English towns in transition, 1500–1700* (Oxford, 1976). p. 19; Penelope Corfield, 'Urban development in England and Wales in the sixteenth and seventeenth centuries' in D.C. Coleman and A.H. John (eds), *Trade, government and economy in pre-industrial England* (London, 1872), p. 62.

48 J.F. Ferguson (ed.), 'Ulster roll of gaol delivery, 1613–18' in *Ulster Journal of Archaeology*, 1st series, i (1853), pp 260–70, ii (1854), pp 25–8.

49 PRONI, T808/15090/1, 8, 16 (I am engaged on an edition of this document); Moody, *Londonderry plantation*, pp 114–15, 209.

50 Below, ch. 15, p. 411–12.

51 NAI, Ferguson MSS, ix, 198; Moody, *Londonderry plantation*, p. 285.

52 Rich journal notes. 1 July 1622 (NLI, MS 8014/v).

53 Moody, *Londonderry plantation*, pp 249. 254, 272.

54 Certificate concerning manor of Dungannon. 1622 (NLI, MS 8014/ ix); PRONI, T808/15090/11; TCD, MS 836, ff 119–9v 121, 133v.

55 NLI, MS 13237/17–20. Licences to collect charitable contributions, issued by patent, a means to deal with disasters, urban and individual, e.g. those to a Derryman and for the 'poor inhabitants' of Enniskillen 'which town has suffered much by fire', both in 1616 (*Cal. Pat. Rolls Ire., Jas I*, pp 304, 308). A system of parish alms was functioning in Derry by at least 1670 (R. Hayes (ed.), *The register of Derry cathedral (St Columb's), parish of Templemore, Londonderry, 1642–1703* (Parish Register Society of Dublin, Exeter and London, 1910), p. 206, also pp 207–9). An example of private benevolence to the poor at Derry, prior to 1637 (Moody and Simms (eds), *Bishopric of Derry and Irish Society*, i, 219) may be taken along with one at Belfast, after 1623, 'being the first money left in that kind' (R.M. Young (ed.), *The town book of the corporation of Belfast, 1613–1816* (Belfast, 1892), p. 233).

56 *Hastings MSS*. iv, 163, 167; TCD, MS 833, ff 265–6v, MS 835, ff 131–2; C.R. Elrington (ed.), *Works of Ussher* (Dublin, 1864), xv, 373–4; PRONI, T808/15090/19.

57 PRONI, T808/15090/21.

58 BL, Add. MS 4576, f. 110; *Cal. Pat. Rolls Ire., Jas I*, pp 107, 182; Moody, *Londonderry plantation*, pp 148, 247–8, 250, 345.

59 PRONI, T808/15090/17, 18, 19, 22.

60 Above, ch. 9, pp 244–5: Moody, *Londonderry plantation*, pp 276–7; *Cal. Pat. Rolls Ire., Jas I*, p. 484

61 CLRO, Great Parchment Book, ff A24–4v; BL, Harl. MS 2138, f. 188. It may be noted that the 'annual revenue' of Kilkenny as recorded in 1628 was £231.17.11 (Charles Vallancey (ed.), *Collectanea de rebus Hibernicis* (Dublin, 1781), ii, 398–412). For the property of the corporation of Kilkenny in 1639 see NAI, Lodge MSS, vi, 278–81.

62 Below, ch. 15, p. 404–5.

63 *Cal. Pat. Rolls Ire., Jas I*, pp 484–5. In 1622 the more important fortifications, where ordnance was located, were Ballyshannon, Derry, Charlemont, Mountjoy, Enniskillen and Mountnorris (List of 'brass' and iron ordnance in 1622 (NLI, MS 8013/vii)).

64 TCD, MS 550, p. 175; see the lists of mayors of Derry and Coleraine in Moody, *Londonderry plantation*, pp 448–50.

65 Bodl., Carte MS 62, f. 195; NAI, R.C. 3/8, pp 54–65; PRONI, T808/15090.

66 Above, ch. 9, pp 243–4; BL, Add. MS 4756, f. 102v; TCD, MS 833, ff 80–80v.

67 BL, Add. MS 19,841, f. 9v.

68 PRONI, T808/15090; BL, Add. MS 19,841, ff 94–5.

69 TNA, S.P. 63/250 ff 69–77v; *Cal. S.P. Ire., 1625–32*, pp 509–11.

70 BL, Sloane MS 3827, ff 62–3v.

[71] *Cal. Pat. Rolls Ire., Jas I*, pp 565, 571. For the functions of the clerk of the market in England see Joan Thirsk (ed.) *The agrarian history of England and Wales* (Cambridge, 1967), iv, 578–9.

[72] PRONI, T808/15090/2a.

[73] R.G.S. King (ed.), *A particular of the howses and famylyles in London Derry, May 15, 1628* (Derry, 1936), nos 85–6, 163; St Columb's Cathedral Chapter House, Tenison Groves MSS; CLRO, Great Parchment Book, ff A8, A8v.

[74] TNA, E190/1334/14, f. 16; Cheshire Record Office, Chester, W.S. 1633. For further supplies of drugs from Chester in 1634 see TNA, E190/1335/1, ff 18, 53.

[75] William Munk, *The roll of the royal college of physicians of London* (London, 1878), i, 170–2.

[76] R. Hayes (ed.), *Register of Derry Cathedral*. p. 110.

[77] TNA, S.P. 28/120, f. 742v.

[78] TNA, S.P. 63/250, f. 77.

[79] TNA, E190/1330/11, f. 24v. It also unloaded at Derry.

[80] TCD, MS 836, f. 115v.

[81] For some discussion see my 'The Ulster plantation in the counties of Armagh and Cavan' (M. Litt. thesis, University of Dublin, 1968), pp 629–38.

[82] Moody, *Londonderry plantation*, pp 448–50; below, ch. 15, p. 415; TCD, MS 832, ff 176–8.

[83] TNA, E190/1330/14, f. 21; E190/1332/1, passim; Derry port books, 1612–15 (Leeds City Council Libraries, Archives Deprtment, TN/P07/ 1/4a–d). As customary, for economy in foot-noting, detailed references within these port books are not cited. (I am engaged on an edition of the Ulster port books at Leeds.)

[84] Lambeth, Carew MS 630, f. 60v; TCD, MS 550, pp 1–2; below, ch. 15, p. 407–8.

[85] TNA, C.O. 388/85/A15 (I am grateful to Dr D. Dickson for the reference).

[86] TNA, E190/1329/9, ff 2, 2v; E190/1334/14, ff 2v–4 (fish shipment to Chester 1607 and 1634); E190/870/8, f. 8 (to Poole, 1611). For some Scottish connections, a visit by an East India Co. vessel and a pirate see BL, Harl. MS 2138, ff 185v–6; Charles Conaghan, *History and antiquities of Killybegs* (Ballyshannon, 1974), pp 65–9.

[87] TNA, S.P. 63/259, ff 215v–25v (I am grateful to Professor M. Perceval-Maxwell for this reference).

[88] Leeds City Council Libraries, Archives Department, TN/P07/l/ 16–18.

[89] H.F. Kearney 'The Irish wine trade' in *IHS*, ix, no. 36 (Sep. 1955), p. 418.

[90] *Hastings MSS*, iv, 163; TCD, MS 832, f. 167; PRONI, D1702/1/27/1; above, ch. 9, p. 245–6.

[91] TCD, MS 833, f. 144; MS 835, f. 48v.

[92] TNA, E190/1330/1, sub 22 July 1612; TCD, MS 833, f. 75, 256–6v.

[93] TNA, E190/1331/8, sub April 1618. He and another Enniskillen merchant also had a connection with Drogheda (above, ch. 9, p. 245–6).

[94] Below, ch. 15, p. 416.

[95] J.J. Marshall, *History of Dungannon* (Dungannon, 1929), p. 119.

[96] Formerly TNA, Manchester Papers, 30/15/2/183 (location now unknown: NLI, Microfilm, Positive 6034).

[97] Certificate to commissioners in 1622 (NLI, MS 8014/viii); M. Perceval-Maxwell, *Scottish migration*, p. 277.

[98] NLI, MS 8014/viii.

[99] NLI, MS 8014/ix.

[100] Below, ch. 16, p. 432; TCD, MS 833, ff 265–6v; Gertrude Thrift (ed.) *Indexes to Irish wills* (London, 1920), v, p. 148 Snapmaker, a maker of dental instruments (OED), but perhaps a snaphance maker.

[101] These examples come from Belturbet and the village of Farnham County Cavan (TCD, MS 832. f. 129; MS 833, ff 148, 295–6v).

[102] TCD, MS 833, f. 268 (Cavan); MS 836, ff 100 (Armagh), 112 (Markethill): MS 833, ff 6–7 Belturbet, here the innkeeper also operated a tanhouse). The dual occupation of butcher and innkeeper is found in Newtownbutler (MS 835, f. 158).

[103] D.A. Chart (ed.), *Londonderry and the London Companies, 1609–29* (Belfast, 1928), p. 105; *Cal. Pat. Rolls Ire., Jas I*, pp 261, 267, 343, 431.

[104] BL, Harl. MS 2138, ff 180, 182, 186; NAI, C.P., U/66; TCD, MS 836, ff 57–7v.

[105] TCD, MS 833, ff 265–6.

[106] TCD, MS 832, ff 223, 227; MS 833, ff 98–9v, 114–6, 189–9v.

[107] Leeds City Council Libraries, Archives Department, TN/P07/1 /4a–d; *Cal. Pat. Rolls Ire., Jas I,* p. 307.

[108] Ibid., p. 306.

[109] PRONI, DOD, 623/7 *Cal. Pat. Rolls Ire., Jas I,* p. 306; County of Huntingdon and Peterborough Record Office, Kimbolton MSS, dd M70/35.

[110] G. Hamilton, *A history of the house of Hamilton* (Edinburgh, 1933), pp 716–7.

[111] PRONI, DOD, 623/6; Perceval-Maxwell *Scottish migration,* p. 275; *Civil Survey,* iii, 393; PRONI, T808/15090/8.

[112] PRONI, T808/ 6461; *Civil Survey,* iii, 401; *Cal. Pat. Rolls Ire., Jas I,* p. 183.

[113] BL, Add. MS 4770, ff 94v, 97.

[114] TNA, E190/1334/14, f. 7v (also 100 calfskins).

[115] Ibid., ff 29, 48v. Port books of this period are often unsatisfactory for the detail of consignments with a high proportion of the goods recorded as 'other wares'.

[116] BL, Add. MS 4770, f. 94v; PRONI, T808/6461.

[117] TNA, E190/1/14, ff 28v, 48v; E190/1136/8, f. 14v, /10, f. 8.

[118] Moody, *Londonderry plantation,* passim.

[119] NAI, Q.R.O., Down Survey trace no. 98.

[120] CLRO, Jor. 30 ff 135v, 138v, Great Parchment Book, ff A1–A26.

[121] Calculations based on 1628 rental (King (ed.), *Howses and famylyes*).

[122] Chart (ed.), *Londonderry and the London companies,* p. 45; Moody and Simms (eds), *Bishopric of Derry and Irish Society,* i, 220; NAI, Lodge MSS, v, 470; Moody, *Londonderry plantation,* pp 392–3.

[123] CLRO, Great Parchment Book, ff A1–A26; Moody, *Londonderry plantation,* p. 251.

[124] TNA, E190/1329/9, E190/1328/11; information supplied by Mr J.D. Galbraith, Scottish Record Office.

[125] For a discussion of the Scottish trade see Perceval-Maxwell, *Scottish Migration,* pp 290–303.

[126] English port books of this period were useful for identifications. The findings here are based on work in progress and are somewhat tentative.

[127] J.H.E. Bennett (ed.), *The rolls of the freemen of Chester* (The record society for the publication of original documents relating to Lancashire and Cheshire, 51, 1906), i, 60; Moody, *Londonderry plantation,* pp 132, 349, 448.

[128] Chart (ed.), *Londonderry and the London Companies,* p. 114.

[129] *Cal. Pat. Rolls Ire., Jas I,* p. 307.

[130] His exports in the year 1614–15, all to Dieppe and Bilbao and valued at £1,212.19.8, were as follows: 93 turns and 3 hogsheads salmon, 60 dicker hides, 57½ cwt. tallow, 1 cwt. 'yarnon' and 3 cwt. wool.

[131] BL, Add. MS 4756, f. 117; NAI, Lodge MSS, vi, 224.

[132] Moody, *Londonderry' plantation,* pp 398–405.

[133] CLRO, Great Parchment Book, ff A1–A26; St Columb's Cathedral Chapter House, Derry. Tenison Groves MSS, extracts from Bramhall's account as sequestrator, 1634–9; R. Hayes (ed.), *Register of Derry Cathedral*: Moody and Simms (ed.), *Bishopric of Derry and Irish Society,* i. 189–90; *Census Ire.,* 1659, pp 123–4.

[134] Includes two Irish names.

[135] Many people appear only with titles such as alderman, also the document is extremely defective.

[136] Moody, *Londonderry plantation.* p. 450.

[137] Derry port book, 25 March–29 September 1644 (NLI, 2559, p. 215); CLRO, Great Parchment Book, ff A16, A17, A24–25, F6.

[138] TNA, E190/1334/14: Moody and Simms (eds), *Bishopric of Derry and Irish Society,* i, 226 –7; CLRO, Great Parchment Book, ff A3–3v, A17, A20v; *Civil Survey,* iii, 106.

[139] TNA, E190/1332/1, E190/1335/1, E190/1336/3, E190/949/1; NLI, MS 2559, p. 215.

[140] Similar Cheshire vessels carried crews of this magnitude (Donald Woodward, 'Ships, masters and shipowners of the Wirral 1550–1650' in *The Mariners Mirror,* lxiii (1977), p. 225).

[141] Moody and Simms (eds), *Bishopric of Derry and Irish Society,* i, 190; R. Hayes (ed.), *Register of Derry Cathedral,* pp 9–64, 70–101, 107–121.

[142] CLRO, Great Parchment Book, f. A1.

[143] J.B. Leslie, *Derry clergy and parishes* (Enniskillen, 1937), pp 31–3; St Columb's Cathedral, Derry, Tenison Grove's extracts from Bramhall's account; Moody and Simms (eds), *Bishopric of Derry*

and Irish Society, i, 231; BL, Harl, MS 2138, ff 185–9. Account should also be taken of garrison soldiers.

[144] TNA, S.P. 63/259, ff 223v–4.

[145] Perceval-Maxwell, *Scottish migration*, pp 308–8; NLI, MS 2559, p. 217.

[146] For Salmon exports to the Straits in 1638–9 see Moody, *Londonderry plantation*. p. 348.

[147] NLI, MS 2559, p. 215.

[148] BL, Harl. MS 2138, f. 185.

[149] NLI, MS 2559, p. 215.

[150] *Cal. S.P. Ire., 1608–10*, p. 209 .

[151] TNA, S.P. 63/259, ff 217v–20v. Average exports of linen yarn over the five years 1635–9, some 106 packs per year, can only be compared with the total from the port book of 1614–15, 31¾per cent packs. (I owe this latter figure to Mr Donald Woodward). Wool exports, for Derry and Coleraine jointly, over the period 1632–40 were more than double their 1614–15 quantity.

[152] Leeds City Council Libraries, Archives Department, TN/P07/1/16–18; TNA, S.P. 63/259, f. 225. The corresponding figures for Coleraine were 0.3–1 per cent and for Dublin 24–38 per cent. Officials at Derry and Coleraine were said, however, in 1637 to under-value the book of rates (BL, Harl. MS 2138, f. 187v).

15

Towns in the Ulster Plantation

I

In the late sixteenth century many English commentators on Irish affairs stressed the importance of establishing towns in Ulster. In 1590 Justice Robert Gardner and Sir Henry Wallop pointed to the peculiar difficulty of reforming Ulster as compared with Munster and Connacht. In the latter there were 'some cuties, many castles [and] towns well walled' whereas in Ulster there were 'very fewe castle, or places of defence, except in Lecale, the Newry and Knockfergus'. They argued that the extension of English authority there could best be achieved by the establishment of fortified settlements on which local government institutions could be based, after the model of Philipstown and Maryborough in Leix and Offaly.[1] Edmund Spenser in 1596 outlined a similar strategy. Garrisoned forts should be established in strategic places, but in addition 'the state of a towne [should be] layde forth, and incompassed' where merchants, artificers and husbandmen of all sorts from England should be placed and to whom charters of incorporation should be granted. He also concluded from Leix and Offaly experience that such settlements would 'in shorte space turne these parts to great comodytie'.[2] Schemes for urban development in Ulster thus had a politico-economic importance. Politically they would be defended settlements, containing garrisons, at strategic places; economically they would be centres of trade providing homes for British craftsmen and merchants. In the closing stages of the Nine Years' War Mountjoy's strategy demonstrated the value of erecting forts in Ulster.

When the colony in Ulster was being planned the importance of establishing towns was therefore recognised. The 'Orders and Conditions' of plantation stated that in each of the six escheated counties 'a convenient number' of market and corporate towns should be established 'for the habitation and settling tradesmen and artificers'.[3] The 'Project' of the plantation, *c.* January 1609, set out the details of this intention – twenty-five corporate towns were projected.[4] The corporate towns should receive rights to hold fairs and markets and other 'reasonable' liberties including the power to return burgesses to parliament. Furthermore land was allocated, about five to ten townlands each, to be granted to the corporations as endowment for urban development. Some were to be new settlements, many were to be developed around existing nuclei, either the recently established forts, or places of traditional Irish occupation. To get them under way it was decided that there should be a 'a leauy or presse' of tradesmen and artificers from England.[5] It was recognised, in effect, that the government in London would have to play a special part in the establishment of the proposed towns. The plantation scheme thus visualised a systematic urbanisation policy for the escheated counties. Nor was it only in government circles that the importance of towns was recognised. An undertaker, Thomas Blennerhasset, who came on a preliminary visit in 1609, asserted that the plantation could not be a success, in terms of security, unless it was based on a structure of 'many goodly strong corporations'.[6]

In spring 1610, however, when the arrangements for the plantation had reached their final stage, it was found that plans for establishing towns had been neglected. It was at least clear that action by London in the despatch of tradesmen or whatever, as envisaged in the 'Project' of plantation, would not be undertaken. It was agreed, nonetheless, that although tradesmen from England would not be 'prest', the projected incorporations should be proceeded with and charters issued 'for that wil draw as well the tradesmen which will come over with the undertakers, as others' to live in them. Besides, the political value of such incorporations was evident; they would return Protestant burgesses to parliament.[7] It was presumably assumed that the attraction of incorporation would be enough to induce sufficient people to come to these places so that charters could be issued and the land allocated for each proposed town could be transferred to corporate bodies.

On 24 July 1610, just as the lord deputy, Sir Arthur Chichester, and the commissioners for the plantation were departing for Ulster to allot the land to its grantees, further directions about towns were issued from London. The commissioners should decide how many houses should be erected for the time being in each town, lay out their sites, and assign land for further buildings. They should ensure that water was conveniently available. No land was to be enclosed and appropriated to any particular householder until the town had been 'conveniently' peopled. One-third of the land allotted to each town might be enclosed at the common charge to make a common meadow, the rest to be left as a commons for cattle. In towns where schools were to be founded, sites should be reserved for that purpose. The deputy should ensure that no lands appointed for towns should be granted for other purposes. The deputy and council were to give instructions for the peopling of the towns and the building of churches and schools 'so far as the means of the country will yield'. When the towns had grown to forty houses they should be incorporated.[8] However, that these instructions left the fundamental problem of procuring residents for the towns unresolved was soon to be apparent. While of interest from a planning viewpoint, on this crucial question they represented not much more than a facile transference of responsibility from London to Dublin.

By the autumn of 1610 only one charter had been issued, that of Cavan.[9] This conveyed to the corporation the allocated lands and established a corporate body of thirteen people of whom only two were products of the plantation. It represented a compromise in favour of native elements whose loyalty was presumably considered dependable. Furthermore Cavan was already an established urban centre. Few of the other proposed centres were comparably developed and, indeed, it would not have been in accord with plantation intentions to issue charters to bodies of people predominantly non-settler in composition. In addition this was done as a result of royal direction of April 1609, the machinery having been put in motion in February 1610, before the directions of July 1610 referred to above. Finally Cavan became the only town actually to receive the town property by charter and is clearly a special case.

That the fundamental problems regarding the establishing of towns in the plantation area remained unresolved emerged in December 1610. After the lord deputy's party had returned to Dublin from Ulster, having allotted the land to its grantees, a series of problems concerning the plantation were submitted by Chichester to the privy council in London. The native Irish, he said, were 'indisposed and unapt' to town life, and he doubted if British tradesmen could be brought to any of the places to be incorporated 'in any due time'. Chichester's suggestion was that some 'principal gentlemen' should be appointed superintendents of the intended corporations to 'draw' settlers there and to maintain order until the towns had increased to a 'sufficient' size when they should be incorporated and authority transferred to the mayors. The privy council accepted this proposal, laying down that an undertaker or servitor near the site of each proposed town should be appointed to build houses for tradesmen, who should hold their tenements from him. The land for the town should be granted in fee farm with a time specified for the performance of his obligations. Incorporation was to follow subsequently.[10]

On the basis of this decision a form of warrant for a fiant granting the lands assigned for towns was drawn up.[11] Grants were to follow a set pattern 'accordings to the artickles layd downe for a burrowe towne'. The lands were to be granted in fee farm under defined rents as well as markets and fairs. The clerkship of the market should vest in the patentee until the town had been incorporated, when it should then come to the chief officer of the town. It was thus a year after many of the major problems of inaugurating the colony had been settled before an expedient for establishing the towns had been devised.

The germ of the superintendency idea, as far as the Irish government was concerned, can probably be found in an arrangement of 27 October 1610 with Sir Richard Hansard of Lifford.[12] However, the agreement concluded in England at the beginning of that year with the city of London whereby it undertook responsibility for establishing two towns in the modern county of Londonderry,[13] and another agreement also reached in London on 18 July 1610 for the establishment of Belturbet in County Cavan, the precise details of which are unclear,[14] but which involved the local grantees, must have contributed to it. Hansard was given a lease for twenty-one years of the fort of Lifford and lands nearby provided that within five years he assign to sixty persons to be inhabitants of the town sites for houses and gardens each to hold their allocation until the expiry of the lease, and also allot areas calculated at 200 acres as a common for the townsmen. There is no reference to prospective incorporation, but it is worth noting that sixty townsmen were considered desirable at this stage. Consistent with the direction of their thinking were other temporary ad hoc arrangements made by the lord deputy and plantation commissioners in January 1611 regarding the land allocated for certain other proposed towns in the plantation counties. It was decided that the land for a new town in Cavan, subsequently Virginia, should be set to a local servitor grantee 'for rent'.[15] A similar arrangement with Captain Basil Brooke was to be made for the town lands for Donegal town.[16] In the cases of the proposed towns at Killybegs and at Lisgoole or Enniskillen local servitors, Sir Henry Foliot and Captain William Cole, were required to set out the land for one year coming 'for the Townes best advantage' and collect rent for the previous half year 'untill other direc'cons shalbe geuen'.[17] The sizes of the corporations envisaged were stated – for Lisgoole or Enniskillen a portreeve, two bailiffs, and forty burgesses, and for Killybegs a portreeve, a bailiff and thirty burgesses; in this respect these orders were in rough accord with the instructions of 24 July 1610. Such arrangements at this stage were necessary since otherwise the town lands would have been islands of land throughout the escheated counties for which, unlike most of the confiscated territory, no grantee had been made responsible.[18]

We have examined so far two stages – the original proposals which necessitated initiatives by the London government, followed by a reconsideration of means and the making of interim arrangements. The next and, as it was to be, definitive phase of decision making about town establishment coincided with the visit to Ireland in the summer of 1611 of

Lord Carew, a former president of Munster, sent by James I to conduct an inquiry into Irish affairs. As part of that enquiry Carew, accompanied by Chichester, examined the plantation at first hand. Broadly, now, the superintendency scheme was being put into effect, though the making of grants of town lands under it was protracted until 1613 and in one case, Killybegs, until December 1615; and the number of proposed towns to be incorporated was reduced from the original number in the 'Project' of plantation. As well, some adjustments in location and other modifications were made.

The reconsidered number and locations of the proposed towns can be found in a document produced by Chichester in the autumn of 1611.[19] Sixteen new incorporations (excluding Derry and Cavan) were now proposed, all except Coleraine and Strabane having featured in the 'Project', though Enniskillen had been substituted for the nearby Lisgoole.[20] While this may have been a more realistic number in terms of what the economy could be expected to sustain, there were other reasons, at least in some instances, for the abandonment of earlier plans. Thus, the establishment of the proposed town in Innishowen was ruled out at an early stage by the nature of the grant of Innishowen received by Sir Arthur Chichester himself.[21] The negotiations with the city of London, conducted independently of the general plantation arrangements and concluding in an agreement of January 1610 whereby it undertook the colonisation of the modern county of Londonderry,[22] also had implications for the urban proposals of 1609. The proposed towns in Loughinsholin barony (then in Tyrone) and at Dungiven were abandoned; the Londoners were to concentrate their efforts on Derry, taken in from Donegal, and designated for development in the 'Project', and on Coleraine, taken in from Antrim, a county not escheated for plantation. In a number of cases the land allocated by the 'Project' for the support of proposed towns was not in fact reserved for this use, and this despite the instructions of 24 July 1610. This may well have militated against the incorporation of some places, for example, Tandragee, though Chichester's list of 1611, when the greater part of the land had been allocated, contained places for which no land was available, and many of these places, for example, Armagh and Charlemont, were subsequently incorporated. Administrative lapses could be circumvented. The reason why many of the proposed towns at places where British forts had been established had no allocation of land can probably be found in a simple administrative confusion. After the defeat of O'Neill reservations of land, perhaps about 1,000 statute acres each, were made for the support of many of these forts, for example, Moyry, Charlemont and Mountnorris in Armagh. It may well have been considered at the time of

planning the plantation that this land should be employed for the support
of the towns and that no further allocations would be necessary. However,
these lands had generally been leased in 1606 and 1607 to the local
commanders, who subsequently became owners of them, without
obligations regarding a town. In the case of Omagh, for example, the lands
around it were granted outright to John Leigh, constable of the fort there,
on 7 July 1610, just before the plantation was got under way.[23] Clearly
factors other than the availability of land specifically granted under the
superintendency system led to the incorporation of a number of these
places. At the same time there was probably a greater likelihood of
incorporation when land was so allocated.

The working out of the superintendency arrangement proved to be
protracted. The initial enthusiasm for the scheme which led to Chichester
issuing a warrant from Lifford on 19 August 1611 at the time of Carew's
survey, for a grant of the land appointed for Rathmullan in Donegal to Sir
Ralph Bingley 'notwithstanding any former caveat or restraintes'[24] was not
followed up. Furthermore, while Carew's survey of the plantation indicated
conspicuous urban beginnings at Derry and Coleraine and indeed Lifford,
elsewhere in the six planted counties only modest efforts were being made,
for example, at Donegal, Charlemont, and Dungannon.[25] It was only from
the beginning of 1612 when preparations for parliament, involving as they
did the creation of new boroughs as a tactic to procure a pliable house of
commons, were being actively pursued,[26] that a series of grants under the
superintendency system was made. The first on 31 January 1612, to Sir
Richard Hansard of the town lands of Lifford, making outright his previous
lease, required him, within four years 'to settle thirty persons, English or
Scots, chiefly tradesmen to be burgesses and hereafter to be incorporated'.
Land allocations, one or two acres each, as well as sites for their houses were
to be made to these, also common of turbary and 100 acres for common
of pasturage was to be available.[27]

Between 4 March 1612 and 22 April 1613 five further grants were made
to patrons or superintendents for the following towns – Dungannon,
Donegal, Enniskillen, Virginia and Augher.[28] The obligations were broadly
identical and generally similar to those of Hansard, except that the number
of burgesses to be settled was further reduced from thirty to twenty. The
time limit for their settlement remained four years, and the patron
undertook within that time to procure their incorporation as a body politic.
The patrons were to build houses or burgages of stone or framed timber 'in
a decent or uniform manner' for these burgesses, to be held for ever in fee
farm. They were to set apart 'convenient places' for the towns, and also for
churches, churchyards, market places, and usually schools. The patron of

Enniskillen, Captain Cole, was required to provide a site for a county gaol. Each burgess should receive small allocations of land as in the case of Lifford. The patrons should allocate land for common pasture, usually thirty acres, which, after incorporation, should be assigned for ever to the 'inhabitants and corporation' for a nominal rent.[29] Inhabitants other than the burgesses, 'cottagers and inferior inhabitants' were envisaged in the patents, but no numbers were defined or obligation to procure them laid down.[30] The patentees were empowered to hold markets and fairs, and courts, and receive their profits. As an essential part of this arrangement the major portion of the land originally intended to be granted to the corporations would now be held permanently by the patrons.

The stipulation that twenty burgesses should constitute the corporations was not, however, adhered to. Concurrently with the issuing of these patents, the privy council in London made regulations,[31] transmitted to Dublin with a royal letter of 26 September 1612,[32] governing the nature and privileges of the corporations of forty 'new boroughs' which were to be created in preparation for parliament. Urban planning in the plantation was thus merged with the more politically-inspired spate of borough-making throughout the island which was a tactic of parliamentary management. The new corporations were to consist of thirteen members, and this despite the obligations on patrons in their grants to procure twenty burgesses.[33] The process of incorporation now proceeded rapidly. Thirteen surviving warrants for incorporation of towns within the planted counties, issued by Chichester, were dated between 30 September 1612 and 20 April 1613.[34] Of these places, two, Mountjoy and Rathmullan, were not incorporated, the incorporation of another, Clogher, did not take place until the reign of Charles I, and the charter issued to a fourth, Coleraine, in March 1613, was superseded by another in June of that year.[35] To each of these warrants a list of the names of the chief officer and burgesses is attached.

The role of the patron or local landlord where no specific grant to a patron had been made, in selecting the original incorporators emerges clearly in some instances. Thus for Donegal there survives a list of the names of the burgesses with a note by Chichester that it was 'delyvered by Cap [Basil] Brookes' on 16 October 1612.[36] Brooke's own name is first, indicating his desire to be chief officer. A further note in Chichester's hand requires that Brooke 'sett down the name of him that he desires to have for the principale officer this yeare', and is followed by the request, in the same hand as the list, presumably Brooke's, that Charles Brooke be appointed 'cheeffe officer'. The warrant for incorporation, issued by Chichester on October 20, embodied Brooke's recommendation, but has an appended note by Chichester to the attorney general instructing that the name agreed on in England for the chief officer be inserted 'in all the warrants.'[37] No such list of names has come to light. The urgency of preparations for parliament seems to have given scope to patrons' wishes. The list of burgesses submitted by Captain William Cole for Enniskillen contained a substantial number of Fermanagh planter landowners, yet despite a note by Chichester that 'these cannot well stand for those he should name must be of the towne, these are undertakers, etc',[38] these people were named as first incorporators in the charter.[39] Thus while Chichester scrutinised the lists he did not rigorously pursue his objections.[40]

Between 27 November 1612 and 29 April 1613 thirteen places in the six planted counties – Dungannon, Strabane, Augher[41] (County Tyrone); Limavady, Coleraine, Londonderry (County Londonderry); Belturbet (County Cavan); Armagh, Charlemont (County Armagh); Enniskillen (County Fermanagh); Ballyshannon, Donegal, Lifford (County Donegal) – received charters of incorporation.[42] Of these, one, Derry, was a re-incorporation, and another, Coleraine, also in the Londoners' plantation, was re-incorporated in June. Derry and Coleraine, by its second charter, were endowed with essentially similar privileges. These charters were more elaborate than those granted to the other towns within the planted counties and elsewhere at this time. They have already been examined comprehensively.[43] This treatment is therefore concerned with the other eleven charters. These charters had an essential simplicity and similarity, being modelled on the 'paper book' of regulations transmitted to Dublin on 26 September 1612 and referred to above. Each town area was created 'one entire and free borough', the inhabitants being incorporated as chief officer (usually called provost or sovereign but sometimes portreeve, bailiff, warden, or burgomaster), the free burgesses, and the commonalty. The free burgesses were twelve in number, except in Enniskillen where fourteen were constituted. The chief officers and burgesses were granted the power of 'perpetual succession', that is to say civic government was vested in a small self-electing group. This body was empowered to elect the two members of parliament each borough might return. Each charter contained the names of the first incorporators, to hold for life unless removed under exceptional circumstances. The chief officer was to take the oath of supremacy,[44] as well as an oath to fulfil his duties, and was to be elected annually by the chief officer and burgesses. The commons or assembly was defined as all the inhabitants of the town and such as were admitted freemen. Each corporation could hold a weekly court of record before the chief officer to hear civil actions, not exceeding the sum of five marks. The right to hold fairs and markets was usual. The corporation might assemble at discretion to make bye-laws, and could impose fines or other punishments should these be disobeyed. The power of the commons was usually limited to participation in such assemblies. The corporations might appoint two sergeants-at-mace and other municipal officers and establish a guild merchant. The smallness of the governing bodies is noteworthy. In England, where there had been a tendency towards closed corporations in the Elizabethan period, bodies of about twenty members were typical.[45]

The most notable features of these charters, perhaps, is that they did not contain a grant of the fee farm of the town. The process whereby responsibility for town establishment came into private hands ensured their subordination to outside authority. While some of the land originally allotted for the towns may have been leased to the corporators as individuals, the fact that the superintendency scheme was adopted meant that it never came to the corporations as a body. Their incomes were thus of necessity severely limited. The financial returns from courts and fairs and markets were small, and patrons also often had parallel rights to hold courts and fairs and markets in their own names.

The composition of the first corporations requires some comment. In most the local landlord or members of his family were amongst the corporators. This influence was particularly strong in Donegal where three members of the Brooke family were included.[46] In a few of the charters local landowners in addition to the patron were represented, but Enniskillen was exceptional in having six of fourteen burgesses drawn from this group. Probably the majority of the corporators had direct connections with the emerging urban settlements, but also were tenants of land nearby. However, more detailed local studies will be needed before a thorough analysis can be made. The over-riding majority were British settlers, but in two instances the old Irish were not totally excluded. Thus the charter of Augher included one old Irish burgess, John O'Reilly, and Dungannon had two, George O'Mullan and Laurence Tallon.[47]

The original plan of 1609 has been criticised before:[48] that the planners sought to develop towns around already existing nuclei; that more attention was paid to the characteristics of individual sites than to the areas to be served by them; that the unequal density of proposed towns probably arose from fear of rebellion, hence more towns were allocated to areas where there were forts, for example the Armagh-Tyrone border, than to others, for example north-west Donegal, where there were not; that in any case the planning was probably done on a county rather than a regional basis. We have already stated that this probably provided for too many towns, but have suggested that the abandonment of some of these had little to do with regional planning. The incorporations of 1612 and 1613 can thus also be seen not as the implementation of a regional scheme. Certain arbitrary features can certainly be detected. The incorporation of Strabane, cross-river as it was from Lifford and not proposed in 1609, was a gesture to the status and vigour of the earl of Abercorn. The abandonment of the incorporation of Rathmullan, Mountjoy, and Clogher, although the process had gone through a number of administrative phases, can probably be accounted for by delays which would not have made their incorporation fulfil the political desideratum of being able to send members to the 1613 parliament.[49]

By 1613, fourteen towns (including Cavan) in the six escheated counties had received charters. In the ensuing years some further initiatives were taken. Thus, in February 1614, the lord deputy issued a warrant for the incorporation of Ballybalfour, now Lisnaskea and the Castleskeagh of the 1609 proposals.[50] In December 1615 a belated grant of land under the superintendency arrangement was made for establishing the town of Killybegs, which was at the same time declared incorporated.[51] In 1617 there was a statement by Chichester that at the inauguration of the plantation, it was intended to make Lisgoole a corporation.[52] These three places had been proposed as towns in 1609. The government may now have been reconsidering these plans, or the appropriate local landlords may have been seeking prestige. However, that only Killybegs was incorporated shows the limits of their concern.

In August 1618 the incorporation of a new town to be at St Johnston in Donegal, a place not previously designated for this purpose, was set in motion. The granting of a piece of concealed, or previously unallocated, land to a prominent undertaker, the Duke of Lennox, was with the condition that he should introduce thirteen English or Scottish men, principally artificers, within four years and build houses for them.[53] This patent recognised that the logic of the decision of September 1612 that each corporation should contain thirteen members was that the minimum number of residents a patron should be required to install was thirteen.[54] The purpose of the proposed corporation was to be (in rough translation) 'as much for defence and garrison of our faithful lieges and subjects in the neighbouring parts as the repressing and restraining of rebels and all our enemies whatsoever'. The incorporation was not, however, proceeded with before 1641 – the Civil Survey describes St Johnston as 'a little village',[55] – though it returned members to the 1671 parliament and thereafter. Another proposal of 1618, equally abortive, was also for another new town. A king's letter of October 15, authorising a regrant to John Murray, later Earl of Annandale, of his extensive lands in south-west Donegal, instructed that a charter should be granted to his proposed town of Murraiston, when built, with powers similar to Coleraine.[56] That these directions came from London – Murray was a gentleman of the bedchamber – probably accounts for the move away from the standard model for incorporations. Murray, however, appears to have acquired Killybegs shortly hereafter,[57] and this probably accounts for his neglect of this scheme.

Even had the government after 1613 wished to establish further corporate towns in the planted counties, it had only limited scope for manoeuvre. Patents of almost the entire area had been issued and so further town building obligations could not be imposed. Initiative for incorporation could only come from local figures, unless there were instances where patronage grants had not been implemented. In the late 1620s and 1630s attention was given to two places which fitted these categories. On 20 April 1629 royal instructions, at the request of the bishop of Clogher, were given for the incorporation of Clogher, County Tyrone.[58] This subsequently took place; although no charter has been located, members were returned to the 1634 parliament.[59] This is the only case of the incorporation of a place proposed in 1609 taking place belatedly as a result of the energy of the local landowner. The other case arose in 1637 when the commissioners for defective titles turned their attention to Ulster. The residents of Virginia – the proposed town midway between Kells and Cavan of 1609 for which the lands allocated had been granted to Captain John Ridgeway as superintendent in 1612 – petitioned Wentworth to cause the then owner, the earl of Fingall, to procure the incorporation of the town and fulfil the other obligations of the 1612 grant. The privy council ordered his compliance but Fingall secured postponements, which, unwittingly by the outbreak of the 1641 rising, deferred the incorporation.[60] Rathmullan, the only other place in this situation, does not appear to have received similar consideration at this time. Thus, before 1641, sixteen towns had been incorporated in the six planted counties, approximately two-thirds of the number proposed in 1609 though coming close to the revised figure of eighteen of 1611.

However, failure to ensure the original number of incorporations is probably less noteworthy than failure to ensure that sizeable towns were developed. While the original intention of government sponsored or impressed immigration to the proposed towns might have been counter-productive in the attitudes of those sent to Ulster, the recession away from it in government policy, understandable enough given the administrative competence and finances of the early seventeenth-century state, deserves emphasis on many counts. We have seen that there was continual lowering of the number of townsmen required. Even the stipulation of twenty in the superintendency grants, where reservations of land allowed to those to be made, was not enforced, and, with the exception of Derry and Coleraine, the minimum requirement for incorporation became thirteen, with, it would appear, no strict governmental ensurance that all these were residents of the place incorporated. Furthermore, if the granting of charters in 1612 and 1613 was intended as a stimulus to urban growth the fact that the corporations received no grants of property militated against their taking steps to this end. The towns became thoroughly dependant on the local landlords some of whom had no obligation to develop them while the obligations of others received little supervision from the central authority.[61] While some were modestly active in promoting urban beginnings, others were remiss. Relations between townsmen and landlords varied; however, in many towns, for example Ballyshannon and Donegal, as late as 1622, the townsmen had no secure tenancies.[62] The private benevolence of Sir Richard Hansard, patron of Lifford, who in his will made provision for the building of a church and a school, and for salaries for the schoolmaster and the officers of the town, was certainly on a scale unequalled elsewhere.[63] That in 1622 the corporation of Strabane petitioned (without effect) to be granted land as a source of income,[64] is a piece of contemporary evidence that these towns were aware of their disadvantageous position. The fact that very few of the towns in the planted counties contained as many as 100 adult British males by 1641, while most had considerably less, was due at least in part to the fact that the government opted out of taking positive action at the crucial time of foundation. Apart from the conspicuous achievements of the Londoners at Derry, with 500 adult males and Coleraine with 300, the only other town to reach sizeable proportions was Strabane with 200. Many of the boroughs were not markedly different in size, character, or independence from the unincorporated villages which grew up throughout the plantation. It is very important, of course, not to minimise the achievements of private settlers, but in leaving urban development – an important aspect of what may be called the institutional side of the plantation – to private initiative the planners incurred some responsibility for the subsequent slow and fitful growth of town life. The establishing of towns, if only because of their defensive potential if walled, was a necessary complement to the introduction of a rural colony.

That there had been a two-fold deficiency in Ulster urban planning was recognised when the later Jacobean plantations were inaugurated. On the one hand civic growth was hampered by the financial circumstances of the corporations; on the other the defensive value of the towns was limited by the fact that, with the exception of Derry and Coleraine, they had not been walled. Attempts were made to rectify both deficiencies. Thus in planning the plantations of Wexford, Longford and Leitrim land was allocated for corporate towns,[65] and the charters of Newborough (Gorey)[66] in 1619 and Jamestown in 1622[67] indicate that the land was granted to the corporations.

In January 1618 royal instructions concerning the plantation of Wexford presented an expedient without burden to the exchequer, to finance the walling of the proposed new corporate town in that county.[68] An annual levy or cotization was to be imposed on landholders there to cover the cost of the walling, to be completed in seven years. In the Leitrim plantation, at any rate, this expedient was adopted,[69] and in 1623 when the walling of Jamestown was underway it was reported that this would 'supply the great defect in the plantation of Ulster where there are no towns walled but Derry and Coleraine.'[70]

II

Apart from the special energy displayed at Derry and Coleraine, the studies of towns in Armagh and Cavan which follow offer a reasonable impression of urban development in the planted counties up to 1641. It is divided into three sections: proposed towns which were incorporated, proposed towns which were not, and other inceptive towns and villages. The treatment is necessarily unsystematic owing to the source material available.

The 'Project' of plantation recommended the incorporation of four boroughs in Armagh and set aside 1,200 acres as then computed as their endowment 'to hould in fee farm as the English and Scottish undertakers.' One, Armagh, was long established, two, Charlemont and Mountnorris, were the sites of recently erected forts and the fourth was to be a new town at Tandragee in O'Hanlon's territory. For Cavan three incorporations were projected and thirty polls of land allotted. Apart from Cavan and Belturbet, a new town was to be erected 'in or neere the mydwaie between Kells and the Cavan', the site to be chosen by the commissioners of plantation.[71] The 1611 list cogitated the abandonment of incorporation of only one of these places, Tandragee in Armagh. Armagh and Charlemont, Cavan and Belturbet in fact received charters.

SOME INCORPORATED TOWNS

ARMAGH
In 1610 Thomas Blennerhasset described the town of Armagh as follows:

> How exceedingly wel standeth Ardmath, better seate for riche soyle there cannot bee, but so poore, as I doe verily thinke all the household stuffe in that citty is not worth twenty pounds, yet it is the Primate of all Ireland, and as they say for antiquitie one of the most

> ancient in all Europe: it is also of so small power as forty resolute
> men may rob, rifle and burn it: were it a defended corporation it
> woulde soone be rich and religious, and the security would make
> one acre more worth than now twenty be. At this present time it is
> a most base and abiect thing, not much better than Strebane, and not
> able to restraine no, not the violence of the woolfe.[72]

Contemporaries concurred with his judgements of its antiquity, ecclesiastical dignity, potential, and present decay. It had suffered a half century of military significance. Furthermore, peculiar historical circumstances had for long made it, although the ecclesiastical capital, unattractive for residence to archbishops whose cultural affiliations cut them off from the northern portion of their diocese. As a monastic centre it had had a distinguished record, but in the altered circumstances of 1610 it could derive no prospects from its monastic tradition.

However, it had potential as a marketing centre and, with the introduction of a Protestant colony, as a revived and re-orientated ecclesiastical centre as well. Its most important new function was as county capital and centre of legal sittings. However, the town which was restored and expanded in the thirty years after the plantation had, in some ways, a much greater continuity with its past, if only because of the smallness of the immigrant population, than Londonderry, a walled and garrisoned town with an important military role. The pre-plantation settlement fell into three areas: the Trian Sassenach to the north, the Trian Masain to the east, and the Trian Mor to the south. Dispersed through these trians or wards, though more densely accumulated in the central ring or hill area, were a series of ecclesiastical institutions of which the cathedral, the abbey of St Peter and St Paul, the Franciscan abbey, St Columba's church, the Culdee priory, and the nunnery of Templefartagh were perhaps the most important.[73] There was thus a nucleus of roads, paths, and sites from which the transformed town could develop.

The town for the most part fell within the manor of Armagh and was traditionally the property of the archbishop. There were small areas which belonged to the abbey – granted to Sir Toby Caulfeild, commander of Charlemont fort, in 1607[74] – and monasteries, the dean, and the vicars choral. Since this account is based almost exclusively on the see records, allowances must be made for marginal incompleteness. The impact of Protestantism was slight before 1610,[75] and apart from the fact that in 1609 it was recorded that the archbishop, Henry Ussher, had recently erected a water mill on the River Callan, there is little evidence of change in the town before the beginning of the primacy of Christopher Hampton in 1613.

In the re-development of the town the building lease was used. Thus in November 1615 the archbishop leased an area of the city, including 'all and singular the houses, ruynous edifices, creats, and ould walls' as well as plots and parcels of lands in the liberties of the town (in an area known as the Bende, an area of 'wast' or common grazing), then occupied by a small number both of Irish and English tenants, to Theophilus Buckworth, bishop of Dromore, and Edward Dodington of Dungiven, a well-known servitor and builder of the walls of Derry.[76] The object was the 'replanting and re-edifying of the decayed cyttie' and the lease was for sixty years.[77] No rent is mentioned; the lease was apparently to empower Dodington, who was the archbishop's agent and seneschal in Tyrone,[78] and Buckworth, who held the rectory of Armagh along with his bishopric,[79] to act on the primate's behalf. They proceeded to lay out the area into plots for houses within the town to each of which twenty acres was alloted from the previously common grazing. Lessees holdings were chosen by lot, each being a site 50 feet in length with land behind 50 feet broad and 150 feet long. The tenant undertook, before 27 September 1618, to build a dwelling house, 40 feet long within the walls, 16 feet broad, the walls to be 15 feet high with gables of brick or stone, the roofs and floors to be of oak, the house to be of two storeys and built of brick or stone and sawn timber 'according to the form of English houses and buyldings'. The garden plot and also the twenty acres should be enclosed after the English manner with a ditch and hedge of two rows of quicksets. Allowances of stone and clay for bricks, and timber for building and lime burning were to be made from the archbishop's lands, and the tenant, who would hold for fifty-nine years, should pay to the archbishop £2 stg rent per annum, and two fat capons at Christmas, the heriot to be 13s 4d.[80]

It should be noted that while longer terms were being granted in building leases in London, the aim was similar, the landlord securing, or attempting to secure, the development of property without major investment but foregoing any sizeable income until the determination of the first lease.[81] It is not clear how many leases were made under this precise scheme, but by this tactic – Dodington soon ceases to be an official of the archbishop – a number of 'plantation' houses were erected in the town. In 1622, apart from an archiepiscopal residence rebuilt and extended at a cost of £160, eight 'fair stone' residences had been erected.[82] The costs of these had varied from £500 to £80. All were held under sixty-year leases, six, with twenty acres of land, at a rent of £2.5.0 each, the other two lessees holding a townland or more and paying rent accordingly. Three of the houses were held by two local clergy. Two others were held by merchants from Drogheda, Andrew Hamlin[83] and Richard Fitzsymonds, himself a landowner in Cavan and with business interests in the Londonderry plantation,[84] and one by Richard Chappell, a substantial leaseholder and agent of the archbishop. Eight other plots and portions of land were held by three tenants, who had as yet not built their houses, one holding five such sites. In 1615 ten people are listed as 'undertakers to build',[85] and by 1622 of twenty people who had so undertaken only seven had fulfilled their obligations, and five plots, a speculation in modest scale, were held by Thomas Dawson, a burgess of the town, who later held land at Moyola (Castledawson) in Londonderry[86] and established an iron foundry there. Four of these twenty were burgesses of the town. Most of the delinquents lived in small houses, mostly of native type, scattered throughout the town.[87] The commissioners of inquiry in 1622 noted this building scheme,[88] but their report in common with those of Carew, Bodley, and Pynnar made no observation on the town.

Up to 1622, then, less than half of those who had undertaken to build had done so. Until 1627, if not later, lands adjacent to the town which it had been decided would be leased to tenants undertaking to build were being let on a yearly basis to native Irish tenantry.[89] Within the town the older Gaelic inhabitants retained their houses on a year to year basis. It will be seen that a change in policy took place later.

In 1615[90] there were on the archbishop's rental ninety-six houses within the town of Armagh. The annual rents (where stated) of these houses with their adjacent gardens varied from 13s 4d to 6s 8d. Fourteen British names occur amongst the tenants. In a very small number of cases more than one house was held in the same tenant's name, though occasionally two tenants, always Irish, held one house.[91] From 1618 dates the only rental of our period from which a street plan can be derived.[92] The street pattern indicates a strong continuity with the pre-plantation town. The houses were mostly of Irish type, and the tenants, while predominantly Irish, appear to have mixed together irrespective of origin. Most of the British tenants lived in houses not markedly different from those of their Irish neighbours, but the occasional British-occupied stone house on its larger site must have stood out. The streets either followed the old roads leading from Armagh in various directions, and named appropriately Monaghan Street (now Navan Street), Dundalk Street (now Irish Street), Newry Street (now Scotch Street), or else were a group of lanes roughly following the contours of the original hill nucleus.[93] Many of the street names were as yet in no way formalised, though it is of interest that English rather than Irish names are given. Street names implying national areas, such as Irish Street, did not formally exist, nor is there clear evidence that the population was tending towards such a segregation.

In all, 123 dwelling houses came to light in 1618, as well as various non-dwelling structures. Twenty-seven houses were held by non-Irish tenants, including a few old English. On most of the sites there were out-buildings of various types as well. A few houses had recently been erected, and it is also clear that there were many sites awaiting development. Some parcels of land adjoining the streets had been newly enclosed. The surveyors indicate that there were further houses on the abbey land, held by Caulfeild, 'of which we can get no certain knowledge.' Two 'shops', held by Irish, are referred to.[94]

We have seen that the building lease as a device to develop the town was being granted from 1615. However, up to the end of Hampton's episcopate in 1624, this had secured the erection of only eight or nine 'plantation' houses. The town was not attracting those capable of the outlay demanded. As much as 500 acres around the town designated for leasing in twenty-acre units, with house sites, to 'gentlemen and tradesmen' remained unleased after the succession of James Ussher.[95] In expectation of applicants this land continued to be let piecemeal to both Irish and British on a yearly basis, the claims to more secure tenure of the traditional occupants being necessarily overlooked.[96] The implication of such a policy for the re-development of the town was, it would seem, the eviction of those whose house areas might be acquired. Accordingly these people – or many of them – it is not possible to state if the entire town had been 'reserved for English that will build' had been let their cottages on a year to year basis. However, two factors appear to have led to the leasing of these houses, or many of them. The first was simply the abortiveness of the building programme. The second was that the greater part of the British population had acquired individual sites or houses which they had expanded or rebuilt. There may also have been a clamour from the Irish for a security of tenure, from the refusal of which, especially if coupled with rent increases, it must have appeared that little could be gained.

The decision to grant leases to the sitting tenants, Irish and British, was taken by James Ussher, though there are about three instances of British residents in the town (other than those with building leases) having leases from before this date.[97] The number of unleased houses at this time is not easily established, complications had been introduced with unrecorded sub-tenancies, and the rentals are not always completely clear. A rental of *c.* 1620 claimed that the potential income from this source was £80.[98] The submissions to the visitors of 1622 restated this figure.[99] However, Ussher has preserved a figure of £60.2.0 from a lost rental, and at his accession a rental for 55 houses or tenants totalled £39.10.0, the range of rents being from £1.15.4 to 6s 8d, the greater number paying either 13s 4d or 10s.

Of these 55, 40 were native Irish.[100] On 10 September 1627, 38 leases were made, each to run for twenty-one years.[101] Some indication of the rent increases resulting can be seen from the fact that the primate's income from these 38 tenancies was £34.1.4 per annum.[102] The tenants should also provide two fat hens each at Christmas, or in some cases two capons. Suit of court and use of the lord's mill was also acquired. One of the thirty-four surviving leases required the building of one 'faire coupled house after the English manner' within five years. At this time some familiar street names occur, Irish Street and Gallows Street. This does not seem to indicate segregation: however, almost all the leases bear a later endorsement 'the tenants being dead and the tenement not meared and bounded, not known where it lyes'. Of these 38 tenants, 25 were British. In May 1628 six further houses were leased, one to a British tenant.[103] The rent from these forty-four tenancies was £39.4.8. In the same year, there were listed 20 'cottages' in the town (6 British) which were unleased, and which appear to have paid similar rents, totalling £5.16.8 per annum. Thus while the decision to grant leases was not extended to all inhabitants, it does seem to have applied to a substantial proportion. In 1639 the archbishop adopted a middleman policy in leasing 'most of the town' for sixty years at £58 per annum to William Hilton,[104] a baron of the exchequer, who was also lessee of the Armagh school lands.

An account of the town based on rentals has unavoidable limitations. However, some list the arrears of tenants as well as the 'charge' due, though to what extent the ratio of arrears to rent payable (in itself difficult to establish given the accounting system) may be taken to indicate the prosperity of the town is doubtful. In 1628 a group of tenants whose quarterly rent was £9.18.5 paid £9.0.9, i.e. were in arrears to the extent of only 17s. 8d.[105] However, in 1629 a rental of all or nearly all the houses, other than 'plantation' houses, reveals that of a quarterly sum of £16.14.7 due, £11.14.3 was paid, and £5.0.4, or 29% of the amount due, was in arrears. In three cases 'pawnes' were taken from tenants, a kettle, a horse-cloth and a cadaw. Thirteen of these tenants, one an Englishman who had left the town, whose rents unpaid came to £1.16.2 were designated as 'not able to pay'. Some had been 'forgiven' their rent by the archbishop, two were widows, and most of their houses were decayed.[106] The surviving rentals for the late 1630s are more difficult to interpret, but the impression is of a somewhat similar situation.[107]

The population of Armagh at the end of our period is difficult to assess. The muster roll of *c*. 1630 lists ninety British male inhabitants of the town and liberties.[108] The archbishop's manor court rolls reveal some additional names.[109] A figure of about 100 British males for the town and liberties can be suggested. There was also, of course, a very substantial number of native Irish living in the town.

The absence of will inventories and corporation records makes analysis of the social and occupational structure of the town impossible, but there is reference to the expected occupations. Most of the leaseholders in 1627 are described as yeomen. There were also two maltsters, Matthew Black and William Rastall. A malthouse was leased to one William McGerr. There was also one glover, Richard Francis, and a tann house was held by a Richard Undelly. The Irish family of Crawley or Croly appear to have been merchants and shopkeepers.[110] Outside the town, Matthew Ussher, a burgess and relative of the archbishop, held a mill. Roger Russell, who made the leases in 1627 on the archbishop's behalf, was a butcher who had previously moved from Moneymore in Londonderry to Armagh. While in Moneymore, an Irish deponent stated in 1627, Russell had frequently harboured rebels and received stolen livestock.[111] Richard Chappell,[112] at one time the archbishop's rent-collector, was lessee of the 'bricke p[ar]ke.' A Scottish merchant in the town, John Rown, in dispute, post 1635, with a supplier who had bought in England £70 worth of 'stuffs', silks, buttons, and other merchandise on his behalf, sold these 'both in his shopp' and in the market place on market days.[113] An Armagh merchant in 1641 had a shop there and also in Loughall.[114] There was also an English innkeeper in 1641.[115]

It was perhaps as a marketing centre that the town had most importance, and much of its life must have had a rural relevance. In 1610 it was noted that Armagh with its markets and courts would be a place of meeting for the colony in the county.[116] The right to hold a market in the town on Tuesdays and two fairs annually in March and August was granted to the archbishop in 1615, and a further fair on 29 June in 1634.[117] The market cross figures prominently on Bartlett's map. There was both a 'new' and 'old' market place in 1627.[118] Being unwalled and with many of the streets following the roads leading from the town, Armagh shaded into the countryside. The land in the liberties and 'demesnes' surrounding was let in small units to many of the townsmen.

Apart from some ecclesiastical restoration, there can have been few buildings or institutions of civic sophistication. A sessions house, jail, and/or house of correction existed, most likely in one building.[119] In 1619 a king's letter had directed that a portion of grounds 80 feet by 40, should be reserved for a sessions house and jail. This should be built at the charge of the town and county, with whatever money had been collected already for that purpose, its custody to be committed to the sheriff of the county.[120] The royal school at Armagh can have developed little before 1641. As a

Protestant ecclesiastical centre the town was revived under Christopher Hampton. In 1622 the cathedral was described as follows

> The cathedrall church of Armagh which was ruined and the steeple thrown down by Shane O'Neale, the steeple built the south and northside walls with fair windows, the south and north isles roof'd and platform'd upon both sides of the church, and the great bell cast by the lo: primate.[121]

The archbishop was non-resident, though he had a house in Armagh, but the dean was not an absentee and a chapter and vicars choral were organised. The abbey had been converted to civilian use.[122] However, possibilities of restoring the old institutions must have been in mind in 1641, and on the evidence of the 1630 muster book the inhabitants were ill-equipped to meet a military challenge. Although the only group in the county to muster a drummer, no more than forty-nine of these men were in any way armed.[123]

The role of the corporation remains entirely indistinct. In January 1611 the lord deputy and plantation commissioners ordered the town to be incorporated and the primate 'dealt with all' to make estates to certain burgesses,[124] but incorporation did not come until 1613.[125] The first sovereign and two of the burgesses were relatives of the archbishop and most of the burgesses were resident in the town. The corporation received no land; also fairs and markets, normal in plantation charters, were not included. Its only source of income was from the right to hold a weekly court of record. The episcopal landlord had been clearly unwilling to forego any rights when the corporation was established. The real source of authority within the town must have lain with the landlord and not the corporation.

CHARLEMONT

Charlemont presents a marked contrast to Armagh. It grew from the fort established by Mountjoy in 1602, near the confluence of the Blackwater and Callan rivers, where there had been no previous settlement. A bridge was built across the river and the garrison was under the energetic control of Sir Toby Caulfeild.[126] In June 1607 the fort, with lands adjacent, was leased to Caulfeild for twenty-one years, to be maintained in good repair.[127] In 1608 Sir Josias Bodley, inspecting the Ulster defences, reported that the fort and bawn were 'much decayed,' but that the governor had undertaken to repair it at a cost of £100.[128]

The original fortress built in two stages is represented on Bartlett's map. Within the defences there were about forty houses, mostly thatched, mostly rectangular, cage work being absent. A wooden bridge with handrails, and also a float on the river is illustrated.[129] There is no evidence of civilian settlement at this point. Charlemont retained its military importance after the plantation. As the place of detention of Conn O'Neill, the capture of Charlemont had a special importance in 1615.[130]

However, Charlemont did not simply remain a fortress, and Caulfeild quickly acquired landed interests in the area. He became owner of the extensive estates of the abbey of St Peter and St Paul in Armagh,[131] was tenant to Trinity College, Dublin,[132] and as well received lands as a servitor in County Tyrone.[133] By the time of Carew's survey of the plantation in 1611 he had built a timber stable, garden and impaled haggard outside the rampart. Also the bridge encouraged traffic, and Carew reported that the 'towne' was 'replenished with many inhabitants of English and Irish who have built them good houses of coples after the best manner of the English'.[134]

In 1613 the settlement was incorporated. The corporation received no grant of land – to have done so would have involved the breaking of Caulfeild's lease of the fort lands'[135] – but it was empowered to hold a court of record, a weekly market, and an annual fair.[136] Another fair and market was granted to Caulfeild in 1622.[137] Steps were taken for the repair of the bridge, which had become dilapidated, in 1626.[138] There is no clear evidence for the size of the settlement by 1641. It probably contained some thirty British households, and was not markedly different in size from some of the other incorporated places in the plantation or indeed from some incorporated landlord villages. Some of the first burgesses or their descendants feature as Caulfeild tenants on his abbey lands in 1630,[139] and in a subsequent list of tenants of the lands nearby which he held from Trinity College.[140]

The relation between property holding in the town and countryside in one case is brought out in a chancery suit of *c.* 1630 between William, Lord Caulfeild, and a tenant, Edward May. The suit concerned terms of rent payment and lease duration and arose in part from William's succession to Sir Toby. May had a sixty-year lease of three townlands formerly abbey land as well as two acres in Charlemont with 'certaine' houses built on it and described as 'subject to ffier and other casualtyes,' and parcels of land around the town varying from fifty to four acres. In the town he also held a horse mill and another tenement with three acres appertaining acquired from a previous tenant under a twenty-one year lease.[141] May, as tenant of land, mill, and cottages, was no doubt one of the more substantial inhabitants, but it also seems clear that the land around the town was being leased in small and irregular quantities to its inhabitants. There was also a tannery in Charlemont by 1641.[142]

CAVAN

Cavan was a place of some standing at the end of the sixteenth century. A map of *c.* 1593[143] shows two principal streets, corresponding to the present Main Street and Bridge Street. It also shows the bridge, the Franciscan monastery, the market cross, the O'Reilly castle, and about fifty houses. An inquisition in July 1601 returned that Mulmory oge O'Reilly was possessed of the castle and town, apart from the castle and land of Walter and Thomas Brady and one water mill.[144] Walter Brady, a landowner and merchant, had been appointed by the crown constable and jailer of Cavan in December 1584.[145] The town had many contacts with the Pale area and the Dublin administration.

Cavan was thus a place of some size by Irish standards on the eve of colonisation.[146] Its incorporation is of special interest because the process was initiated before the arrival of colonists. In February 1610 Chichester directed the attorney-general to draw up a fiant for a charter and submit it for his consideration.[147] This appears to have been neglected by Davies so in October the deputy repeated his instructions, recommending that the charter should follow that of Kells and directing that the new corporation be granted 500 acres of land allotted to it.[148] The charter was issued on 15 November 1610.[149] The land granted amounted to some 683 statute acres.

The incorporation of Cavan presented it with a governing body distinctively different from the other Ulster corporations. The first sovereign, Walter Brady, and the two portreeves, Owen (Mor) Brogan and Farrall M'Eregules, were old Irish as were most of the corporators, though Brady was thoroughly anglicised, and only two of the twelve burgesses, Hugh Culme, constable of Cloughowter and a grantee under the plantation, and James Murray, were settlers. Walter Talbot, who, like Culme, did not live in the town, represented the old English landed interest. The area of the borough was to be within a one-mile circumference of Walter Brady's house, but the castle of Cavan and two polls of land appertaining to it were to be exempt from its jurisdiction. The sovereign was to have powers as ample as the sovereign of Kells. The corporation might appoint a recorder or town clerk and also a sergeant of the mace. They might build a 'common hall or tolts hill'. The sovereign was to be a justice of the peace within the bounds of the town. The oaths of officers were laid down and recited. The sovereign was to take the oath of a justice of the peace, the oath of allegiance and an oath to fulfil his duties. There might be a three-weekly court with jurisdiction to the extent of £20. A weekly

market and fairs were also included in the charter. In January 1611 the
deputy and plantation commissioners directed that the justices of assize on
their next circuit should ensure that the sovereign took the oath of allegiance
according to the charter.[150]

From the fragmentary evidence available it seems that the corporation
retained much of its old Irish character up to 1641.[151] In 1627 the sovereign
was Patrick Brady,[152] and in 1628 Nathaniel Dardes, a burgess of old
English origin who died *c.* 1630 and who had taken the oath of supremacy
in 1612,[153] held the office.[154] It may be, however, that in the 1630s the
colonial interest began to achieve a prominence. In 1633 Alan Cook, lay-
chancellor of the diocese of Kilmore and member of parliament for the town
in 1634,[155] features as 'Superior Ville sive Oppid' Cavan',[156] and in the
following year Lawrence Moore was sovereign.[157] In 1628 the portreeves
were William Moore,[158] who held this office also in 1627, and William
O'Brogan.[159] In 1633 a certain John Dowdall, a palesman in origin, held
one of these posts, though at this time the clerk of the court of the town,
Edward Foherton(?), belonged to the incoming element.[160] In 1633, the
recorder, William Clifford, was British.[161] Of eighteen people whose names
survive as burgesses or freemen between 1627 and 1634 nine were Irish or
old English and nine were British. One of these, John Gibson, was a Dublin
merchant. It is difficult to say if the tendency towards British dominance in
the town was further advanced by 1641. However, the sovereign then was
Stephen Allen, who lived in Cavan abbey,[162] and John Whitman, a
merchant, had also been sovereign.[163] After the plantation the castle of Cavan
and the abbey had come into British hands. The former was leased to Sir
Thomas Rotherham, the overseer of fortifications, in 1616,[164] and later
became the property of Sir Oliver Lambert,[165] a local plantation owner. The
abbey was granted to Sir Thomas Ashe, also a plantation grantee, in 1611.[166]

In comparison with Belturbet, which appears to have been larger,[167] Cavan
had a special interest for native Irish elements. In 1636 a report on the state
of the Catholic diocese of Kilmore stated that although there was no city in
the diocese there was, however, one town – 'oppidu . . . unicum' – Cavan,
where there had been, while the Catholic religion flourished, a Franciscan
monastery: yet even now some fathers of the order lodged in private houses.[168]

In its early years the borough was rent by dispute, both internal and
external. In 1612 commissioners for adjudicating land disputes in the
plantation decided and 'quieted' differences between the townsmen, as well
as disputes for land between them and three neighbouring undertakers.[169]
Internal contention appears to have continued, however, and Bodley in
1613 found 'little show of any purpose'. Two or three houses of lime and
stone had been built by the townsmen, who were otherwise 'at a non

plus'.[170] In 1622 it was found that dissention still prevailed, hinging on the use of the town land, and detrimental to the progress of the corporation.[171] The use of the corporation land remains obscure. A number of freehold grants of small areas along with houses were made by the corporation from September 1611. Much of the land – about 500 acres – had come into the hands of Walter Brady's family, and Robert and Patrick Brady are recorded as owners in 1641.[172] The effect of this, however achieved, was that the Bradys were now in a somewhat similar position to the patrons of other towns. The corporators in March 1635 petitioned the house of commons for redress; the outcome is not known, but in July 1641 Patrick Brady petitioned for redress against the corporation.[173]

In 1610 the town was composed, seemingly, of two streets. However, in 1611 a 'vicus novus' or 'new street' 'leading from the high crosses unto the Gallows Hill'[174] features in corporation deeds.[175] High Street also appears, but this may be an alternative name.[176] However, expansion seems to have been slow. By 1613 only two or three new houses were built.[177] Evidence survives of nineteen freehold grants from the corporation of property in the town and its environs between September 1611 and August 1634, seventeen of them between 1624 and 1634. Seven were to British. Some must have been of houses already in existence. The rent payable to the corporation in a few cases where known was either 6d. sterling or 8d. Irish. Grants of land from the corporation in six instances ranged in size from one to four acres. All corporation grants were on the condition that no part should be alienated to any person other than a burgess or freeman of the town.[178]

Between 1632 and 1639 thirteen Cavan freeholders, one of whom, Thomas Newman, lived in Dublin, sold their property to John Gibson, a Dublin merchant, who also in 1634, as a freeman of Cavan, was granted a 'house-roome' from the corporation. An absentee thus appears to have made himself perhaps the largest property owner in Cavan, buying out British and Irish proprietors in almost equal numbers. For twelve properties he paid £345.6.8 stg, in all perhaps £360. The largest component was the property of Patrick McDonagh O'Brogan, a merchant. In all he bought fifteen houses or messuages, and six freeholds in land amounting to sixteen acres.[179]

The muster roll of c. 1630 lists twenty-seven townsmen.[180] Two lived outside the town and three had old English names. Only three were armed. However, leases and deeds of town property, mostly in 1627, provide evidence in witnesses' signatures of forty British, of whom only six appear on the muster roll, who must have lived in the town or close by, and of under thirty Irish and old English residents. There were thus perhaps some fifty British males in the town by 1641.

Cavan was unwalled, though there was a 'town ditch',[181] and it was a market centre. William Cole, a miller present in 1641,[182] would have served both town and countryside. The first sovereign, Walter Brady, was a merchant, but also held land nearby. Few of the inhabitants have their occupations defined. Mahun O'Brogan was also a merchant of some standing in 1611. Patrick McOwen O'Brogan and Patrick McDonagh O'Brogan were of the same occupation, though the latter sold his property, some of which he had acquired from British townsmen, to John Gibson. By 1632 Walter Brady's house was held by John Whitman, an English merchant. In the early 1630s the names of three British merchants occur: one Nicholas Garnett, living outside the town. Hamnet (or Hamlet) Steele was an innkeeper, whose wife in 1639, previously Brennan, was the widow of another British settler. Another establishment, the 'Signe of the Bull', along with four acres of land, was held by Lawrence Dardes, son of Nathaniel the sovereign, and it was mortgaged in 1633 for £40 and sold outright in 1638 for a further £48.[183]

Cavan was, then, a small county and market town, neither a military nor an ecclesiastical centre. Its political structure indicates how much of the old remained in the plantation period. Yet it is evident that both the economic and political balance was changing before 1641. The corporation, as we have seen, clearly had some authority within the town. In the 1620s it resisted a private claim to hold markets there deriving from a patent of 1603.[184] In a list of 'chief gents in Ulster' of about 1625 the sovereign of Cavan was included amongst the fifteen leading people in the county.[185]

BELTURBET

The destruction of the English privy council records for this period leaves the terms of an arrangement made by it for the establishment of Belturbet on 18 July 1610[186] a matter of conjecture. It would seem, however, that the land allocated for the town was granted to Stephen Butler, one of the undertakers in the barony of Loughtee, in August 1610 with building and settling obligations, and that the other undertakers in the barony were required to procure settlers for the town. They were also to build a church.[187] It received its charter in March 1613, Stephen Butler himself being the first chief officer.[188]

By the time of Carew's survey in 1611 Butler and Sir Hugh Wirrall, another undertaker, were living there. Also they, and another grantee, had had boats built there, one of which would carry 'twelve or fourteen' tons.[189] Bodley in his survey of 1613, stated that the corporation 'goeth well forward'. Butler, Wirrall, 'and others the undertakers thereof' had appointed their freeholders for the town, many of whom had already built their houses there.[190] Pynnar in 1618-19 found in the town 'houses built of cage-work all inhabited with British tenants, and most of them tradesmen, each of these having a house and garden plott, with four acres of land, and commons for certain numbers of cows and garrans'.[191]

That the inhabitants were dissatisfied in their relations with Butler is evident, however. They appealed to the lord deputy and council and received an order in their favour.[192] On 20 May 1618 Butler granted the town lands, except one acre called the 'Tile Kill Yard,' to the corporation along with a weekly market and court of record and two fairs at a rent of £1.10.0.[193] In 1622, however, the commissioners then surveying the plantation found that although there were thirty-four houses all with British inhabitants, there was complaint that allocations of land had not been made. Many of the corporation claimed not to have heard of the council order, but with this knowledge at their disposal they seemed more satisfied and Butler and they 'promised future love and amitie one towards another'. The commissioners hoped this would encourage 'that well begune corporacion which is fitt to be cherished' and stated that there was a 'great store' of Protestants in and about the town. They recommended that a church should be built there.[194] Subsequent relations with Butler remain obscure, but there were difficulties about the corporation in the 1670s.[195] There is little detailed evidence about the composition of the town. In 1613 Richard Allsop, merchant, of Lisduff, County Cavan, and Margaret Smith of Dublin received licences to keep taverns in Belturbet and Cavan.[196] In 1622 the parish minister lived there, though no church had been built.[197] In 1624 during an insurrection scare it emerges that the town had constables and a watch.[198] By 1641 Belturbet was a place of some size and substance, and more Protestant in character than Cavan. Bishop Bedell's son, William, writing after the Restoration, described Belturbet in his father's time as being 'the only considerable town in the whole county', but which 'yet was built as one of our ordinary market-towns here in England, having only but one church in it.' Cavan, however, was 'not so big by one-half' as Belturbet.[199] The depositions of 1641, if one can accept deponents' own definitions of their occupations, reveal that there were, of British settlers, living in the town in 1641 at least five merchants, one baker, two carriers, one gun smith, one felt-maker, one shoemaker, and one innkeeper who also had a tannhouse.[200] Some of these also held land. Indeed some substantial landowners lived there, for example, Thomas Tailor, who was a freeholder and leaseholder on a number of estates in the barony of Loughtee.[201]

TOWNS WHICH WERE NOT INCORPORATED

MOUNTNORRIS

In origin and development Mountnorris was akin to Charlemont.[202] The fort there was established in 1600, and by 1611, Carew, who regarded it as a place of 'special importe … and fit to be mayntained and supported', reported that English and Irish inhabitants had 'resorted' there and built 'good' houses 'after the manner of the Pale, which is a greate releafe, saftie, and comforte for passengers between the Newrye and Armagh'.[203] In 1605 the fort and associated lands were leased to Captain Henry Adderton,[204] and, after his death in 1611, the fort and cumulatively lands in the vicinity came into the hands of Francis Annesley, later Lord Mountnorris.[205] No lands were specifically reserved for the proposed town, however; hence, although a warrant for a grant of such lands to Annesley was drawn up,[206] there were no obligations binding him to procure incorporation. The subsequent development of Mountnorris remains obscure.

TANDRAGEE

Tandragee proposed for incorporation in 1609 was not, unlike Mountnorris, included in Chichester's list of 1611. Although its incorporation was thus officially dropped, it became, under the tutelage of the grantee in whose estate it was located, Sir Oliver St John, a typical planter village consisting of thirty-five 'English-like houses' in 1622.[207]

VIRGINIA

Virginia, the proposed town midway between Kells and Cavan, failed to be incorporated, it would seem, for a number of reasons. Although a grant under the superintendency system of the lands allotted to it was made to Captain John Ridgeway in 1612, by 1613, the operative date for incorporation, though the name had been chosen otherwise, there was 'nothing done'.[208] Shortly afterwards a change of ownership, whereby the town lands and the adjoining estate came to Hugh Culme, a servitor owner elsewhere in the county, brought little energy in urban beginnings. By the 1620s when the estate had come into the old English hands of Lucas Plunkett, subsequently earl of Fingall, there were less than ten British settlers resident there. Discontinuity of ownership had doubtless accounted for this slow growth. By the 1630s there were twenty British residents, who attempted to secure incorporation, but prevarications by Fingall caused this to be deferred. Virginia was in the anomalous position of being the only proposed corporation in the planted counties to have come into old English ownership.[209]

OTHER INCEPTIVE TOWNS AND VILLAGES

Lurgan, on the Brownlow estate in north Armagh, became a sizeable settlement. It contained a church and a mill and grew up close to the landlord's house. A list of inhabitants and their occupations dating from 1622 is unusually informative.[210] Lurgan then consisted of forty-seven houses, two occupied by Irishmen, one a cooper and another who was stated to be 'conformable.' Of the remaining residents there were one each of masons, butchers, carpenters, tanners, smiths, weavers, and tailors. There were two coopers, four joiners, three turners, and two shoemakers. Each had a house in the town and usually small areas of land. The other residents apart from a labourer who held two acres were on the whole defined as yeomen or husbandmen.

For his village of Clancarny or Markethill, also in Armagh, Sir Archibald Acheson listed thirty-six resident householders for the commissioners examining the plantation in 1622.[211] These included three shoemakers, three weavers, one baker, and one carpenter. The commissioners noted of one, Patrick Sherry, that he was 'an Irish man and goes not to church.' That the town had some arrangements for the maintenance of order can be seen from the fact that one resident, Edward Johnson, is listed as constable.

While there is less information about village development in Cavan a similar picture emerges. By the end of the 1620s Bailieborough was a village of fifteen 'English-like houses planted and inhabited with British families'.[212] Shercock, then Persecourt, contained eighteen 'English-like' houses,[213] Killashandra had thirty-four houses with British residents,[214] and Moynehall had twenty-four 'and more, all inhabited with Englishe and Britishe families'.[215]

Perhaps the most obvious common characteristic of the towns in Armagh and Cavan prior to 1641 is their limited size. At the same time they were developing centres containing a variety of tradesmen and serving the surrounding countryside. Much of their physical fabric was obviously British, especially those which originated as forts. But not all of them had such an origin. Cavan and Armagh had considerable Gaelic antiquity and retained much of their indigenous character. Most seem to have attracted Irish as well as immigrant inhabitants. Many of those which were incorporated were not markedly different in size, character, or independence from the unincorporated landlord towns or villages. If to the Irish the new corporations symbolised an altered dispensation, the flimsiness of that symbolism, their pregnability, was demonstrated in 1641. Nevertheless the urban beginnings made in the previous thirty years have had, in varying scale, a continuity to the present day.

APPENDIX

Proposed towns 1609	Proposed towns 1611	Towns incorporated and dates
Dungannon	Dungannon	Dungannon, 27 November 1612
Clogher		Clogher c. 1629–34
Omagh	Omagh	
Loughinsholin		
Mountjoy	Mountjoy	
	Strabane	Strabane 18 March 1613
		Augher 15 April 1613
Limavady	Limavady	Limavady 30 March 1613
Dungiven		
	Coleraine	Coleraine 28 June 1613
Derry	*Derry*	Londonderry 29 March 1613
Lifford	Lifford	Lifford 27 February 1613
Ballyshannon	Ballyshannon	Ballyshannon 23 March 1613
Killybegs		Killybegs 14 December 1615
Donegal	Donegal	Donegal 27 February 1613
Raphoe		
Rathmullan	Rathmullan	
Dowagh in Innishowen		
Lisgoole		
Castlekeagh		
middle way between Lisgoole and Ballyshannon }		
	Enniskillen	Enniskillen 27 February 1613
Cavan	*Cavan*	Cavan 15 November 1610
Belturbet	Belturbet	Belturbet 30 March 1613
midway between Kells and Cavan }	Lough Ramor	

421

Armagh	Armagh	Armagh 26 March 1613
Mountnorris	Mountnorris	
Charlemont	Charlemont	Charlemont 28 April 1613
Tandragee		

Italicisation indicates that incorporation had taken place by this time.

[1] Cambridge University Library, MS KK, 1 15, vol. 1, ff 5–8.
[2] W.L. Renwick (ed.), *A view of the present state of Ireland by Edmund Spenser* (London, 1934), 165–6.
[3] G. Hill, *An historical account of the plantation in Ulster* (Belfast 1877), 88.
[4] 'Ulster Plantation Papers' no. 74, in *Analecta Hibernica* 8 (1938), 286–96. The version in W. Harris, *Hibernica* (Dublin, 1770) refers to only twenty-three proposed towns.
[5] 'Ulster Plantation Papers' no. 74, in *Analecta Hibernica* 8 (1938), 288.
[6] T. Blenerhasset, 'A direction for the plantation in Ulster', in *A contemporary history of affairs in Ireland* I, i ed., J.T. Gilbert (Dublin, 1879), 317–26.
[7] The National Archives, London, State Papers [henceforth TNA, SP] 63/228, ff 172–3 (*Cal. S.P. Ire., 1608–10*, 415–16).
[8] Lambeth Palace Library, Carew MS 629, ff 66v–7v (*Cal. Carew MSS, 1603–24*, 56–7); *Cal. S.P. Ire., 1608–10*, 488.
[9] This excludes the incorporation of Derry in 1604, which preceded the plantation plan.
[10] Lambeth Palace Library, Carew MS 629, ff 68–72 (*Cal. Carew MSS, 1603–24*, 141–2; *Cal. S.P. Ire., 1611–14*, 36–7). The dating of this document in the Carew calendar is incorrect and misleading. The propositions were sent to England on 11 Dec. 1610 and returned on 19 May 1611.
[11] 'Ulster Plantation Papers' no. 52, in *Analecta Hibernica* 8 (1938), 260. The document is undated. The suggested date, 1610?, is probably too early, it is clearly related to the decision discussed previously.
[12] *Cal. Pat. Rolls Ire., Jas I*, 182.
[13] T.W. Moody, *The Londonderry plantation* (Belfast, 1939), 36, 41, 62–83, 133–8.
[14] The English privy council registers for this period have been destroyed.
[15] 'Ulster Plantation Papers' no. 27, in *Analecta Hibernica* 8 (1938), 242.
[16] Ibid., no. 28, 245.
[17] Ibid., 244–5.
[18] However, there is no indication that similar arrangements were made for the other places.
[19] Lambeth Palace Library, Carew MS 629, ff 43–6v (*Cal. Carew MSS, 1603–24*, 134–6). See Appendix. Another document of this period, used by Carew, envisaged five, rather than four, corporate towns (unnamed) for Donegal (ibid., f. 41).
[20] W.C. Trimble, *The history of Enniskillen*, i (Enniskillen, 1919), 6–10, 161–70.
[21] *Cal. S.P. Ire., 1608–10*, 580; *Cal. Pat. Rolls Ire., Jas I*, 153, 161, 169, 173.
[22] *Cal. Carew MSS, 1603–24*, 36–8.
[23] *Cal. Pat. Rolls Ire., Jas I*, 165. The lands previously allocated to the fort of Mountjoy, a place designated for incorporation in both 1609 and 1611, and like Omagh not subsequently incorporated, were leased in June 1610 to the local commander (ibid., 176).
[24] Bodleian Library Oxford, Carte MS 62, f. 19 (*Cal. S.P. Ire., 1611–14*, 96). Abstract of patent in G. Hill, *Plantation in Ulster* (Belfast, 1877), 325–6.
[25] *Cal. Carew MSS, 1603–24*, 75–9, 220–30.
[26] T.W. Moody, 'The Irish parliament under Elizabeth and James I' in *Royal Ir. Academy Proc.* 45C (1939–40), 53–7.
[27] *Cal. Pat. Rolls Ire., Jas I*, 206–7. Sixty 'inhabitants' had been required by his lease.
[28] Ibid., 217, 219–20, 232, 236, 256.
[29] The calendared versions of these patents vary in detail. A transcript of the patent for Enniskillen appears in Trimble, *History of Enniskillen*, i, 166–70. Here the patron was also required to provide for 'ten other burgages of inferior place', and engage in a substantial building programme.

[30] The city of London may be regarded as patron of Derry and Coleraine; however, the obligations it entered into were very much more demanding. At Derry 200 houses were to be built and room left for 300 more, and at Coleraine 100, with space for a further 200 (*Cal. Carew MSS, 1603–24*, 36).

[31] These have not been found, owing to the destruction of the privy council records. However, they are referred to in the warrants for incorporation. See endnote 34.

[32] *Cal. S.P. Ire., 1611–14*, 285–7.

[33] In one case, Lifford, recommendations by the patron and townsmen transmitted to the lord deputy at the beginning of August about the charter, assuming a corporate body of twenty, were therefore now overruled (Bodleian Library, Oxford, Carte MS 62, ff 211v–13v).

[34] Bodleian Library, Oxford, Carte MS 62, ff 143, 145, 147, 159, 161,163, 167, 191, 195, 201, 209, 214, 221 (*Cal. S.P. Ire., 1611–14*, 308, 300, 338, 288, 293, 302, 299, 336, 304, 294, 294, 300, 295). The calendared versions contain many inaccuracies.

[35] On Coleraine see Moody, *Londonderry plantation*, 138–9.

[36] Bodleian Library, Oxford, Carte MS 62, ff 223–3v.

[37] Ibid., f. 221.

[38] Ibid., ff 201–3.

[39] For biographical details of them see Trimble, *History of Enniskillen*, i, 181–2.

[40] The substitution, in the charter of Ballyshannon, of one name for another, in the warrant of incorporation, stated to have taken place by a local historian (E. Maguire, *Ballyshannon, past and present* (Bundoran and Ballyshannon [*c.* 1920], 71) did not take place. The author was misled by an error in transcription in *Cal. S.P. Ire., 1611–14*, 288, see Bodleian Library, Oxford, Carte MS 62, f. 159.

[41] Anomalously, though indicating the speed with which incorporation was pushed through, the charter of Augher was issued some days before the grant of the town lands to the patron.

[42] Transcripts of many of these charters are in Royal Irish Academy [hence forth RIA], 24 Q 7, 10, 11, 13 and National Archives of Ireland [henceforth NAI], RC 3/2, 4, 5, 7, 8.

[43] Moody, *Londonderry plantation*, 122–42.

[44] There had been some dispute about this in 1612 (*Cal. S.P. Ire., 1611–14*, 288).

[45] A.G.R. Smith, *The government of Elizabethan England* (London, 1967), 96–7. For a recent discussion of one such charter, that of Congleton in Cheshire of 1625 see W.B. Stephens (ed.), *History of Congleton* (Manchester, 1970), 64–71.

[46] Bodleian Library, Oxford, Carte MS 62, f. 221.

[47] The warrants of incorporation of Mountjoy and Rathmullan included one and two old Irish names respectively (ibid., ff 161, 163), but these places were not incorporated.

[48] G. Camblin, *The town in Ulster* (Belfast, 1951), 19–21.

[49] As it was, both Augher and Charlemont were disfranchised because their charters were granted after the issue of writs of election (*Cal. S.P. Ire., 1611–14*, 498).

[50] Bodleian Library, Oxford, Carte MS 62, f. 343. It was to receive the privileges contained in the recent charters, except the right of sending burgesses to parliament.

[51] *Cal. Pat. Rolls Ire., Jas I*, 300, see also p. 436.

[52] Ibid., 413.

[53] NAI, RC 3/4, ff 88–93 (*Cal. Pat. Rolls Ire., Jas I*, 403). The patent contained stipulations about the plan of the town.

[54] In this context the patent of Killybegs which required the patron 'to build twenty houses and to assign lands for the burgesses who are to be twelve in number' (ibid., 300), represents a compromise position in relation to the earlier patronage grants.

[55] *Civil Survey III*, 23.

[56] *Cal. Pat. Rolls Ire., Jas I*, 433, see also pp 483, 488.

[57] NAI, Chancery Pleadings, W, no. 65.

[58] *Cal. Pat. Rolls Ire., Chas I*, 464–7, 544.

[59] For some discussion see J.J. Marshall, *Clochar na righ* (Dungannon, 1930), 50–52; Earl of Belmore, *Parliamentary memoirs of Fermanagh and Tyrone* (Dublin, 1887), 144.

[60] National Library of Ireland [henceforth NLI], Fingall Papers, MS 8032/1, 2, 3. For some discussion of this see my 'An Ulster plantation town – Virginia' in *Breifne* (1970), 43–51.

[61] Although it only happened in one instance, the entrusting of town development to private individuals made it possible that by sales towns could come into the possession of people not considered appropriate agents of plantation development. Thus Virginia and the neighbouring

plantation estate was acquired by the old English Lucas Plunkett, subsequently earl of Fingall, in 1622 and was described in 1642 as 'a towne of the trayter the Earl of Fingall' (J. Hogan (ed.), *Letters and papers relating to the Irish Rebellion* (Dublin, 1936), 150).

[62] V. Treadwell, 'The plantation of Donegal – a survey', in *Donegal Annual*, vol. 2, no. 3 (1953–4), 513.

[63] TCD, MS E. 3. 6, p. 205. The statement that the chief officer of Enniskillen received a salary of £100 per annum (Trimble, *History of Enniskillen* (1921), 721–2), has no foundation in the charter, nor could any such financial arrangement have been made at this time. This must have arisen in the eighteenth century.

[64] NLI, MS 8014/X.

[65] *Cal. Carew MSS, 1603–24*, 370, 380; *Cal. S.P. Ire., 1615–25*, 231, 303.

[66] *Cal. Pat. Rolls Ire., Jas I*, 445.

[67] NAI, RC, 3/4, ff 62–73v; (*Cal. Pat. Rolls Ire., Jas I*, 521).

[68] *Cal. Pat. Rolls Ire., Jas I*, 412, 'to the end that the town may be of better use to the King and more safety for his subjects … than other ordinary towns of the kind have been.'

[69] *Cal. S.P. Ire., 1615–25*, 336; *Cal. Pat. Rolls Ire., Jas I*, 512, 567.

[70] *Cal S.P. Ire., 1615–25*, 449.

[71] 'Ulster Plantation Papers' no. 74, in *Analecta Hibernica* 8 (1938), 294.

[72] T. Blenerhasset, 'A direction for the plantation in Ulster', in *A contemporary history of affairs in Ireland*, I, i, ed., J.T. Gilbert (Dublin, 1879), 321.

[73] G.A. Hayes-McCoy (ed.), *Ulster and other Irish maps, c. 1600* (Dublin, 1964), iii. On the origin of the trians see J. Stuart, *Historical memoirs of the city of Armagh* (Newry, 1819), 143–4.

[74] *Cal. Pat. Rolls Ire., Jas I*, 102. This was a lease, in February 1610 he received an outright grant (ibid., 159).

[75] *Cal S.P. Ire., 1603–6*, 317–23, 328–30.

[76] Moody, *Londonderry plantation*, 275.

[77] Armagh Public Library [henceforth APL], cardboard box, 'old leases of primate's', lease not found, but referred to in lease from Buckworth and Dodington to John Hall, 20 Dec. 1615.

[78] Armagh Archiepiscopal Registry [henceforth AAR], A. 2a. no. 28, f. 28.

[79] J.B. Leslie, *Armagh clergy and parishes* (Dundalk, 1911), 42, 113, 205.

[80] APL, in box 'old leases of primate's'. Lease between Buckworth and Dodington, and John Hall of Armagh, 20 Dec. 1615. This lease, while the only one of its type to survive, is clearly a standard one drawn up with gaps for the entry of tenants' names.

[81] See L. Stone, *The crisis of the aristocracy, 1558–1641* (London, 1965), 357–63.

[82] AAR, Visitation book, 1622, B. Ib. no. 193, p. 1; Rental, 1622, with amendments by James Ussher, *c.* 1627, Armagh Rent Rolls, A. 2a. 28/13.

[83] Hamlin was mayor of Drogheda in 1609 (*Cal. S.P. Ire., 1608–10*, 140).

[84] Moody, *Londonderry plantation*, 151, 173.

[85] AAR, A. 2a. 28/10, p. 36.

[86] Moody, *Londonderry plantation*, 239, 372.

[87] AAR, A. 2a. 28/11, Civitas ac villa de Armath (rental of 1618).

[88] NLI, Rich papers, MS 8013/9.

[89] AAR, A. 2a. 28/13.

[90] The date of the first surviving rental.

[91] AAR, A. 2a 28/10, pp 28–31; Liver supervisor de anno 1615 pro ter Primat.

[92] AAR, A. 2a 28/11: Civitas ac villa de Armath, a general survey of the town of Armagh by Mr Thomas Grant, Xpfer Bent[ley], William Harris and Patrick Croly, the 25 Sep. a.d. 1618.

[93] H.D.McC. Reid, *The historical geography of Armagh* (unpublished M.A. thesis, Queen's University, Belfast 1954).

[94] AAR, A. 2a, 28/11, passim.

[95] AAR, A. 2a. 28/13, p. 41: The true revenue of the temporalities belonging to the archbishopric of Armagh … at the decease of Christopher Hampton. This document contains meticulous notes and observations appended by Ussher, *c.* 1627.

[96] Ibid., passim.

[97] AAR, A. 2a. 28/13, p. 3, also list of counterparts of leases made by Christopher Hampton, ibid., 43–55.

[98] L.P. Murray (ed.), 'A rent-roll of all the houses and lands belonging to the see of Armagh' in *Archivium Hibernicum* 8 (1941), 100.

99 AAR, B. Ib. no. 193, p. 2.
100 AAR, A. 2a. 28/13, p. 5.
101 Thirty-four of the counterparts of these leases have survived, one being in Ussher's own hand (AAR, E.I.e.).
102 AAR, A. 2a 28/19, p. 3; ibid., 20, 5–6.
103 AAR, A. 2a. 28/19, p. 3.
104 AAR, A. Ib. 31 (Walter Dawson's rental, 1713), p. 3.
105 AAR, A. Ib. 29/1, 2–3.
108 AAR, A. Ib. 29/2, 1–2.
107 AAR, A. Ib. 29/5, 6, 7, passim.
108 British Library [henceforth BL], Add. MS 4770, ff 41v–3.
109 APL, Archbishop's manor court rolls.
110 AAR, bundle of leases, E.I.e.
111 TNA, SP 63/244, ff 145–6v (Cal S.P. Ire., 1625–32, 216).
112 Memorial tablet in Church of Ireland Cathedral, Armagh.
113 NAI, Chancery Pleadings, U. 66 (document damaged).
114 TCD, MS F. 3. 7, ff 57–7v.
115 Ibid., f. 100.
116 Cal. S.P. Ire., 1608–10, 406.
117 APL, John Lodge MS G. III. 23, p. 5.
118 Referred to in leases, 1627.
119 TCD, MS F. 3. 7, f. 249.
120 AAR, A. Ib. no. 26, pp 206–7.
121 AAR, B. Ib. no. 193, pp 26–7.
122 TCD, MS F. 3. 7, ff 42–3.
123 BL, Add. MS 4770, ff 41 v–2v.
124 'Ulster plantation papers' no. 27, in Analecta Hibernica 8 (1938), 243.
125 RIA, MS 24 Q 7, pp 160–72; Cal. Pat. Rolls Ire., Jas I, 255 (heading only); Stuart, Armagh, 640–46 (translation).
126 Earlier writings have been mainly concerned with the military importance of Charlemont, e.g. J.J. Marshall, History of Charlemount fort and borough ... and Mountjoy fort (Dungannon, 1921); J.W. Hanna, Annals of Charlemont (Armagh, 1846).
127 Cal. Pat. Rolls Ire., Jas I, 102.
128 J. Buckley (ed.), 'Report of Sir Josias Bodley on some Ulster fortresses in 1608' in Ulster Journal of Archaeology, 2nd series 16 (1910), 62.
129 Hayes-McCoy (ed.), Ulster and other Irish maps, c.1600, iv and p. 7.
130 Cal. S.P. Ire., 1615–25, 82.
131 Cal. Pat. Rolls Ire., Jas I, 229.
132 TCD, MSS Room, box of College leases under D.
133 Hill, Plantation in Ulster, 316.
134 Carew MS 630, f. 60v.
135 He became owner of the fort and lands in 1623 (Cal. Pat. Rolls Ire., Jas I, 562–3).
136 RIA, MS 24 Q 10, pp 104–15; Marshall, Charlemount and Mountjoy, 14–15 (translated abstract).
137 APL, John Lodge MS G 111 23, p. 5.
138 C.R. Elrington (ed.), Works of Ussher (Dublin, 1864), XV, 273.
139 BL, Add. MS 4770, ff 43–4.
140 TCD, Muniment Room, Mahaffy collection, Drawer G. folder 1.
141 NAI, Chancery Pleadings, I, 65 (damaged bill).
142 TCD, MS F. 3.7, f. 215.
143 Reproduced in P. O'Connell, The diocese of Kilmore (Dublin, 1937), 301.
144 NAI, Calendar to exchequer inquisitions, Ulster, Cavan, (7) Eliz., 17–24.
145 Cal. Fiants Ire., Eliz., no. 4547.
146 Davies described it in 1607 as a 'poor Irish town' (H. Morley, Ireland under Elizabeth and James I (London, 1890), 374).
147 Bodleian Library, Oxford, Carte MS 61, f. 485 (Cal. S.P. Ire., 1608–10, 390).
148 Ibid., f. 497 (ibid., 514).
149 RIA, MS 24 Q 10, pp 130–52; T.S. Smyth, The civic history of the town of Cavan (Dublin, 1938), 18–21 (abstract).

[150] 'Ulster plantation papers' no. 27, in *Analecta Hibernica* 8 (1938), 243.

[151] The main source for what follows is a collection of leases and deeds or abstracts of them in NLI, Farnham Papers, D 20409–20475, and MS 11490/3, 4.

[152] Indenture, 20 Sep. 1620, between corporation of Cavan and Terence O'Reilly (NLI, D 20409–20475).

[153] 'Ulster plantation papers' no. 69, in *Analecta Hibernica* 8 (1938) 277. Here he is listed with a group of tenants of Stephen Butler, a local undertaker.

[154] Indenture, 1 Aug. 1628, between corporation of Cavan and Lawrence Dardes (NLI, D 20409–20475). 155. H.F. Kearney, *Strafford in Ireland, 1633–41* (Manchester, 1959), 257–8.

[156] Indenture, 13 Sep. 1633, between corporation of Cavan on the one hand and William Clifford and James Gray on the other (NLI, D 20409–20475).

[157] Indenture, 28 Aug. 1634, between corporation of Cavan and John Gibson (NLI, D 20409–20475), Moore may have been Irish.

[158] Indenture, 20 Sep. 1627 between corporation of Cavan and Terence O'Reilly (ibid.).

[159] Indenture, 29 Aug. 1628, between corporation of Cavan and William Moore (ibid.).

[160] Indenture, 13 Sep. 1633, between corporation of Cavan, on one hand, and William Clifford and James Gray on the other (ibid.).

[161] Indenture, 29 Aug. 1628, between corporation and William Moore (ibid.).

[162] TCD, MS F. 3. 3. ff 173–4.

[163] TCD, MS F. 3. 4, ff 273–4v.

[164] *Cal. Pat. Rolls Ire., Jas I*, 313.

[165] Ibid., 454. He was required to build a strong house or castle.

[166] Ibid., 199.

[167] T.W. Jones (ed.), *Life and death of William Bedell* (London, 1872), 62.

[168] P.F. Moran (ed.), *Spicilegium Ossoriense* (1st series, Dublin, 1874), 208.

[169] TCD, MS F. 1. 20, ff 16, 17v, 19.

[170] Historical Manuscripts Commission [henceforth HMC], *Hastings MSS*, iv, 162.

[171] BL, Add. MS 4756, f. 104.

[172] NAI, Book of Survey and Distribution.

[173] *Commons Jn., Ire.*, 17 March 1635, 105; 14 April 1635, 117; 15 July 1641, 257.

[174] Indenture, 13 March 1632, between Patrick Brady on one hand, and Thomas Brady and Nicholas Garnett on the other (NLI, D 20409–20475).

[175] Indenture, 1 Sep. 1611, between corporation of Cavan and Mahun O'Brogan (ibid.).

[176] Indenture, 30 May 1634, between Lawrence Dardes and John Gibson (ibid.).

[177] HMC, *Hastings MSS*, iv, 162.

[178] NLI, D 20409–20475, MS 11490/4.

[179] NLI, D 20409–20475, MS 1490/3, 4.

[180] BL, Add. MS 4770, f. 22v.

[181] Indenture, 28 Aug. 1634, between corporation of Cavan and John Gibson (NLI, D 20409–20475).

[182] TCD, MS F. 3. 4, ff 226–6v.

[183] Ibid.

[184] *Cal. Pat. Rolls Ire., Jas I*, 12; NAI, Chancery Pleadings, 2B. 30. 120, no. 96; *Inq. Cancell. Hib. Repert.*, ii, Cavan (68) Chas I.

[185] Public Record Office of Northern Ireland, T808/15261.

[186] Referred to in NAI, Lodge, Records of the rolls, vi, 169.

[187] HMC, *Hastings MSS*, iv, 163; Hill, *Plantation in Ulster*, 465–6 (Pynnar's survey).

[188] *Cal. Pat. Rolls Ire., Jas I*, 255; Bodleian Library, Oxford, Carte MS 62, f. 167.

[189] Lambeth Palace Library, Carew MS 630, f. 62.

[190] HMC, *Hastings MSS*, iv, 163.

[191] Hill, *Plantation in Ulster*, 465–6. A conveyance in 1641 indicates that small acreages were associated with houses in the town, as well as common rights (NLI, D 10025).

[192] Referred to in BL, Add. MS 4756, f. 102v.

[193] NAI, MS Co. 1822, Lodge, Records of the rolls, vi, 169; *Cal. Pat. Rolls Ire., Jas I*, 423.

[194] BL, Add. MS 4756, f. 102v.

[195] NLI, MS D 7340.

[196] *Cal. Pat. Rolls Ire., Jas I*, 261.

197 AAR, B. Ib. no. 193, pp 144–5.
198 *Cal. S.P. Ire., 1615–25*, 479–80.
199 T.W. Jones (ed.), *Life and death of William Bedell* (London, 1872), 62.
200 TCD, MS F. 3. 3, 4 passim.
201 TCD, MS F. 3. 3, ff 97–7v.
202 Hayes-McCoy, *Ulster and other Irish maps, c. 1600*, 11.
203 Lambeth Palace Library, Carew MS 630, f. 60v.
204 *Cal. Pat. Rolls Ire., Jas I*, 78.
205 Ibid., 203, 207, 272.
206 'Ulster plantation papers' no. 58, in *Analecta Hibernica* 8 (1938), 265–6.
207 *Inq. Cancell. Hib. Repert.*, ii, Armagh (7) Jas I.
208 HMC, *Hastings MSS*, iv, 160.
209 For a more detailed examination see my 'An Ulster plantation town – Virginia' in *Breifne* (1970), 43–51.
210 TNA, Manchester Papers, 30/15/2/183.
211 NLI, MS 8014/9.
212 *Inq. Cancell. Hib. Repert.*, ii, Cavan (18) Chas I.
213 Ibid., (19) Chas I.
214 Ibid., (24) Chas I.
215 Ibid., (25) Chas I.

16

An Ulster Plantation Town, Virginia

I

This examination of the early history of the town of Virginia seeks to pinpoint in an extreme case one of the defects of the plantation in Ulster – its inadequate urban basis. Although Virginia owes its origin to the plantation scheme, it was described in 1642, when the plantation was being subjected to the trial of arms, as 'a towne of the trayter the Earl of Fingall'.[1] That it had come into old English hands was peculiarly anomalous, how and with what effects is set out below, but except in this the development of Virginia during the plantation is not unique, and indeed that this could happen follows logically from the evolution of government policy on the establishment of towns in the Ulster plantation. It will be valuable then to set out the early history of this one town against a background, briefly outlined, of the urban proposals, and their modification in the Ulster plantation scheme.

II

At the planning stage of the plantation the importance of inaugurating towns was fully recognised. The 'Project' of the plantation, produced at the beginning of 1609, embodied the details of this intention – in all twenty-five towns were to be established in the six confiscated counties. Some were to be completely new settlements, others were to be developments on previous sites, forts or places of traditional Irish occupation. It was intended that these towns should be given corporate status, and land was allocated, some five to ten townlands each, to be granted to the corporations to provide an income for their development. In order to establish these towns there should be a 'leavy or presse' of tradesmen and artificers from England.[2] It was accepted, in other words, that the establishment of towns should demand positive action by the state.

One year later, in the spring of 1610, it was found that although many aspects of the plantation had been by then considered in detail, arrangements for the foundation of towns had been neglected. To the Dublin government, confronted with the task of getting the plantation into operation, it now seemed that action by London, in the despatch of tradesmen or whatever had become unlikely and the question they posed was whether if tradesmen were not to be 'pressed' from England, corporations should be established at all. The London government thus pressed by Dublin decided that the projected incorporations should be proceeded with – that charters should be issued – 'for that will draw the tradesmen who will come over with the others'.[3]

In July 1610, just as the lord deputy, Sir Arthur Chichester and the plantation commissioners (members of the Irish privy council) were departing to Ulster to allot the land to its new grantees, further directives were issued from London. The plantation commissioners were to decide on the number of houses to be built in each town, and set out sites for churches, market places, and the like. The lord deputy and council were to give instructions for the peopling of the towns and the building of churches and schools 'so far as the means of the country will yield'. When the towns had grown to forty houses they should be incorporated.[4]

These instructions represented in reality not much more than a facile transference of responsibility from London to Dublin. In December, after the land had been allotted to grantees, the Dublin government submitted a series of problems to the privy council in London for their advice and direction. One of these revealed that the founding of towns still remained a difficulty to which no satisfactory solution had been found. The lord deputy's suggestion was that some 'principal gentlemen' should be appointed 'superintendents' of the corporations to 'draw' settlers there and to maintain order until the towns had increased to 'sufficient' size when they should be incorporated and authority transferred to the mayors. The privy council accepted this proposal, laying down that an undertaker or servitor near the site of each proposed town should be appointed to build houses for tradesmen, who should hold their tenements from him. The land for the town should be granted to the planter in fee farm with a time specified for the performance of his obligations, incorporation to take place subsequently.[5]

On the basis of this decision steps were taken for the granting of the lands assigned for towns to neighbouring planters. A form of warrant for the fiant of a grant of town lands was drawn up, presumably about mid 1611, whereby grants were to follow a set pattern 'accordinge to the artickles layd down for a burrowe towne'.[6] It was thus a year after many of the major problems of inaugurating the colony had been settled, and when almost all the land had already been granted, that a means to establish the towns had been found. One clear outcome of this arrangement whereby landlords rather than the government were made responsible for establishing the towns was that the major part of the land initially assigned as endowment for proposed corporations now came into private hands.[7]

This initial recession in policy is reflected also in the fact that only fourteen towns (not including Virginia) eventually received charters, only somewhat more than half of the number originally proposed. The charters of these towns had an essential simplicity and similarity.[8] Civic government was vested in a small and self-electing body of twelve burgesses and a chief officer. It was these who should elect the two members of parliament each incorporated town might return. Each corporation might hold a weekly court to hear minor civil actions. Rights to hold fairs and markets were also usual.[9]

One of the most notable features of these charters was that they, necessarily, did not contain a grant of the fee farm of the town and of the lands originally intended as its endowment. The process, outlined above, whereby responsibility for town establishment came into private hands ensured their subordination, in varying degree, to local outside authority. The incomes of the corporations were thus from the start severely limited. Thus the retreat in government policy at the outset, in deciding to entrust the founding of towns to individual settlers, requires emphasis. To do better would probably have stretched the competence and finances of the contemporary state, but in leaving urban development to private initiative, the planners incurred some responsibility for the subsequent slow and fitful growth of town life. The establishment of towns, if only because of their defensive potential especially if walled, was of little less importance than, and a necessary complement to, the inauguration of a rural colony.

III

In the Cavan section of the 'Project' for the plantation of *c.* January 1609[10] it was proposed that three urban centres for the county should he developed, each to be endowed with land. These were Cavan and Belturbet, places of previous settlement and of Gaelic name, and 'a third towne to be erected in or neere the mydwaie between Kells and the Cavan', the site to be chosen by the commissioners of plantation.[11] Ten polls or townlands were allotted for each of these proposed corporate towns.[12] It remains to be seen how the proposed new town fared under the modified arrangements, discussed above, for town establishment.

Captain John Ridgeway, a brother of Sir Thomas Ridgeway, the Irish vice-treasurer, who was made patron of the town, was granted land nearby as a servitor in the barony of Castlerahen, on 18 December 1610.[13] He took out his patent as patron of the town, to be 'called Virginia', some eighteen months later in August 1612.[14] The patent included some five polls or townlands approximately 1,297 statute acres, and, it may be noted, appreciably less than the amount specified in the project of plantation.

The obligations of town patrons may be seen in his case. He undertook to 'plant and settle' on one of these townlands – Aghanure[15] – within four years, twenty persons, English or Scottish, chiefly artificers, who should be burgesses of the town which within the same time (i.e. before August 1616) should be incorporated. These prospective burgesses were to be 'accommodated' with houses and lands, ten to receive two acres each and ten one acre, in an area to be called the 'Burgess field', and a further thirty acres was to be allotted as a common to the town. The patron was to allot 'convenient places' as sites for the town itself, and also for a church and churchyard, a market place and a public school. The patentee was licensed to hold a weekly market (on Thursdays) and an annual fair, to receive the tolls, and the profits of a court of pie-powder, and he and his heirs to be clerks of the market.[16] Other inhabitants than the burgesses, 'cottagers and inferior inhabitants' were also envisaged in the patent but no numbers were defined or obligation to procure these laid down.

Although by 1611, when the first government-commissioned survey of the Ulster plantation was conducted, Ridgeway had imported a number of artisans to his estate,[17] at the time of the next government survey that of Sir Josias Bodley made in 1613, coincident, as it happened, with the incorporation of a number of Ulster boroughs, only the site of the proposed town, and the name Virginia had been chosen, otherwise there was 'nothing done'.[18] Before 1619 Ridgeway had sold his estate to Captain Hugh Culme, the obligation to build the town, and the townlands, being thus transferred.[19] Culme's connexion with County Cavan pre-dated the plantation. He was constable of Cloughowter castle,[20] and in 1610 he was provost-marshal of the county 'and parts adjoining'.[21] He easily made the transition to landownership in the county with the plantation, and his acquisition of Ridgeway's property is one example of his energy at this time. From Culme the beginnings of settlement at Virginia can be traced. On the evidence of Pynnar's survey – the next in the sequence of government inquiries – conducted between December 1618 and March 1619, he had erected eight timber houses and placed in them English tenants. There was also present a minister 'which keepeth school and is a very good preacher'.[22] At this point Virginia was similar to many other modest villages being established under planter tutelage, throughout the escheated counties. The stipulation in Ridgeway's patent to import twenty residents had not been obeyed, however, despite this incorporation could probably have been procured. The failure of the incipient town to receive a charter was probably due, on the one hand, to the discontinuity arising from the transfer of responsibility from Ridgeway to Culme, and on the other to government laxity in the detailed supervision of the plantation scheme. The political importance of the Ulster corporations was that their members re-inforced the new English interest in the Dublin parliament. Virginia could not have been incorporated for the 1613 parliament since on Bodley's evidence in that year no progress in its erection had been made. No parliament was held thereafter – until 1634 – to give impetus to government interest in its incorporation.

Commissioners in 1622, examining the progress of the plantation, heard complaints from the inhabitants, Culme being absent at the time, that they had no security of tenure. This 1622 return mentions only five stone and clay houses inhabited with 'poore' families, though it states that two more houses were being built.[23] In 1622 also an inquiry – or visitation – into the state of Protestantism in Ireland was conducted. This report, dealing with the parish of Lurgan, stated that the church – at Lurgan – was 'ruinous', and recommended, to rationalise the parochial centre with the inceptive town, that 'the place fitt for the building of a church is Virginia'.[24]

Another and definitive change of ownership came in this same year placing the estate around the town, and Virginia, in the hands of the old English Lucas Plunkett, baron Killeen and subsequently earl of Fingall, who owned land nearby.[25] Thus ten years after Ridgeway's patent market forces had placed the town in Catholic hands.

It was under Plunkett that the inhabitants (or some of them) received grants of title to their houses and pieces of land in the area. Thus on 25 January 1625 the Rev. George Creighton of Virginia and his wife received a fee-farm grant of their house and three roods of land 'inclosed and marked forth' at a rent of 5s. 4d. per annum.[26] Later, on 30 June 1626, Plunkett leased to Creighton and seven other named residents of the town 'together with the rest of the freeholders of Virginia', jointly, two of the townlands which were to have been allotted to the corporation, as well as the profits of the fairs and markets for sixty-one years at £17 per annum rent.[27] One of those named was a weaver, another a mason, and a third a 'brasior' or brass worker. Another, David Kellett, was subsequently a landholder in the area.[28] The granting of leasehold security to the residents had thus awaited the end of James's reign and after.

The fact that the town had not been incorporated became an issue when the commissioners for defective titles, one of the instruments of Wentworth's administration, turned their attention to Ulster. An inquiry into the extent of Plunkett property in County Cavan was held in September 1637.[29]

In March 1638 Creighton on behalf of the townsmen petitioned Wentworth to cause Christopher Plunkett, Lucas's successor, to procure the incorporation of the town. The matter was referred to Lord Dillon and Sir Gerald Lowther, chief justice, and heard by them in the presence of both parties in July. They advised that Plunkett, then earl of Fingall, should surrender the five polls of town land and receive a regrant for the purpose of incorporating the town. The corporation was to include a provost and nineteen burgesses, the first members of which were listed by name, had been the petitioners of March, and were all British. These may well have been all, or the majority of the British residents; however the number must have arisen from the fact that Ridgeway's patent had stipulated that the governing body after incorporation should have twenty members. The corporation, they further ordered, should receive the right to hold two fairs annually (on 26 May and 6 October) and a weekly market (on Thursdays) under rent to the crown, as well as the town lands and the fishing of Lough Ramor at an annual crown rent of £2.6.3. They went on to order that after land had been reserved for public buildings – a church, a minister's house, a school, a schoolmaster's house, a market place, and a town hall – the remainder, divided into equal proportions, should be granted to the twenty burgesses, to be held of the earl of Fingall in free burgage at the yearly rent of twenty shillings.

To effect this it was ordered that a commission should be issued to the bishop of Kilmore (William Bedell) and others to lay out the town and lands on these principles and define places for 'convenient lanes and ways' in and about the town. The earl of Fingall should himself build the church before 9 February 1640[? –41], and enter into a bond of £4,000 to perform the stipulations of the order as it concerned him.[30] On August 7 this adjudication was ratified in the council, and the bishop of Kilmore, Luke Dillon, Sir James Craig, and Thomas Fleming were appointed planning commissioners. The date of the proposed fair on October 6 was altered to November 6, and the rent for the market and fairs was to be £2.[31]

The commission was accordingly issued to the bishop and his associates, emphasis being placed on defining the dimensions of the church, the thickness of its walls, and that it should be built of lime and stone and slate-roofed.[32] The building of the church, it may be noted, had been recommended by the ecclesiastical visitation of 1622. Upon the return of the commission Fingall, on 7 December 1639 by order of the lords justices and council, was directed to enter into bond to fulfil his obligations.[33]

However, although the lands had been laid out to the settlers, various difficulties arose and the earl attempted to defer fulfilment of certain parts of the order. The problem was further discussed at the council in the spring.

The outcome was that it was decided that Fingall should be given three years from that date (13 February 1640) for erecting the church, that he should receive all arrears and rents up to 1638 due on those parts of the town lands which had not then been leased to the inhabitants of the town, and that the grant of the market and fairs to be made to the corporation should not terminate his rights to hold those fairs and markets which had been contained in Ridgeway's patent.[34]

In making this come-back and achieving the postponement of his building obligation until the spring of 1643, Fingall had unwittingly achieved a much longer exemption. The 1641 rising broke out, too, before the town was incorporated. Although the townsmen pressed their case in the courts of claims at the restoration they were unsuccessful. They then sought redress in the court of chancery in 1668–70, and being there unsuccessful presented a petition to the house of commons with the same result.[35]

By an interesting combination of circumstances Virginia thus did not achieve corporate status, and at least some, and probably all, the building plans were frustrated. Up to 1641 Virginia was a simple dwelling centre, like many other plantation villages, though it was somewhat strange, yet in the argument of this paper by no means provided against in the government's modified plans for urban genesis in the Ulster plantation, that a projected corporation came to have an old English landlord.

[1] Hogan (ed.), *Letters and papers relating to the Irish rebellion*, p. 150.
[2] 'Ulster Plantation Papers' no. 74, in *Analecta Hibernica*, viii.
[3] *Cal. S.P. Ire., 1608–10*, pp 415–16.
[4] *Cal. Carew MSS, 1603–24*, pp 56–7; *Cal. S.P. Ire., 1608–10*, p. 488.
[5] Lambeth Palace Library, Carew MSS, vol 629, ff 68–72 (*Cal. Carew MSS, 1603–24*, pp 141–2; *Cal. S.P. Ire., 1611–14*, pp 36–7). The dating of this document in the Carew calendar is incorrect and misleading. The propositions were sent to England on 11 Dec. 1610 and returned on 19 May 1611. (The instructions in Carew MSS, vol 629, ff 16–189v [*Cal. S.P. Ire., 1611–14*, pp 63–7] are in reply to further queries sent over with Bourchier and brought back to Ireland by Carew on 13 July 1611.)
[6] 'Ulster Plantation Papers' no. 52, in *Analecta Hibernica*, viii. The document is undated. The suggestion [1610?] seems too early. It was probably drawn up following (or perhaps just before in expectation) the receipt on 19 May 1611 of the directions from London, and before August 19 when the first grant (for the town of Rathmullan in Donegal to Sir Ralph Bingley) was authorised (Bodleian Library, Oxford, Carte MSS, vol 62, f. 19; *Cal. S.P. Ire., 1611–14*, p. 96). For the warrant for a grant of a borough (Mountnorris, to Sir Francis Annesley) see 'Ulster Plantation Papers' no. 58 in *Analecta Hibernica*, viii.
[7] For the precise obligations on the grantees, as exemplified in the case of Virginia, see above p. 431.
[8] For the more complex charter of Londonderry, see T.W. Moody, *Londonderry Plantation* (Belfast, 1939), pp 122–38.
[9] For many of these charters see RIA, Charters of Irish towns, vols i–iv.

[10] 'Ulster Plantation Papers' no. 74, in *Analecta Hibernica*, viii.

[11] Ibid.

[12] Ibid.

[13] *Cal. Pat. Rolls Ire., Jas I*, p. 186.

[14] Ibid., p. 236. One reason for the delay can be found in an administrative error. On 11 April 1611 a dispute between Ridgeway and Sir Thomas Ashe about the ownership of some of the land assigned for the town arose. Ashe had acquired some land in Cavan before the plantation. This dispute arose because his prior claim had not been thoroughly examined before the land concerned was allocated to Ridgeway. The settlement arranged in 1611 ('Ulster Plantation Papers' no. 33, in *Analecta Hibernica*, viii) would have taken some time to work out. Such errors in detail were not uncommon throughout the plantation. No systematic buying out of prior interests as in Londonderry took place in Cavan or the other planted counties. Ridgeway was in fact associated tentatively with the proposed town from an earlier stage, it had been decided on 8 January 1611, in view of the delay in finalising arrangements for town establishment to let the town land to him 'for rent' (ibid., no. 27). This was technically no more than a *custodiam*, a temporary lease. However the fact that it was made one month after the proposal of 11 December 1610 for the 'superintendant' system had been sent over to England probably implied a willingness on the part of the Dublin government that if the patron system were accepted in London Ridgeway would be made responsible for establishing the town. Another reason for the delay in taking out the patent seems to be that there was dispute as to where the town should be established. The order of 8 January 1611 suggests that at this stage the town was intended 'to be erected at Ballaghana', an important site where there was an O'Reilly castle. However this area had been granted to Ridgeway on 18 December 1610 without preference to building the town (*Cal. Pat. Rolls Ire., Jas I*, p. 186). The choice of the new location – the present site – probably arose from his determination to hold on to all the land he had already received.

[15] For the Gaelic name of the site see T.F. O'Rahilly, 'Notes on Irish place names' in *Hermathena* XLVIII (1933), 197–8. On the outbreak of the rising in 1641 local insurgent opinion favoured the restoration of the old name (M. Hickson, *Ireland in the seventeenth century* (London, 1884), ii, 392).

[16] *Cal. Pat. Rolls Ire., Jas I*, p. 236. Protection for the town was provided in the stipulation that no persons should 'sell by retail within three miles of the town without licence' (ibid.).

[17] Lambeth Palace Library, Carew MSS, vol 630, f. 69.

[18] Historical Manuscripts Commission, *Hastings MSS*, iv, 160.

[19] G. Hill, *An historical account of the plantation in Ulster* (Belfast, 1877), pp 457–8 (Pynnar's survey).

[20] *Cal. S.P. Ire., 1608–10*, p. 80.

[21] Ibid., p. 512.

[22] Hill, *Plantation in Ulster*, pp 457–8. Hill suggested that this was the Rev. Benjamin Culme, brother of Sir Hugh, who was in 1619 appointed dean of St Patrick's, Dublin. The incumbent was in fact the Rev. George Creighton (J.B. Leslie, Biographical succession list of Kilmore, unpublished, NLI, MS 2685, p. 283).

[23] BL, Add. MS 4756, f. 101.

[24] Armagh Archiepiscopal Registry, MS B. 1b. no. 193, pp 146–7.

[25] NLI, J. Ainsworth, Reports on private collections, vol. 1, no. 6, p. 127.

[26] Indenture, 25 January 1625, between Plunkett and Creighton (NLI, Fingall Papers, MS 8026).

[27] Indenture, 30 June 1626, between Plunkett and Creighton and others (ibid.).

[28] *Inq. Cancell. Hib. Repert.*, ii, Cavan, (51) Chas I.

[29] Ibid., (54) Chas I.

[30] Document endorsed: '1637, Proceedings at Council Table when, Wentworth was Lord Deputie' (NLI, Fingall Papers, MS 8032/1).

[31] Ibid.

[32] Ibid., MS 8032/2.

[33] Ibid.

[34] Order to lords justices and council, 13 February 1639 [–40] (ibid., MS 8032/1).

[35] Ibid., MS 8032/1, 2, 3.

17

John Franckton (d. 1620):
Printer, Publisher and Bookseller in Dublin

John Franckton was the first person to engage in the practice of printing and bookselling in Ireland over a reasonably extended period, which embraced the first two decades of the seventeenth century. His career in Ireland falls into two phases, the first from 1600–1603 being during the later years of the Nine Years' War, the latter taking up much of the reign of James I. The object of this paper is to examine his work and to comment on its significance. Although his name in either its short or extended form (Francke or Franckton) was not very common in later sixteenth-century England, his precise origins there have not yet been firmly established. However, since his primary function in Ireland was to do government printing in Dublin, the first known item of which was a proclamation published in August 1600, it seems likely or not impossible that he had been recruited in London by Lord Deputy Lord Mountjoy after the latter's appointment earlier that year. Since the exercise of executive authority in England, and so in Ireland, was based on a mix of sources which included proclamation and statute law (with the former aptly conveyed in the phrase 'government by proclamation'), and since in Ireland parliament in recent times had had a smaller role in the formulation of policy than in England (the first parliament to draw membership from the entire island being that of 1613–15), the printing of proclamations was clearly to be the most important and routine part of Franckton's work. However, what else he did both by way of public and private printing must be considered as well, and attention also given to his role as bookseller. He died in Dublin in October 1620.

In the first phase of his career in Ireland Franckton had not enjoyed any security of tenure, but was paid for his work as it was accomplished. At first he worked 'at the Bridge' or Bridge foot in the house of William Ussher (later Sir William) there, who had been clerk of the privy council since 1594. From 1603 he was in St Patrick's Street and, now more established, in Castle Street from 1605.[1] While Franckton took control of the equipment of his predecessors, he was not without problems arising from its efficiency. One of his authors indeed, in 1602, felt constrained to offer an apology for faults in the print: 'impute them not', he said, 'to the skilfull printer but to the stumpeworne letter'; only since the printer's 'return from London with new letters' had the work gone forward satisfactorily.[2] Franckton had however succeeded adequately in the printing of proclamations for publication. In his first year he produced two of these, both directly related to the Nine Years' War. The first, dated 10 August 1600, but of which no copy has been located, forbade the importation and sale of powder and arms without license, while the second, of 22 November, offered a reward to whoever should 'bring in' Hugh O Neill, earl of Tyrone, 'alive' – preferably – or 'dead'.[3] For the printing of each of these – 'divers' copies in the latter case – Franckton (still called Franke) received individual payments by concordatum (or 'reward') of £3.6.8.[4] Related (since O Neill and his confederates had sought Spanish support and suggested that Ireland be joined to the Spanish monarchy) was another of 10 March 1603 – the first in which he spelled his name as Franckton – forbidding merchants to trade to Spain, with whom England remained at war until 1604, without licence, so that carriage of letters, messages and emissaries could be prohibited.[5] Another group of proclamations printed by Franckton in these years, beginning with one of 20 May 1601, concerned the debasement and regulation of the Irish currency and its exchange between Ireland and England. For printing 'a great number' of the first of these 'for establishing the new monies' – of which 300 had been ordered to be produced – he received £10 in payment.[6] Although it will be shown that Franckton printed many more proclamations than investigation heretofore has revealed, his government work for much of both 1602 and 1603, including what he was paid for printing the New Testament in Irish, cannot be recovered in full detail since records of payments at that time are incomplete.

All this work in printing proclamations was, by its nature, practical and utilitarian. However, those who brought Franckton to Ireland may have intended for him a larger purpose. Argument in print, in contrast to contemporary European conflicts, had played little part in justification of either rebellion or government policy in sixteenth-century Ireland. As it happened, neither the Earls of Kildare as lord deputies prior to direct rule in 1534 had established a printing press in Dublin nor had any of the great lords of Gaelic Ireland, such as O Neill or O Donnell, now towards the end of their heydays, ever managed to promote one, in Renaissance fashion, within their own territories. Also, for its part, government printing in Dublin (since the mid-sixteenth century) had been only intermittent. However, with the emergence of Hugh O Neill's proposals for the future government of Ireland in 1599 some response was deemed to be necessary. One such, defending the existing order, was prepared immediately by Thomas Jones, bishop of Meath, but it remained unprinted.[7] It would seem that by now it was thought preferable that Franckton should continue with the printing of the New Testament in Irish, already begun by his predecessor William Kearney, and this was published in 1603.[8] In addition, Franckton (under that spelling of his name) had also printed one substantial tract, *A friendly caveat to Ireland's Catholics*, by John Rider, dean of St Patrick's Cathedral in Dublin, of which the 'epistle dedicatorie' was dated 14 September 1602, which was more a defence of Protestantism than specifically an answer, as it could scarcely be, to O Neill's demands, now somewhat redundant, for what would be in effect a form of home rule government with the requirement also that people in Ireland should be Catholic only.[9]

By 1603, then, Franckton had established himself as more than a printer of proclamations, but not all proclamations concerning Ireland had their origin in Dublin. This is particularly the case with the announcement of the succession of James I. In this instance copies of the English proclamation of 24 March 1603, printed by Robert Barker the king's printer in London, were sent to Dublin where they arrived on 5 April, when Lord Deputy Mountjoy gave order 'forthwith' that 'James the VI'th of that name, king of Scotland' should be proclaimed king of England, Scotland, France and Ireland, 'which was done the same day according to the effect of a proclamation sent hither out of England for that purpose'.[10] Reporting next day to the privy council in London on what had been done, the lord deputy and privy council stated that proclamations of like tenor were now to be imprinted in Dublin.[11] On 15 April, when a larger body of assentors had been convened, the king was proclaimed as ruler 'by law, by lineal succession and undoubted right' before this assembly, which itself constituted, as had happened in England, a great council, and proclamations bearing their names were then ordered to be printed for more widespread distribution in Ireland.[12] The names consenting included those of the lord deputy and privy council (i.e. the government, whose powers had been renewed); John Tirrell, the mayor of Dublin; seven of the old English nobility of the Pale, Gormanston, Dunsany and Killeen amongst them; Hugh, earl of Tyrone; and a number of prominent military men.[13] Although no original appears now to survive, many copies of this proclamation must have been printed by Franckton. While some opposition to the succession arose immediately thereafter in towns such as Waterford and Cork with 'some saying we will not have a Scot to be our king' and with a friar in Navan, County Meath reported as protesting that James was '*Rex Scotiae*' and '*est hereticus*' (that he was a heretic), the reign of James I came to be the period in which the rule of the Dublin government over all Ireland was consolidated, and Franckton's work over the ensuing fifteen years throws light on the principal ways in which this took place.[14]

There was also an after-matter in 1605, though not one in which Franckton was involved: James I's abortive project for a full union of England and Scotland. This, which had implications for the king's style, was also publicised in Ireland. To begin this unification of both countries ('since the isle within itself hath almost none but imaginary bounds of separation'), he had announced by proclamation in London on 20 October 1604 that his style should now be king of Great Britain, France and Ireland.[15] In March of the following year Lord Deputy Sir Arthur Chichester, who had taken up office one month before, asked if this should be published in Dublin too, and if so that some of the proclamations should be sent over. This had in fact no practical constitutional effect for Ireland, though from about now the notion of Ireland as the 'third kingdom' or as one of the 'three kingdoms' (to be a focus of identity for many in Ireland as a part of the greater whole for centuries to come) was coming to be established; the English proclamations were duly publicised in Dublin in May and Franckton was not called upon to reprint them.[16]

In 1604, Franckton, now well established, sought to have his *de facto* position as king's printer in Ireland confirmed by the security of patent. The sequence of events is somewhat protracted. In March he procured a fiant, which initiated the process, authorising a patent to him of the office of king's printer in Ireland 'to hold in the same ample manner and form as the king's printer in England' and to be held during 'pleasure', while on 8 October he obtained a revised one, to hold during 'good behaviour' (seemingly an improvement) which ordered that he receive a fee of £8 per year. In between had come a warrant from Lord Deputy Sir George Cary (a short-term appointee) on 10 July 1604 ordering that the second fiant be drawn up, which specified that he should hold the office for life with no one else to practise the trade of printer or stationer in Ireland unless Franckton himself should appoint deputies.[17] No final patent in this sequence seems with certainty to have been enrolled, but, as will be seen, one was granted in 1609 by which time he had accomplished a good deal of work.[18] However, Franckton was defined clearly as king's printer on proclamations from 1605.

In the ensuing years Franckton was to print a substantial number of proclamations all of which shed light on the great growth of governance and its various directions in Jacobean Ireland, especially during the lord-deputyship of Sir Arthur Chichester between February 1605 and 1616. Some in particular are worthy of note. Two of these, both of 20 February 1605, signalled the full ending of the Nine Years' War. One revoking commissions of martial law (though with a number of exceptions) was balanced by another forbidding the carrying of arms under pain of confiscation and five days imprisonment (though with exemption for, amongst others, gentlemen of the Pale and merchants, provided they had permission).[19] Others of great importance followed. One of 11 March 1605 had a dual intent, so as 'to establish the Commonwealth of this realm' for the future. The first part of it offered pardons for offences prior to the king's accession, with a scale of fees for procuring them, provided those pardoned took an oath of allegiance, while the second dealt with the rights of the lesser landowners in those former Gaelic lordships, especially in Ulster, whose lords had recently received title to 'great skopes and extents of land'. The lesser landowners should have certainty of tenure, with defined rents for their tenancies, and be no longer subject to the demands for 'cutting and coshering' of their lords, who also might not claim them as 'their natives and natural followers' since all now should be the 'free, natural and immediate subjects' of the king and not the subjects of 'any other lord or chieftain whatsoever'. In short, since the circuits of the assize judges had now been extended for the first time ever over all Ireland, all should henceforth be governed under one legal system. Henceforth as well, it was proclaimed, those remaining loyal would be protected, while any making 'any defection' would be rigorously prosecuted.[20] To make the proclamation more fully comprehensible in the distant parts to which it was addressed, it was ordered that it should be printed also in Latin and Irish.[21] Another of some moment was issued on 15 July 1606. This, which announced the forthcoming sitting of the commission for defective titles, was designed to make known a new initiative with regard to landownership. Although it was to have the effect, contrary entirely to what might have been expected, of leading to partial plantation in some counties, the objective was not only that all land title in Ireland should be secure (and revenue-generating), but also that land should all now be held under one system of law. Those who held land, many of them outlying old English, by uncertain title, must surrender and have their titles confirmed by letters patent. Also, those who held land by 'the Irish custom of tanistry' or just by 'long continuance of possession', i.e. Gaelic lords or lesser gentlemen, might surrender as well (under a commission of 19 July 1605) and have their titles now secured too by regrant.[22] A further proclamation, printed by Franckton, announced the renewal of this commission on 19 June 1609.[23]

Other proclamations dealt with important immediate events. Thus he printed three proclamations, one of them a reprint of the English one of 15 November 1607, arising from the Flight of the Earls, of which only one, that of 9 November 1607, survives.[24] Others dealing with immediate events at this time were one against Richard Nugent, baron Delvin, of 23 November 1607,[25] and two, of April and July 1608, occasioned by O Doherty's rising.[26] One entire group of proclamations printed by Franckton, none of which has been located, all prorogations, arose from the holding of the parliament of 1613–15.[27] That parliament legislated for the payment of a land tax or subsidy, to be collected now for the first time ever, from the whole of Ireland, and the act (of which just one copy is now known to survive) which authorised this was printed by Franckton in 1615.[28] Franckton also printed two proclamations in 1612 and 1613, one following English practice, which defined wages and prices, the other containing a range of civic regulations, on behalf of the then lord mayor of Dublin, Sir James Carroll, and while he himself was one of the city's two sheriffs.[29] The last government proclamation surviving under his imprint, one of 25 April 1618 by direction of Lord Deputy Sir Oliver St John (Chichester's successor) and his privy council, was one which announced the setting up of a registry of births, baptisms, marriages and burials for Ireland.[30] Since proclamations were, in effect, enunciations of government policy, Franckton's work in this capacity was of much immediate importance. An impression of the number of proclamations that he actually printed can be gained from the appendix. He was equipped to print them in the normal black letter type by January 1603 but not in June 1602 or before.

Much of what Franckton printed dealt with matters of religion. The Nine Years' War had raised the issue of religion in Ireland to high prominence and the authorities now became agitated as to how reformed religion might at last be extended beyond those who already practised it so that for all uniformity in religion with England might prevail in Ireland too.[31] Franckton's printing work indicates the diversity of tactics that were turned to after the war, all of them as it turned out largely ineffective if only because the Dublin government lacked that sufficiency of power to drive all forward together with full rigour. What Franckton had already printed, the New Testament in Irish and John Rider's tract (for the printing of which Rider had presumably paid out of his own income), was a contribution in that direction.

Rider, an Oxford graduate and a man of some learning who had published an English-Latin dictionary in 1589, had been dean of St Patrick's in Dublin since 1597. Later, as bishop of Killaloe from 1612, he argued for the liturgical use of the Irish language there to attract Irish speakers. His *A friendly caveat to Ireland's Catholics* was mainly an exposition of the Protestant 'position' on the issue of transubstantiation carried out by reference to 'apostolic warrant' and the practice of the early church in its first five hundred years. Other 'positions', as he saw them, which differentiated Anglican from Catholic thought – on services in the vernacular, on purgatory and prayers for the dead, on images and praying to saints, on the nature of the Mass and on the papal claim to temporal power over all rulers and their subjects – were set out also early in the work but not enlarged on because of the problem of printing a bigger work. Addressed to the 'Reverend Fathers, the holy Jesuits, seminaries and all other Priests', it was designed for the literate English speaking laity mainly amongst, it can be assumed, the Dublin populace and that of its hinterland. He also suggested, writing as he was just after Kinsale, in a preface addressed to them, that clergy of the opposite persuasion should not keep silent on what he saw as a political parallel were Spanish rule to be established. Conditions, he said, in the kingdom of Naples and the dukedom of Milan under Spanish authority did not bode well for people in Ireland were it too to come under Spanish control. Finally in an 'epistle dedicatorie' to Lord Deputy Mountjoy seeking patronage and protection for his book, he promised in turn to praise God for 'those honourable victories against the insolent Spaniards and perjured rebels' that he had achieved. He went on to hope that 'you may not only suppress rebellion but abandon superstition' and both 'plant in the church truth and in the commonwealth peace'. 'For', he said, 'subjection without religion is but temporising, and till religion be seated in the heart, look for no sound subjection generally and perpetually in the land'. But Mountjoy was withdrawn and returned to England in May 1603 before such weighty matters could be attended to.

One tactic that was adopted, early in Chichester's administration, came in a proclamation of 4 July 1605 issued from London 'By the king' and printed in Dublin by John Franckton. Noting that 'a great number of Jesuits, seminary priests and other priests made by foreign authority do range up and down in that our kingdom' endeavouring 'to alienate the hearts of our subjects from us by insinuating and breeding a distaste in them both of our religion and civil government' and even (as it claimed) 'taking upon them the ordering and deciding of causes both before and after they had received judgements' in the law courts, it proclaimed that they should depart before 10 December ensuing, none to come there or return thereafter.[32] When it was re-issued by the lord deputy and council and again printed by Franckton – on 13 July 1611 (proof clear that it had been ineffectual on its first appearance), Andrew Knox, now bishop of Raphoe in Ulster, expressed the hope, in retrospect an optimistic one, that if energy and diligence were devoted to all fronts it should be possible 'within a little space and by the grace of God to reclaim the people'.[33] Later, when a convocation of the Church of Ireland meeting alongside parliament produced the *Articles of religion* of 1615, a work of definition, Franckton was appointed to put them into print.[34]

Plate 17.1 *Leabhar na nUrnaightheadh gComhcoidchiond*. Baile atha Cliath, 1608.
[Book of Common Prayer, Irish, Dublin, 1608]

In bibliographical terms Franckton's most important religious publication, along with the New Testament, must have been the Book of Common Prayer in Irish. By the nature of the endeavour, it took some time in preparation. Some time before 30 September 1607 William Danyell (as he was called) 'preacher', charged with its translation, had received a government payment of £26.13.4 'in consideration of his travel and charges employed in the province of Connaughte by the lord deputy and council to translate the book of common prayer into the Irish tongue for

Plate 17.2 *Leabhar na nUrnaightheadh gComhcoidchiond*. Baile atha Cliath, 1608.
[Book of Common Prayer, Irish, Dublin, 1608]. Signature 2E2

the benefit of the Irishry',[35] the latter the common term, by contrast with 'the Englishry' (which stood for those of old English origin and English-speaking), used for those mainly of Gaelic descent in Ireland. The objective, in short, was that the liturgy should be available in each of both languages spoken in Ireland. Daniel, otherwise Ó Domhnuill, a graduate of Emmanuel College, Cambridge, had been a Fellow of Trinity College, Dublin and was promoted to be archbishop of Tuam in 1609. Although the title-page is dated 1608, publication was delayed until he had completed the 'Epistle dedicatorie' on 20 October 1609.

In the 'Epistle dedicatorie' (written in English) addressed to Chichester, Daniel, still retaining a residence at St Patrick's Close in Dublin, expressed his hopes for it. Past glories in religion in Ireland, as indeed 'in all other Christian kingdoms', had long, he insisted, 'since the time that Sathan was set at liberty' been darkened and debased. But now there was 'great hope that … this kingdom may flourish in the same mercy that the neighbour kingdoms do and may see greater glory than ever it hath seen heretofore', since God had caused – even 'in the depth of our discomfort and despair' – 'a most glorious star to arise out of the North', James I, to promote it. If at first sight prospects might seem uncertain, with many 'wicked seducers' still in evidence and churches themselves laid waste, yet, he felt, God had made the way plain now 'by causing our wars to cease'. Moreover 'the blessed Trinity hath already founded a College upon our eastern shore wherein learning and religion begins to flourish' and he doubted not but 'that in God's good time, by the means thereof' and of other schools, 'the chiefest means of reformation, the country that doth now sit in darkness, shall in time see great light, to their everlasting comfort'. He commended Chichester for maintaining there 'divers poor scholars of the country birth' and for initiating this endeavour. Realizing that a liturgy in 'an unknown tongue can leave no blessing behind it, as both the Apostle teacheth and this poor church can certify by woeful experience', he had 'imposed' on Daniel 'the burden' of translating it 'the liturgy of the famous Church of England' into the 'mother tongue' both 'for the comfort of the mere Irish churches' and to confound those who led 'the ignorant' to believe 'that our divine service is nothing else but the service of the devil'. He now asked the lord deputy to 'send it abroad into the country churches, together with the elder brother the New Testament', there to be 'fostered and fomented.' Earlier in the 'epistle dedicatorie' of the Irish New Testament, also Daniel's work, addressed to James I, he had stressed that the 'quietness and peace of kingdoms' consisted chiefly in religious uniformity and lamented that through long delay in producing it the mere Irish had been deprived 'of this heavenly comfort and means of their salvation'. This, moreover had culminated in the recent 'universal flood of rebellion' that had 'overflowed the face of the kingdom' when 'both the unnatural barbarous rebel and the proud bloody Spaniard, under the colours of the Romish Antichrist' had 'proclaimed themselves absolute lords of the land' and had indeed 'cast lots for the lives, lands and goods of those few that professed either religion or subjection unto God and his annointed'. Thus, advancing the reformation was not without political importance too.

Since the liturgy of the Church of Ireland followed that of the Church of England, the text used for the Irish translation of the Book of Common

Prayer was that of the prayer book of 1604 published following the Hampton Court conference at the beginning of the king's reign. Some brief comments on both are necessary. One of the features of the English reformed liturgy lies in its treatment of saints. These had proliferated greatly prior to the reformation with many days being observed as holy days.[36] Since it was felt that these celebrations could lead to behaviour unseemly to a religious festival as well as impeding labour and on the grounds that only those religious occasions which were biblical should be celebrated their number had been greatly reduced. By Elizabethan times, twenty-seven days, along with all Sundays were commonly listed in the prayer books as those 'to be observed for Holy days and none other'. These included events in the life of Christ from the Annunciation to the Ascension and the feasts of the Apostles such as St Matthew, and of the Evangelists, St Mark, St Luke and St John. In the ecclesiastical calendar printed in the prayer books these days were done in red letter – a printing technique – and services for these red letter days, as well as Sundays, with collects, epistles and gospels, appeared in prayer books from the time of Edward VI onwards. Later, at the Restoration, their number was increased to twenty-nine with the addition of the conversion of St Paul and St Barnabas and then also the term 'holy day' gave way, generally, to 'feast', listed now in 'a table of all the feasts that are to be observed ... through the year'.[37] All this was in some contrast to the attitude to saints and their invocation in the post-medieval Catholic world, where, although they were now to be subject to Counter-Reformation validation, saints and their hagiography may well have been coming to have an increased importance in the piety of the *era sanctorum*, to be useful even, too, in the minds of some as a 'hammer and a dagger against heretics'.[38] During the reign of Elizabeth it became customary as well to insert in the calendar, also in red letter, the dates of the monarch's birth and accession, given the royal role as defender of the church's reformed doctrine and its erastian nature.[39] In addition, services for certain 'solemn days' were brought in at the Restoration.

In Daniel's (or Ó Domhnuill's as he gave his name on the New Testament) translation, the calendar, then, followed the English one, though stripped of much of the residuum from the middle ages which remained in calendars printed in English prayer books. However, in the text he made some modifications. Thus, for example, and with indications of his theological leanings, he used '*An Minisdir*' (the Minister) in all cases where the English prayer book had continued to use 'Priest' as well as 'Minister' for clergyman. In the headings of the services he also made some alterations. In this way he linked two accepted days of observance to the festivals of two saints, though primarily as a means of identifying the former. Hence he made *La fheile Muire na feile brighde* (i.e. that particular feast of Mary that falls around the time of Brigid's day) the heading in the collects, epistles and gospels for the day of the Purification of St Mary the Virgin. He also rendered the feast of the Annunciation (Lady Day on 25 March) as *La fheile Muire na feile Padraig*, i.e. that feast of Mary that falls around the time of Patrick's Day which may also have been seen as the octave of St Patrick's Day. In short, the dates of these two feasts of the Blessed Virgin were themselves identified by reference to the days of St Brigid and St Patrick.[40] In the calendar he subtly altered the day of the Purification (2 February) to 1 February which was St Brigid's Day. Amongst other renditions, he styled the Circumcision (1 January) as *La Nodlog beag*, the day of little Christmas, and, still in January, he termed the Epiphany (6 January) as *La chind an da la dheag*, (the day of the end of the twelve days). For the feast of Philip and Jacob on 1 May or May Day he used the purely secular *La Bealltaine*, while for 1 November, the feast of All Saints, he combined secular with religious with the form *La Samhna no feile na nuíle naomh*. In the calendar as Franckton printed it, the king's accession day and birthday (24 March and 19 June) both appeared but not in red letter as in editions of the prayer book printed in England.[41]

Some handwritten insertions into the calendar in the Trinity College Dublin Library copy dating most likely from the Restoration lead one, by way of brief diversion, back to the 'solemn days' earlier referred to. Additional forms of service 'appointed' for three 'solemn days' (now all in red letter also) had been incorporated into English prayer books at the Restoration on foot of approval and order of Charles II of 2 May 1662. All three – 5 November, for the Gunpowder Plot in 1605; 30 January for the execution of Charles I 'the Martyr' in 1649, which led to the abolition of an episcopal church in England; 29 May, the day of the 'birth and return' (in 1660) of Charles II, which restored episcopacy – were important in their different ways for the survival and 'deliverance' (itself a word with strong biblical resonance) of the Church of England.[42] For Ireland there was now to be one extra solemn day. Its origins lay in an act of the Restoration parliament in Dublin which provided that 23 October – the day in 1641 when (due entirely to God's 'infinite goodness and mercy') the plot to seize Dublin and other centres was discovered – should be kept and celebrated as an 'anniversary thanksgiving', with all to attend morning prayer and abstain from labour.[43] On clerical initiative a special form of service for this occasion was prepared, and eventually the king was moved to issue a warrant, as he did on 15 August 1666, that all four forms of prayer be printed and published and annexed to the Book of Common Prayer of the Church of Ireland. Congregations in Ireland, then, could not only commemorate their common inheritance with England but also an averted disaster of their own. These services may have appeared in some copies of the Book of Common Prayer published in Dublin in 1666, the first specifically printed in English for the Church of Ireland,[44] as they certainly did in other editions printed there later, but since prayer books imported from England also continued to be used in Ireland the conducting of the 23 October service may not have been as widespread as was intended. While this is to stray a little further than an investigation of Franckton's work may strictly require, it serves to account for these handwritten additions in that copy of his Book of Common Prayer in Irish. Finally, in these handwritten insertions in the prayer book, the English saint, St Swithun, was also now included. The title-page border that Franckton used for it was architectural, but it was of a standard – and very handsome – sixteenth-century Mannerist design rather than being strikingly new and classical.[45] It varied, however, from those then used for prayer books in England and may well have been intended to convey the strength of royal authority which now lay behind its publication. He re-used it to convey similarly the authority of statute in 1615. With it was printed also both the royal arms and those of Lord Deputy Chichester. The Prayer Book's utility for conducting services fully in Irish was, however in one respect – through the absence of a Psalter – severely limited; the psalms had not yet been translated.[46] For printing it and for 'his furnishing for the same' Franckton received a payment of £40.[47] The printing of these publications had been the contribution of Franckton's press to advancing the Reformation in Ireland.

Franckton's career as a publisher, private as well as public, extended further than this. Thus in 1608 he produced a *Book of rates* for Ireland, a government publication which gave the valuations on which customs duties, now being organised on an all-Ireland basis, on commodities imported and exported through the ports should be calculated.[48] In 1606 he had reprinted Sir Robert Cecil, earl of Salisbury's *An answer to certain scandalous papers, scattered abroad under colour of a Catholicke admonition*, a vindicatory tract of a topical nature arising from the Gunpowder Plot, which had been first published in London by Robert Barker, the king's printer there.[49] This reprint is an early example, as it turned out, of what was to become, with all its cultural significance in terms of demand and its supply in Ireland, a regular Dublin publishing practice.[50] Franckton was also to do some legal publishing. Sir John Davies's *Le Primer report des cases et matters en ley ...*, published in 1615, was an account of some of those fateful law cases that he had prosecuted during his time as attorney-general. Two years later a law book by John Merick, an English lawyer now appointed as feodary for Connacht and Clare in the court of wards, followed. This, *A compendious collection and breefe abstract of all the auncient English-statutes now in force within Ireland* dedicated to the judges in Dublin, was an alphabeticized handbook of more than four hundred pages (and the forerunner of others of its kind) seen by its author as a timely production published just when English law, to replace 'the tyrannical Irish customs', was being extended beyond its medieval limits to apply over Ireland as a whole. He had endeavoured, he said, 'in respect of the poverty of this distressed kingdom, to couch' it in 'so small compass and little volume' – an octavo – that both for its 'price and portableness' it should be accessible to both the rich and poor. It was to be sold at Franckton's shop in Castle Street and 'anywhere else with the author's license'.[51]

A work of a genre long familiar in England, the almanac, came also from Franckton's press in 1612. Almanacs contained a wide range of information in succinct form: calendars, summary historical chronologies, practical information on, for example, fairs and markets, and astrological prognostications for the ensuing year. Their astrological content, which in some ways inter-related with the new science, remained strong until the later seventeenth century, when it began to give way to scientific scepticism. Their chronologies, often dated from the creation, provided the reader with outline knowledge of history and they also tended to record instances of progress or innovation: recent achievements or improvements were often noted.[52] William Farmer, whose *Prognosticall almanacke* for Ireland Franckton printed in 1612, described himself as a chirurgeon and a practitioner in the mathematical arts. He had also been preparing chronicles of recent events in Ireland under the patronage of Sir Arthur Chichester.[53] In 1587 he had published an almanac and prognostication designed for Ireland in London and part of another, London-printed, for 1614 also survives.[54] Whether during Franckton's time these almanacs were published simultaneously in Dublin and London is a matter for speculation. Farmer's 1612 almanac had many characteristics. In his calendar, he gave the dates 'three-fold': by the 'old and usual' one; by the new Gregorian calendar of 1582 (as he had done promptly in 1587), for the convenience of travel and business; and by one of his own calculation 'more exact and more true' he claimed because he had 'cast away' thirteen days. His chronology of 'memorable things done in this kingdom of Ireland' linked England and Ireland, while references to the king also brought Scotland to notice. Amongst recent events noted were the defeat of the Spanish Armada, the battle of Kinsale and the building of Trinity College, while the last entries referred to the printing of the New Testament in Irish 'by John Franckton, now the King's Printer in ... Ireland', the accession of James I and, finally, the translation of the Book of Common Prayer at the instance of Lord

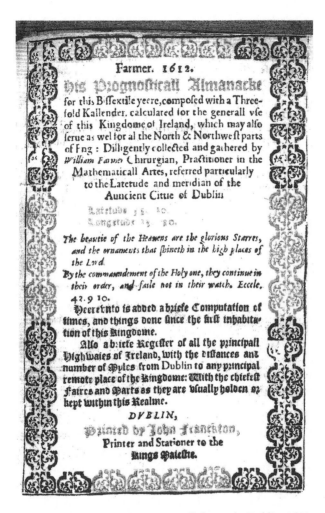

Plate 17.3 W. Farmer, *His prognosticall almanacke*. Dublin, 1612

Deputy Chichester who had 'caused it to be printed and dispersed throughout the churches of this kingdom'. Farmer's prognostication dealt mainly with the weather and he also provided a section on 'physical elections' which aimed to give the best astronomical conditions for particular medical treatments or indeed agricultural activities. Thus one should geld cattle 'in the wane of the moon, being in aries, or in sagitarius or capricorn'. In presenting all this, however, Farmer allowed space for a critical outlook: lest it seem distasteful to 'any good christian', he had given these times of elections – derived from the ancient practitioners of medicine – until 'another doctrine' may be found to overthrow them. Two final sections gave his almanac a further utilitarian character. Not only did he give the dates of fairs and markets throughout Ireland, but he also supplied a list, with the distances involved, of the routes from Dublin to 'the chiefest' towns in each province, done, 'in regard of this new plantation', to be for the benefit of all who do 'daily repair hither as strangers to inhabit'. That some of these were underestimates, as Dublin to the 'new city' of Derry via Dundalk and Omagh at 110 miles, is a comment on the exactitude of knowledge of Ireland at that time. In producing this almanac Franckton used a number of fine ornaments and also Chichester's and the royal arms, but in a note explained that since he had ventured it to test the market he had not printed it with red letters 'altogether' on this occasion.[55]

And there was a little more. Another work, *A consideration upon death, conceived through the decease of Robert [Cecil] late earle of Salisburie*, by E.S., a quarto printed by Franckton in 1612, survives only in the Middle Temple Library, London.[56] Its title, however, is suggestive of its contents: a type of meditative or reflective literary work in prose or verse not unfamiliar to its time. Its location, moreover, might also suggest who E.S. was. He might just have been Edward Sibthorpe, for a time with an interest in plantation land in Ulster and brother of Christopher Sibthorpe, a judge in Dublin who had trained in the Middle Temple and whose own works were also acquired by its library.[57] If this be plausible, then *A consideration upon death* could enjoy the distinction, chronologically at least, of being amongst the earliest pieces of literary writing published in Dublin by a person of new English background in Ireland. Finally, a medical work, on the study of disease, by an Irish author was published by John Franckton's deputies – and successors – in 1619, just as his career was coming to an end.[58] This, his *Pathologia haereditaria generalis sive de morbis haereditariis tractatus spagyrico-dogmaticus*, a duodecimo of some 130 pages, by a cultured and ambitious doctor, Dermitius Meara and dedicated fulsomely to Lord Deputy Sir Oliver St John, drew on the ancients, Galen and Hippocratus, as well as the more modern medical thinking of Paracelsus (d. 1541) and was prefaced by a splendid Latin epigram by John Kelly, a Trinity College graduate and Fellow, which praised its author's learning.[59] It can be seen then that with Franckton's work there, the practice of book publishing in Dublin was now established, albeit very slenderly and in a specific direction. He had printed, alongside his work with proclamations, over a typical range of areas of contemporary publication: pamphleteering, religious, legal and medical amongst them. That he had produced more which has not survived is not impossible, especially works of an ephemeral nature.

Franckton was also a bookseller or stationer, getting his supplies in London, which can be traced for a number of years in the surviving port records of Chester, then the principal port for the shipment of goods from London to Dublin. Thus on 23 October 1602, as John Francktone of Dublin printer he paid subsidy there on 12 reams of paper and 2 rolls of parchment and also on 10 reams of printed books in quires and 40 small printed books.[60] In the following year he brought over a much larger stock. Late in July he brought 40 reams of printing paper, 5 reams of books unbound, 3 dozen of coarse parchment skins to bind books and half a gross of either primers or pennars on all of which he paid the customs subsidy, and also two small firkins of printing letters and one small firkin of ink, which were 'allowed' to him custom's free as 'provision'. It is worth noting that on the same ship, the *Nightingale* of Chester, which regularly plied the Chester/Dublin route, Lucas Challoner, D.D. 'overseer of Trinity College near Dublin' also conveyed, 'for the use of the said College', one dryfat and two barrels of books 'to the value of' (i.e. probably their customs' valuation) £100, which – a large quantity indeed – were also 'allowed for the said College as provision', while a month later, Franckton not being the only importer of books, the palesman Sir Christopher Plunkett shipped in by means of his servant Walter Skolley commodities which, along with coal, included trunks and other containers holding books as well as apparel for his wife and children.[61]

In 1607 Franckton's supplies both of paper and books were much more substantial. That year also he was engaging in some other mercantile activity when he shipped in 100lbs of that new luxury commodity tobacco – leaf and cane – along with 3½ shortcloths at the end of January. In May/June and also November he made his imports of books and paper. Now a free citizen of Dublin, his shipments through Chester were organised by Thomas Tomlinson, a Chester factor, and he was exempt from paying subsidy there. In the summer 100 reams of printing paper and 30 reams of ordinary paper were laded, along with 17 rolls of parchment and also 7 dozen of inkhorns, 7lbs of hard wax and a half-hundredweight of both gall and copperas. Robert Panting, a Dublin merchant, was also importing paper that year and had included 30 reams of pott paper amongst a varied range of commodities imported in May. Franckton's book imports took place on both occasions and accumulated in all to 2¾ maunds of books both bound and unbound.[62] The maund, a type of basket which held forty reams, had become the established measure for customs purposes for books imported to or exported from England and the valuation per maund for their calculation tended to be in the region of £10. In the early seventeenth century calculations can show a maund of books to have been some 10 hundredweight (half a ton) in weight, though, later, in 1702 it was defined as holding 8 hundredweight.[63] Hence, one can get a good impression of the quantity of books involved in these importations. When in October 1610 the Dublin city authorities noted that Franckton had 'lately brought out of London' one dozen of buckets which it was thought should be acquired for fire control, it seems likely that he had returned then from a now regular book-buying – and paper-buying – visit, whatever their quantity may have been.[64]

When the Dublin book trade can be traced again, in 1614, it was not Franckton who was directly involved, but one John Gillam. It seems unlikely that Gillam was an independent bookseller in his own right; more probably he was acting on Franckton's behalf. Gillam can only first be defined with accuracy in 1625 when he was admitted to the franchise of Dublin city as a bookbinder who was apprentice to a fellow bookbinder, William Wight.[65] Wight first appears in the record as a bookbinder in November 1607 when, 'having done good service to the state', he received a government grant of £6.13.4 'for his better enabling to buy some tools and other instruments to execute that place'.[66] All that could suggest that Wight was working alongside Franckton and Gillam must have had a similar link. At any rate it was Gillam rather than Franckton who was importing books to Dublin in 1614. The activities of all three must, however, have interconnected and the increasing number of such people in Dublin is significant in itself. Gillam brought supplies from England on two occasions in that year, in May and in November, bringing in one maund of books unbound in May along with 30 reams of ordinary paper and in November a quarter maund of books similarly unbound without other additional commodities.[67] While Gillam's imports in 1614 were smaller than Franckton's had been in 1607, they may indicate, on the other hand, that a practice of importing books from London twice a year for sale in Dublin had now become common. While what precise titles all these books may have been cannot emerge from this kind of evidence, for those who read or owned them, perhaps mainly if not exclusively the growing new English element in Dublin and elsewhere in Ireland, they were the marks – and influences – of a culture shared in common with people in England itself. One purchaser at least can be disclosed: Franckton sold some books to Trinity College, Dublin, in 1608 and one of those remains there still in Franckton's binding.[68]

This provides the context within which Franckton, then at the peak of his career in Ireland, was granted a patent of his office on 3 May 1609. This conferred upon him the position of king's printer general in Ireland, to hold, to himself and his assigns or deputies, during good behaviour, with an annual fee or stipend of £8 (the figure for 1604) to begin from Easter past. He might print all 'books of statutes, grammars, almanacs, acts of parliament, proclamations, injunctions, Bibles and books of the New Testament and all other books whatsoever as much in the English, Irish or any other language' which were authorised to be printed and sold in England, provided that they were not 'contrary, repugnant or scandalous to our laws or government … of … England, Scotland or Ireland'. He was also given sole licence and authority to bind and sell all such books, and all other books permissible for sale in England and Ireland, whether they had been printed in England or in Ireland or anywhere else, again provided that they be not 'contrary, repugnant or scandalous', as expressed above. It is thus very essential to recognize that within this lay an important element of press regulation and control. Franckton's patent, moreover, also conferred a monopoly of printing and bookselling upon him. No other person in Ireland might, without Franckton's license, either print or sell any such books, those doing so to be subject to a penalty payable to him and to suffer their forfeiture, unless they had themselves received a licence 'well and lawfully' to do so. Franckton might also take and employ, 'for reasonable wages and hire', such workmen or apprentices 'to work in the said art and mistery of printing and bookbinding' as he should require.[69] A payment to him of his salary for this year has also been detected.[70]

The granting of his patent effectively recognised the position that by now he had established for himself. If, as can be shown, since Dublin was after all not the only port in Ireland, books in modest quantity from England were entering many parts of Ireland, including the plantation north, during Franckton's time, either in the hands of merchants or through many individuals bringing their own with them directly, then his monopoly of bookselling was, not surprisingly, somewhat less than watertight.[71] But that can scarcely detract from his importance. He was the first bookseller with a shop and publisher of books for any length of time anywhere in Ireland. What his income may have been overall cannot be established.

The end of Franckton's career was both somewhat misfortunate and a testimony to his own success. In 1618 the Company of Stationers of London, seeing prospects for themselves as printers and booksellers in the new Ireland now steadily being re-created, intervened, and secured the right for three of its members, Felix Kingston, a prominent and prolific London printer, Matthew Lownes and Bartholomew Downes, to replace him on its behalf. The change-over was fully completed by July 1620. It was claimed that Franckton was not wealthy enough – which may well be true – to retain, or expand, his position and that he was now subject to 'infirmities, both of body and mind'. Clearly anyhow he had been ageing, since he died in Dublin in October 1620.[72] In March 1618 the lord deputy and privy council were ordered by the English privy council to ensure that the transition be effected without impediment, since the Company had already undertaken to send over a person of 'skill and ability' to both occupy the 'place' of printer in Ireland and also to 'settle a factory of booksellers and bookbinders' in Dublin 'to furnish the kingdom plentifully' in that regard. The new grant should therefore proceed, they were told, as for the 'great good of that realm and his majesty's subjects there' so that nothing necessary should be wanting 'for the plantation of learning, civility and religion amongst them'. While, given economic depression in the early 1620s, this new departure was not to prove just as spectacular as had been forecast, Felix Kingston with 'some others' was in Dublin by June 1618 and somewhat later it was Robert Young, subsequently a printer of much importance in London and to hold also the office of king's printer for Scotland, who was to receive payment for government printing there.[73]

Uncertainty about Franckton's date of birth makes it impossible to say what age he was when he died. Efforts to trace his origins in England proved disappointing at the last moment, when proof emerged that the wrong person was being pursued.[74] People of his surname, generally in its Francke form, can be found in the sixteenth century mainly in the midlands and in southern and eastern England, some of them bearing arms as gentlemen similar to those ascribed to him on his funeral certificate in 1620, which records his death using both spellings.[75] He was no doubt a relative of an Edmond Francke who appears in the records of the Stationers' Company of London in 1602.[76] Pollard's suggestion that he had had two wives seems well founded. Since his daughter Elinor, necessarily then twenty-one years old, received the freedom of the city of Dublin in April 1613,[77] a first marriage early in the 1590s to a wife who died either in Dublin or before his arrival there is likely. His second wife was found in Ireland: in October 1606 he was himself admitted to the freedom of the city 'as husband of Margery Laghlin, daughter of William Laghlin freeman' and at the instance of Thomas Jones, archbishop of Dublin and lord chancellor.[78] His children, Roger and Jane, were admitted in 1630 and 1639 respectively. In Dublin he himself had been one of the sheriffs for the year 1612–13.[80] Apart from his role as printer of proclamations, themselves indicators of the decisive change being brought about in the Ireland of his time, Franckton's importance in the intellectual history of Dublin and indeed of Ireland cannot be overlooked. He can be claimed to have been the father of publishing and bookselling in Dublin and as the person from whom a continuing practice in these activities sprang.

Government Printing Payments to John Franckton, 1 April 1600–31 March 1602 and 1 October 1603–31 March 1619

These have been extracted from The National Archives (UK), AO1/287/1081–/291/1091 and known surviving copies have been given their STC number.

1 April 1600–31 March 1601

For printing of proclamations for restraint of powder and arms to be brought into the realm or to sell the same without special license.

66s. 8d.

For printing like proclamations wherein was promised a reward to him that should bring in Tyrone alive or dead (STC 14147). 66s. 8d.

1 April 1601–31 March 1602

For printing a great number of proclamations for establishing the new monies to be current in Ireland (STC 14147a). £10

1 October 1603–30 June 1606

For printing two several proclamations, one for establishing fine silver coin in this realm and reducing the base monies to a third part thereof (STC 14151) and the other for proportioning the rates of victuals and all other commodities. £6 13s. 4d.

For printing a proclamation dated 7 December 1603 commanding all his Majesty's subjects according to the tenour of a former proclamation to receive the monies of the new standard as well for payment of rents and debts as for all manner of payments whatsoever. 66s. 8d.

For printing a proclamation dated 15 January 1603[–4] commanding all his Majesty's subjects according to the tenour of a former proclamation to receive the monies of the new standard, certifying withal that his Majesty had caused an exact trial to be newly made of the same upon the oaths of all the officers of the mint. £5

1 July 1606–30 September 1607

For printing … three proclamations, one forbidding the bringing of powder and other munitions to this kingdom by any merchants dated 10 March 1605[–6] (STC 14156), one other concerning surrenders (STC 14157), and the last for decrying the harp shilling to 12d Irish (STC 14148).

£16

1 October 1607–30 September 1609

For printing of five several proclamations, the first concerning the decrying of the piece of the twelve pence to the sixteen pence Irish, the second concerning the Earls of Tyrone and Tyrconnell their departure out of the kingdom without license, the third concerning his Majesty's seizure of their lands (STC 14159), the fourth touching Tyrone and Tyrconnell first printed at Westminster (STC 8409) and after printed in Ireland the fifth concerning the Lord of Delvin's escape out of Dublin castle (STC 14160).

£25

For printing the Book of Common Prayer in Irish for the instruction of the ignorant and barbarous people[81] and for his furnishing for the same (STC 1643). £40

For printing the proclamation against Sir Cahir O Doherty and Phelim Reough McDavid (STC 14161) and for printing certain rates for his Majesty's customs in that kingdom (STC 14128.3). £8

For printing of proclamations of the overthrow of Sir Cahir O Doherty and of the bringing in of his head (Reprinted in London in STC 18786).

£6 13s. 4d.

For printing of proclamations touching matters of surrender of lands and seignories (STC 14162) and one to forbid archbishops and other ecclesiastical persons to make away their livings. £8 17s. 9d. ob.

1 October 1609–30 September 1611

For printing a great number of proclamations dated 10 June 1610 forbidding all persons (except merchants) to go beyond the seas without license and that no nobleman or gentleman should send their sons, friends or kinsmen into any foreign country without license. £6 13s. 4d.

For printing the book of rates for customs (STC 14128.3) and two proclamations one dated 12 December 1610 concerning intrusions and the other dated 13 July 1611 for the departure of priests and friars out of the realm and for the repair of the subjects to the parish churches (STC 14163).

£26 13s. 4d.

1 October 1611–30 September 1613

For printing by direction of the state sundry proclamations dated

21 December 1611 for raising the rates of the gold coins according to his highness pleasure, every of them containing three sheets of paper.   £5

For printing of six several proclamations for his Majesty's service.   £40

1 October 1613–30 June 1616
For printing several proclamations for proroguing the last parliament and one other proclamation for stay of pipe staves.

£60

1 July 1616–31 March 1619
For printing five hundred proclamations for banishing of seminary priests and Jesuits.   £13 6s. 8d.

1 April 1619–31 March 1623 (Franckton's successor)
Robert Young printer employed by the lord deputy and council in printing sundry proclamations for his Majesty's service.   £20

---

[1] M. Pollard, *A dictionary of members of the Dublin book trade 1550–1800 based on the records of the Guild of St Luke the Evangelist Dublin* (London, 2000), p. 225.

[2] J. Rider, *A friendly caveat to Ireland's Catholics* (Dublin, 1602), sig. A4.

[3] Abstracts of such of the Irish proclamations, both in printed and in manuscript form, as had been then located are printed in R. Steele, *Tudor and Stuart proclamations 1485–1714*, v.2 (Oxford, 1910). That of 22 November 1600 is STC 14147 and Steele no. 159.

[4] TNA, AOI/287/1081 f. 84v; *Cal. S.P. Ire., 1600*, Ernest George Atkinson, (ed.) (London, 1903), p. 450; *Cal. S.P. Ire., 1600–01*, Atkinson, (ed.) (London, 1905), p. 165.

[5] STC 14150.

[6] TNA, AOI/288/1082 f. 87; *Cal. S.P. Ire., 1600–01*, p. 351.

[7] Hiram Morgan, 'Faith and fatherland or Queen and country', in *Dúiche Néill* 9 (1994), pp 9–65.

[8] STC 2958.

[9] STC 21031.

[10] *A repertory of the inrolments on the patent rolls of chancery in Ireland commencing with the reign of James I*, J.C. Erck, ed., v.i, Part 1 (Dublin, 1846), p. 16; *Cal. S.P. Ire., 1603–6*, C.W. Russell and John P. Prendergast, eds (London, 1872), p. 1.

[11] *Cal. S.P. Ire., 1603–6*, pp 10–11.

[12] Ibid., pp 21–2.

[13] *Cal. Pat. Rolls Ire., Jas I*, facsimile repr. (Dublin, 1966), pp 418–19.

[14] *Cal. S.P. Ire., 1603–6*, pp 18–20, 22–57, 62–63.

[15] *Stuart royal proclamations I: Royal proclamations of King James I, 1603–1625*, J.F. Larkin and P.L. Hughes, eds (Oxford, 1973), pp 94–98.

[16] *Cal. S.P. Ire., 1603–6*, pp 266–7, 278–9.

[17] National Archives of Ireland, Lodge MS 26, p.185; Bodleian Library Oxford, MS Carte 61, f. 74.

[18] No patent to Franckton at this time can be found in the calendar of patent rolls. One possible reason for non-enrolment might be financial: to avoid payment of his annuity in an age of financial stringency and to continue paying him for his work on a piecemeal basis. Indeed he was one of those called upon to make a loan towards paying the army in 1606.

[19] STC 14152 and 14153.

[20] STC 14154.

21 *Cal. S.P. Ire., 1603–6*, p. 267
22 STC 14157.
23 STC 14162. Some of the quotations are taken from this latter proclamation.
24 The English one is STC 8409. The Irish one of November 1607 is STC 14159.
25 STC 14160.
26 The first is STC 14161. The second, of 7 July 1608, is reprinted at the end of *The overthrow of an Irish rebel …* printed in London in 1608 (STC 18786).
27 On these, see the list of payments made to Franckton at the end of this paper.
28 STC 14133.
29 STC 14164 and 14165.
30 STC 14168.
31 See, for example, *Cal. S.P. Ire., 1603–6*, pp 241–2.
32 STC 14155.
33 STC 14163; *Cal. S.P. Ire., 1611–14*, C.W. Russell and John P. Prendergast, eds (London, 1877) pp 80–82.
34 STC 14260.
35 TNA, AO1/289/1087, f. 33v.
36 For a thorough examination of late medieval religious observance in England see Eamon Duffy, *The stripping of the altars* (New Haven and London, 1992).
37 This and what follows has been based on an examination of many sixteenth- and seventeenth-century prayer books.
38 Carlos M.N. Eire, *From Madrid to purgatory: the art and craft of dying in sixteenth-century Spain* (Cambridge, 1995), p. 509. For the revival of saints in Anglicanism in the eighteenth and nineteenth centuries see Nicholas Orme, 'St Endellion and all that', in *Church Times* 30 October 1998, p. 13.
39 See David Cressy, *Bonfires and bells: national memory and the Protestant calendar in Elizabethan and Stuart England* (Berkeley and Los Angeles, 1989) for a study the conclusions of which could probably shed light on the thought processes of Protestants in Ireland too.
40 I am most extremely indebted to Pádraig Ó Riain of University College Cork for his advice to me on this matter, which has been followed.
41 It is possible, however, that the reason for this was that Franckton had some difficulty in printing in red letter.
42 The failure of the Gunpowder Plot was celebrated earlier and had been in red letter from at least the early 1620s. A service for the 'dreadful' Fire of London appeared in a prayer book published in Oxford in *c.*1683.
43 14 & 15 Chas II, cap. 23.
44 They do not, however, appear to be in either the copy in Trinity College Dublin or in that in the British Library.
45 I am very indebted to Dr E. McParland for his advice on this point.
46 William Reeves, *The Book of Common Prayer according to the use of the Church of Ireland: its history and sanction* (Dublin, 1871), p. 37.
47 TNA, AO1/290/1088, f. 52.
48 STC 14128.3.
49 The London edition is STC 4895 and the Dublin one STC 4895.3.
50 On this in general, as it developed, see M. Pollard, *Dublin trade in books, 1550–1800* (Oxford, 1989).
51 STC 17836.3.
52 Bernard Capp, *Astrology and the popular press: English almanacs, 1500–1800* (London and Boston, 1979), passim.
53 STC 443.5; E.R.M'C. Dix, 'A Dublin almanack of 1612', in PRIA 30 C (1913), pp 327–330. One of ;'s[sic] chronicles of contemporary affairs appears in W. Harris, *Desiderata curiosa Hibernica* v.1 (Dublin, 1772).
54 STC 443 and 443.7.
55 For Franckton's ornaments see E.R.M'C. Dix, 'Ornaments used by John Franckton', in *Transactions of the Bibliographical Society* 8 (1907), pp 221–7.
56 STC 21487.5.

57 I am grateful to Stewart Adams of the Middle Temple Library for giving me information about Christopher Sibthorpe's works which are held there.

58 STC 17762.

59 I am grateful to F.J. D'Arcy for his help with the epigram.

60 TNA, E190/1328/20 (unfoliated).

61 Ibid.

62 TNA, E190/1329/9, ff 7v 10, 11, 19.

63 Calculated from *Records of the court of the stationers' company 1602 to 1640*, W.A. Jackson, (ed.) (London, 1957), p.141; *A collection of several acts and statutes relating to her Majesty's revenue of Ireland*, C. Young, (ed.) (Dublin, 1702), p. 287.

64 *Calendar of ancient records of Dublin*, J.T. Gilbert, (ed.) (v.1–7) and Rosa Mulholland Gilbert, (ed.) (v.8–19), 19v. (Dublin, 1889–1944 (hereafter cited as CARD), v.2, p. 534.

65 Ibid., v.3, 183.

66 TNA, AOI/290/1088 f. 48v; *Calendar of state papers, Ireland, 1608–10*, C.W. Russell and John P. Prendergast, eds (London, 1874,) p. 74.

67 TNA, E190/1330/11 ff 21v, 37.

68 Pollard, *Dictionary*, p. 226.

69 *A repertory of the inrolments on the patent rolls chancery in Ireland commencing with the reign of King James I*, J.C. Erck, ed., v.1, Part 2 (Dublin, 1852), pp 605–06; M. Pollard, 'Control of the press in Ireland through the King's printers patent, 1600–1800', in *Irish Booklore* 4, no. 2 (1980), pp 79–81.

70 TNA, SP. 63/230, f. 207.

71 I am engaged in a study of this over an extended period.

72 NLI, G.O. MS 66, f. 96.

73 *Acts of the privy council of England 36* (1618–19), pp 64–66; TNA, AO1/291/1092, f. 49. For this next phase see Pollard, *Dictionary*, pp 541–4 and R. Gillespie 'Irish printing in the early seventeenth century', in *Irish Economic and Social History* 15 (1988), pp 81–8.

74 I am indebted to Vernon Hood, Susan Campbell and also Angela Downton of Worcestershire Record Office, for their genealogical assistance.

75 B. Burke, *The general armory of England, Scotland, Ireland and Wales* (London, 1884), pp 375–6; NLI, G.O. MS 66, f. 96.

76 *Records of the court of the stationers' company 1576 to 1602, from register* B, W.W Greg and E. Boswell, eds (London, 1930), p. 85.

77 CARD, v.3, p. 38.

78 CARD, v.2, p. 468.

79 CARD, v.3, pp 242, 365. Another daughter, Jeneta, was married to a merchant (ibid., p. 374).

80 CARD, v.3, pp 27–28.

81 The most succinct meaning of 'barbarous people' may simply be those not ordered by our laws and conventions.

18

The Bible and the Bawn: an Ulster Planter inventorised

The most enduring changes brought about in early seventeenth-century Ulster were the introduction of Protestantism and the decision to carry out a plantation there. In origin neither coincided exactly with the other, but they soon came to interlink. The final plan of plantation in 1610 produced on the whole a regional scheme for the allocation of the confiscated lay land in the six forfeited counties there – Cavan, Fermanagh, Donegal, Londonderry, Tyrone and Armagh – whereby, using the barony as a unit, English grantees were allocated to some areas, Scots to others, and those Irish who were restored, placed alongside servitors or former military men, to yet other areas.[1] A crucial agent in the extension of the structures of Protestantism into much of Ulster was George Montgomery (d. 1621), who had already, in 1605, been appointed bishop of Derry, Raphoe and Clogher.[2] A Lowland Scot who had obtained preferments in England both before and with the union of the crowns in 1603, and more an ecclesiastical administrator than one who had sought solely to organise a mission (now anyhow of uncertain success) to the Gaelic Irish, his achievement, from one perspective, was to establish the Church of Ireland in his northern dioceses on a sound economic basis. Having been appointed a commissioner for planning the plantation, he secured, before his own removal to the diocese of Meath, with which he was allowed to retain Clogher, in 1610, a significant endowment of lands for the episcopate within the plantation dioceses, some of which, albeit formerly of an ecclesiastical character, might otherwise have gone to lay settlers, as well as of glebe land for the parish clergy. His proposal that a university be established at Derry, on the other hand, came to naught, but the endowing of grammar schools, one in each county, may have derived from his suggestion. Also, in order to begin the establishment of Protestantism at parochial level in his dioceses, he got permission to bring over nineteen 'painful preachers', English and Scottish, to be employed 'for planting the churches in those northern parts'.[3] One of these, the subject of this chapter, was the Rev. Edward Hatton. In his case, not an entirely typical one, both Protestantism and plantation – the Bible

461

and the bawn – came to overlap, since he became the owner of a plantation estate. Some of them became an administrative elite amongst the new Protestant clergy in Ulster. One, John Tanner, was to be made bishop of Derry in 1613 and died there in 1615. Another, James Heygate, a Scot, was made archdeacon of Clogher diocese and lived at Clones, County Monaghan.[4]

I

Edward Hatton was admitted as a sizar to Pembroke College, Cambridge, in 1585 and took his MA from St Catherine's in 1597.[5] He would have been born, therefore, about 1568 or a little later; his place of birth cannot readily be established. He bore in his coat of arms core armorial elements used by the larger Hatton family, which had originated in Cheshire and moved downwards in England in the course of time.[6] Origins for him in Cheshire could be quite plausible, though a possible identification with an Edward Hatton of Gravesend in Kent – which would make him a nephew of Lord Chancellor, Sir Christopher Hatton – can be no more than a possibility.[7] He was ordained for the diocese of Norwich in August 1591 and instituted as rector of Brampton (which he surrendered in 1601) in August 1592, and he became vicar of Westhall in February 1597, both being contiguous parishes in north-east Suffolk.[8] Three of his children, Edward (who may have died young), James and Susanna, in that order, were baptised in Westhall between December 1595 and December 1602.[9] His first wife, Anne Beaumont, was probably of a Suffolk family.[10] The fact that the patron of the vicarage was the dean of Norwich gave him a link to the deans, and so to George Montgomery, who held the deanship of Norwich from 1603 by royal nomination, in addition to a rectory in Somerset where he forged West Country links.[11] Hatton was himself also made a prebendary of Norwich cathedral in 1604, but in the following year relinquished it, in exchange for one of Southwell, in favour of Thomas Jegon, master of Corpus Christi College, Cambridge, and brother of the then bishop.[12] Another factor drawing Hatton towards Ireland might well have been contact with his successor in Brampton, William Flowerdew. Not only was another Flowerdew to be a Virginia planter, but Thomas Flowerdew, from Hethersett near Norwich, was to be a grantee of a plantation estate in Ulster in 1610.[13]

In Ireland in the 1620s he was be to called 'a master of arts of ancient standing' and 'a grave preacher', and – a little earlier – a minister who was 'a good teacher of the Word of God'.[14] Being at Cambridge in the period of theological controversies of the 1580s, he must surely have come under the influence of Lancelot Andrewes, whose lectures on the Ten Commandments at Pembroke embraced recommendations on a proper preaching style. That he may have tended towards moderation, however, may account for him taking his MA in 1597 from St Catherine's, Cambridge, whose master then, Edmund Hound, was a man of moderate views.[15] As against that, it was said of him (in common with about a third of the clergy in Suffolk at that time) in Bishop Redman's diocesan visitation, also in 1597, that 'he weareth not the surples'. Here too it was noted that while 'he preacheth' – unlike many – he did not 'catechise the youth'.[16] Later, in 1604, he was to be listed among the graduate clergy of the diocese who were 'of honest life' and 'able to catechise' and did not appear in any list of those who were subject to criticisms, though it was noted of him, under Westhall, that he had conducted one marriage there 'without license or banes asking'.[17] While he was certainly no outright nonconformist opposed to episcopacy, Hatton's own precise theological reasoning on any subject is not known since none of his sermons was reproduced in print. That at any rate he aspired to some continuing learning can be seen when, on a return journey from England to Ireland in July 1620, the commodities he brought with him included 'books for his study'.[18] Although the precise nature of these books is unknown, they symbolise a process of cultural transfer into an Ulster whose growing number of English residents now shared a common culture with England itself.

Hatton's Ulster appointments were to be in Montgomery's diocese of Clogher, but he was also favoured, perhaps as security to fall back on in the event of any new Ulster crisis, with two parishes (one a vicarage) in the diocese of Meath.[19] Monaghan became his base, where, to stiffen control over a county whose land ownership had been remodelled among local lords and freeholders in the settlement of 1591, an English seneschal had been put in place, to hold also by lease the lands nearby which had formerly pertained to the lordship's MacMahon ruler, which function was now abolished.[20] In the aftermath of the failure of the Nine Years' War, that settlement had been restored, though with modifications which increased the share of new English ownership, with Sir Edward Blayney, commander of the forces there, receiving a lease of Monaghan and this associated land in January 1607, which (except for the castle or fort), with additional lands, was granted to him outright in June 1611.[21] There a small colonising outpost was now in the process of growing up, building houses in the emerging town and erecting a new parish church. It was in the town of Monaghan that Hatton was placed, and where he was to be 'most commonly resident'. He also held the parishes of Tyholland and Galloon, the latter including part of plantation County Fermanagh within its bounds.[22] This alone illustrates the problem of extending Protestantism into Ulster at this time: a lack of clergy in sufficient supply. England, even with Scotland now, did not have a sufficient or willing pool to draw from; Trinity College, Dublin, was only at an infant stage. To have sought alternatively to employ the pre-existing Irish clergy in numbers (though some few did adjust) in an Ulster where recent rebellion had had profound linkages to religion would have presented mutual incompatibilities. From now, in fact, two churches were to emerge in Ulster, with the Catholic one retaining religiopolitical connections with continental Catholicism and with the former Ulster lords and their descendants in Europe in the aftermath of the Flight of the Earls. Hatton officiated and lived in his Meath diocese parishes from time to time as well as having a curate there. But the curate was his nephew Bartholemew Hatton, a 'reading minister', and he also had a parish of his own. In Ulster in 1622 he was 'of late without a sufficient curate'. Curates too were in short supply. A further problem concerned the church fabric. While on the eve of his appointment the church in Monaghan was in good order and that of Tyholland, a parish in which in any case much land still continued in Catholic occupation, was then 'repaired', that of Galloon was, like many others, 'in decay'.[23] What was to happen in regard to church buildings in this area in the longer term is of some interest. In fact by 1622 a new church was to have been built under the aegis of James Heygate at Clones, itself the nub of a substantial monastic estate granted in lease at its dissolution in 1587 to Henry Duke, and now coming to be actively colonised under his successors.[24] Also, as Newtownbutler developed as a centre of settler population, a new church was built there by the 1630s.[25] For the same reason, the pre-existing chapel at Magheraveely, location, as will be seen, of a small plantation village, may also have been put to Protestant use. Where new churches could best be built to suit the emerging pattern of plantation had been made a matter for investigation in the later 1620s. Thus although the proposal at the time of plantation that a new church should be built for each plantation estate was on the whole not acted on at the time, a process of rationalisation in church location was beginning to receive some attention.[26] These churches were also very much an element in the town planning of the time.

When Hatton first came to Ireland is not clear; some initial hesitancy about being placed in Ulster may well have affected him, given residual uncertainties about Spanish intentions in the aftermath of the Flight of the Earls. Only when the new Jacobean Ireland seemed of more certain creation, and with plantation in Ulster coming into being too, did he fully commit his future to it. In November 1614 he returned from a visit to

England (via Chester to Dublin) bearing goods including books for the bishop of Meath, and having surrendered his Suffolk living.[27] He was replaced in Westhall in July 1614.[28] Thereafter he immersed himself in settler society in Ireland. His son and heir James was sent to Trinity College, Dublin, where he graduated in 1619, and was eventually to succeed him in the church, though as rector of Galloon solely. A glimpse of him can be obtained in 1627, when, a curate and 'a man of reasonable good gift in pulpit' and then employed as schoolmaster to the children of Sir William Stewart in County Tyrone, he was expected to preach an assize sermon before the judges in Enniskillen, in what must have been the new church there, then nearing completion.[29] A daughter, Martha, was to marry another clergyman of the diocese, the Rev. James Slack, while another daughter married Nicholas Willoughby, who became tenant of some of the Clogher episcopal land. When a second wife was required, she also came from settler society: Anne Piggot of Kilmainham, County Dublin, was probably a relative of an Elizabethan captain of that surname.[30] As a figure in church administration, Hatton appears as chancellor of the diocese of Clogher in January 1614, and when he died in 1632 he was archdeacon of Ardagh. Also since the late Elizabethan creation of counties in Ulster had now been made effective, it emerges that he had been a justice of the peace of both Counties Monaghan and Fermanagh.[31] Somewhat materialistic in outlook, or ambitious as a married clergyman with children to provide for, and committed to the English view that a radical new beginning in Ulster through plantation should be made, he had also become owner of a Fermanagh plantation estate.

Under the plan for plantation in Ulster, the forfeited secular land in the barony of Clankelly, County Fermanagh, previously owned in gavelkind under Maguire rulership principally by the MacMulrooneys, MacDonaghs and MacDonnells, was allocated both to English undertakers (five in all) and, as part of a larger educational endowment, to Trinity College, Dublin, and also – unusually, since those Irish who were restored to land under the plantation were normally gathered together in other baronies alongside army officer grantees (themselves not formally required to plant their estates with settler tenantry) – to one Irish grantee, Brian MacMulrooney, presumably head of his sept.[32] The grantee of one of these undertakers' estates, one of a group from East Anglia, Robert Bogas, had been slow to take out his patent, and indeed by 1613 his allotment of land had 'neither tenants, cattle nor building', nor had he himself arrived.[33] A neighbouring estate had been granted to Thomas Flowerdew, Hatton acquired Bogas's estate, much of it in Clones parish. Bogas came from the Stour valley in south Suffolk, a pasture region, commercialised through the cloth trade and prone to advanced Protestantism.[34] The earliest contact between them can be traced to 1614, on Hatton's return to England. On 24 May Hatton purchased the estate from Bogas for probably quite a small sum and under an arrangement which may have left Bogas with some residual interest.[35] They may have recruited jointly some tenantry for it from Suffolk at the same time. The estate in question was, by the assessed measurement of the time, a 1,000 acre one – a 'small proportion' in the plantation scheme of things – made up of great and little tates (Ir.? *táití*), the ancestors of the modern townlands, which had been grouped together, for the purposes of issuing the patents, on the appropriate barony map in the series prepared during the survey of the plantation counties in 1609. Its modern statute acreage was some 2,867 acres, or 4.5 square miles. However, by established convention the occupants of many townlands had rights of use over hilly and other land, their 'barrs [Ir. *barra*, tops] and mountains', to the north.[36]

The land granted to Brian MacMulrooney, adjoining the Bogas estate – just under 400 statute acres (granted as 240) but with 'barrs' also – came to Hatton by another route and reveals other linkages. Acquired by Hugh Culme, originally from Devon, who had been a captain in the English army in Ireland since the later stages of the Nine Years War and who had been granted an estate, not far distant, in County Cavan, it was bought for £120 from him by Hatton who mortgaged it to raise money in February 1621 [–/2?] to Nicholas Willoughby (b. 1586), another Devonian, for £160 stg 'of pure silver coin'.[37] Willoughby, who at this time lived in County Meath, was not only a Montgomery connection (arising from the latter's West Country days), being related to his wife, but his mother had been a Culme. In Ireland under Montgomery's aegis, he was already since 1614 tenant of some of the episcopal land in Fermanagh, on which he later came to live at Gortnacarrow, and, as has been seen, he was to marry Hatton's daughter and remain closely intertwined in his affairs.[38]

Under Hatton's ownership, plantation proceeded on the main estate. As one of the undertaker category, he was required under the regulations to plant settler tenantry there (in a defined social structure) who should replace the Irish, who had to be removed. Since it was a small proportion, the newcomers should consist of a minimum of ten families including his own. He was also bound by regulation to build for himself, and to 'draw' his tenants to build nearby 'as well for their mutual defence and strength as for the making of villages and townships'.[39] Investigations some years after he became owner reveal that by then, although it is not possible to pin person to place, all or most of the land had been let to British – English and Lowland Scottish – tenants, with Hatton himself retaining an area in

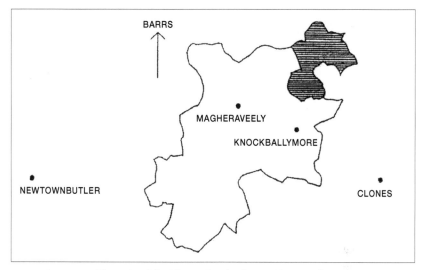

Plate 18.1 The Hatton Lands, County Fermanagh;
lands granted to Brian McMulrooney are hatched

demesne. An inquiry in 1618–19 found two freeholders, five lessees and eight cottagers 'of British birth' (mainly English, as will be seen) planted there, or fifteen families, with amongst them 'not above twenty men in all'. This had increased to twenty-one families (which included Hatton's), with some thirty men, including servants, by 1622.[40] The site of his own stronghold, at Knockballymore, strategically located beside a pre-existing 'thoroughfare' and at a river to power his 'water-mill for corn', had been chosen to be as close to Clones (1½ miles away) as possible. Here he had built an 'excellent strong house and bawn' of stone and lime construction: the bawn (a defensive courtyard), with three flanker towers, measured in 1622 as 70 ft square and 14 ft high, with the house within 70 ft long and, in an apparent error in transcription, described as five storeys high. A later description had the bawn as 68 ft square, and the house – 60 ft long by 28 ft wide – 31 ft high, i.e., to the ridge.[41] In essence, therefore, it must have been a two-storey house with a pitched roof, with a floor area of about 1,700 square feet. By the standards of Ulster plantation architecture, house and bawn were of about average size, conforming well to the plan laid down. The house can be taken to have followed recent English styles in that it was storeyed and chimneyed, while the entity as a whole – called, as was usual, a castle – was, above all, a small privately constructed fort, flankered for protection, with the residence, at once a castle (on its side) and a house, built lengthwise within a taller outer wall and domesticated with windows, probably mullioned and square-headed, on its inner side. Neither building cost nor artisan/contractor's identity can be recovered.

In the matter of his estate village, the plan was less adhered to. Here beginnings were made, not at Knockballymore but at a more centrally located spot about a mile further inwards along the same 'thoroughfare' at Magheraveely, the site of a small church which was a chapel of Clones parish. Here too Hatton was empowered in April 1618, for a yearly fee of £1 stg (in addition to his quit-rent of £5.6.8 on the estate and £2.1.4 on the MacMulrooney lands), to hold a Saturday market and two annual fairs. Here he had also built, but this time timber houses, with a village of eight 'cottagers' now in existence. Although the occupations of these – the skilled poor of the plantation – are not to be found, this was primarily a settlement for artificers of various kinds, each with a house, a 'garden plot' or 'backside' and 'four acres of land'. It also became an administrative centre. Not only was the court leet of the manor held at Magheraveely, but inquisitions ordered by the central administration were occasionally taken there also, with the chapel probably used as their location.[42]

The tenants on the estate, despite the requirement that all should live in villages for security, as well as in the interests of ordered planning and social regulation, came to live on the whole in dispersed settlement on their holdings, their housing generally unremarked on. Some, with a number of townlands, held more land than others, and were thus becoming, with their fellows on other estates, a gentry (below the ranks of the actual landowners) in the settler society. One such was Clinton Maund. A man with some money to invest located in the northern portion of the estate and having for a time some interest in the MacMulrooney lands nearby, he had erected a substantial stone-built house specially noted in 1622, and indeed to have its dimensions recorded, so striking was it – long but low – at the end of the decade.[43] By implication, the houses of the tenantry at large were not substantial structures, and so initially they may not have been people of any great wealth.

When these settlers were mustered for training in the use of arms in about 1630, forty-four males attended, mostly with swords and pikes, though with eighteen unarmed.[44] If, to take account of some few absentees or because some families (if they had children old enough) might have been represented by only, one member, some increase should be made, then fifty to sixty might be the truer figure. This, mainly due to the fact that the estate village had remained small (since, overshadowed by close proximity to Clones and given the much greater growth of Newtownbutler, each equidistant from it by some 3 miles, it had not developed as a trading and processing centre), indicates rather low-intensity plantation, with about one adult male settler per 50 acres. The economy of the estate was largely pastoral, though (despite rainfall levels) with considerable tillage and haymaking taking place as well.[45] Two possible sources of recruitment for some of these tenants already suggest themselves: East Anglia and indeed Hatton's own personal connection, and the English West Country. A smaller group, Armstrongs among them, had Lowland Scottish names; some others may have been from the north of England. A few, Thomas Seaton, Sebastian Cottingham and John Slack, were, perhaps not surprisingly, in view of the ownership of the estate, relatives of other clergy.

While for the Irish the implications of plantation could not but be profound, their position on this estate is by no means fully clear. For them also there was to be some divergence from prescription. All were not just simply removed, though some – perhaps even a fairly considerable number – might well have moved to the nearby college lands which were much less planted. Some had grazing let to them by the settler tenantry (probably on annual subtenancies), but were seemingly fewer in number than on neighbouring estates where there were fewer settlers.[46] At another level, apart from these grazing farmers interspersed with the settlers on some townlands, Irish workmen may well have been employed in the varied labours on the land, not least in whatever new improvements were being carried out by way of enclosure – hedging and ditching – for tillage or meadow fields or of outward bounds of farms.

Edward Hatton was recorded, as having died in the town of Monaghan in 1632 with his plantation at this stage.[47] Three at least of his children survived him: James, now his heir, who may have supervised the estate as well as being a curate, Martha Slack, and Willoughby's wife, probably either Susanna or Mary. He had also added further to his possessions by obtaining the lands of one of the County Monaghan freeholders, Edmund Oge MacMahon, who died in 1621. Acquired to advance his daughter, these lands were held by her husband Willoughby in 1641.[48]

If the son (in particular) had clearly benefited from his father's decision to come to Ireland, the father also left problems to his successor. Bogas's widow, Anne, made claims for her 'thirds and right of dower', which came to litigation in 1638 after James Hatton had died. At the time of probate of his father's will James was immediately confronted by proceedings in the prerogative court, by his father's widow, Anne, concerning her rights, which resulted in a chancery suit between them. By the time of James's death she was receiving a jointure of £40 stg out of the estate. Controversy between himself and Willoughby over his mortgage of the MacMulrooney lands was eventually resolved by arbitrators, but only after his death.[49]

James Hatton died prematurely in May 1637. What emerges about him is that he had been an improver. In his will he stated that he 'would have' his executors – Willoughby, John Heygate (son of the Rev. James, now bishop of Kilfenora, who had himself also purchased an estate in Clankelly, and who died in 1638), and his own son Edward, then aged six – 'go forward with the building [a new house apparently] I have begun on Knockballymore'. To link himself with the new urban development at Armagh (as a potential regional capital) promoted by Archbishop James Ussher, he had already in 1634, following an initiative by his father, acquired a lease for a house there, adjoining 'the new sessions house', and 20 acres allotted to it.[50] He had also held new houses by lease in Monaghan, probably acquired by his father. His will was a revealing document in many respects.[51] He was to be buried within the church in Clones close to his wife, who had predeceased him. Something of his theological position may be found in its introductory phrasing, albeit a familiar formula: he bequeathed his soul 'unto almighty God, assuring myself through the merits, death and passion of Jesus Christ his only Son and my only Saviour to obtain remission of all my sins and life everlasting'.

He disposed of the manor of Knockballymore to his eldest son, Edward, while the MacMulrooney lands were to go to his younger son, James. His leases of houses in Monaghan and Armagh, some of which had been applied by his father to the benefit of Martha Slack, should pass to his daughter Jane. She should gain possession from his executors when fourteen, while the sons, whose tuition should lie with the executors, should succeed at eighteen. Members of his immediate family also received bequests: his 'sister Slack' should get £20 stg and two of her daughters, one now married to a settler in County Cavan, £10 each, to be paid out of ensuing rents. His cousin Edward Hatton was to receive £5. The sum of £4 a year should be expended on a young boy called Webster to 'bring him up to writing and reading' until he was fifteen, when £10 should be paid to apprentice him to 'some good trade'.

Through James's will, two important figures also come to light. One was agent of the estate, a native Irishman: James left £10 to his 'old servant' (a witness to the will, competent and literate in English) Patrick O'Brien, 'who hath spent his youth with me and done me faithful service'. Since James had succeeded his father as rector of Galloon, the other may well have been his curate there and was certainly his successor: to Edward Howe he left all his books. Howe, one of a second generation of clergy now coming to the fore, was at this precise time, in an orientation towards Scotland followed later by Edward Slack (son of two English-born parents and also from Fermanagh), in the final stages of his studies at Glasgow University, *alma mater* alike of both Heygate and Montgomery, where he was defined as 'Anglo-Hibernus'.[52] Hatton left the adjudication of the dispute between himself and Willoughby over the MacMulrooney lands to Edward Aldrich and Nicholas Sympson, two prominent settlers in this region and 'especial friends unto us both', under the umpirage, if necessary, of George Baker or Barker of Dublin, probably a lawyer. The names of witnesses to his will, as well as those mentioned in it, show something of the circle of which he was part in the settler society of Fermanagh, Monaghan and Cavan, just as the earlier mortgage between his father and Willoughby (then in the Pale) had revealed, interestingly for its time, some old English links: an Edward and a John Dowdall were witnesses to it.

Since new patents now had to be taken out under Wentworth's administration, Aldrich and Sympson proceeded fairly swiftly to their adjudication in April 1638. Willoughby stated that he had lived in the castle, or part of it, for eleven years, and although Edward Hatton and his family came there from Monaghan from time to time and had kept servants there, he had never demanded any rent, nor had he redeemed the mortgage. He had dealt with millers there and had spent £80 on 'building, repairing and fencing of the said castle, outhouses and lands', and had received no portion from Hatton with his wife in marriage. The decision arrived at by Aldrich and Sympson, whereby Willoughby should retain the tenancy of two of MacMulrooney's four great tates and be paid £50, reveals also who then occupied them: one was in the hands of Willoughby and Patrick O'Brien; the other was held by an Irishman, Redmond Maguire, a typical Irish grazier.[53] Two further developments in the colonisation of the estate may also have taken place during James Hatton's ownership. William Bignall, millwright, living on the more overcrowded Newtownbutler estate nearby in 1630, had moved – in a still fluid situation to another of these MacMulrooney townlands in the 1630s, from which he was to be dislodged in 1641.[54] Another newcomer to the estate at large, ejected also in 1641, exemplifies the East Anglian connection. Simon Crane – of a surname with a Bogas link – who was registrar of Clogher diocese as well, may be taken to have been a relative of the Rev. Felix Crane, another clergyman who now lived at Castleblayney (where a new church was also built, the old one being put to Catholic use) and who had been curate of Brampton in 1603.[55] For his part, Willoughby (the younger single-function man of affairs who may have somewhat dominated Edward Hatton), may in fact only have moved to his new house at 'the Carrow', some miles away, at about the time that James Hatton succeeded.

James Hatton had died, however, at a fateful time, as the countdown to the War of the Three Kingdoms was beginning. The settlers on the estate were apparently mostly 'put out' of houses and lands in the terror which accompanied the easily understandable attempt at repossession in 1641. Those from it who were killed then included (as far as certainty can allow) Maximilian Tibbs, high constable of the barony; Miles Acres, possibly born in Westminster, where there were Hattons, in 1599;[56] Peter Maddison, a witness, by mark, to James Hatton's will; Thomas Ashton; Thomas Seaton (a Scot); and Sebastian Cottingham.[57] The churches at Clones, Newtownbutler and Monaghan were burnt and various clerical libraries destroyed.[58]

Willoughby and O'Brien, together at the outbreak of the rising, were among those who fled to Dublin. It fell to the latter, occupying a crucial role since James Hatton's death, to leave the only account of what the income from the estate – some £200 per annum – had been at this time. To Edward Hatton was owing rents of £198.10.4 per annum and other debts of £176. 18.6 and to his sister, Jane, small sums.[59] O'Brien, an Irish Protestant, went on to die as an army lieutenant. He too, it emerged, had acquired some Irish freeholder land in Clones parish, County Monaghan, which Willoughby survived to claim as his 'executor or heir'.[60] By then the Irish attempt at counter-revolution in all its aspects had been defeated and plantation in Ulster was restored. Hatton ownership in direct male line did not, however, prove enduring. Hatton's son Edward had not survived; his son James had died young. They had not in the best of times been a strong family; the first Edward, despite his energy, had been unwell in 1622. By the Restoration, the estate had passed to the ownership of William Davies by right of marriage to James Hatton's daughter Jane, who himself died in 1662.[61] The Hattons had been in at the start of a major transformation in Ulster, but they did not survive to found a dynasty there. Their story, however, serves as a case study in the exercise of power on one estate in plantation Ulster. It also indicates in microcosm not only the difficulties of implementing both plantation and Protestantism in Ulster, but also the degree of success being achieved in both areas. Whatever interrelationships between settlers and native Irish as may have been developing were mostly shattered by the outbreak of the rising of 1641.

II

The value of the document which accompanies this account of the Hattons as planters lies in its, virtually unique character. It derives from the litigation between James Hatton and his father's widow in the Court of Chancery in Dublin, forming part of his answer to her bill.[62] However, its actual production arose from a commission out of the prerogative court, to appraisers nominated by both parties, to establish the value of the estate at the time of Edward Hatton's death. The document bears heavily the marks of the damage it sustained in 1922 and is also incomplete. In full, it would have given a list of all the tenants on the estate. The importance of what remains of it lies in the fact that whereas the sizes of plantation landlord houses in Ulster are well known, the number of rooms within them is not, while a systematic recording of the contents is very rare indeed, owing to the very limited survival in Ireland, unlike England, of probate inventories. An added bonus lies in the record of the mixed agriculture practised on the land directly farmed in the neighbourhood of the 'castle', as well as in the hints it gives both to linen and woollen industries and to the presence of English and Irish cattle. There were a lot of horses. The values given for all items are extremely useful. The inventory might also be used to assess the 'civility' of an Ulster rural landowner's residence, though with the precaution that it had not in this case been lived in continuously by one family. It is a very English document both in the words used for some of the rooms – parlour, chamber – and in the fact that the values are given in sterling and not in Irish currency. In the following transcription illegible words and characters are denoted by empty square brackets; in some instances putative readings are given in angle brackets.

A scedule inventory and particular of all the goods chattles and cattles leases debts sperate and desperate which were the said Edward Hatton's at the day of his death and belonging to him which any ways came unto this defendants hands or to his knowledge being truly [ ] prized and valued as be herein set forth by commission out of the prerogative court by such apprizors as were nominated by the parties, plaintiff and defendant, as followeth:

Imprimis, *in the parlour*	£	s.	d.
2 long tables vizt one being a drawing table	1	10	0
1 great cubbord and a liv'y cyubbord	1	0	0
2 chairs, two dozen of joyne stooles	1	2	[ ]
[ ] cushens		2	0
2 old carpets and a brekar		[ ]	0
2 pistols		15	0
5 pikes one without [ ]			6
1 long fowling piece		10	0
22 pounds of course yarn		7	0
1 pestel and mortar		3	4
In the room at the stayres head			
3 flock beds and bowlsters		15	0
4 old caddows		10	0

	£	s	d
1 feather bed and bowlster	1	0	0
1 old bedsted		2	0

In the old chamber over the hall

	£	s	d
2 feather beds, 2 bowlsters and pillows	3	0	0
2 bedsteds and hangings	1	0	0
3 caddows, 1 blanket	1	0	0
1 flock bed		5	0
1 truckle bedsted		2	0
1 livery cubbord		7	0
1 small table and 2 chairs		3	0
1 carpet		3	0
1 chest and 1 old trunk		6	0
1 warming pan		3	0
1 old cushion stool and a pair of bellows, fire shovel and thongues and 1 iron grate	5		0
1 old watch out of temper		10	0
Silver plate in the said room:			
1 great double salt weighing 31 oz. at 4s. the ounce	6	4	0
4 brass candles weighing 45 oz. at 4s. the ounce	9	0	0
4 small bowls, whereof 3 wine bowls weighing 31 oz. at 4s. the ounce	6	4	0
15 spoons weighing 24 oz. at 4s. the ounce	3	16	0
1 little gilt salt without a cover weighing 9 oz. at 4s. the ounce	1	16	0
1 gilt sugar dish weighing 15 oz. at 4s. the ounce	3	0	0
1 small aquavite cupp weighing 2 oz.		8	0

In the chamber over the kitchen

	£	s	d
2 feather beds and 6 feather pillows	2	0	0
2 old coverlets		6	0
2 old caddows and 1 blanket		8	0
1 old bedsted and old curtens		2	6
3 trunks and 4 chairs		10	0

In the chamber over the brewhouse

	£	s	d
2 truckle bedsteds and 1 old bedsted		4	0
1 old spinning wheel		1	6
1 old rotten trunk		1	0

In the chief chamber
[the document is badly damaged at this point]

1 pair of iron racks		6	8
2 spitts		2	0
2 dozen and a half of pewter dishes	1	10	0
1 pewter bason and yewer		5	0
6 sawcers 6 pottingers 6 old chamber pots,			
2 [ ] candlesticks		11	6
2 flaggon pots of pewter		10	0
2 pewter basons and a cullendar		4	0
4 brass candlesticks		10	0
2 old brass pots and chefing dish		17	6
2 small brass pans		6	8
1 dripping pan		3	6
2 little iron pots		5	0
1 chopping knife, a basting ladle, a grater,			
a frying pan and a grid iron		4	6
9 pitch forks, 8 wooden hay rakes		2	6
1 churn, 5 milk tubbs and a basket		5	0
1 old trunk 1 old c [ ]		2	0
1 scimmer 1 marking iron, a cleever and a beef fork		3	6
[ ]		10	0
2 cheeves full of course wool		3	0
some hops and an old bag		10	0
1 close stool and pan, 1 other close stool and pan		7	0
2 stone jugs		8	0
1 pail and a small firkin		1	0
9 flat milk cheeses		4	0
8 small c[ ]s of rendered tallow		12	0
Lyning [linen] praysed:			
10 pair and 1 sheets Irish cloth old and new	3	3	0
1 white English cloth for sheets		10	0
1 diaper table cloth, cubbord cloth and tweel and			
diaper for another small table cloth	1	1	0
7 Irish cloth towels		7	0
2 dozen and 8 napkins Irish cloth		10	0
8 old piltcheeres		12	0
2 old cubbord clothes		2	0
5 old table cloths for a small round table		5	0

In the studdy

1 chair and 1 old cushion		<5>	6
1 desk		3	4
40 books great and small	3	0	0
1 <piece> of old gold waight		2	0

In the buttery

5 hogsheads	7	6
2 barrels and 1 firkin	7	0
2 <powdring tubs>	2	0
1 brass pan	13	4
2 small pails	1	0

In the kitchen

1 old washing tub, 1 pair of pothooks 2 hangers	2	6

In the deary

A boulting tub, a churn, 4 small tubbs with other implements as milk bowls and old barrels	5	0

In the brewhouse

1 old furnace	1	6	8
2 kevers		6	8
1 open hogshead, a coole <pip> measure and a pail		[ ]	0
Plowe implements:			
6 iron chaynes with coulters, 2 socks, 2 plow implements		16	0
2 spades			6

Corn praysed and hay

Corn in the haggard	30	0	0
Hay in the haggard	10	0	0
Barley in the barn	1	0	0
4 barrels of wheat threshed in the house	1	6	0
6½ barrels of oats		<13>	0

Corn in ground

5½ barrels of wheat sown	2	15	0
6½ barrels of bear		12	0
Hay in blackwater meadow		15	0

Cattle praysed

16 oxen praysed	27	0	0
17 cows	24	0	0
12 heifers and a bullock	8	5	0
2 bulls	2	0	0
6 calves	1	10	0
6 Irish cows	4	10	0
Another cow	1	0	0

Horses mares and colts

1 dune colt 3 years old	1	0	0
1 small gray mare colt 3 years old		15	0
1 bay mare colt 3 years old		15	0
2 black yearling colts	1	0	0
6 old working mares	6	0	0
1 old hipt mare and 2 yearling colts	1	0	0
1 bald gelding with 4 white feet	4	0	0
1 old grey gelding	2	10	0
1 chesnot horse and a rawe horse	<4>	0	0
4 hogs	1	0	0
1 bore, 1 sow and 2 pigs		15	0

This chapter is offered in less than adequate tribute to Aidan Clarke, to remind him of his years in Northern Ireland, though with the hope that his memory is not too acute in points of detail.

[1] The exception was the Londonderry plantation.

[2] Henry A. Jefferies, 'George Montgomery, first Protestant bishop of Derry, Raphoe and Clogher (1605–10)' in Henry A. Jefferies and Ciaran Devlin (eds), *History of the Diocese of Derry from Earliest Times* (Dublin, 2000), pp 140–66.

[3] *Cal. S.P. Ire., 1615–25*, p. 253.

[4] J.B. Leslie, *Derry Clergy and Parishes* (Enniskillen, 1937), pp 6–7, 274; *Cal. S.P. Ire., 1606–8*, p. 427; Leslie, *Clogher Clergy and Parishes* (Enniskillen, 1929), p. 42; *Irish Patent Rolls of James I; facsimile of the Irish Record Commissioners' calendar prepared prior to 1830*, with foreword by M.C. Griffith (IMC, Dublin, 1966), p. 326; Armagh Public Library, Visitation Book, 1622, pp 172–3.

[5] John Venn and J.A. Venn, *Alumni Cantabrigienses*, part 1 (4 vols., Cambridge, 1922–27), II, p. 331.

[6] Bernard Burke, *The General Armory of England, Scotland, Ireland and Wales* (London, 1884), p. 4, 67; BL, Add. MS 19,646.

[7] J.P. Rylands (ed.), *The Visitation of Cheshire in the year 1580* (Harleian Society, 18, London, 1882), pp 114–15.

[8] Norfolk Record Office, Norwich, MS DN/Reg. 14, book 20, ff 210, 248v, 295v.

[9] Suffolk Record Office, Lowestoft, MS 163/D1/l (unfoliated).

[10] NLI, G[enealogical] O[ffice] MS 68, p. 180, MS 69, p. 109.

[11] Ian Atherton, Eric Fernie, Christopher Harper-Bill and Hassell Smith (eds), *Norwich Cathedral: church, city and diocese, 1096–1996* (London and Rio Grande, 1996), pp 513–14; W.C. Trevelyan and C.E. Trevelyan (eds), *Trevelyan Papers*, III (Camden Society, 1st series, 105, London, 1872), pp 35–6, 44–72.

[12] John Le Neve, *Fasti Ecclesiae Anglicanae*, corrected and continued by T. Duffus Hardy, II (Oxford, 1854), p. 498.

[13] Norfolk Record Office, Norwich, MS DN/Reg. 14, book 20, f. 295v; *Cal. Pat. Rolls Ire., Jas I*, p. 167.

[14] Armagh Public Library, Visitation Book, 1622, p. 178; George Hill, *An historical account of the plantation in Ulster at the commencement of the seventeenth century, 1608–20* (Belfast, 1877), p. 483.

[15] H.C. Porter, *Reformation and Reaction in Tudor Cambridge* (Cambridge, 1958), pp 209, 346, 391–8. I am indebted to Professor D. MacCulloch for this reference.

[16] *Diocese of Norwich, Bishop Redman's Visitation 1597: presentments in the archdeaconries of Norwich, Norfolk and Suffolk*, (ed.) J.F. Williams (Norfolk Record Society, XVIII, Norwich, 1946), pp 19, 127, 152. Hatton was formally licensed to preach in 1604–5.

[17] Norfolk Record Office, Norwich, MS DN/VIS 3/3, ff 68, 101v.

[18] TNA, E190/1332/l, ff 25rv.

[19] Leslie, *Clogher clergy*, p. 59.

[20] For the settlement of Monaghan see 'Fiants of the reign of Queen Elizabeth', nos 5621–80 in *The Sixteenth Report of the Deputy Keeper of the Public Records in Ireland* (Dublin, 1884), appendix IX, pp 184–94.

[21] *Cal. Pat. Rolls Ire., Jas I*, pp 95, 103, 199.

[22] Armagh Public Library, Visitation Book, 1622, pp 178–9.

[23] HMC, *Report on the Manuscripts of the late Reginald Rawdon Hastings* (4 vols., London, 1928–47), IV, pp 154–6; NAI, Book of Survey and Distribution, County Monaghan, pp 112, 129–32, 156–8.

[24] 'Fiants Ire., Eliz.', no. 5042; Armagh Public Library, Visitation Book, 1622, pp 172–3.

[25] TCD, MS 835, ff 36rv, 176rv.

[26] T.W. Moody (ed.), 'Ulster plantation papers', *Analecta Hibernica*, 8 (1938), p. 286; *Inq. Cancell. Hib. Repert.* (Dublin, 1829), II, Fermanagh (11) Chas I.

[27] TNA, E 190/1330/11, f. 37.

[28] Norfolk Record Office, Norwich, MS DN/Reg. 16, book 22, f. 49v

[29] G.D. Burtchaell and T.U. Sadleir, *Alumni Dublinenses* (2nd edn, Dublin, 1935), p. 380; *The Spottiswoode Miscellany*, I (Edinburgh, 1844), pp 121–2.

[30] NLI, GO MS 68, p. 180.

[31] *Cal. Pat. Rolls Ire., Jas I*, p. 519; NLI, GO MS 68, p. 180.

[32] *Cal. Pat. Rolls Ire., Jas I*, p. 186.

[33] HMC, *Hastings MSS*, IV, p. 166.

[34] D. MacCulloch, *Suffolk and the Tudors: Politics and religion in an English county, 1500–1600* (Oxford, 1986), pp 7–52, 179–80.

[35] *Inq. Cancell. Hib. Repert.*, II, Fermanagh (5) Chas I.

[36] *Cal. Pat. Rolls Ire., Jas I*, p. 167; *Inq. Cancell. Hib. Repert.*, ii, Fermanagh (5) Chas I. The modern acreage has been calculated from the Ordnance Survey.

[37] NAI, RC 5/28, pp 44–8.

[38] *Trevelyan papers*, III, pp 78, 89–90,101–4; *Cal. Pat. Rolls Ire., Jas I*, p. 519.

[39] T.W. Moody (ed.), 'The revised articles of the Ulster plantation, 1610', *Bulletin of the Institute of Historical Research*, 12 (1934–35), pp 178–83.

[40] Hill, *An historical account of the plantation in Ulster*, pp 483–4; BL, Add. MS 4756, f. 105.

[41] *Inq. Cancell. Hib. Repert.*, II, Fermanagh (5) Chas I.

[42] *Cal. Pat. Rolls Ire., Jas I*, p. 367; TCD, MS 835, f. 265; BL, Add. MS 4756, f. 105; *Inq. Cancell. Hib. Repert.*, II, Fermanagh (5) Jas I (1623), (5) and (10) Chas I (1629–30). A piece of land here was technically claimable by the bishop, but Hatton was allowed to use it.

[43] *Inq. Cancell. Hib. Repert., II*, Fermanagh (5) Chas I. It was 86 ft long by 20 ft wide and 16 ft high.

[44] BL, Add. MS 4770, f. 59v.

[45] This impression is based on the 1641 depositions.

[46] BL, Add. MS 4756, f. 105. An indication of who some of these Irish were can be gleaned from TCD, MS 835, ff 142, 179, 210.

[47] NLI, GO MS 68, p. 180.

48 'Fiants Ire., Eliz.', no. 5644; *Inq. Cancell. Hib. Repert.*, II, Monaghan (17) Chas I, and Fermanagh (5) Chas I; NAI, Book of Survey and Distribution, County Monaghan, p. 71.
49 *Inq. Cancell. Hib. Repert.*, ii, Fermanagh (43) Jas I; NA, CP/S25.
50 On the development of Armagh at this time see above, ch. 15, pp 405–12.
51 NAI, RC 5/28, pp 49–54. His funeral entry is in NLI, GO MS 70, p. 179.
52 *Munimenta alme universiatis Glasguensis: records of the university of Glasgow from its foundation till 1727*, (ed.) C. Innes (4 vols., Maitland Club, Glasgow, 1854), III, pp 90, 92; TCD, MS 835, ff 29rv, 120rv. Howe was dislodged from Galloon in 1641.
53 NAI, RC 5/28, pp 55–63.
54 BL, Add. MS 4770, f. 63v; TCD, MS 835, ff 47v–8.
55 TCD, MS 835, ff 198rv; Armagh Public Library, Visitation Book, 1622, pp 178–9; Norfolk Record Office, Norwich, MS DN/VIS 3/3, f. 66.
56 A.M. Burke (ed.), *Memorials of St Margaret's Church, Westminster: the parish registers, 1539–1660* (London, 1914), p. 62.
57 TCD, MS 835, ff 35, 82v, 174, 265–6.
58 Ibid., f. 198v.
59 Ibid., ff 82rv, 203.
60 NAI, Book of Survey and Distribution, County Monaghan, p. 158.
61 NLI, GO MS 70, p. 339; Aidan Clarke, *Prelude to Restoration in Ireland: the end of the Commonwealth, 1659–60* (Cambridge, 1999), p. 183.
62 NAI, CP/S25.

19

Chester and the Irish Book Trade

The influences of books from England on cultural change and the Anglicisation in process in early modern Ireland can have been of no mean significance. The book trade has been largely neglected, yet English port books provide valuable evidence about its dimensions. Since much of the trade of London (the primary source of book imports) with Dublin and a number of other east coast ports was normally channelled through Chester, what follows is a sample of the material available deriving from the overseas port book of Chester for the year Christmas 1680 to Christmas 1681.[1]

In addition to details of the ship, and usually its destination, port books record the merchant's name and the commodities on which he paid duty. The list extracted below is of those making shipments of books, referred to in no more detail than 'printed books' and measured in the hundred weight. Addresses of those consigning the books are not given, but in most cases it was clear that the intended destination was Dublin. Only one, Francis Garnett, who also dealt in tobacco pipes, had books on a ship with a clearly defined alternative destination – Carrickfergus.[2] The names are presented in alphabetical order along with the number of times the individual had traded that year and the quantity of books involved.

Four stationers emerge as the giants of the Dublin book trade for this year – Patrick Campbell (later to suffer the enmity of the London bookseller John Dunton[3]); Eliphal Dobson, this year made free of the Guild of St Luke the Evangelist, the guild of cutlers, painter-stainers and stationers; James Malone, a member of the guild since 1672; and John North, who was a charter member of the Guild of St Luke on its establishment in 1670, having been free of the Stationers Company of London since 1655.[4] All four had associations with publishing and printing, their names appearing at various times in the imprints of Dublin printed books.[5] Two other substantial importers, Samuel Helsham and Andrew Crook, the latter the son of John Crook, a London stationer who had been a bookseller in Dublin in the 1640s and king's printer there in the 1660s, were to become joint king's printer there within the next few years.[6] Another printer the Rev. Thomas Bladen, dean of Ardfert and son of William Bladen (d. 1663), bookseller and king's printer in Dublin since the

1630s, had kept up a printing business in Dublin despite the monopoly of the king's printer.[7]

Of the other persons named in the port book as importing books in this year, seven can be found in various capacities in the records of the stationer's guild.[8] A number can also be found in the imprints of Dublin printed books.[9] Some, such as Dobson, Campbell and Malone, are known from later evidence to have been Dublin booksellers.[10] John Foster practised in a bookshop known as 'the Dolphin'.[11] Other, important booksellers, however, can now be identified. From the scale of their operations these must include Joseph Howes[12] and Robert Simpson, along with Matthew Dowling and William Winter. Of these Dowling, along with a number of the smaller men, was not a member of the stationer's guild. Two book importers, Mathias of St Werburgh's and Ashton of Kevin St, can be identified as glovers.[13] Whitwood appears to have been a Londoner with Irish printing connections whose trade in books to Ireland now becomes apparent.[14] It is likely that the rest were Dubliners.[15] William Powell's name suggests a connection with an important printing family.

Book importation was not confined to dealers. Light is also thrown on the activities of collectors. John Parker, Church of Ireland archbishop of Dublin, brought back books on two occasions. Sir Robert Reading, a minor government official and a landowner through his marriage with the dowager countess of Mountrath some twenty years before, was a man of scientific interests who corresponded with Martin Lister, joined the Dublin Philosophical Society in 1684 and read papers, one of which was published, before it.[16] A third, George Tollett, who was a mathematician working in Dublin and a founder member of the Dublin Philosophical Society in 1683, imported books in such quantity (6½ cwt) as to suggest that he may have operated as a bookseller as well.[17]

In comparison with their equivalents of a century before, who were general merchants including books amongst their merchandise, most of those importing books to Ireland for sale at this time brought no other commodities. Of the four larger booksellers, each importing *c.* 10 cwt and above, only one, John North, brought other commodities on one of three occasions. Only nine of the 28 people involved also imported additional commodities.[18] James King, for example, who traded on two occasions, brought in tobacco pipes as well as iron and silk, in addition to a small quantity of books. Thomas Ashton brought as well as books two dozen 'shovels shod'. Tobacco pipes or tobacco were brought by a number, including Powell, Glegg and Garnett as well as James King.[19] Overall it seems clear that bookselling, or bookselling with printing connections, had by now become a much more specialised occupation.

Two further points remain to be made. The office of king's printer in Ireland conferred the sole right not only to print but to import and sell books in Ireland.[20] It is clear that by 1681 this monopoly of importation had broken down. The total of some 5½ tons of books despatched from Chester to Dublin in that year is an impressive one and suggests that more books were on sale in Ireland than has heretofore been thought.[21] The second point is also of some interest. Unlike their sixteenth-century predecessors, who were for the most part merchants descending from the old Anglo-Norman colony of the middle ages, the book importers presented here were heavily new English. They included different varieties of Protestant – Eliphal Dobson was a 'great dissenter' with a creaking wooden leg,[22] Campbell was a Presbyterian[23] – but there were few Catholics amongst them. Certainly, few recognisably old Dublin names stand out. The Fosters may perhaps stem from that tradition and probably also Matthew Dowling,[24] but only James Malone can be surely identified as a major Catholic bookseller and printer.[25] This was in itself a form of control which made the effective ending of the king's printer's monopoly largely irrelevant.

Book Importation through Chester, 1681

Name	Number of Occasions	Quantity in Hundredweights
Thomas Ashton	1	¼
Dr Thomas Bladen	1	2½
Patrick Campbell	4	11½
Andrew Crook	1	3
Eliphal Dobson	3	11¾
Ma[thew] Dowling	1	6
George Foster	2	2
John Foster	1	7
Francis Garnett	1	3
Henry Glegg	1	1½
Joseph Glover	1	1½
Humphrey Hanwell	1	1
Samuel Helsham	1	3½
Joseph Howes	2	6
Robert Ince	1	¼
James King	1	¼
James Malone	3	9¾

Mortimer Mathias	1	1
William Mendy	1	2
John North	3	10½
John Parker, Archbishop of Dublin	2	3
William Powell	1	¼
Sir Robert Reading	1	2
Robert Simpson	1	4
George Tollett	1	6½
William Whitwood	1	1½
Joseph Wilde	1	1
William Winter	1	6½

1. TNA, E190/1343/3.
2. Garnett appears as a Drogheda merchant name in the earlier seventeenth century (for example, NAI, R.C. 6/2, p. 57) and it may have been for there that these books were intended.
3. John Dunton, *The Life and Errors of John Dunton* (London, 1818), II, 491–508 (I owe this reference to Dr Sean Connolly).
4. Mary Pollard has most generously provided me with the information given here and in footnote 8, which derives from the records of the Guild of St Luke the Evangelist (NLI, MS 12122, 12123).
5. The information on imprints given here and below (footnote 9) has also been provided by Mary Pollard.
6. M. Pollard, 'Control of the Press in Ireland through the King's Printer's Patent 1600–1800', *Irish Booklore*, IV, 2 (1980), 84–9.
7. Ibid., pp 32–5.
8. George Foster, John Foster, Joseph Howes, William Mendy, Robert Simpson, Joseph Wilde and William Winter. Campbell, Crook, Dobson, Helsham, Malone and North appear also in these records. Mendy was presumably son of William Mendy of Dublin, bookseller, who died *c.* 1673 *Reports of the Deputy-Keeper of the Public Records in Ireland, 26* (1895), App. p. 595.
9. Bladen, Campbell, Crook, Dobson, both Fosters, Helsham, Howes, Malone, Mendy, North, Simpson, Wilde, Winter and probably this William Whitwood. For further detail about printing in Dublin at this time see E.R.McC. Dix, *List of Books, Tracts, Broadsides, etc. printed in Dublin from 1601 to 1700*, Parts III and IV (Dublin, 1902, 1905).
10. Especially Dunton, *Life and Errors.*
11. E. MacLysaght, *Irish Life in the Seventeenth Century*, (3rd ed. Shannon, 1969), p. 217.
12. Presumably son of Robert Howes of Dublin, stationer, who died *c.* 1672 (*Rep. DKPRI 26*, App. p. 434).
13. From their wills: Mathias, 1684 (*Rep. DKPRI 26*, App. p. 588); Ashton, 1716 (P.B. Eustace (ed.), *Registry of Deeds, Dublin: Abstracts of Wills*, I (IMC, 1956), p. 53).
14. Dunton refers to 'rolling and honest Whitwood' (*Life and Errors*, I, 292).
15. Robert Ince, for example, was chosen to be one of the auditors of the city's accounts in October 1681 (J.T. Gilbert (ed.), *Calendar of Ancient Records of Dublin*, V (Dublin, 1895), 224).
16. L.J. Arnold, 'The Restoration Land Settlement in the Counties of Dublin and Wicklow' (unpublished Ph.D. Thesis, University of Dublin, 1967), pp 202, 226; K.T. Hoppen, *The Common Scientist in the Seventeenth Century* (London, 1970), pp 42, 138, 223, 240.
17. Hoppen, *Common Scientist*, pp 20, 25–7, 116, 120–21, 146, 151. 157–8, 235.
18. Ashton, Garnett, Glegg, Hanwell, Ince, King, North. Powell and Tollett.
19. King (d. 1727), a relative of Archbishop William King, and Glegg (d. 1720) may be identified as Dublin merchants. See Eustace, *Abstracts of Wills*, I, 24; A. Vicars (ed.), *Index to the Prerogative*

Wills of Ireland, 1536–1810 (Dublin, 1897). In the later 1690s King was involved in a Dublin printing controversy (Marsh's Library, Dublin, MS Z3.1.1/88: I owe this reference to Miss Pollard).

20 Pollard, 'Control of the Press in Ireland'.
21 Bound books exported from England to Ireland in 1681 were valued at £1,000 (F. Brewster, *New Essays on Trade* (London, 1702), p. 87.
22 Dunton, *Life and Errors*, I, 238.
23 R. Munster, *The History of the Irish Newspaper, 1685–1760* (Cambridge, 1967), p. 69.
24 His names suggests a connection with Luke Dowling, the most prominent Catholic bookseller in Dublin in the early eighteenth century (Munster, *Irish Newspapers*, pp 27, 122, 135).
25 On Malone (d. 1721) see Munster, *Irish Newspapers*, pp 13, 24, 121–2.

INDEX
of principal personal names and place names